IMPLEMENTING SAP R/3 SALES AND DISTRIBUTION

Implementing SAP R/3 Sales and Distribution

Glynn C. Williams

McGraw-Hill
New York San Francisco Washington, D.C.
Auckland Bogotá Caracas Lisbon London
Madrid Mexico City Milan Montreal New Delhi
San Juan Singapore Sydney Tokyo Toronto

McGraw-Hill

A Division of The ***McGraw-Hill*** *Companies*

2 3 4 5 6 7 8 9 0 DOC/DOC 0 5 4 3

ISBN 0-07-212404-0

The sponsoring editors for this book were Simon Yates and Sharon Linsenbach and the production supervisor was Clare Stanley. It was set in New Century Schoolbook by D&G Limited, LLC.

Printed and bound by R.R. Donnelley & Sons Company.

This book is printed on recycled, acid-free paper containing a minimum of 50 percent recycled de-inked fiber.

CONTENTS

PREFACE

This book is designed to help you implement the SAP *Sales and Distribution* (SD) module. It is a compilation of notes, tips, and tricks I have learnt in various implementations.

After completing projects I found myself with a bunch of notes, OSS numbers, and virtually a whole spectrum of advice gleaned from wonderful individuals with whom I have had the pleasure of working with.

This coupled with an accumulation of quick referral notes and other pieces of paper eventually ended up with my carrying a portable library of folders and files.

After compiling the information I had collected into a coherent structure, I was approached by numerous friends and colleagues to share this information with them. Thus came the decision to publish this book. You will find it a valuable source of trustworthy advice given in an easy-to-access format, with direct answers. Instead of having to read ten pages to obtain one point, my desire is that you find ten points in one page.

This book is not only directed at the consultant implementing the SAP SD module, but is also a valuable tool for the IT/IS department left to maintain the system post implementation.

This book is not a remake or copy of the help files SAP offers, nor is it in any way directed or controlled by SAP—nor does it intend to replace SAP training.

It will however enhance your knowledge of the SD module in SAP by providing easily accessible implementation guides, fantastic time saving tips, as well as direct, easily accessible information on the dos and don'ts of implementing and maintaining the sales and distribution module of SAP.

Should you wish to contact the author or offer feedback on this book, please send an e-mail to `sapsd@attglobal.net`.

Chapter 1 SAP Basics, Organizational and Master Data

In this chapter you will start your road map with SAP. We will begin with basic data such as how SAP functions and where it access the information in the system. We will go through the different versions of master data, material, customer, organizational, and all related data.

We will cover basic fields and tables, their usage, and how to make the most of them. We will also cover what master data is transferred into the sales order and various forms of master data grouping.

Chapter 2 Sales Document Flows

This is one of the largest sections, it covers all different types of sales documents, starting where we left off in the previous chapter. We learn about the different document types, how they are set up as well as what makes them function. We learn about item categories how they control the item being sold and schedule lines and how they control critical data such as deliveries and how they impact other modules. We also deal with copying control between documents in SAP, leading the reader through to the delivery stage.

Chapter 3 Deliveries and Invoicing

In this chapter we cover the deliveries and invoicing functions, this includes route determination and packing. You will learn how the system controls a delivery, as well as collective invoicing and collective deliveries. It is in this chapter that we cover the availability checking process and the transfer of requirements. You will also cover the intercompany business scenarios, and how they function.

Chapter 4 Basic Functions

This chapter alone is extensive enough to have its own book, it is not as basic as it sounds. In it we cover virtually all the extras that make up the sales process. This includes pricing and the condition technique. As well as the determination of partners, texts, output and the all too important credit management. We end off with a look at requirements and formulas, and how they integrate into pricing and copying control.

Chapter 5 Cross Functionality

A large proportion of what you need to know involves cross functionality, namely, how the SD module interfaces with other modules. In this chapter we will learn about basics in the logistics information system, how to create reports using the standard structures SAP has, and how to create our own structures, to report on what we would like to see. We also learn about user exits and new fields in pricing. As well as various ABAP enhancements, for example the creation of ones own user menus. We finish off with batch jobs, ABAP queries and a list of sundry tips which we are sure will be useful to you.

ACKNOWLEDGMENTS

A book of this proportion would not have been possible without the support of family, friends and colleagues. I would thus like to say thank you to my darling wife, Wendy, for her support in the creation of this book. Wends, you are an angel. Sincere thanks to one of the best SD consultants, Keenan Jones, for his superb proofreading and advice throughout the stages of this book. Special mention also goes to Keenan for the work he contributed in Chapter 5 with regards to Batch inputs and ABAP Queries.

I would like to thank Casim Mithani, and my colleagues at Avnet, Germany, for their enthusiasm and support of this project, as well as to say thank you to SAP South Africa, especially to Chris Holden and Ingrid Johanson for permitting me to work on their systems in order to meet the deadlines for this book. Special thanks also to Simon Yates and Sharon Linsenbach of McGraw-Hill, as well as to Beth Brown, for their support and assistance. And finally to my Lord Jesus, thank you—for everything.

CHAPTER 1

Introduction to SAP Sales and Distribution

The name SAP, being a German company, is an acronym for "Systeme, Anwendungen, Produkte in der Datenverarbeitung." This is translated into English as "Systems, Applications, and Products in Data Processing."

The SAP system consists of a complex integration of different modules or applications, each representing part of the basic business process. These modules are described a little later in this section. SAP runs on a fourth-generation programming language called *Advanced Business Application Programming* (ABAP).

The SAP Graphical User Interface

SAP has also developed a user interface called the *SAP graphical user interface* (SAPGUI), which runs on Windows 3.1/95/98/NT, Motif, OS/2 presentation manager, and Macintosh. All SAPGUIs look identical, regardless of the operating system on which they are running. This interface varies according to the version of SAP or SAPGUI you are running; however, the difference in appearance is minimal. The appearance of the screens and menus is configurable. These topics will be covered in the last chapter of this book.

The basic SAP screen is shown in Figure 1-1. This screen will be referred to as [S000] because it is obtainable by using transaction code [S000].

Figure 1-1
The basic SAP screen

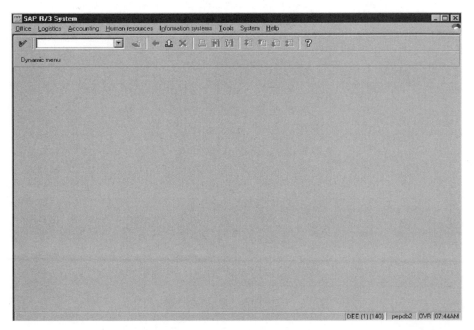

The Application Integration

SAP is an *enterprise resource planning* (ERP) software product capable of integrating multiple business applications, with each application representing a specific business area. SAP homogeneously produces a product that is capable of great depth in a specific application or area while still being part of the overall bigger picture.

These applications update and process transactions in real time, thus allowing seemingly effortless integration and communication between areas of a business. Thus, one can create a sales order and observe the update order values in a *sales information structure* (SIS) immediately, without having to wait for day-end or month-end processing. (SIS is covered in Chapter 5, "Cross-Functional.")

Customizing Tools

The cornerstone of SAP is its ability to be configured to meet the needs of your business. This is done by customizing or adapting the system to your business requirements, which is the process of mapping SAP to your business process. A business process would be, for example, a sales order entry or delivery creation.

This process of mapping SAP to your business process is generally time-consuming and costly, as one needs to fully understand the business process procedures, find a solution in SAP to meet these requirements, and then customize the solution within the system. The basis for this book is to teach you how to develop and enhance the Sales and Distribution module of SAP to its fullest potential using these tools in order for you to effectively meet your business requirements.

Since SAP Version 3, the *reference implementation guide* (IMG) for R/3 customizing has been available. Until this version, customizing had to be done in the menu paths of the system with considerably more hassle. For the purpose of this book, we will be using SAP Version 4.0b as a reference. Figure 1-2 shows an example of the IMG or customizing screen, which we will call the IMG in future.

This screen is the backbone for SAP and the entries placed in it determine how the system functions. We will be using this screen extensively for the purpose of configuring the SD module.

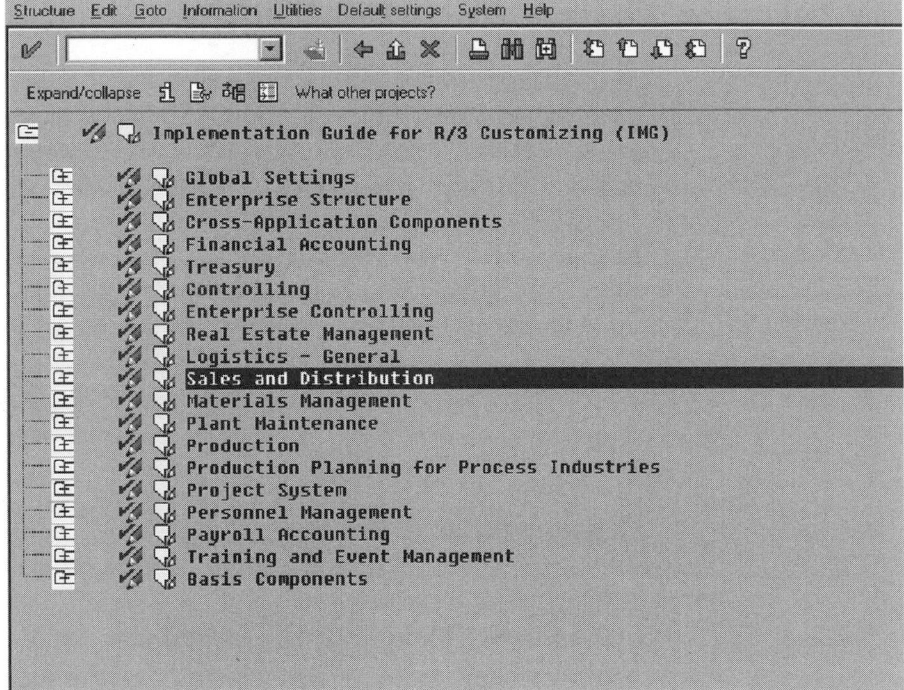

Figure 1-2 The IMG or customizing screen

R/3 Applications Overview

R/3 applications are categorized into three core functional areas: logistics, financial and human resources. Of these three functional areas, there is a further subdivision into applications or modules. In addition to these applications, SAP creates *industry-specific solutions* (ISs), which are, as the name defines, created tailor-made for a specific industry. A few examples of these would be

IS-OIL	The SAP industry solution for oil companies
IS-T	The SAP industry solution for telecommunications
IS-B	The SAP industry solution for banks
IS-Retail	The SAP industry solution for retail

In addition to these industry solutions of which there are currently 19, standard cross-application components are available, such as the SAP Business Workflow. This tool is not dedicated to one unique application or module; it can be used throughout the system to integrate and automate R/3 processes. The following is a brief description and overview of a few of the major functional areas in SAP.

Financial Applications

This functional area contains the necessary information on profitability analysis, general ledger accounts, and information on reporting using the *executive information system* (EIS). This area contains the following modules:

FI	Financial Accounting
CO	Controlling
EC	Enterprise Controlling
IM	Investment Management
TR	Treasury

Human Resources

This area contains the following modules:

PA	Personnel Administration
PD	Personnel Development

These modules include support on salary and payroll administration as well as areas such as work schedule models. This core functional area is very country-specific, due to country-related taxes, employee benefits, and employment laws.

Logistics Applications

Logistics is the largest of the three functional areas. It includes, among others, the following modules:

SD	Sales and Distribution
MM	Materials Management
WM	Warehouse Management
PP	Production Planning
LO	General Logistics
QM	Quality Management

We will be focusing on the Sales and Distribution module of SAP, SD.

The Sales and Distribution Module (SD)

It cannot be stressed how important this module is or the impact that it has in the structure of SAP. It integrates with every other R/3 application including FI, CO, MM, PP, and so on.

The SD module is made up of multiple components. We will cover all these components and how to configure the majority of them in the system. Here is a brief list of these:

SD-MD	Master data
SD-BF	Basic functions subdivided into multiple components, such as pricing, output, and so on
SD-SLS	Sales
SD-SHP	Shipping
SD-TBA	Transportation
SD-FTT	Foreign trade
SD-BIL	Billing
SD-CAS	Sales support
SD-EDI	Electronic data interchange
SD-IS	Information systems

SAP Basics

This book contains a few guidelines that can offer instant understanding and promote ease of use. Firstly, all transaction codes are shown with square brackets, such as [SPRO]. When you see this flag ➤ next to a paragraph, it denotes a tip or trick. These tips and tricks are fantastic time-savers and have been gathered the hard way. Be sure to make the most of them.

Basic Transaction Codes

Transaction codes are the short path to a specific screen in SAP. They are found by selecting System: Status, as the following example in Figure 1-3 shows.

Here the transaction code is [OVS9], which is the change view for customer groups. By the way, the [SPRO] transaction code is the shortcut for the business IMG.

The standard menu path is always described from the logistics screen (unless specifically stated from the IMG). An example of using the menu path to access the Sales and Distribution environment in the system is shown in Figure 1-4.

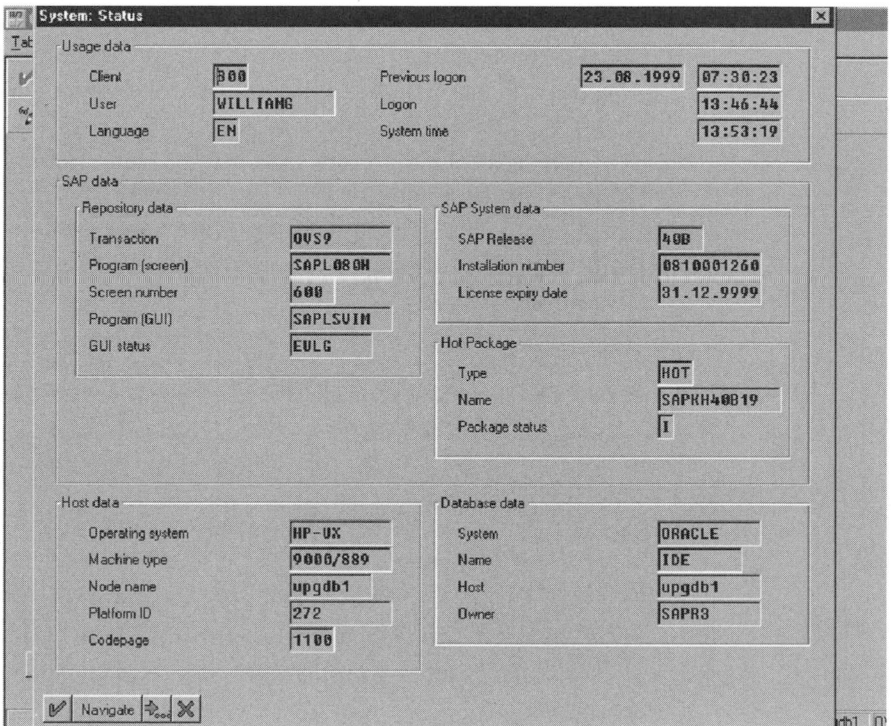

Figure 1-3
The System: Status screen

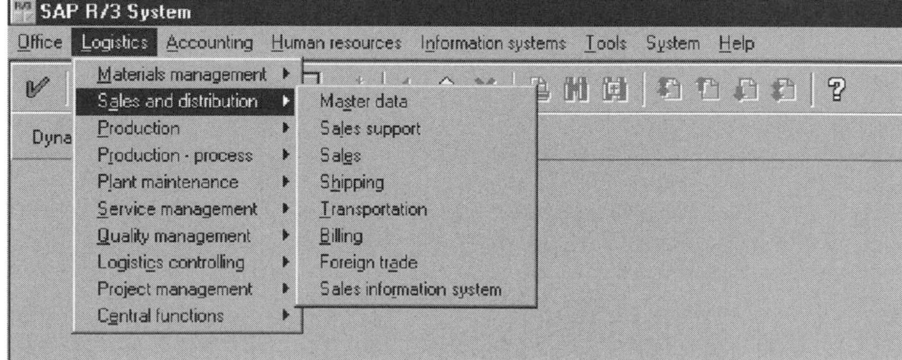

Figure 1-4
Using the Logistics menu to access the Sales and Distribution environment

Thus, the menu path to get to the IMG from the Logistics screen, or [S000] as in the example of the SAPGUI, is as follows: Tools, Business engineering, Customizing.

Please refer to Chapter 5 to read about creating your own transaction codes. Table 1-1 shows codes you will be accustomed to using:

Naturally, there are hundreds of such codes and it would be irrelevant to list them all now; generally, SAP groups transaction codes into its componants. For example [VAOO] will give you the sales overview screen, whilst [VAO1] will give you the create sales order screen, [VAO2] the change sales order, [VAO3] display sales order, etc.

Note as transaction codes call up screens, there must be a link from the screen you are trying to access to the relevant screen you wish to call up; thus, you will not be able to use the transaction code VA00 whilst in the IMG. As a general rule, you can access every screen from [S000] the logistics screen.

TIP: *To save time transferring between screens to call up a transaction, you can utilize the short commands to move quickly around the screens while calling up a transaction at the same time. For example, here is a list of transaction codes or prefixes:*

/N	moves you back from any screen into the logistics screen.
/Nxxxx	moves you from anywhere into transaction xxxx.

Table 1-1
Basic transaction codes

Code	Description
VS00	Master data
VC00	Sales support
VA00	Sales
VL00	Shipping
VT00	Transportation
VF00	Billing
VX00	Foreign trade
SPRO	Enterprise IMG

/NVA00	moves you from anywhere into the Sales screen.
/O	generates a session list.
/Oxxxx	opens transaction code xxxx in a new session.
/OVA00	opens Transaction VA00 in a new session with the sales front-end screen.

TIP: *A few other functions crucial to easily using the system are the function codes:*

F1	*Help*
F9	*Technical info (used from within the Help screen of the field or after you have used F1)*
F4	*Possible entries or matchcode for the field you are accessing*

To briefly explain, a *matchcode* is a comparison key. It enables you to locate the key of a particular database record by entering a field value contained in the record. The system then displays a list of records matching the specifications for you to select from. An example of this would be searching for the customer number in a sales order. Should you select F4, you would have the option to select a suitable matchcode to obtain the customer number you are after, as shown in Figure 1-5 below.

Figure 1-5
Selecting a matchcode to obtain a customer number

Customers by country/company code

Country
City
Search term
Name
Customer
Company code

Restrict display to 500

Alternatively, you may select F5 from within this selection screen, which brings up the Search Help Selection screen for you to select a different matchcode, as we see in Figure 1-6.

These function codes are to be used from a specific field, such as the customer group field. Pressing F1 brings up the screen shown in Figure 1-7.

Subsequently pressing the F9 function key or hitting the Technical info button will give you the Technical Information screen, shown in Figure 1-8.

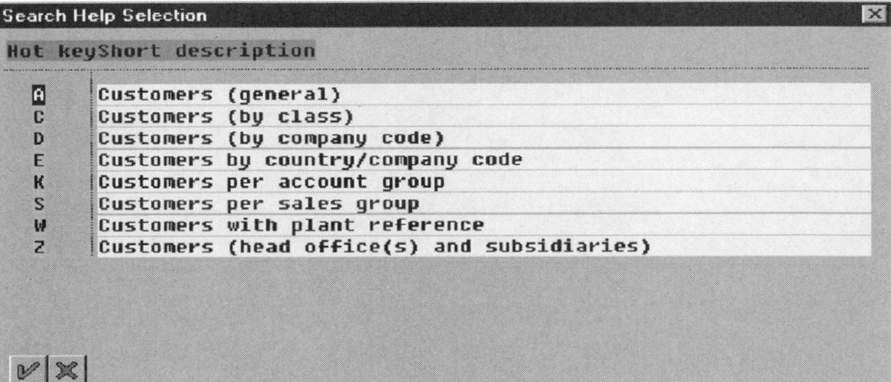

Figure 1-6
The Search Help Selection screen for selecting a different matchcode

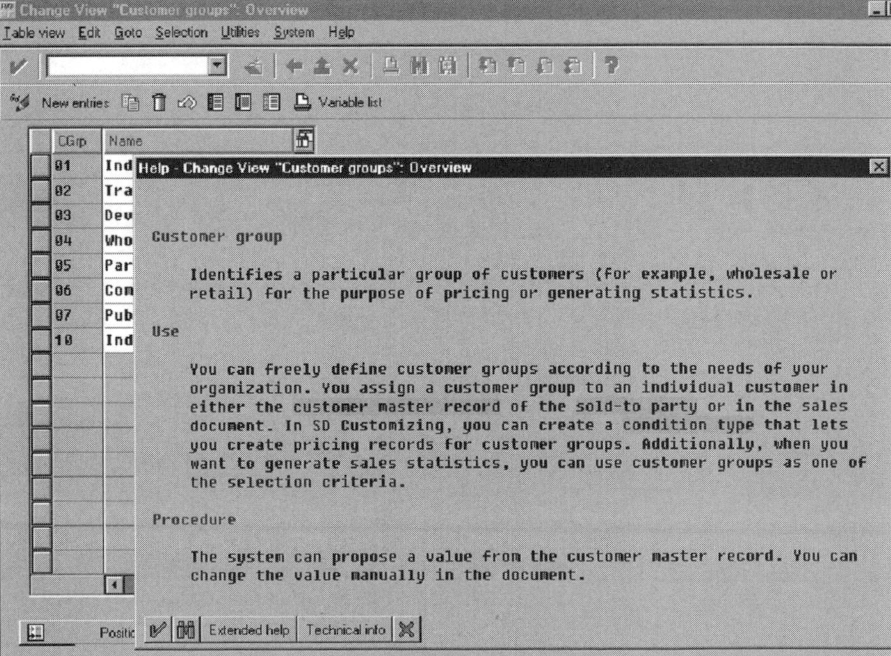

Figure 1-7
The Change View "Customer groups" screen

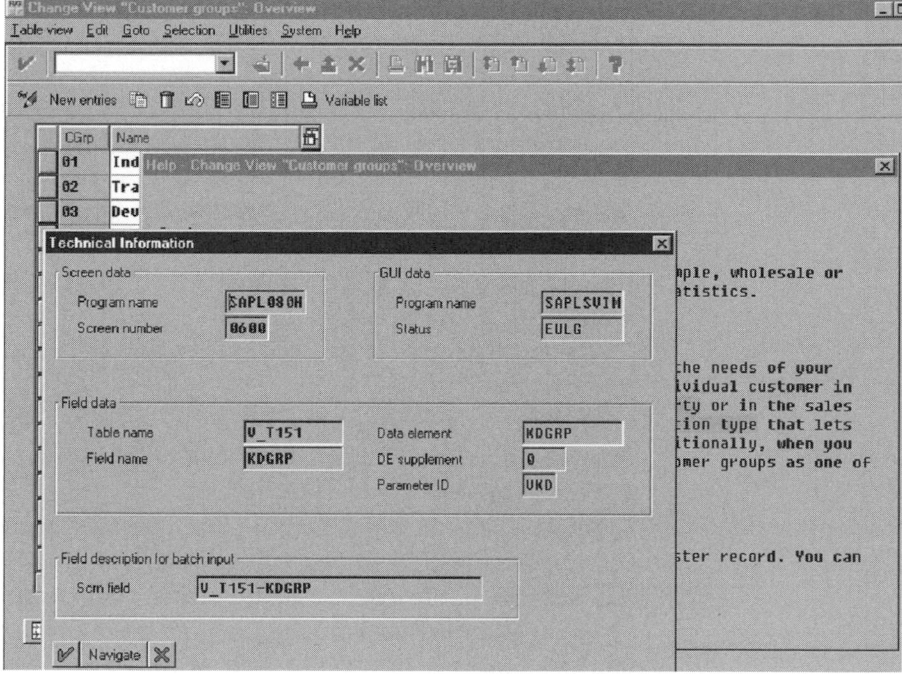

Figure 1-8 The Technical Information screen

The Structure of SAP SD Master Data

Master data forms the basis of the SD processing. Master data is the responsibility of all modules, as each module has an element of it. However, the SD master data will be accessed by many other modules other than SD, such as PP, FI, and CO. The structure of this master data represents how the system is to perform in the future. It is the highest level of data and thus it has the largest effect on the standard business process. Master data in SD is divided into three main areas:

Organizational Data This is the structure of the company, whereby each area of the business is represented by a hierarchical element. For example, a sales area is constructed of a sales organization, a distribution channel, and a division. The Finance module uses the highest form of master data, which is the "company code." The SD module integrates with this company code via the sales organization. Thus, due to the link between the sales organization and the company code in Finance, SAP knows which company code to post a sales transaction to. This is based on the sales organization in the sales order.

Customer and Material Master Data As goods and services are sold by the company, for which the organizational data has been maintained, we need to represent this material and service data in our system as well as maintain and represent all our different sold-to parties and partners.

Document Master Data Business transactions are stored in the form of documents. These SD documents are structured in such a way that all the necessary information is stored in a systematic way.

Global Settings This area defines the country keys and currencies. This data is application-independent; however, these settings are a prerequisite for handling all business transactions.

One of the most fundamental principles to grasp when dealing with the SD module of SAP is to understand where information is coming from and at what time in the transaction it is accessed. This information can be found by debugging SAP or running an SQL trace (both of those topics will be touched on lightly in Chapter 5). However, with a little understanding, you can spot issues and narrow investigations to solve problems with little effort.

Generally, SAP looks from the highest level of data to the lowest. Thus, when creating a sales order, it will look at the organizational master data first, followed by the customer master data, followed by the material data, when entered, and all the while it checks various document master data.

This is a very light overview of tracking master data in SAP. As we go through the configuration of the data, we will automatically cover this in more detail. A rule of thumb would be, "as input is added, it is checked by the system from the highest level of master data to the lowest." Thus, if you are in a sales order and enter a material, the system will check organizational data first, followed by customer data (checking for customer material information records). It then checks the material data, perhaps for the minimum order quantity, and finishes with document data, perhaps to determine if this material is valid for this item category in the sales order.

Organizational Data

You must set the organizational data in SAP before you can process SD transactions. For example, without a sales organization, it is not possible to create a sales order in SAP. This data reflects the structure of your business. Every transaction occurs within this structure. The organizational data is like the steel girders in a building, so setting them up correctly is essential to a sound structure.

The more thought you give to the organizational structure, the easier SAP SD will be to configure and use. You should understand the business and the SD configuration in order to set up a sound organizational structure.

Summary

Here you define your sales organizations, distribution channels, sales offices, sales groups, shipping points, loading points, and transportation planning points.

Menu Path

To follow the path, you go to the IMG Enterprise structure, Maintain structure, Definition, Sales and Distribution. One can see the menu path in the IMG from Figure 1-9.

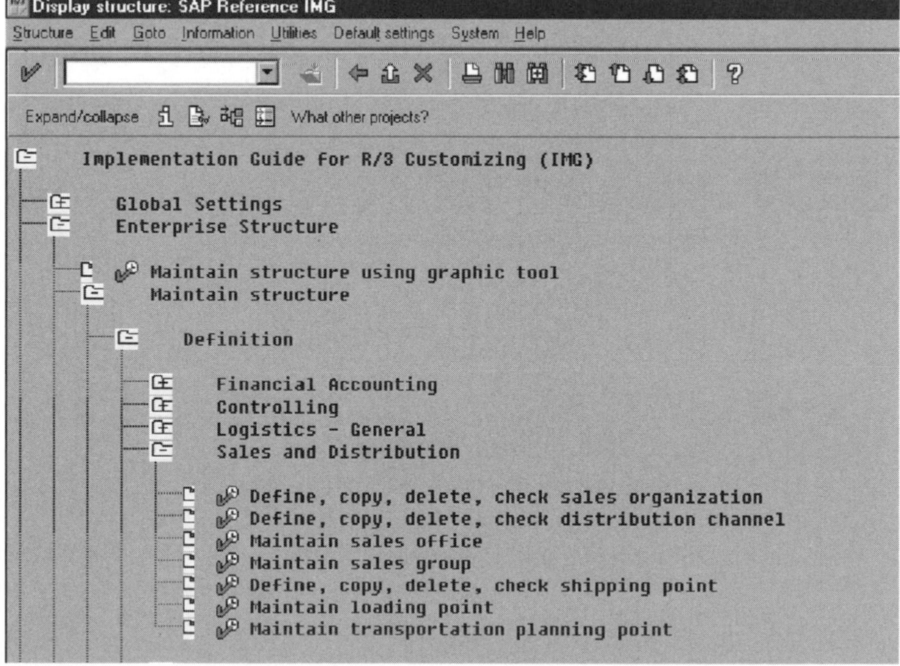

Figure 1-9 The menu path for SD Copyright by SAP AG

A *sales organization* is an organizational unit that sells and distributes products, negotiates terms of sale, and is responsible for these transactions. A *distribution channel* is a channel through which materials or services reach customers. Typical distribution channels include wholesale, retail, and direct sales. You can assign a distribution channel to one or more sales organizations. A customer can be delivered from multiple distribution channels. A material master record can be maintained with different sales organization and distribution channel views, allowing different data to be accessed.

A *division* is a product group that can be defined for a wide-ranging spectrum of products. You can make customer-specific agreements for every division, such as partial deliveries, pricing, and terms of payment. Within a division, you can carry out statistical analyses or set up separate marketing. Please note that divisions are utilized in SD but they are defined and maintained in IMG, Enterprise structure, Maintain structure, Definition, Logistics general.

Figure 1-10 shows a basic organizational structure. In Sales Organization 1000, SD business transactions can be carried out for distribution channel 10 and 20 and division 01 and 02. In Sales Organization 2000, transactions can only be processed through distribution channel 10 and division 01 and 02. Likewise, transactions in Sales Organization 3000 can only be done through distribution channel 10 and division 01.

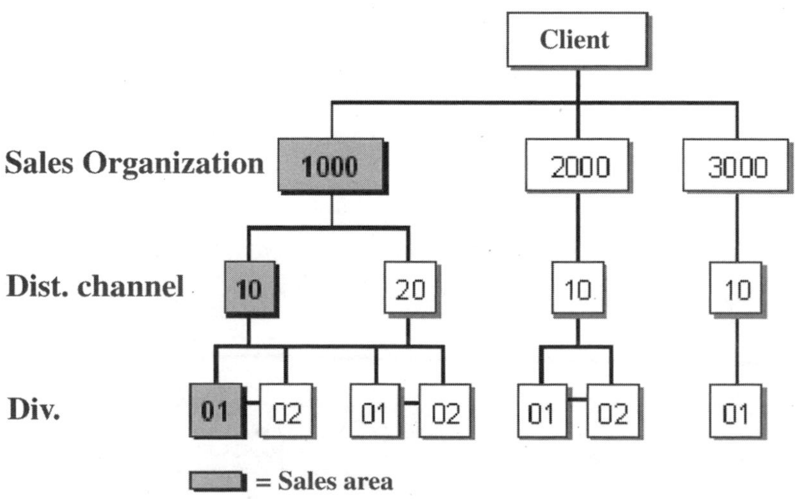

Figure 1-10
A basic organizational structure in which different sales organziations utilize some of the same distribution channels and divisions

TIP: *Sales organizations should be kept to a minimum, so try to have one per company code. Only have another sales organization if the company sells completely differently in a particular area. For example, sales processed in Great Britain would be handled differently than sales processed in Ireland, even though they would have the same company code. A good rule of thumb is that if the material can be sold in both sales organizations and there is one company code, then there should only be one sales organization.*

Master data records are multiplied by each additional organizational element you have. Thus, 10 customer master records with two sales organizations, two distribution channels, and two divisions would have a total of 80 customer master record sales views. Add another sales organization and you have 120 customer master record sales views.

Adding divisions does not multiply the material master views, but it does multiply the customer master sales views. Add a division to our 80 customer master views and we suddenly have 120 customer master sales views. However, add the division to the material and we still end up with 80 material master views. (Please refer to common distribution channels and common divisions later on in this chapter.)

A *sales area* is compiled of the following data: a sales organization, a distribution channel, a division. A sales area may be used for reporting purposes; all data relevant for sales can be defined by a sales area. For example, you can define pricing according to a sales area or do your sales information analyses per a sales area.

Inside every organization is a team responsible for sales. This team can be complex, allowing its own structure to be determined based on its actions in order to optimize its functions. This internal organizational structure has the following elements:

Sales Office Geographical aspects of the organization in business development and sales are defined using the term "sales office." A sales office is in turn assigned to a sales area. If you enter a sales order for a sales office within a certain sales area, the sales office must be assigned to that area.

Sales Group The staff of a sales office may be subdivided into sales groups. For example, sales groups can be defined for individual divisions.

Salespersons Individual personnel master records are used to manage data about salespersons. You can assign a salesperson to a sales group in the personnel master record.

Organizational Structures in Accounting

A client can have one or more company codes. Each company code is its own legal entity in finance. One or more sales organizations are assigned to a company code. The data would have the structure as shown in Figure 1-11.

Organizational Structures in Materials Management

A *plant* is where stocks of a material are kept. A storage location is, as the name says, a storage area for the stock in a plant. One or more plants are assigned to a company code, and one or more storage locations are assigned to a plant. The data would have the following structure as displayed in Figure 1-12.

Shipping points are defined in the SD organizational master data setup. They are the top level of the organization in shipping. Deliveries are always initiated from exactly one shipping point. A shipping point is assigned one or more plants and can be subdivided into several loading points.

A *loading point* is a voluntary entry. It is merely a subdivision of a shipping point. A loading point is manually entered into the header data of the delivery. For the moment, it is best to leave the transportation planning point until we discuss shipping in Chapter 4.

Now that you understand the data, go ahead and define your data in the following area in the IMG: Enterprise Structure, Maintain Structure Definition, Sales and Distribution.

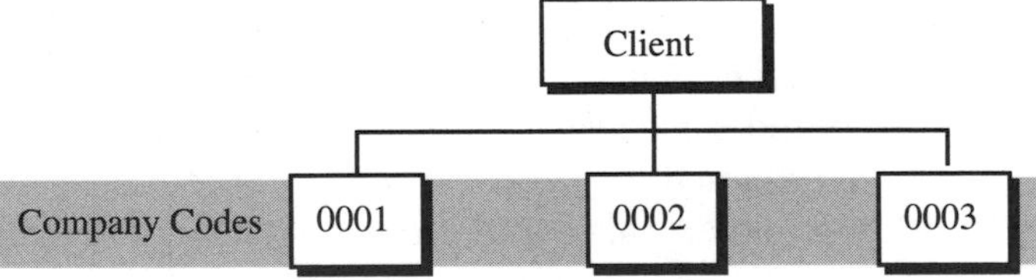

Figure 1-11 Company code data structure Copyright by SAP AG

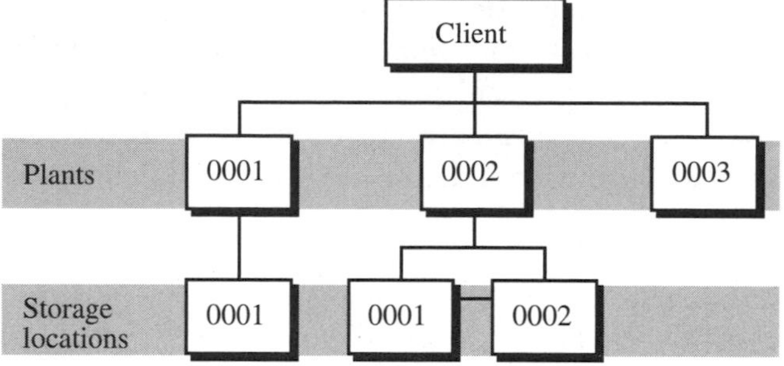

Figure 1-12
Plant and storage location structure
Copyright by SAP AG

Assignment of Organizational Data

In the assignment of organizational data, you create the linking that integrates the different modules in the system. This is best shown by the assignment of sales organizations and plants. A plant, although always linked to one company code, can be linked to several sales organizations (see Figure 1-13).

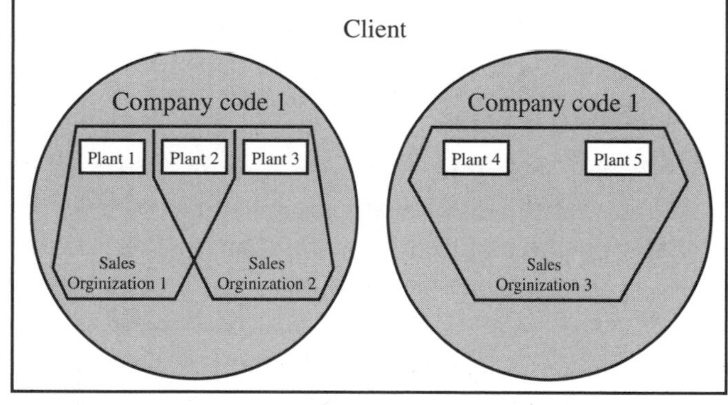

Figure 1-13
Plants 1, 2, and 3 belong to company code 1. Sales organization 1 uses plants 1 and 2, Sales organization 2 uses plants 2 and 3. Sales organizations 1 and 2 can make cross-company sales for goods from plants 4 or 5.
Copyright by SAP AG

After you have defined your data and the other modules have defined theirs, such as FI for company codes and MM for plants, it is time to assign the SD organizational data. To assign the data you have just created, follow this path: Enterprise structure, Maintain structure, Assignment, Sales and Distribution. We will cover the credit control area assignment in detail in Chapter 4.

NOTE: *Shipping points are not assigned here, so please refer to Chapter 3.*

Master Data for the Customer

The customer master record is the basis for all sales transactions as well as deliveries and payments. It represents the data relevant to the entity being dealt with. The basic customer master records we create are

- The sold-to party record
- The ship-to party record
- The bill-to party record
- The payer record

Other important customers are created, such as inter-company customers (that is, the customer master record), which represent the sales entity purchasing between company codes within the same client. Also important is a one-time customer, which is a customer master record that represents all partner functions and is used as a general customer for all the cases for which you do not want to create a new specific master record. An example would be a customer who orders stock from you once every two years.

Menu Path

The path to create is as follows: Logistics, *Sales and Distribution* (SD), Master data, Business partner, Sold to party, create.

Transaction Code

[VD01] is the customer master record for sales view creation. [XD01] is the central customer master record creation with company code data.

When you create a customer master record, the system knows which fields to turn on and off by using the assigned **account group**.

The account groups are defined in Finance. However, they can be accessed by going to the IMG, Financial Accounting, Accounts receivable and accounts payable, Customer accounts, Master records, Preparations for creating customer master records, and then Define account groups with screen layout (customers) [OBD2] as described later in this chapter.

When creating the customer master record [VA01], you are faced with the screen in Figure 1-14.

The Customer Change master record initial change screen is displayed in Figure 1-15.

General data, like addresses and telephone numbers, is maintained for every customer. This data is only identified by the customer number, not by the company code or sales area. Maintaining the data is possible from both the accounting view and the SD view using transaction [VD02] or [XD02] to change.

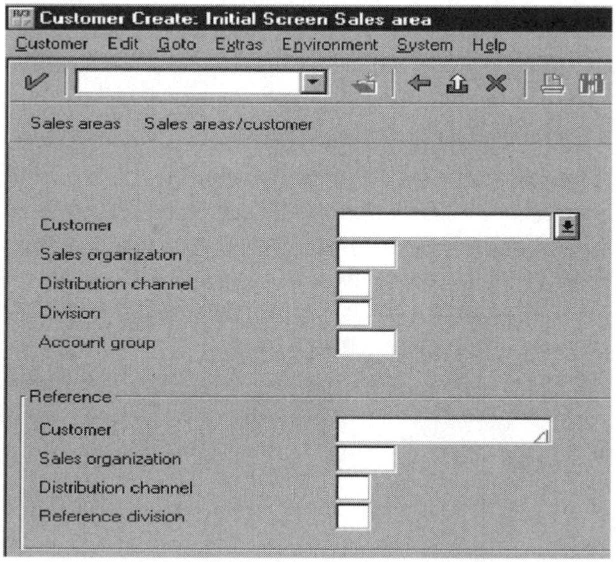

Figure 1-14 The Customer Create: Initial Screen Sales area screen

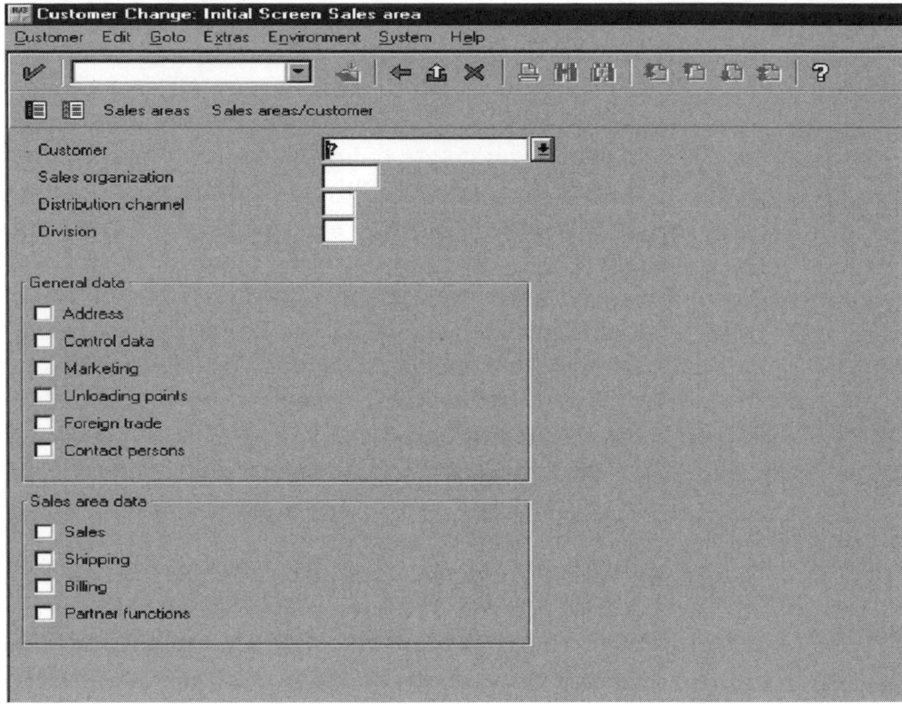

Figure 1-15 The Customer Change: Initial Screen Sales area screen

Company code data is only of interest to the accounting department. It includes, for example, information on insurance or account management. This data applies to only one company code. Transaction code [XD01] is used to create customer master data with company code-relevant data.

Sales and distribution data is only of interest to the SD area. It includes, for example, data on pricing or shipping. This data only applies to one sales area and therefore is dependent on the sales structure (sales organization, distribution channel, and division). When changing a customer master record from transaction [VD02], click the Customer/Sales areas button. This will provide a list of sales organization distribution channels and divisions for you to select from.

You would not have different customer numbers if your customer is serviced by more than one company code. Nor would you have different customer numbers if your customer is serviced by more than one sales organization. It is possible, however, to have different data for the same customer number in different sales areas. Examples of general data in the customer master record would be the following: Address, Control data, Marketing, Payment transactions, Contact person, and Unloading points.

An example of company code-specific data in the customer master record would be data on accounting information, payment transactions, correspondence, insurance, and withholding tax, credit management is linked to the customer master but will be covered in Chapter 4 later.

Company code data only applies to one company code. If you edit the customer master record, you must specify customer number and company code in order to access the screens containing company code data using transaction code [XD02].

TIP: *As the customer master record is copied into the sales order as well as referenced from the sales order for LIS and SIS, it is worth spending the time and effort carefully planning the usage of each key field that is copied into the sales order. Most of the important fields I have listed in Table 1-2.*

Although these are by no means all the master records you can report on, they are the most common of the available fields. Other fields exist, and if required, you can add extra fields to the customer master record. Don't be liberal in your use of fields; often you may realize you have a need for the field shortly before go live once you start the reporting specifications.

To briefly summarize

- The account group defines what fields are available in the customer master records.
- A sold-to party only needs sales-relevant data. However, a sold-to party can also be created as all the partner functions.
- The ship-to party only needs shipping-relevant data, such as unloading points and so on.
- A payer is the individual or company who settles the invoices for a service or for delivered goods.
- The bill-to party need only have the basic data such as address and output fields.

Table 1-2

Customer master field usage

SAP Table and Field Name	Description	Key	Entries
RF02D-KUNNR	**Customer number**	Assigned to each customer	Customer-specific
RF02D-VKORG	**Sales organization**	Assigned per company code	Company code-specific
RF02D-VTWEG	**Distribution channel**	Assigned to sales organization	As Defined
20			
RF02D-VSPART	**Division**	01	As Defined
KNVV-BZIRK	**Sales district**	0000001	As Defined
KNVV-BKBUR	**Sales office**	000001	As Defined
KNVV-VKGRP	**Sales group**	001	As Defined
KNVV-KDGRP	**Customer group**	01	As Defined
KNVV-KLABC	**ABC classification**	A	As Defined
KNVV-KONDA	**Price group**	1	As Defined
KNVV-PLTYP	**Price list type**	A	As Defined
KNA1-BRSCH	**Industry**	0001	As Defined
KNA1-BRAN1	**Industry code**	00001	As Defined
KNA1-KUKLA	**Customer classification**	A	As Defined
KNVV-KVGR1	**Additional data customer group**	01	As Defined
KNVV-KVGR2	**Additional data customer group**	02	As Defined
KNVV-KVGR3	**Additional data customer group**	03	As Defined
KNVV-KVGR4	**Additional data customer group**	04	As Defined
KNVV-KVGR5	**Additional data customer group**	05	As Defined
	Customer Hierarchy	This will be dealt with in Chapter 4.	

The Material Master Data

The material master data is used by the system to represent the data pertinent to the product or service your company is selling or producing. It is configured much the same way as the customer master record with different views.

Menu Path

The menu path is as follows: Logistics, Sales and distribution, Master data, Products, Material, Other material, create.

Transaction Code

The code here is [MM01]. You are presented with the screen as shown in Figure 1-16. You will notice a mandatory field is the material type; this material type is similar to the customer account group in the way it governs what fields are relevant for data and that it controls to some extent how the material behaves. Another mandatory field is the industry type.

Figure 1-16
The Select View(s) screen

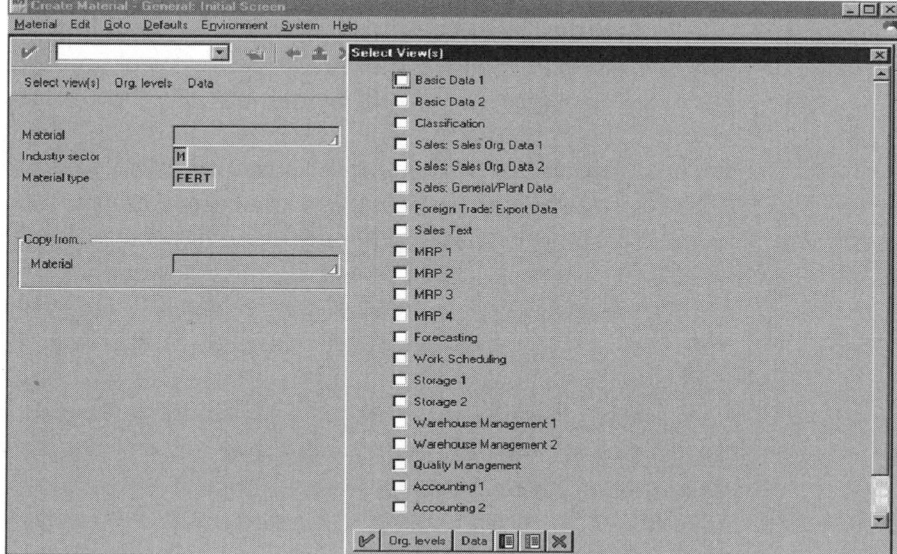

An example of material types are as follows:

HAWA Trading goods

NLAG Non-stock materials

VERP Packaging materials

DIEN Services

These are merely a few; it is possible to create your own versions of these material types, but this should be done in MM.

NOTE: *A mandatory material type is necessary in this [MM01] screen as this is the selection screen to create all types of materials. Should you follow the standard menu path and create, for example, specifically trading goods, the system does not need a material type entered, as it is defaulted by the system.*

As you can see, you have the option to create references to already created materials. This is a popular solution, should you wish to copy the data from one material into another that is similar.

You are provided with a number of views from which to select. Like the customer master record, you have sales views as well as accounting views. A few relevant material master views are as follows:

Accounting This screen contains the valuation and costing information. Examples would be standard price, past and future price, and moving average cost price.

Materials Requirements Planning (MRP) 1,2,3,4 Theese screens provide information for material requirements planning (MRP screens) and consumption-based planning/inventory control/availability checks. Examples are safety stock levels, planned delivery time, and reorder levels for a material. A crucial field value for MM, PP, and SD is the MRP type; MRP will be covered with the schedule line categories in Chapter 2.

Purchasing Data here is provided by purchasing for a material. Examples include the purchasing group responsible for a material, over- and underdelivery tolerances, and the order unit.

Storage This screen contains information relating to the storage/warehousing of a material. Examples would be the unit of issue, batch management, and storage conditions.

Forecasting Here you'll find information for predicting material requirements. Examples include how the material is procured, the forecasting period, and past consumption/usage.

Sales and Distribution These views are most relevant for the SD team. It covers information pertinent to sales orders and pricing. Examples would be the delivering plant, taxes, pricing reference material, and the item category group. The availability check indicator is represented here as well, which controls how the system determines if stock is available for a sales order and when it will become available. These subjects are covered in detail in Chapter 2.

The pricing reference material is where you can enter a material for which you have a material master record and prices in your system. You can use the pricing reference material as a reference for the material you are busy creating or editing.

The item category group is of utmost importance to SD; it covers how the material behaves from the sales quotation right through to the invoice. In fact, all sales documents are dependent on this fields value. It will be covered in item category determination in Chapter 2.

Material Master Units of Measure

As a material can be stored, transported, and sold in various units of measure, in the SAP R/3 system, you can define various units of measure that are maintained in the SD screens. However, you only need to maintain the fields of the units of measure if they deviate from the base unit of measure. You can enter the following units of measure in the SD screens:

Base Unit of Measure This is the unit of measure used as a basis for all transactions. All quantity movements in other units of measure, should any exist, are converted automatically by the system in the base unit of measure.

Alternative Unit of Measure If a product is managed in the base unit of measure "piece," but is sold in the sales unit "box," you must define the conversion factor. The alternative unit of measure can define, for example, that one box of this material contains five pieces.

Sales Unit The unit of measure in which materials are sold is referred to as a sales unit (for example, piece, box, or bottle). The value you define in the material master record is proposed during business transactions relevant for sales. You can replace them with other alternative units of measure in the sales order.

Delivery Unit The delivery unit refers to the unit in which materials can be delivered. Only exact multiples of the delivery unit can be delivered. For example, with a delivery unit of 30 bottles, 30, 60, or 90 bottles can be delivered, but not 100 bottles.

Quantity Specifications

SAP uses two different quantity specifications for the material master record.

Minimum Order Quantity The minimum order quantity refers to the minimum quantity the customer must order. A warning message appears if the minimum order quantity is not reached during order entry.

Minimum Delivery Quantity The minimum delivery quantity refers to the minimum quantity you must deliver to the customer. This quantity is automatically checked during delivery processing. A warning message appears during delivery processing if you enter a delivery quantity lower than the minimum delivery quantity.

Although the material master record does not explicitly fall into the SD modules area, it is still worthwhile exploring the fields available in it as well as what and how the values in the fields affect the SD process. Whenever a material master field affects a transaction or process, we will highlight the impact such settings will have.

Customer Material Information Records

Customer material information is information on a material that applies to a specific customer. An example would be a customer's description of your material. You can record this customer-specific information for a material in a customer-material information record.

The data in the customer material info record has priority when master data is copied into SAP. A customer material information record is the highest level of data the system copies into the sales order as far as absorbing data relevant to the specific combination of customer and material that you have.

Menu Path

The path is as follows: Logistics, Sales and distribution, Master data, Agreements, Customer material information, Create. It can also be accessed from the relevant customer master record within the customer master record inside [VA02]. You would select Environment, Cust.material info.

Transaction Code

The code here is [VD51]. This data is dependent on the relative sales areas. That is, data created specifically for Sales Organization 1000 will be different from that of Sales Organization 2000. Figure 1-17 shows the screen you are faced with when creating a customer material info record.

1. Enter the material that you store in your plant or sell.
2. Enter the customer's product name or description.
3. Select the entry and then select details by clicking on the magnifying glass icon.
4. You now have the relevant entries on the sale and shipment of this particular item. Of special importance is the plant as seen in Figure 1-18.

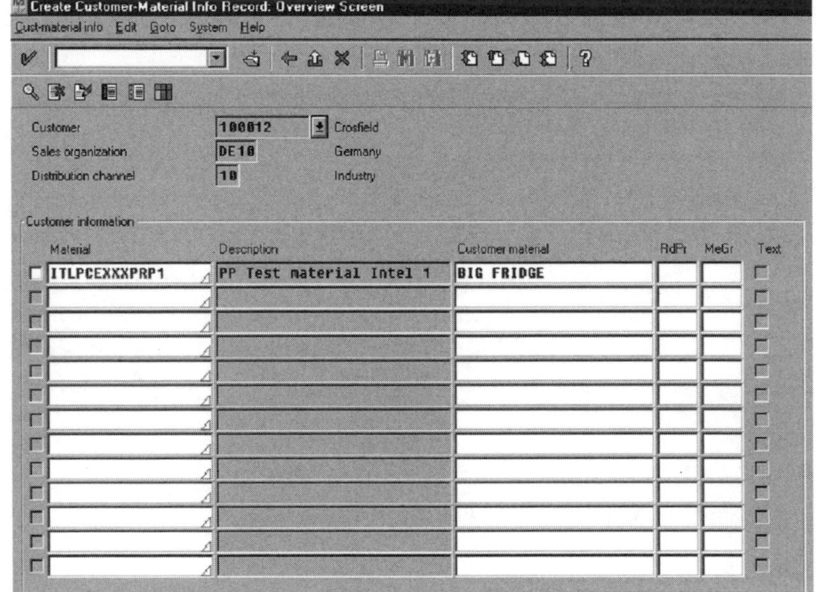

Figure 1-17 The Create Customer-Material Info Record: Overview Screen

TIP: *The system copies the plant data into the sales order from the relevant entries in the master records based upon the following priorities:*

1. *Customer material information master record*
2. *Customer master record*
3. *Material master record*

Thus, the customer material plant entry will be copied and remain in the sales order for that particular line, unless otherwise manually overridden.

Another important entry is the Delivery priority. This field is used when creating the delivery in order to determine for whom deliveries are created/grouped. It can be used as a selection parameter and can also used for rescheduling. As the rescheduling process in SAP is a complex one, it is advised that you do not alter the process or use this field for any purpose other than what it was created for. You are faced with the screen shown in Figure 1-18 when creating a customer material information record.

Figure 1-18
Creating a Customer Material Information Record

Create Customer Material Info Record : Item Screen

Cust-material info Edit Goto System Help

Material	ITLPCEXXXPRP1	PP Test material Intel 1
Sales organization	DE10	Germany
Distribution channel	10	Industry
Customer	100012	Crosfield

Customer material

Customer material	BIG FRIDGE
Customer description	
Search term	

Shipping

Plant	
Delivery Priority	1 High priority
Minimum delivery qty	10 PCE
Batch split allowed	

Partial delivery

Part.dlv./item		Underdel. tolerance	%
Max.part.deliveries	9	Overdeliv. tolerance	%
		Unlimited tolerance	

When creating a sales order, you have the option of merely entering the customer's material in the sales order, and the system will bring the linked material to this information record.

NOTE: *The customers material must be entered in the Customer Material field. Otherwise, the system will try to search for a valid material in your system or a material determination record. Material determination will be covered in Chapter 3.*

TIP: *Make sure the relevant indicator is set on the sales document type in order for the system to read this customer material information record. See Chapter 2.*

Master Data Sharing, Common Distribution Channels, and Common Divisions

You can define common distribution channels and divisions. This is possible for two areas of SAP, for all master relevant data, and for all condition relevant data.

Menu Path

The path is as follows: IMG, Sales and distribution, Master data, Define common distribution channels. You can also go to IMG, Sales and distribution, Master data, Define common divisions.

Transaction Code

The code here is [VOR1]. The IMG menu path is shown in Figure 1-19.

After creating the organizational structure and relevant master records you want to use as the masters, that is, in the distribution channels and divisions you are going to use as a reference, you can group distribution channels and divisions separately for master data (which combines customer master and material master records), group condition records, or both master data and condition records.

Let's say you have a product range that is not different for the four different distribution channels you have (the channels could be telesales, retail, industry, and wholesale.) Neither is there a difference in the customers' details when they purchase through one or the other. Thus, you will not want to create a multiple of four views of customer master and material master records. Merely create the customer master records and material master records in one of the distribution channels, such as retail. Then assign the other distribution channels you created in the organizational structure setup to this one.

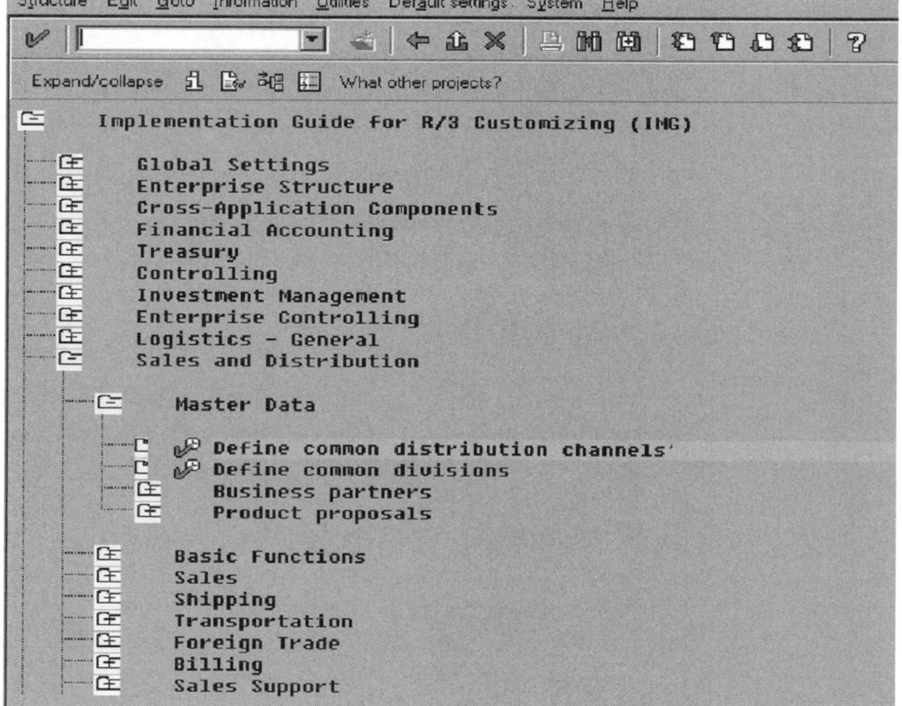

Figure 1-19 The common distribution channels and divisions menu path

TIP: *Don't forget this means you can only create or change master data in the distribution channel that is being referenced. In the scenario above, this means you can only change data for the retail distribution channel. Even if you should access a customer or material master in change mode, press F4 (possible entries), and select telesales, industry, or wholesale, you will receive a message "Sales area is not defined . . . "*

TIP: *The same is true for the sharing of conditions. If conditions are shared, you need only create a condition in the distribution channel or division you are using as the reference. Obviously, this only pertains to conditions that have the distribution channel and/or division in their key, such as a price based on sales area.*

Customer Groups

The customer group is a grouping of customers that is configured under master data in the IMG. After defining the group and allocating it a two-digit alphanumeric key, you can assign the group to the customer master record. The customer group is a wonderful field that is copied into the header and item level of the sales document.

Menu Path

The menu path is as follows: IMG, Sales and distribution, Master data, Business partners, Customers, Sales, Define customer groups.

Transaction Code

The transaction code here is [OVS9]. Simply assign a two-digit alphanumeric key to the text description that would best define your customers' grouping. Now proceed to the customer master record [VD02] sales screen and enter the appropriate customer group. If you want this field to be a mandatory field, that is, no customer master record can be created without this entry, you can define the category for the customer master records by referring to the procedure a little later.

The customer group is a field that can be used to generate statistics as well as to create condition records, such as pricing, should you wish to offer discounts per customer group for example, international, but not per customer group for example, domestic.

Sales Districts/Customer Districts

Sales districts, also referred to as *customer districts*, can be geographical areas or regions. They can also function as master data fields that are copied into the header and item data of the sales order. They too can be used for statistics purposes as well as for pricing.

Menu Path

The menu path is as follows: IMG, Sales and distribution, Master data, Business partners, Customers, Sales, Define sales districts.

Transaction Code

The code here is [OVR0]. Create a new entry that is an alphanumeric key of up to six characters. Enter a description that is easily identifiable in order to prevent confusion in the assignments of the sales districts in the customer master record.

To assign sales districts to the customer master record, proceed as follows to the Customer Sales screen, as shown in Figure 1-20.

Customer Master Record Fields

Customer master records are made up of many fields. These fields may all be necessary in some business practices and may be unnecessary in others. Some fields may be crucial in order to ensure the consistency of data throughout the system, such as in the customer's pricing procedure indicator. Others may be not as critical. In order to control the customer master field input, you may indicate which fields are necessary.

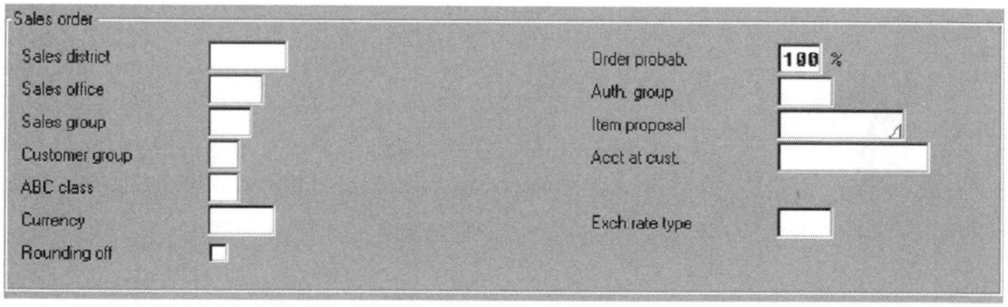

Figure 1-20 The customer sales screen

Menu Path

The path is as follows: IMG, Financial accounting, Accounts receivable and accounts payable, Customer accounts, Master records, Preparations for Creating Customer Master Records, Define account groups with screen layout (customers).

Transaction Code

The code here is [OBD2]. The customer master record is controlled via the account group. To configure your own account group, always copy an initial SAP standard account group. By always copying the standard component, the system copies all underlying assignments. The process is as follows:

1. Highlight the account group by selecting the one you wish to copy, such as 0001.
2. Select the Copy button, shown in Figure 1-21.
3. Change the account group number starting with the letter Z, such as Z001. SAP uses this prefix for all upgrades in order to ensure it does not overwrite client-specific entries.
4. After you have selected your changes, press the Save button (see Figure 1-22). Should you select the newly created account group or a client specifice account group you want to make the alterations for and press the Magnifying Glass button, shown in Figure 1-23, you will be faced with an overview screen, shown in Figure 1-24. This overview screen corresponds to the three areas of data kept in the customer master record.

TIP: *Don't forget to allocate this new account group into the list of allowed account numbers for partner determination. Otherwise, you will not be able to create any customer master records using this new account group (partner determination will be covered in Chapter 4).*

Should you select the newly created account group or a client specifice account group you want to make the alterations for and press the magnifying Glass button, shown in Figure 1-23, you will be faced with an overview screen, shown in Figure 1-24. This overview screen corresponds to the three areas of data kept in the customer master record.

For the purpose of this example, we would like to make the customer group field mandatory in order to ensure that the users who create the sold-to parties do not leave out this field, which can be used for generating statistics. Select the sales data by clicking on it and then select Edit field status. Now double-click on the sales group, Sales, as shown in Figure 1-25.

Figure 1-21
The Copy button

Figure 1-22
The Save button

Figure 1-23
The Magnifying Glass button

Figure 1-24
The field status overview screen

Figure 1-25
Selecting the Sales group for editing purposes

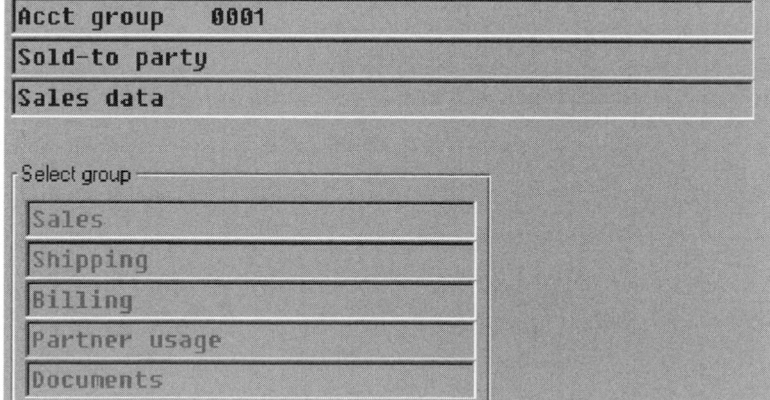

After double-clicking on Sales, you are presented with an overview screen where each field represented in the customer master record is available. Each field has four radio buttons from which to select. Only one button can be selected at one time. These buttons indicate if the associated field is

- Surpressed
- A required entry
- An optional entry
- Grayed out or displayed

To show the differences of the field values, the customizing entry for the sold-to party has been changed to look as shown in Figure 1-26.

This produces the following results on the customer master record's sales view. Notice in Figure 1-27, by comparing to Figure 1-22, how the sales district (customer district) has disappeared. The customer group now has a required entry, indicated by the ?, and the sales group is no longer changeable, but merely displayed. After completing the necessary changes to the account group of the customer master record, you may save your data.

Figure 1-26 Editing the Sales group

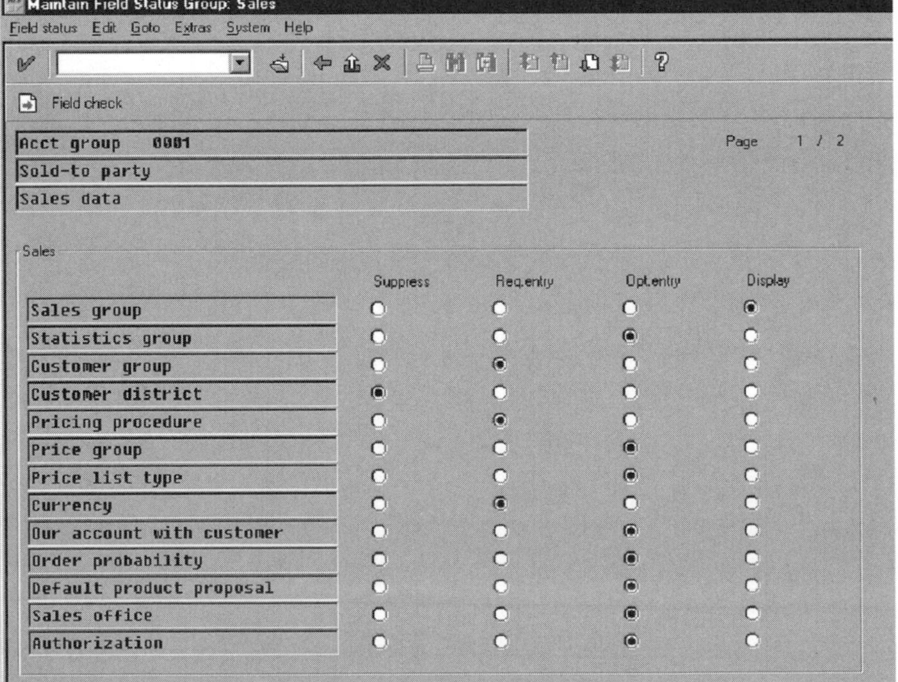

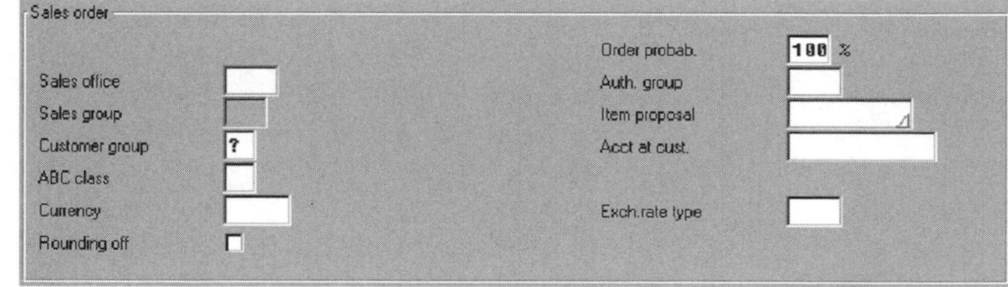

Figure 1-27
The results of the changes to the Sales group

Basic SAP R/3 Tables and Fields

Information is stored in SAP R/3 in a sequence of tables and fields. This information is then copied into the relevant documents or areas of the system when called up. The underlying structure of SAP is a fourth-generation programming language called ABAP. We are not to interested in the ABAP programming at this time, but in order to implement the SD module effectively, it is a necessity to know and understand the basics of how the information is stored and when it is accessed. From time to time, we will refer to a few ABAP basics and their impact on the SD module.

Menu Path

The path is as follows: Tools, ABAP workbench, Select dictionary.

Transaction code

The code here is [SE11]. Because this book is not intended to cover ABAP, we will not be discussing areas that are not pertinent. However, take note of the [S001] ABAP Workbench screen, as shown in Figure 1-28, as we will be referring to it often.

Once you are in the [SE11] view, you are presented with the display shown in Figure 1-29. In it you can enter the table you want to see. For our example, we will use the table VBAK. This view is also accessible in display mode using the transaction SE12.

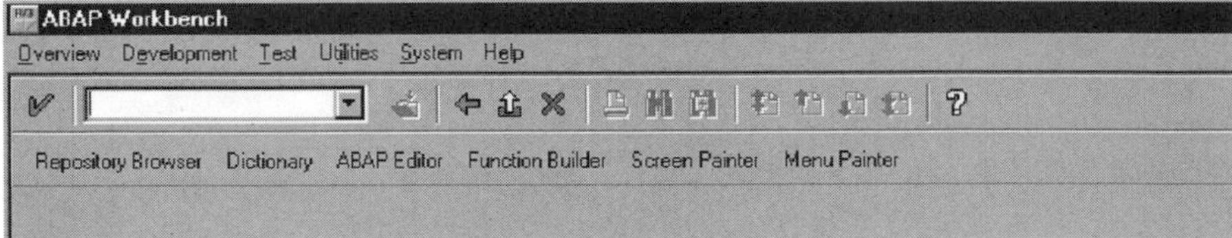

Figure 1-28 The [S001] ABAP Workbench screen

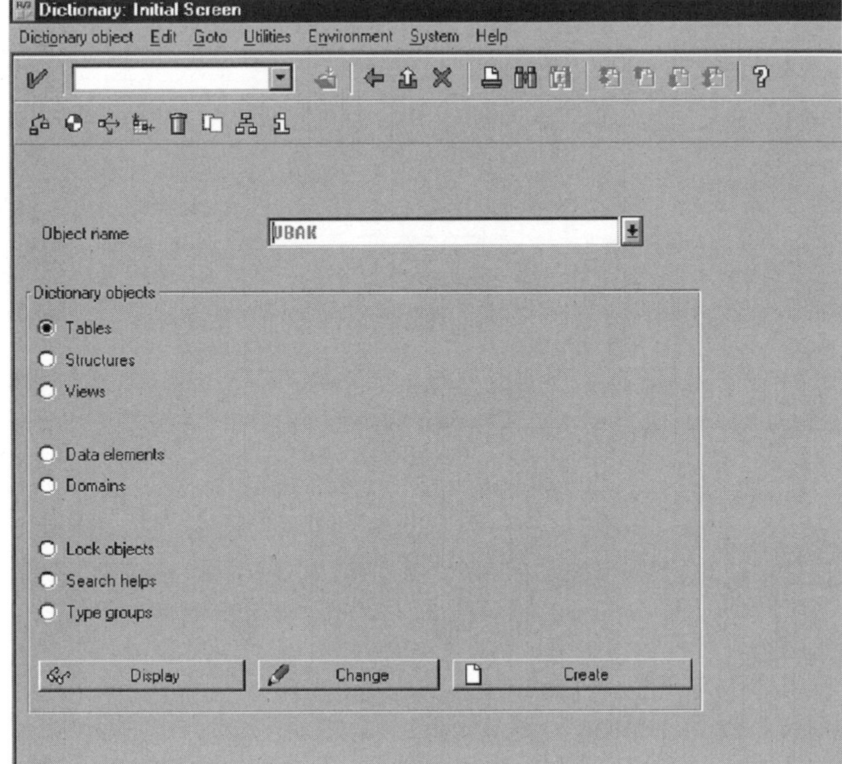

Figure 1-29 The Dictionary: Initial screen

On the left side of Figure 1-30, you will find the respective fields that exist in the table you selected. A field usually has a five-digit name as well as a description that the system uses in the user interface. This description is the data element you see on the right-hand side. The field has characteristics such as a data type and length.

The following tables are often referred to in the SD module.

VBAK Order header

VBAP Order item

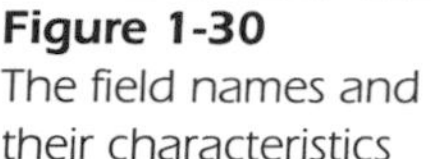

Figure 1-30
The field names and their characteristics

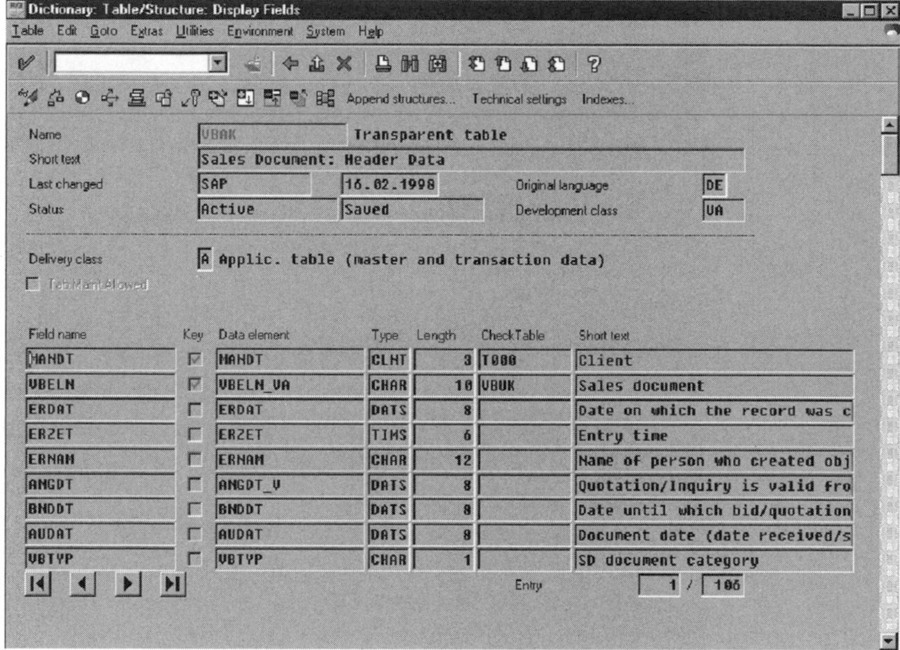

VBEP Order schedule line
LIKP Delivery header
LIPS Delivery item
VBRK Billing header
VBRP Billing item
VBPA Partners
VBUK Status header
VBUP Status items
VBKD Business data
VBFA Document flow

The use of tables is used further in Chapter 5 on data elements. Should you wish to see the entries of the table, go to Utilities-table contents or to [SE16]. In [SE16], enter the table name if you used transaction [SE16]. Otherwise, you will be prompted with the data of the table you are accessing from the data dictionary.

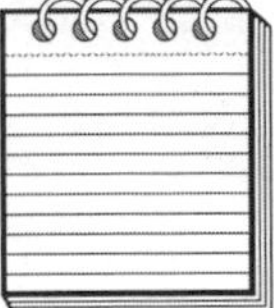

NOTE: *In Settings, User parameters, as shown in Figure 1-31, you can select the field name or field text. The field text will offer you the data element as the field description, which is easily understandable, but it may not offer you the reliability you are seeking. (It is easy to mistakenly confuse two fields using text displays.) On the other hand, the field name is the actual field SAP uses and calls up in ABAP programs. Thus, it may be a reliable source to access information.*

Once you have selected the table you wish to read, you may restrict the tables of certain fields. Remember to restrict your entries by setting a maximum number of hits (in SAP Version 3 onwards) or a restrictive search, for example, from Sales Organization 1000 to 2000. Otherwise, you may end up reading every entry in the data base, which can cause slow system performance.

Many fields are important to the SD module, and we will cover them and their associated tables throughout this book. It is worthwhile to access these table structures and familiarize yourself with them as soon as possible. A few crucial fields are

KUNNR Sold-to party

VBELN Document number

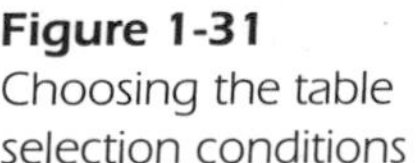

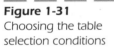

Figure 1-31 Choosing the table selection conditions

NETWR	Net value
MATNR	Material number
ERDAT	Date
AUART	Document type

If you do not have the required data (field names) in the selection screen from [SE16], go to Settings, Fields for selection. Then select your fields as shown in Figure 1-32.

Naturally, not all fields are in all tables, as SAP stores information at different levels. Organizational data and header master data are read from header master tables and populated into the documents. A selection of master data tables is as follows:

Here are the customer master tables:

- KNA1 Customer master header data
- KNB1 Accounting views
- KNVV Sales views

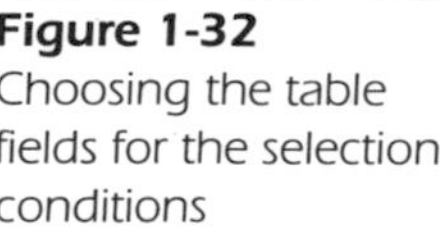

Figure 1-32
Choosing the table fields for the selection conditions

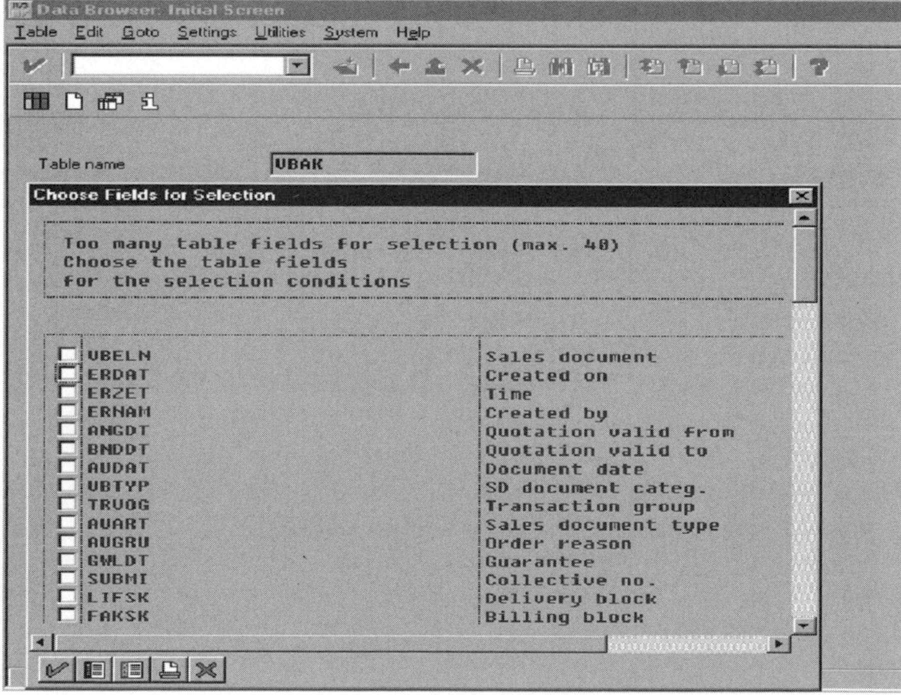

Material master is divided into multiple tiers:

- MARA Highest level of data
- MBEW Data referring to accounting
- MVKE Data referring to sales
- MARC Data referring to the plant level
- MARD Data storage location

The packaging tables are as follows:

- VEKP Shipping units header
- VEPO Shipping units item

Finally, here are two tables that we will refer to often in Chapter 5:

- VBUK Document header status
- VBUP Document item status

TIP: *To discover the field and table name of a specific field, place your cursor on the desired field and press F1, Help, followed by F9, Technical Information as seen previously in Figure 1-8.*

CHAPTER 2

Sales Documents

Sales documents are the core components of SAP's selling process and *sales and distribution* (SD) Module. A sales document defines how the data is to function, how it is to be displayed, the pricing that happens during the output, and so on. It is the heartbeat of the sales environment.

Each sales document is divided into three levels:

- **Header-level data (table VBAK)** is responsible for master data, such as customer material master as well as sales area and organization data. In the *implementation guide* (IMG), the Document Type settings control how this sales document functions. This is controlled by a sales document type, such as TA (OR-English).
- The **item-level data (table VBAP)** is responsible for material item data, such as the order quantity and material number. This is controlled by the sales item category, such as TAN.
- The **schedule line data (table VBEP)** is responsible for delivery dates and delivery quantities. This is controlled by the schedule line category, such as CP.

Each level has its own controlling data, such as delivery blocks, and each will be discussed separately in this chapter.

When you do an [SE16] for either of these tables, the system will give you a list of the table entries per document number or range of numbers.

To configure a sales document type, we will start with product proposals.

Item Proposals (Product Proposal)

Item proposals are used when certain materials are ordered. An item proposal is a list of materials and order quantities that can be copied into the sales order. Items can also be selected from a list and copied into a sales order.

Menu Path

The path is as follows: Logistics, Sales and distribution, Master data, Products, Item proposal, Create.

Transaction Code

The transaction codes here are [VA51] to create and [VOV8] to configure. Item proposals are sales area-specific. They can be referenced when creating the sales order. By entering the item proposal on the Sales View screen of the customer master record. Each time a sales order is created, the system automatically promotes the item proposal to be selected. This can greatly speed up order entry times by the sales people.

When entering materials in an item proposal, the entry of a *bill of materials* (BOM), a single item that is made up of one or more components, will not explode as usual as in the sales order. Instead, you should only enter the header material of the BOM. This way, the system will copy it into the sales order and explode it once it is in the order. For example, if we sold a computer, the BOM would include a monitor, keyboard, and hard drive.

This document type introduces you to the configuration of the system. To configure this sales document, proceed as follows, as shown in Figure 2-1: IMG, Sales and distribution, Master data, Item proposal (product proposal in version 3).

Item proposal is the same as product proposal and often SAP uses the two terms interchangeably. You will not find a document type called Item

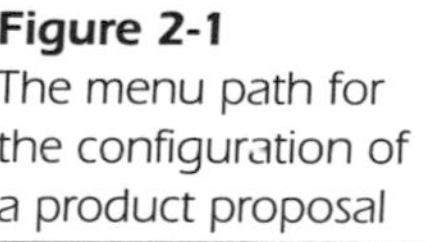

Figure 2-1
The menu path for the configuration of a product proposal

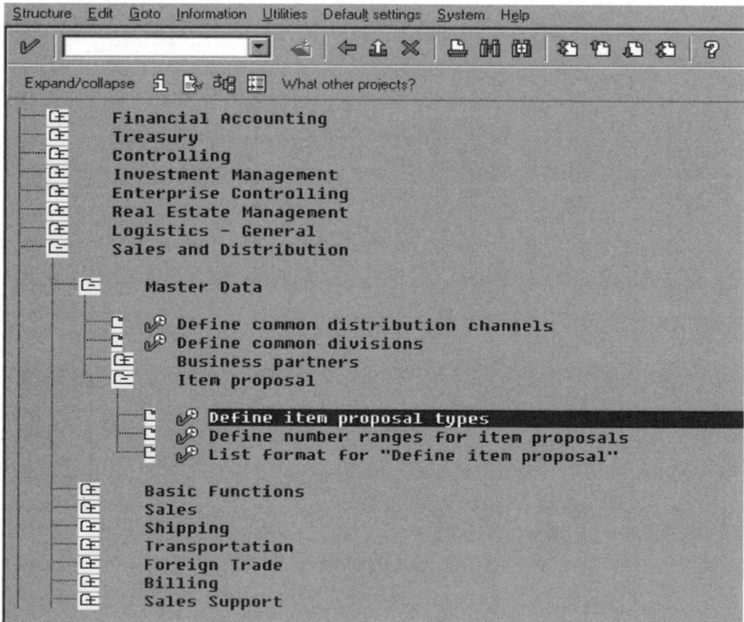

proposal; however, you will find the document type product proposal. Don't worry about confusing the two.

The list of document types you have shows all the relevant sales document types in the system. We will look at them in detail later. To start your introduction to sales documents, we will go through the configuration settings in this product proposal first. Select document type MS—Product proposal. You are then presented with the screen shown in Figure 2-2.

This screen tells us the following. Note for the purpose of this example we will only refer to the filled entries.

- The control data is "D." The document category controls how the document behaves in the system; it is predetermined in SAP and may not be added to.
- The document is not blocked.
- It has an internal and external number range key, which we will refer to later.
- The item number increment on the sales order is the sequence in which items in the order are numbered, which is 10.

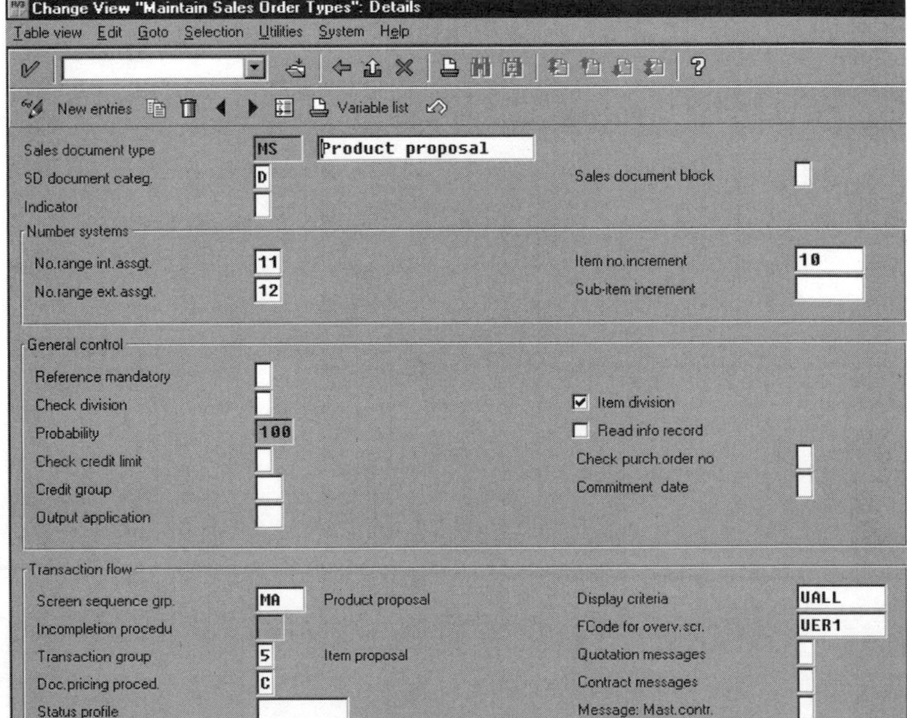

Figure 2-2
Starting with the configuration settings in this product proposal

- Document probability is at 100%. (It is best to leave this field at 100% for sales documents unless you wish to plan your material requirements based upon this setting and the respective setting in the customer master record. It is not possible to change the value of this field for product proposals, as a product proposal is merely a planning tool and is not valid for deliveries or invoicing.)
- The Item division field controls whether the system proposes the items division from the material master record or from the header data of the sales documents entries. Flagged indicates it is looking at the materials division.
- Screen sequence, display criteria, and function code for overview screens are all values that can be manipulated. They control how the interface is represented in the sales document. That is, should you want the system to propose a different screen for quotations as for orders, you can change these entries or specialist screen overviews can be created.
- Transaction group controls the data to be updated in the respective tables for each transaction of the respective document type.
- The Document pricing procedure is a indicator that determines what pricing procedure the system will use in this sales order. For the purpose of product proposals, it is indicating "free." Refer to pricing procedures in Chapter 4, "Basic Functions," for further data.

Page down and you will have the following screen display (see Figure 2-3).

Of interest is the Shipping section, which displays no delivery type. This means this document type cannot create a delivery. Also of interest is the Billing section, which shows no order-related billing type and no entry for delivery-related billing either. This means this document type is not billed or invoiced in any way.

Paging down to the bottom of the document type will give you the following display, as shown in Figure 2-4. We will go over these settings in Figure 2-4 once they are used a little later.

Now the document type is created we need to follow these steps:

- Go to [VA51] and create the proposal.
- Go to [VD02] and change the customer master record to include the proposal you created in the sales view. Then enter the proposal number.
- Go to [VA01] and create your sales order. Select Edit, Propose items.

You can select Propose default, with or without a quantity, and offer a selection list.

After completing the section, you will have completed the settings relevant to creating and utilizing a product proposal document type.

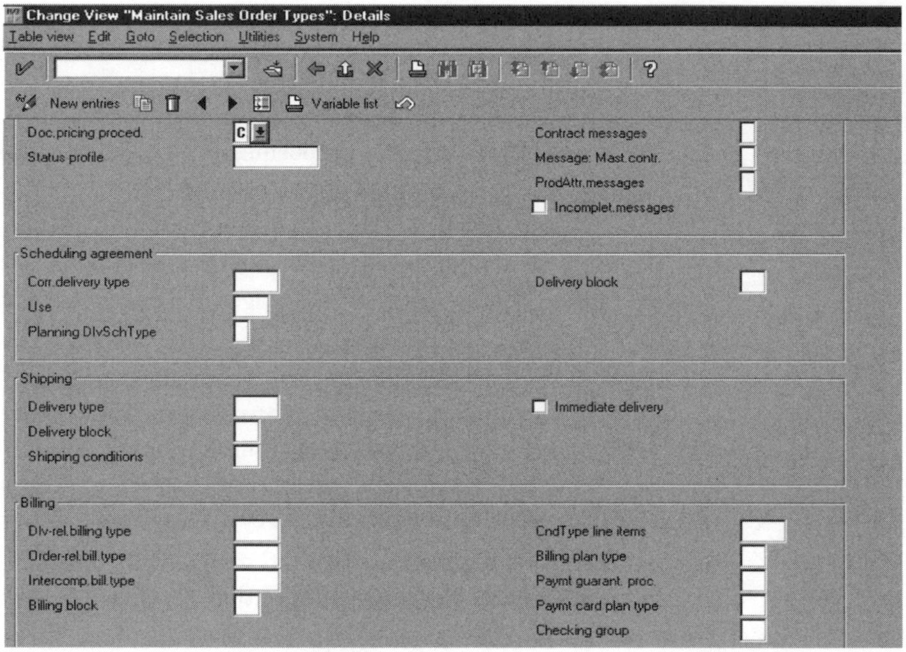

Figure 2-3 Further settings in the Change View "Maintain Sales Order Types": Details screen

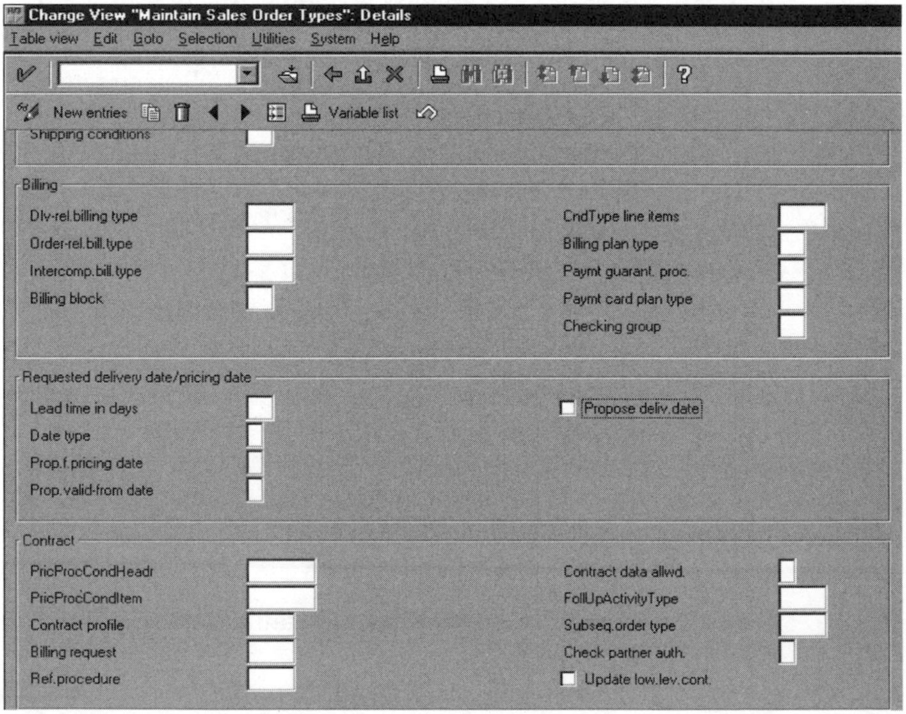

Figure 2-4 The final categories in the the Change View "Maintain Sales Order Types": Details screen

Number Ranges

Number ranges are used in all modules throughout SAP. They define the valid range of numbers for an object, whether it is a customer master record (for which you assign the number range to the customers account group) or whether it is for an sales document type. The procedure is the same.

Menu Path

Number ranges are assigned throughout the system; however, for the purposes of this example we will look at assigning number ranges to sales document types. Here is the path to follow: IMG, Sales and distribution, Master data, Item proposal, Define number ranges for item proposals.

Transaction Code

The code here is [OVZA] or [VN01], and so on. Two forms of number ranges exist:

Internal. The system automatically proposes the number range and the next available number to be used.

External. The system enables the user to specify the number in the number range he or she wishes to use.

In the overview screen, as seen in Figure 2-5 below, select the change intervals button, with the pencil icon, as shown in Figure 2-6.

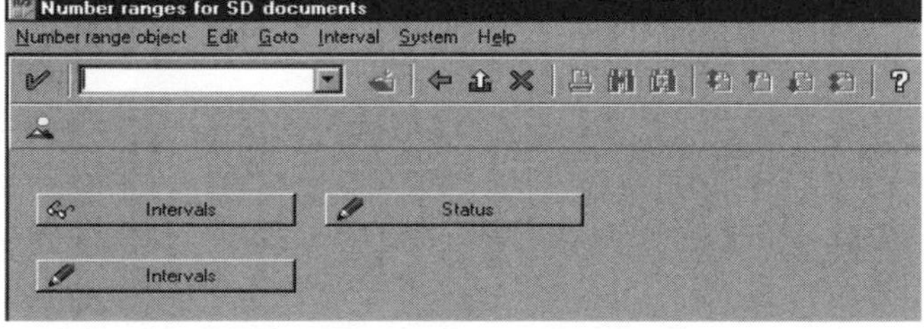

Figure 2-5 Changing the intervals in the Number ranges for SD documents screen

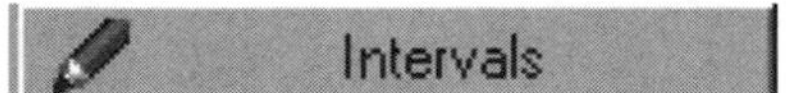

Figure 2-6 The change intervals button

You are then presented with the number range interval key. Remember that the product proposal used item number range 11 for internal and 12 for external. You can see the relevant sequence here. To create a new number range, first find the exact requirements of the business; they may want the number range to be shared by numerous document types. Thus, it must have a large interval. Find a interval that is not yet used and select the button shown in Figure 2-7.

Now enter your alpha numeric key (for example, 70) followed by the from and to numbers for the range. Also indicate if the number range is internal or external. In most document types, you may only want to use an internal number assignment.

After creating your number range, you may assign it by accessing the object you are creating it for, such as the document type MS.

TIP: *Should you be doing any data conversion of old documents such as sales documents into new SAP R/3 documents, ensure that your external number range assignment interval matches the external document number range for which you are doing the data conversion.*

Number ranges are manually transported through clients. A client is the environment you are operating in; you could be in the development environment, the quality or production environment, or client.

When transporting number ranges, the intervals you have in the client that you are exporting to will be deleted first. Then the number range and assigned status will be created in the new client. Also note that the number range assignments to document types or other objects are not transported with this manual transport.

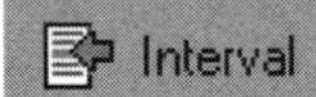

Figure 2-7
The insert interval button

Basic Sales Order Cycles

A sales order is a contractual agreement between a sales organization and a customer (sold-to party) for the supply of services or products over a specific period of time and in certain quantities. A sales order copies all relevant information and master data from the customer master record and the material master record for a specific sales area. It can be created with a reference to a preceding document, such as a quotation. Should a document refer to a preceding document, the initial data is copied into the new document; thus, for example, the information of a quotation is copied from the quotation into the sales order. This data is then transferred into the delivery document type, which uses the delivery or shipping information to create a delivery note. Following the goods issue, the information is passed on to billing, if billing is necessary. (Integration with other modules can happen throughout the process. An interface with warehouse management, for example, could happen during the delivery process.) The basic sales order process would look like Figure 2-8.

As we saw from product proposals, each document (quotation, order, delivery, or invoice) is represented by a key document type. For example, a standard delivery is LF and a standard invoice is F2.

Sales document types can also be translated into other languages; thus, a sales order may be TA (German) or it may be OR (English). SAP has a language translation table where you can determine what a user should enter. For example, if a user is logged on in English, the system will propose OR automatically. Should the user enter OR, the system knows to use document

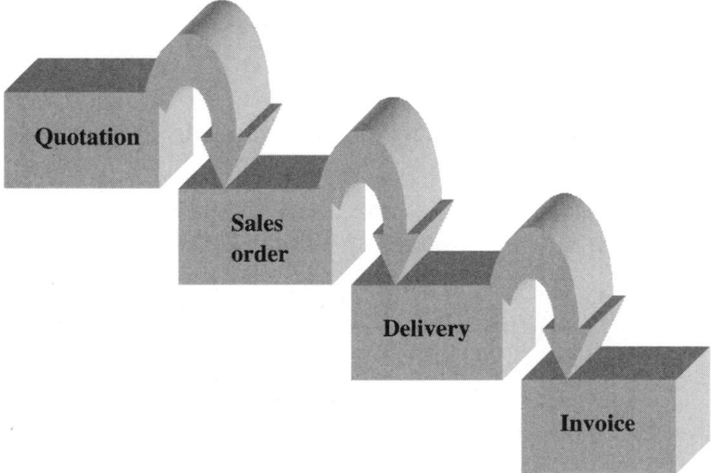

Figure 2-8 The basic sales order process

type OR and not TA. This is done by going to IMG, Sales and distribution, Sales, Sales documents, Sales document header, Convert language for each sales document type.

We will use the unconverted German version of sales document types unless otherwise specified. Thus, the previous document flow would look like the following representation of document types:

AG , TA , LF , F2

We will map out the sales document flows valid for each section during the description of the section.

Sales Document Types—Header Level

The header of the sales document type defines the core header process of the sales order. These include the pricing procedure, the delivery types, and the billing types assigned to the sales document. We will focus on the configuration of the standard basic sales order process, which is TA, LF, F2 for now.

Menu Path

The path is as follows: IMG, Sales and distribution, Sales, Sales documents, Sales document header, Define sales document types.

Transaction Code

The transaction code here is [VOV8]. When dealing with the configuration of sales document types, generally one of two functions is performed. One either creates a new document type or wishes to alter an existing document type. It is recommended you follow a couple of basic guidelines:

- When creating a new document type, one should always reference the document type that suits the closest match to the one you are aiming to create. For example, should you need a new sales order document type, you should copy document type TA. Once you have copied the document type, the system copies all assigned data, such as item category and schedule line category determination and copying rules.

- When wishing to alter an existing document type that is not created by you or your business, (in other words, it is still SAP standard), it is better for you to copy the document type and assign it a new name as if it were a new sales document type you were creating. Let's say you want to change the pricing procedure determination indicator for document type TA. It would be better to copy TA and then make the changes.

We will now look at the configuration settings necessary for a sales order document type. When copying or creating a new document type, one must be sure the name range selected begins with the letter Z. SAP enables the use of objects beginning with the letter Z, as it is an indicator in release upgrades not to overwrite any created data. To copy a sales document type, select the document you wish to copy and press the button in Figure 2-9.

The sales document type configuration settings screen, as shown in Figure 2-10, indicates the following details.

- The document type is OR; its description is "Standard order." If copied, change the name to ZZOR or something similar.
- The document category is C, meaning a sales order document type, rather than a quote, or item proposal, etc.
- The sales document is not blocked for processing.

Figure 2-11 continues with the document type configuration settings:

- The internal number range interval is 01.
- The external number range interval is 02.

Figure 2-9
The copy button

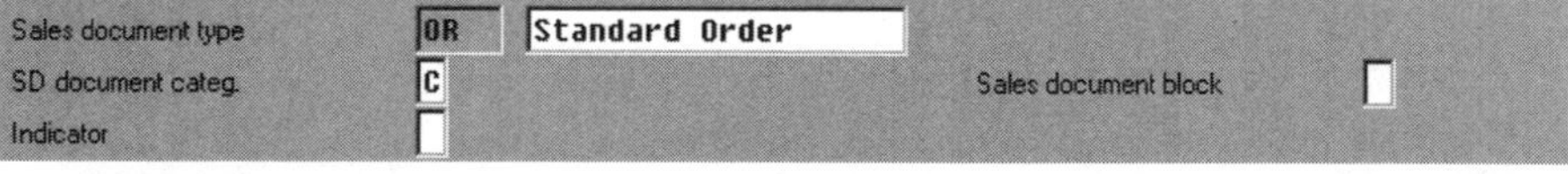

Figure 2-10
Sales document type configuration settings

Number systems
No.range int.assgt. 01
No.range ext.assgt. 02
Item no.increment 10
Sub-item increment

Figure 2-11
Saes document type—Number assignments

- The items in the sales order increase in increments of 10; the subitems increase in intervals of 1 (as the field is blank).

Figure 2-12 continues with the general control of the sales document, which controls the following:

- The document does not have a mandatory reference before an order can be created, such as "reference to a quotation is mandatory."
- The division of the material or item is copied into the sales order.
- There is no check to see if this division is equal to the header division.
- The probability of this order being completed and fulfilled is 100 percent.
- The system must read the customer material info record, if one exists.
- The credit limit check is set at D, which means automatic processing using credit group 01, being the group assigned to sales orders. Credit management will be covered in Chapter 4.
- The system must not check the purchase order number.
- The output application is assigned for sales. Output determination will also be covered in Chapter 4.
- The commitment date is not checked. The commitment date will be recalculated if changes are made to the material, quantity, requested delivery date, or delivery time. The availability check will be covered later in this chapter.

Figure 2-13 displays the data relevant to the transaction flow of the sales document:

- The screen sequence group controls the way data is displayed, and in what sequence.
- Whilst the display criteria determines what items in the sales order are displayed, example all items or only header items.

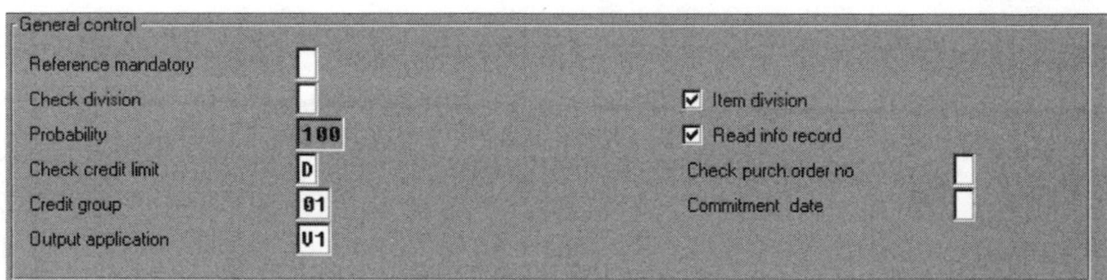

Figure 2-12 Sales document type—General control

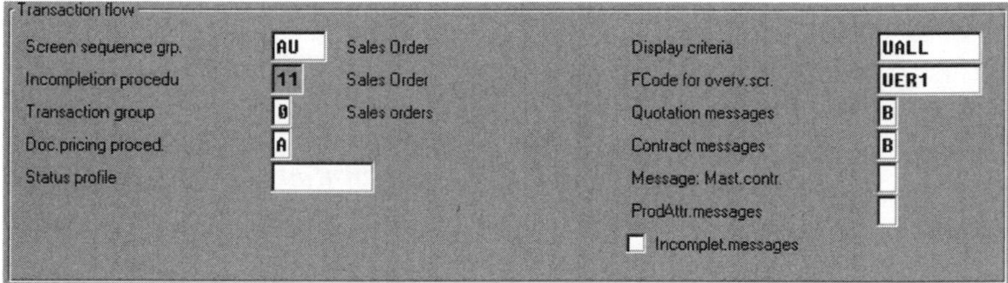

Figure 2-13 The data relevant to the transaction flow of the sales document

- The incompletion procedure at sales document header is 11. See incompletion procedures Chapter 4.
- The function code for overview screens is the function code which determines what data and layout you see in the sales order.
- The transaction group determines what indices must be updated with reference to this sales order.
- Quotation messages and contract messages are set with a indicator B, as quotations and contracts and master contracts are the three preceding key document types, you may want the system to give you a warning if you are creating a order whilst for example open quotations still exist. This setting "B" checks to see if the item is available on any other quotations or contracts for this sold to party.
- The document pricing procedure is "A" this indicator plus the indicator on the customer master and the relevant sales area determine which pricing procedure to use. See Chapter 4 pricing.
- Status profile is used to assign a status profile to the particular document type it is also assigned at item category level.
- Message master contract check to determine if any master contracts exist whilst you are creating a document type "contract."
- Product attribute messages—the system can error or warn to check manually entered products for the attributes to see if the ship to party accepts them. In the cases automatic material entry such as, material determination this check is ignored.
- With the incomplete messages indicator as blank—the system will inform you at the time of saving that the document is incomplete however you will still be able to save the document.

The scheduling agreement area, as shown Figure 2-14, is used by scheduling agreement document types as follows:

- The correction delivery type is used for scheduling agreements.

- The usage field is used to indicate what the customer uses the material for on the sales order. This entry will be copied into all items or may be placed into items individually in the sales order.
- The planning schedule is used for scheduling agreements in case the system should use *just-in-time* (JIT) processing or forward the demands on to *material requirements planning* (MRP).
- If a delivery block must be automatically set for scheduling agreements, a blank entry indicates no delivery block.

By referring to the shipping screen in Figure 2-15, we can see the following data:

- The standard shipping screen indicates that this document type is relevant for delivery, and the delivery type to be used is LF.
- No automatic delivery block is entered in the sales order.
- The shipping conditions are proposed by the customer master record. Should an entry have existed in this field, this entry would have taken precedence and overwritten those found on the customer master record. The shipping condition value is used to determine the shipping point. See Chapter 3, "Deliveries and Invoicing," for more information on shipping point determination.
- The immediate delivery indicator is not set. If this flag is set it creates a delivery in an immediate update after saving the sales order. Thus, if set for each sales order you create, the delivery is created and a delivery number is allocated as well. The delivery is not completed and the picking, packing (if relevant), and goods issue must still be carried out.

Figure 2-14 The sales document type scheduling agreement area

Figure 2-15 The shipping screen

Figure 2-16 is the billing section of the sales document type:

- This document is relevant for invoicing, and for delivery-related invoicing, the system uses invoice document type F2.
- If an order-related invoice is possible, the system will use document type F2 as well. It is not recommended, however, to use both order-related and delivery-related invoicing for the same sales order document type, as this may cause confusion with the people using the system later.
- The Intercompany billing document type is IV.
- There is no automatic posting of a billing block on the sales order, but it may be necessary to have a billing block for credit notes, which we will look at later.
- The Condition Type for line items, for example, EK02, must be equal to the one allocated on your pricing procedure and must have the indicator on the condition type of Q (see the pricing information in Chapter 4). This condition is used to determine the cost of the line item.
- The Billing plan type is either *periodic billing*, in which the entire value is billed in full on each billing plan date, or *milestone billing*, in which the total value to be billed is distributed between the individual billing plan dates (the value billed on each date can be a fixed amount or a percentage).
- The Payment guarantee procedure indicator on the customer master record indicates to the system which form of guarantee procedure to use for this sales document. These are risk management settings. For more information, see the section on credit management in Chapter 4.
- The Payment card plan type is an essential setting, should you want your system to accept payment cards in the sales order process.
- The Checking group is used to determine how the system carries out the checking of payment card data.

Figure 2-16
The billing section of the sales document type

Billing

Dlv-rel.billing type	F2	Invoice	CndType line items	EK02
Order-rel.bill.type	F2	Invoice	Billing plan type	
Intercomp.bill.type	IV	Intercompany billing	Paymt guarant. proc.	01
Billing block			Paymt card plan type	03
			Checking group	01

In Figure 2-17, you can see the settings that affect the picking, pricing, and delivery dates:

- The Lead time in days is the proposal of what the requested delivery date in the sales order should be. It is recommended that this be left as a zero in most instances.
- The indicator, Propose delivery date, is set to propose the current date as the delivery date. You should choose one of the two settings.
- The Date type enables the user to set the format of the delivery schedule line date for internal system use. It may be left empty.
- The Proposal for pricing date enables you to specify the valid from date for the pricing of the reference document, the requested delivery date, or the current date.
- The Propose valid from date enables you to determine when the valid from date for pricing should be. This is used for example in quotations.

This section, displayed in Figure 2-18, refers to contract details:

- Pricing procedure conditions at the header level (`PricProCondHeadr`) refers to contract conditions. (Contracts will be covered later in this chapter.)
- Pricing procedure conditions at item level (`PricProcCondItem`) refers to contract conditions.
- Contract profile is a default setting that will propose defaults for the contract you are creating, such as validity dates. (Contract profiles will be covered later in this chapter.)
- Billing request is associated with contracts.
- Reference procedure is used for master contracts to determine which data is to be copied or proposed for lower level contracts. The referencing procedures are configured with master contracts later in this chapter.

Figure 2-17 The requested delivery date/pricing date settings

Requested delivery date/pricing date

Lead time in days: 7
Date type:
Prop.f.pricing date:
Prop.valid-from date:
☑ Propose deliv.date

Figure 2-18
Contract settings

Contract
PricProcCondHeadr
PricProcCondItem
Contract profile
Billing request L2
Ref.procedure
Contract data allwd.
FollUpActivityType
Subseq.order type
Check partner auth.
Update low.lev.cont.

- The Contract data allowed field controls what data is to be copied over contract item data from header contract data. Don't forget, if you do not want contract data for this sales document type, leave the field blank.
- The Follow-up activity type is used to initiate and assist in the speedy creation of a sales activity worklist, such as a follow-up phone call or sales letter.
- A subsequent order type is assigned here, should you define a follow-up action for the contract. For example, if you wish your contract to create a quotation one week before the contract end date, you would specify what type of quotation document type (such as AG) that would be.
- The Check partner authority field is used by the system to check the partner type creating a release order against the contract. Only those partners with the partner function AG (sold-to party) or AA (sold-to party for release orders) or higher level partners in a hierarchy are allowed to create release orders.
- The Update lower level contracts field is used by the system to update lower level contracts if you are changing the master contract. These changes are then passed down to the lower level contracts via workflow. Should this field not be set, the system will only update the lower level contract when it is reprocessed.

The Assignment of Sales Areas to Sales Documents

There may be a need to assign sales documents to specific sales areas. For example, a different sales document is used for all sales orders from a specific sales organization.

Menu Path

The path here is IMG, Sales and distribution, Sales, Sales documents, Sales document header, Assign sales area to sales document types.

Transaction Code

The code here is [OVAZ]. You may assign reference sales organizations as well as reference distribution channels and divisions. Do not confuse this referencing with the assignment of common distribution channels and common divisions. The referencing done here is only used by the system to determine which sales documents are permitted for which sales areas. If all sales document types can be used by all sales areas, leave the assignment fields blank.

Create Order Reasons for Sales Documents

You can create the reasons as to why a customer is purchasing or using a sales document. This is helpful in determining the trigger that creates the sales order. The order reason can be a "sales call" or a "good price," while processing returns can be due to "poor quality" or "material ruined."

Menu Path

The path here is IMG, Sales and distribution, Sales, Sales documents, Sales document header, Define order reasons.

Transaction Code

The code here is [OVAU]. You create the order reasons for the business, the standard sales order cycle, the returns cycle, and any other sales process you may need. The order reason can be used for the *logistics information system* (LIS); thus, you can report on or use this field in a matrix for sales information.

TIP: *Should the order reason be a crucial field for your reporting, you can assign it to an incompletion log for the particular sales order. That way, no sales order can be saved or further processed until the order reason has been filled. Incompletion logs will be covered further in Chapter 4.*

Item Categories—Sales Document Types

The item category is one of the most important key fields in the SAP sales cycle. It controls the sales document and affects the schedule line category. The item category of the sales order affects the delivery and finally impacts the billing process as well. Keeping to our basic sales flow, we will look at the integration of the item category into the following document flow for now:

TA, LF, F2.

Menu Path

The menu path is as follows: IMG, Sales and distribution, Sales, Sales documents, Sales document item, Define item categories.

Unlike the sales document type that is entered manually on the sales order, the item category is automatically determined by the system. The system uses the key field of the material master record, the "Item category group," as the main indication of how the system will determine the item category in the sales order. The system uses this field in combination with the sales document type, such as a TA sales order. It is these two indicators plus an indicator depicting the usage of the item category (for example, is this item a product selection?) and an indicator that ascertains if another higher level item exists that determine the item category in the sales order document. This is best seen in Figure 2-19.

This process is found in *item category determination*, which is done after you have created your item categories. To assign the item categories, follow the IMG to Sales and distribution, Sales, Sales documents, Sales document item, Assign item categories [VOV4]. Figure 2-20 is a view of this customizing screen.

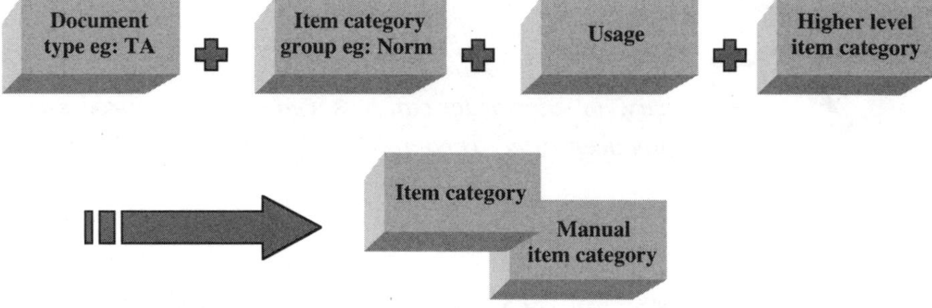

Figure 2-19 Determining the item category in the sales order document

Change View "Item Category Assignment": Overview

Table view Edit Goto Selection Utilities System Help

New entries Variable list

SaTy	ItCGr	Use	HLevItCa	DfItC	MItCa	MItCa	MItCa
OR	NORM			TAN			
OR	NORM		TAE	TAE			
OR	NORM		TAG	TAN			
OR	NORM		TAM	TAN			
OR	NORM		TAN	TANN			

Figure 2-20 Customizing the item categories

Back in IMG, go to Sales and distribution, Sales, Sales documents, Sales document item, Define item categories. We define the following areas in the item category. In this example, we will use the standard item category TAN, as shown in Figure 2-21 through Figure 2-25.

Again copy and change the name, as required, beginning with the letter Z, such as ZTAN. Assign a description.

The business data of the item category, as seen in Figure 2-22, controls the following:

- The Item type is the controlling indicator to the system for standard items; leave the field blank.
- The Completion rule is used to determine when the item is deemed to be complete. For standard processing, this too can be left blank. However, should you wish to utilize these rules, you must ensure you have set the "Update document flow" indicator in copy control (copy control will be covered later).
- The Special stock indicator should be set for items that are processed as special stock. For example, should you use consignment stock at your customer's site, this indicator should read W. For standard processing, it may be left as blank.

Figure 2-21 Defining the item category TAN

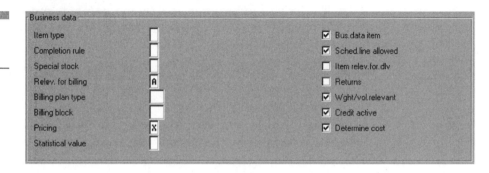

Figure 2-22 The Business Data settings

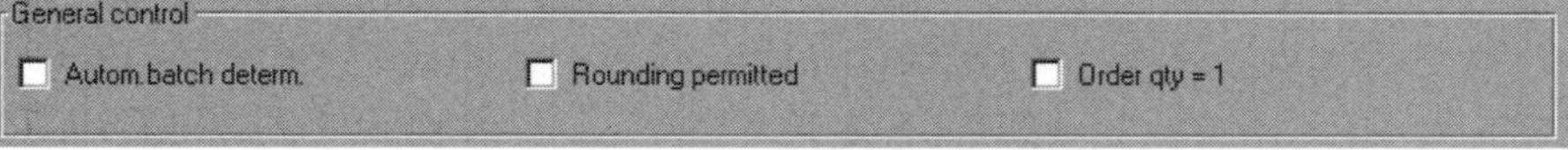

Figure 2-23 The General control area

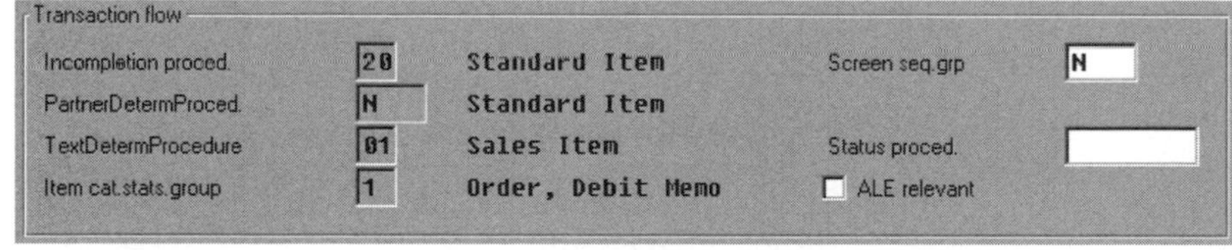

Figure 2-24 The Transaction flow settings

Figure 2-25 The settings for Bill of material/configuration

- The Relevant for billing category works in conjunction with your billing type categories to determine if this item is relevant for delivery-related or order-related billing. Thus, a setting of A here and a setting for delivery-related billing of F2 on the sales document type would indicate from the sales order that this item is relevant for a delivery and then an invoice.

- The Billing plan type defines if the item does milestone or periodic billing (see Chapter 4 for more on pricing).
- The Billing block indicator is used to block each item of this category for billing.
- The Pricing indicator is used by the system to propose if this item category is relevant for pricing. It would not make sense to indicate a text item for pricing.
- Use the Statistical value flag if you want the system to calculate the total values of all items at the header level or, on the other hand, not to include the value of the item.
- The Business data item field is used if the item's business data should be different from the business data at the header level. Business data is a group of sales details, shipping details, and billing details found at both the item and header level.
- Schedule line allowed is used to determine if this sales item category is permitted a schedule line. This is one of the most important item settings, as it determines if the item is relevant for delivering or not. Schedule line categories will be covered later on in this chapter.
- Item relevant for delivery causes the system to copy the item from the sales order into the delivery note. This, however, should not be set for standard items, as a standard item would have a schedule line and thus be able to be determined as relevant to a delivery. This setting should be used to copy such items as text items.
- Should the item be a returns item category, such as REN, then the returns flag should be set.
- Weight volume relevant is an indicator that tells the system if weight and volume are relevant and if the system should calculate these fields for these characteristics.
- Credit active indicates that this item is relevant for credit record updating and credit statistics. (Credit management will be covered in Chapter 4.)
- Determine cost is a indicator that tells the system to use the condition type VPRS on the pricing procedure to indicate the cost price of the item.

The General control area in Figure 2-23 affects the following:

- Automatic batch determination enables the system to carry out batch determination for this item at the time of the sales order. Batch determination is the process whereby one allocates a material batch to a item. This can happen at the time of the order, at the time of the delivery, or even in the warehouse management module.
- Rounding permitted is used to set the allowance for rounding this particular item. Rounding is set in the customer material information record or the material master record and enables the system to round the order quantity up or down to make a specific package size. For example, a material's base unit of measure is one unit, but the sales order must create orders in layers, where one layer is equivalent to five units. Thus, the system will round the order quantity from, say, two units up to five units in the sales order.
- Order quantity is equal to one. This is self-explanatory. Set this indicator if you want your sales item to be limited to a quantity of one per line item.

The Transaction flow data in Figure 2-24 controls the following:

- The Incompletion procedure at the line-item level, which is explained in the incompletion procedures in Chapter 4.
- The Partner and Text Determination Procedures, which are described in Chapter 4.
- The Item category statistics group, which is used by the logistics information system to indicate which item categories are relevant for statistical updating. This is used in sales reporting. You can assign statistics groups to each of the following: item category, sales document type, customer material, shipment type, and transportation service agent. When you generate statistics in the LIS, the system uses the combination of specified statistics groups to determine the appropriate update sequence. This update sequence in turn determines for which fields the statistics are generated.
- The Screen sequence group is used to control which screens you see when displaying a line item.
- The Status procedure is a key that indicates a status profile, as discussed later in this chapter. A status profile may be assigned at header and item levels.
- The ALE relevant is an indicator for *Application Link Enabling*.

Figure 2-25 shows the settings for a BOM or a configured item. It is best to leave this section until we cover BOMs later on in this chapter.

Figure 2-26 is relevant for value contracts:

- The Value contract material may have a material number entered here. Should the user not enter a material at the line item level for a value contract, the system can then copy this material into the value contract item. This is useful for copying the material-relevant data, such as tax determination, into the value contract.
- Should the value contract's target quantity be exceeded, the system will respond according to the indicator set at the contract release control field.

This sales item category is then used by the system to determine the schedule line category. It is also used by the system in conjunction with the MRP type of material to determine the requirement type or requirements class, which primarily controls the execution of the availability check and transfer of requirements.

It is possible to create your own item category groups (the component of the material master that determines the item category in the sales order.) To create an item category group, you proceed to IMG, Sales and distribution, Sales, Sales documents, Sales document item, Define item category groups.

An item category group can then be assigned to a material type as a default. Thus, each material you create that is based on a particular material type can have a defaulted item category, which is then manually changeable in the material master record. This can be allocated in IMG, Sales and distribution, Sales, Sales documents, Sales document item, Define default values for material types.

An item category's usage can be defined, but I have not found a need to create any more than what the system has as a standard. These usages are

Figure 2-26 The settings for contracts

Change View "Item Category Assignment": Overview

Table view Edit Goto Selection Utilities System Help

New entries Variable list

SaTy	ItCGr	Use	HLevItCa	DfItC	MItCa	MItCa	MItCa
OR	LUMF			ZZ01			

Figure 2-27 Promoting a standard item category. (The header item)

determined when creating a sales order and the system determines, for example, that due to product selection or material determination, you have a substituted item, such as PSEL, PSA1, or PSA2. It will then use the item category determination to propose an item category.

The higher level item is another determining factor in item category determination. The system finds a higher level item category by looking at any linkage of items and then tracing the path back to the main item category. As stated earlier, a BOM is a product that, when sold, includes many other parts.

In a BOM, you have a header item, usually an item category group, such as LUMF. This would promote a standard item category, such as ZZ01 (see Figure 2-27). Since this item category begins with Z, it would be self-created. In the configuration of the BOM, the sub-items assigned to it may be standard parts (a keyboard can be sold on its own) and are capable of being resold as normal items if sold alone (see Figure 2-28). Thus, they would have a standard item category group of NORM. However, if sold as part of a BOM, the keyboard would be part of the total computer sold. The item category must now act differently and would need a new item category, such as ZZ02, as shown in Figure 2-29. This would be represented in the following item category determination structure and further down in the table.

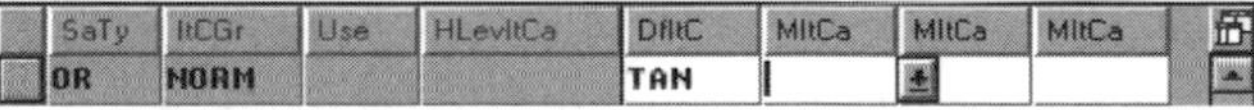

SaTy	ItCGr	Use	HLevItCa	DfltC	MItCa	MItCa	MItCa
OR	NORM			TAN			

Figure 2-28
A new category is created when sub-items are resold as normal items.

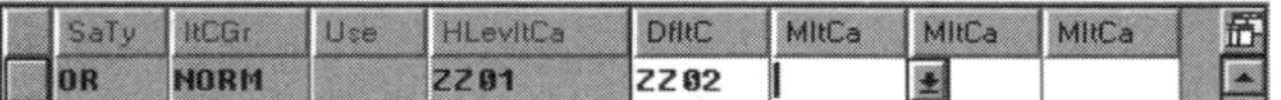

SaTy	ItCGr	Use	HLevItCa	DfltC	MItCa	MItCa	MItCa
OR	NORM		ZZ01	ZZ02			

Figure 2-29
If sold as part of a BOM, a sub-item would be part of the total computer sold. The item category must now act differently and would need a new item category, such as ZZ02.

The previous structure would determine that no matter how many sub-items of item category ZZ01 there were (in our example, a BOM header), the proposed item category would always be a ZZ02 (presuming the document type is OR, there is no item category usage and the item category group is NORM).

Schedule Line Categories—Sales Document Types and the Schedule Line

The schedule line category is used by the system to determine if the item is relevant for delivery. Only those items that have schedule lines assigned will have a delivery created for them. The deliveries are created for the dates and quantities assigned to the respective schedule lines. Keeping to our basic sales flow, the schedule line category will be integrated into the following document flow:

TA, LF, F2

Menu Path

The path is as follows: IMG, Sales and distribution, Sales, Sales documents, Schedule lines, Define schedule line categories.

Transaction Code

The code here is [VOV6]. Only two assignments are represented in the IMG: firstly, to create or define the schedule line category, as seen in Figure 2-30, and secondly, to assign it. We will first look at the schedule line category and its characteristics.

This schedule line category is the standard CP, which is relevant for MRP. It has a alphanumeric two-digit key as well as a short description. The business data section of the schedule line category defines the following:

- A **delivery block** that is automatically created for this schedule line category. You can specify a delivery block for any of the following:

  Sales document type

  Schedule line category

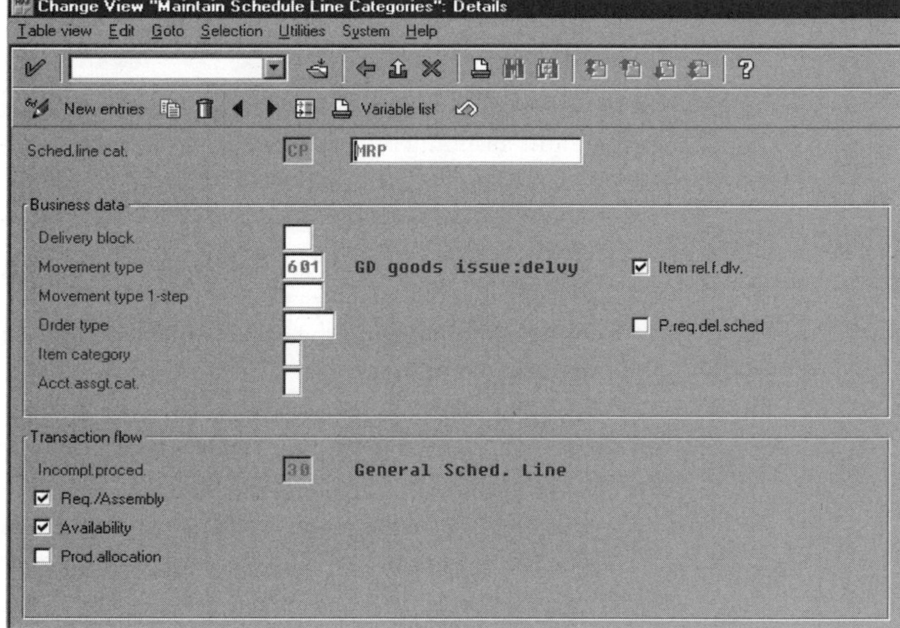

Figure 2-30 Creating or defining the schedule line category

Delivery type

Shipping activities

- For every movement of stock in the SAP system, there is a **movement type** that represents this. For example, a movement of stock between plants has a movement type. However, this type represents the movement of stock for our schedule line category CP, which in turn we will assign to our item category TAN, a standard item category that represents a material to be sold to a customer. Thus, our goods movement is a movement from our stock as a sale to our customer. It would be correct to leave this field blank for items with no stock movement. Also, should this schedule line be assigned to a return item category, you should ensure the movement type here is relevant for returns, such as a goods receipt.
- The **movement type 1 step** is used when two goods movements need to happen for a schedule line category.
- The **order type** is the assignment of the purchase requisition type to the schedule line that enables the system to automatically create a purchase requisition for this schedule line category.

- The **item category** is not to be confused with the sales document item category. This is the item category of the purchasing document or purchase requisition.
- The **account assignment category** is used to determine which account assignment is necessary for the item.
- The **item relevant for delivery** indicator must be set to indicate to the system that this schedule line category is delivery-relevant.
- The **purchase requisition delivery scheduling** indicator must be set if you want the system to predetermine the delivery dates of the schedule line based on the expected receipt times generated from the purchase requisition.
- The **incompletion procedure** is covered in Chapter 4, (it is the assignment of the fields that renders a schedule line incomplete).
- The **requirements/assembly** indicator is used to transfer the requirements for the material. Thus, the demand will be shown in the stock requirements list. This will be covered later in this chapter.
- The **availability check** indicator is used by the system to determine if this item is relevant for availability checking. Please refer to availability checking later on in this chapter.
- Should product allocation be active for this schedule line category, activate the **product allocation** indicator.

When creating the schedule line category, it is worthwhile to follow the naming conventions used by SAP in order to avoid confusion. You must also ensure the objects you create have the prefix Z to avoid being overwritten by a release upgrade.

In the standard SAP R/3 system, the key of the schedule line categories contains the following information concerning its usage: The schedule line category follows a naming convention as shown in Table 2-1 and 2-2. In the STD version the first character defines the document type, and the second character defines the document type's usage with MRP.

Table 2-1

Schedule line category naming convention (first character)

First Character of the Key	Usage
A	Inquiry
B	Quotation
C	Sales order
D	Returns

Table 2-2 Schedule line category naming convention (second character)

Second character of the key	Usage
T	No inventory management with services
X	No inventory management with issue of goods
N	No planning
P	MRP
V	Consumption-based planning

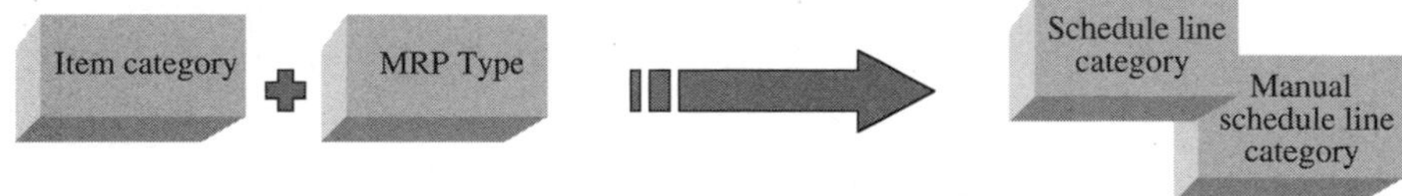

Figure 2-31 The schedule line category determination process

Figure 2-32 The MRP procedure screen

Thus, CP stands for sales order with MRP.

Schedule Line Category Determination

The schedule line category determination is carried out automatically by the system, as displayed in Figure 2-31. The item category of the sales order line item, plus the MRP type found on the material master MRP 1 screen, is displayed in Figure 2-32.

This process is configured in IMG, Sales and distribution, Sales, Sales documents, Schedule lines, Assign schedule line categories, as shown in Figure 2-33.

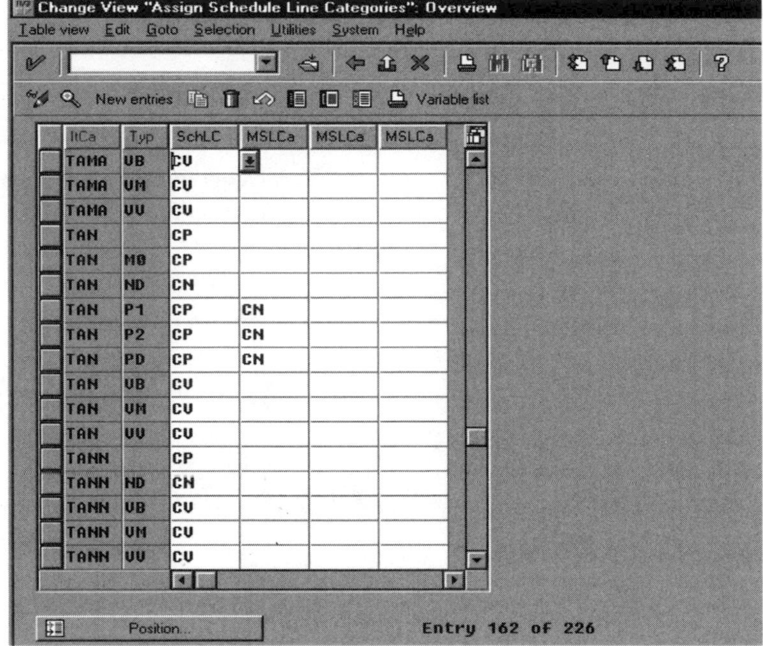

Figure 2-33
The Assign schedule line categories screen

Overview of a Sales Document

We have now been able to configure the basic backbone of the sales document. We have the customer and material master data as well as the determination item categories and schedule lines.

Menu Path

To create a sales order, go to Logistics, Sales and distribution, Sales, Order, Create.

Transaction Code

The code is [VA01]. Select your newly created order document type, as in Figure 2-34. In this example, we are following the standard sales document types OR (English for document type TA).

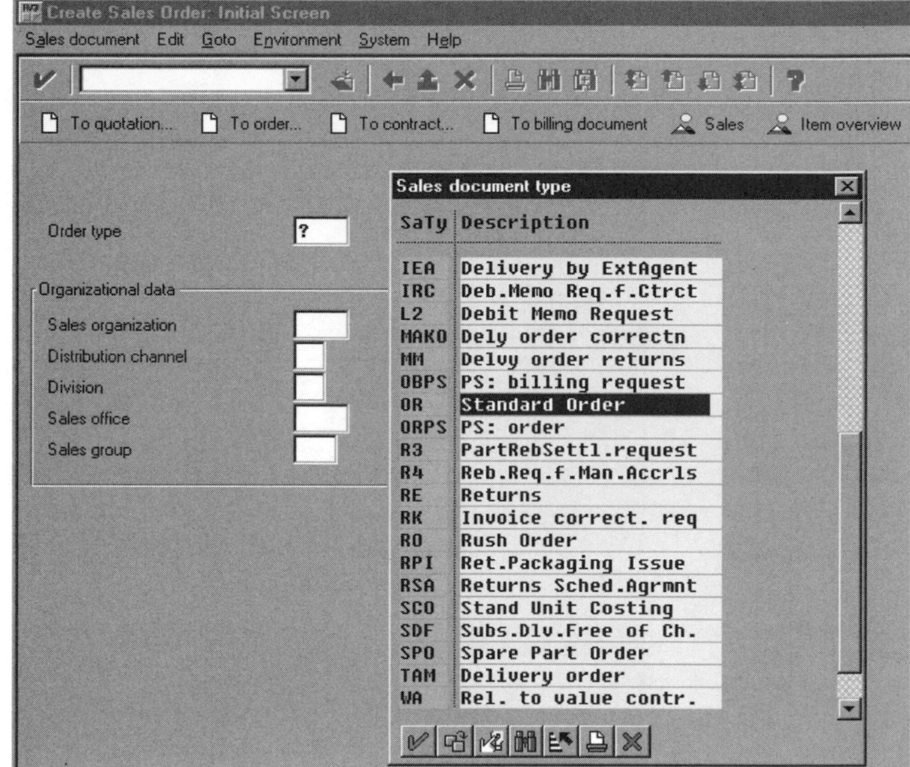

Figure 2-34 Selecting your newly created order document type

You can enter your sales area in this previous front screen. I personally like to leave this front-end without a sales area and, after entering the sold-to party, have a selection screen to select the sales area I am working from. (This is only advisable if you have not restricted your sales document to a specific sales area and if your sold-to party is created for more than one sales area.)

SAP Version 2 with the standard GUI standard sales order front-end has an appearance similar to Figure 2-35. SAP Version 3 standard GUI sales front-end has a similar appearance to Figure 2-36.

We will be working with SAP version 4.0B, which has an almost completely revolutionized sales order front-end with the standard GUI. Utilizing page tabs to facilitate ease of use, the 4.0B version is shown in Figure 2-37.

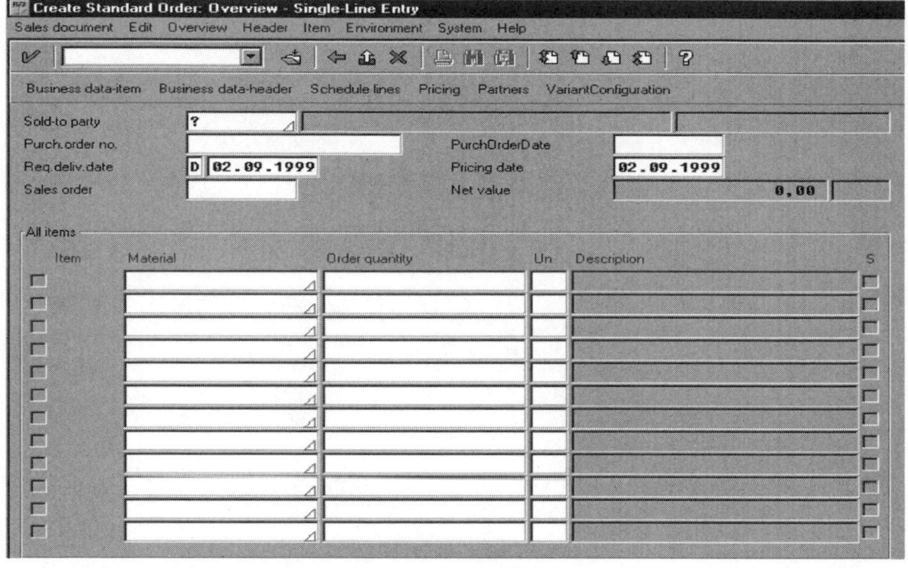

Figure 2-35 Overview of the single-line entry standard order, version 2

Figure 2-36 The standard GUI sales front-end, version 3

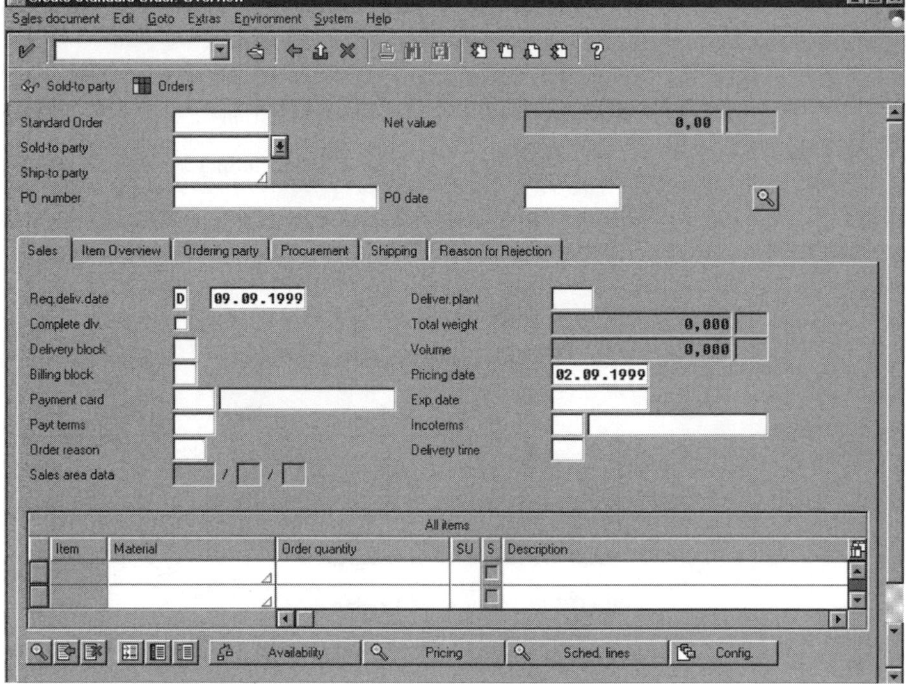

Figure 2-37
The 4.0B version sales order front-end with the standard GUI

The sales order has many fields, and accessing them is not hard. One can merely use the transaction code [SE12] for a table example, VBAK. However, determining which fields are represented on the sales order tables and which are important to the sales and distribution configuration team are two different issues.

What I have done is index the most important table and field names as shown in Table 2-3, as well as indicate where the entry originated in the sales order. This makes a valuable referral to use for pricing, analysis, and virtually any area that involves the condition technique.

Table 2-3

Index of important sales document tables and fields, with organization

Table and Field	Description	Origination
Organizational data		
VBAK-VKORG	Sales organization	Chosen
VBAK-VTWEG	Distribution channel	Chosen
VBAK-SPART	Division	Chosen
VBAK-AUART	Sales document type	Chosen
VBAK-KALSM	Pricing procedure	Customer indicator plus document indicator plus sales area
Header data		
KUAGV-KUNNR	Sold to party	Customer master record
VBAK-VKBUR	Sales office	Customer master record
VBAK-VKGRP	Sales group	Customer master record
VBKD-PRSDT	Pricing date	Entered, copied, or automatic
VBAK-AUDAT	Document date	System entry
VBAK-AUGRU	Order reason	Entered
VBAK-WAERK	Document currency	Customer master record
VBKD-KONDA	Price group	Customer master record
VBKD-BZIRK	Sales district	Customer master record
VBKD-KDGRP	Customer group	Customer master record
VBAK-VSBED	Shipping condition	Customer master record
VBKD-INCO1	Incoterms	Customer master record
VBKD-ZTERM	Payment terms	Customer master record
VBAK-LANDTX	Departure country	Country of plant
VBAK-STCEG_1	Destination country	Country of ship-to party
VBKD-PERFK	Billing schedule	Customer master record
VBKD-ABSSC	Payment guarantee procedure	Customer indicator plus document indicator
VBKD-BSTKD	Purchase order number	Entered
VBAK-KVGR1 through to 5	Additional data	Customer master record

Item data		
VBAP-PSTYV	Item category	Automatic
RV45A-KWMENG	Order quantity	Entered
VBAP-MATNR	Material	Entered
VBAP-MATWA	Material entered	Entered
VBAP-CHARG	Batch number	Automatic
VBAP-PMATN	Price reference material	Material master record
VBAP-PRODH	Product hierarchy	Material master record
VBAP-MATKL	Material group	Material master record
VBAP-WERKS	Plant	Cust. material info record or customer or material master
VBAP-VSTEL	Shipping point	Plant plus shipping conditions plus loading group
VBAP-ROUTE	Route	Automatic or manual
VBAP-LPRIO	Delivery priority	Customer material info record or customer master
VBAP-KDMAT	Customer material	Customer material info record
VBAP-MVGR1	Additional data	Material master record through to 5
VBAP-POSNR	Item number	Automatic
Schedule line		
VBEP-POSNR	Schedule line	Automatic
VBEP-ETENR	Schedule line number	Automatic
VBEP-ETTYP	Schedule line category	Automatic
RV45A-ETDAT	Delivery date	Automatic or manual
VBEP-WMENG	Order quantity	Entered
VBEP-BMENG	Confirmed quantity	Automatic
VBEP-MBDAT	Material availability date	Automatic
VBEP-LDDAT	Loading date	Automatic
VBEP-WADAT	Proposed goods issue date	Automatic can be changed in delivery

continues

Table 2-3
Continued

Table and Field	Description	Origination
	Schedule line	
VBEP-TDDAT	Transportation date	Automatic
VBEP-VSTEl	Shipping point	Plant plus shipping point plus loading group
VBEP-BWART	Movement type	Schedule line category

Copy Control

Copy control is used by the system to determine what document types, item categories, and schedule line categories (the three tiers of the sales document type) can be copied into each other or referenced. This includes all three tiers of data allowed into and from delivery documents and/or billing documents.

Menu Path

For sales documents, the menu path is IMG, Sales and distribution, Sales, Maintain copy control for sales documents. The options are copying control: sales document to sales document [VTAA] and copying control: billing document to sales document [VTAF].

For deliveries, the menu path is IMG, Sales and distribution, Shipping, Maintain copy control for deliveries (copying control: sales document to delivery document) [VTLA].

For billing, the menu path is IMG, Sales and distribution, Billing, Billing documents, Maintain copy control for billing documents. The options are copying control: sales document to billing document [VTFA], copying control: delivery note to billing document [VTFL], and copying control: billing document to billing document [VTFF].

Overview

It cannot be stressed how important it is to take careful note of your copy control rules. The following common scenarios give examples of the copying control you will need. These are in no way the only process flow models you will have or need, but they highlight the basic principles of copying control.

Scenario A (Standard sales order)

Quotation, Sales order, Delivery, Invoice

(Sales) → (Sales) → (Delivery) → (Billing)

This basic scenario will need the copying rules set up to enable a sales document type to be copied into another sales document type (Quotation → Sales order), a sales document type to be copied into a delivery (Sales order → Delivery), and finally a delivery to be copied into a billing document (Delivery → Invoice).

Scenario B (Returns Process)

Please refer to the returns procedure later in this chapter for an explanation of the returns process.

Invoice → Returns Sales order → Returns delivery → Credit for returns

(Billing) → (Sales) → (Delivery) → (Billing)

Scenario C (Credit memo process)

Please refer to the Credit procedure later in this chapter for an explanation of the credit process.

Invoice → Credit memo request → Credit memo

(Billing) → (Sales) → (Billing)

Copy Control for Sales Documents

At the header level, we can see in Figure 2-38 the document types that can be copied into one another, such as OR into OR or TA into TA (German). This is a SAP standard setting that is used in order to create a sales document with reference to another sales document.

If you wish to create a sales order without having to recreate all the item lines, you can simply copy the data by creating the order with reference to another sales order. In the procedure where we define a product proposal, you set up the copying rules that enable a product proposal to be used as a reference when creating a sales order.

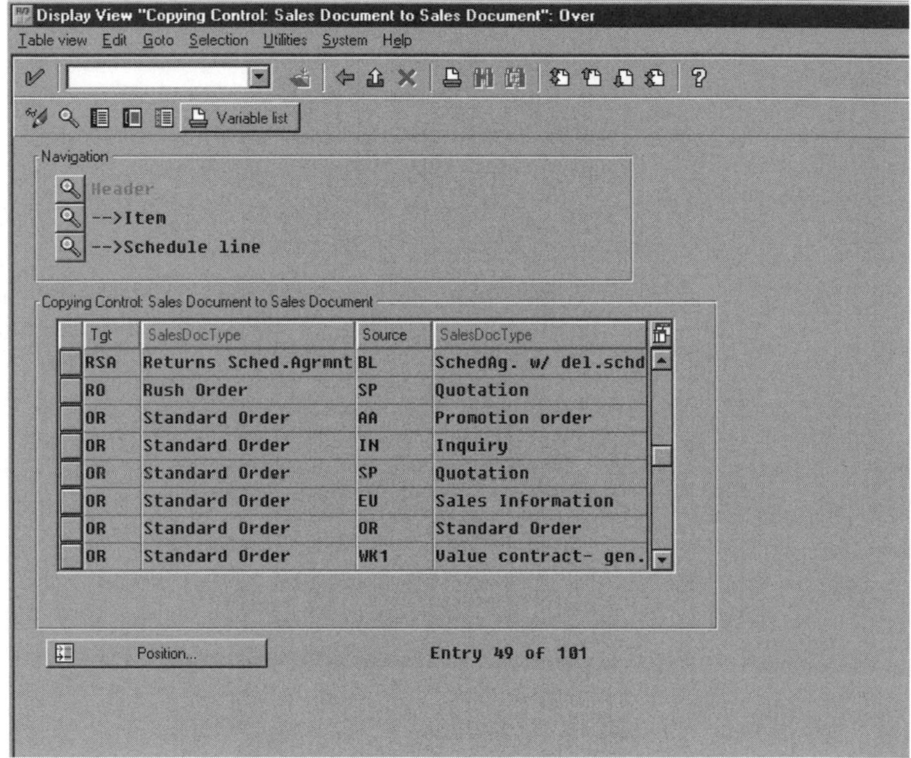

Figure 2-38
The document types that can be copied into one another.

NOTE: *The document type as well as the schedule line and item data must already be configured prior to configuring the copy control rules.*

NOTE: *When creating a sales document, item category, or schedule line category with reference to an existing object, such as another sales document, item category, or schedule line category, the system automatically creates the copying control rule to be equivalent of the item you are copying. For example, let's say you create a new sales order document type, ZZOR, made with reference to the standard document type OR. The system will automatically copy all item categories and schedule line categories that were previously assigned to OR and assign them as relevant to ZZOR.*

By selecting the document type that we would like to configure or change and then pressing the button shown in Figure 2-39, we can see the configuration for the header transfer of data.

Copying rules are set up at the header level for sales documents, deliveries, and invoices. They are set up at item levels for sales documents, deliveries, and invoices too, but they are only set up for schedule line levels for sales document types. If we select the button in Figure 2-40, which resembles a selection option available in Figure 2-41, we will find the following screen shown in Figure 2-42.

In this example, we note the item categories for which we have created copying control rules. By selecting TAN, for example, we have the actual nuts and bolts of the copying control at item level.

By referring to Figure 2-43, we can see the following settings:

- We have the source document type OR and the target document type OR, as well as the source item category TAN and the target item category TAN.
- The copying requirements are rules or certain criteria that must be met before the copy can take place. This example has the copying requirements 303, "always an item" (requirements and formulas will be covered in Chapter 4).

Figure 2-39 Magnifying Glass button

Figure 2-40 Display item

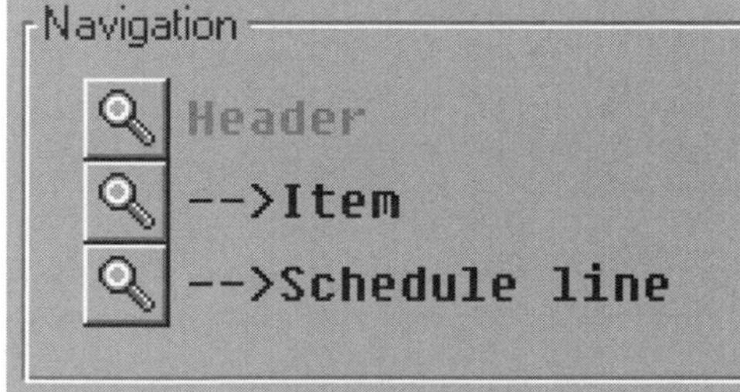

Figure 2-41 Navigation, display Header, Item or Schedule line

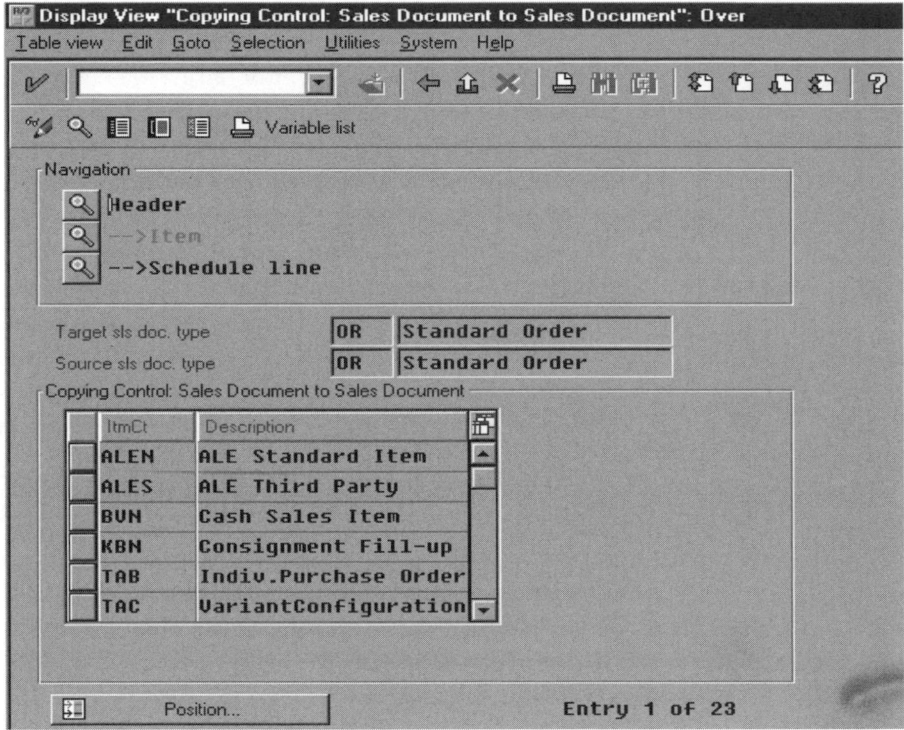

Figure 2-42 Copying control from sales document to sales document

- Three data transfer routines are in control of copying data between items. Our example has the following: (Again, refer to Chapter 4, "Basic Functions.")

1. DataT	151	General item data
2. DataT	102	Bus.data/item compliance
3. DataT	002	Partner item

- The FPLA field is a routine that checks certain billing plan requirements have been met and then copies relevant billing plan data into the proceeding document. The setting used in this example is 251, "conditions."
- The indicator copy schedule line must be set, should you wish the data of this items schedule line to be transferred to the new document. Be sure to also create the schedule line copy control rules.
- The update document flow indicator tells the system to keep a record of the preceding document in the document flow of the sales order or document you are creating. It would not be wise, for example, to have

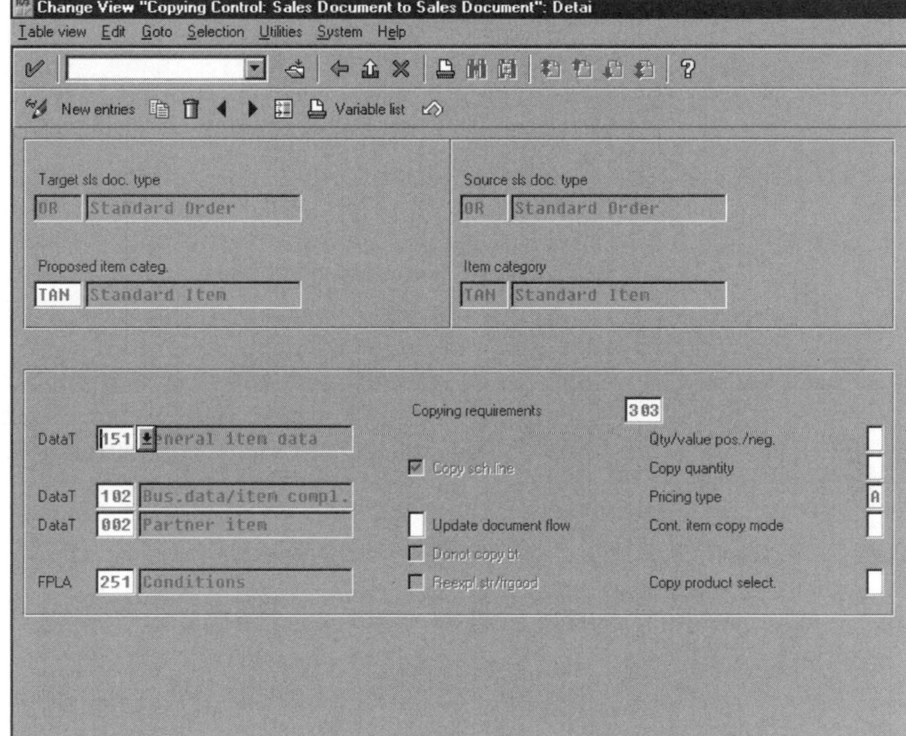

Figure 2-43 The settings for copying control at item level

the flow updated when made with reference to another sales order; otherwise, there may be confusion in tracing the document flow, but it would be recommended to have a document flow updated when creating a sales document (for example, a credit memo) with reference to a billing document. This way, you can see the faulty invoice for which you are creating the credit memo.

- There is another indicator "do not copy batch." This is self-explanatory; set this indicator if you do not want the system to copy the batch number of the material into the following document.
- The indicator Reexplode structure/free goods is used when you wish the system to redetermine the BOM in the proceeding sales document. Thus, the system does not copy the actual BOM from one sales document into another, but by controlling the copy rules for the main item in the BOM; the system can copy a header BOM item into the proceeding document, which then reexplodes itself.
- It is best to leave the Qty/value positive/negative field blank.

- Copy quantity is again best left blank when copying from a sales order to another sales order, as there is no affect on the quantity. However, in copying between the following, it would be advisable to follow the standard rules:

  Quotation to Sales order: Positive

  Contract to Return: Negative

  Sales order to Sales order: No effect

  - The pricing type is an extremely important field. It is worthwhile keeping this entry in mind when creating your pricing condition types. As a rule of thumb, you should have all item categories for a particular sales document with the same settings. You may generally use pricing type B, "carry out new pricing," or G, "copy pricing elements unchanged and redetermine taxes."

NOTE: *When using condition B, all manual pricing condition types are lost.*

If you want a particular condition type to be placed in the invoice and not the sales order while still copying the data from the sales order, you can use the standard copying rule pricing type G, "copy pricing elements unchanged and redetermine taxes." Set the condition type condition category to L, "generally new when copying."

When using copying rule pricing type G, the following condition type categories are redetermined:

D	Taxes
C	Volume-based rebate
I	Intercompany billing conditions
R	Invoice list conditions
L	Condition types with condition category L
G	Cost conditions
E	Cash discount conditions

TIP: *When copying rules are being defined, you may refer to OSS note 24832, which I have found to be useful:*

- The copy control for material in a value contract governs how the system is to allow the copying of an item in a value contract.
- The copy product selection indicator should be left blank if you wish the system to carry out a new product selection in the target document you are creating.

When selecting schedule line, as displayed previously in Figure 2-40, you are presented with the same layout of the screen, with the source and the target schedule line category for that particular sales item category and particular sales document type. You again have a data transfer and requirements assignment.

When copying from a billing document type into a sales document type, you again have the same screen layout yet *without* the following:

- Copy quantity
- Contract item copy
- Copy product selection
- Reexplode structure free goods

When copying from a sales document into a delivery document type, you again have header and item data, yet no schedule line data, as the schedule line data is actually not copied into the delivery. The delivery is actually a result of the schedule line and actually replaces the schedule line. Thus, all the schedule line data has been used to create and form the basis of the delivery document.

When copying from a sales document into a billing document or from a delivery document into a billing document, the same data is required at the header level. In Figure 2-44, we use a delivery document header to a billing document header.

The source and target document types are shown, but we also have a field for requirements that determine, for example, if one invoice should be created from a single delivery or if multiple deliveries are to be allowed on one invoice. You can also select if you want the system to redetermine the export data or to copy the export data from the delivery document.

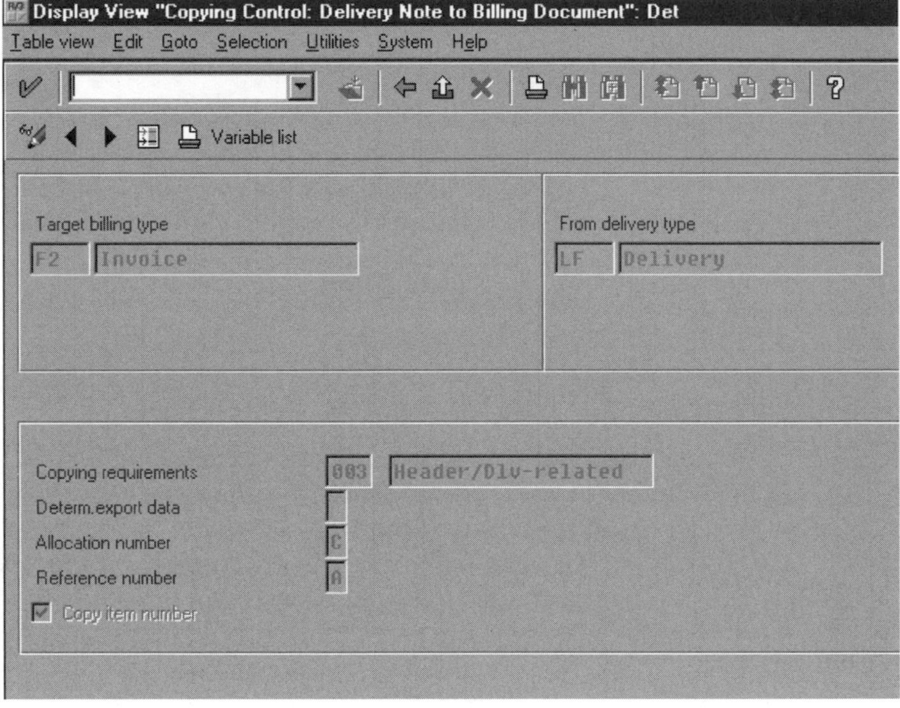

Figure 2-44 Using a delivery document header for a billing document header

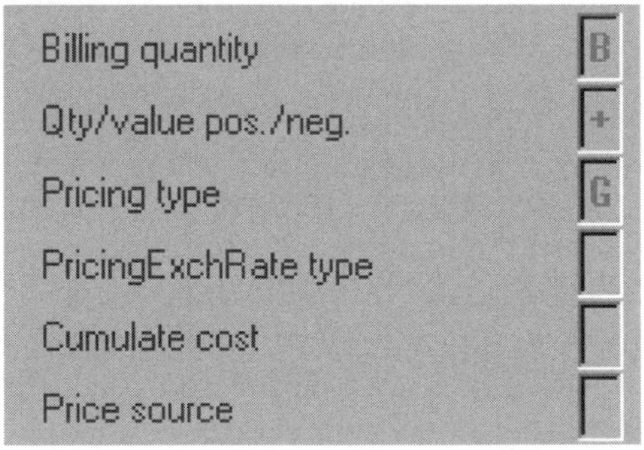

Billing quantity B
Qty/value pos./neg. +
Pricing type G
PricingExchRate type
Cumulate cost
Price source

Figure 2-45 Further copy control settings

At the item level of the copy control, you have the item data copying rules as well as a requirement allocated to the transaction. You also have the following settings, as shown in Figure 2-45.

- Billing quantity is equal to the quantity you want to use in deliver-related billing. It should be set to B, indicating delivery quantity less invoiced quantity.
- The quantity value being positive or negative determines how the value taken from the source document will affect the billing documents, such as

  Delivery to Invoice: Positive

  Delivery to Cancellation: Negative

  Delivery to Pro-forma invoice: No effect

- The pricing type is governed by the same rules as in the sales document. However, the pricing exchange rate type is used by the system to determine which date to use as the basis for the exchange rate.
- The cumulate cost indicator determines if the cost (usually condition type VPRS) is to be rounded up from the sub-items to a main item. This is used in BOMs to determine if the costs are passed up to the header item. This is especially needed if the sub-item is not relevant for billing.
- The price source indicator determines where the system obtains its pricing values. If blank, this indicates the values are found in the sales document.

In copying one billing document into another, such as from an invoice into an invoice cancellation, the same determining values are used and the same rules apply.

A crucial interface with the copy control rules is the assignment of the delivery document type in the sales order document type, as well as the invoice document type assignment in the sales order document type. As you will see in the billing, the invoice cancellation type is also assigned to the billing document type.

TIP: *When using intercompany billing and credit or debit memos, it is not possible to copy from a credit memo request or debit memo request into a intercompany invoice. Rather see OSS note 63459 and the information on the credit memo process later in this chapter.*

Rebates in Kind and Free-of-Charge Items

Do not mistake rebates in kind with the rebate procedure in SAP R/3. Rebates in kind are merely free-of-charge items that are allocated to another standard item in a sales order. The simple process is assigning a free-of-charge item category to a higher level item category. The standard version of SAP R/3 has a free-of-charge item category TANN, as shown in Figure 2-46. (This is not to be confused with the standard item category of TAN.)

Item category TANN that is free of charge item is not accessed in standard item category determination, as the standard item category determination will allocate item category TAN. The item category determination will propose TANN only if selected manually or if allocated to the main item as a sub-item on the sales order. As soon as an item of category TAN is assigned as a lower level item (with no specific usage), it will be allocated as TANN and thus as a free item, as seen in the configuration settings of Figure 2-47.

To assign a normal item to a higher level item in a sales order, proceed to the double-line entry view of the sales order if using SAP Version 3 and below. If using Version 4 and above, proceed to the item overview screen and

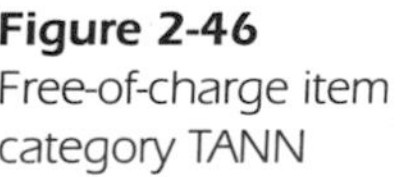

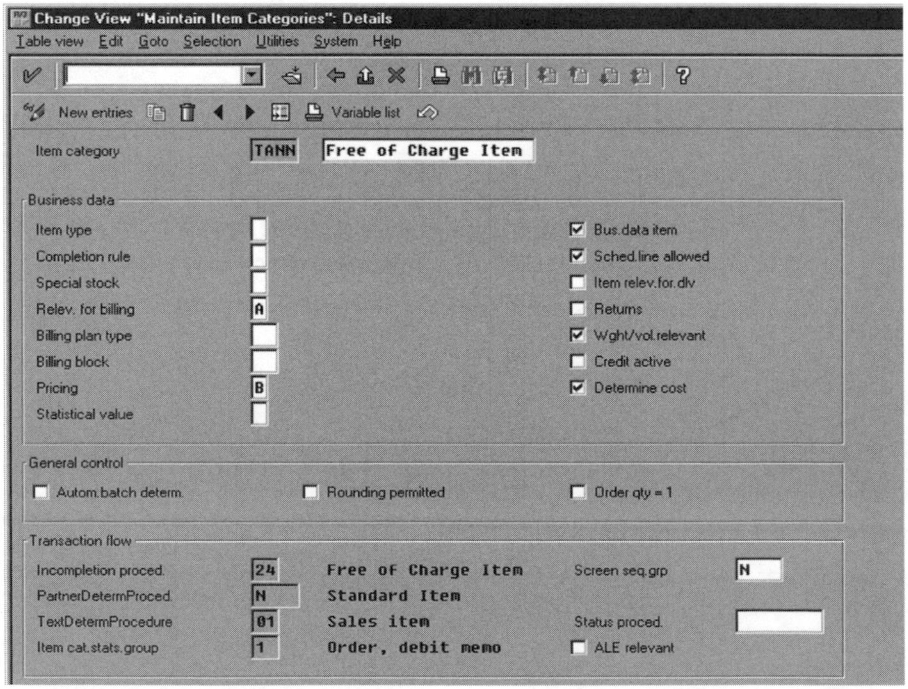

Figure 2-46
Free-of-charge item category TANN

SaTy	ItCGr	Use	HLevItCa	DfltC	MItCa	MItCa	MItCa
OR	NORM			TAN	TAP	TAQ	TANN
OR	NORM		TAC	TAE			
OR	NORM		TAE	TAE			
OR	NORM		TAG	TAN			
OR	NORM		TAM	TAN			
OR	NORM		TAN	TANN			
OR	NORM		TANN	TANN			
OR	NORM		TAP	TAN			

Figure 2-47
Item category TAN may be manually changed to TANN. However, should a standard item of category TAN be assigned as a lower-level item to another standard item, it will automatically assume the new item category of TANN.

Sales | Item Overview | Ordering party | Procurement | Shipping | Reason for Rejection

Req.deliv.date D 29.09.1999 Deliver.plant

All items

Item	Material		First date	Plnt	ItCa	HgLvlt	Batch	CnTy	Rate	Curr.
10	1300-260	D	29.09.1999		TAN			PR00	100,00	GBP
20	1300-260	D	29.09.1999		TANN	10		PR00	100,00	GBP

Figure 2-48
Assigning the lowest level item to the higher level item

enter the original material as well as the material you want to give away for free. Assign the lowest level item to the higher level item, as displayed in Figure 2-48. You will be informed via a warning message that the item category will be redetermined.

This process is especially useful when the business is selling standard materials and allocating a free-of-charge service to specific materials. In the case of using service materials, don't forget they are not delivered; thus, they will need a new free-of-charge item category and possibly a new schedule line, depending on your business requirements.

Sales Document "Order" Types

Many sales document types exist, and you have the ability to create endless more. However, the sales document types we will focus on are the standard processes most commonly used in SAP SD. These documents encompass their own business process procedures. The document flows we will look at are the following: the quotation, special sales orders such as the cash sale process and the rush order process, credit and debit cycles, and the returns and free of charge subsequent deliveries process. We will also look at the new document type as of Version 4.0, which is the invoice correction request. That is a combination of the credit and debit document. Following this, we will look into contracts and scheduling agreements.

Menu Path

The path is as follows: IMG, Sales and distribution, Sales, Sales documents, Sales document header, Define sales document types.

Transaction Code

The code here is [VOV8].

The Inquiry Sales Document—Sales Document Type AF (In English)

The sales inquiry is actually a request for a quotation. It is a non-obligatory request for sales information. The inquiry can relate to materials and services, and is sent to a specific sales area. The inquiry comprises of materials and/or services that can have schedule lines and delivery dates.

When configuring the sales document type for inquiries note the following: After an inquiry, you can create a quotation. Should your business decide to use inquiries, ensure you have the sales document category "A" for inquiries. No reference is necessary and should not be mandatory. The transaction group should be 1 for inquiries, and the screen sequence group can be different than the standard sales process. The SAP standard screen sequence group is AG.

If you are utilizing inquiries, be sure to have the item category determination set up for Inquiries as well as the schedule line category determination. Do not forget the copy control rules, should you wish a quotation to be created subsequent to a inquiry. The standard item category for inquiries is AFN.

The Quotation—Sales Document Type AG (QT in English)

The quotation is a sales document type that comes before the sales order and after an inquiry. It is used as a proposed agreement of a price and quantity for a particular material or service for a particular date. Most quotations have a validity date.

The quotation can include pricing and schedule lines. It can also have output assigned and credit checks assigned. A quotation is usually copied into a sales order. Depending on the customizing entries, you can copy the pricing elements, the header data, and the material and order quantities into the sales order.

When configuring the sales document type for inquiries note the following: Your quotation should have sales document category "B." This sets all relevant document types to read the customer material info record. Thus, set the indicator to "read info record." The screen sequence group can be set as AG, which is the SAP standard for quotations. The transaction group should be set as "2."

It is also proposed that you set the indicator for open quotations. The indicator can read the item or header levels to indicate to the user, when he or she is creating a new quotation, that an open quotation exists for the customer, if set at the header level, or for the material, if set at the item level.

Do not forget to set the item category determination and schedule line category determination as well as the copy control rules, such as from a quotation to a sales order. The standard item category used in quotations is AGN.

Order Probability

When a sales inquiry or quotation is created, you may want to know whether or not the customer will follow through with a purchase. The system uses an order probability percentage from the customer master record and combines it with the order probability percentage of the sales document type. The combination of the two percentages results in an order probability percentage, as displayed in Figure 2-49. This percentage is available for lists of sales documents; thus, you can create a list of sales quotations that has the highest probability of being confirmed first.

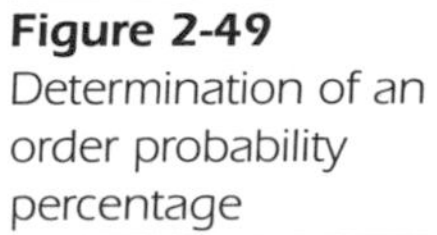

Figure 2-49 Determination of an order probability percentage

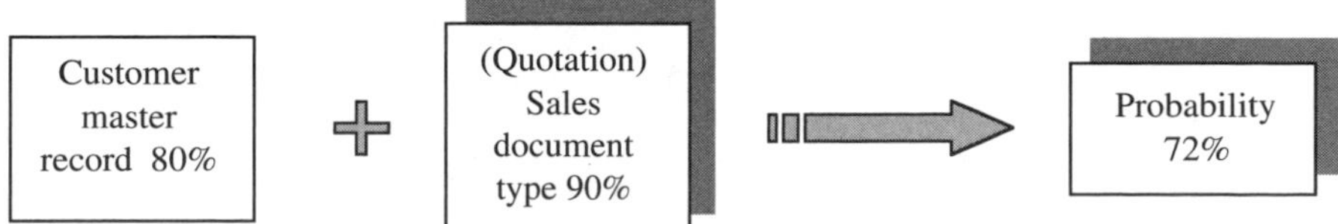

Special Sales Document Types—The Cash Sale Process

One uses the cash sale process displayed in Figure 2-50 when the customer places the sales order and picks up and pays for the goods at the same time. Thus, the system automatically proposes the current date in the sales order as the date for the delivery and billing. Once the sales order is saved, the system then creates a delivery automatically and prints out a cash sale invoice that can be given to the sold-to party. This cash sale invoice is a form created via output determination (see Chapter 4) of the systematic invoice, which must be created using the standard process.

The delivery can be relevant for picking (see Chapter 3 for delivery and picking processes), or if the goods are not to be picked, the delivery can have the goods issue automatically happen in a batch process and then the billing can occur. Note the billing follows the standard process.

The Rush Order Process (Document Type SO)

In the rush order process displayed in Figure 2-51, the customer places the order and collects the items immediately or we ship the materials immediately. However, we only invoice the customer later.

The system automatically creates a delivery when we save the sales order, but no invoice is printed. Instead, the system follows the standard procedures for creating the invoice. Both the rush order process and the

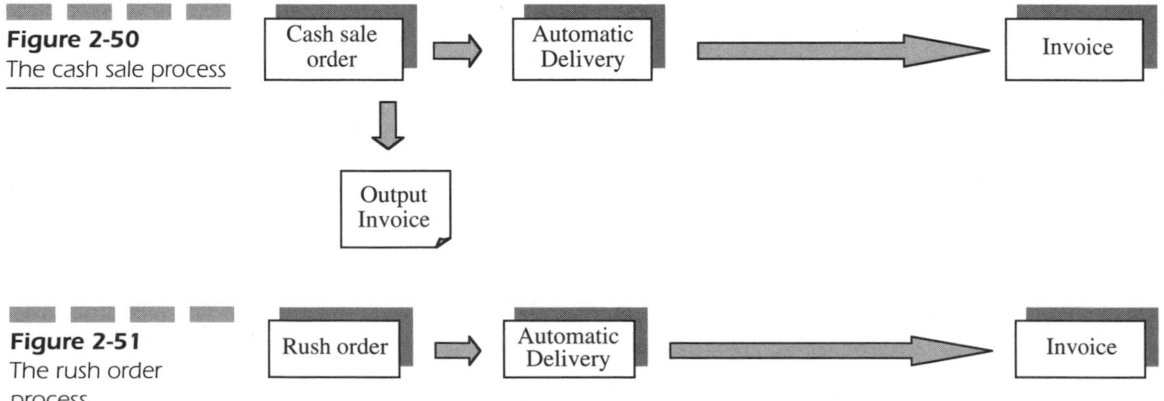

Figure 2-50 The cash sale process

Figure 2-51 The rush order process

cash sale process utilize the shipping conditions passed on from the sales document. The shipping conditions in turn are used to determine the shipping point and the route. (As we will see in later chapters.)

The Credit Process—Sales Document G2

The credit procedure displayed in Figure 2-52 generally follows two business procedures, the first being the scenario where the customer returns products previously purchased and requires a credit. This we will look at in the returns process. The second general form of credit procedure is when the customer is credited without reference to a return.

This would be used in the following examples. The customer discovers the products we sent him are defective and the costs to initiate a return delivery would exceed the costs obtained in rehabilitation or repair of the product. Thus, we instruct the customer to scrap the material and we subsequently issue a credit note.

The second commonly used process is when the customer is overcharged for a product or service and we issue a credit for the difference. Again there is no movement of material. When configuring the sales document type "credit memo request," note the following: You can automatically set a billing block that can be released by an authorized person prior to the billing. It is the billing which in turn is the actual creation of the credit note.

You should also set a mandatory indicator that the credit memo request can only be created with reference to the invoice document that originated with the problem. That way, you ensure traceability. It is also possible to select an order reason on the credit note, which can provide the reason why the credit was given. The standard item category used by credit memos is G2N. (Don't forget in the copy control to ensure "update document flow" is activated when copying from an invoice to a credit memo request.)

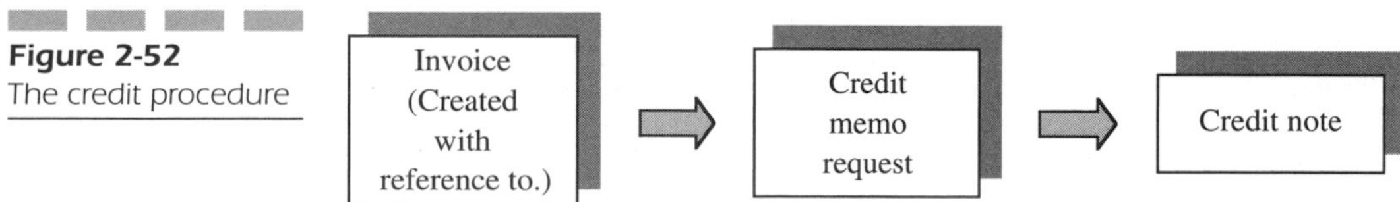

Figure 2-52
The credit procedure

TIP: You may not wish to credit for everything, such as the entire freight charge from one invoice. You can instead have a new returns pricing procedure in the credit memo request that is similar to the standard pricing procedure you use, but not have the freight condition type. Thus, the standard values are copied over, excluding freight. However, this new pricing procedure may have an additional manual condition type, such as "total transfer costs credit," which can be manually entered in the credit memo request (refer to the pricing information in Chapter 4).

The Debit Process — Sales Document L2 The debit process displayed in Figure 2-53 is used when we charge a customer too low a resale price for a material or service. We then create a debit memo request and invoice it using standard billing procedures.There is no movement of material.

When configuring the sales document type debit memo request, note the following: You can automatically set a billing block that can be released by an authorized person prior to the billing being carried out. This, however, is not commonly used when we are charging customers. The billing is the actual creation of the debit note. You can also set a mandatory indicator so that the debit memo request can only be created with reference to the invoice document that originated with the problem. That way, you ensure traceability. It is also possible to select an order reason on the debit note, which can offer the reason why the debit was given.The standard item category used by debits is L2N.

TIP: *Rather than merely debit the customer for the disputed amount, it is recommended in almost all instances to credit the customer for the discrepancy in full and create another standard sales order to invoice, with the correct amounts for the original disrupted sales order. This procedure can be followed for all disputed short-priced orders and overpriced orders, thus resulting in one standard solution.*

Figure 2-53
The debit process

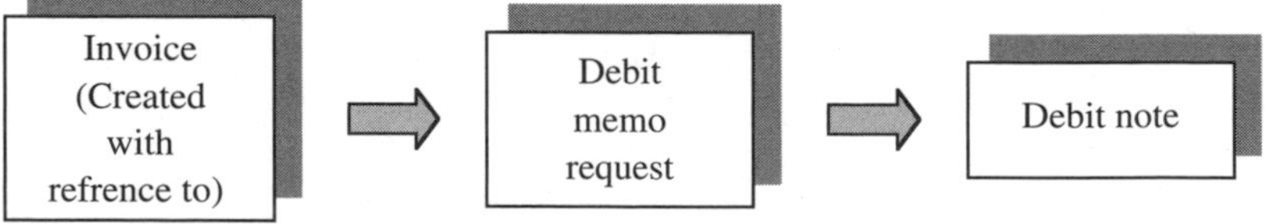

TIP: *As already discussed, should you be using an intercompany sales process and want to create a intercompany credit or debit memo originally created from a credit or debit memo request, you will experience difficulty as this is not a standard procedure until SAP Version 4.5.*

Standard SAP will not enable the creation of intercompany invoices for order-related billing documents. Instead, see OSS note 63459. The basic concept of this OSS note is that you need to assign a output type to the external invoice (the customer's credit or debit, output type ZZIV) at the header level. This output type then needs to be activated via a run of the print program RSNAST00 and the intercompany credit or debit will be created. This process is well supported by SAP and you should not worry about its implementation. The procedure will then look similar to Figure 2-54 for credit memos.

The Returns Process — Sales Document Type RE

The returns process displayed in Figure 2-55 is different than the standard credit process in that a delivery is made. Although we cannot map all the functionality you may require in the physical process, such as goods receipts and warehouse management movement, we will look at the basic flow of the returns order procedure.

The returns order can be created with reference to an invoice to ensure traceability of the process. It may be worthwhile ensuring this is mandatory when creating the returns order type. It may also be worthwhile ensuring

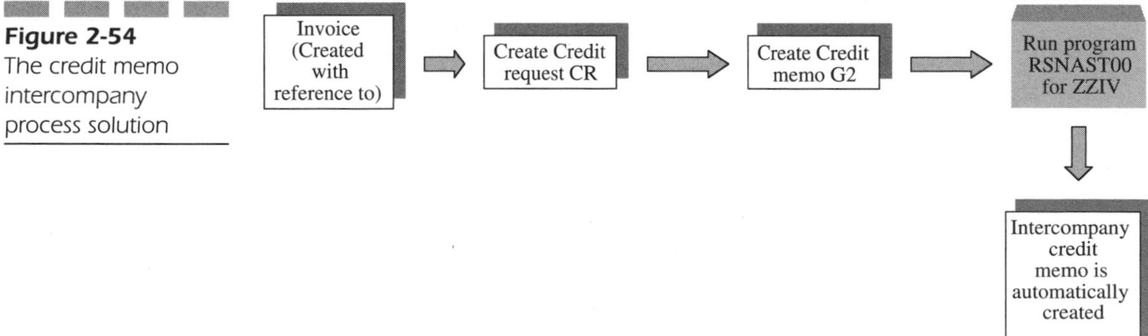

Figure 2-54 The credit memo intercompany process solution

the returns order reason was entered on the sales document. Thus, it may be necessary to add this in an incompletion procedure. You may want to copy the pricing from the invoice back into the sales order.

NOTE: *There is no need to indicate a negative value in the copying control rules, as the system sees the document type as a return. It automatically posts the entries in the finance document as opposite entries on the ledger. By using the same pricing values, you ensure a reversal of the externally created invoice.*

It is advisable to have a billing block assigned to the return order to prevent a credit for returns being created until an authorized person releases the billing block. Go to Sales, Sales documents, Sales document header, Define sales document type in the billing block field in the billing section.

Once the returns delivery is created, the material is receipted back into our plant. The material should use a goods movement back into stock that inspects the stock, such as blocked stock, before placing it back into available stock to be consumed by the next sales order that places a demand for the material in the plant.

TIP: *It is advisable to indicate a shipping condition that is specifically used for returns. Thus, all return deliveries or goods receipts can be done by a specific shipping point (see shipping point determination in Chapter 3). This is useful when running the delivery due list. You can select only to process the returns deliveries, as well as offer better visibility of stock movements.*

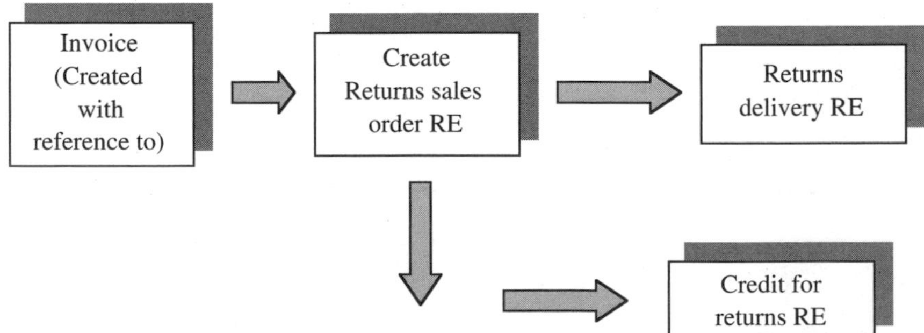

Figure 2-55
The process flow for returns

The standard item category used by returns is REN. The process flow for returns is shown in Figure 2-55.

After the creation and goods issue of the delivery, the billing block is removed from the sales order and the invoice is created with reference to the sales order. This way, you can create a credit for the return in the sales order, which in turn has the order quantity copied from the preceding invoice.

Free-of-Charge Subsequent Deliveries—Sales Document Type KN

If the business does not want to credit the customer for the return, it is possible to instead issue a free-of-charge subsequent delivery. Such a delivery, shown in Figure 2-56, is a sales order document type that must refer to a previous sales document type, such as a returns order or a contract.

Be sure, however, that the sales document you are using as a reference, if no longer valid due to this free-of-charge delivery, has its line items rejected. Should they not be rejected, it is possible that the return can accidentally create a credit memo.

You do not have to use Create with reference to free-of-charge subsequent deliveries if you enter the order type and then choose Enter. When creating the sales document using [VA01] a dialog box will appear where you can enter the number of the order to which you are referring.

It is advisable to have a delivery block ensuring the sales order is released before a delivery can be created and materials shipped to the customer. This can be set in the sales document type automatically. Go to Sales, Sales documents, Sales document header, Define sales document type. Then enter the value in the delivery block field. No invoice is created or necessary, as the items are free (see the section on billing in Chapter 3). The standard item category is KLN.

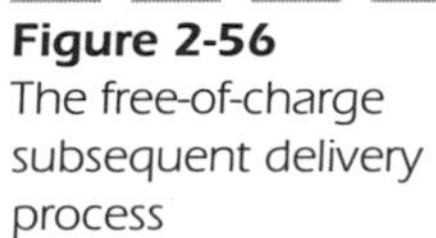

Figure 2-56
The free-of-charge subsequent delivery process

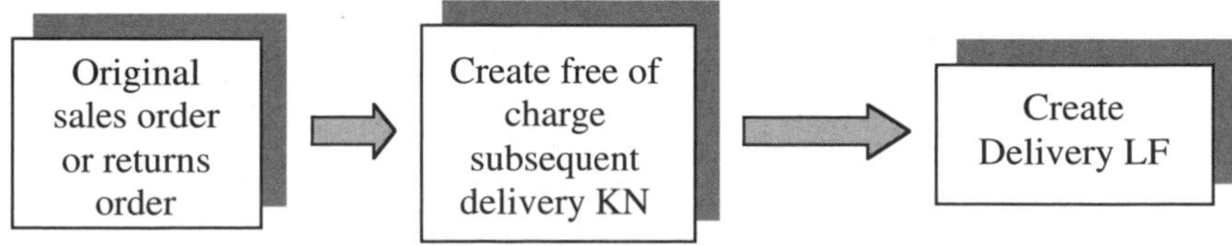

Free-of-Charge Delivery—Sales Document Type FD

A free-of-charge delivery, displayed in Figure 2-57, is used to send samples or free products to your customer. The delivery is actually a sales document type that is only relevant for deliveries and not invoicing; as in a free-of-charge subsequent delivery, you can issue a pro forma invoice if required. The delivery type used is the standard delivery type LF.

Again, it would be advisable to have a delivery block automatically set for the sales order; thus, no delivery can be made until this block is released by an authorized person.

Invoice Corrcction Request—Sales Document Type RK

As of 4.0, SAP has a new document type called an *invoice correction request*. This document proposes a new way of processing complaints and issuing credit and debit memos. The document enables you to correct the quantity and/or the price for one or more items in an invoice.

Each invoice correction request that is made in reference to an invoice contains two items for each item in the invoice (you cannot create an invoice correction request in reference to a sales or delivery document type). The first item is the copied value and quantity copied from the invoice; this item appears as the credit item. The second item is the debit item, which represents the correct quantity and/or value. Should you change this second debit item due to a new pricing or whatever reason, the difference of the two would automatically be passed on to billing as either a credit or debit memo. It would be advisable to set an automatic billing block on the sales document type. As in a number of instances, you may wish to credit the customer. This may require authorization before the credit/debit is issued.

The billing document type assigned to the invoice correction request is order-related, a G2 (credit memo), and has the characteristic as K, which indicates a credit memo request. The system creates a credit memo for a

Figure 2-57
The free-of-charge delivery process

positive total value and a debit memo for a negative total value. If the invoice correction request is characterized as a debit memo request, that is, the document type RK has a characteristic as L and has order-related billing assigned to it in the form of an L2 or debit memo, the opposite occurs.

The title of the printout for the credit or debit memo depends on the characteristic that has been assigned to it (sales document category) and not the total value, as shown in Figure 2-58.

The copy control at the item category level from the billing document to the invoice correction request must have the pricing type E (adopt pricing components and fix values), as shown in the Figure 2-59.

NOTE: *Due to the classification type D of the sales document type RK, an additional two fields are generated in the copy control at the item level, as shown in Figure 2-59. These are a second item category proposal and a second pricing type. Both of these fields relate to the debit memo item in the invoice correction request.*

The document flow appears as follows in Figure 2-60.

Contracts in SAP SD

Numerous business relationships relate to contracts or agreements with customers and the represented business, based upon material, price, and quantity over a fixed period of time. They facilitate planning on behalf of the business and guarantee a fixed-price agreement with the customer. These contracts are represented in the SAP system as outline agreements.

Sales document type RK Invoice correct. req
SD document categ. K Sales document block
Indicator D

Figure 2-58 The printout title for the credit or debit memo depends on the characteristic assigned to it that is the SD document category.

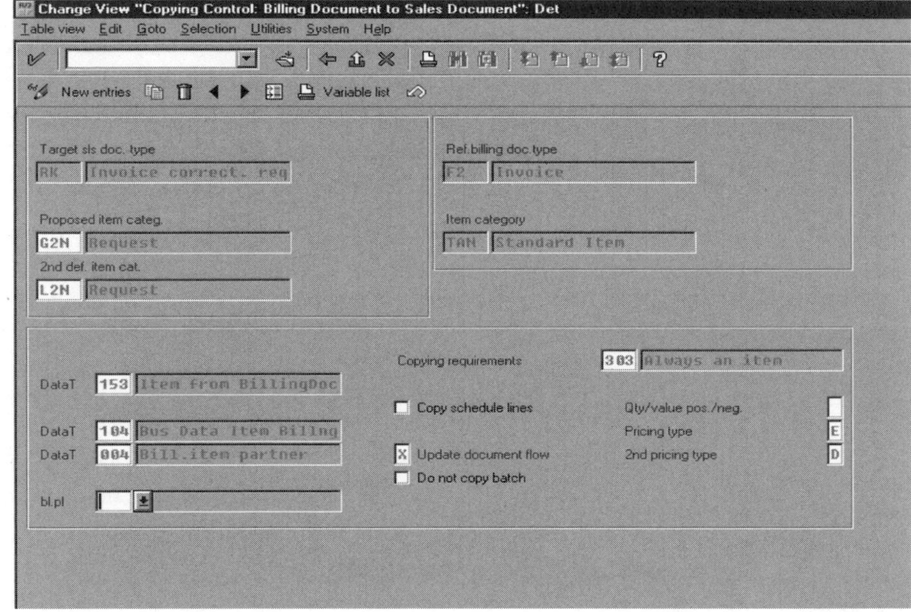

Figure 2-59
The copy control at the item category level must have the pricing type E.

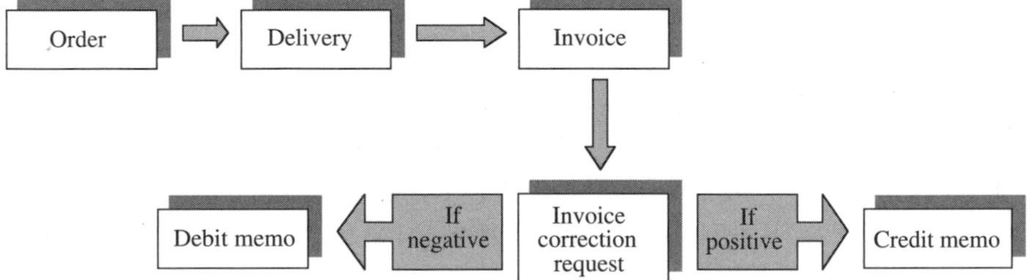

Figure 2-60
The document flow process

These outline agreements take the form of quantity contracts, value contracts, service contracts, and group master contracts, which are a new functionality offered as of SAP Version 4.0.

NOTE: *It is advisable to use a different number range for contracts, as this ensures ease of use when searching for documents and referencing to contracts later.*

The area in the IMG for configuring the contracts process is the same as the standard sales document types, unless specifically stated. Thus, to configure the contract document type, proceed as follows: IMG, Sales and distribution, Sales, Sales documents, Sales document header

Quantity Contract Process

The quantity contract takes place after the quotation but before an order. They are mainly used to limit the quantity in demand by the customer and to offer special pricing. Generally, quantity contracts are used when the demand for a material is greater than the available supply, and the business has to implement measures to limit the supplied quantity evenly between its customers for this material.

Sales Document Type Is KM

The quantity contract does not transfer the requirement. This means

- That it does not create a need for stock from the warehouse (in reserving stock through available-to-promise processing)
- That it does not require production to make the stock to satisfy the contract
- That it does not require material management to purchase the stock to satisfy the contract (if it is a trading good)

The requirement is placed on the warehouse, production, and materials management when the order is created in reference to the quantity contract. The contract itself has no schedule lines, but it does have a validity date. It also enables the customer to have a special price per material. Based on a limited quantity, this quantity decreases each time an order is made by the quantity of stock ordered.

Quantity contracts have no schedule lines or specific delivery dates. Because they do not go to a delivery, they go to an order and then a delivery (an order from a contract is called a release order). Once the contract validity date expires or the customer has purchased the full quota of stock, the contract expires and a new one must be created.

A contract is made, say, with an order value/quantity of 1,000 items. Then each order that the customer places with reference to this contract will decrease the available quantity of this contract. This applies if you have set the "Update document flow" indicator on the item category in the copy control rules. If this is not set, the customer can order as much as he would like, without regard to the contract quantity being updated. This is useful for blocking standard order types for a customer; he is only allowed to order on a certain order type, such as ZOR, which refers to the contract only. Thus, this customer is limited to only ordering 1,000 items. A quantity contract also has validity periods and can have cancellation rules.

To create one, go to Log, SD, Sales, Outline agreement, Contract, Create [VA41]. To make a Release order, go to log, SD, Sales order, Create sales document, Create with reference to contract.

NOTE: *After a release order has been created, it will automatically decrease the amount of the available quantity for the customer to purchase. This will be seen when viewing the contract and when creating new orders.*

Set up the quantity contract and service contract by going to IMG, Sales and Distribution, Sales, Sales doc., Sales Document header.

The quantity contracts have their own pricing procedures, texts, and partners. Like any other document type, they also have their own item categories. Also, don't forget to set up the copy control to other order document types you may be using as release orders.

Service and Maintenance Contract Process

The service contract is an interface and a legal agreement between the receiver of the service and the business supplying the service. It is used beneficially by the business for initiating automatic billing of routine services at regular intervals, for example, and can determine if a cancellation request of the contract is valid. It is used beneficially by the receiver of the service as a contract he can claim, with easy access to requests for service and set prices on specific services.

Sales Document Type Is WV

Generally, a service contract need not have a call-off or release order, nor does it need to be created with reference to other sales documents. For a service and maintenance contract, no delivery is necessary; due to the process being the offering of a service, no materials are relevant for delivering.

A service contract should have its own specific pricing procedure compared to the standard one that may be used by the business (see Figure 2-61). This is due to the fact that the distribution of services may be controlled very differently to that of the distribution of materials.

Let's look at the sales document header in the IMG, Sales and distribution, Sales, Sales documents, Sales document types. By looking at the contract settings of the sales document type, we note the following: The contract profile available for assignments in contracts is predefined as a profile defaulting validity dates and cancellation procedures in the contract. We will cover contract profiles later.

The reference procedure is used for master contracts to determine which data is to be copied or proposed into lower level contracts. The referencing procedures are configured with master contracts later in this chapter.

The Contract data allowed field is a critical field used by the system in contracts. As contract data, validity periods and cancellation data may be kept at the header as well as the item level of the contract. This field indicates to the system what to do when data differs between the header and item levels. With the Contract data allowed set at X, the system will not copy any changes you make in the header level to the item levels. This is also true even if the data at the header and line items were identical prior to the header data being changed. With the setting at Y, the system automatically copies all header data from the header into the item in the contract, but only if the header and item contract data were identical prior to the changes.

Figure 2-61
A service contract should have its own pricing procedure.

Contract

PricProcCondHeadr	PABR01	Contract data allwd.	X
PricProcCondItem	PABR02	FollUpActivityType	0002
Contract profile	0001 One-year Contract	Subseq.order type	
Billing request	IRC	Check partner auth.	
Ref.procedure		☐ Update low.lev.cont.	

The follow-up activity type speeds up the creation of follow-up activities. For example, the follow-up sales activity type 0002 (telephone call) is specified for sales document type WV (service contract). You can create a follow-up activity worklist for contracts by choosing Outline agreement, Contract, Subsequent functions, Follow-up actions and then maintain the selection criteria as required. Then select all contracts with the follow-up action "Create sales activity" and choose Edit, Follow-up actions. A dialog box is then displayed that proposes the sales activity type 0002. Select Save and the follow-up sales activities for the selected contracts will be created automatically. In this case, a workflow will be sent to the user to make the sales call.

Should the follow-up action have been to create a quotation, you would need to enter a quotation document type in the field Subsequent order type. Then when you select Outline agreement, Contract, Subsequent functions, Follow-up actions, the system will propose the order type you entered in this field. The Check partner authorization field determines which partners are authorized to release a contract. Should no check be performed, you may leave the field blank.

Partners for Release Orders The release partner is the sold-to party (partner function AG, the German standard) of the contract or it may be a partner in the contract that has a partner function of AA, which is the partner function of an authorized release partner. This is the standard checking rule A.

In the standard checking rule B, the system checks if the partner wanting to be released from the contract is a lower level customer in the customer hierarchy. You can also create multiple ship-to parties for the specific contract. The standard (German) ship-to party partner function is WE, but you may have more than one ship-to party; thus, you may assign ship-to parties with the partner function AW.

Assign both the release sold-to parties and the release ship-to parties to the sold-to party of the contract in the customer master record. Thus, when you create the individual contracts, the system will propose these assigned partners. Please also refer to partner determination in Chapter 4 where this configuration is explained.

The Update lower level contracts field need not be initiated, as the contract in question is not a master contract. This field is used by the system to update lower level contracts, should the data you are changing be the master contract. These changes are then passed down to the lower level contracts via workflow. If this field is not set, the system will only update the lower level contract when it is reprocessed.

The Contract Profile The contract profile is explained in three categories: contract profiles, contract validity dates, and cancellation procedures. These are defined by proceeding to IMG, Sales and distribution, Sales, Sales documents, Contracts, Contract data, Define contract profiles. To define your own contract profile, select a standard contract profile and copy. An example of a contract profile is shown in Figure 2-62.

You have a contract start date and end date. In this case, the start date is the acceptance date and end date is the start date plus the validity period. The contract also has a validity for one year. These dates are defined in the IMG, Sales and distribution, Sales, Sales documents, Contracts, Contract data, Define rules for determining dates. The cancellation procedure is defined in IMG, Sales and distribution, Sales, Sales documents, Contracts, Contract data, Control cancellation, Define cancellation procedures.

For each cancellation procedure, you must assign a cancellation rule. This cancellation rule, as shown in Figure 2-63, in a procedure defines two basic aspects:

1. The date of earliest cancellation for the start date plus the validity period rule 08 (for example, five years).
2. The period of notice, which is the period before the end of the contract for which a cancellation notice must be entered (here this is three months), failing which an automatic extension of the contract is valid for another year. The customer then has to submit a cancellation request three months prior to the end of the next cancellation period, which here is one year.

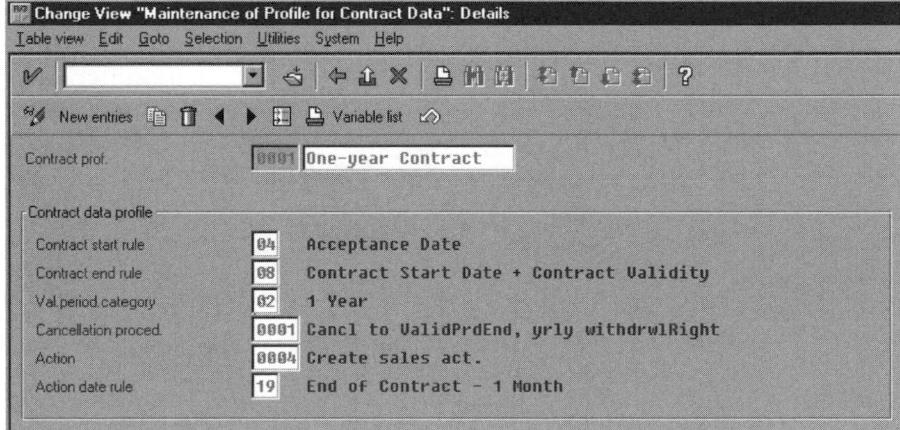

Figure 2-62
A contract profile

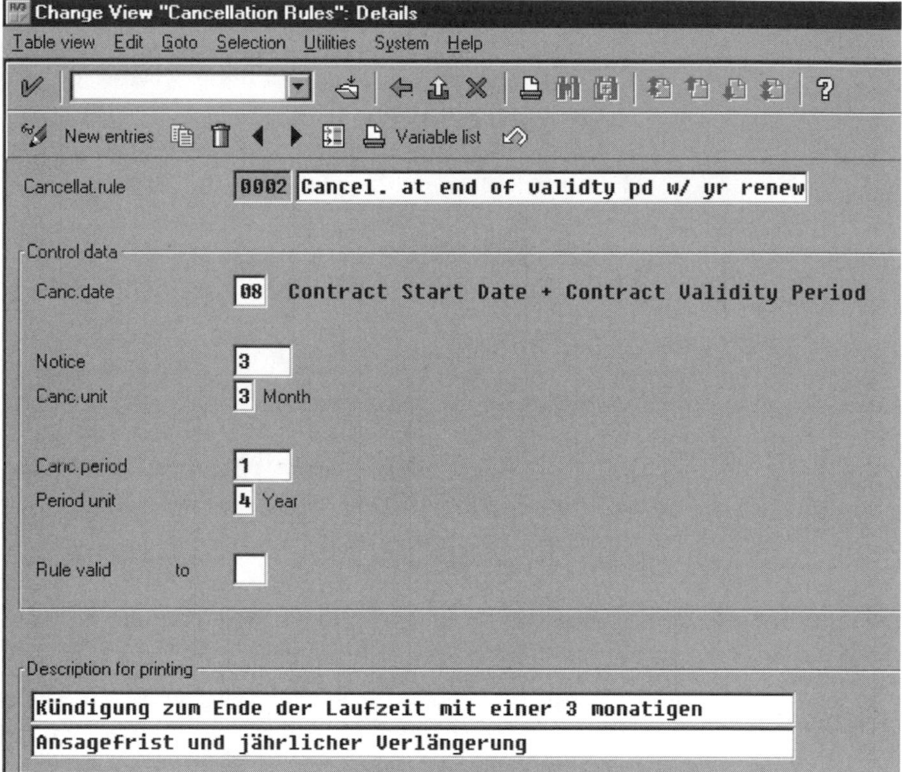

Figure 2-63
Configuring the cancellation rule

The cancellation rule is defined in IMG, Sales and distribution, Sales, Sales documents, Contracts, Contract data, Control cancellation, Define cancellation rules and then assigned in Assign cancellation rules and cancellation procedures. Due to these settings, the system can automatically enter the validity period and date determination in the contract. This is done by assigning the contract profile to the sales document type representing the contract, such as WV.

The item category used by service contracts is very important. It is best to understand the process to be mapped before customizing. This is due to the fact that the service item can be any one of the following:

- A service task
- It may be time, charged for a technician's hourly rate.

The standard item category for a service is WVN. You may need additional item categories, which will possibly be the case, due to the multiple types of items available on a service contract. Remember to copy this standard and change the necessary fields.

The standard item category has been created to represent an item, which is a service that is carried out and billed periodically. The standard item category has a completion rule C, which determines the item to be fully referenced when the target quantity is fully reached. This particular item category is relevant for order-related billing, according to a billing plan, and utilizes billing plan type 02, which indicates periodic billing. This item category does not enable any schedule lines.

SAP provides standard material types for service items. These material types are DIEN and KMAT. DIEN is the material type generally used for standard services.

After setting up the relevant document type and item categories, proceed to mapping the copying control rules. Create the service contract by proceeding as follows: Logistics, Sales and distribution, Sales, Outline agreement, Contract. Then select the respective contract you wish to create, such as WV. Enter the relevant details including the material and target quantity.

Value Contract Process

The value contract is similar to the quantity contract in that it limits material or services to a customer. However, instead of limiting due to the quantity of stock, the contract and its ceiling is based upon a total value.

The value contract is created and maintained the same way as the other standard contracts and document types, yet SAP has created its own configuration menu path in the IMG. The only reason why I can see that this was done is to assist in the implementation of online documentation, making the documentation readily available by merely double-clicking on the function in the IMG. Nonetheless, should you wish to configure this contract by using the menu paths created for it in the IMG, proceed as follows: IMG, Sales and distribution, Sales, Sales documents, Contracts, Value contract.

The sales document type is WK2 for a specific material or WK1 for assortment modules.

An Assortment Module

An assortment module is a order entry tool that displays a list of materials and services that can be released from a value contract. It has a validity date and a restriction that only the materials and services that belong in the same sales organization and distribution channel for which your release order is being made will be displayed.

To create a assortment module, as displayed in Figure 2-64, proceed as follows: Logistics, Sales and distribution, Master data, Products, Value contract assortment module, Create. Press enter and you are faced with the following screen.

Enter a short description for the material assortment module. Then enter the materials and their respective validity dates.

Now that the background is done, one can continue creating the value contract. You do not need to utilize an assortment module; you may instead create a value contract per a product hierarchy range, or you may create a value contract per material.

As already stated, two types of value contracts exist in SAP. They are referred to as the standard value contract and the material-related value contract.

Specifics of the Standard Value Contract WK1 This value contract should be used for the majority of instances when a contract is based upon the total value of an assortment of materials according the particular customer. You can specify a product hierarchy or an assortment module for value contracts of this type.

Specifics of the Material-related Value Contract WK2 This value contract should be used when you need the functionality of a value contract, yet when using this type of contract, you are restricted to using it for one material. This one material is usually a configurable material. The contract length can be different here at the item level than at the header level.

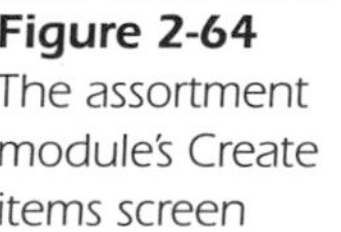

Figure 2-64
The assortment module's Create items screen

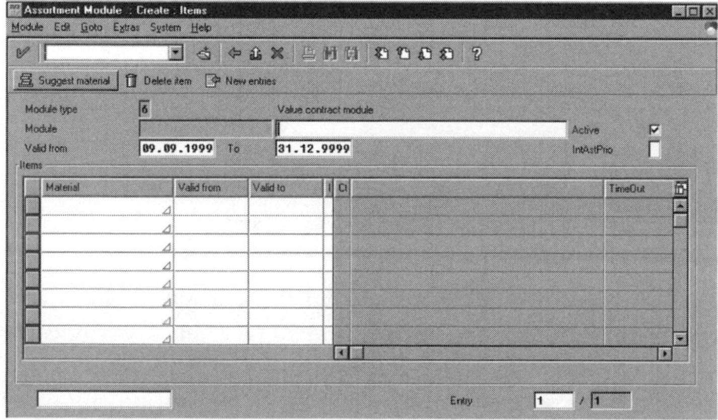

Similarities of the value contracts WK1 and WK2 Both of the value contracts have a header level and an item level. None of the contracts have a schedule line level. Thus, neither of these contracts are responsible for delivering products. Each of the value contracts has a release order, which is based on the total value.

The release orders are standard order types created with reference to the contract. The sold-to party must correspond to that of the value contract, or it must be a release partner. This is also true for the ship-to party.

To configure the value contracts, follow the standard procedure from the IMG, Sales and Distribution, Sales, Sales doc., Sales Document header. Or, as already explained, go to IMG, Sales and distribution, Sales, Sales documents, Contracts, Value contract.

The value contracts WK1 and WK2 have their own number range, so try to keep all contract number ranges equal to facilitate ease of use. They both have the sales document category G (contract).

They both also have a pricing procedure assigned to them. The value contract can have a billing type assigned to it, should order related billing be necessary. Refer to Chapter 3 for billing information. Specific contract data, as defined previously in quantity contracts, can also be selected and assigned.

Do not forget the copy control rules from sales document type WK1 or WK2 to TA, as well as item category WKN to TAN being a standard item category (the standard item category for WK1 contracts) or WAN being a release order item category. This is in order to allow release orders for the value contract. The standard item category for WK2 contracts is WKC.

NOTE: *When configuring the item categories, it is proposed that you select completion rule E for the contract item category. Indicating the item is deemed to be complete when the total target value is reached.*

In the configuration of the item category, should the item be relevant for billing, enter the billing indicator and refer to Chapter 4. Due to there being no schedule lines permitted, be sure *not* to select the schedule lines allowed.

The value contract material is a material that you can add to the item category. It is necessary for value contracts that have no one specific material, but rely on a material assortment or product hierarchy. The value contract material is used to derive taxes and update statistics. Be sure that the material you enter here has the correct item category determination. The item category group on material master plus the sales document type will propose the item category.

The contract release control, which is set at the item category level, defines if the item must give an error, a warning, or no response when a complete contract is being used as a reference to create a release order. A setting of "A" here is recommended.

The release order can be created in any currency. The system automatically converts the currency of the release order to that of the currency in the value contract on the pricing date of the release order.

The value contract is deemed as complete once the total value is reached, the validity period has been met, or a reason for rejection has been entered for the line items. Do not forget that you can control how the system must respond by changing the setting in the item category WKN. Here you can define a warning message, an error message, or no reaction required from the system. No reaction from the system results in the system accepting the contract and allowing the release order, should you wish to create a release order for a contract that has already expired.

To create a contract, proceed as follows: Logistics, Sales and distribution, Sales, Outline agreement, Contract. Then select the respective contract you wish to create, such as WK1.

Figure 2-65 shows a standard value contract WK1, created for three materials. It has a call-off value for each material as well as a validity date for the contract.

Figure 2-65
A standard value contract, WK1

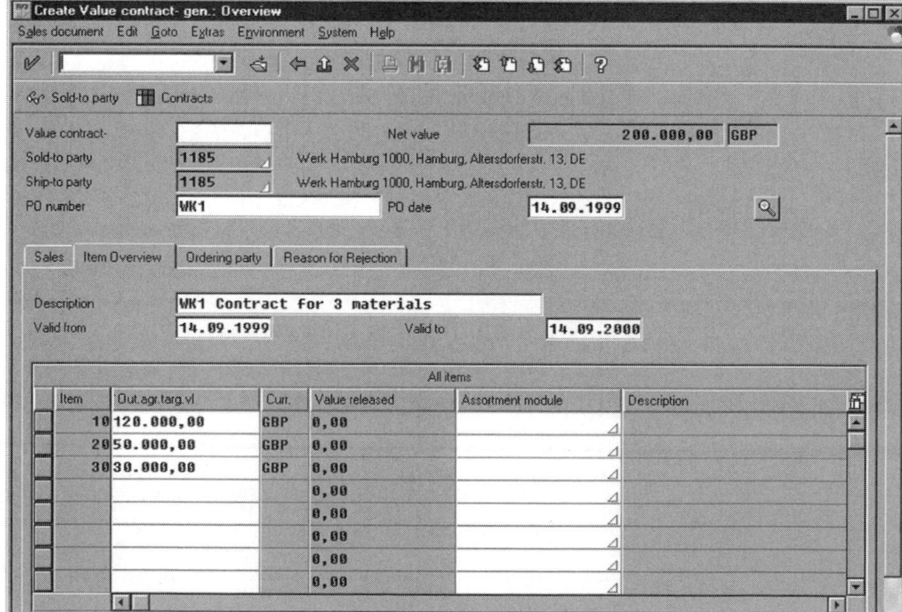

After creating the contract, you may call off from it using a *release order*. To do this, proceed as follows: Logistics, Sales and distribution, Sales, Order, Create. Then select the button to contract.

Enter the contract number, as displayed in Figure 2-66, followed by the call-off party. If no call-off party is entered, it will be proposed automatically. After selecting Copy, the system will propose that you indicate which material you wish to copy into the release order.

In the selection screen, when processing from a WK1 contract, select the Enter material button, as shown in Figure 2-67.

Proceed with entering the material and call-off quantity you wish to call off from, being sure it is in the product hierarchy if you have selected one in the value contract. Following this, select the green arrow, indicate the material you have just selected (it will have a small green icon attached to it), and press copy.

By selecting the Expand assortment button in Figure 2-68, the system allows you to display a list of materials in the assortment module from a selection list. Select the material and enter a required selection quantity. Use the selection list function to return to the selection list. Again, indicate

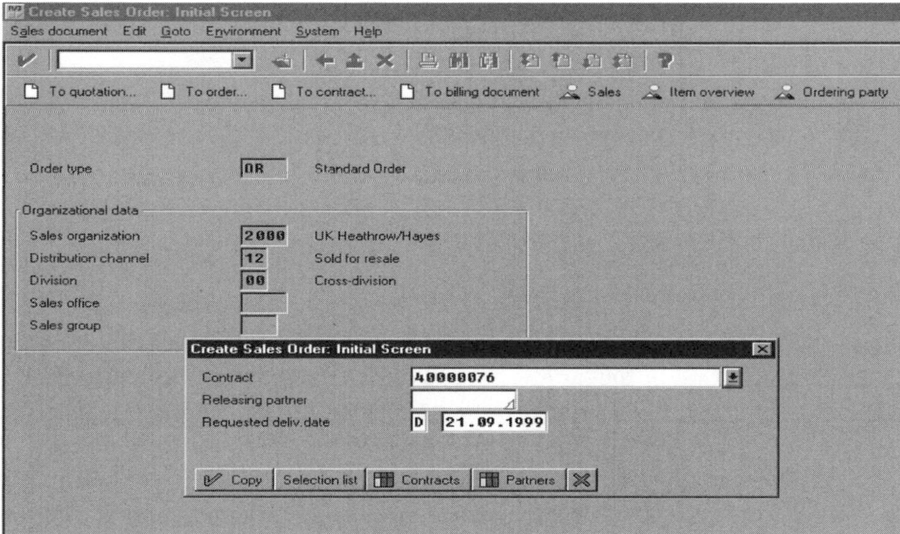

Figure 2-66 Entering the contract number

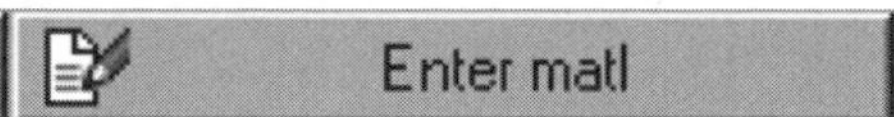

Figure 2-67 The Enter material button

Figure 2-68 The Expand assortment button

the material you have just selected (it will have a small green icon attached to it) and press copy.

In the selection screen, when processing from a WK2 contract, press copy and enter the release quantity you wish to call off. After creating the release order, the system will then update the value contract by the value that was called off.

The release order value is calculated automatically and updated into the value contract. The remaining value in the contract is the original value less the combination of the total of open order and delivery values and the total of the items already invoiced. Should there be any negative process flows, such as returns or rejected line items of the release order, the system takes this into account with the automatic update of the value contract.

NOTE: *You can only have one release order refer to a contract. Thus, you cannot have a release order for both a quantity contract as well as a value contract.*

Master Contracts

A master contract consists of other contracts that are grouped as lower level contracts. Thus, the master contract has the general data that is relevant for all lower level contracts over a specified period. Contracts are grouped in order to ensure that all data in the lower level contracts remain consistent and that terms granted in the master contract are copied into all lower level contracts.

The documents that can be grouped under a master contract are as follows:

- Quantity contracts
- Value contracts
- Service contracts

A master contract contains header data as well as the billing plan data, the partners data, business data, and contract data. To understand and configure a master contract, it is important to understand the desired functionality of contract grouping.

Contract grouping is the process whereby several lower level contracts are linked to one master contract to ensure data consistency. When you link a lower level contract to a master contract, the header data of the master contract are passed down into the lower level contract.

NOTE: *For this to happen, the lower level and higher level contracts must be assigned to the same sales area. Also note that you cannot assign a hierarchy of contracts together. You can only have one master contract with many lower level contracts assigned to it.*

To group contracts, you must first determine the referencing requirements. Proceed as follows: IMG, Sales, Sales documents, Contracts, Master contracts, Define referencing requirements, Define reference sales document types. In this activity, you assign the contracts that can be referenced by the main master contract. Note that you can create other master contract document types in the same way that you can create other sales document types. We will cover the data required in the master contract document type a little later.

The process of assigning reference document types is beneficial if you want to only allow quantity contracts to be assigned to a particular master contract.

This screen example in Figure 2-69 shows the contract types on the left that use the GK master contract as a source. That is, they reference the GK contract.

Now that the document assignments are done, the most crucial procedure is defining the referencing procedures. Its path is IMG, Sales, Sales documents, Contracts, Master contracts, Define referencing requirements, Define referencing procedures. There should be no need for you to create a new reference procedure, as displayed in Figure 2-70, but if you should require one, follow these steps:

1. Select the sample procedure as delivered in the standard system.
2. Copy the procedure and rename it. Select "copy all" from the pop-up box, as shown in Figure 2-71, to copy all subsequent entries. It is always recommended to copy all the subsequent entries and to delete the entries not required afterwards.

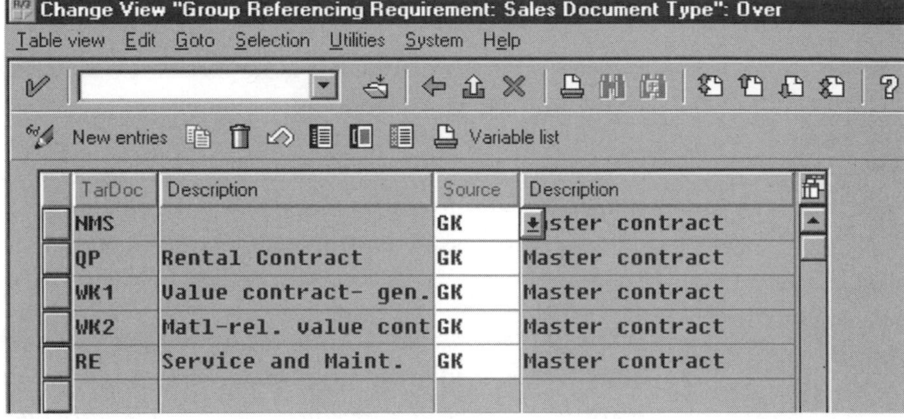

Figure 2-69
Contact types that which reference the master contract

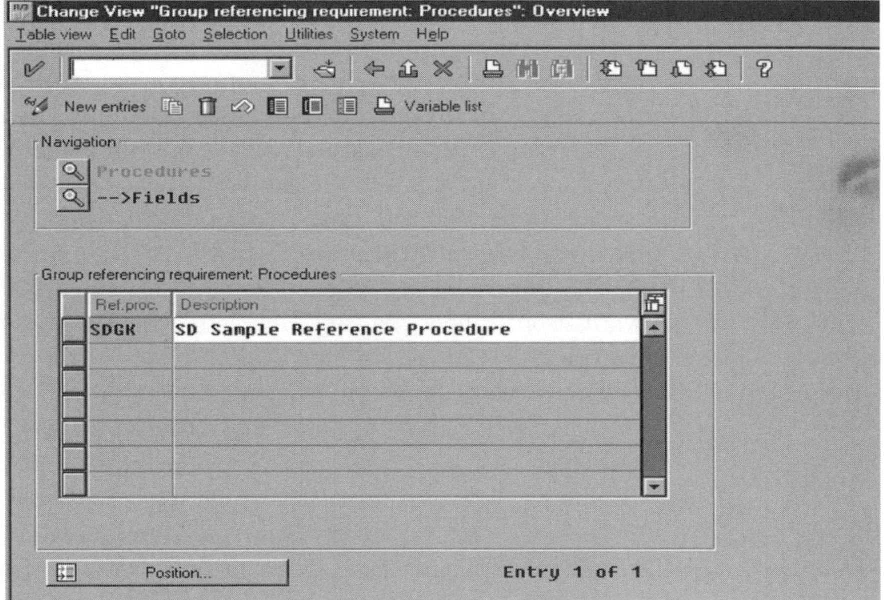

Figure 2-70
A new reference procedure

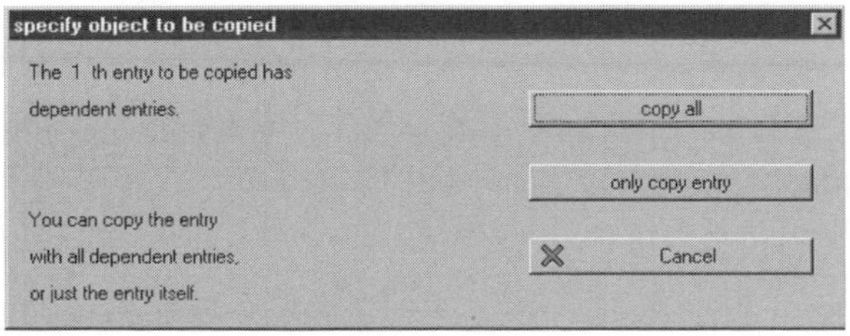

specify object to be copied

The 1 th entry to be copied has dependent entries.

copy all

only copy entry

You can copy the entry with all dependent entries, or just the entry itself.

Cancel

Figure 2-71
Specifying the objects to be copied

3. Select the procedure and select the button fields.
4. You are presented with the table displayed in Figure 2-72.

You will notice that this screen enables you to enter or delete certain table and field entries. As you are familiar with tables and field names from Chapter 1, "SAP Basics, Organizational and Master Data," you can use the transaction [SE12] to read the short text of the field entries of a certain table.

The data represented here is divided into five columns. Column 1 and 2 are the table and field names respectively. Column 3 is a partner column, the partner representing a function of the customer, such as the ship-to party (see partner determination in Chapter 3.) Column 5 indicates if the system is to give a message to a lower level contract each time it wants to update this lower level contract with data from a master contract. Column 4 has the copy rules assigned to it that are as follows:

A indicates the contract must have the same value in the field for the higher and lower level contract. Should these fields not match, that is, if you change the value in the field of the lower level contract, the

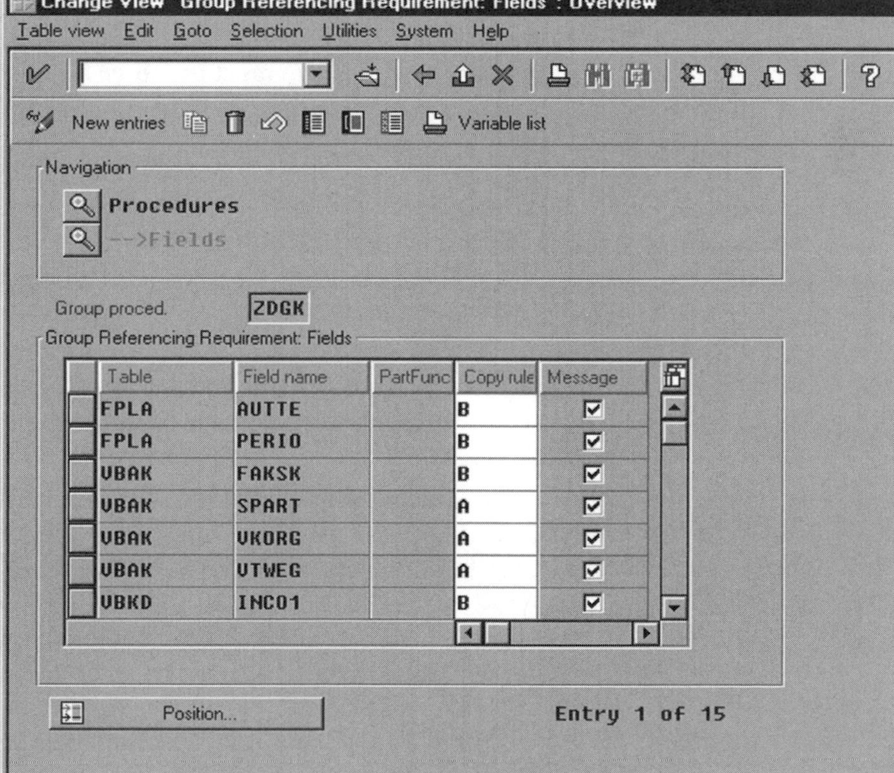

Figure 2-72 The Group Referencing Requirement fields

reference will no longer be carried out. Thus, the contracts will not be allowed to be linked.

B indicates the value in the field is to be copied from the master contract and cannot be changed in the lower level contract. Thus, fields deviating in the lower level contract are not allowed.

C indicates proposal fields; this occurs when the master contract copies or proposes data into the lower level contract, but the value of these fields is allowed to be overwritten in the lower level contract. If you change one of these fields in a master contract, the system will only copy the proposal fields into the lower level contract if the value of both the master and lower level contracts was equal before the master contract was changed. This is referred to as standard application logic.

Now that we have defined the background of the master contracts, we need to define the document type and the associated process. Proceed to define the sales document types. The standard sales document type is GK. To create or change this document, remember to select, copy, rename, and save. Ensure the document type has the following configuration entries:

- The SD document category must be a 0 for the master contract.
- The screen sequence group must be GK or a copy of GK.
- The transaction group must be 4 to represent a contract.
- You may wish to select the Contract messages field and enter a value of A, which will cause the system to propose a list of master contracts for you to select from with the same header data, should one already have been created.
- The contract profile should represent the date procedures you want to have defaulted.
- The reference procedure is the same reference procedure as defined in the master contract reference tables and fields earlier with the copy rules A, B, and C.
- The update lower level contract field is crucial. This field, if selected, will cause the associated lower level contracts to be updated immediately after a change has occurred in a higher level contract according to the rules specified in the referencing procedures; this is carried out via workflow. Should this field not be indicated, the system will only update a lower level contract once that contract is called for processing.

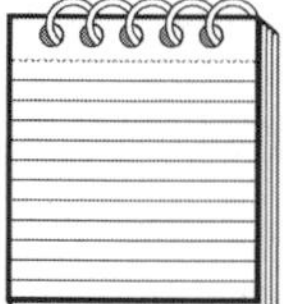

NOTE: *In the automatic updating via workflow, when the fields value is set and the system finds an error in the updating, the user who changed the master contract will receive a workflow item, enabling him to make the changes in the lower level contract manually.*

No delivery type or billing type is necessary, as the master contract is not relevant for deliveries or billing documents.

Also do not forget to set up the copy control rules at the header level only, as no items or schedule line data exists. To link a contract to a master contract, proceed as follows: Logistics, Sales and distribution, Sales, Select outline agreement, Create. Here you create a master contract. It is recommended that you create a master contract first and then proceed with creating the other individual lower level contracts. You can then assign the lower level contracts to the higher level contract.

The master contract has the following overview screen, as displayed in Figure 2-73. You can see it does not have any item details and you can also see the reference procedure. Once a lower level contract has been assigned to a master contract, you can no longer assign another reference procedure to the master contract.

After assigning the lower level contracts to the master contract, you are nearly finished with the master contract process. The only remaining data

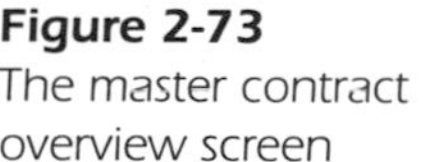

Figure 2-73
The master contract overview screen

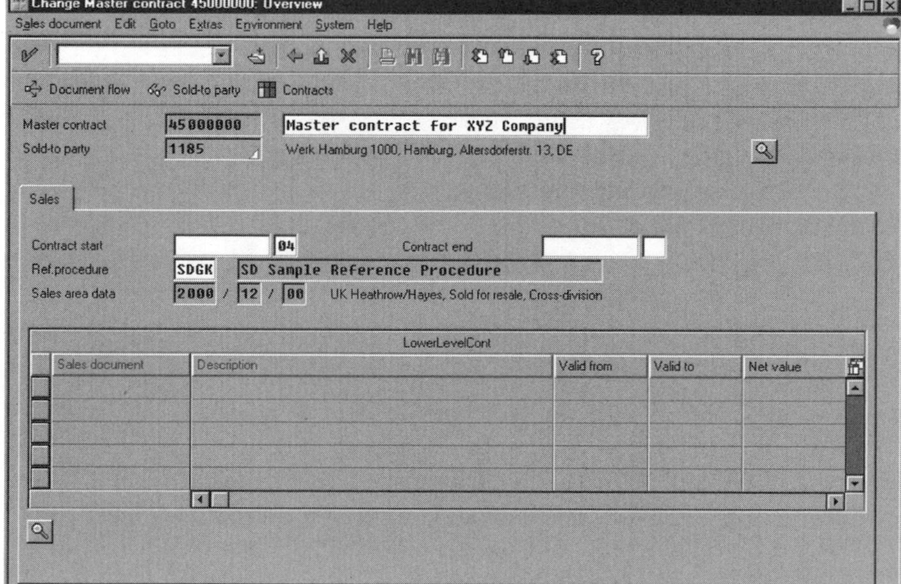

to configure is the workflow, which is issued once a contract is to be updated. A workflow is a sequence of steps that are processed either by people or automatically by the system. Generally, workflow is controlled by a specialist workflow resource; thus, we will not be looking into the configuration of workflow objects, as it is beyond the scope of this book. We will, however, look into the simple task of assigning agents to the workflow task. Proceed as follows: IMG, Sales, Sales documents, Contracts, Master contracts, Activate workflow for master contracts, Activate event linkage. Press enter. Page down until you reach the workflow object type for master contracts, which is BUS2095 (see Figure 2-74).

Select the object and press display. You are presented with the following screen, as shown in Figure 2-75.

Select the Enabled indicator as shown in Figure 2-75 and save.

Then proceed to IMG, Sales, Sales documents, Contracts, Master contracts, Activate workflow for master contracts, Maintain assignment of agents (see Figure 2-76).

Select Task, Display, followed by Additional data, Agent assignment, Maintain. You are presented with the following screen, as shown in Figure 2-77.

Select Change customer contract on screen and hit the button shown in Figure 2-78.

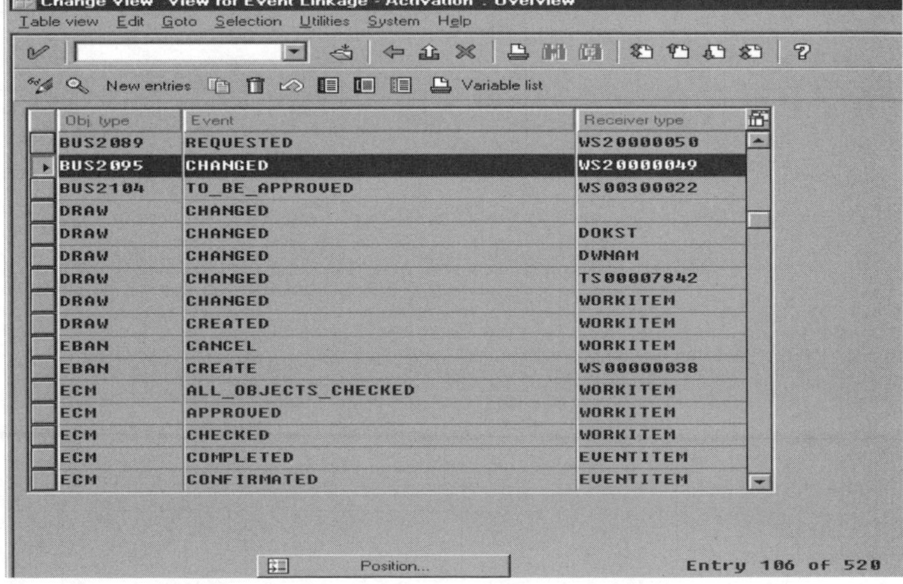

Figure 2-74 Locating BUS2095, the workflow object type for master contracts

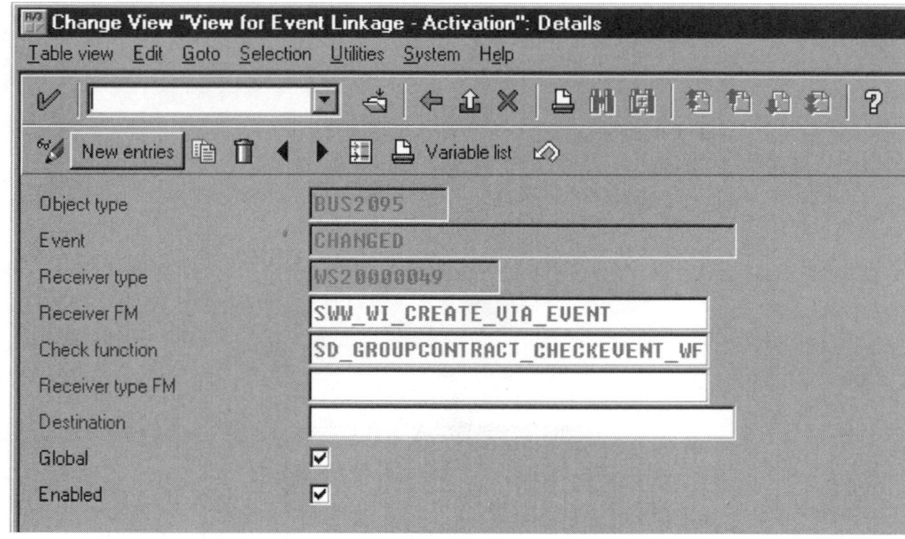

Figure 2-75
Changing BUS2095

Select a user and then enter the user ID of the person whom you want to receive the workflow, as shown in Figure 2-79.

Now the user ID is assigned to the workflow object and the master contract configuration is completed.

Consignment Stock Process

In the consignment stock process, a business allows stock or materials to sit at the customer's site or allows stock that is reserved for the customer to sit at its own site. This is done through an agreement that the customer will sell or consume as many of these materials as he can. Only after the customer has consumed or sold anything will the business issue a invoice. Should the customer not want to sell or consume any more material, he informs the business and it returns their stock.

NOTE: *All requirements transferred from consignment sales orders to materials planning are transferred as individual requirements. This occurs regardless of what availability checking group indicator is set on the respective material master record.*

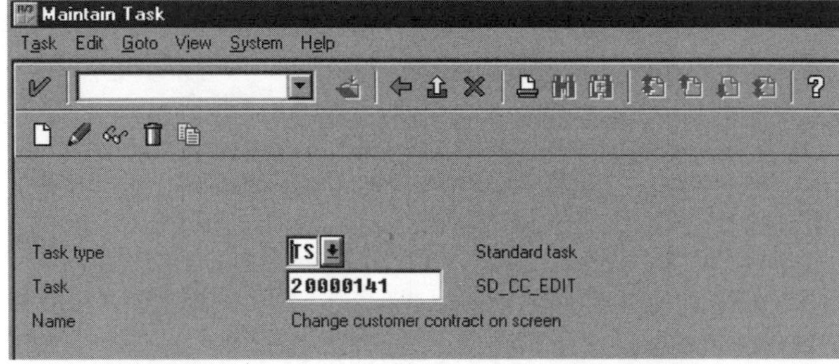

Figure 2-76 Maintaining the assignment of agents

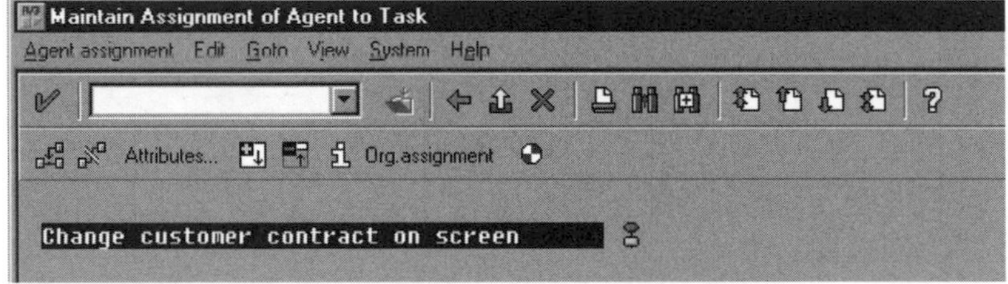

Figure 2-77 Changing the customer contact on screen

Figure 2-78 Select node

The Stock Consignment stock is monitored in our system by individual customer and material. The consignment quantity is controlled separately from the available stock for standard sales orders. This type of stock is refereed to as *special stock*. Other forms of special stock are returnable packaging.

The Consignment Fill-up The business delivers stock, as displayed in Figure 2-80, to a customer on consignment. This process is called the *consignment fill-up*. The consignment fill-up uses a standard sales order document type KB. This KB order type is then followed by a standard delivery LF.

The consignment fill-up sales document type KB and all other consignment-related sales document types should have the sales document category setting C (sales order). It is also advisable to use a different number range, as

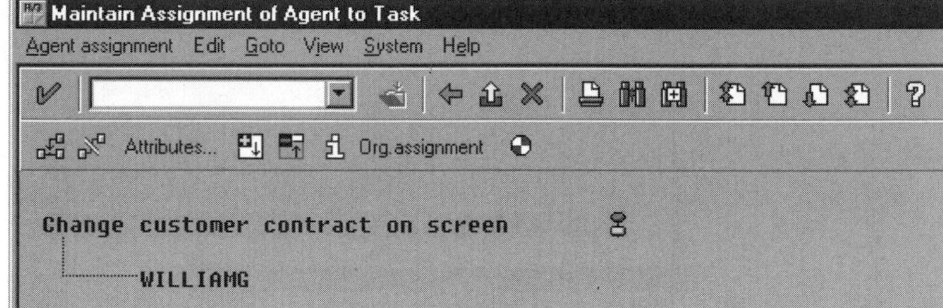

Figure 2-79 Specifying the user who will recieve the workflow

Figure 2-80 The consignment fill-up process

you will want the consignment sales process to be highlighted as a different sales procedure to the standard sales cycle.

TIP: *It is also advisable to refrain from reporting on these fill-ups for statistical purposes, as bookings as these fill-ups in no way indicate a sale. To report on bookings and billings, you should use the consignment issue process.*

The delivery type used is the standard LF; see Chapter 3.

The big changes to the standard sales order process are the following. Due to the customer not being billed for any of these items, no invoice is relevant. Thus, the sales document type setting, whether it be for order-related or delivery-related billing, should show no billing document relevant.

The item category that is the standard for consignment fill-ups, KBN, should be set as not relevant for billing as well as set for no pricing. Thus, the business data of the item category should look similar to Figure 2-81.

NOTE: *The item does allow schedule lines. This is a fundamental element in the consignment process. The schedule line category determines how deliveries are to perform and what types of goods movements are carried out. The standard schedule line categories to be used are E0 and E1.*

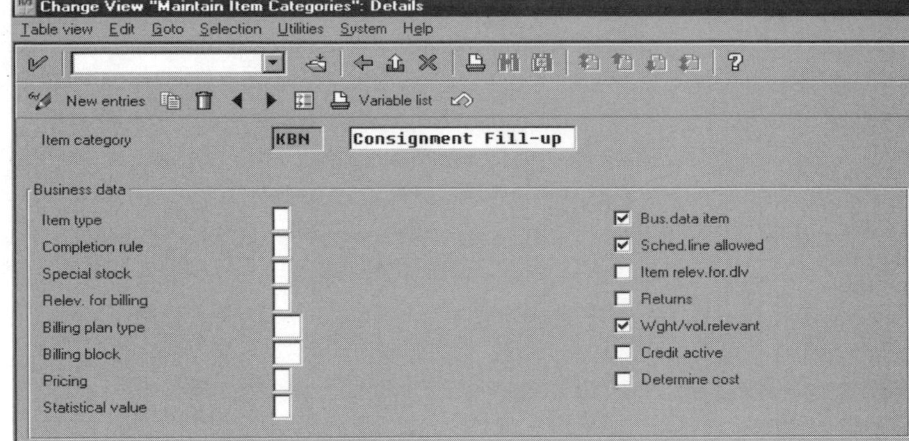

Figure 2-81
The consignment fill-up item category

Change View "Maintain Schedule Line Categories": Details
Table view Edit Goto Selection Utilities System Help
New entries
Variable list
Sched.line cat. E1 StoTranToCons. w. AC
Business data
Delivery block
Movement type 631 GI consgmt: lending
Item rel.f.dlv.
Movement type 1-step
Order type
P.req.del.sched
Item category
Acct.assgt.cat.
Transaction flow
Incompl.proced. 30 Deliv-Rel.Sched.Line
Req./Assembly
Availability
Prod.allocation

Figure 2-82
Schedule line category E1 uses MRP and availability checking.

Schedule line category E1, as displayed in Figure 2-82, is used with *materials requirement planning* (MRP) and uses availability checking.

The schedule line states the item is relevant for deliveries and when the delivery happens, the item must use movement type 631. Movement type 631 is the key that, at the time of goods issue, posts the stock into a special consignment category in the delivering plants stock for that particular customer and material (Chapter 3 will cover delivery processes).

Do not forget to set up the sales document copying control for the sales document, item category, and schedule line category. You may wish to assign a delivery block to the sales document type KB, as this will automatically propose a delivery block before the materials are shipped to the consignee. Thus, you are able to monitor what stock you are sending and if it is authorized.

After completion of the customizing entries, create a sales order [VA01] using document type KB for a specific material and customer. To create a consignment fill-up order, proceed as follows. Go to Logistics, Sales and distribution, Sales, Create, and then enter the order type. Next proceed with the delivery and goods issue.

To view the stock the customer has on consignment, you can use transaction code [MB58] or transaction code [MMBE]. You can also use the menu path Logistics, Materials management, Environment, Stock, Stock overview.

Enter the material and the plant, which delivers the material, as shown in Figure 2-83. Press execute and you will be see a list of stock for that material in the plant. Should you not select a plant but merely enter the material and select execute, the system will propose material in all the plants within a company code.

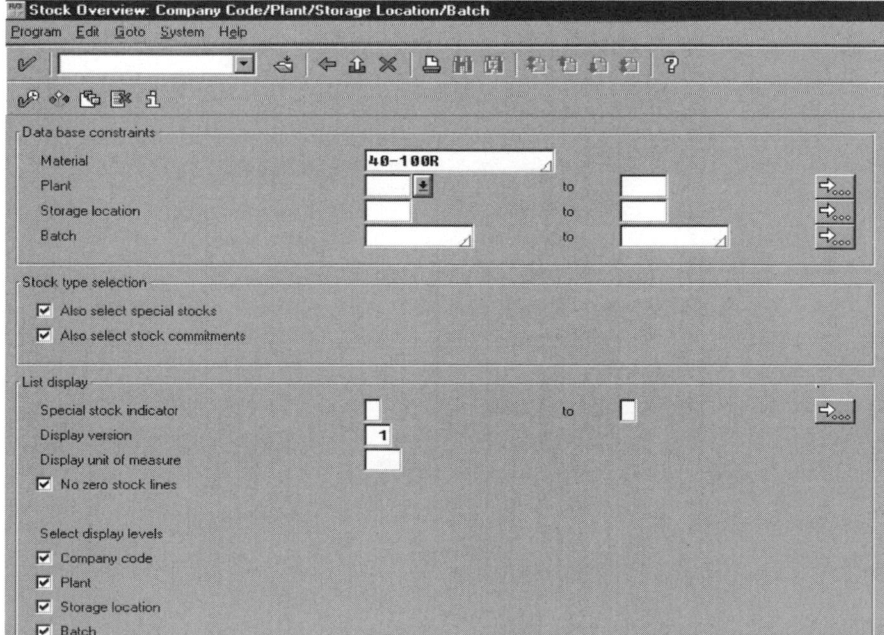

Figure 2-83 Entering the material and plant information

You are then presented with the stock overview screen, as shown in Figure 2-84. This screen shows the material, its description, and its type, in this case a HALB. It also shows its unit of measure as well as the total stock available for the company code, 1000.

Should stock be available and be on consignment at the customer, you will see an entry shown in Figure 2-85, with the consignment stock total represented at a customer as well as the batches that make up that total.

Should you double-click on Cnsgmt at customer, you will receive the following, as displayed in Figure 2-86. This indicates the consignment stock quantity at the customers site as well as who the customer is.

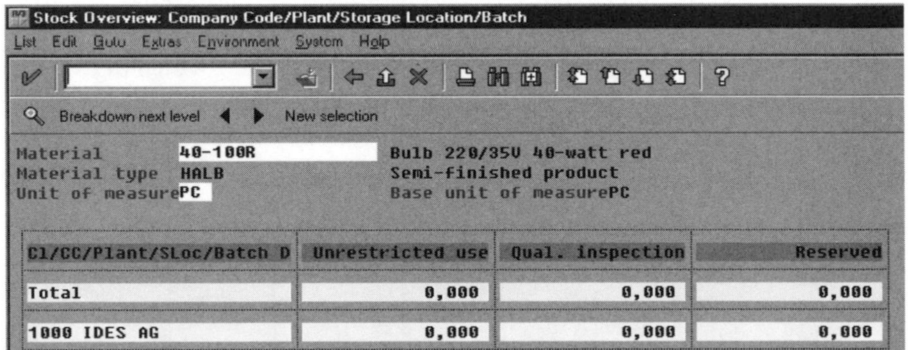

Figure 2-84 The stock overview screen

Cnsgmt at customer	202,000
199907BE	2,000
199907US	200,000

Figure 2-85 Consignment at the customer information

Stock type	Stock
Customer 100012	
Crosfield	
Unrestricted use	202,000
Qual. inspection	0,000
Restricted-use	0,000

Figure 2-86 Customer and the consignment stock quantity information

NOTE: *When a consignment fill-up is carried out, the system checks the available quantity of stock in the delivering plant to see if this quantity can be met. When the system proceeds with a consignment issue or consignment pick-up, the system checks the stock represented at the customer's site to see if there is an available quantity.*

Now that we have completed the consignment fill-up, the consignee may consume the material or sell some. He then indicates to us that this has happened, usually after it has actually occurred. Because the business is usually only informed after the consumption happens, it is not sensible to have any checking in the consignment issue cycle. For example, there is no need to have a billing block or a delivery block. It is possible to have an automatic credit check for consignment issues as you determine open items that are unpaid. A manual credit check should be done on the consignee *before* every consignment fill-up is done, however, should a fill up already be carried out, it is not physically possible to stop the consignee from consuming stock at his site, should he fail his check, as he usually only informs the business after he has consumed one stock.

The Consignment Issue The customer only pays when he sells or consumes the materials. The business issues the sale to the consignee via an order type KE. A standard LF delivery is then done followed by the invoice. This process flow is displayed in Figure 2-87.

The consignment issue document type KE is again a sales document with category C. It has a standard delivery type LF. This document type is relevant for billing and should be relevant for delivery-related billing using a standard delivery type F2.

The standard item category used is KEN. This is relevant for billing as well as pricing. It has schedule lines and should determine the cost of the item. Thus, the item category control for business data should appear as displayed in Figure 2-88.

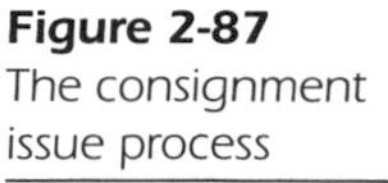

Figure 2-87
The consignment issue process

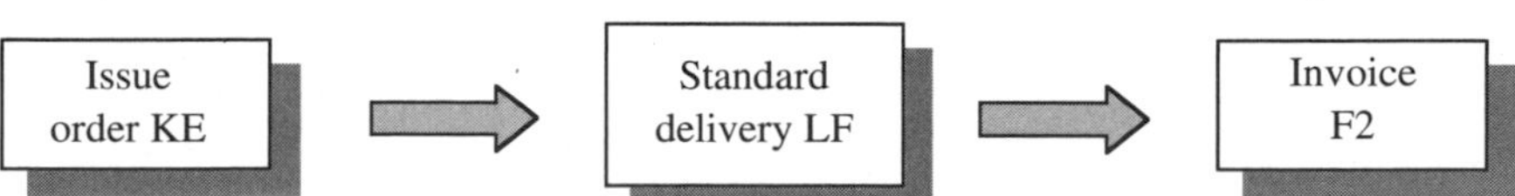

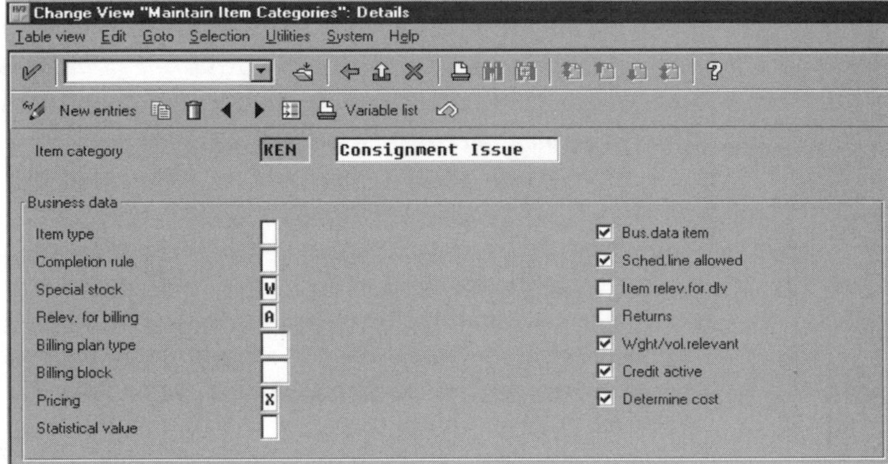

Figure 2-88 The item category control for business data for item category KEN

NOTE: *The special stock indicators are used to indicate that the material being controlled must be controlled as special stock. For consignment, the special stock indicator used is a W. The standard schedule line categories used are C0 and C1.*

Schedule line category C1 does an availability check and performs materials requirements planning. It uses goods movement 633, which checks for available consignment stock at the consignee's site. The schedule line is relevant for deliveries. To create a consignment issue order, proceed as follows: Logistics, Sales and distribution, Sales, Create, and enter the order type. Then proceed through to the invoice.

Once stock has been consumed from the customer's consignment stock, that is, the delivery has been made and the goods issue posted, the stock overview [MMBE] screen will represent this transaction by showing a lower available quantity available in the customer's consignment for that particular material.

The Consignment Return This process should not be confused with the pick-up of the materials. The consignment return is a sales process flow that represents faulty materials or the product consumed or sold by the consignee. The consignee puts the stock back into his consignment stock as faulty and requests a credit note for returns. The process flow is shown in Figure 2-89.

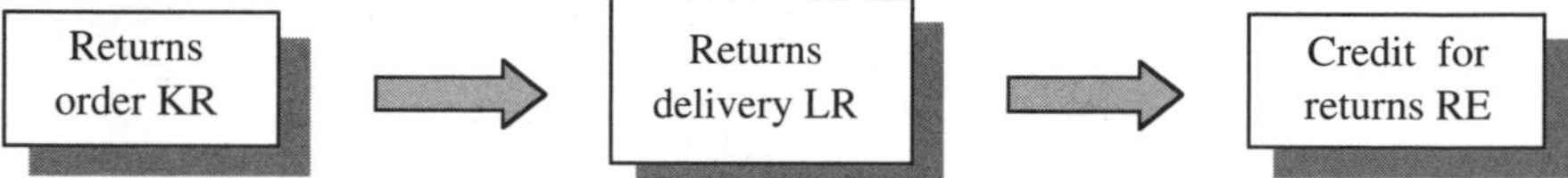

Figure 2-89 The consignment return process

TIP: *You may wonder why the material is simply not returned into stock. A rule of thumb is that for every outward process, there must be an equal inward process. This is to ensure that material postings back into stock and financial postings are balanced. It also assists in the balanced inward and outward updating of logistics information systems.*

The sales document type KR has a sales document type category H, which indicates a sales return document. The return should also have a different number range for the visibility of returned items. The returns document type should also promote a special shipping condition that causes a special shipping point to be used in shipping point determination, which, as discussed in sales document types, can be used to process all return deliveries.

I would suggest all return order document types be restricted to a mandatory reference procedure. Thus, an M would be assigned, indicating a reference to an billing document. Do not forget to assign the reference document in the copying control rules and make sure you select the update document flow in the copying control rules. This will ensure a direct path through the consumption and returns of stock.

Should one wish to utilize a different return pricing procedure for all return process flows. Enter a different document pricing procedure indicator. The assigned delivery type is LR. The delivery-related or order-related billing type should be RE. It is valid to automatically propose a billing block in order to check if the credit is authorized and valid. Thus, assign the standard billing block 08 here.

The item category in the sales document that is passed through to the invoice is KRN. Item category KRN also has the special stock indicator W to indicate the consignment process. The item is also relevant for delivery-related billing and is valid for pricing. The item category business data screen will have the following appearance, as shown in Figure 2-90.

The standard schedule line category used in the system for consignment returns is D0, which uses the standard movement type 634. Being the receipt of the customer's consignment, the item is relevant for delivery. However, no transfer of requirements should be carried out and no availability check should be done. This is due to the fact that we are receiving the

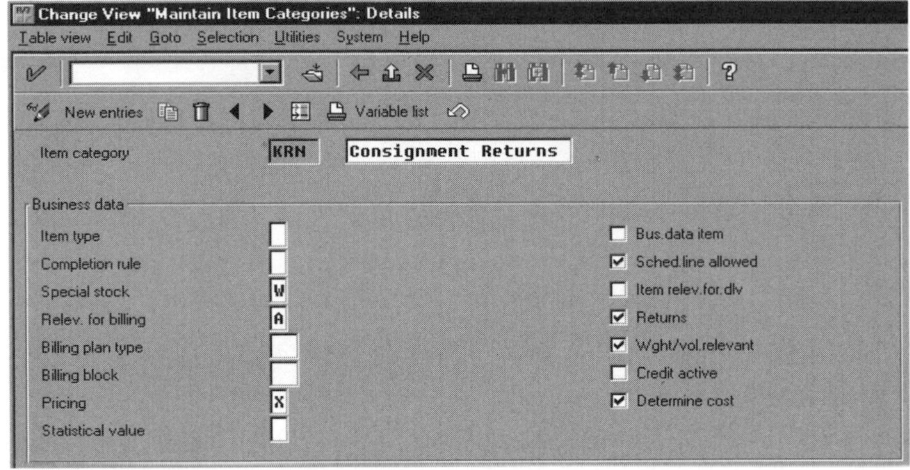

Figure 2-90 The item category business data screen for item category KRN

goods back into our plant. We cannot do an availability check, as the articles are moving back into the customer's site, nor does it make sense to transfer requirements to our materials management.

The stock is moved back into the customer's consignment stock, not our plant. The logic is that the customer will call us to pick up the unused goods and simply consume other material in their stock that is not faulty. Thus, the customer's consignment stock will increase by the quantity he returned. To create a consignment returns order proceed as follows: Logistics, Sales and distribution, Sales, Create, and then enter the order type. After creating a returns order for 10 pcs and posting the goods issued, the stock overview screen shows the consignment amount as being increased by 10 pcs, as shown in Figures 2-91 and at batch level in Figure 2-92.

The Consignment Pick-up The consignment pick-up process is the last and final process linked to the consignment procedure. It is responsible for the picking up of faulty materials as well as the picking up of excess materials not yet consumed by a consignment issue. The sales document type KR should have the SD document category C, being a sales order. The process is outlined in Figure 2-93.

Depending on your business, it may be beneficial to have a mandatory reference. This will restrict all consignment pick-ups from being made unless they make reference to a fill-up order type. You can restrict the reference to being mandatory and to an order type, thus setting C, and then further control the referencing procedure by using the copying control rules. Again, in the copying control rules, indicate the document flow.

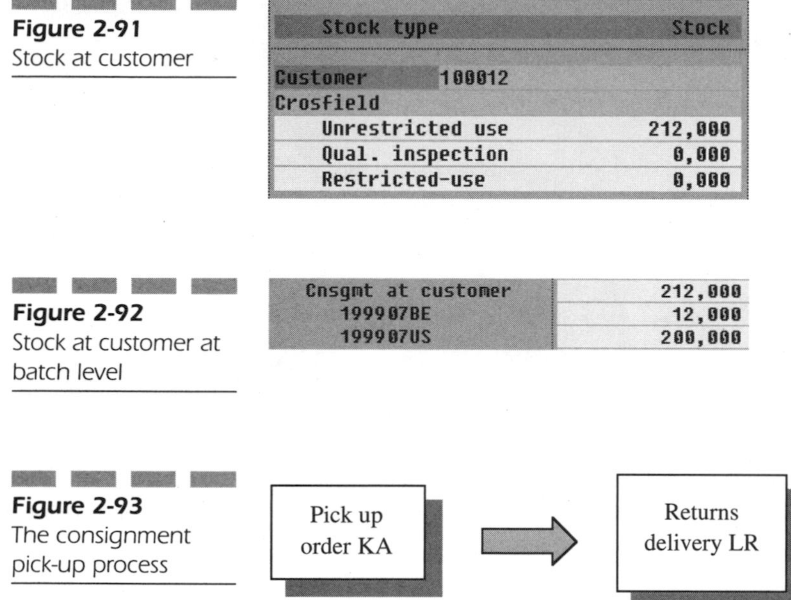

Stock type	Stock
Customer 100012	
Crosfield	
Unrestricted use	212,000
Qual. inspection	0,000
Restricted-use	0,000

Figure 2-91
Stock at customer

Cnsgmt at customer	212,000
199907BE	12,000
199907US	200,000

Figure 2-92
Stock at customer at batch level

Figure 2-93
The consignment pick-up process

As the stock is coming back into the warehouse or plant, you will want a specific returns shipping point to be automatically determined. Assign the special shipping conditions you use to determine this (see the shipping point determination section in Chapter 3).

No invoice is necessary, as the goods are not changing ownership. The materials in the fill-up are still the possession of the business and remain in their possession until the goods issue process is carried out in a consignment issue. The goods issue is the trigger that transfers ownership from the business to the consignment consumer.

The standard item category for consignment pick-ups is KAN. The business data screen of the item category is displayed in Figure 2-94.

The standard schedule line categories of the consignment pick-up process are F0 and F1. We will look at F1, as shown in Figure 2-95, keeping in line with the observance of a materials planning movement process. Schedule line category F1 is relevant for delivery as well as a transfer of requirements and an availability check. It has SAP standard movement type 632.

Do not forget the availability check is done against the stock on the customer's consignment. To create a consignment pick-up, proceed as follows: Logistics, Sales and distribution, Sales, Create, and then enter the order type. Next, proceed with the delivery and goods issue.

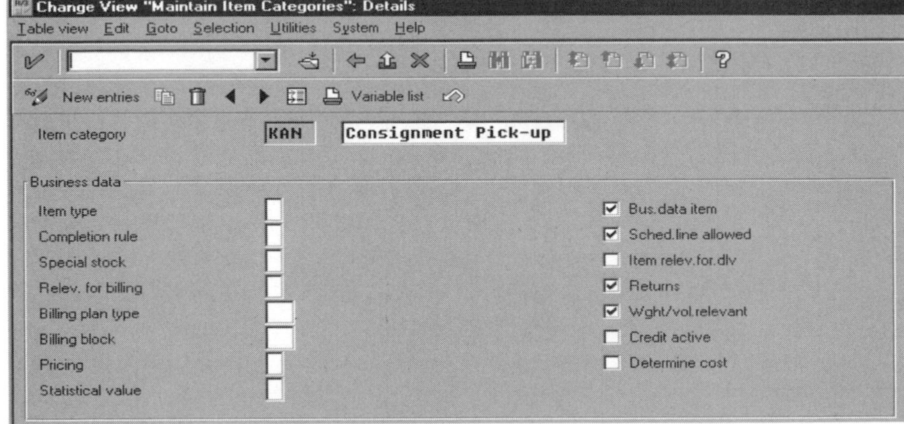

Figure 2-94 The business data screen of the item category KAN

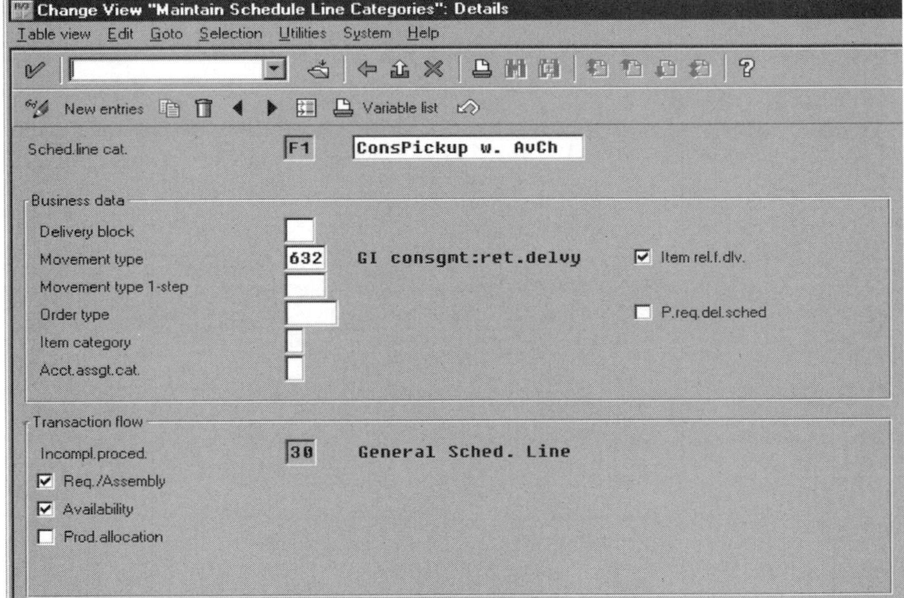

Figure 2-95 The standard schedule line category, F1

After goods issue, if you proceed to the stock overview screen, you will notice that the material available at the customer's consignment has decreased by the quantity picked up. In this example, I created a pick-up of 210 pcs.

This is shown at the batch level in Figure 2-96 and at the customer level in Figure 2-97.

Cnsgmt at customer	2,000
199907BE	2,000

Figure 2-96
Stock at customer at batch level

Stock type		Stock
Customer	100012	
Crosfield		
Unrestricted use		2,000
Qual. inspection		0,000
Restricted-use		0,000

Figure 2-97
Stock at customer

The Consignment Process

The complete consignment process can be seen in Figure 2-98.

As previously discussed, SAP has a standard overview for consignment and returnable packaging (for more on returnable packaging, see Chapter 3). This overview lists all the consignments for all materials in all plants for all customers. It is an invaluable tool in a comprehensive overview of goods on consignment. It can be accessed by going to Logistics, Materials management, Inventory management, Environment, Consignment, Consignment at customer, and then execute [MB58]. The overview is shown in Figure 2-99. This overview shows the material and respective quantities as well as the respective customer.

TIP: *Consignment stock processes can work across borders and company codes. However, you may experience difficulties when trying to accommodate certain legal regulations such as intrastat and exstrastat requirements in Europe. For this process, SAP has developed an invoice named WIA. It is relevant for EU border invoicing only. It is accessed via the billing indicator on the item category as J. This is only necessary for goods movements across E. U. borders where there is no invoice to show values. This would be relevant for KAN and KBN item categories.*

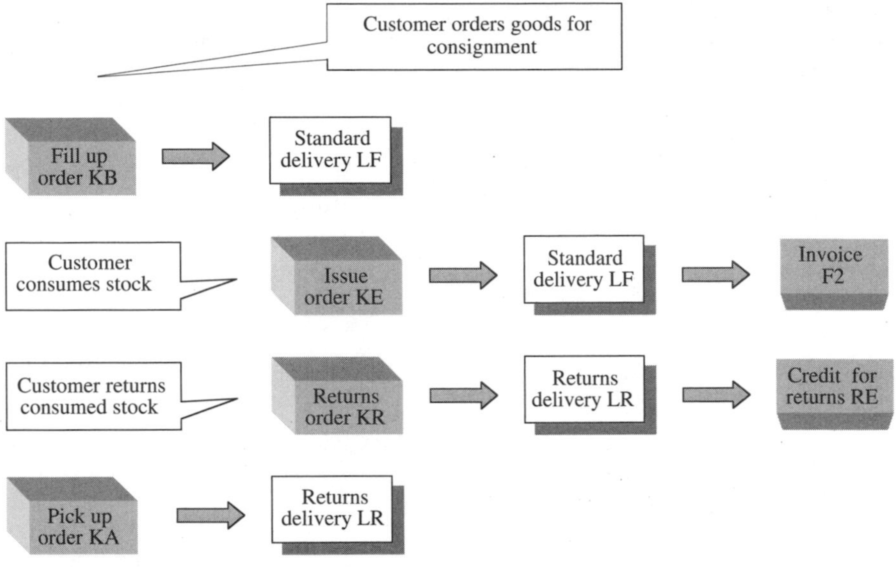

Figure 2-98
The complete consignment process

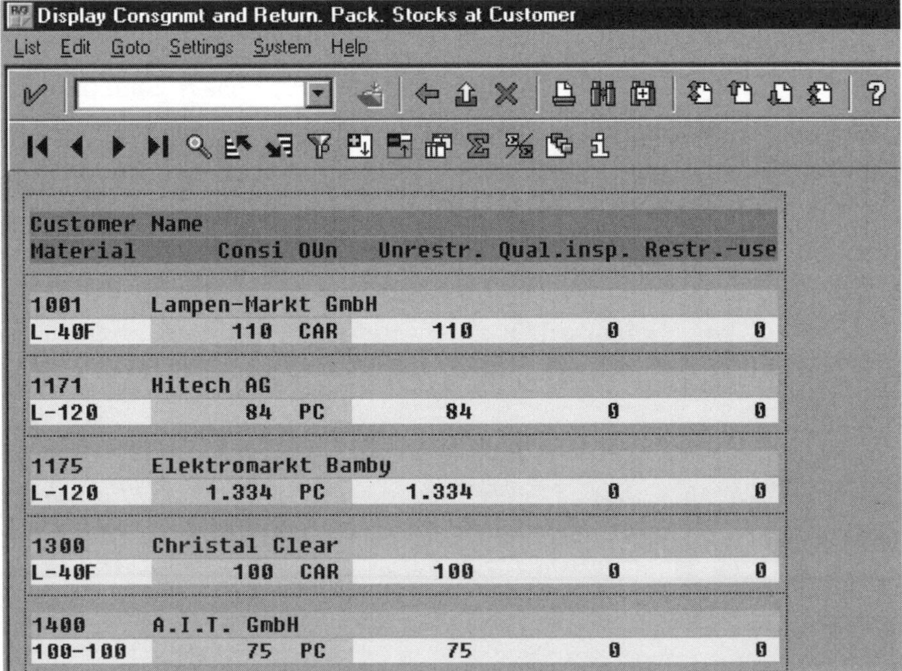

Customer Material	Name Consi	OUn	Unrestr.	Qual.insp.	Restr.-use
1001	Lampen-Markt GmbH				
L-40F	110	CAR	110	0	0
1171	Hitech AG				
L-120	84	PC	84	0	0
1175	Elektromarkt Bamby				
L-120	1.334	PC	1.334	0	0
1300	Christal Clear				
L-40F	100	CAR	100	0	0
1400	A.I.T. GmbH				
100-100	75	PC	75	0	0

Figure 2-99
A standard overview for consignment and returnable packaging

Scheduling Agreements

Scheduling agreements are outline agreements that the business has with a customer. They contain delivery dates and quantities to be delivered. These dates are then entered as schedule lines in the delivery schedule of the agreement. The scheduling agreement is processed by delivering the schedule lines as they become due.

To configure scheduling agreements, proceed to IMG, Sales and distribution, Sales, Sales documents, Scheduling agreements with delivery schedules, define schedule line types.

Schedule line types are not schedule line categories. Schedule line types are used for information purposes only. Should you need to create one, follow the standard process of copying and changing a SAP standard. We will be focusing on *just-in time* (JIT) delivery scheduling. Proceed to IMG . . . Maintain planning delivery sched. Instruct./splitting rules. The planning delivery schedule is an internal delivery schedule used to plan requirements more efficiently. It is subdivided into three sections:

Defining planning delivery schedule instructions. These instructions determine the characteristics of the planning delivery schedule.

Rules. These define the split of schedule line quantities between the different days in the planning delivery schedule and the forecast delivery schedule.

Assignment. This is concerned with splitting rules for planning delivery schedule instructions. You may have more than one splitting rule for each instruction. You can thus assign a date type and a splitting rule range, which will allow the system to carry out the splitting rules in sequence.

In the overview screen in Figure 2-100, some standard SAP examples are shown.

Proceed by setting up the planning delivery schedule instructions first. This determines if schedule line categories are relevant for deliveries and how the planning delivery schedules are to be generated. Note schedule lines in the planning delivery schedule replace those in the forecast delivery schedule with regards to planning relevance, and if required, delivery relevance.

The two examples of SAP1 and SAP2 are useful in explaining the overview of this functionality. SAP1 indicates that the schedule lines in the planning delivery schedule are relevant for delivery and should replace

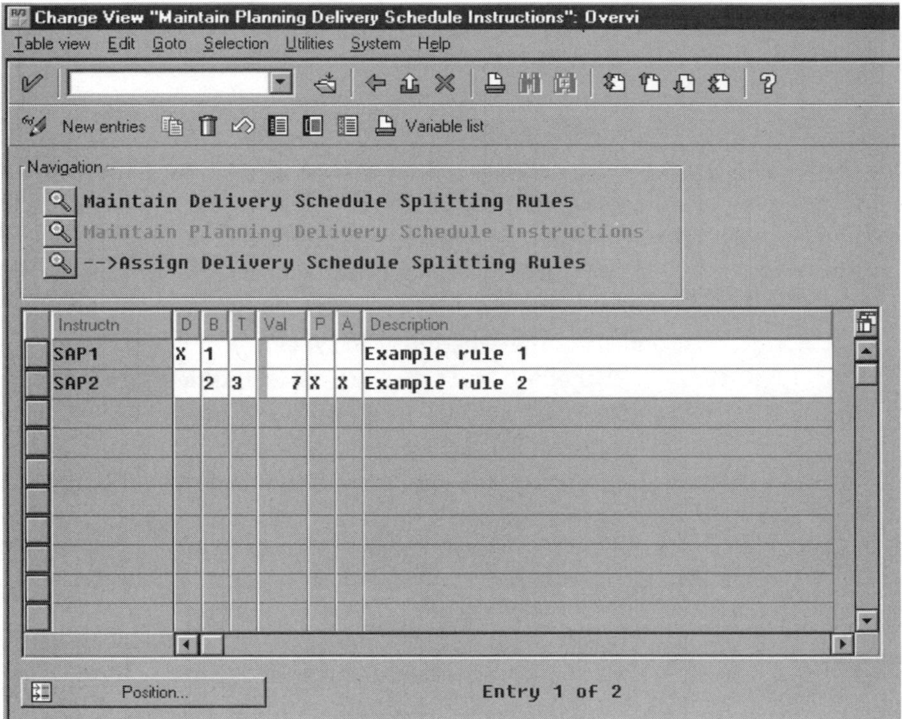

Figure 2-100
SAP1 and SAP2 serve as standard examples

the schedule lines in the forecast delivery schedule, should their dates lie outside the dates of the JIT delivery schedule. This is indicated by a "X" in the column "D."

Column "B" is crucial; it indicates the baseline date used by the system for the planning of delivery schedules. Should no date be entered here, the system will not generate any schedule lines in the planning delivery schedule. You may select date type 1, which sets the delivery schedule date as the base date, or date type 2, which selects the planning delivery schedule generation as the base date.

Column "T" represents the date type for the validity period of the delivery schedule split. It is used to indicate if the validity period is measured in weeks or months. The validity period is the period of time in weeks or months that the delivery schedule split is valid. The system does not take into account the schedule lines in the forecast delivery schedule; its date lies after the validity end date. The associated column Val represents the value in units in order to determine the end date of the validity period. Thus, example SAP2 has a date type of 3, which is months, and a value of 7, or seven months after the baseline date of column "B."

Column "P" indicates whether the system should adopt schedule lines from a previous planning delivery schedule when generating a new one. It would only be valid for those schedule lines occurring after the validity end date of the delivery schedule split. Column "A" indicates if the system should automatically generate a planning delivery schedule when a forecast delivery schedule is created.

Proceed to maintain the delivery schedule splitting rules. Highlight the Instruction SAP2 and select Assign Delivery Schedule Splitting Rules. Here you define the split share sum into daily periods, as shown in Figure 2-101. Should you have an initial schedule line quantity of 600 pieces using split rule SD1, that schedule line will be divided up into three equal schedule lines of 200 pieces each (600 divided by 3). Each set of 200 pieces will be delivered on Monday, Wednesday, and Friday, respectively.

TIP: *It is easier to make the splits add up to 100; that way, you are working with a percentage of the total schedule line quantity. For example, the split rule SD2 adds up to 100, so you would assign 15 percent of the schedule line quantity to be delivered on Mondays, 30 percent on Tuesdays, and so on.*

The column "H" defines the holiday rule for the delivery schedule split. You can select to treat the holidays as workdays or you can choose to have the schedule line quantity move to the last preceding workday. You can also choose to have the system split the quantity via the remaining days according to the delivery split.

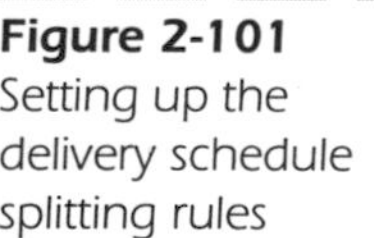

Figure 2-101 Setting up the delivery schedule splitting rules

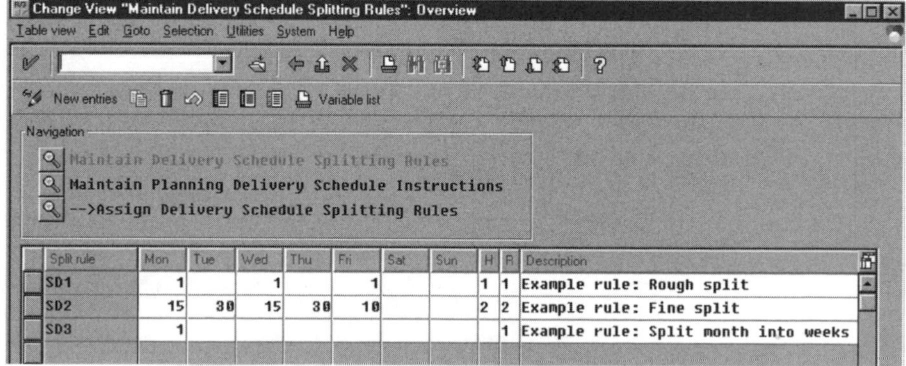

NOTE: The calendar used to define the holidays and workdays is the calendar of the ship-to party. The system uses the calendar of the schedule agreement items, unloading point as the calendar. This calendar may be changed using the assigned user exit C_CALENDAR. User exits will be covered in Chapter 5, "Cross Functional."

Column R represents the rounding rule for schedule line quantities. You may select to round up to three decimal places according to the sales unit or you may round up to a multiple of the delivery-rounding quantity.

After you have defined your delivery schedule splitting rules, assign them a brief description for ease of use later. After you have completed this task and saved, proceed back to Maintain Planning Delivery Schedule Instructions. Select the instruction again, such as SAP2, and then select Assign Delivery Schedule Splitting Rules.

The split rules we have defined, such as SD1, are now assigned to a date range again using weeks and months as the date type followed by the range of this date type. Thus, in Figure 2-102, the date range is eight weeks for split rule SD2 from the start of the base line date.

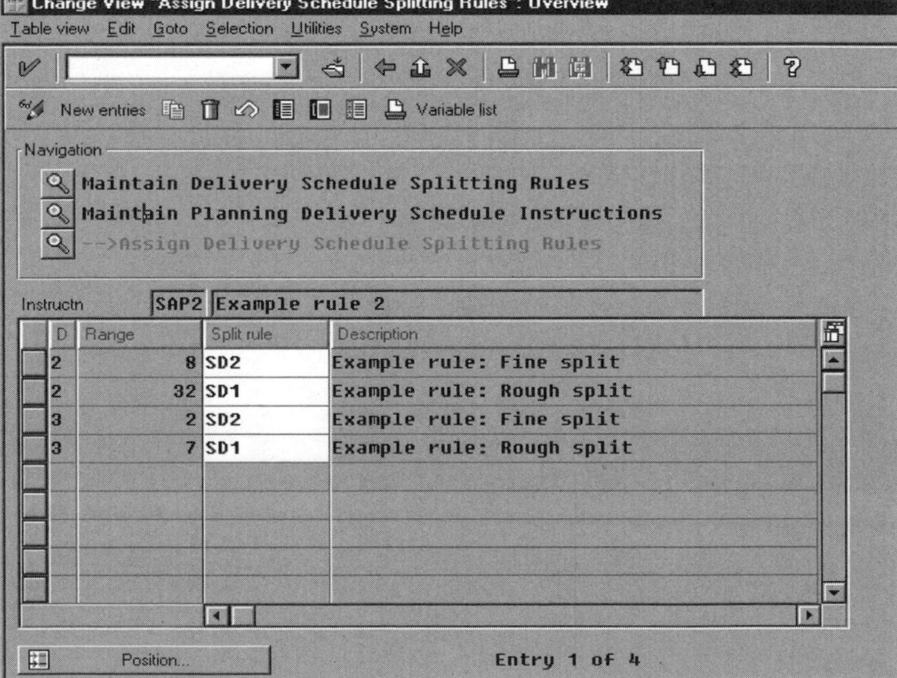

Figure 2-102 The date range is eight weeks for split rule SD2.

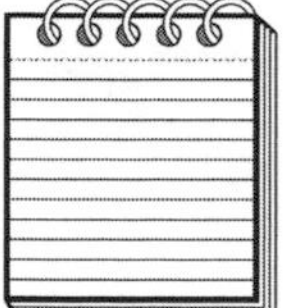

NOTE: *Although the split rule range and the delivery schedule split influence schedule line splits, the split validity period overrides the splitting rule range in every case.*

The standard sales document type for scheduling agreements is LZ. This LZ sales document type is configured in the same process as all other sales document headers. Note that this sales document type has the following changes to the standard order sales document. The BL document type must have E as the SD document category, indicating a scheduling agreement. It too has a different screen sequence group using the standard LL.

The pricing procedure can be the same as that of the standard sales orders; thus, you can leave the document pricing procedure indicator or set it as the same as for standard sales orders. The transaction group must be three, indicating this sales document transaction is a scheduling agreement.

The sales document type has the following section with relation to scheduling agreements, as shown in Figure 2-103.

The correction delivery type is LFKO. The usage indicator can be any indictor you set. The value set here will default into all scheduling agreements at the header level and thus will be copied into all items. The planning delivery schedule type is the key entry that defines how the schedule lines are to be controlled. This value is proposed when creating a scheduling agreement. Standard deliveries are created for the scheduling agreements. Thus, the delivery type used is LF.

The standard billing type is used as well. However, just as you may copy and change the sales document types, you can also copy and change the delivery and billing documents, should this be necessary.

The standard item category is LZN. LZN behaves like a standard item category. It is relevant for delivery-related billing as well as pricing and it does allow schedule lines. The schedule line categories used are as follows:

CP: Deterministic MRP

CV: Consumption MRP

CN: No MRP

CN does no availability check and no MRP. Although CP is the standard schedule line category, posting requirements through to materials planning and doing the availability check, CV is also a standard schedule line category that does an availability check, but it does not post the demand through to MRP.

Figure 2-103 The sales document type's scheduling agreement settings

Change SchedAg. w/ del.schd 30000045: Overview
Sales document Edit Goto Extras Environment System Help
Document flow Sold-to party Orders
SchedAg. w/ del 30000045 Net value 130.583,00 DEM
Sold-to party 2002 Sapsota AG, Altersdorferstr. 13, DE
Ship-to party 2002 Sapsota AG, Altersdorferstr. 13, DE
PO number 5500000038 PO date
Sales Item Overview Ordering party Procurement Shipping Reason for Rejection
Valid from Valid to

Item	Material	Rounding qty	SU	Description	Custo
10	AZ2-600	10	PC	Klimaanlage	AM2-

Figure 2-104a Scheduling agreement front end

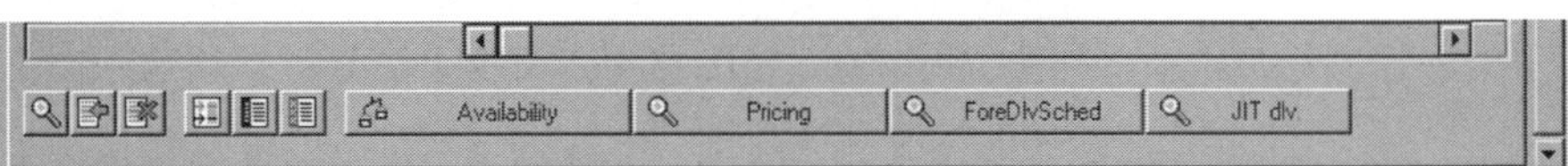

Figure 2-104b Scheduling agreement front end, item selections

Proceed with creating the scheduling agreement by going to Logistics, Sales and distribution, Sales, Outline agreement, Scheduling agreement, Create, and then enter the order type, such as LZ. Enter the relevant data, such as the customer and material numbers, as well as the order quantities for the materials. The scheduling agreement appears as shown in Figure 2-104a with the selection buttons at the foot of the document front end as represented in figure Figure 2-104b. To enter the delivery dates for the item, select the Times and go to Item schedule lines.

The schedule line screen is different in appearance, as shown in Figure 2-105.

NOTE: *Deliveries are automatically created from the schedule line of the scheduling agreement. These deliveries happen when the delivery due list is run on the same date as the schedule line is relevant for deliveries. You can also create the delivery manually [VL01] or by following the procedures in Chapter 3.*

A useful button in the 4.0 version is displayed in Figure 2-106. By clicking it from the schedule line screen, you will receive an overview of the deliveries carried out, the deliveries still to be carried out, and an overall status.

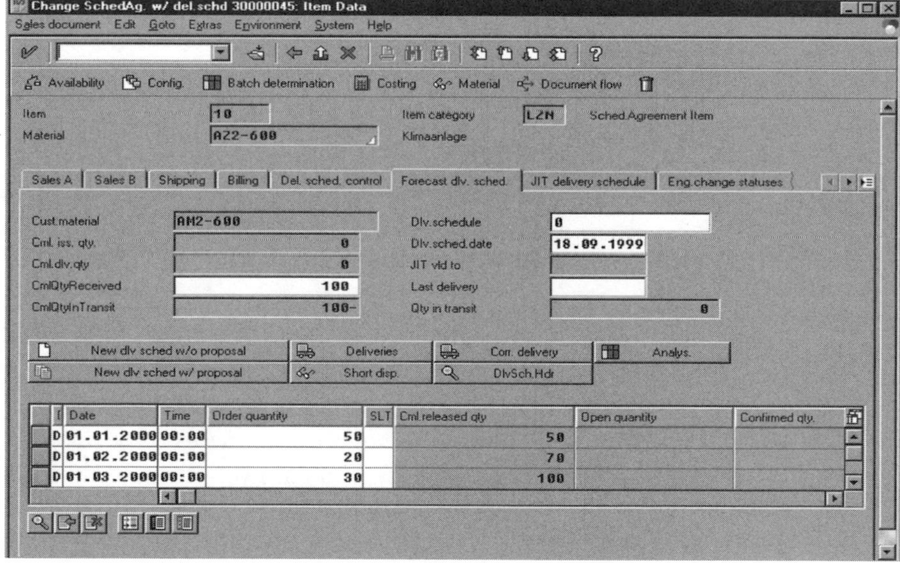

Figure 2-105 Scheduling agreement item data

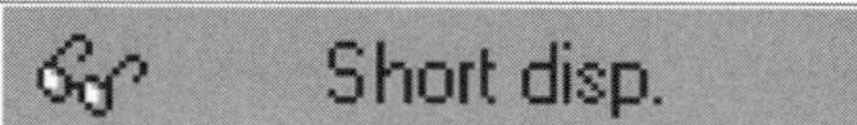

Figure 2-106 The Short disp. button in the 4.0 version

Sales Document Lists

Lists are used throughout the system to generate an overview of documents displayed in a certain style and totaled by a certain parameter. You will use lists in all document processes from inquiries through to invoices. As the procedure is standard throughout, I will concentrate on the configuration of one example, that is, sales order lists.

The Background Configuration

To configure sales document lists, should you be using a version of SAP prior to Release 4, you must use the following guidelines. If you are using Version 4 and above, you can skip this section. Otherwise, proceed as follows: IMG, Salesand distribution, Sales, Lists, Define list layout for sales orders. Then select the display variants and you are presented with an option to choose between four display groups:

By purchase order number

By partner

By material

By material and partner

This selection is necessary, as you will be creating a list of sales orders (a display variant) based on the option the user selects as his entry or display group. We will use Partner. Select create from the display as seen in Figure 2-107.

Name the display variant, keeping the SAP name range starting with Z (see Figure 2-108). Then name the variants description. Although I have named mine in the previous example after a company, it is also beneficial to name them according to the data displayed, such as "Sales Doc. Item Cat. Partner." The data you select in the access type and the additional information will determine what type of data you can select for the list display variant.

After pressing enter, you come across a blank selection screen. Press the Insert before . . . button shown in Figure 2-109.

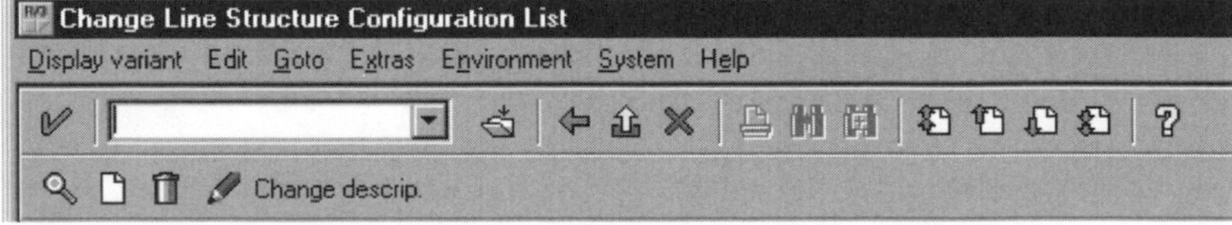

Figure 2-107 Creating a list of sales orders based on the user's entry or display group

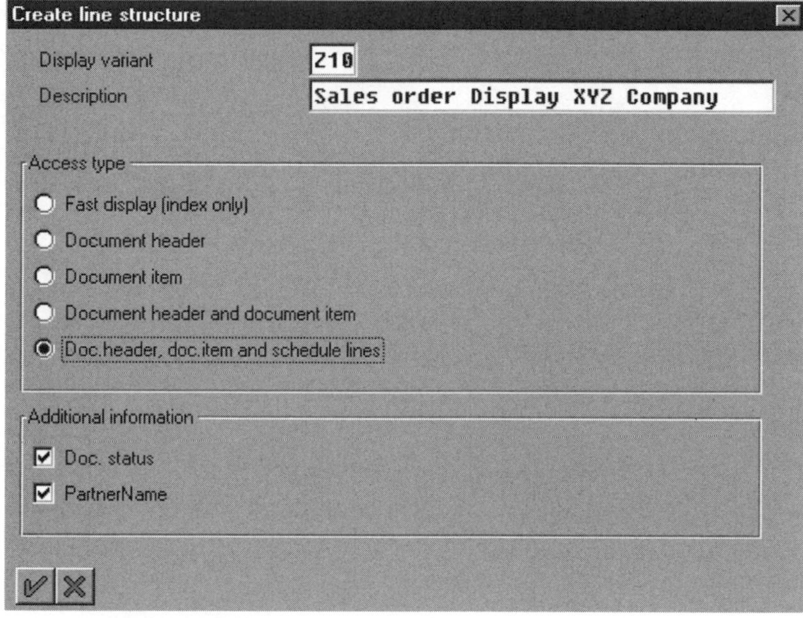

Figure 2-108 Naming the display variant, keeping the SAP name range starting with Z

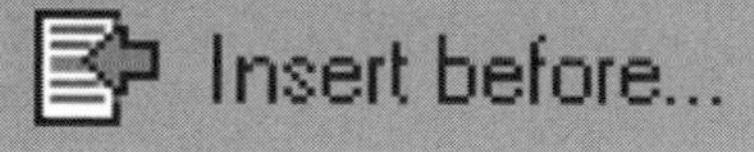

Figure 2-109 The Insert before . . . button

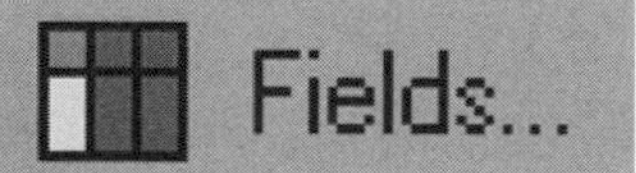

Figure 2-110 The Fields . . . button

It is highly unlikely you will want to enter your field name directly into the selection box, so select the Fields .. button, shown in Figure 2-110. You will then be prompted with the Field List screen to select your fields (see Figure 2-111).

After selecting the fields, press copy. The fields I have selected for this exercise are as follows:

KUNNR	Sold-to party
VKORG	Sales organization
VTWEG	Distribution channel
SPART	Division

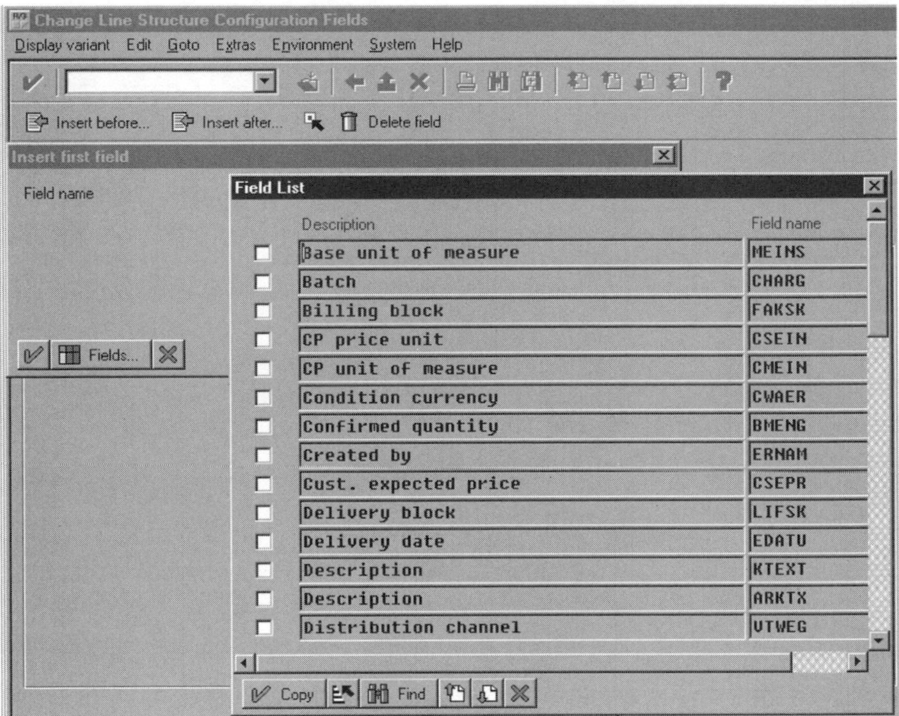

Figure 2-111
The Field List screen

MATNR	Material
WMENG	Order quantity
AUART	Sales document type

After creation of the display variant, you have the option to create a totals variant. This is used to sum up quantities and values in a list. To create a totals variant, proceed with the same procedure as shown previously.

After completing a totals variant, return to the display variant you created and select the display variant. Go to Environment, Total variant allowed, Create. Enter your totals variant, press enter, and save. Now to utilize your variant. Return to the logistics screen: Logistics, Sales and distribution, Sales, Order, List. Enter the sold-to party. Press enter. You are now presented with a list of sales orders for that particular sold-to party. If the variant in the display is not the same variant you created, select Settings, Display variant, Choose.

For SAP R/3 Version 4.0 and Above In Version 4.0 and above, the system uses the ABAP List Viewer tool. To proceed, you will need to determine the update of the partner indices. Do this from the relevant list section that you wish to configure. Again, we will use sales orders. Go to IMG, Sales and distribution, Sales, Lists, Define list layout for sales orders. After pressing enter, select Partner indexes, select the partner function, and press enter. After updating the partner index, you may want to update the index for existing documents; if this is the case, run the report RVV05IVB.

Next, you will want to access all the additional fields you may require for the display variant. Proceed to the List in customizing and select Field selection and additional fields. Now select the fields you want to use as additional fields.

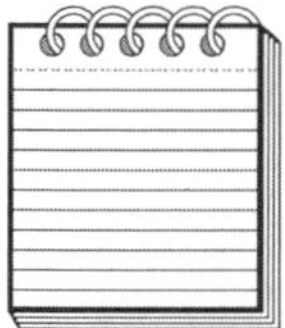

NOTE: *This old list functionality will no longer be available as of SAP version 4.0C.*

The new version of the list is shown in Figure 2-112.

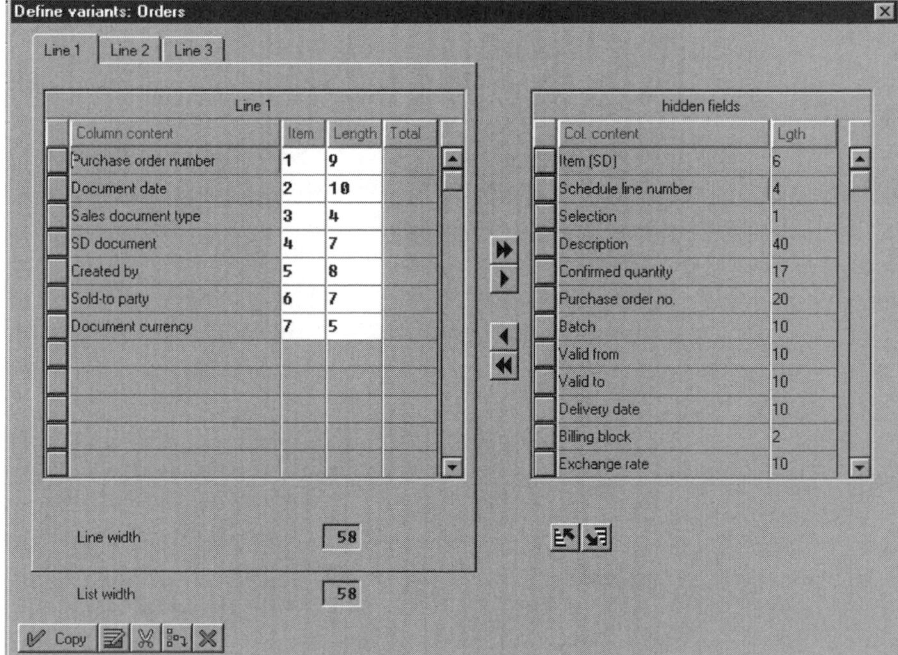

Figure 2-112 The Define variants: Orders screen

You can transfer fields to be used in the variant by selecting the left arrow button and transfer fields out of the display variant by selecting the right arrow button.

Blocking Reasons

In the creation of sales orders or sales documents, you can block the document type from being processed or used by a specific customer. This block on the customer master record can be set for all sales areas or for just specific sales areas. This is specifically useful when wishing to block blacklisted customers or customers with a poor credit history.

Menu Path

To assign the blocks to the relevant sales document types, go to IMG, Sales and distribution, Sales, Sales documents, Define, and assign reasons for blocking.

Transaction Code

Here you assign to the sales document types [OVAL] to the sold-to party master record [VD05] now that you have created the sales document blocks and assigned them to the relevant sales document types. Proceed in assigning the sales document blocks to the specific customer master records, as displayed in Figure 2-113. Go to Logistics, Sales and distribution, Master data, Business partner, Sold-to party, Block/unblock.

I have not been able to create these blocks using the IMG, as the table TVAST has no maintenance object in SAP version 4.0b. Should this be the case in the system you are using, you may enter the values manually by proceeding as follows. Use the transaction code [SM31], as displayed in Figure 2-114, and select Maintain, as seen in Figure 2-115.

Now create your entries. Return back to the assignments in the IMG and assign the relevant document types. Then proceed with the assignment of the document block to the customer master records.

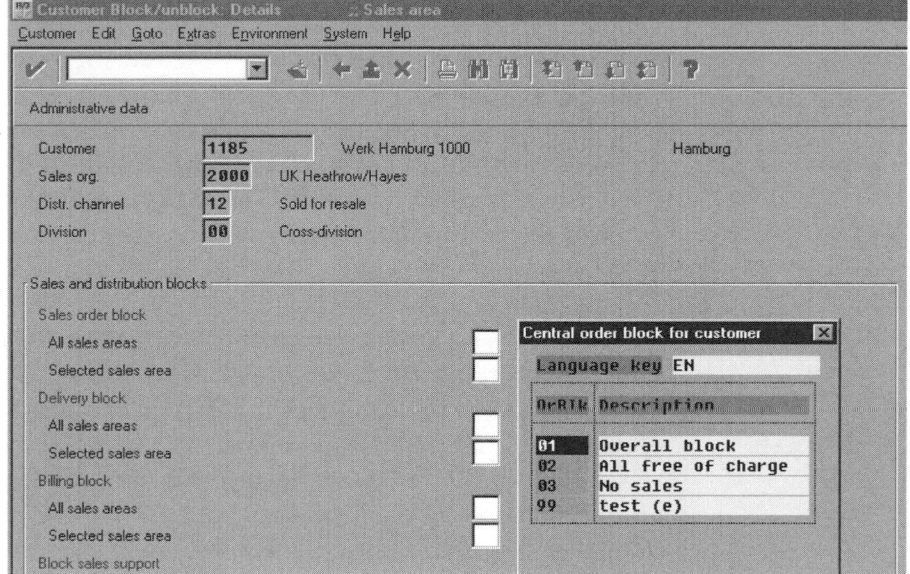

Figure 2-113 Assigning the sales document types to the specific customer master records

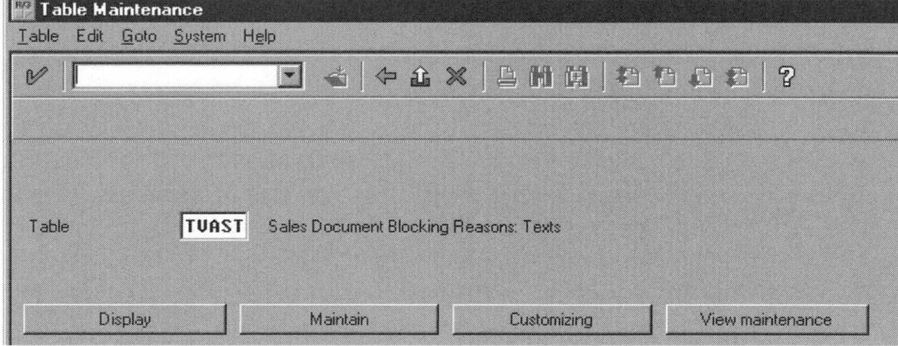

Figure 2-114 Using the transaction code [SM31]

Figure 2-115 Selecting Maintain

Bills of Materials (BOMs)

The *Bills of Materials* (BOM) process can be complex and dependent on Sales and Distribution as well as other modules such as Materials Management or Production Planning. I have explained the Sales and Distribution parts that contribute to the BOM process and that a BOM is a collection of materials that make up a product. A computer, as shown in Figure 2-116, could be called a BOM. The header item or main item, the computer, could be constituted of many subcomponents or subitems: a hard drive, a keyboard, and a monitor. It is these subitems of the BOM along with the header item that make up the BOM. When the customer places his order, he orders the header of the BOM only and the subitems are automatically included in the sales order.

Due to the BOM having header and item levels, the system does not process pricing, inventory control, and delivery processing at both levels. This would be futile; for example, there is no need to price at the header level for the entire computer and then again at the item level for all the subitems. Thus, BOM processing is divided into two different ways of being processed, namely, at the main item level if the material is assembled or at the component level if the material is not assembled.

Main Item Level Processing

The material master records should have the item category group ERLA in the Sales 2 screen of the finished product. In this case, the associated subitems

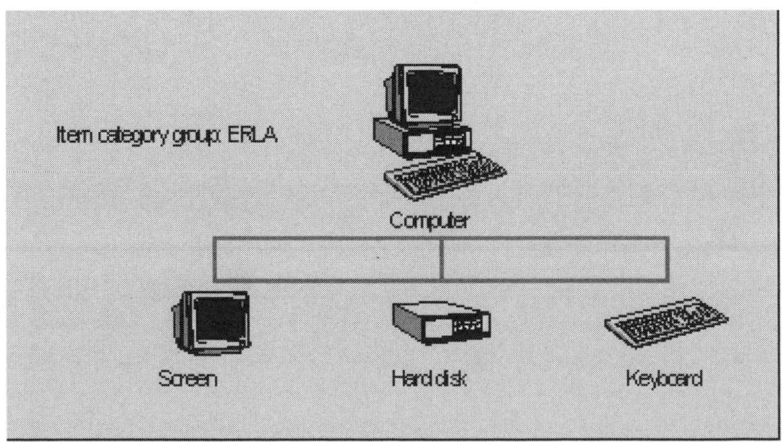

Figure 2-116 A computer can be an example of a BOM. Copyright by SAP AG.

function only as text items, and thus are not relevant for delivery. This process ensures that pricing, inventory control, and delivery processing is carried out at the header level that is for the finished product only (see Figure 2-117).

Subitem-Level Processing

If you would prefer to have the subitems be responsible for pricing, inventory control, and delivery processing, enter the item category LUMF on the material master record in the Sales 2 screen. This ensures the subcomponents are relevant for processing. To ensure all the components can be delivered at the same time, use the functionality of the delivery group.

The Delivery Group The subitems of a BOM may be available at different times due to the lead times in procurement (MM) and production (PP). You can use the delivery group to indicate that all the subitems must be delivered together. This means that the subitems must be delivered as a group. You indicate on the item category whether a delivery group applies.

Should the subitems be relevant for delivery at different times, the system will automatically deliver these partial deliveries whenever they are available and the delivery due list is run. This could be disastrous, however. If the customer has ordered a computer and we deliver a keyboard to him one day followed by a monitor the next, he will not be too happy. Thus, if a delivery group is assigned to the item category of the subitems, the system will determine the latest schedule line of the items and confirm the delivery date according to that last schedule line.

For a delivery group to perform correctly, the following prerequisites must be met:

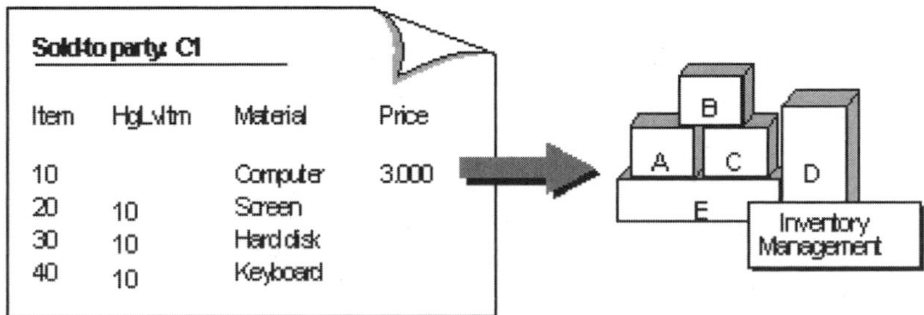

Figure 2-117 The sales order's relationship to inventory management Copyright SAP AG

- The delivery group can only contain one BOM.
- It cannot contain any fixed quantities.
- It cannot contain any items that have partial delivery indicator C (one-time delivery).
- It cannot contain any partially delivered items.
- It can only contain items that can be at least partially delivered.
- It can only contain items that have a maximum of one requested schedule line. In the header item category used for the BOM, ensure that you have indicated the relevant delivery groups, as shown in Figure 2-118.

A delivery group can be viewed in the sales document by accessing the Shipping overview of the sales order, as shown in Figure 2-119.

In the above example, the delivery group 1 will be available for delivery on 25.08.1999.

NOTE: *The system only checks the delivery group before creating the delivery or processing the delivery due list. Once the date is met, the system does not check to see if all the materials can be delivered. Thus, if you have a delivery group, as in the previous example, and run the delivery due list, the system rejects or finds an incomplete line item in the delivery. The unrejected lines will still be shipped and the incomplete or rejected line will still be open.*

Should you wish to create a BOM that is to be relevant for sales, proceed as follows: Logistics, Sales and Distribution, Master data, Products, Bills of mate-

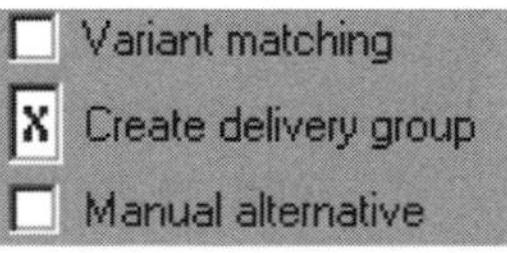

Figure 2-118 Indicating the relevant delivery groups

All items

Item	Material	Deli	DlvDateForGrp.	S	Delivery date	Mat.av.dt.	Loading date	Plnt	Shipp	Route
10	ADVPRGAM28F01015!A	1	25.08.1999	☐	25.08.1999	25.08.1999	25.08.1999	IE01	IE1I	
20	ADVAM28F010150PC	1		☑	25.08.1999	25.08.1999	25.08.1999	IE01	IE1I	
30	PRODUCTIONLAB	1		☑	25.08.1999	25.08.1999	25.08.1999	IE01	IE1I	

Figure 2-119 The Shipping overview of the sales order

rial, Create. Ensure that the item category determination will be correctly configured for the item category groups you plan to use in the BOM you are defining. Also ensure that your material master records are created with the correct item category groups and are maintained in the correct plants. Proceed with entering the material and entering the relevant plant and usage. Usage 5 indicates the BOM is relevant for sales and distribution documents.

Now assign the material master records and quantity to this header material. Select the Material item button, as shown in Figure 2-120.

You reach an overview screen of materials and validity periods, as in Figure 2-121.

After the BOM has been created, save it. You can then create the sales order, in which you will see the BOM explode. Follow the standard sales order process. Enter the header material, press enter, and the system will automatically display the subitems of the BOM.

Make-to-order Production (MTO) *Make-to-order production* (MTO) is a process whereby the business carries out a production cycle for a product that a customer wishes to purchase compared to the usual business process where a business has a large quantity of products it tries to sell to consumers. In make-to-order production, the exact product sold is not generally stored on the shelves. The product could be very similar and merely change a portion of its form for different sales orders.

Generally, there are two ways to process make-to-order production, namely MTO using the project system and MTO using the sales order. As the project system is beyond the scope of this book, we are interested in the make-to-order process using the sales order.

Figure 2-120 The Material item button

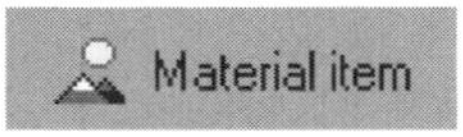

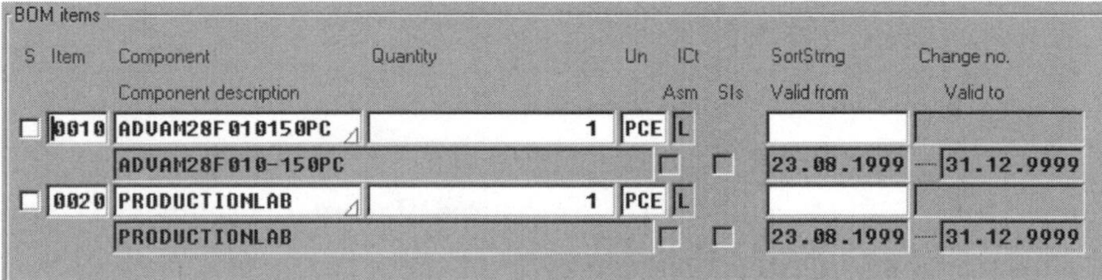

Figure 2-121 The BOM items screen

Make-to-order Production—Using the Sales Order For make-to-order production using the sales order, all costs and revenues involved for an order item are held collectively at that item. A particular settlement rule is used that can be changed manually to transfer costs to profitability analysis.

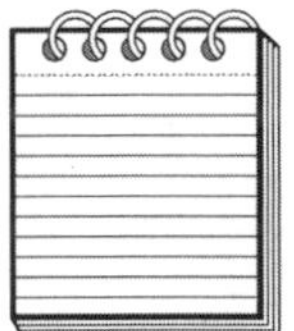

NOTE: *Up to SAP Version 3.0, the system uses the item category to determine the requirements type; thus, special item categories are used to control make-to-order production.*

Make-to-order production is largely a production planning configuration. It is also controlled by the requirements type, which is determined by three things:

a. The strategy group on the material master MRP screens of the material

b. The MRP group on the MRP screens

c. The item category and MRP type

SAP searches in this order until it finds the requirements type to use for the sales order item. The last option is configured under IMG, Sales and distribution, Basic functions, Availability check, and Transfer of requirements. A requirements type is just a link to something called a *requirements class*. A requirements class contains all the information used by production and costing to produce a product. For example, there is a requirements class for make-to-stock, for make-to-order, for production consuming a planning material, for lot-size production, and so on. These are just different ways to handle production and production planning. So if the requirements type that is determined from 2a-c is linked to a requirements class that is defined as make-to-order, then the order becomes a make-to-order object.

When you create the production order (Logistics, Production, Production control, Order), you have to create using the sales order. A few things happen to the production order:

a. The BOMS (like a recipe) and routings (like the steps in production) are copied into the production order (much like customer and material data is copied into a sales order).

b. The order is released for production.

c. When it is produced, the order is confirmed (that is, what was actually produced, much like a delivery is what was actually sold).

d. After that goods receipt, the made items are put into the warehouse.

Note that in goods receipt the stock is *not* receipted into unrestricted warehouse stock, but into the sales order stock. This is special stock indicator E. In the same way as when you have consignment stock at a customer, you have the special stock indicator W (and returnable packaging as V), so you have order stock as E. When you look at the stock overview report [MMBE], you will see that the stock receipted from production does not increase the warehouse stock, but you can see it under the sales order.

When you create the delivery at the time of goods issue, the stock is issued out of the order to the customer. You create the delivery and invoice normally. Note that the delivery does an availability check against the stock just for that sales order, so you cannot create the delivery until the goods receipt from production. That is why the account assignment is set to the order. When you receipt stock, your stock asset goes up by the cost of production, but in make-to-order, there is no increase in stock, so instead the costs are assigned to the order. This will be defined by the Production Planning and Controlling modules.

There is also a special case that you should be familiar with. If you have a variable product or a product that can be defined by the customer in the order, you must use make-to-order with variant configuration. If a business sells aluminum rods, the customer can order any length and diameter. The business, however, cannot create a material master for each possibility of length and diameter. Instead, we create a configurable material (type KMAT). We create a class to describe this material. A class contains characteristics, which are the various things that describe the material. Then we can use classification (a central function in SAP) to configure the material in the order.

In the previous example, we create a class called Billet, because aluminum rods are also called billets [CL01] (use class type 300, for variant materials). We have two characteristics: a length and a diameter. So, we create two characteristics [CT01] that describe the rods and assign them to the class Billets.

We then create a KMAT called Billet and a configuration profile called Billet Configuration (Logistics, Materials management, Material, Environment) and assign this to the KMAT billet. When you create the order for a KMAT, the order will branch to the configuration screen (access it using Item, Configuration), and the user can enter the diameter and length that the customer needs. Thus, you have one material master for possible hundreds and thousands of materials.

Obviously, variant configuration is always make-to-order, since the customer is ordering a specific product that applies to him or her only. So, when you create a KMAT, the item category group is 0002, which proposes item category TAC that has a requirements type linked to a requirements class for make-to-order. The account assignment in the requirements class is E for the sales order, which means the costs and stock are assigned to the sales order.

TIP: *that if you create an order from a preceding document (for example, a quote), the production order will define the customer requirement as the quote and assign the stock to the quote, not the sales order. This is usually not good. The only way around this is to define a requirements type for the item category of the quote as not make-to-order and the requirements type of the item category as make-to-order. This means that you cannot use the strategy group and the MRP group, since the material is the same on the quote and the order, so the same make-to-order requirements type will be determined. You must use the item category and the MRP type. For the quotations item category, indicate make-to-stock, and for the order item category, indicate make-to-order requirements type.*

Individual Purchase Orders

A purchase order is a demand for stock that the business places with a vendor. Individual purchase orders are used when a customer orders materials from the business that is not in stock,and must be obtained from a vendor.

During the sales order entry, the system automatically creates a purchase requisition, which the purchasing department converts to a purchase order. The vendor ships directly to you, unlike in third-party orders where the vendor ships directly to the customer (see Chapter 3 for third-party business processing).

The material type setting in the material master record controls whether a material can be used for internal or external production. However, the control of the material, promoting the system to automatically create a purchase order at the time of the sales order, is controlled by the item category group held in the Sales 2 screen of the material master record. SAP has a standard item category group BANC, which one can allocate to the material. This will cause the item category TAS (third-party) or TAB in the standard system. Item categories TAB and TAS have the special stock indicator "items at hand." The item business data screen is shown in Figure 2-122.

As it has no relevance for a BOM, the bill of materials and configuration section of the item category is empty, as well as the item category data on value contracts.

As you know, the item category in the sales order controls the schedule line category and how the material behaves. Sometimes businesses require

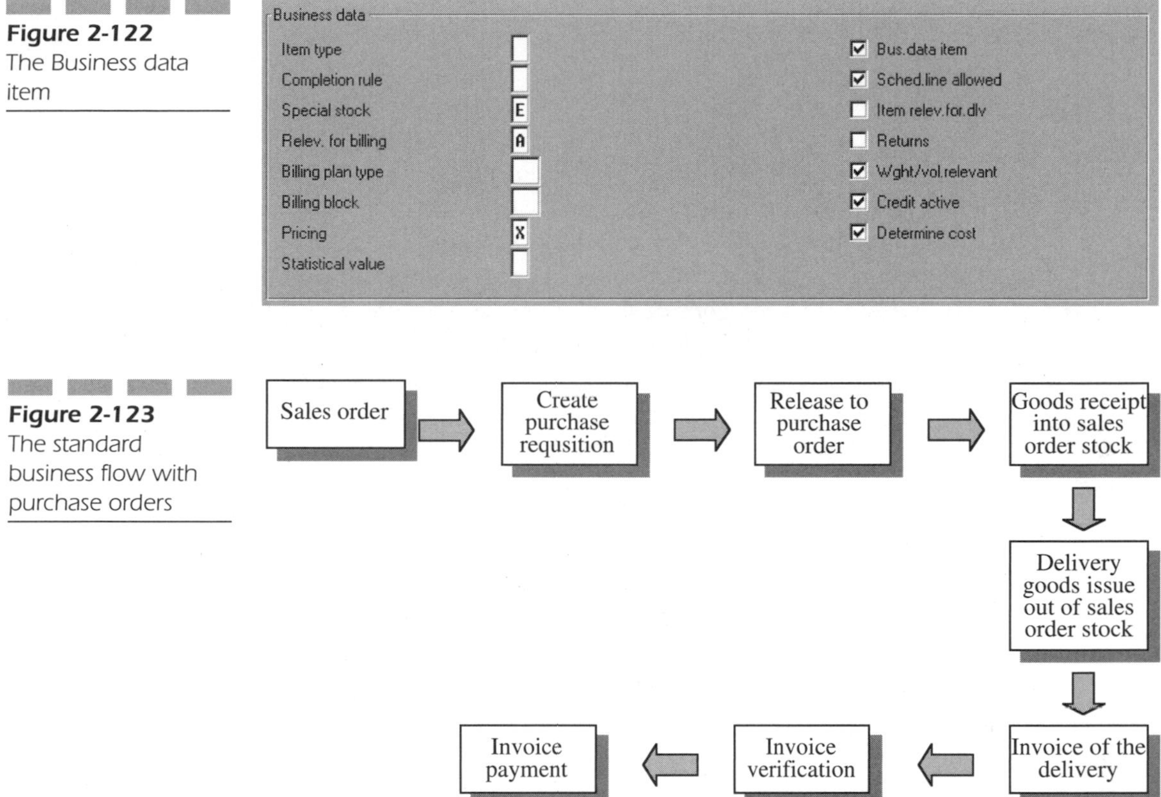

Figure 2-122 The Business data item

Figure 2-123 The standard business flow with purchase orders

a material that is normally produced to have an individual production order to be created for it at the time of the sales order. Should this be the case, you can allocate the item category TAB (or a similarly created item category) as a manual entry for the sales order in item category determination. Thus, at the time of the sales order, simply changing the item category manually from TAN to TAB will cause an individual purchase requisition to be created.

For each individual purchase order item, the system will create an individual purchase requisition item, but if the individual purchase order item has multiple schedule lines, the system will create multiple purchase requisition items for each schedule line quantity.

To display the purchase requisition number on the sales order, proceed by selecting the sales line item for which a purchase requisition is to be created. Select Item, Schedule lines, Quantities/dates. Select the schedule line and then Edit, Procurement. The standard business flow is displayed in Figure 2-123.

CHAPTER 3

Deliveries and Invoicing

Introduction to the Condition Technique

The condition technique is the single largest configuration technique used in the *Sales and Distribution* (SD) module. Knowing how the condition technique operates will allow you to understand how the system reacts in different scenarios. The condition technique is used in pricing, text determination, output determination, and material determination, basically anywhere you have a condition record. The condition technique is used by SAP to find a choice from among a number of alternatives. SAP makes the choice based on conditions, therefore the name condition technique.

For example, let's say SAP must find a price for a product, but a number of prices can exist for the product. There could be the list price that applies to that group of products, a special price for that customer, or a specific price for that product.

What product is being sold, who it is being sold to, and the product group the product belongs to are all called *conditions*. They are specific situations that apply to that sale. Different conditions (for example, different products) will have different prices. The different conditions and the prices associated with each are stored in SAP in *condition records*.

When SAP must find a price, it finds all the prices that meet the conditions in the sale. This process of finding a price is also called *determining a price*. Once SAP has determined all the prices that apply, it must decide on which one to use. SAP uses an access sequence to decide on which price applies. The access sequence is simple; it is the order in which SAP must search.

For example, search first for the price of a customer. If one is not found, continue looking at the other conditions for a product price. If a price is still not found, look for a product group price.

Conditions are grouped together in *condition types*. You can therefore have condition types for prices (which contain the conditions customer price, product price, and product group price), discounts, and so on. Condition types are grouped together in a *determination procedure*. A determination procedure is simply a process of finding something using the condition technique. That is, a determination procedure contains a number of condition types. Each of these types is linked to an access sequence. For each condition type, SAP searches all the conditions in the order of the access sequence until it finds a value. The result of the search is a value for the condition.

The previous explanation shows the condition technique in pricing, but you will see it is used in many other areas of SAP, such as account determination. Whenever a sale is posted to accounting, SAP must find (or determine) the account to which the revenues and discounts are posted.

Therefore, a determination procedure is used to find the accounts, called the *account determination procedure*. This procedure contains a condition type to find which account to post to based on the conditions of the sale. The condition type searches all the records that contain accounts for the conditions that match the sale in the order of the access sequence. As soon as it finds a record that matches the conditions, it returns a condition value, in this case the GL account.

The condition technique is used because you may want to post to different accounts under different conditions. For example, sales of a certain material can go to one revenue account, sales of other materials to a different account, export sales to another, and local sales to yet another. Depending on all these conditions (the material, types of sale, and so on), SAP can find a different account. The condition technique is used to find the right account under the right conditions. The condition technique is therefore SAP's method of determining which value to use under which circumstances or conditions (see Figure 3-1).

Material Determination or Product Selection

Material determination is a method in SAP SD to determine the material to be used in the sales order. Material determination uses the condition technique to swap one material for another when certain conditions apply. In other words, it is possible to use the condition technique to substitute one material in the sales order for another.

Material determination is triggered by the material entered in the line item of the sales order. This material can be used to automatically swap

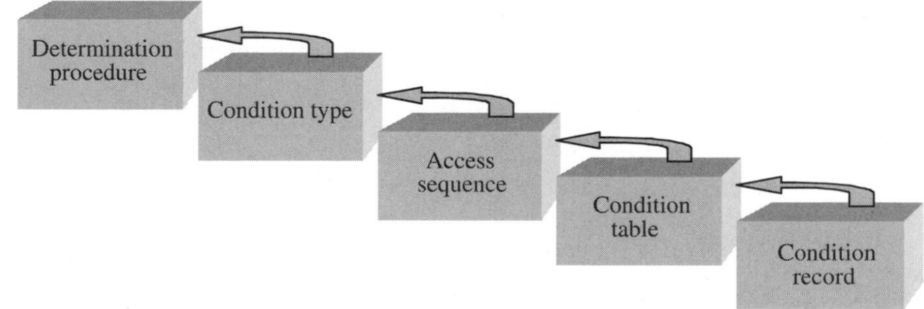

Figure 3-1 The condition technique

one of the business' products for another during certain periods, such as Christmas time, using a specially wrapped product. It can also be used to swap a customer's part number for the business' part number. Material determination can also use a pop-up window with a number of products the user can select from.

Menu Path

For customizing, go to IMG, Sales and distribution, Basic functions, Material determination, Maintain prerequisites for material determination. Proceed to define the type of material determination.

Transaction Code

The code here is [VB11] to create a material determination condition record. Go to Logistics, Sales and distribution, Master data, Products, Material determination, Create.

Material determination is specifically useful should you wish to swap your customer's part number automatically for your own at the time of the sales order. This also enables you to swap your own part number for another part number over a specific season, such as Christmas. The customers will then receive a specially wrapped product, compared to the standard product and packaging.

Material determination is also useful when an old product is becoming obsolete or a new product is to be released by your company at a specific date. Material determination can automatically swap the old product for the newer product at the time of the sales order automatically based on a validity date.

Material determination, sometimes referred to as *product selection*, can be automatic or manual. This is useful when the customer may not want the specially wrapped product at Christmas; he may prefer the standard product. Thus, certain configuration options are available to you:

1. You may configure the system to automatically swap the one material for another (for example, obsolete products).
2. You may configure the system to automatically swap one material for a number of other materials, the one material being determined based on which one is available.
3. You may configure the system to swap the material for a number of materials, where the user is presented with a list to choose from.

For example, option 1 may be the swapping of an obsolete product or it may be the swapping of a customer's part for one of the business' parts.

Material determination uses the condition technique to determine the outcome in the sales order. Begin the configuration of material determination at [OV12] and define the type of material determination as illustrated in Figure 3-2.

Should you want a new material determination condition type, remember to copy the standard and change its name to Z . . .. For the purpose of this example, we will use the standard *condition type* A001. The condition type is assigned to an access sequence. You need not have a validity date here, as it is a better option to constrict your entries with validity dates in the logistics screens when you create your condition records.

NOTE: *The access sequence must exist before you can assign a condition type to it. In this example, access sequence A001 is assigned to condition type A001.*

Now proceed to Maintain access sequence as shown in Figure 3-3. Select the access sequence and select access. You are presented with the following screen shown in Figure 3-4.

Note the entry has an AcNo column (access number) as well as a Tab column (table key), a description, and a requirement. An access sequence is a sequence of steps that the system follows in order to obtain a condition record. The condition record has a value that is assigned to it in the logistics front end.

The access number is the order in which the system will read the access sequence. For example, if we had access number 10, 20, 30, or 40, the system would start with the lowest entry, which is access 10. It will then try and process everything assigned to step 10. Should it not be able to process line 10, it will proceed to line 20, and so on. Should it reach line 40 and still not be able to process it, the system will conclude that no condition record exists for this condition type.

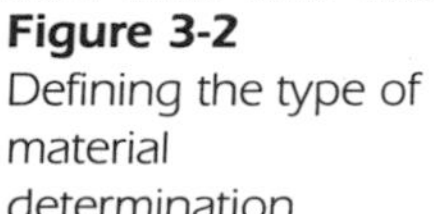

Figure 3-2
Defining the type of material determination

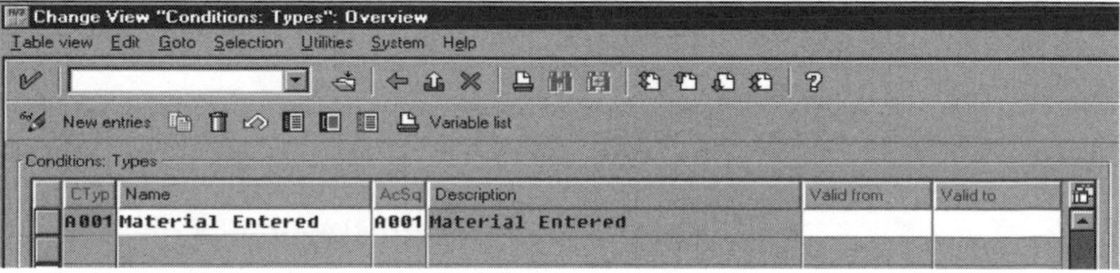

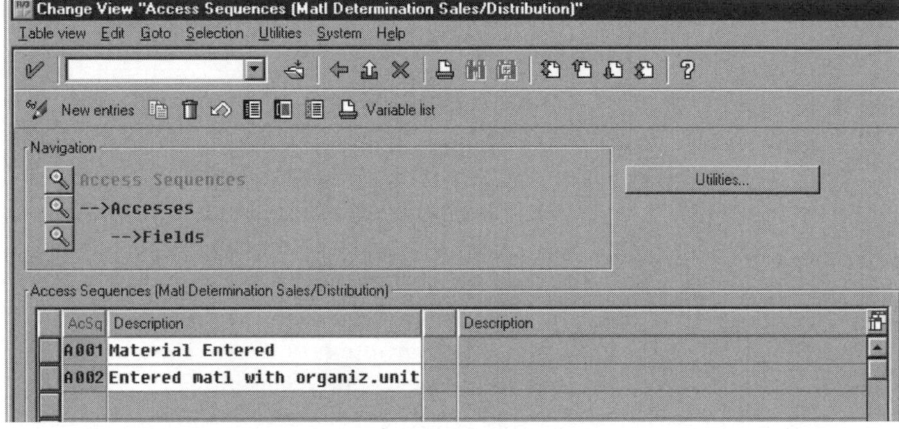

Figure 3-3 Maintaining the access sequence

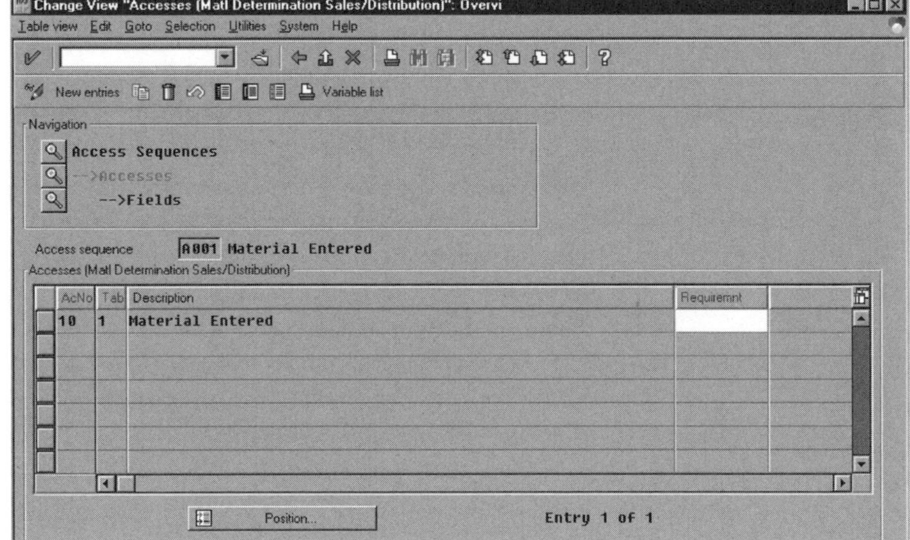

Figure 3-4 The Accesses (Matl. Determination Sales/Distribution) table

In the previous example, there is only one access. Thus, should the system not find a record for this access, it will not carry out material determination. The table key used is 001. Table 001 is described as the material entered. A *condition table* is merely a tabulated combination of fields that are assigned to the access sequence. Table 001 has only one entry, which is Material Entered. To see these condition tables, proceed to Condition Tables, Display material determination. Then enter 001 in the table selection and press Enter. You are now presented with Condition Table 001, as shown in Figure 3-5,

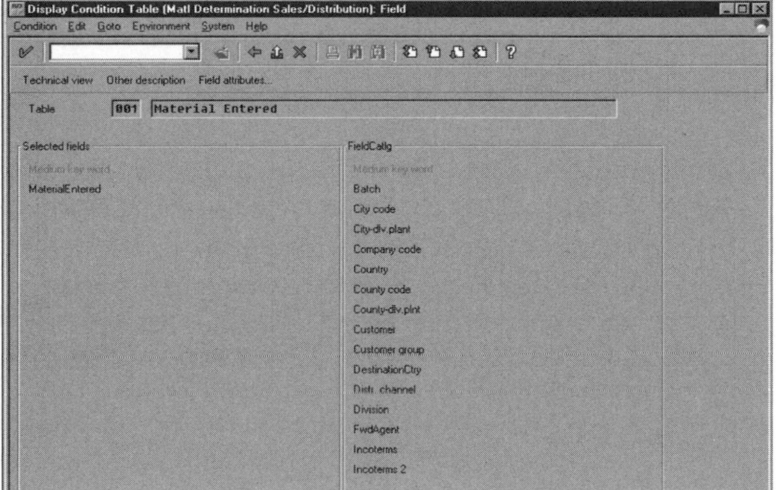

Figure 3-5
Condition Table 001

Figure 3-6
The actual SAP field name being selected

Figure 3-7
Display fields

which is merely a "Material Entered" field that has been selected from a list of fields in the field catalog. This field catalog is a list of allowed fields for material determination. It is maintainable; that is, you can add more fields to it for selection. This will be covered in more detail in the section on pricing.

Should you select the technical view, you will see the actual SAP field name being selected, as shown in Figure 3-6.

Now proceed back to the Maintain access sequence. On the right hand side of the description, you have a column for a requirement. This requirement is similar in theory to those you used in copying control. That is, it restricts entries being accessed. The system will look at the access line, read the requirement, and if the scenario fails the requirement, it will proceed to check the next access. However, in our example, as there is no "next access," it will not proceed to find a condition record. Should you wish to see which fields are used in the Condition Table, select the access and press the magnifying glass button, shown in Figure 3-7.

You will have the following display as shown in Figure 3-8.

Now proceed to Maintain procedure for material determination. This is the determination procedure.

Select the Procedure A00001, as shown in Figure 3-9, and select Control. You will be presented with a determination screen, as shown in Figure 3-10. The same basic layout is used in pricing (just enhanced a bit further) as in many other areas.

This procedure again has steps that can range from 01 up to 999. The step further breaks down into a counter, which is like a mini-step in a step. For example, the system could have a step 10 counter 1, a step 10 counter 2, and a step 10 counter 3. It would then execute these steps in that sequence.

A condition type is assigned to the determination procedure. A requirement can also be entered for the Condition Type, again as a check to see if it must be accessed. In this example, there is no limitation in the form of a requirement.

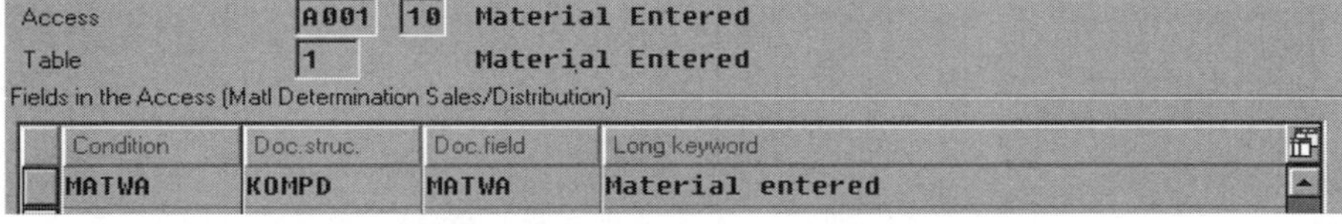

Figure 3-8 Displayed fields in the access

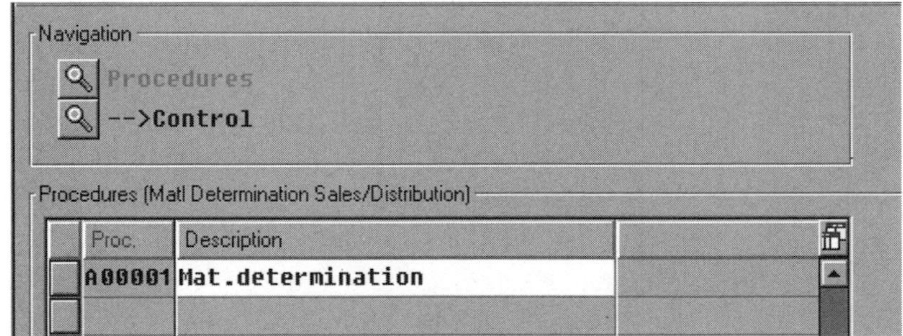

Figure 3-9 Selecting the procedure A00001

Procedure A00001 Mat.determination

Procedure (Matl Determination Sales/Distribution)

Step	Cntr	CTyp	Description	Requiremnt
10	0	A001	Material Entered	

Figure 3-10 Selecting Control brings up a determination screen

Now that the determination procedure has been done, you need to assign this determination procedure to a sales document type for which you want the material determination be carried out. Proceed to Assign material determination to sales document types. By assigning the material determination procedure to the sales document type you are initiating, that material determination is active whenever a sales document type of that sort is proposed. Generally, I find you may want all the document types to be active for material determination as it would cause the user community to be confused, should they have different results using different sales orders (comparing a quotation to an order, for example).

Now all that is left of the condition technique is for you to create a condition record for the respective Condition Type A001. To create a Condition Type, you may follow the path: Logistics, Sales and distribution, Master data, Products, Material determination, Create. Then follow these steps:

- Enter the material determination type, such as A001
- If you select "Key combination," you will see the condition tables in the access sequence. Select our example material entered.
- Create your condition record, as shown in Figure 3-11.

This completes the introduction to the condition technique. I have explained it in a way that is easy to follow and progressive, but is not the simplest of methods to implement. After you have become confident with the condition technique, the best procedure I find to follow is

1. Put the fields you need into the field catalog.
2. Create the condition tables you need.
3. Create the access sequence you need.
4. Assign the condition tables to the access sequence.
5. Create the condition types.
6. Assign the access sequence to the condition types.

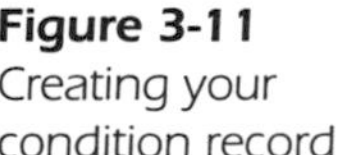

Figure 3-11 Creating your condition record

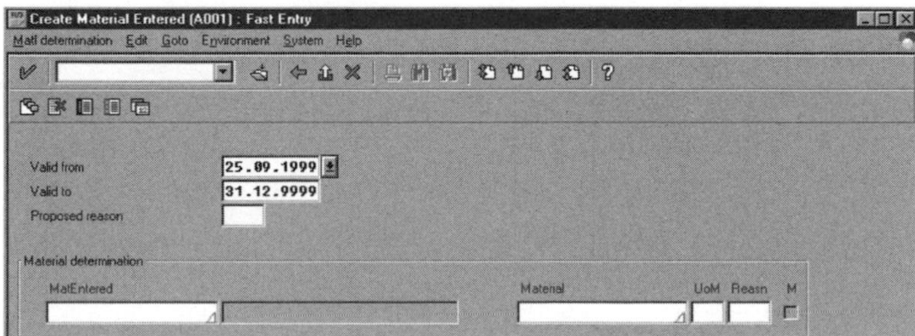

7. Create the determination procedure (if necessary) and assign the condition types to it.
8. Assign the determination procedure.
9. Lastly, create your condition records.

As mentioned, this completes the introduction to the condition technique. However, for material determination, you need a *substitution reason*. A substitution reason is a rule that controls the material determination's execution.

You define substitution reasons in IMG, Sales and distribution, Basic functions, Material determination, Define substitution reasons.

The substitution reason in Figure 3-12 has a four-digit key and description that is used as a reference in the condition record. Attached to this key in customizing, as previously, is a set of rules.

The first column is Entry. It controls whether you would like the system to print the name or number of the original material on the order confirmations, or the substituted material's name or number. The next column is the warning indicator, which, if set, will indicate a warning message to the user that a material determination is about to take place. The strategy column is used to promote if the substitution should be automatic or if the proposed material determination items should be displayed via a pop-up box for selection.

NOTE: *When using material determination, you may enter the material to be swapped in the standard Material Entered (MatEntered) column of the sales order. However, when using the customer material information record, you can only enter the customer's material in the customer material field of the sales order. Thus, should you be using material determination to propose automatic swapping of the customer number automatically one to one, be careful not to use the customer material information record, as this may confuse the user as to where he should enter the data.*

SbstReason	Description	Entry	Warning	Strategy	Outcome
0001	Advertising campaign	☐	☐		
0002	Customer material	☐	☐		
0003	Internat.Article No.	☐	☐		
0004	Availability	☑	☑		A
0005	Promotion	☑	☐	A	

Figure 3-12
A substitution reason with a four-digit key and a description used as a reference in the condition record

NOTE: *The automatic substitution that happens in the background only occurs according to the availability check (if you select a subitem). Thus, should you have four products for the system to do a automatic substitution on, and you have stock of one of them and not the other three, the system will propose and consume that one for which you have stock. This can cause problems due to the fact that if this one material is procured correctly, due to it having a demand on it to be consumed, it may be automatically filled up, causing a continual circle where only this material is used and the other three are not consumed.*

Unfortunately, you are in a bit of a predicament as the pop-up box for manual selection only offers the material numbers and not the available stock on hand. Thus, it is impossible for the user to make an informed choice as to which material to use. Apparently, from Version 4.5 onwards, SAP will show the available stock in the pop-up box for selection. However, the ABAP code is very integrated and not worth moving into a previous release, such as 4.0.

The outcome column enables you to decide whether or not the proposed item from material determination should automatically replace the existing material or if it should be displayed as a subitem in the sales order. Remember that if you use the outcome subitems, be sure to configure your item category determination correctly. That is, the main item that is being substituted should have the product selection higher-level (PSHP) item as the usage indicator, and the subitem material being displayed as a subitem should have the usage indicator PSEL. An example of item category determination would then be as illustrated in Figure 3-13.

NOTE: *Only one schedule line is proposed by the system for the line item which automatic substitution occurs for when the item is a represented as a subitem.*

Figure 3-13
An example of item category determination

OR	NORM	PSEL	TAX	TAPS			
OR	NORM	PSHP		TAX			

TIP: Do not change and do not allow the user to change or delete any entry the system has found when using the automatic substitution as a subitem. Due to the method SAP uses in determining the substituted product, should you, for example, delete the subitem proposed by the system, it will not be fully deleted and may still have entries in table VBBE. Thus, you will still have requirements sitting in the stock overview allocating stock to the particular subitem, even though it does not exist in the sales order. If you find yourself in this unfortunate predicament, refer to OSS note 87944.

Proceeding back to the material determination condition record, we can create a one-to-one automatic swap by selecting the settings shown in Figure 3-14 and the condition record shown in Figure 3-15.

The result you have in the sales order is as shown in Figure 3-16.

Lastly, when using a one-to-one automatic swapping of materials, the material entered does not need to be created in the system. However, should you use the outcome displayed as subitems, both materials need to be configured in the system.

Figure 3-14 Creating a one-to-one automatic swap

SbstReason	Description	Entry	Warning	Strategy	Outcome
0001	1:1 automatic swop	☐	☑		

Figure 3-15 Selecting the condition record

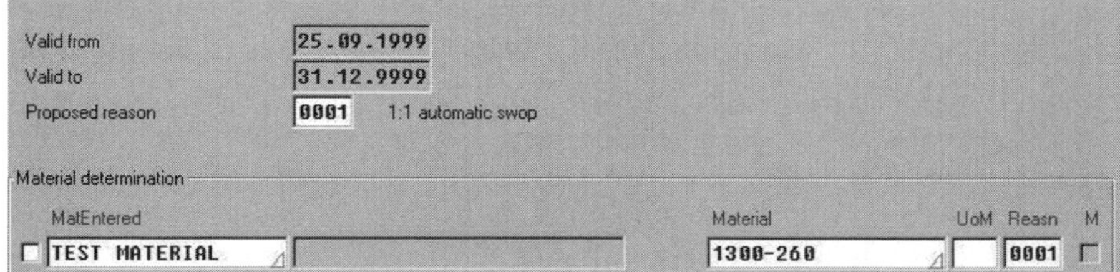

Figure 3-16 The result of the test material

TEST MATERIAL 1

W: Material 1300-260 found on the basis of entry TEST MATERIAL: Reason 1:1 automatic swop

Material Listing and Exclusion

Material listing and exclusion is used in order to list the products or services specific customers may or may not purchase. For example, you may list products that a specific customer may not buy or conversely you may list only the products that the customer can select. Material listing and exclusion uses the condition technique to determine its values and procedures.

Menu Path

The menu path for material listing and exclusion is as follows: IMG, Sales and distribution, Basic functions, Listing/exclusion.

Since material listing and exclusion uses the condition technique, in order to determine the procedure it uses, we will use the configuration procedure of the previous section, that is

1. Put the fields you will need into the field catalog.
2. Create the condition tables you will need.
3. Create the access sequence you will need.
4. Assign the condition tables to the access sequence.
5. Create the condition types.
6. Assign the access sequence to the condition types.
7. Create the determination procedure (if necessary) and assign the condition types to it.
8. Assign the determination procedure.
9. Lastly, create your condition records.

Here we will discuss these steps in more detail.

1. Put the fields you will need into the field catalog. Then go to Maintain allowed fields for listing/exclusion and add any additional fields you will need for the condition tables you are planning to create. You can do this by selecting the button "New entries." Press F4 and you will have a list of fields per table to add to the field catalog. As an example, you can double-click on the entry you wish to add to the list of available fields (see Figure 3-17).
2. Create the condition tables you will need. Go to Maintain condition tables for listing/exclusion and create the condition table you will be using in the access sequence, such as condition table 001. Condition

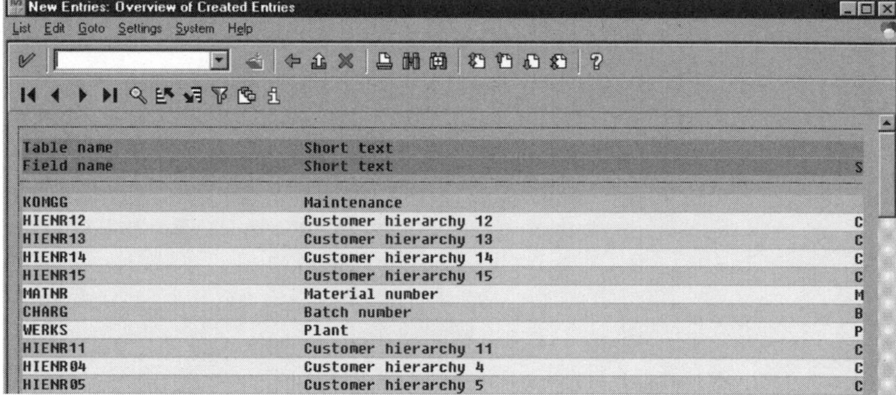

Figure 3-17
A list of fields per table to select and add to the field catalog

table 001 is the SAP standard and is customer and material. Should you be creating your own entries, make sure to use a naming convention, followed by your business, such as 900 onwards. Be sure never to change the standard. Select entries to add to your table by double-clicking the fields on the right.

TIP: *By clicking other descriptions four times, you will receive the long text version of the field's name (or data element, which will be covered in Chapter 5, "CrossFunctional"). This usually provides further descriptions of the field properties. Also be sure to check the technical name of the field as well as access the table where the field exists, such as VBAP. Then compare the entry with the technical view of the field in the field catalog.*

3. Create the access sequence you will need.
4. Assign the condition tables to the access sequence. Go to Maintain access sequences for listing/exclusion. Here you can copy an existing access sequence and change the name of the created access sequence. Should you do this, all subsequent entries such as tables and fields will also be copied. Alternatively, should you not want to copy the access sequence, you may create your own. Either way, after creating or copying and changing, select the button Accesses.

   In our example, we will use the access sequence A001 and call it Listing. This does not mean we can use this access sequence only for listing; we can also use this access sequence for exclusion too, but in order to keep to the customizing rules we will have an individual access sequence for listing and exclusion. After selecting accesses, we are faced with the following screen (see Figure 3-18).

Thus, the table assigned is 001 and the selection is customer and material. Save your data.

5. Create the condition types.
6. Assign the access sequence to the condition types. Go to Maintain listing/exclusion types. Here you assign your condition type to the respective access sequence you have just created. There should be no need to create more condition types than those offered in the standard system for Material listing and exclusion. However, should there be a need to create one, copy an SAP standard condition type and assign it your access sequence, as shown in Figure 3-19. Save before proceeding to step 7.
7. Create the determination procedure (if necessary) and assign the condition types to it. Go to Procedures for maintaining listing/exclusion. In this section, you create your material listing and exclusion determination procedures by developing a determination procedure such as A00001 for listing (see Figure 3-20).

Figure 3-18 The Access sequence listing table

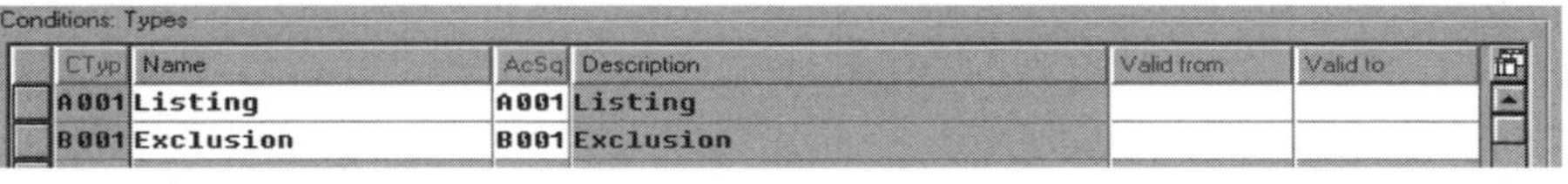

Conditions: Types
CTyp Name AcSq Description Valid from Valid to
A001 Listing A001 Listing
B001 Exclusion B001 Exclusion

Figure 3-19 Copying an SAP standard condition type and assigning it to your access sequence

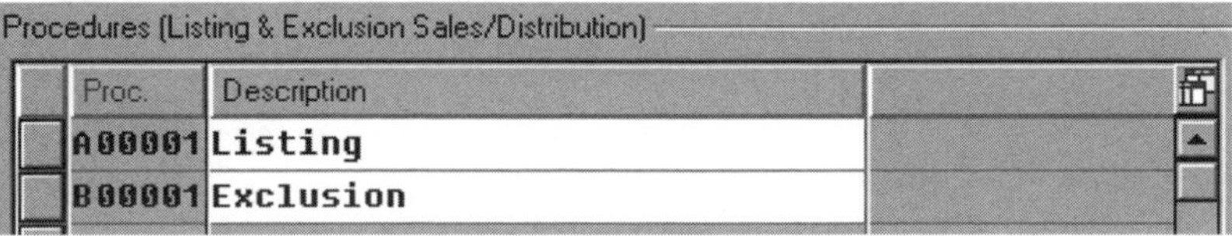

Procedures (Listing & Exclusion Sales/Distribution)
Proc. Description
A00001 Listing
B00001 Exclusion

Figure 3-20 Creating your material listing and exclusion determination procedures by developing a determination procedure

By selecting the procedure and the Control button, you can assign your condition type to the procedure. Then save the entries.

8. Assign the determination procedures. Go to Activate listing/ exclusion by sales document type. Here you assign the determination procedures you have just created to the respective sales document types. You may want one sales document type to be relevant for material listing, but not relevant for material exclusion. Generally, you should assign material listing and material exclusion procedures for the same sales document type. An example of the assignment is shown in Figure 3-21.

   After saving the entries, proceed to Step 9.

9. Create the condition records. All condition records are created in the logistics overview screens, not in the customizing or IMG screens. Then proceed as follows: Logistics, Sales and distribution, Master data, Products, Listing and exclusion, Create. Enter the listing or exclusion condition type. We will use listing condition type A001. Select the table you are entering a record for, if you have more than one table in the conditions access sequence. Press Enter and add the values for your customer and the materials he is allowed to order. Then save your data (see Figure 3-22).

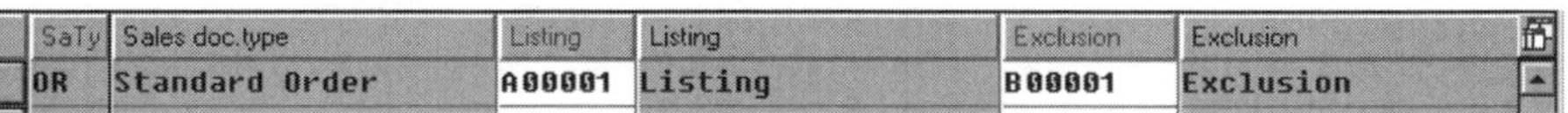

SaTy	Sales doc.type	Listing	Listing	Exclusion	Exclusion
OR	Standard Order	A00001	Listing	B00001	Exclusion

Figure 3-21 Assigning the determination procedures

Customer	1185	Werk Hamburg 1000
Valid from	25.09.1999	
Valid to	31.12.9999	

Conditions

Material	
1300-260	HD Rear shock absorber
AS-10	Pallet
AS-100	Aluminium wheel 7,5 * 16
AS-20	Basic pallet
AS-200	ALuminium-lid
AS-30	Intermediate layer

Figure 3-22 Creating the condition records

TIP: *When creating the sales order, the system will first check to see if the material the customer is ordering is allowed for the sales area in which the order is placed. Then it checks to see if the material is excluded for that customer and lastly it checks to see if the material is on a list of allowed materials for the respective customer.*

TIP: *The system will check the listing and exclusion of the sold-to party first; if it finds a listing or exclusion for the sold-to party, it does not check further. However, should it not find a entry for the sold-to party, it then proceeds to check if a listing or exclusion is created for the payer. If no entry exists for either the sold-to party or the payer partner roles of the customer master record, the customer may order any product created in the sales area for which the order is being created.*

Materials Requirements Planning and Transfer of Requirements

At the time of a sales order, a line item in the sales order creates a schedule line. The schedule line represents the customer's intended delivery date and quantity to be delivered. This information is transferred (a *transfer of requirements*, TOR) to materials requirements planning. Materials requirements planning is then able to determine if there is enough quantity of stock available for the scheduled delivery date. The TOR is closely integrated with the *Materials Management* (MM) and *Production Planning* (PP) modules; thus, it must be configured in association with the respective teams.

Menu Path

The menu path is as follows: IMG, Sales and distribution, Basic functions, Availability check and TOR , TOR .

As described earlier, the schedule lines in the sales order transfer the requirements through to *materials requirements planning* (MRP). You can then select the documents on which you would like the TOR to happen. For example, you may not wish any TOR to happen for quotations, but you may want the TOR to happen for standard sales orders.

The TOR aims to ensure that the materials ordered are ready for the requested delivery date. The TOR can be set for individual requirements or for collective requirements. The indicator can be set in the material master record in the sales/plant view. Individual requirements are, as the name implies, an individual transference of demand to MRP for each schedule line. An advantage of this is that the availability overview [CO09] will show the order quantity, the sales document number, the item number, and the requirements class (discussed later) for each schedule line for which a demand has been created. Collective requirements are a collective grouping of requirements created either daily or weekly that are transferred to MRP. The documents created in collective requirement processing cannot be individually identified from the availability overview.

To access the availability overview screen, proceed as follows: Logistics, Materials management, Environment, Stock, Availability overview [CO09] (see Figure 3-23).

In the previous example, we see that material AM2-730 (an onboard computer) has a stock of 99,000 pieces available. We will be referring back to this screen often.

Collective requirements are useful to a business that deals with a large volume of sales orders per day, as it allows the business to have a clearer view of the availability overview. It also speeds up the response time within the system.

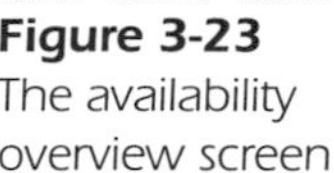

Figure 3-23
The availability overview screen

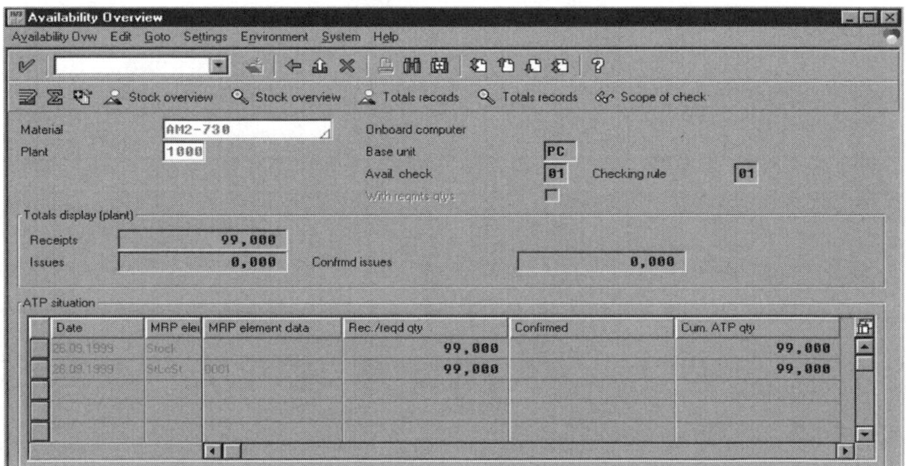

TIP: *The system will automatically create individual requirements for materials with collective requirements indicated on the material master for transactions that create special stock. Examples of this would be consignment, returnable packaging, or make-to-order stock.*

Essentially, the same control elements are used for the TOR as are used for the availability check. The TOR is dependent on the following data:

- The requirements type
- The requirements class
- The checking group
- The schedule line category

The requirements class is the key factor in the TOR. It is based on the requirements type for the sales document. These requirements classes are also used in PP, so be sure to involve PP and MM in any changes you envisage in the SD module. The requirements type and eventually the requirements class are determined in the strategy group, so all changes made there should also be coordinated with PP. The strategy group can be found in the material master [MM02] MRP 3 view under planning.

For TOR to be carried out, you need to ensure a few criteria are met:

- A plant must be assigned to the sales document line item level.
- The schedule line category must be switched on for the TOR.
- The TOR must be switched on at the requirements class level.
- A checking group must be defined and allocated to the material master record in the sales/plant view in the availability check field.

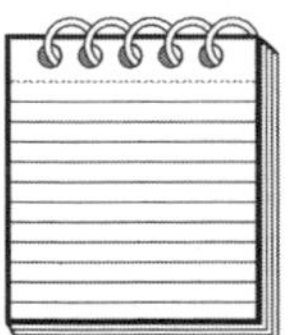

NOTE: *When the TOR is switched on at the requirements class level, it can be switched off at the schedule line level. However, you cannot switch on the TOR at the schedule line level if it is switched off at the requirements class level.*

Settings for the TOR specific to the schedule lines are only relevant for sales documents, such as the sales order. In the shipping documents, however, the settings for the requirements class apply. The requirements class is determined from the requirements type of the material. An example of how the TOR is carried out is shown in Figure 3-24.

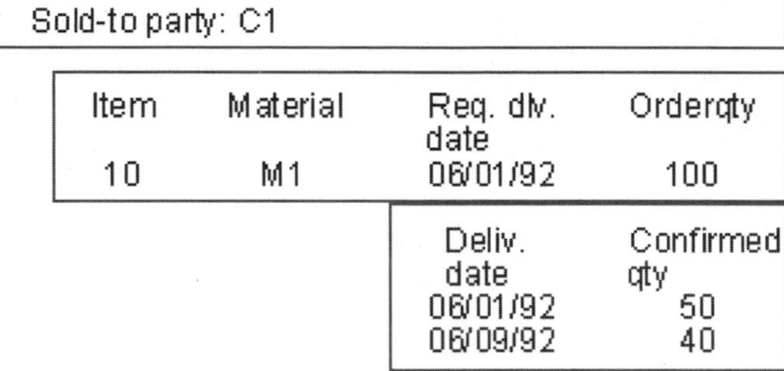

Sold-to party: C1
Item
Material
Req. dlv. date
Orderqty
10
M1
06/01/92
100
Deliv. date
Confirmed qty
06/01/92
50
06/09/92
40

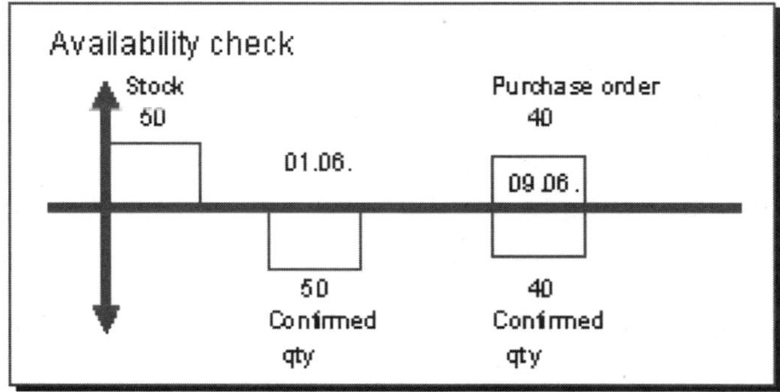

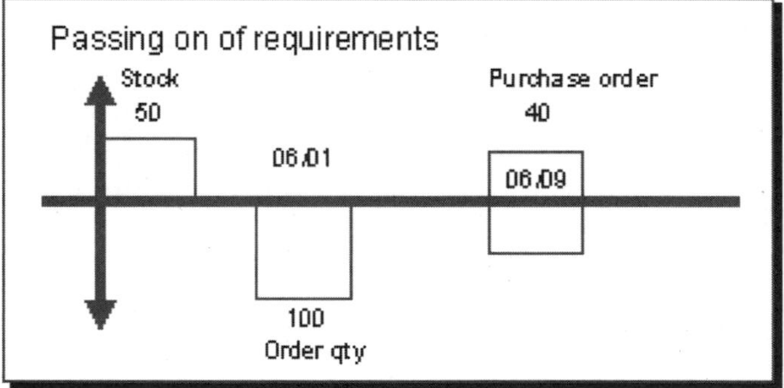

Figure 3-24 Carrying out the TOR Copyright SAP AG

Let's say the customer orders 100 pieces for the requested delivery date of 06/01 /92. Block A represents the availability check, which shows the confirmed quantities at the schedule line level. Block B represents the passing of requirements, which shows the passing of the demand for 100 pieces for 01/06 /92. The result would be the confirmed quantities as confirmed in the schedule lines with an open order quantity of 10 pieces, which could be procured from a purchase order.

Consumption Modes

The consumption mode defines whether and in which direction on the time axis from the requirements date the consumption of customer requirements with planned independent requirements should occur. The requirements date corresponds to the date when the sales order items were created. One has the following options:

- No planning consumption
- Backwards consumption only: starting from the requirements date, backwards consumption is carried out within the relevant consumption period.
- Forwards consumption only: starting from the requirements date, forward consumption is carried out within the relevant consumption period.
- Backwards/forwards consumption: starting from the requirements date, backwards consumption is performed first. Then, if no planned independent requirements can be allocated before the requirements date, forward consumption is performed. Both procedures are carried out for the relevant consumption period.
- Forwards/backwards consumption: Starting from the requirements date, forward consumption is performed first. Then, if no independent requirements can be allocated after the requirements date, backwards consumption is performed. Both procedures are carried out for the relevant consumption period.

Planning Materials

It is possible to create a common planning material and assign similar materials to it. Independent requirements are created for the planning material to cover the requirements that are expected for the materials assigned to the planning material. Thus, customer requirements for these materials are consumed by the independent requirements of the planning material. This means that you do not have to create independent requirements for each material.

You assign the planning material to the materials on the *MRP 3* screen. You must also enter the appropriate strategy group for planning with planning materials on the *MRP 1* screen.

TIP: *You cannot perform a TOR from the sales or delivery documents when using a planning material. Rather, the actual requirement from the order or delivery consumes the independent requirement of the planning material. The independent requirement is thus reduced. Then when MRP is run, requirements are created for the order or delivery and for the balance of the independent requirement.*

For example, let's say we have an independent requirement of 100 tons and an order of 20 tons. The order becomes a requirement of 20 tons, and the independent requirement is reduced to 80 tons. The total requirement is still 100 tons.

The Stock Requirements List

The stock requirements list is the central table for planning and stock control. It is accessed via various menu paths, but the most straightforward method is as follows: Logistics, Materials management, Inventory management, Environment, Stock, Stock requirements list [MD04].

Figure 3-25 is an example of individual requirements. You can clearly see the order number or the delivery number as well as the line item and schedule line placing the demand on plant 0001. The first line displays the avail-

Figure 3-25
An example of individual requirements

Stock/Requirements List: Individual Lines

List Edit Goto Settings Environment System Help

On Vendor Customer

Material TESTMAT1 MOTMC326D

Plant 0001 MRP type PD Material type ZSTD Unit PCE

Date	MRP element	St	O	MRP element data	E	Rec./reqd quantity	Available quantity	Deliv.	Stora
28.09.1999	Stock						6.098		
26.05.1999	PurOrd			4500000739/00010	07	1.100	7.198		0001
26.05.1999	Order			0000001414/000010/0001		10-	7.188		
31.05.1999	PurOrd			4500000772/00010	07	950	8.138		0001
01.06.1999	PurOrd			4500000796/00010	07	415	8.553		0001
07.06.1999	Deliv.			0080000787/900002/0000		5-	8.548		0001
07.06.1999	Deliv.			0080000787/900001/0000		80-	8.468		0001
07.06.1999	Deliv.			0080000787/900003/0000		4-	8.464		0001
07.06.1999	Deliv.			0080000787/000010/0000		11-	8.453		0001
21.06.1999	Order			0000002007/000020/0001		10-	8.443		
21.06.1999	Order			0000002007/000010/0001		10-	8.433		
22.06.1999	Deliv.			0080001038/900001/0000		10-	8.423		0001
02.07.1999	Deliv.			0080001194/900001/0000		11-	8.412		0001
02.07.1999	Deliv.			0080001194/000010/0000		19-	8.393		0001

able stock in the plant. The next line shows a purchase order, which is booked into available stock, increasing the stock level to 7190. The following line shows the result of TOR from a sales order for a quantity of 10 pieces. Line 6 shows a delivery placing a demand for five pieces of stock for 7/6 /99. This demand is placed on stock in storage location 0001.

TIP: *Another view of stock that is invaluable to the interpretation of the available stock and the situation of stock levels in a plant is the stock overview (previously used in consignment stock [MMBE]).*

This view will show you the total stock per company code, then plant followed by storage location, and finally a breakdown per batch. A useful tool here is the material movements, which can be viewed by selecting the stock line and proceeding to Environment, Material movements.

NOTE: *You may find from time to time that you may have inconsistencies between the stock requirements list [MD04] and the actual placed orders. This can be solved by implementing OSS note 25444.*

This OSS note explains the possible reasons for the inconsistencies. Most inconsistencies are generally caused by poor user training, resulting in poor usage of the system. The note proposes implementing a report ZSDRQCR21 that will regenerate all the requirements for a particular material in a particular plant. I have found this report to be very useful.

Configuring the Transfer of Requirements

Note that as the TOR is closely linked to the materials management module, we will be focusing on the SD configuration areas only. Proceed as follows: IMG, Sales and distribution, Basic functions, Availability check and TOR , Transfer of requirements, Define requirements classes.

The requirements class is the controlling factor for the availability check and the TOR for all sales documents types. The system uses the entries at the requirements class level as a default and brings the data into the sales order. The schedule line category is used to fine-tune the settings at the requirements class level.

1. Generally, SD will not need to create a new requirements class for a standard business process. However, should a new requirements

class be necessary, simply copy and rename the class that resembles the requirements class you need. Be sure you rename the class using the SAP-standard name range that begins with a Z.

A useful tip is to select the requirements class you want to configure and then select the Display button represented by a magnifying glass. This will produce an easily configurable overview of the indicators you may set at the requirements class level. As the standard, the 041 requirements class is displayed in Figure 3-26.

Use the indicators to select if this requirements class must carry out an availability check and/or a TOR. Once the requirements class has been created, proceed to define the requirements types.

2. Define the requirements types. A requirements type is allocated to a single requirements class, but a requirements class can be allocated to more than one requirements type. The requirements type is displayed in the sales order. It is based on the item category and the MRP type of the material. It is possible to change the requirements type at the time of creating the sales order. Assign the requirements

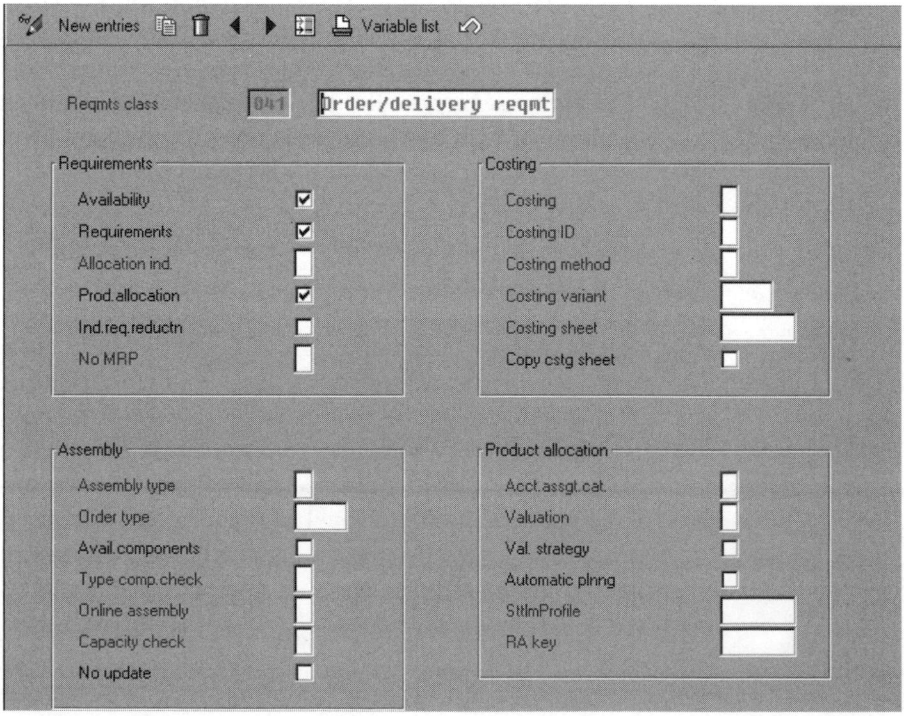

Figure 3-26
The 041 requirements class

class you created to a requirements type. Once this assignment has been made, proceed to determine the requirement types.

3. Here you assign the requirements type to the relevant item category in the sales order and the MRP type found on the material master record. The MRP type is used in the material master to determine how a material is planned for automatic reorder point planning, manual reorder point planning, or forecast based planning. Generally, the system uses the following process to determine the requirements type, as shown in Figure 3-27.

   However, the system uses a predefined search strategy to determine the requirements type:

1. First, an attempt is made to find a requirements type using the strategy group in the material master.
2. Then if the strategy group has not been maintained, the system will determine it using the MRP group.
3. If, however, the MRP group has not been defined, the system uses the material type, instead of the MRP group, when accessing the corresponding control tables.
4. If no requirements type is found here, the system assumes a special rule and attempts to find a requirements type with the aid of the item category and the MRP type.
5. If this is not possible, a last attempt is made to find a requirements type with the item category only.
6. If the last attempt fails, the system declares the transaction as not relevant for the availability check or TOR.

   Should you not want this strategy to be used to search for a requirements type and instead would like the system to immediately determine the requirements type based on the item category and MRP type as you assigned them, you can select an alternative search strategy where you assign the requirements type (see Figure 3-28). For this particular example, you would select a 1, which determines that the source is used as the item type and MRP type strategy.

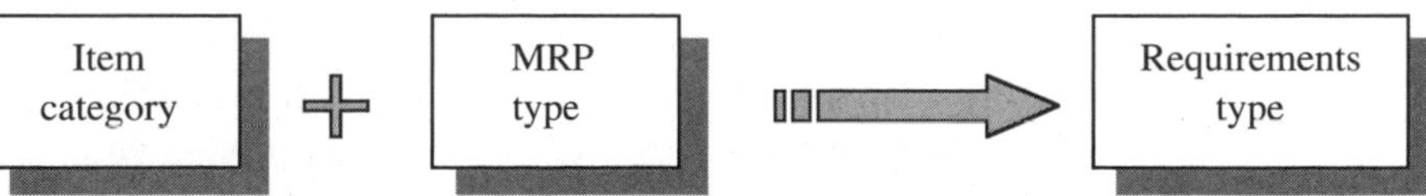

Figure 3-27 The requirements type process

Figure 3-28 Selecting an alternative search strategy

ItCa	Typ	RqTy	Q	Requirements type description
TAN		041		Order/delivery requirement
TAN	ND	041		Order/delivery requirement
TAN	P1	041		Order/delivery requirement
TAN	P2	041		Order/delivery requirement

Figure 3-29 Indicating the schedule line category for the TOR availability check and/or product allocation

SLCa	Description	AvC	Rq	All.
AN	ALE Standard	☐	☐	☐
AT	Inquiry sched.line	☐	☐	☐
BN	No MRP	☑	☐	☐
BP	MRP	☑	☑	☐
BT	No inventory mgmt	☐	☐	☐
BV	Consumption MRP	☐	☐	☐
C0	ConsgtIssue/w/o AvCh	☐	☐	☐
C1	ConsgtIssue/w. AvCh.	☑	☑	☐

Once this assignment has been made, proceed to the Define procedure for each schedule line category menu.

4. As discussed previously, the TOR and the availability check can be fine-tuned at the schedule line category level. Note that this only allows you to deactivate a setting at the schedule line level only if it is already set at the requirements class level. Thus, you can select that a particular requirements class be active for the availability check or TOR and then decide that you do not want the schedule line to transfer requirements at the schedule line level. However, you must have selected the requirements class as relevant for TOR before trying to activate it at the schedule line level. Proceed with indicating which schedule line category will be available for the TOR availability check and/or product allocation. Note that the product allocation is also controlled in the requirements class (see Figure 3-29). After completing this, proceed to the Block quantity confirmation in the Delivery blocks menu.

5. Block quantity confirmation in delivery blocks is shown in Figure 3-30.

   This is used to block the reservation of the TOR from MRP. In standard sales order processing, the system transfers the requirements to MRP, but in some cases you may need to block a

Figure 3-30 Block quantity confirmation in delivery blocks

transaction due to a bad result of the credit check, for example. In cases where the transaction is blocked, the requirement still sits in MRP and still reserves a quantity. This often is unfavorable; thus, you may indicate here that the system does not reserve the stock. It will still transfer the requirement to MRP but will not reserve the quantity.

You can set a limit on the number of days you would want the system to postpone this block on confirmation of requirements. This can be carried out by setting a number of days to the block in the Def.period column.

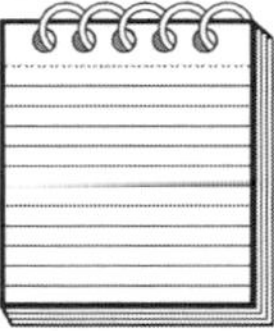

NOTE: *This postponement period will only affect the order confirmation if the postponement falls within the confirmation period. For example, if a material is ordered on the 01.10 and confirmed for the 02.10 and the period for the block is 10 days, the resulting confirmed date would be 11.10. However, should the original schedule line only be confirmed in 20 days, the block would have no affect on the sales order. Once the block is removed in the document, the system will do an availability check and confirm quantities with respective dates.*

6. Maintain requirements for the TOR. In the same way as requirements are used in access sequences, that is, a number of preconditions must exist for the transaction to be carried out, requirements can be used to determine that the TOR to MRP is not carried out unless a number of conditions are met. A good example of this would be the standard SAP requirement that you can assign "102," which prevents reservations from being carried out in the event of a credit block. You can also set requirements at the Maintain requirements for purchase and assembly orders menu.

   In standard sales order processing, a purchase order may need to be created in order to meet the demands of the customer. This purchase order is used to purchase new stock in order to meet the demand on MRP for a particular customer's sales order.

Here you define requirements that must be met in order for the purchase order or assembly order to be created. An example is the standard SAP requirement 101, which will cause a purchase order or assembly order from being created, should a credit block exist on the sales order.

This completes the SD module's task of configuring the TOR. The TOR is closely associated with the availability check. They should be planned and configured at the same time.

Availability Check

The availability check is an integral part of the business process. It determines if the desired delivery quantity can be met on the desired date. The availability check takes into account the respective activities that must be carried out before a delivery can take place. This includes the scheduling for picking or packing times and the time taken to produce or obtain the material as well as many other background functions.

Menu Path

The menu path here is as follows: IMG, Sales and distribution, Basic functions, Availability check and TOR, Availability check, Availability Check with ATP Logic or Against Planning.

Backorder processing is the processing of a backorder, which in itself is a sales order that has not been confirmed in full or not confirmed at a certain delivery date.

Rescheduling is a proposal of how confirmed quantities already assigned to sales orders can be reassigned to other orders that have a higher priority, such as an a earlier delivery date.

ATP stands for *available to promise*. It is the process of checking the available quantities of a material. The ATP quantity is equal to warehouse stock plus the planned receipts (incoming stock) minus the planned issues (outgoing stock). ATP takes into account all movements into and out of the warehouse. If selected, it can check the stock examined for ATP that can be safety stock, stock in transfer, stock in quality inspection, and blocked stock, although the planned receipts and planned issues of the stock associated with ATP may be purchase orders, purchase requisitions, planned orders, production orders, reservations, dependent reservations, dependent requirements, sales requirements, and delivery requirements. If the business produces special stock such as made-to-order goods or consignment stock, the ATP check is done against the special stock.

Replenishment lead time (RLT) is the time needed to produce the requested stock. It can be the time taken by the business to produce a material or the time taken to externally procure the material from a vendor. This includes the goods receipting time; thus, the RLT is the time taken for the material to become available. RLT is only used when doing an ATP check. The value of the RLT for a material is specified on the material master record. It can be determined in one of two ways:

- *The RLT for an* externally procured material. This is determined based on the total of the processing time for purchasing, the planned delivery time, and the goods receipt processing time. These settings can be made on the Purchasing and MRP 2 views of the material master record.
- *The RLT for an* internally procured material. This is based on the in-house production time, found in the MRP 2 view, and the goods receipt processing time or alternatively on the total replenishment lead time, which is found in the material master record on the MRP 3 view.

NOTE: *If a sales order is created, there is no available stock, and the ATP check is set to include RLT, the system will automatically confirm the desired quantity for the end of RLT based on whether the material is externally or internally procured. Thus, should you have an order for 100,000 pieces of material XYZ and the system has no available stock, it will still give a confirmed date according to the end of the lead time. Should there be partial stock available, the system will confirm this partial quantity and move the remaining quantity to the end of RLT. Thus, it does not do an availability check outside of the RLT. If RLT is three days for a specific material, it will not do an availability check outside of those three days, as it automatically thinks it will definitely have stock on the fourth day.*

To examine stock on hand, proceed to Logistics, Sales and distribution, Sales, Environment, Availability overview [CO09]. To examine stock on hand from a created order, proceed to change mode [VA02] schedule line, Environment, Availability.

There are three types of availability checks. The first is the availability check on the basis of the ATP quantities, as previously described. The second is the availability check against product allocation, which from SAP release 3.0F onwards enables an availability check against product allocation, allowing a predefined distribution quantity of products to customers. The third availability check is the check against planning. This is not a check against sales orders (a pull business cycle in which a sales order pulls demand through the system to confirm the order), but rather a push business flow where quantities are produced in line with expected sales quantities independent of sales orders.

Configuring the Availability Check through Checking Groups

The checking group defines what type of requirements we will pass on. Do we record summarized requirements daily or requirements in the stock requirements list weekly? Or do we record individual requirements for each sales order, line item, and schedule line in the stock requirement list?

The advantages of individual requirements over summarized requirements are as follows:

- Backorder processing is possible for individual processing.
- We can access the order and line items and schedule lines in MD04. This gives one greater control over the available stock and the requirements placed on the stock.

The disadvantages are that there may be slightly more impact on system performance as each demand is placed immediately into the stock requirements list.

Do not forget the system automatically uses individual requirements for special stock movements such as consignment stock, returnable packaging, and so on, even if summarized requirements have been selected.

The checking groups are configurable, yet SAP standard uses the following checking groups:

01 to represent daily requirements

02 to represent individual requirements

The checking group plus the checking rule determines how the availability check is to be performed. The checking group is found on the material master record MRP 3 view.

Checking Rule

The checking rule is used to control the scope of the availability check for each transaction in sales and distribution. The control of the availability check is defined by the checking group on the material master record and the checking rule representing the transaction. The checking rule may be configured in the system depending on the application or module, but in the sales and distribution module, it is predefined.

Schedule Line Category

The availability check can be fine-tuned at the schedule line level in the same way as the TOR is carried out at the schedule line level. Those schedule lines that are not relevant for an availability check can be switched off at the schedule line level by ensuring the availability check indicator is not flagged.

Delivery Item Category

The delivery item category can be used to control whether an availability check takes place in deliveries.

Requirements Class

The requirements class, as used in the TOR, controls the relevance for the requirements planning strategy and the requirements consumption strategy. It is also responsible to determine if an availability check is to be performed for the material on the basis of the ATP quantity and whether the TOR is passed on.

Requirements Type

The requirements type refers to the requirements class and its features. The requirements class is assigned to the requirements type in the TOR.

Required Data for the Availability Check to Be Carried Out

In order for the availability check to be carried out, the following data in addition to the configuration entries, described later, must be defined in the system:

- The availability check must be switched on at the requirements class level. Refer to the TOR configuration process [OVZG] (see Figure 3-31).
- For the availability check in the sales document, the indicator must be set at the schedule line category level [OVZ8] (see Figure 3-32).
- A requirements type must exist by which the requirements class can be found. Again refer to the TOR [OVZH] (see Figure 3-33).
- A plant must be defined in the sales order for the line item. It can either be automatically proposed by the system from the customer, the customer material information record, or the material master record. It can also be entered manually in the document.
- A checking group must be defined in the material master record in the MRP 3 screen in the *Availability check* field (see Figure 3-34).

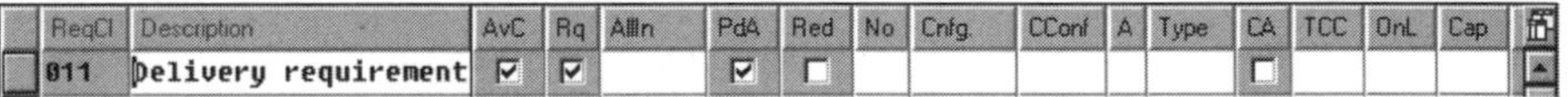

ReqCl	Description	AvC	Rq	Allln	PdA	Red	No	Cnfg.	CConf	A	Type	CA	TCC	OnL	Cap
011	Delivery requirement	☑	☑		☑	☐						☐			

Figure 3-31 Switching the availability check on at the requirements class level

SLCa	Description	AvC	Rq	All.
CP	MRP	☑	☑	☐

Figure 3-32 Setting the indicator at the schedule line category level

RqTy	Requirements type	ReqCl	Description
011	Delivery requirement	011	Delivery requirement

Figure 3-33 A requirements type must exist so that the requirements class can be found.

Figure 3-34
A checking group must be defined in the material master record in the MRP 3 screen in the *Availability check* field.

Av	Description	TotalSales	TotDlvReqs	Block QtRq	No check	Accumul.	Response	RelChk
01	Daily requireme	B	B	☐	☐			
02	Individ.require	A	A	☑	☐			

Figure 3-35
You can choose between the standard SAP checking groups of 01 for summarized requirements or 02 for daily requirements.

Configuring Entries of the Availability Check and Defining Checking Groups

Proceed to IMG, Sales and distribution, Basic functions, Availability check and transfer of requirements, Availability check, Availability Check with ATP logic or against planning, Define checking groups.

You can use the standard SAP checking groups of 01 for summarized requirements and 02 for daily requirements or you can create your own entries (see Figure 3-35). Should you create your own, do not forget to copy and name them using the SAP allocated range beginning with a Z.

The columns total sales and total deliveries in Figure 3-35 are selection options whereby you can configure a checking rule to sum up requirements to post to MRP either individually or by day or week. Do not forget that by selecting the summarized requirements you will lose out on the connection to the individual sales order and associated line item in the stock requirements list [MD04]. Note column 5, Block QtRq; set this block if you want several users to be able to process the material simultaneously in different transactions without blocking each other.

The No check indicator is used when you want a material to not be relevant for an ATP check; thus, no check is carried out for the material with a checking rule indicating "no check." For materials that there is a high quantity of stock for, it would be impossible and unnecessary to validate the available quantity.

Defining a Material Block for Other Users

The Block checkbox is an indicator that enables you to block the particular material from being checked for availability if it is already being checked at the same time by another user (see Figure 3-36). This block serves a valuable purpose in that, should the block not be set, two users can confirm the same quantity for the same material at the same time.

You cannot change the field value for the initiator of the availability check, such as A-order or B-delivery note, as in the configuration menu.

Defining the Default Value for Checking Groups

We have defined the checking groups, which are introduced into the sales order based on the setting in the material master record. However, should no entry exist in the material master record, one can set a default value per material type and plant. This default value will be used by the system based upon the material type of the material master record and the plant in the sales order, unless an entry exists in the material master record, whereby it will be overwritten by the material master checking group.

Controlling the Availability Check

In this section, you tell the system what stock on hand and what inward and outward movements of stock it must take into account when performing the availability check (see Figure 3-37).

These settings are based on the checking group that is assigned to the material master record and the checking rule that is predefined and assigned to the sales and distribution transaction. The carry out control for the availability check must be maintained for both the sales order and delivery, as shown in Figure 3-38. This is due to the fact you may want to include specific stock or incoming stock for the sales order, yet at the time of the delivery only include physical stock on hand waiting to be shipped.

Figure 3-36 Various Block settings for different materials

AvailCheck	Description	Initiator	Block
01	Daily requirements	A	☑
01	Daily requirements	B	☑
01	Daily requirements	C	☐
02	Individ.requirements	A	☑

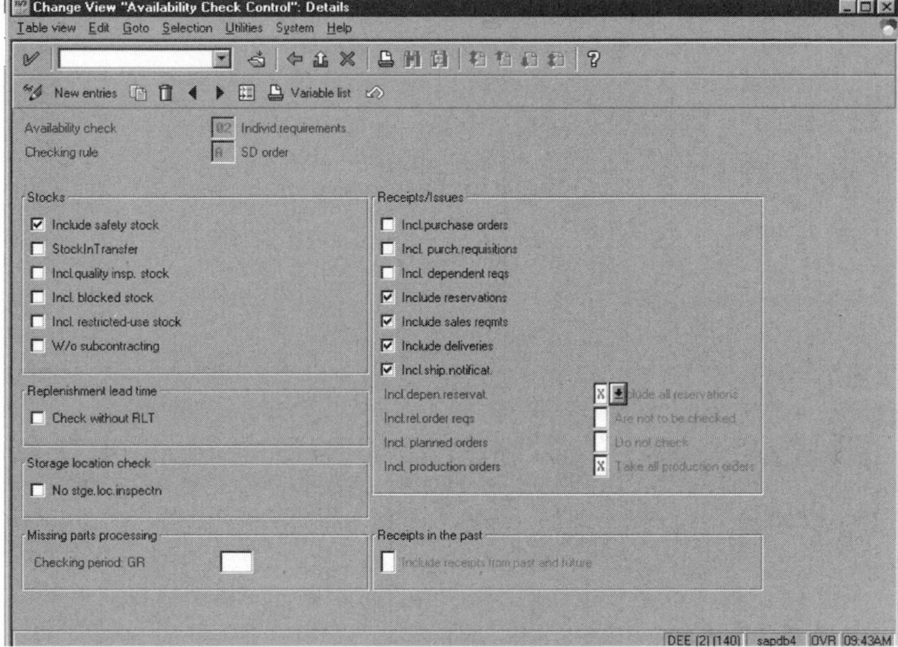

Figure 3-37
The settings for the availability check

Figure 3-38
Maintaining the carry out control for the availability check for both the sales order and delivery

Av	Description	ChR	Checking rule
02	Individ.require	A	SD order
02	Individ.require	AE	SD order; make-to-order stock
02	Individ.require	AV	SD order; returnable packaging
02	Individ.require	AW	SD order; consignment
02	Individ.require	B	SD delivery
02	Individ.require	BE	SD delivery; make-to-order sto
02	Individ.require	BO	Backorder processing
02	Individ.require	BV	SD delivery; returnable packag
02	Individ.require	BW	SD delivery; consignment

Select the indicator, should you wish to take the respective stock into account when carrying out the availability check, such as

- Safety stock
- Stock in transfer
- Quality inspection stock
- Blocked stock

Now select the planned inward and outward movements of stock you would like to take into account when doing an availability check:

- **Include sales requirements** is used to include the requirement based on a sales transaction that could have been previous orders placed for the material or even quotations.
- **Include deliveries** is used by the system to include requirements passed on from a delivery document for this material.
- **Include reservations** is used to determine if the system should take into account the reservations of stock for this material.
- **Include dependent requirements** is used by the system to indicate if dependent requirements such as components of a production order are taken into account.
- **Include purchase requisitions** is used by the system to determine if it should use the requisition for purchasing to obtain more stock in the availability check.
- **Include purchase orders** is slightly better than purchase requisitions as it tells the system to include actual orders placed for more stock.
- **Include shipping notifications** is used by the system to include confirmed purchase orders, ensuring that stock is coming into the plant or warehouse.

You can then check dependent reservations and release order requirements, planned orders, and production orders.

It is also possible to indicate to the system that you would like the availability check not to check the stock at the storage location level. Should you set this indicator, the system will automatically use the check based on the plant. We covered replenishment lead time earlier on. Should you *not* want the system to automatically check the replenishment lead time, you may indicate so here.

The business now needs to define the elements necessary to be included in the availability check. No one can define what your specific business would need to include or exclude in the check, but a few tips in making these decisions would be the following:

- When controlling the availability check at the time of the sales order, a purchase requisition does not necessarily indicate the stock requested by it is going to come in to the plant.
- A shipping notification, which is a confirmed purchase order, on the other hand is a good indicator you will be receiving stock at a certain date.

- Should you select shipping notifications as an element for the availability check in the sales order, be careful if selecting it for the delivery. You may discover you actually did not receive the stock and may be creating a delivery with no materials in the plant or warehouse.
- Both sales and delivery requirements are taken into account in the availability check in sales documents. However, in deliveries, only the delivery requirements are taken into account and there is a danger that quantities reserved in the sales documents are considered to be available by the availability check in the deliveries This results in the deliveries being created and the material availability dates of the materials in the sales order being pushed out.

Transportation Scheduling

The entries in the carry out control of the availability check control the data you tell the system to take into account when carrying out the availability check to meet a specified delivery date. The customer specifies a delivery date on the schedule line of the sales order. The business must determine if it can carry out the associated functions in procuring the requested quantity and delivering it to the customer by the requested delivery date in the sales order. The business functions required to be performed before a delivery date can be met are the following:

- Procuring materials, such as for obtaining materials from a supplier
- Planning the transportation to obtain space on a ship, for example
- Selecting and packing the items
- Loading the materials
- Transporting the materials to the customer

This process of scheduling the business process from the requested delivery date backwards in order to meet a specified delivery date is called *backward scheduling* (see Figure 3-39).

If a customer's requested delivery date is on the 20th of January for a sales order it places on the 14th of January, the system carries out backward scheduling from the date of the requested delivery date. Let's say the transit time (the time taken to move the materials to the customer's site) is four days and the loading time in the warehouse is one day. The transportation lead time (the time taken to schedule the containers or shipping companies to move the materials) is one day, which usually falls into the

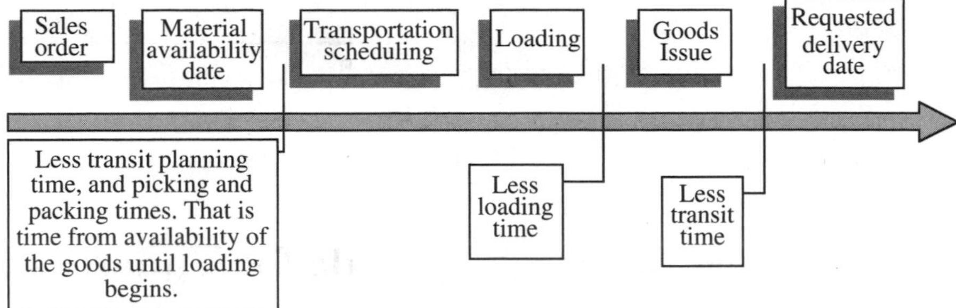

Figure 3-39 The backward scheduling process

time taken for the material to become available. We now have a delivery date of January 20th, less four days, less another day, less another day, which gives us the 14th of January. Should the material be available on the 14th, we could confirm a delivery date of the 20th.

However, should the materials not be available on the 14th, and indeed if the system finds the materials will only be available at a later date, it immediately carries out *forward scheduling*, projecting the earliest possible delivery date based on the scheduling of the business process from the material availability date forward. Forward scheduling takes the availability date of the material in the future and adds the business processing scheduled times required to meet the requested delivery date. Thus, should the stock be available on the 18th in the previous example, the materials will arrive at the customer's site on the 18th plus six days, (4+1+1) = the 24th, less the time taken for transportation lead time, one day, as this step could have been carried out during the period waiting for the materials' availability. Therefore, the delivery date based on forward scheduling would be the 23rd of January.

Carrying on with the configuration of the availability check, we have already ensured the availability check is "switched on" at the requirements class level as well as for each schedule line category.

Determining the Procedure for Each Delivery Item Category

In this step, you switch off the availability check for specific delivery item categories, as shown in Figure 3-40. This should be done for returns deliveries.

ItCa	Description	Avail.check off
REN	Standard Item	X

Figure 3-40
Switching off the availability check for specific delivery item categories

Checking the Rule for Updating Backorders

The checking rule used here is the same checking rule as configured in the carry out control of the availability check. This checking rule is used in the availability overview [CO09] and during backorder processing [CO06]. We will cover backorder processing later on in this chapter.

Defining Default Settings for the Results of the Availability Check in the Sales Order

Here you define the default setting according to the sales organization, distribution channel, and division (sales area). As shown in Figure 3-41, if you should automatically fix the date and quantity of the delivery date, and thus the resultant material availability date, and you select this indicator, the delivery dates are fixed in MRP. However, should you not select the fixed date and quantity and can speed up the supply of the materials into your plant, the resultant material availability date is more favorable and you can reschedule the dates in order for them to obtain a more favorable delivery time.

The availability check rule is a rule defining what the result of the availability check in the sales order should be. This can take the form of either a pop-up window where the user can select either a delivery proposal or a complete delivery or it could take the form of the system automatically selecting a delivery proposal, a one-time delivery, or a complete delivery without a pop-up window being shown.

TIP: *The availability checking rule set here not only determines what the user sees when carrying out an availability check online; it also determines the result of the availability check in background mode. The entry in parentheses defines how the system behaves in background mode (see Figure 3-42). Background mode can be active during any batch rescheduling that you carry out.*

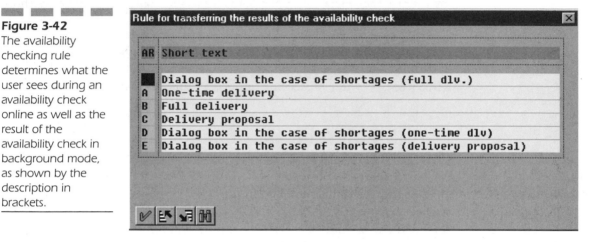

Sales org.	Distr. chl	Division	Fixed date and qty	Avail.check rule
0001	01	01	☐	E
0020	01	01	☐	E

Figure 3-41 Defining the default setting according to the sales organization, distribution channel, and division

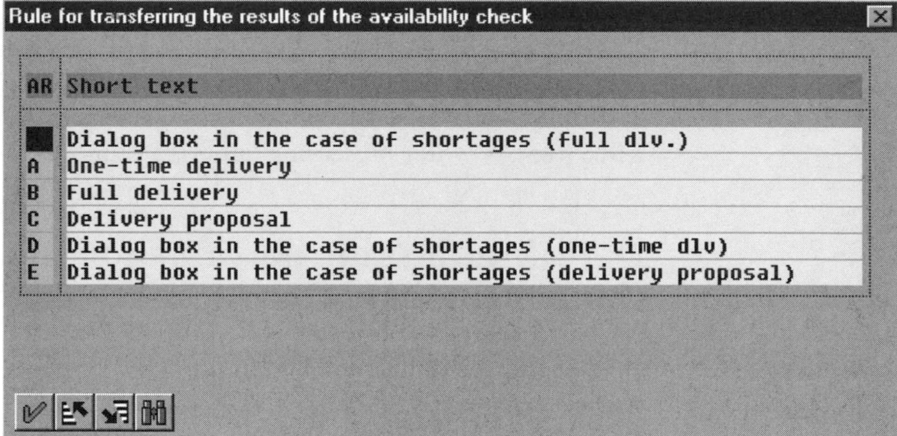

Rule for transferring the results of the availability check
AR Short text
Dialog box in the case of shortages (full dlv.)
A One-time delivery
B Full delivery
C Delivery proposal
D Dialog box in the case of shortages (one-time dlv)
E Dialog box in the case of shortages (delivery proposal)

Figure 3-42 The availability checking rule determines what the user sees during an availability check online as well as the result of the availability check in background mode, as shown by the description in brackets.

One-time delivery The system will try to confirm material for there requested delivery date. Should it not be able to confirm stock for the requested delivery date, it will confirm a value of zero.

Complete delivery The system will only confirm a delivery date on a date when the entire scheduled, ordered quantity for that line in the sales order is available. For example, should the quantity ordered be 100 pieces for an order on January first with a requested delivery date of January first and you have 90 pieces available, the system will wait until 100 pieces can be confirmed, which may be at the end of the lead time for the material. If the lead time is one month, the complete delivery will only be made on the first of February.

Delivery proposal Here the system will confirm the quantity it has available for the requested delivery date. It will then create another confirmation for the resulting outstanding material for the end of the lead time or for when new stock will be available. Using the previous example, the system will confirm the 90 pieces immediately, use forward scheduling to propose the delivery date (plus six days, for example), and will then confirm a second delivery date for the remaining 10 pieces at the end of the lead time that is February the first.

An example of this dialog box in the Availability Check Overview screen for the user to select from is shown in Figure 3-43.

You can select an availability check across plants from the availability control screen by selecting Goto, Other plants. This will display a selection for the user to select the other plant he wishes to check. Note only those plants in which the material is maintained will be displayed.

TIP: *By selecting Goto, Scope of check in the Availability Control screen, the system will display the automatic control of the availability check, that is, the selections of stock availability.*

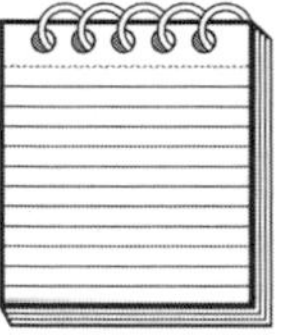

NOTE: *You may receive two specific messages when carrying out an availability check on a line item. One may be a "product allocation found changes to the confirmation." This means that the customer purchasing the stock has exceeded his allowed quantity and the product allocation has limited the quantity he may consume for this material or for this particular line item. It is possible to see his allocated quantity by proceeding from the availability control screen to Goto, Product allocation. This will also show his consumed quantity and the quantity he still has available to consume. We will cover product allocation later.*

One-time delivery on requested delivery date: not possible
Date 07.10.1999 Confirmed quantity 0

Complete delivery
Date 08.10.1999

Delivery proposal
Date 08.10.1999 Confirmed quantity 300

Figure 3-43 The one-time delivery on requested delivery date section

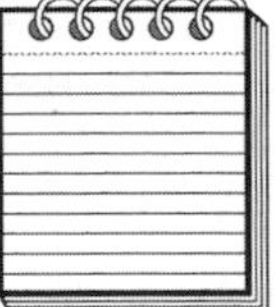

NOTE: *The other message you may get is "no feature combination exists . . . ." This message is also linked to product allocation, yet this message will mean that no availability check will be carried out. This is because the system has tried to do an availability check according to product allocation yet has found errors in the process setup. These errors could be that the customer is absent from a planning hierarchy (used in product allocation) or an incorrect schedule line category is being used to allocate according to product allocation, but neither the customer nor the transaction are relevant for product allocation.*

Delivery Document Types

A delivery document type is similar to the sales order document type in that the settings control how a delivery is to be carried out at the highest level. The structure is very similar to a sales document type in that a delivery type has a delivery item category assigned to it. A delivery is the next logical step in the standard business process flow. The SAP delivery is the documented means of preparing for a movement of goods.

Menu Path

The path here is IMG, Sales and distribution, Shipping, Deliveries, Define delivery types.

Transaction Code

The code here is [0VLK]. The SAP delivery is usually the next logical step proceeding a sales document type. Sales document types that normally proceed with a delivery document type include standard sales orders, standard return orders, and scheduling agreements. However, a delivery is not restricted to being created from a sales document type. The delivery document type has fewer control settings than the sales document type, which can be seen in Figure 3-44.

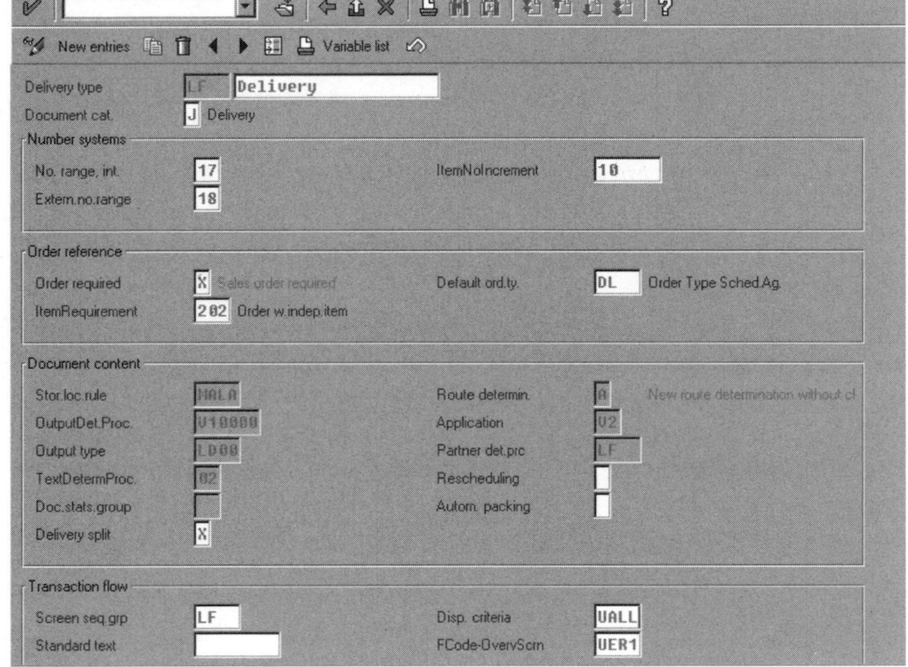

Figure 3-44 The delivery document type settings

Number Ranges

Here you assign the particular number range your delivery will follow as well as the item incrementation in the delivery document type. You can create the number ranges relevant for delivery documents by proceeding to IMG, Sales and distribution, Shipping, Deliveries, Define number ranges for deliveries [VN01]. After creating the interval, refer to the section on defining number ranges. If necessary, you can assign your delivery document number range to the document type.

Order Reference

You can also indicate if the system should enable the particular delivery to be created without reference to a sales order document type. Should you allow this delivery to be created without such a reference, you must specify a pseudo-sales documents type in the Default order type field. This will cause the system to use the control data set for this referenced pseudo-document type.

TIP: *When it is necessary to have a specific goods movement assigned to a delivery that has no sales document type used as a reference, your pseudo-sales document type must have an item category followed by an assigned schedule line category. It is this schedule line category that must have the assigned goods movement. Be sure when creating document types and objects in SAP to copy the standard and change the name beginning with the permitted naming convention Z.*

An example of a pseudo-sales document would be when the warehouse asks for a specific delivery that must not be created from a sales order but will use a special goods movement type. This goods movement type, such as 901, is used to show the return of stock to a supplier. You would configure this by copying a standard delivery type. An example would be LF and you would name it ZLF. You would then copy a sales document type, such as TA, and name it ZTA, followed by copying an item category TAN and naming it ZTAN. Finally, you would copy a schedule line category such as CP and name it ZCP. Assigned to this schedule line category would be the movement type 901. You would then assign the sales document type ZTA to the delivery type ZLF as the default order type. Do not forget your individual settings in the relevant document types and item categories as well as the copy control settings. The specific control of the item categories in the delivery will be covered a little later.

We will not go into a lot of detail on the delivery types item requirement, other than it is a requirement that must be fulfilled before an item can be processed in a delivery created without reference to a sales document type.

Document Content

Most of the fields in the document content screen are not configurable from this view. They are mostly determined in individual settings that allocate the settings to the delivery document type. They are shown in the delivery document type for ease of use and control. Only the delivery split, rescheduling, and automatic packing indicators are controllable from this screen.

The *storage location rule* specifies how the system determines the picking/storage location when you create a delivery without entering a picking/storage location for the item.

The *output determination procedure* and output type are used by the system in allocating output to the delivery document type. This output will be covered in Chapter 4, "Basic Functions," and may take the form of delivery or shipping notes.

The *text determination procedure* is used by the system to determine where texts are allocated from in the delivery. We will cover text determination later in Chapter 4.

The *document statistics group* is the determining field that updates the *logistics information structures* (LIS). It is not possible to assign a value to this field, but you can assign a value to the delivery document type in the control settings for LIS, which we will cover in Chapter 5. Note it is only advisable to assign a statistics group value to those deliveries and delivery items that do not contain a reference to an order.

You can assign a *delivery split* per warehouse number. That is, items belonging to different warehouse numbers will be split into different deliveries.

The assignment and control of *route determination* will be covered in Chapter 4.

The settings for the *application* are internally used by the system to allocate output, such as output used for sales orders or delivery documents.

The *partner determination* is also not available in the delivery document type. It is set in the assignment of document types to the partner's determination procedure. Partner determination procedures will be covered in Chapter 4.

The *rescheduling* indicator is used to reschedule backlog deliveries. It will be covered a little later in this chapter.

The *automatic packing* indicator controls if the packing proposal should be adhered to and if the items in the delivery automatically are packed or not.

Transaction Flow

The *screen sequence group* determines the screens and their sequence for a certain delivery type.

The *display criteria* controls the data display for the delivery items. For example, you can limit the display to only main items and to suppress all items dependent on main items.

The *function code overview screen* controls the overview screen that is to be displayed first during delivery processing after you have entered data on the initial screen. For example, you may specify that you enter information immediately into the picking screen in the delivery.

The *standard text* field is not used in 4.0B.

The key SAP standard delivery document types are as follows:

Standard delivery	LF
Delivery without reference	LO
Returns delivery	LR
Replenishment delivery	NL

The standard SAP version of a delivery that can be made without reference to a sales order is delivery type LO.

Delivery Item Categories and Determination

A delivery item category is similar to the sales document item category in that it controls how the item is to behave in the document type. Generally, the delivery item category has the same naming convention as the sales document item category from which it is determined, yet it has its own control features.

Menu Path

The menu path is IMG, Sales and distribution, Shipping, Deliveries, Define item categories for deliveries.

Transaction Code

The code here is [0VLP]. Firstly, we need to discover from where the delivery item category is determined. If an order item or a schedule line is copied into a delivery, the item category used in the sales order is also copied. For example, if a TAN item category is used in the sales document type, the system will propose a TAN in the delivery document as well. For items independent of orders in the delivery (for example, packaging material that is entered in the delivery) or for deliveries that have no reference to a sales document, the item category is determined by the delivery item category determination table.

This item category is thus determined, as in Figure 3-45, by the *delivery type* plus the *item category group* of the material plus the *usage* of the item plus the item category of the *higher level* item, much in the same way as the item category determination procedure in the sales order.

To configure this delivery item category determination, proceed to IMG, Sales and distribution, Shipping, Deliveries, Define item category determination in deliveries.

NOTE: *The SAP system will still need an underlying schedule line category. Thus, should a delivery item category be able to copy a item category from a sales order, a schedule line category must still be maintained in order for the system to propose the correct goods movement type and subsequent financial postings for the goods movement. The availability check in the delivery is still carried out and controlled by the delivery item category.*

The delivery item category determination is especially useful for assigning batch items to standard delivery items. For example, should you carry out batch determination in the delivery, you can assign a delivery item category to an item that has a usage of CHSP, a batch split. An example using ZZ01 is shown in Figure 3-46.

Figure 3-45
The item category is determined.

DlvT	ItCG	Use	ItmC	ItmC	MItC	MItC	MItC	MItC	MItC	MItC	MItC	MItC
LF	NORM			DLN								
LF	NORM	CHSP		TAN								
LF	NORM	PACK		DLN	DLX	DLP	KEN					
LF	NORM	PSEL	TAX	TAPS								
LF	VERP			DLN								
LF	VERP	PACK		DLN	DLX	DLP	KEN					
LO	DIEN			DLX	DLX							

Figure 3-46
Assigning a delivery item category to an item that has a CHSP usage

DlvT	ItCG	Use	ItmC	ItmC	MItC	MItC	MItC
LF	NORM	CHSP		ZZ01			

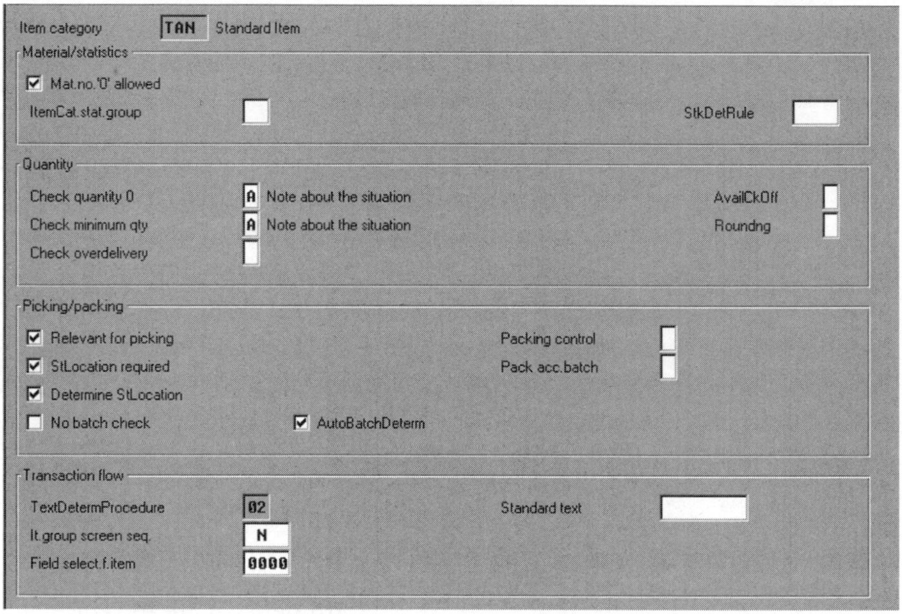

Figure 3-47
The delivery item category settings

Item category TAN Standard Item
Material/statistics
Mat.no.'0' allowed
ItemCat.stat.group
StkDetRule
Quantity
Check quantity 0 A Note about the situation
Check minimum qty A Note about the situation
Check overdelivery
AvailCkOff
Roundng
Picking/packing
Relevant for picking
StLocation required
Determine StLocation
No batch check
AutoBatchDeterm
Packing control
Pack acc.batch
Transaction flow
TextDetermProcedure 02
It.group screen seq. N
Field select.f.item 0000
Standard text

The delivery item category is represented by the settings shown in Figure 3-47.

The *check quantity of 0* specifies whether you can create an item that has a zero quantity and, if you do, how it is to react with a warning or error message or no message at all.

The check *minimum quantity* is a check carried out against the minimum order quantity on the material master record and the customer material information record. The response from the system can be a warning or an error message.

It is possible to create an over delivery, so the *check over delivery* indicator is used to display a warning message or an error message, should the delivery quantity exceed the limit in the customer material information record or the limit placed in the sales order.

You can switch the *availability check off* for a delivery item by selecting the indicator AvailCkOff.

The *rounding indicator* determines if the system should round up or down or leave the results as they are in the case of a correlation of multilevel *bills of material* (BOM) in the delivery if the nonavailability of a particular partial BOM in another partial BOM were to cause decimal positions.

The *relevant for picking* indicator is used to activate the picking relevance for a particular item. This item is then available in the picking list and to be transferred to warehouse management. It would not be advisable to make all items relevant for picking; for example, you would not pick service items such as a technician's hours. Generally, unless you do physical picking from the warehouse, you do not need picking. Picking is therefore not required for nonstock, value, and service items.

The *storage location* required indicates a storage location must be entered for this item before the delivery can be completely processed. Likewise the *determine storage location* is an indicator used by the system to indicate automatic determination of the storage location for the delivery item.

The *no batch check* ensures the system does not check to determine if the batch entered in the delivery line item exists in the system or not. Thus, should you enter a batch in the line item while the batch is not in the system, the system will accept it anyway.

The *automatic batch determination* indicates to the system to carry out automatic batch determination in the delivery of this line item. (Automatic batch determination can happen at the line item level in the sales order or the delivery.)

The *packing control* indicates to the system that the line item can be packed, must be packed, or cannot be packed. Should "must be packed" be selected, the materials must be packed before goods issue can happen.

The *pack according to batch* is an indicator selecting packing according to a batch split or to the main item only.

The *text determination* procedure is not maintainable and will be covered in Chapter 4.

The *screen sequence group* is again used to determine the screens used in the delivery and the order in which they appear.

The *field selection for* item is used to control which fields appear on the item screens for each delivery item category.

The *standard text* field is not used in 4.0B.

The item categories of a delivery are referenced from the sales order. Thus, item category TAN in the sales order proposes item category TAN in the delivery. The SAP standard version uses item category DLN as the standard item category used in the system to represent an item in a delivery without reference to a sales order. You can also define a delivery split according to specific criteria in the copy control rules. In the formation of the data transfer, you can set up splitting criteria. Splitting criteria and the usage of ZUK in pricing will be covered later in this chapter.

Deliveries can be sorted by 10 additional criteria in combination with the shipping point, delivery creation date, and the selection of sales orders or stock transport orders when running the delivery due list [VL04]. These 10 additional criteria can be selected by using the Additional Criteria button. Note that you can also run the delivery due list per sales area, incorporating the sales organization. You can do this by selecting "organizational data."

A little tip when creating a variant to run the delivery due list program SAPMV50S is that you can select between sales and purchase orders, as shown in Figure 3-48.

This is merely a incorrect display. The system is selecting between sales orders and stock transport orders. Thus, purchase order should read stock transport orders. You may refer to Chapter 5 for information on the creation of variants for batch jobs.

You can see in Figure 3-49 how SAP copies data from a sales order into a delivery. The system copies data equally from the header- and item-relevant shipping data into the same delivery. Thus, if you have item details for the header and item data that are equal, such as the same ship-to party, the same plant, and the same shipping point, the system will copy the item and its schedule line into a combined delivery. However, should one of the items in the sales order have shipping details that are not equal, such as a different ship-to party, the system will create a new delivery note for that particular item.

Shipping Point Determination

Shipping points are independent organizational units that are linked to a plant and represent the point of departure or receipt of materials. A plant may have many shipping points. A delivery is created from one shipping point only.

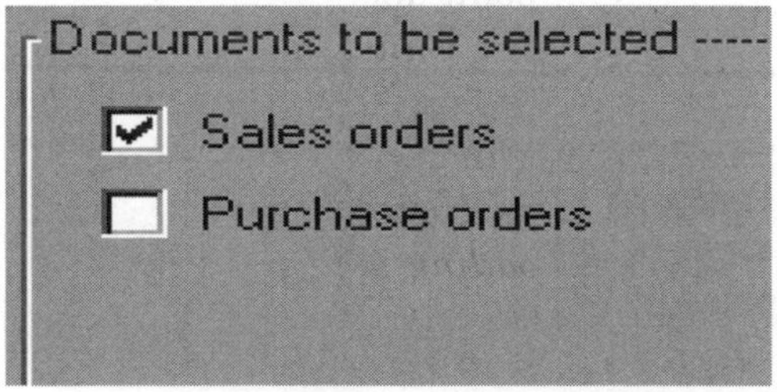

Documents to be selected

☑ Sales orders

☐ Purchase orders

Figure 3-48
Selecting between sales and purchase orders

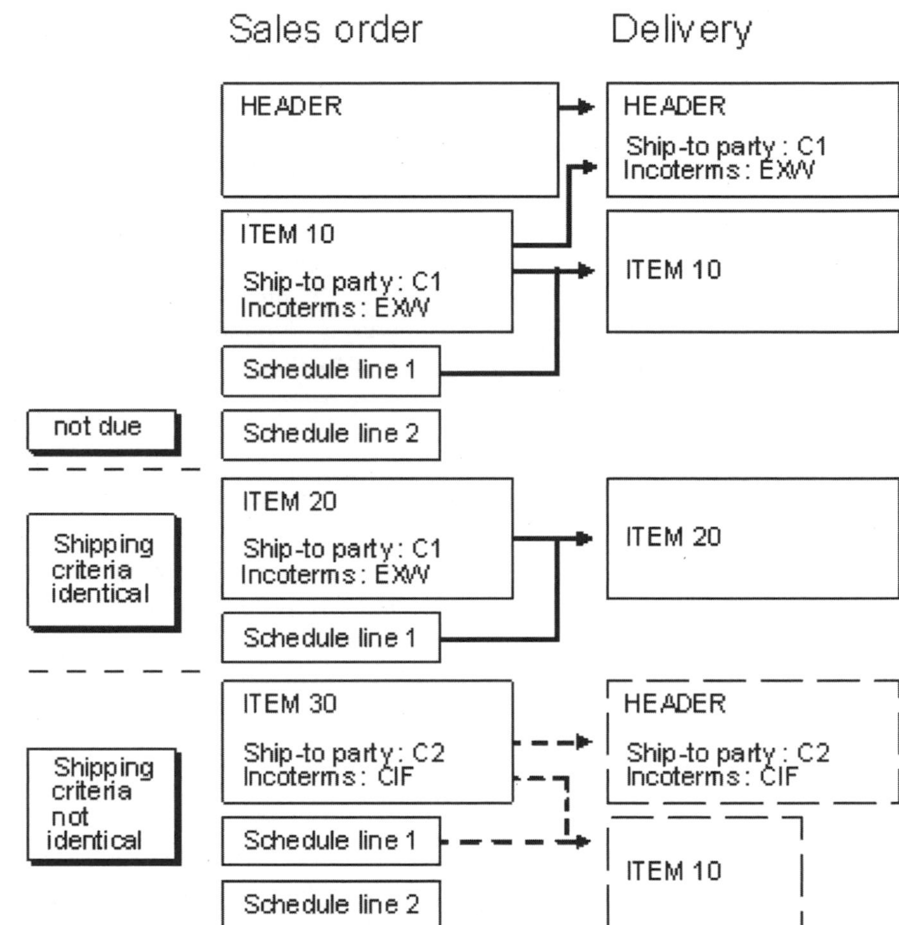

Figure 3-49 The process of copying data from a sales order into a delivery Copyright SAP AG

Menu Path

The menu path here is IMG, Sales and distribution, Shipping, Basic shipping functions, Shipping point determination.

The shipping point is the central key to a delivery; no delivery can be made without one. The shipping point is determined by the system based on the *shipping conditions*, which are either entered manually in the sales order or are copied from the customer master record. The shipping point is also determined by the *loading group,* which is copied from the material master record, and the *delivering plant* of the line item in the sales order. This is illustrated in Figure 3-50.

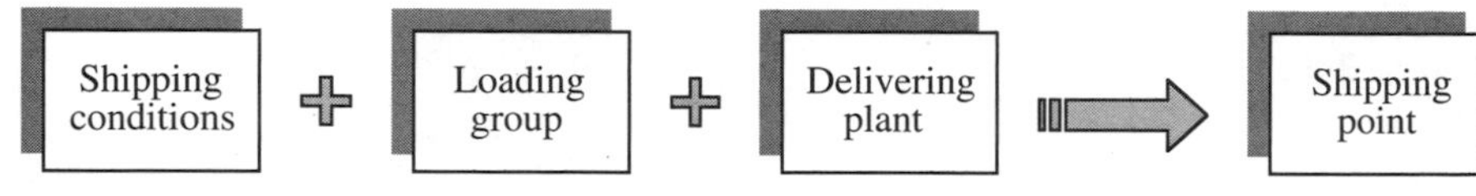

Figure 3-50 The shipping point determination process

TIP: *Should a customer ask for a complete delivery, it makes sense that you should not have multiple shipping points manually entered for each line item in the sales order, or else the customer will receive multiple deliveries.*

TIP: *As each delivery is created via a shipping point, and each run of the delivery due list is made with reference to a particular shipping point, you may want to have an express shipping point. This way, you can run the due list every half an hour for one shipping point only to create deliveries for that particular plant. Likewise in the sales order, the user knows that if he manually enters a specific express shipping point, he will have the delivery created within half an hour. The remainder of the deliveries may be created via the delivery due list in the normal processing run.*

Configuring the Shipping Point Determination

At this point, we define the shipping conditions. The shipping conditions are entered in the customer master record in the shipping screen. These settings are then copied into the sales document and are used to determine the shipping point. The shipping conditions can be manually changed in the sales order, or they can be defaulted to a particular sales document type. Should they be defaulted to a particular sales document type, the system will ignore the setting on the customer master record.

Proceed with copying a shipping condition and changing the name to represent your requirements using the prefix Z. The shipping condition is a two-character alphanumeric key, as shown in Figure 3-51.

Now we define shipping conditions by the sales document type. As discussed, the shipping conditions defined by the sales document type override the shipping conditions automatically proposed by the system from the customer master record. This is useful in returns.

SC	Description
01	As soon as possible
02	Standard
03	Collect. processing
04	Transport Service

Figure 3-51 Shipping condition descriptions

SaTy	Description	SC	Description
RO	Rush Order	10	Immediately
OR	Standard Order		

Figure 3-52 Express shipping points for express sales documents such as rush orders

In returns processing, a returns delivery must be made with a shipping point that represents the incoming goods. It would not be recommended to use the same shipping point for returns or receiving goods as you do for outgoing deliveries. Thus, you can assign all returns sales document types their own returns shipping conditions and promote a returns shipping point.

Having a returns shipping point allows greater visibility in the system and in the plant of material movements. This also allows the processing of the delivery due list for returns orders only.

TIP: *Another reason for assigning a shipping condition to a sales document could be to automatically propose your express shipping point for express sales documents such as rush orders. This is shown in Figure 3-52.*

Loading Groups

The loading group is used in the determination of the shipping point and is copied from the material master record.

TIP: *As a delivery is not possible without a loading group, it is recommended that you indicate the field loading group of the material master record as a mandatory field. This way, no material master record can be created without a respective loading group.*

Figure 3-53 Four-character loading groups

LGrp	Description
0001	Crane
0002	Forklift
0003	Manual

Figure 3-54 Assigning the proposed shipping point and the allowed manual shipping points to the shipping condition, loading group, and plant

SC	LGrp	Plnt	PrShP	MShPt	MShPt	MShPt	MShPt	MShPt	MShPt
01	0001	0001	0001						
01	0001	1000	1000						
01	0001	1100	1100						

The loading group in Figure 3-53 is a four-character alphanumeric key. You may copy a standard and rename it.

Assign Shipping Points

As the first step in this process, it is worthwhile doing a background check on your organizational data. Ensure your correct delivering plants have been maintained in the system as well as the correct shipping points. Go to IMG, Enterprise structure, Maintain structure, Definition, Sales and distribution, Define, Copy, Delete, Check shipping point. Also ensure you have allocated your shipping points to the respective plants by going to IMG, Enterprise structure, Maintain structure, Assignment, Assign shipping point to plant.

Now proceed to IMG, Sales and distribution, Shipping, Basic shipping functions, Shipping point determination, Assign shipping points. Assign the proposed shipping point and the allowed manual shipping points to the shipping condition, loading group, and plant (see Figure 3-54).

Delivery Process

It is possible to create a delivery either individually via the menu path, individually from the sales document, or via the delivery due list.

To create an individual delivery document, one uses the menu path logistics by going to Sales and distribution, Shipping, Delivery, Create [VL01]. Enter the shipping point, the selection date, and the sales document number, should the delivery be created with reference to a sales document.

To create a delivery via the sales document, proceed from the sales document overview screen to Select-sales document, Deliver.

To create a delivery via the delivery due list, proceed from the logistics screen and go to Sales and distribution, Shipping, Delivery, Create collective processing [VL04]. You will notice when using the delivery due list that you can select for processing both sales orders as well as stock transport orders. When using the delivery due list, you can restrict your entries and thus you can have further selection criteria that narrow down the selection of the documents for which deliveries must be processed. The selection criteria are shown in Figure 3-55.

You can also select your criteria using a specified sales area or sales organization. This can be done by selecting the organizational data button.

TIP: *When creating individual deliveries, you may find the system does not create an individual delivery, due to one or a combination of reasons. Generally, the help message offered in these cases is not beneficial in discovering the problem in order to fix it. In cases where you would like a more detailed explanation of the problem, it is advisable to use the delivery due list [VL04] and then only select the individual sales order you would like to process. The system will then offer you a more detailed note on the problem being experienced.*

When having problems creating a individual delivery, it is worthwhile checking the following:

- *Is the sales document number correct?*
- *Is the shipping point selected equal to the one on the line item in the sales order?*
- *Has the line item in the sales order already been fully delivered?*
- *Does the schedule line have a confirmed quantity and date?*
- *Is the selection date correct? The selection date should be equal to or later than the confirmed delivery date at the schedule line level in the sales order.*

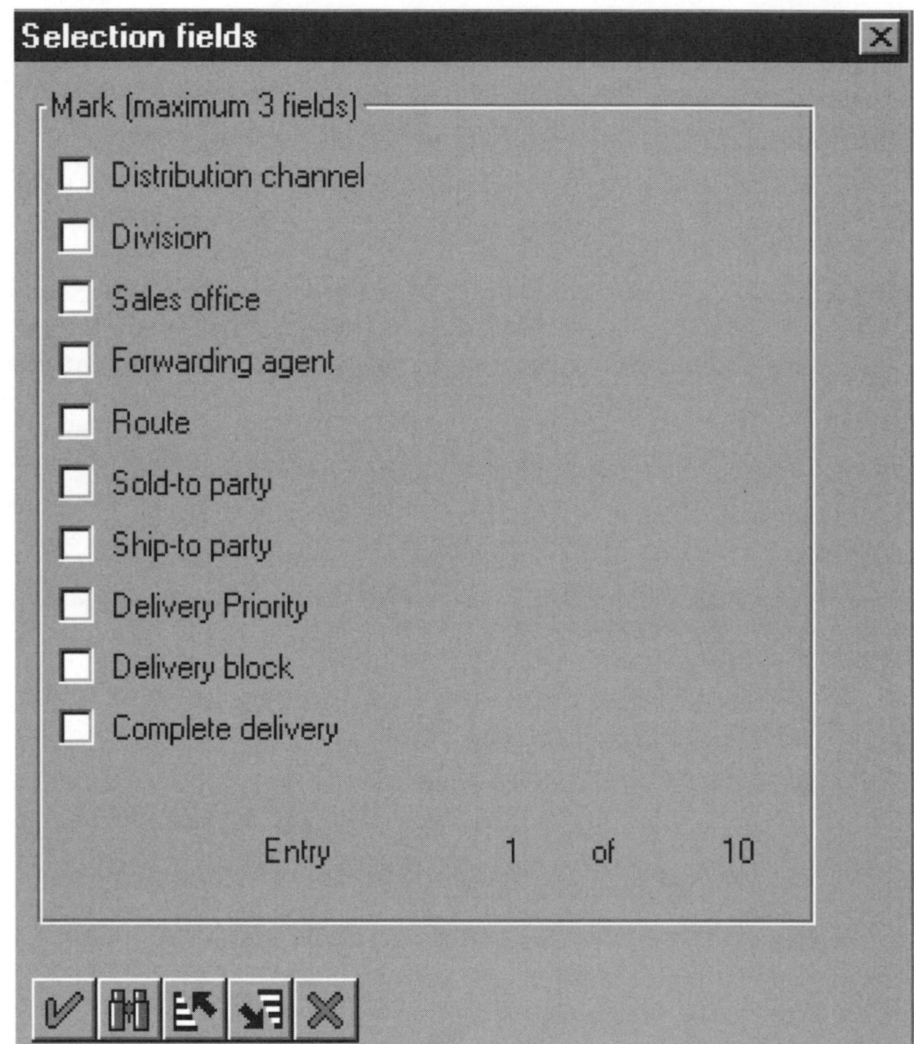

Figure 3-55
The Selection fields dialog box

- *Is there a delivery block on the line item in the sales order?*
- *Is there a delivery block on the schedule line in the sales order?*
- *What is the status of the sales order and the line item in question? This can be seen from the sales order by selecting Goto, Header, Status or Goto, Item, Status. Figures 3-56, 3-57, and 3-58 show three examples of statuses in the sales order.*

TIP: *Using the transaction code [SE16], one can use table VBAKUK, which is actually a combined view of the selected fields from the VBAK and VBUK tables. However, it enables you to access the statuses of the sales documents as well as generate queries of data at the header and item levels.*

Picking and Interfacing with Warehouse Management

Picking is the process where the stock is selected from the storage facility to fulfill a delivery. One needs to pick the correct quantity of the right items for the delivery.

Menu Path

The path to follow here is IMG, Sales and distribution, Shipping, Picking.

First, not all items are relevant for picking. You may have items such as text items or return items that are not picking-relevant. Picking is always carried out from a particular storage location. Thus, for a delivery to be

Delivery status	Not delivered

Figure 3-56
A not-delivered delivery status

Rejection status	Nothing rejected
Delivery status	Fully delivered

Figure 3-57
A fully delivered status

Rejection status	Everything rejected	
Delivery status	Not delivered	Completed

Figure 3-58
An status in which nothing is delivered.

picking-relevant, a storage location must always be entered. If interfacing with warehouse management, the storage location in the delivery determines which storage location to use in the warehouse.

Item Categories Relevant for Picking

Here you indicate to the system which item categories are relevant for picking. This indicator can either be set here or when defining the delivery item category. Should the item not be relevant for picking, it is not necessary to have a storage location determined for the item either. Thus, when creating the delivery item category, you would not need to indicate "determine storage location" or "storage location required."

Confirmation Requirements

It is possible to set a requirement not allowing goods issue to be posted until all items on the delivery have been successfully picked. This setting is based on the shipping point and will indicate that the items on the delivery note be confirmed for picking (see Figure 3-59).

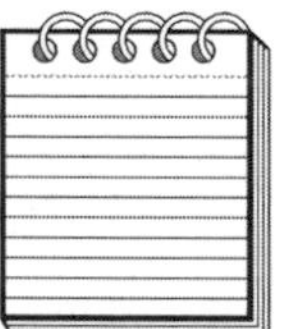

NOTE: *If you want only certain items to be relevant for picking in a specific shipping point, you may use the user exit USEREXIT_LIPS-KOQUI_DETERMINE in Program MV50AFZ3.*

Interface with Warehouse Management

In SAP, you can create a warehouse for a storage location. This means that all movements within that storage location need to be managed using the *warehouse management* (WM) functions in SAP. You define warehouses in

Figure 3-59 Shipping point assignments

ShPt	Description	C	Short text
0001	Old shipping point 0001		No confirmation
1000	Shipping Point Hamburg		No confirmation

the enterprise structure for materials management. You also assign the warehouses to storage locations in the menu path for assignments. If you have defined a warehouse in SAP and assigned it to a storage location, and you use this storage location in a delivery, then you must use warehouse management to do the picking for that delivery.

The process of placing goods in the warehouse is as follows. The goods are received in the interim storage area for goods receipts (for example, from production). A transfer order is then created in WM to move the goods into the warehouse. This tells the warehouse staff where to put the stock. When the stock is put into the warehouse in the correct place, the transfer order is confirmed, which tells SAP that the goods have been moved out of the interim storage area (the loading and unloading area) into the warehouse.

Later when you want to deliver the stock, you need to fetch it out of the warehouse. You can create a transfer order from the delivery and SAP will choose stock from the warehouse to be delivered. This choice is based on a number of inventory methods, such as *last-in, first-out* (LIFO) and *first-in, first-out* (FIFO). The transfer order will instruct the warehouse staff where to get the stock from and to deliver it to the interim storage area for goods issue.

Once all the stock has been picked, the transfer order is confirmed, which informs SAP that the stock has been taken out of the warehouse and made available for loading in a loading bay or another such place. If you created the transfer order from a sales delivery, SAP will confirm that the delivery has been picked when you confirm that you have fulfilled the stock quantity in the transfer order. It can now be loaded onto the truck and goods issued.

Picking can be done on an interface with the WM module of SAP. Should this be the scenario, once the delivery is created, you need to create a transfer order. You can create a transfer order from the delivery within the delivery select delivery by going to Save and subsequent functions, Transfer order. It is also possible to create a transfer order for a delivery by proceeding from the logistics screen by going to Materials management, Warehouse management, Transfer order, Create, for Delivery.

After the transfer order number has been created, it is necessary to confirm the transfer order by proceeding to Transfer order, Confirm transfer order. This transfer order would carry out the picking automatically. A brief overview is illustrated in Figure 3-60.

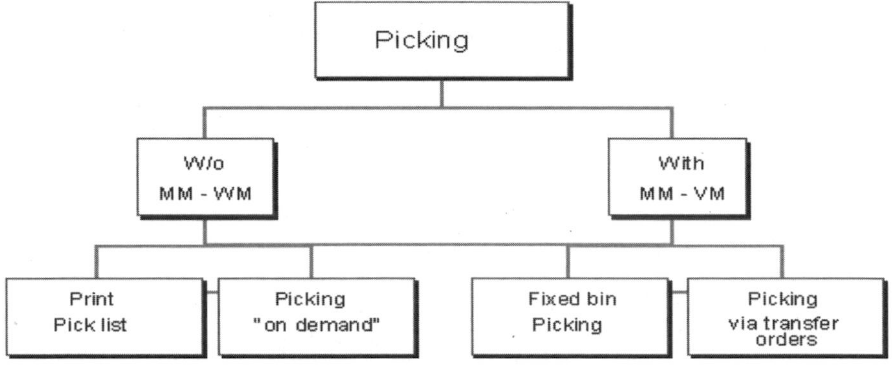

Figure 3-60
An overview of the picking process

Picking Requirements

Here you can define your own requirements that must be met before picking can be carried out. SAP uses the standard requirement 111, which restricts picking to be carried out only after checking and passing the credit check. Should you wish to create your own picking requirement, you can create one using a number in the range from 500 upwards.

Determine Storage/Picking Locations

The entry maintained here is copied into the delivery header data. This entry here enables the system to determine the storage location automatically, should the storage location not have been maintained in the delivery manually. Proceed in assigning a storage location rule, such as MALA to the delivery document type.

Define Storage Conditions

The storage condition is a two-character alphanumeric key that is used by the system to indicate the storage conditions for a material. This field is then used in combination with the plant and shipping point to determine the storage location.

Assign Picking Locations

The picking location is the storage location. The system bases the automatic determination of the storage location on the combination of the determination rule MALA. This is assigned to the delivery document type that combines the shipping point, the delivering plant, and the storage condition on the material master record to determine the storage location, as shown in Figure 3-61.

Blocking Reasons

The SAP Sales and Distribution module has many areas available for blocking. The "shipping blocks" are one of the most commonly used. These shipping or delivery blocks can be manually entered or automatically proposed in the sales order and the delivery documents.

Menu Path

The path here is IMG, Sales and Distribution, Shipping, Deliveries, Define reasons for blocking in shipping.

Transaction Code

The code here is [OVLS] and delivery blocks must be removed manually from the sales order.

Delivery Blocking at the Header Level

Delivery blocks can be assigned manually in the sales order by entering the desired block in the header's shipping view of the sales document. Should

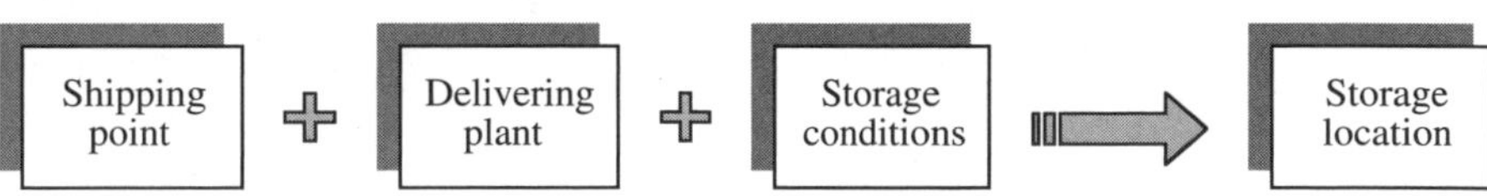

Figure 3-61
The storage location determination

you desire the block to be automatically proposed for specific sales document types, you can set the delivery block in the sales document type for which you want to automatically block. This is done in the Shipping area of the Define sales document types menu, as shown below in Figure 3-62.

However, this delivery block is only effective if this delivery block has been assigned in the respective delivery document type.

Delivery Blocking at the Schedule Line Level

Delivery blocks are also available at the schedule line level. These are simply delivery blocks that are manually entered in the sales document at the schedule line level. It is possible to have the system automatically propose a delivery block in the sales document for particular schedule lines. This can be done by allocating the delivery block to the Define schedule line categories menu (see Figure 3-63).

This delivery block at the schedule line level is always effective, regardless of whether the delivery block is assigned to the respective delivery document type or not. The schedule line category block is very useful, as it is not copied into the sales document item. This enables you to create a sales order and to manually set the delivery block for schedule lines due for delivery with a delivery date of over one month. You can still allow deliveries for unblocked schedule lines to be created within the month, although both sets of schedule lines originate from the same line item.

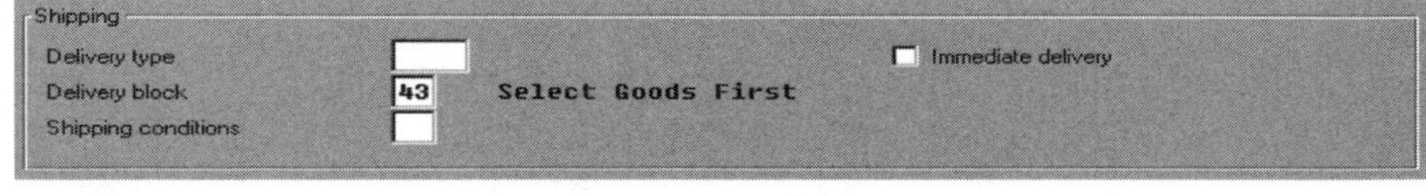

Figure 3-62 The Shipping area of the Define sales document types menu

Business data
Delivery block 05 Check free of ch.dlv

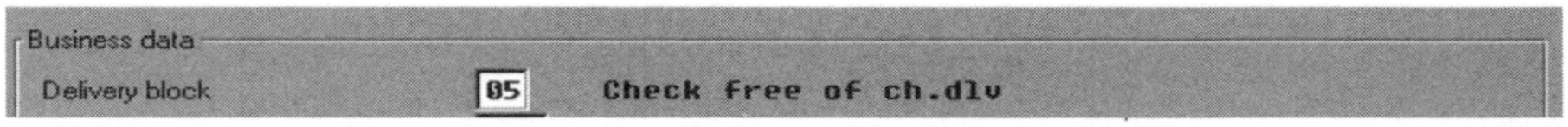

Figure 3-63 Setting the delivery block at the schedule line level

Delivery Blocks at the Customer/Header Level

You can also block a customer master record for a particular sales area, or for all sales areas as far as deliveries are concerned. This is done in [VD05] (see Figure 3-64).

Configuring the Delivery Blocking Reasons

Proceed to Deliveries: Blocking reasons/Criteria. In this IMG activity, as shown in Figure 3-65, you assign the effects of the blocking reasons on the sales documents and associated functions. If you indicate a "X," you are selecting the function.

By selecting to block orders in the first column, the system will take the customer master delivery block set in [VD05] and copy the block into the sales order. Note that once this block is manually removed in the sales order and a delivery is created, the system does not recheck the customer master blocking in the delivery. Should you delete the block from the customer master record, the respective blocks must still be manually removed from all sales documents created prior to the deletion of the block.

By selecting the blocking of "Conf," you are setting a block on the confirmation of requirements in the sales order. This is useful for customers whose credit is in question. You can set the system to propose schedule line dates with confirmation dates and confirmed quantities. However, when a delivery block is set, the system will automatically reset the confirmed

Figure 3-64
You have the ability to block all sales areas or only certain ones

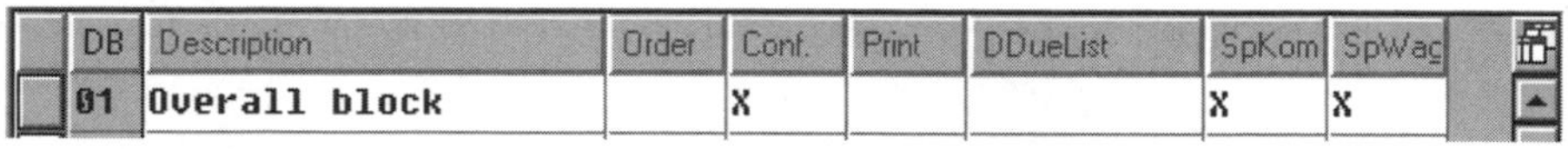

Delivery block
All sales areas
Selected sales area

Figure 3-65
Assigning the effects of the blocking reasons on the sales documents and associated functions

DB	Description	Order	Conf.	Print	DDueList	SpKom	SpWac
01	Overall block		X			X	X

quantities to zero, thus allowing the stock to be free for other sales orders. You can also set an indicator causing all printouts, such as order confirmations, not to print sales items for which a delivery block has been set.

You can stop a sales document from having a delivery created by the delivery due list by setting the delivery due list indicator. If the indicator is set, the system will not create the delivery when using the delivery due list. It will only allow the delivery to be created manually. Thus, it is possible to deliver such sales orders, but only individually and manually.

"SpKom" is the picking block; you can set this indicator if you want to block picking from being carried out. "SpWag" is the goods-issue-blocking indicator; with this set you will not be able to post goods issue until the block is manually removed.

Now proceed to Delivery blocks. Here you assign which delivery blocks are assigned to which delivery document types. If you recall, a delivery block in the sales order at the header level is only effective if the delivery block is assigned in this table, as shown in Figure 3-66.

Packing

Packing is carried out at the item level. You can determine that a specific item is to be mandatorily packed or will be packed when necessary. This packed item then in turn may be packed again into a shipping unit, which in turn may be packed into another shipping unit, thus creating a multilevel procedure.

Menu Path

The path here is IMG, Sales and Distribution, Shipping, Packing.

DB	Description	DlvTy	Description
01	Overall block	LF	Delivery
02	Political reasons	LF	Delivery

Figure 3-66
A delivery block in the sales order at the header level is only effective if the delivery block is assigned in this table.

Packing by Item Category Packing is carried out at the item level. Thus, some items may need to be packed and other items may be forbidden to be packed. Each item category that needs packing must have its corresponding setting at the item category level. For those item categories that need packing, set the indicator to an **A**. For those item categories that cannot be carried out, set the indicator to a **B.** For those item categories that do not have to be packed, yet packing can be carried out, leave the assignment blank (see Figure 3-67).

You may select that, should there be a batch split in the delivery, the system is to pack the main item with an accumulated batch quantity or the batch split items only. Should you wish the main item to be packed, leave the Pack main item field blank.

Packing Requirements You may want to create a requirement for packing. This requirement performs the same way as all other requirements in the SD module, in that the criteria stipulated must be met in order for packing to be carried out. An example of a requirement here could be that no packing is to be carried out for items that have a credit block.

Shipping Material Types In order not to be confused, we will call these descriptions types. Each shipping material is assigned to a shipping material type. The shipping material type controls the shipping material. The SAP standard system comes with shipping material types truck, container, and ship. Should you want to create your own, simply copy an existing type and assign a four-character, alphanumeric key with a text description, as shown in Figure 3-68.

Figure 3-67
Leaving the packing assignment blank

ItCa	Description	Packing control	Pack ma
TAN	Standard Item		

Figure 3-68
Creating your own shipping material type

ShMtT	Description
V010	Crates (domestic)
V020	Crates (Export)
V030	Std. cartons (mid.)
V040	Std. cartons (big)
V050	Pallet cartons

By selecting the shipping material type and selecting details, you can see the assigned data, as shown in Figure 3-69.

The output determination procedure and associated output type determines what output can be sent during packing, such as a packing list or packing slip. The shipping element category is used to define different types of shipping material types. For our example, we have the shipping material type crates, category C-packing.

Material Groups for Shipping Materials

In this activity you create material groups for shipping materials. Note the shipping or packing material must have a material master record created in the system. This material master record is to use the material type VERP, which is the SAP standard for packing. You can then assign the material group for the shipping material in the shipping materials master record. The shipping material group is also assigned to standard items that are to be packed. This enables similar materials to be grouped together. For example, the materials may all be able to be packed into a carton; thus, a shipping material group, Carton, is necessary for shipping materials (as shown in Figure 3-70). However, the standard products being packed into the cartons may be fragile; thus, there may be a need to call a group Fragile. This assignment of Fragile would be on the basic data screen of the standard item in the material master record.

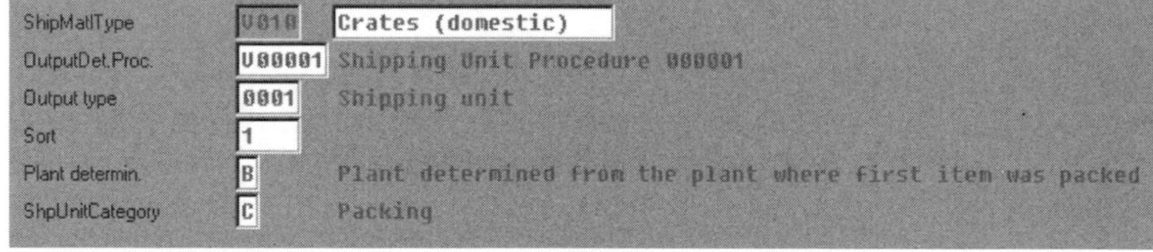

Figure 3-69 Finding the assigned data by selecting the shipping material type and selecting details

GrpS	Description
C010	Container
G010	Skeleton box
K010	Carton (middle)
K020	Carton (big)
K030	Crate (domestic)

Figure 3-70 A list of shipping material groups

Allowed Shipping Materials

In this activity, you allocate which shipping materials can be packed into which other shipping materials (see Figure 3-71). Since not all packing is interchangable (you can't place a crate in a cardboard box, for example), the groups are allocated to the types. That is, the shipping material group on the material master record, small box, is allocated to the shipping material type.

Due to this assignment, you may have the following on the initial material master, material type FERT, which the customer purchases. For example, for material AZ2-600, you may have the shipping group M020 Monitors board/computer (on the basic data 1 screen), as shown in Figure 3-72.

In the allowed shipping units table, you may have the setting material shipping group M020 Monitors board/computer (shipping material type), V030, Std. cartons mid (see Figure 3-73).

In the material master record, a standard carton can have any name, such as PK - 100. Using material type VERP, which is packaging material, you can have the shipping group K010-Carton (middle), as shown in Figure 3-74.

Mat.grp SM	Description	ShpMatlTyp	Description
C010	Container	V110	Ship
G010	Skeleton box	V080	Containers
G010	Skeleton box	V090	Waggons
G010	Skeleton box	V100	Trucks
K010	Carton (middle)	V060	Pallets type A
K020	Carton (big)	V060	Pallets type A
K030	Crate (domestic)	V070	Pallets type B

Figure 3-71 Allocating which shipping materials can be packed into which other shipping materials

Figure 3-72 The packaging material data setting

M020	Monitors/board comp.	V030	Std. cartons (mid.)

Figure 3-73 The allowed shipping units table

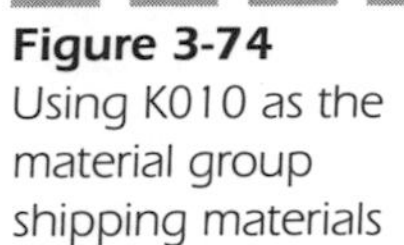

Figure 3-74
Using K010 as the material group shipping materials

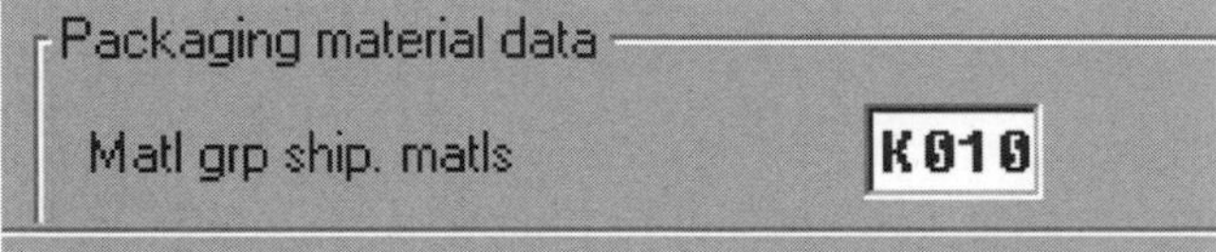

Figure 3-75
The packaging material data

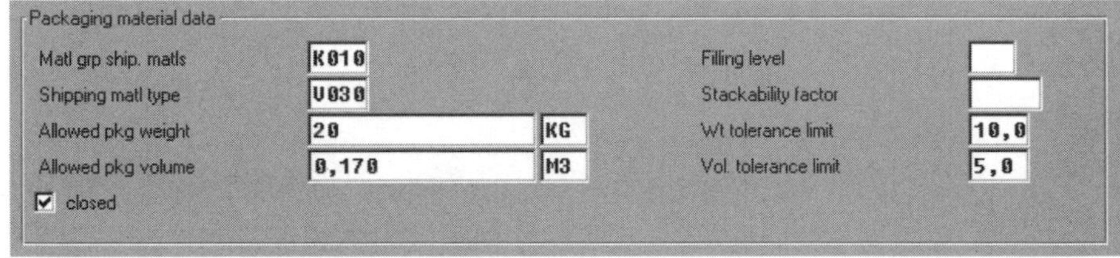

Figure 3-76
Packing for V060 - Pallets type A

	K010	Carton (middle)	V060	Pallets type A

The key that links the two materials is found in the material master record in the Sales general/plant data screen (see Figure 3-75). This shows the shipping unit for the material you are creating and the shipping material type to which it corresponds.

In our example, only those finished goods materials that have K010 as the material group for packing can be packed into shipping materials (VERP) that are defined as V030 shipping materials. The material group on the sales/plant data screen of a material therefore determines the allowed shipping materials (VERP) using the Allowed shipping materials table. Similarly, the material group on the sales/plant data screen of a shipping material (VERP) also defines the allowed shipping materials (VERP) into which it can be packed. This is packed into V060 - Pallets type A (see Figure 3-76).

In the VERP material master record "pallets type A," you have the assignment P010. In the material master sales general/plant data section, you have the following assignment, as shown in Figure 3-77.

As seen below, P010 can be packaged into V090 - Wagons (see Figure 3-78).

Now we create a sales order for 80 pieces of the original material AZ2-600, as sold to the customer. We create the delivery and begin packing. Select the Packing button on [VL02] or from inside the initial delivery proceed with Edit, Packing. You will be faced with a split-level screen with the lower portion of the screen showing items relevant to be packed. You can then select the shipping units in the higher portion of the screen into which

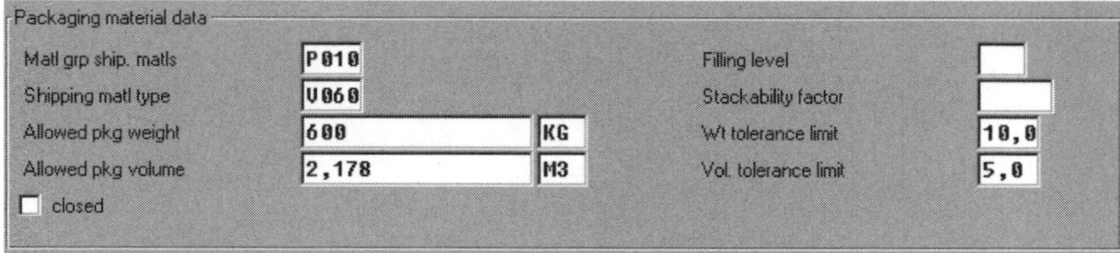

Packaging material data

Matl grp ship. matls	P010		Filling level	
Shipping matl type	V060		Stackability factor	
Allowed pkg weight	600	KG	Wt tolerance limit	10,0
Allowed pkg volume	2,178	M3	Vol. tolerance limit	5,0
☐ closed				

Figure 3-77
The assignment P010's settings

P010	Pallet type A	V090	Waggons

Figure 3-78
Wagons packaging for P010

All shipping units

Vol. to	Total volume	Tare volume	ShipMatlType
5,0	0,351	0,151	V060
5,0	0,200	0,200	V030

Figure 3-79
The shipping material type in packing within a delivery

All shipping units

Shipping unit	Shipping mat.	Description
817	PK-095	Pallet 110 x 110 x 12,5 Type A
814	PK-100	Special carton high tech

Figure 3-80
Packing in a delivery

the material must be packed. You then pack the items from the lower portion of the screen into the shipping units in the higher portion of the screen. The system uses the allowed weight and volume of the materials from the material master record.

In the packing screen, go to Edit, Pack items. You will see, once all the items have been packed, how the system followed the customizing procedure, that is, how it packed the original material into a V030, which was packed into the V060 (see Figures 3-79 and 3-80).

By selecting the now-packed shipping unit and clicking on the Contents of the shipping unit button, you will see what items are packed in the shipping unit and their details. By selecting the highest shipping unit level in our example, the pallet PK-095, we can view an example similar to Figure 3-81.

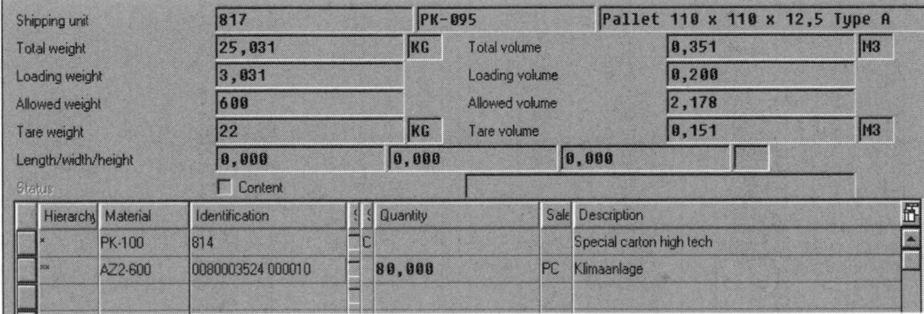

Figure 3-81
Selecting the highest shipping unit level in our example

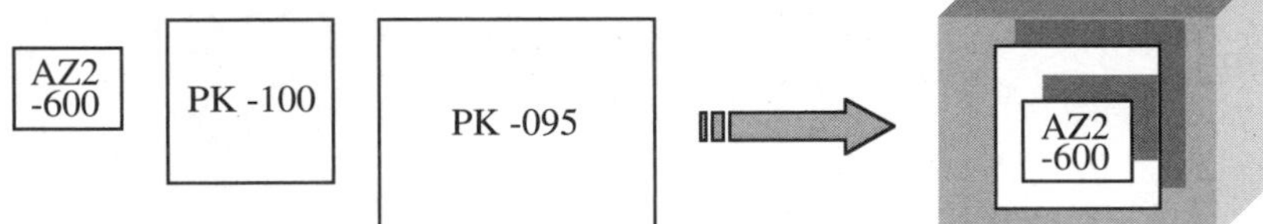

Figure 3-82
Our three individual materials are packed into one shipping unit.

This figure shows us the details of the shipping unit as well as the hierarchy of materials packed into it. The AZ2 - 600 is packed into the PK-100, and both of these materials are packed into the selected shipping unit. Thus, our three individual materials are packed into one shipping unit, as shown in Figure 3-82.

Shipping Unit Supplements

SAP has assigned five additional fields that can be accessed from the packing screen; these five additional fields are VEGR1 through VEGR5. They should be treated in the same way as the five additional fields found on the customer master and material master records. These fields are useful in designing extra functionality, which you may need to build into SAP. By having these fields available for maintenance and checking, you can use the entries for condition records, for formulas, or requirements.

Please refer to Chapter 5 for details on data elements. The maintenance of data elements enables one to change the text description seen in the system of the field, such as the "shipping unit group" to, for example, the "color of the box."

Returnable Packaging

Not all packaging materials are inexpensive enough for the cost of the sale to include the cost of the packaging as well. One may have packaging materials that are valuable, and should a customer decide to keep or destroy the packaging items, he should reimburse the business.

Thus, returnable packaging is used in the process whereby the business sells items to the customer. These items are packed into shipping units, such as boxes and crates. The customer can then keep the boxes or crates up to a certain period of time and then must return the items. Should the customer not have returned the shipping units specified by that set date or should he have destroyed the shipping units, the business may bill the customer.

Details

The stock you deliver has special packaging materials. This packing is kept at the customer's location but will remain the property of your company. He must return the packing to you within a period of time or be billed for it. The stock is recorded automatically as special stock at the customer's location. This special stock can be seen using the Stock overview screen; [MMBE] returnable packaging has the stock indicator of V.

You can also view returnable packaging at the customer's site by proceeding from the logistics screen and going to Materials management, Inventory management, Environment, Consignment, Consignment at customer, and then select returnable packaging at customer (see Figure 3-83).

An example would be Figure 3-84, which shows PK - 095 and PK - 100 at two customer sites.

The sales order functions as normal; there is no special order type, but one can use the sales order view of a double-line entry. This enables you to view the main item and the returnable packing stock, shown as the lower

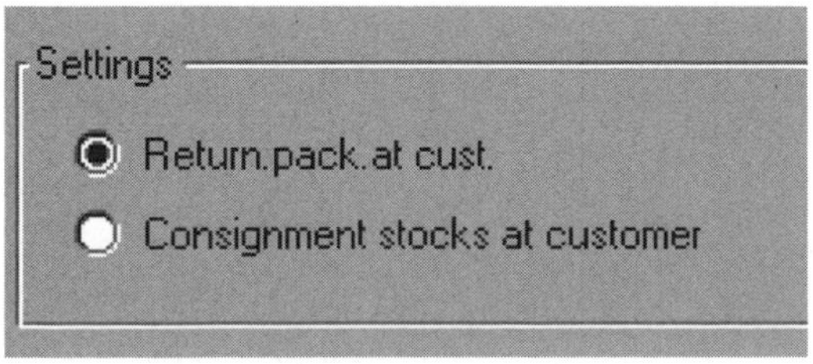

Figure 3-83 Selecting returnable packaging at customer

Figure 3-84
PK - 095 and PK - 100 at two customer sites

Customer Material	Name LnObj	OUn	Unrestr.	Qual.insp.	Restr.-use
1900	J & P				
PK-095	1	PC	1	0	0
PK-100	2	PC	2	0	0
2001	SAPSOTA AG				
PK-095	3	PC	3	0	0
PK-100	3	PC	3	0	0

level item to the item it packs. This is merely for display and traceability in the sales order; the packaging material may also be the main item of a sales order.

The packaging's material master record should use the material type VERP for packaging and the item category group LEIH. The item category group LEIH is the SAP standard for returnable packaging.

If you enter a packing proposal in the order (by going to Edit, Packing proposal from within the order document), it is copied into the delivery. If you enter the item category in the shipping unit (selected from the shipping unit from the Edit, Packing proposal screen, and then selecting the General header data button), SAP will create a delivery item in the delivery for the shipping material from the packing proposal, even if you have not entered it as an item in the sales order.

For example, if you enter TAL (the item category for returnable packaging) in the shipping unit header, then when you create the delivery, SAP will also create an item TAL for that shipping material in the delivery. When you goods issue the delivery, SAP will record that this shipping material has been issued to the customer and must be returned. Note that you only have to price the returnable packaging in the returnable packaging issue order document. It does not need to be priced in the sales order and cannot be in this method.

Proceed with the normal packing configuration. The returnable packaging material follows the same rules as a standard material, in that you must define a item category for it as well as the necessary copy control rules. The SAP standard is to use item category TAL. The process flow used in returnable packaging is shown in Figure 3-85.

Should you wish to create your own sales document item categories, you can copy and change the SAP standard that uses the item category LAN for the returnable packaging pick-up and the item category LNN for the returnable packaging issue. Do not forget to give your returnable packaging material a price.

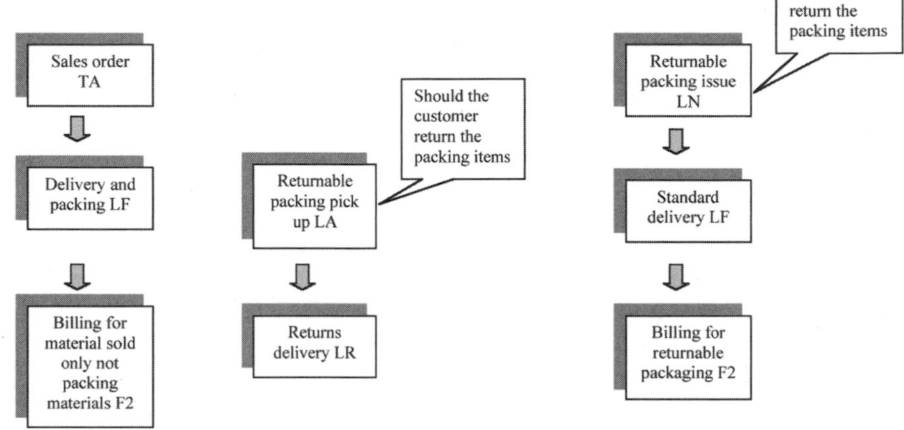

Figure 3-85
The process flow in returnable packaging

Special Stock Partners

A special stock partner is a partner that is assigned to the customer master record in the sales order. This partner need not be the sold-to (SP), ship-to (SH), bill-to (BP), or payer (PY) partner. However, this partner may be the partner who actually consumes the materials.

For example, should a large organization have a central depot where all consignment stock goes, then the consignment stock is shipped directly to each customer's plant as needed (see Figure 3-86). The central depot would be registered in the system as a partner. For both returnable packaging and consignment stock, you can have special stock partners. You must first create a new customer for them using the same account group as if you were creating a sold-to party. One must then assign these special stock partners to the relevant sold-to parties' customer master records. The special stock partners have the partner function key SB. When materials are consumed by the special stock partner, should there be any consignment stock or returnable packing, the system automatically picks up the special stock partner and records the stock in the system as being stored at their site. You can view these allocations of stocks in the same way as previously discussed [MMBE] and [MB58].

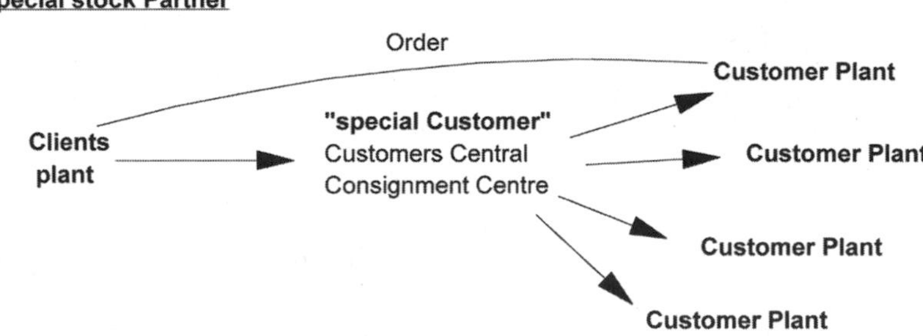

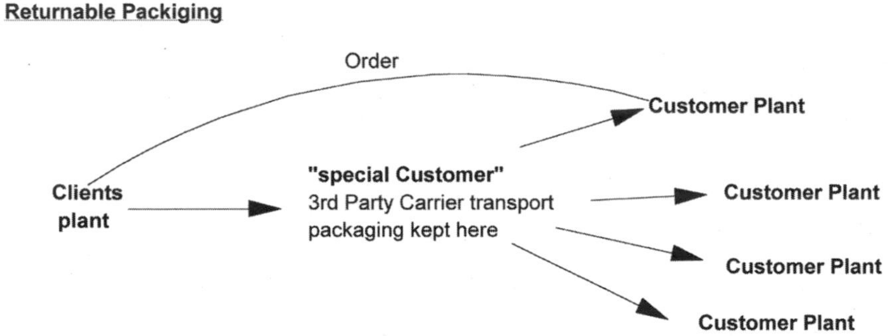

Figure 3-86 The special stock partner process

Route Determination

Route determination is automatically proposed for each sales document item in the sales order. It is a process whereby one can assign a specific route with transportation legs using different shipment types and carriers. Route determination can also be predetermined in the delivery; this will use the weight group of the item that can, if defined, propose a different route to be used.

Menu Path

The menu path here is IMG, Sales and distribution, Basic functions, Routes. Before one can assign the route determination to be used by the system, one needs to define the data that is used in the route determination. This background data will be covered in this section.

Define Routes

The modes of transport are self-explanatory. They may be, for example, road or plane. You define the mode of transport used in the business and assign a two-character alphanumeric key with a meaningful description, as shown in Figure 3-87.

Now let's define the shipping types. The shipping types are the actual vehicles used to transport the materials and can be defined as a train, or mail, and so on. In this assignment, you assign the shipping types along with the previously defined modes of transport (see Figure 3-88).

The next step is to define the transportation connection points. Transportation connection points, as shown in Figure 3-89, can be airports, railway stations, and border crossings. They define points where transportation types connect or where a transportation type crosses a border.

After completing the transportation connection points, you can proceed with defining the routes and stages. In this activity, one defines the route with its associated route stages and transportation connection points (see Figure 3-90).

Figure 3-87 Define the mode of transport and assign a two-character alphanumeric key

ShTy	Description	SType
01	Street	
02	Train	
03	Ship	

Figure 3-88 Assigning the shipping types along with the previously defined modes of transport

CA	Description	MdTr	Description	STPG
01	Truck	01	Street	0001
02	Mail	06	Postal Service	0002
03	Train	02	Train	0003
04	Ship	03	Ship	0004

Figure 3-89 Defining the transportation connection points

Points	Description	Cust.off.descr.
BERLIN	Berlin, Germany	
CLERMONT	Clermont-Ferrand	
DRESDEN	Dresden, Germany	

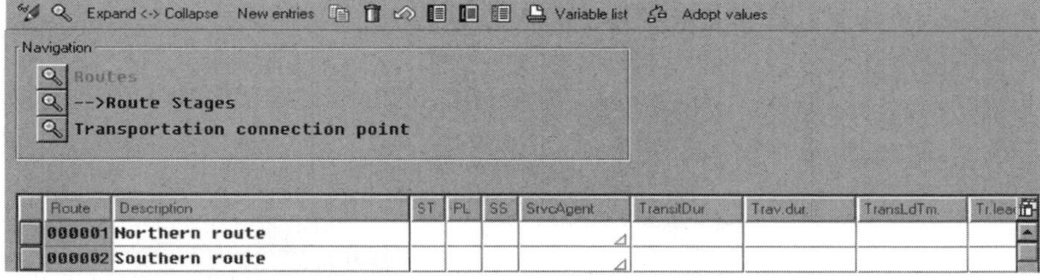

Figure 3-90 Defining the route with its associated route stages and transportation connection points

Double-column

Figure 3-91 The Double-column button

Now let's define a route that is a six-character alphanumeric key with a description. For the defined route, you can set a forwarding agent or carrier as well as define the transit times and the transit lead time, which is the number of days required for organizing a shipment for an item that is to be delivered via a certain route. One can also specify the distance to be traveled and the total transit duration. Do not confuse the settings when defining the route here. The transit duration in calendar days and the transit planning time in hours and minutes are used by the system to define delivery dates and timing. The system does not use the transit duration in hours and minutes for transportation planning and scheduling. After defining the route, proceed with defining the route stages and select the Double-column button, shown in Figure 3-91.

Now select your departure point from the list of transport connection points previously defined (see Figure 3-92). Then select your destination point, such as an airfield, which also originates from the connection points previously defined. Proceed with a new entry and continue with the assignments.

The truck icon in Figure 3-93 represents a vehicle that may be a truck, train, ship, or plane. The icon in Figure 3-94 represents a load transfer point. The icon in Figure 3-95 represents a border crossing point.

Now that the route has been defined, you can proceed with an optional step of maintaining the stages for the routes. This can be carried out for each individual leg, but once you have many routes in the system and you need to define some "global" changes, you can proceed to maintain stages for all routes.

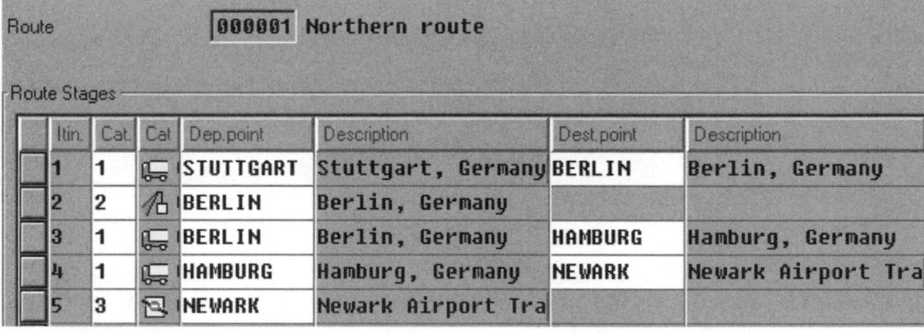
Route 000001 Northern route

Route Stages

Itin.	Cat.	Cat	Dep.point	Description	Dest.point	Description
1	1		STUTTGART	Stuttgart, Germany	BERLIN	Berlin, Germany
2	2		BERLIN	Berlin, Germany		
3	1		BERLIN	Berlin, Germany	HAMBURG	Hamburg, Germany
4	1		HAMBURG	Hamburg, Germany	NEWARK	Newark Airport Tra
5	3		NEWARK	Newark Airport Tra		

Figure 3-92 Selecting your departure point from the list of transport connection points previously defined

Figure 3-93 Vehicle icon

Figure 3-94 The load transfer point icon

Figure 3-95 The border crossing point icon

In the selection screen, enter the data you wish to change. In this example, I have entered all stages defined as transport legs for route 000001, which offers me the following transport legs, as shown in Figure 3-96.

One can now expand these legs and select all of them. You will notice a red traffic light. After selecting them all, click on the change icon (the pencil button). This will offer you a number of attributes that you can now select and change. These changes will be assigned to all the originally selected legs. For example, one can set the shipping type to truck. Then select the execute button.

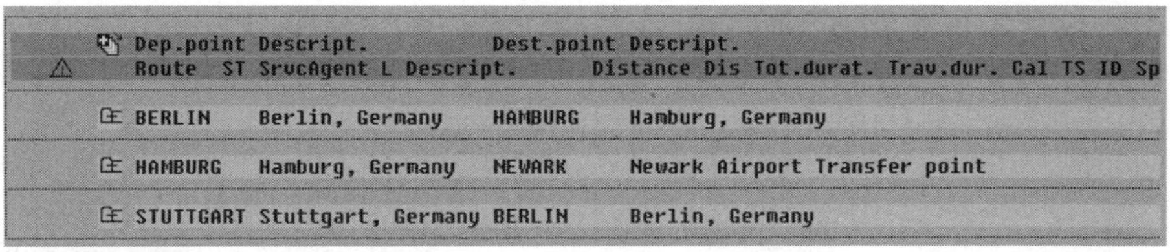

Dep.point	Descript.	Dest.point	Descript.
Route ST SrvcAgent L Descript.		Distance Dis Tot.durat. Trav.dur. Cal TS ID Sp	
BERLIN	Berlin, Germany	HAMBURG	Hamburg, Germany
HAMBURG	Hamburg, Germany	NEWARK	Newark Airport Transfer point
STUTTGART	Stuttgart, Germany	BERLIN	Berlin, Germany

Figure 3-96
The available transport legs

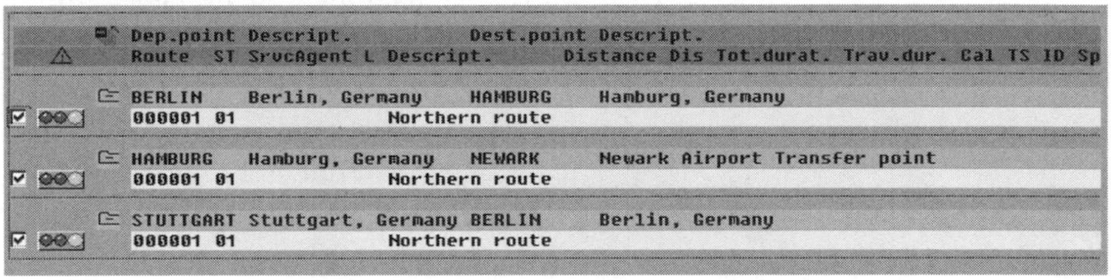

Dep.point	Descript.	Dest.point	Descript.
Route ST SrvcAgent L Descript.		Distance Dis Tot.durat. Trav.dur. Cal TS ID Sp	
BERLIN	Berlin, Germany	HAMBURG	Hamburg, Germany
000001 01	Northern route		
HAMBURG	Hamburg, Germany	NEWARK	Newark Airport Transfer point
000001 01	Northern route		
STUTTGART	Stuttgart, Germany	BERLIN	Berlin, Germany
000001 01	Northern route		

Figure 3-97
After selecting all the items and saving, the traffic signal indicates green.

You will now notice the traffic signal is displayed as yellow. After again selecting all the items and pressing Save, you will notice the traffic signal indicates green, as shown in Figure 3-97. This signaling is merely there for one to use as an indicator as to which items have been processed and which are still to be processed when working with a large number of entries.

Now that the routes have been maintained, you can proceed with defining the route determination.

Route Determination

Route determination occurs in the SAP system based on the following items:

- The country and departure zone (taken from the shipping point)
- The shipping conditions in the sales order
- The transportation group of the material master record
- The country and receiving zone of the ship-to party
- The weight group (optional)

The SAP system then copies the route as proposed in the sales order into the delivery document header. The route already determined in the sales order and copied into the delivery can be predetermined in the delivery document. This predetermination uses the weight of the materials and must be indicated for each relevant delivery document type in customizing.

Now define and assign the transportation zones. You will be faced with an overview screen, as shown in Figure 3-98, which at first glance does not seem to tell you much.

This overview screen is used often for route determination (we will refer to it as the route overview screen for our navigation purposes.) From the route overview screen, proceed with the influencing factors to Zone for route determination, in which you divide a country up into transport zones. A customer exists in a transport zone and so does a shipping point. SAP determines the route for moving from a shipping point in one zone to a customer in another zone (also taking into account other conditions like the weight, shipping conditions of the customer, and the loading group of the material). Here you assign all the zones that you require in route determination. Each zone has a description and an assignment to a country key. This country key is later used to determine what zones are relevant for what shipping points.

After defining the relevant zones, proceed from the route overview screen to Influencing factors, Departure centre/zones. In this assignment, you assign the departure zone to the shipping points you use. Note the shipping point is maintained for a plant and the plant resides in a country; you must also enter the country key of the shipping point here. This country key, as shown in Figure 3-99, determines what departure zones you are allowed to select from, based on the previous settings.

After defining the transportation departure zones, you can now proceed with the definition of the transportation group. From the route overview screen, go to Influencing factors, Transportation groups. The transportation groups, as shown in Figure 3-100, are assigned to the material master record sales/plant view. This transportation group is then copied into the delivery item.

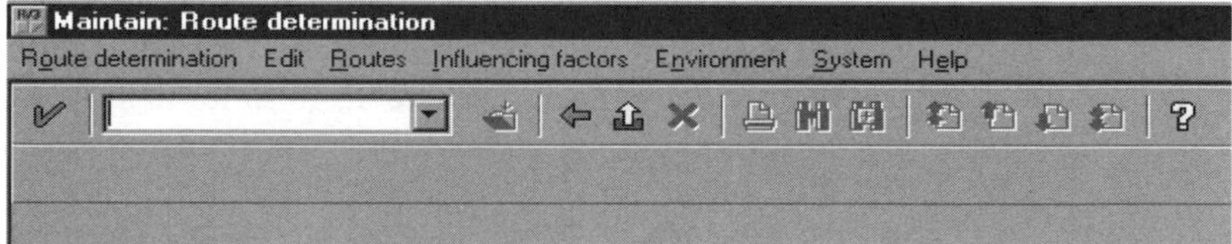

Figure 3-98 The Route determination overview screen

Figure 3-99 The country keys determine what departure zones you can select from.

Shippng point	Ctry	Depart.zone
0001	DE	D000020000
1000	DE	D000020000
1100	DE	D000010000

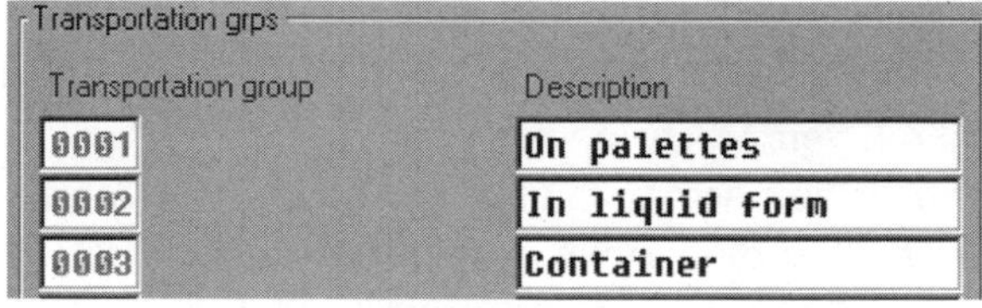
Transportation grps

Transportation group	Description
0001	On palettes
0002	In liquid form
0003	Container

Figure 3-100 The transportation groups

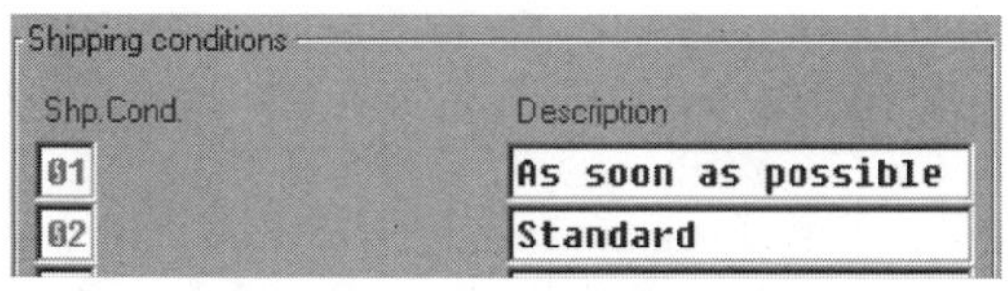
Shipping conditions

Shp.Cond.	Description
01	As soon as possible
02	Standard

Figure 3-101 The shipping conditions which will be allocated to the customer master record or sales document

TIP: *Because the transportation group is a prerequisite for the determination of the route, it is advisable to include it as a mandatory field for the material master record to ensure that during the maintenance of the material the field empty is never left empty.*

Proceed with defining the shipping conditions. From the Route overview screen, go to Influencing factors, Shipping conditions.

The shipping conditions are held in the customer master record (see Figure 3-101). They are used to define the route determination as well as determine the shipping point. One can assign a shipping condition to a sales document; if this has been maintained, the system will not copy the shipping condition from the customer master record.

Now you can define the shipping point determination in the sales order. From the route overview screen, go to Routes, Route determination. Here you can create the route determination based on the shipping point and the destination country, as shown in Figure 3-102.

The shipping point is used to determine the country and zone of origin, and the destination country is then used to propose all related zones as previously configured. In Figure 3-103, we will use shipping point 1000 for destination country AT.

This assignment can now have all the proposed routes for further combination of the shipping condition and transportation group. We can now assign the route we previously maintained to this determination. Should you wish the route in the delivery to be predetermined, proceed with defin-

Figure 3-102 Creating the route determination based on the shipping point and the destination country

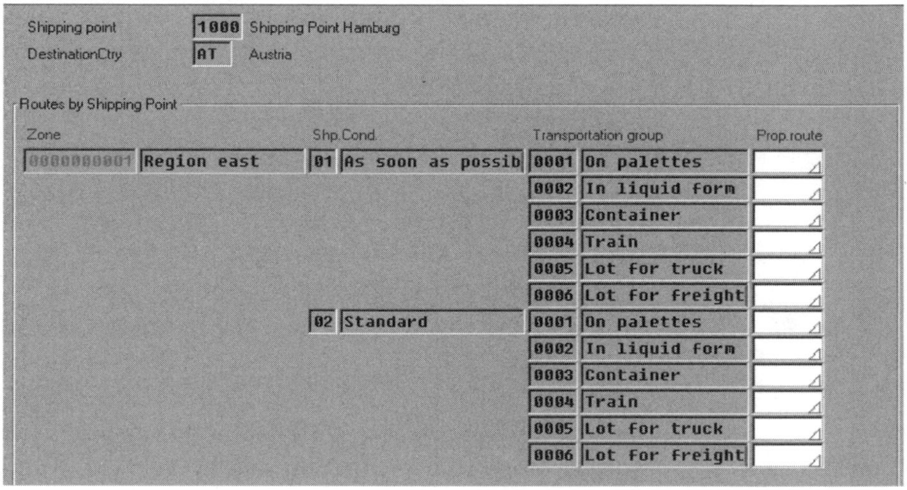

Maintain: Route determination

Route determ. For Shipping point

To Country

Figure 3-103 Using shipping point 1000 for destination country AT

Shipping point 1000 Shipping Point Hamburg

DestinationCtry AT Austria

Routes by Shipping Point

Zone		Shp.Cond.		Transportation group		Prop.route
0000000001	Region east	01	As soon as possib	0001	On palettes	
				0002	In liquid form	
				0003	Container	
				0004	Train	
				0005	Lot for truck	
				0006	Lot for freight	
		02	Standard	0001	On palettes	
				0002	In liquid form	
				0003	Container	
				0004	Train	
				0005	Lot for truck	
				0006	Lot for freight	

ing the route determination by the delivery type. You can now assign one of the following indicators:

- Blank, which indicates no new check
- A, which indicates new route determination without a check
- B, which indicates new route determination with a check

The check performed is the comparison of the proposed route with the actual routes allowed. Go to Define route determination by delivery type and then to Routes allowed actual routes for delivery.

In this assignment, you merely assign additional routes to the proposed route that the system determines automatically. These additional routes can be entered manually or they can be used to determine if they are valid in the predetermination of the route in the delivery.

Proceed to the Define weight groups menu from the route overview screen and then to Influencing factors, Weight groups. You can use the weight group to further refine the route determination in the delivery. For example, let's say the customer shipping condition is "as soon as possible." It makes sense to send the stock by air, but this might be too expensive if the weight is more than 50 kilograms. So, you can say for this shipping condition to the customer, if less than 50 kilograms, use the route that has a transportation type by air; if over 50 kilograms, use a road or sea route. The weight group can therefore be used to determine the route, taking into consideration the weight of the delivery. This is very important when sending stock by rail or truck.

It is generally cheaper to send the stock by truck, rather than rail, if the quantity is small, but for very large quantities, it is usually cheaper to use rail. For the smaller quantities, determine a route that is defined for road shipments; for large quantities, determine a route that is defined for rail shipments. Weight groups should be defined with a short meaningful description, as displayed in Figure 3-104.

TIP: *Always use the weight group as defined in "up to . . .," as this offers a greater ease of use later.*

Now you can proceed with defining the route determination as it occurs in the delivery documents by selecting an entry and maintaining it, or in creating a new entry. You will have the following overview screen in Figure 3-105.

Thus, route determination can be defined based on the factors shown in Figure 3-106.

Posting Goods Issue

Goods issue is posted for a delivery once the goods are transferred into the hands of the carrier; that is, the ownership of the goods leaves the business

Figure 3-104 Weight group settings

Weight groups

Weight group	Description
0001	Up to 1 kg
0010	Up to 10 kg
0100	Up to 100 kg
9999	Over 100 kg

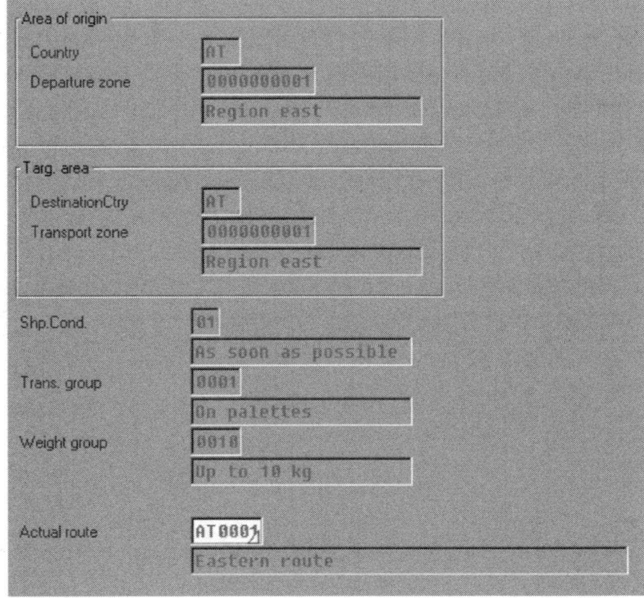

Figure 3-105 Defining the route determination for the delivery documents

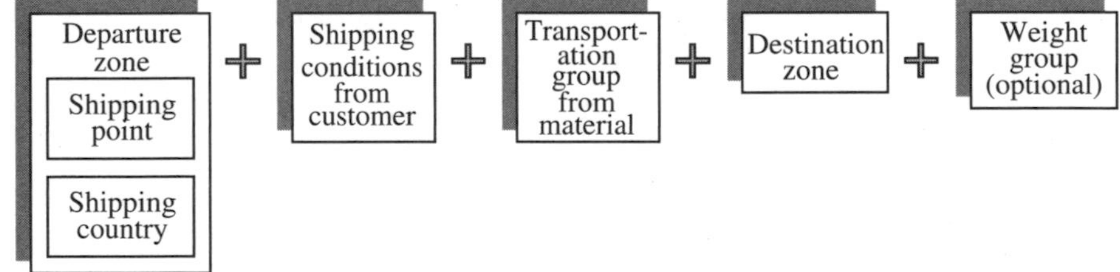

Figure 3-106 The factors on which route determination is based

and transfers to the carrier. The carrier then relieves himself of ownership of the goods once the customer signs for the articles. Once goods issue is posted in a delivery, the system updates numerous records.

The posting of goods issue causes the system to update the *stock quantities*. That is, the warehouse or plant stock is decreased by the quantity of goods that have left the warehouse.

The system also automatically updates the posting to the *general ledger accounts*. Based on the account determination for the inventory posting, the system decreases the value of the stock on hand and increases the cost of goods sold. Later, when the invoice is created, SAP will update the revenue accounts and the amount to be received from the customer. This completes the sales transaction from an accounting perspective.

The system also updates the requirements in the stock requirements list. Once goods issue has occurred, there is no longer a need for a customer's delivery requirement to sit in [MD04]. The system then proceeds to update previous documents with a status displaying that goods issue has been posted. The system updates the deliveries relevant for billing and adds the delivery, if billing-relevant, to the *billing due list*.

From SAP Version 4.0, one can cancel a goods issue posting. To do this, proceed from the logistics screen and go to Sales and distribution, Shipping, Goods issue, Cancellation. Enter in the selection criteria you want and hit the Execute button. You will then see the deliveries that match your selection criteria. Select the deliveries you want to cancel and press Cancel/Reverse.

Invoice and Billing Processes

The business can now create invoices for the customer for the materials or services rendered. The billing process can be order- or delivery-related and may include the billing of standard deliveries as well as the creation of debit and credit memos.

Menu Path

The menu path here is IMG, Sales and distribution, Billing, Billing documents, Define billing types. The billing document is similar to the delivery document in that it has header and item levels, but no schedule line level, as in the sales documents. Thus, one must configure the header document type and the relevant item categories.

Billing Document Type

You can maintain a billing document type or create your own by copying and changing the billing type key. Remember when creating your own document types to use the name range beginning with Z . . .. The header data of a billing document defines how the invoice is to behave. It has the standard number range assignments, but note that the billing document only uses internal assignments. It is not possible to have an external number range for a billing document.

The General Control Data

The General Control data, shown in Figure 3-107, includes the *sales document category*, which defines what type of document the system is using. The SAP standard for invoices is M. One must also assign a transaction group 7 for billing documents and 8 for pro forma invoices. The invoice list type represents the document type that can be used to create invoice lists for this billing document. This list type can be relevant for rebates and indicate that the billing document type is relevant for statistics and should update the logistics information system.

Once a billing document is created and saved with no errors, the system will automatically post the document to accounting. You can place an automatic *posting block* and the system will only post the billing document once you release it by selecting Logistics, Sales and distribution, Billing, Billing document, Change, Release to accounting.

Cancellation Data

The cancellation data, as shown in Figure 3-108, is used by the system when a document type you are defining is cancelled. The system will automatically use the *cancellation billing type* as well as any *copying requirements* you maintain here.

The SAP standard invoice cancellation type for F2 billing documents is S1 as well as SV for a cancellation of a cash sale. If you recall, a cash sale has sales document type BV followed by a billing document type BV.

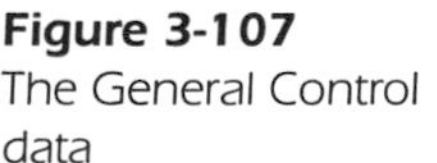

Figure 3-107
The General Control data

General control

SD document categ.	M	Invoice	☐ Posting block
Transaction group	7	Billing documents	☑ Statistics
Billing category			
Document type			
Negative posting	A	Negative posting for sam	
Branch/Head office		Customer=Payer/Branch=so	
Credit memo w/ValDat	☐	No	
Invoice list type	LR	Invoice list	
Rebate settlement			☑ Rel.for rebate
Standard text			

Cancellation
Cancell.billing type S1 Invoice Cancellation
Copying requirements
Reference number
Allocation number

Figure 3-108
The cancellation data

Account assignment/pricing
Account determ.proc. KOFI00 Account Determination
Doc.pricing proced.
Acc. det. rec. acc.
Acc. det. cash. set.
Acc. det. pay. cards A00001 Standard

Figure 3-109
The account assignment and pricing control area

Account Assignment/Pricing Data

The account assignment and pricing control area, as shown in Figure 3-109, is used by both the account determination and pricing determination. The *account determination procedure* is used by the system to propose which general ledger accounts entries must be posted. The *document pricing procedure* indicator is used to determine pricing in conjunction with the sales area and the customer pricing procedure indicator. Both of these determination procedures will be covered in Chapter 4.

Output/Partners/Text Data

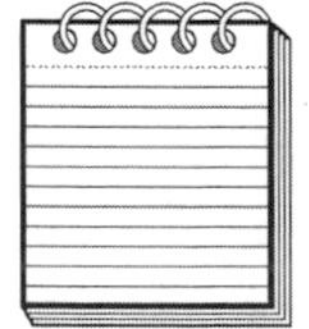

NOTE: *The billing document has header and item levels, but the billing document does not have a configurable item level. Rather, the data entered in the header document type is used by the system in determining the output, partner, and text determination of the item level.*

The *output determination* procedure, which is assigned to billing document types and the application the output is assigned to, that is, V3, indicating billing is assigned here (see Figure 3-110). The header and item *partner determination* key specifies the group of partner functions the system proposes automatically for a billing document of this type. These

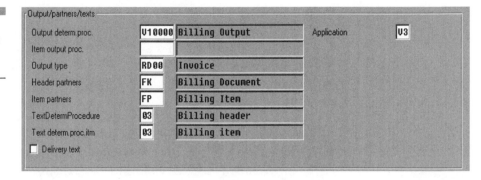

Figure 3-110
The output, partners and text procedure assignments

Output/partners/texts

Output determ.proc.	V10000	Billing Output	Application	V3
Item output proc.				
Output type	RD00	Invoice		
Header partners	FK	Billing Document		
Item partners	FP	Billing Item		
TextDetermProcedure	03	Billing header		
Text determ.proc.itm	03	Billing item		

☐ Delivery text

header partners may be mandatory for the sold-to party as well as the bill-to party and payer partner, but the ship-to party may be an optional entry. The *text determination* procedure for the header and item level are also assigned to the billing document header. The output, partner, and text determinations are covered in Chapter 4.

The SAP standard uses, amongst others, the following billing types:

F1: Order-related invoice

F2: Delivery-related invoice

F5: Pro forma invoice for sales orders

F8: Pro forma invoice for deliveries

G2: Credit memo

L2: Debit memo

RE: Credit for returns

S1: Cancellation invoice

S2: Cancellation credit memo

IV: Intercompany invoice

The item categories found in the billing document are copied from the preceding document. Thus, item category TAN in the delivery will be copied as item category TAN in the billing document.

Special Billing Document Types

The *pro forma invoice* uses billing type F8. It is an invoice that does not post any financial amounts into any general ledger. It is used in information purposes only. An example of using a pro forma invoice would be to accompany the shipment of products across a border post. The invoice would be used to represent the actual value of the articles. The actual invoice can be sent to the customer via post. Another example of using a pro forma invoice would be when a customer needs to be sent an invoice representing the value she must claim from a superior authority before the business sends her the actual payable invoice.

The *standard cancellation invoice* for a F2 invoice is the billing type S1. The cancellation invoice is used when one discovers that a billing document has errors on it and needs to be cancelled and recreated.

The *intercompany invoice* will be discussed later. It represent the internal invoice used between two company codes belonging to the same business. It is an internal invoice in the fact that it is not passed on to any external sold-to party or partner.

As you know, it is possible to have order-related billing as well delivery-related billing. Examples of commonly used order-related billing documents would be

- Credit memos
- Debit memos
- Invoice correction request

For all billing documents like standard document types, it is necessary to maintain the copy control rules.

Consolidated Invoicing and Copy Control for Billing Documents

Billing documents can be created individually; that is, you can create an invoice for each sales order or billing document. Billing documents can also be created and consolidated; the invoices are accumulated and created collectively, for example, on one day of the week. Thus, when all relevant data is equal, the system can combine multiple deliveries or sales document into one invoice. This is maintained by using a combination of the factory calendar and copying rules.

To create consolidated invoicing for a customer, one must first define the factory calendar the payer is using (factory calendars will be covered in Chapter 4). This factory calendar is then to be assigned to the billing view of the customer master record for the payer. The billing calendar may indicate one day of the week as a working day; thus, the system will only propose creating billing documents for this party once a week. This does not mean that the deliveries and sales orders will be consolidated into one billing document. The copy control may require the invoices to be split (such as if the payment terms are different), but it also means that the billing documents will be created on that day.

The copy control for billing documents is split into three overall copy control rules. They define copy rules for header and item levels between sales documents:

- *Sales document to billing document* This is used for credit memos and debit memos that have no delivery document.
- *Delivery note to billing document* This is the most widely used copying rule and covers the standard sales process.
- *Billing document to billing document* This is used by the system to determine copying control between an invoice and an intercompany invoice, for example.

As the copy control definition and maintenance is equal for all three types, we will only use the delivery note to the billing document as an example. Using this, we can fabricate an example whereby we have created five sales orders for the customer. Of these five sales orders, we have created two deliveries due to the fact that the shipping point on one of the sales orders was different. Now we have the scenario whereby two deliveries of delivery type LF are to be billed.

Looking at the copy control rules from delivery type LF to billing document type F2, as shown in Figure 3-111, we can select the relevant item category levels.

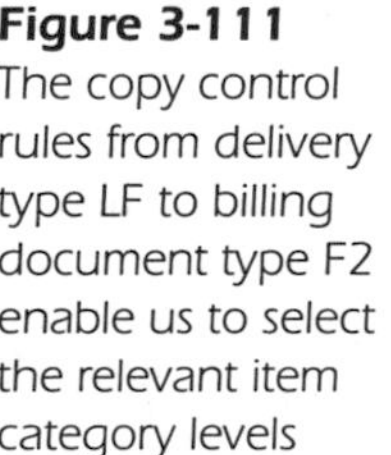

Figure 3-111
The copy control rules from delivery type LF to billing document type F2 enable us to select the relevant item category levels

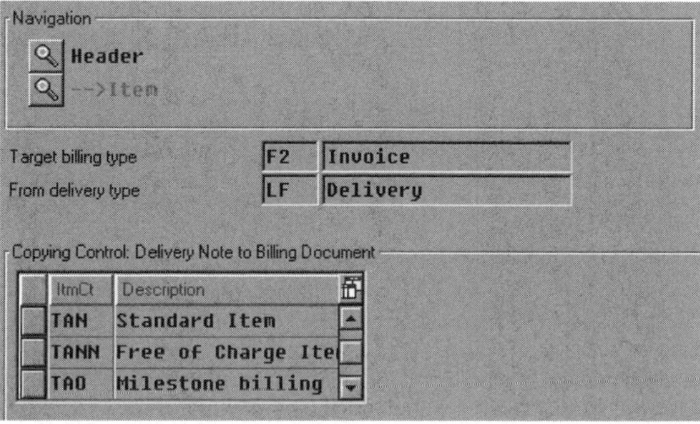

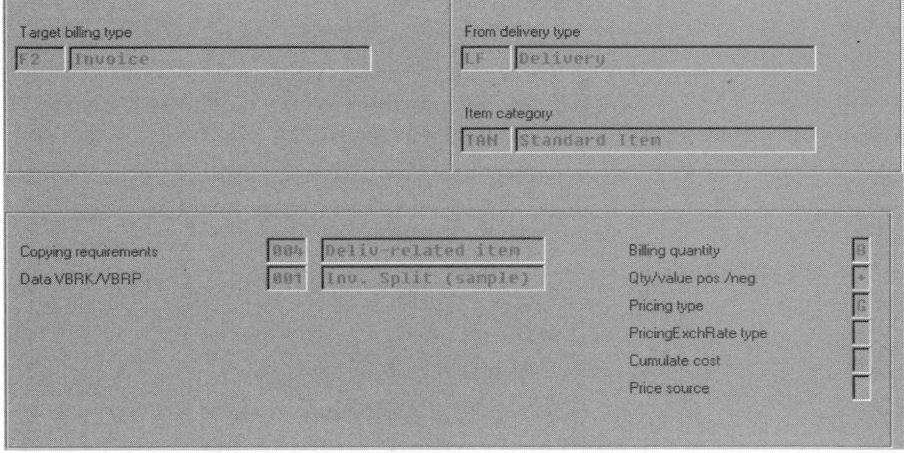

Figure 3-112 Target billing type information

Using the TAN example, we have a similar view to the copy control rules, as found in the sales documents (see Figure 3-112). However, we have a *billing quantity* value that determines the quantity of items to be invoiced. For example, setting B provides the invoice with the delivery quantity less the already-invoiced quantity. The pricing type used determines what type of pricing the system is to automatically use. The requirement field is used as a standard; that is, all elements requested by the requirement must be fulfilled in order for the billing document to be created.

The data that is important to an invoice splitting or invoice combination is the entry in the field data VBRK/VBRP. Table VBRK is the billing header and table VBRP is the billing item. The key entered here is used by the system to defining splitting rules. For our example, the two deliveries created from five sales orders can be split into individual billing documents, each one representing a sales order, or the deliveries can be combined to form one billing document.

To create a splitting rule, proceed to [VOFM] and select Data transfer, Billing documents. Copy the standard 001-Inv, Split (sample). This is done by merely overwriting the number, such as type 900 over 001, and pressing enter. Note you will need an access key, as displayed in Figure 3-113, for the object you wish to create.

The focus of this book is not ABAP; thus, we will not go into the programming of ABAP and the related commands. However, it is worthwhile noting that the data copy routines used here are merely comparisons of tables and fields in ABAP. The system compares the values in the header VBRK table and item VBRP table, as displayed in Figure 3-114, if any comparisons are defined.

Figure 3-113
An access key is needed for the object you want to create.

Please enter the key for the object: R3TR PROG RV60C900
SAP Release: 40B
Access key:

Figure 3-114
Comparing the values in the header VBRK table and item VBRP table

```
*----------------------------

form daten_kopieren_901.

* Kopfdaten
* VBRK-xxxxx = ............


* Positionsdaten
* VBRP-xxxxx = ............

```

In addition to the comparisons, SAP has a standard internal table called ZUK. In this table, you can define fields that must be compared and found to be equal before an invoice may be combined.

In Figure 3-115, table ZUK is comparing

- VTWEG, the distribution channel
- BSTKD, the purchase order number
- SPART, the division

Thus, those deliveries that do not have the same entry in the fields will be assigned individual invoices. In our first example of five sales orders and two deliveries, should any of the header data or the three defined fields be unequal, the system will create an individual invoices.

NOTE: *ZUK is a string field of 40 characters that is stored on the billing header table (VBRK). Therefore, the maximum length of the fields assigned to ZUK must be 40 characters.*

Figure 3-115 Table ZUK is comparing VTWEG, BSTKD, and SPART.

```
* zusätzliche Splitkriterien
  data: begin of zuk,
                modul(3) value '905',
                vtweg like vbak-vtweg,
                bstkd like vbkd-bstkd,
                spart like vbak-spart,
            end of zuk.
  zuk-spart = vbak-spart.
  zuk-vtweg = vbak-vtweg.
  zuk-bstkd = vbkd-bstkd.

  vbrk-zukri = zuk.

endform.
```

Should a customer then define that he wants to have consolidated invoicing, his billing schedule date must resemble the dates he wants to be billed on, and he must realize he will have his invoice split according to the splitting requirements set globally. The invoice split is defined according to the combination of document types and thus does not take the sold-to party or associated partners into account.

Invoice Lists

At specific time intervals or dates, invoice lists can be created. Invoice lists are merely a list of billing documents that is either individual and/or collective and these documents are combined into one document for a particular customer.

Menu Path

The menu path to follow is IMG, Sales and distribution, Billing, Billing documents, Invoice lists.

Two types of invoice lists are available in the SAP standard system:

For invoices and debit memos: **LR**

For credit memos: **LG**

An invoice list has header and item data. One cannot change the details of the invoices once they are in the invoice list. For invoice lists to be used, the following prerequisites must be maintained:

1. Condition type RL00 [factoring discount] and the tax condition MW15, if required, must be maintained and placed in the pricing procedure.
2. An invoice list type must be assigned to each billing type that you want to use to process invoice lists. The two invoice lists that can be used are LR and LG. Should you need an additional billing document type for invoice lists, copy the original and rename it beginning with a Z.
3. Proceed to assign the invoice list type for each billing type. Here you assign the invoice list type to be used by the associated billing document types, as shown in Figure 3-116.
4. Copying requirements must be maintained between the billing document and the invoice list document. The system does not carry out copying at the item level for billing documents. The standard copying requirement used in invoice lists is 016.
5. A customer calendar must be defined specifying dates on which invoice lists are to be processed, such as once every two weeks. This is assigned to the customer's billing view in the customer master record.
6. Output the condition records for condition types LR00 and RD01.

Figure 3-116 Assigning the invoice list type to be used by the associated billing document types

Bill.type	Billing type	InvListTyp	Invoice list type
B1	Rebate Credit Memo		
B2	Rebate Correction		
B3	Rebate Part Settlmnt		
B4	Rebate Manual Accrls		
BM1	Debit Memo Agreemnt		
BM3	Debit Memo Agreemnt		
BV	Cash Sale	LR	Invoice list
F1	Invoice	LR	Invoice list
F2	Invoice	LR	Invoice list

We will leave the output assignments and condition type assignments in their respective determination procedures until we cover these determination sections in Chapter 4.

To create an invoice list, proceed from the logistics screen and go to Sales and distribution, Billing, Invoice list, Create. Proceed with entering each billing document separately. Alternatively, proceed with Logistics, Sales and distribution, Billing, Invoice list, Edit work list and enter the selection criteria to the invoice list. Then select the Display individual invoice list button. Proceed with selecting the billing documents and then go to Invoice list, Save. An invoice list created from a combination of two individual billing documents would then look like Figure 3-117.

By selecting the pricing header, one can see the factoring discount as well as the factoring discount tax assigned to this invoice list, as shown in Figure 3-118. The total payable is 69.448,50 DEM.

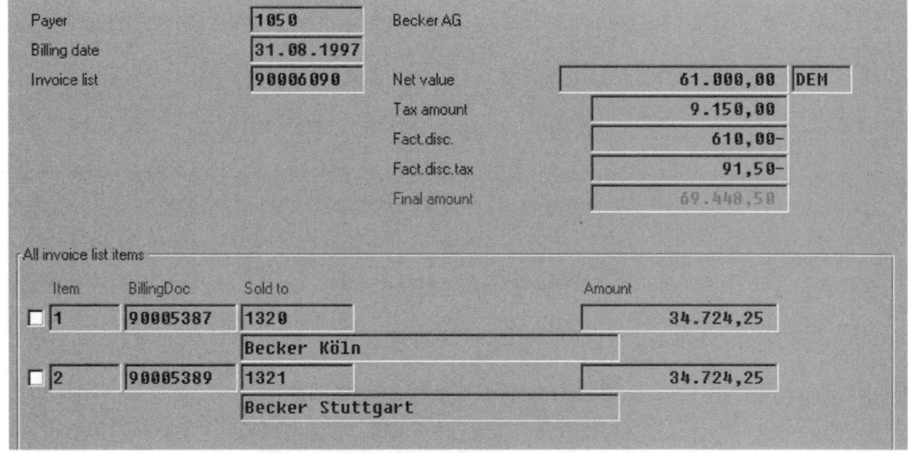

Figure 3-117 An invoice list created from a combination of two individual billing documents.

Net value in DEM 610,00-
Tax amount 91,50-

Conditions

CnTy	Name	Rate	Curr.	by	UoM	Cond.value DEM
RL00	Factoring Discount					610,00-
MW15	Fact.Discount Tax	15,000	%			91,50-

Figure 3-118 Selecting the pricing header enables one to see the factoring discount and the factoring discount tax.

Billing Plans

The SAP system uses two billing plans. The first, *milestone billing,* is a final billing in full at a particular milestone, according to items sold or services rendered. An example of this would be a project milestone, such as when an architect's blueprint is finished, for which the service is invoiced. The alternative billing plan is *periodic billing*, which uses a predefined date proposal that bills the customer at periodic intervals. An example of this would be billing for rental of an object.

Menu Path

The menu path here is IMG, Sales and distribution, Billing, Billing plan, Define billing plan types.

The difference between milestone billing and periodic billing can be described as follows. Milestone billing bills an amount distributed between dates until the total value is billed. Periodic billing bills a total amount for each date until a predefined end date is reached. Proceed with maintaining the billing plan types for *periodic billing*. In this view, you assign data to a relevant periodic billing plan type (see Figure 3-119). You assign a start date, which may be the start date of the rental contract, as well as an end date, which may be the contract's end date.

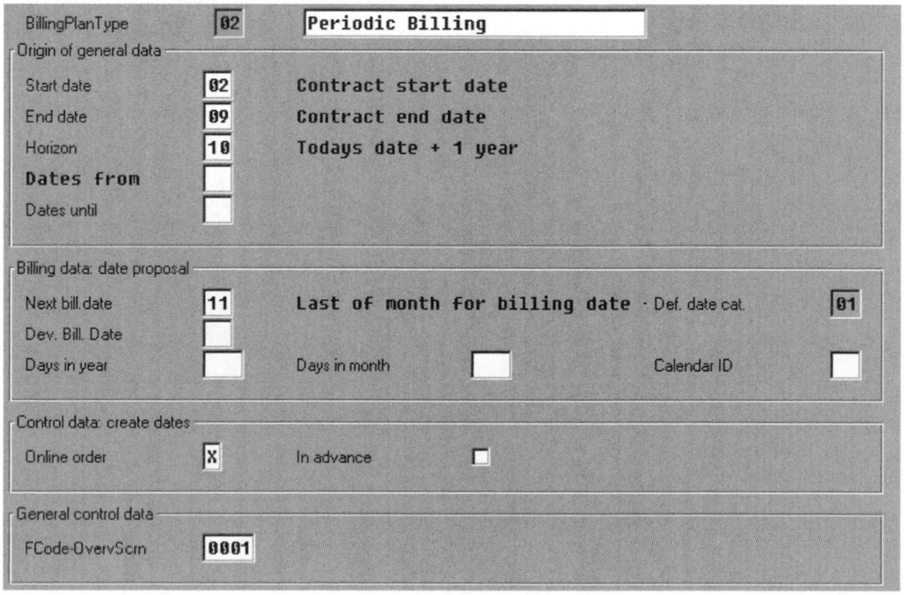

Figure 3-119 *Assigning data to a relevant periodic billing plan type*

BillingPlanType 02 Periodic Billing

Origin of general data
Start date 02 Contract start date
End date 09 Contract end date
Horizon 10 Todays date + 1 year
Dates from
Dates until

Billing data: date proposal
Next bill.date 11 Last of month for billing date · Def. date cat. 01
Dev. Bill. Date
Days in year · Days in month · Calendar ID

Control data: create dates
Online order X · In advance

General control data
FCode-OvervScrn 0001

The next billing date can be set, defining the billing dates for periodic billing. The previous example refers to "the last of the month for the billing date." You can assign a deviation billing date, which is a rule that can be set to determine that the customer is billed a period of time prior to the billing date as determined by the system.

In the control data, one can set the deadlines to be created automatically in the sales order as well as define that the system should bill in advance by indicating this in the In advance field. Should this indicator not be set, the system will automatically bill in arrears. For example, should you want to bill the customer for the upcoming month's rental, set this indicator. One can then define which screen the system will use as its overview screen after entering data on the initial billing plan screen. Then proceed with maintaining the billing plan types for milestone billing.

This screen, as shown in Figure 3-120, is similar to Figure 3-119, the one for periodic billing; however, due to there being less data relevant for periodic billing, the only settings required here are the start date, usually set as today's date, the date category, the on-line order indicator, which determines if the system automatically creates the billing deadlines, and the overview screen.

Proceed to the Define date descriptions menu. These date descriptions are merely used for informational purposes. Create a four-character alphanumeric key with a meaningful description and then go to the Define and assign date categories menu. In this assignment, as displayed in Figure 3-121, you assign a date category, previously undefined, to the previously defined billing plan type using an example of milestone billing. You then create a date category.

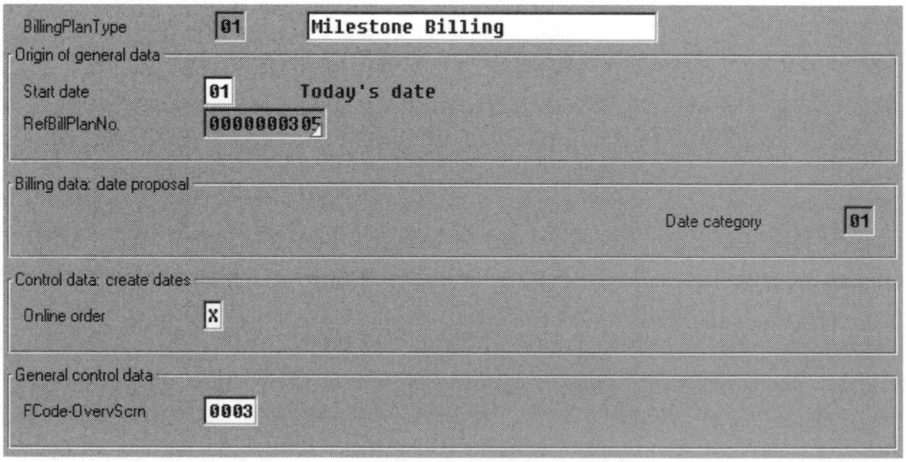

Figure 3-120 Assigning data to a relevant milestone billing plan type

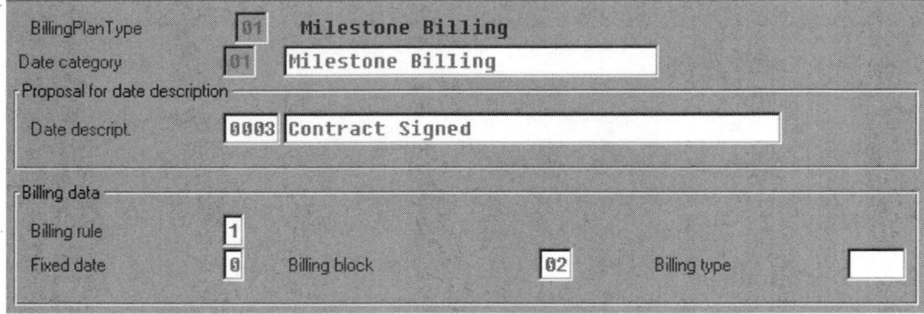

Figure 3-121 Assigning a date category to the previously defined billing plan type using milestone billing

Figure 3-122 Setting a value billing rule

Then assign a created date category with a description for the billing plan type. Next, assign a date description, as previously defined, and assign the billing rules. A value billing rule is used by the system in taking the full billing amount, such as $10,000, and dividing it up into partial amounts, such as $3,000, $2,000, $4,000, and $1,000. The milestone billing based as a percentage would determine percentages of the total billing amount to be billed such as 30 percent, 20 percent, 40 percent, and 10 percent. One can then set the *default date category* to be used per billing plan type. This is done in the *allocate date category*. The system will use this value as a default (see Figure 3-122).

Milestone billing has an allocation for date proposals. These milestones are defined in the settings for maintaining date proposals for billing plan types. As seen previously in milestone billing, the milestone billing plan has a reference billing plan type. In this view, one can maintain the dates defined in the milestone billing plan type. Periodic billing does not have a need to define milestone dates, as it determines its billing date by following a repetitive procedure until finally reaching a termination date. By selecting Maintain dates, you will be faced with a screen in which you can enter the relevant dates and assignments in percentages or in a total value (see Figure 3-123).

Should one select the date and press Display, you will be faced with a controlling screen (see Figure 3-124).

Of particular importance in this screen is the billing rule. This defines if the billing dates should be percentage- or value-based. One can also define if a billing block should be automatically proposed or not.

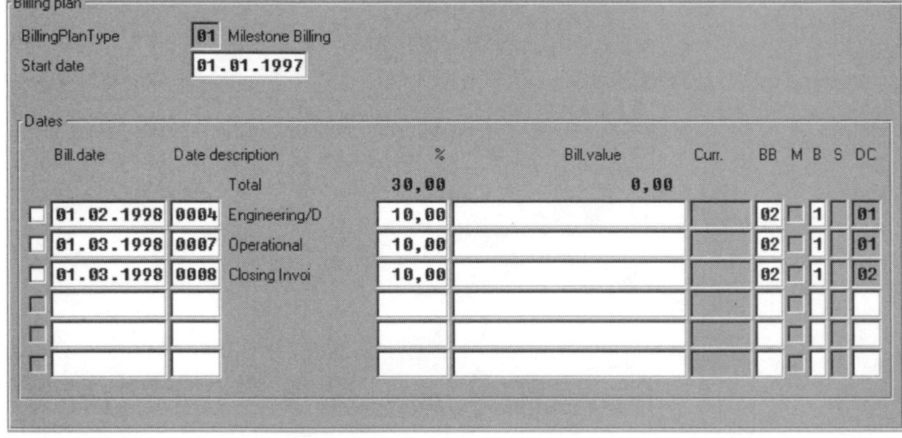

Figure 3-123 The Billing plan screen where you can enter the relevant dates and assignments in percentages or in a total value

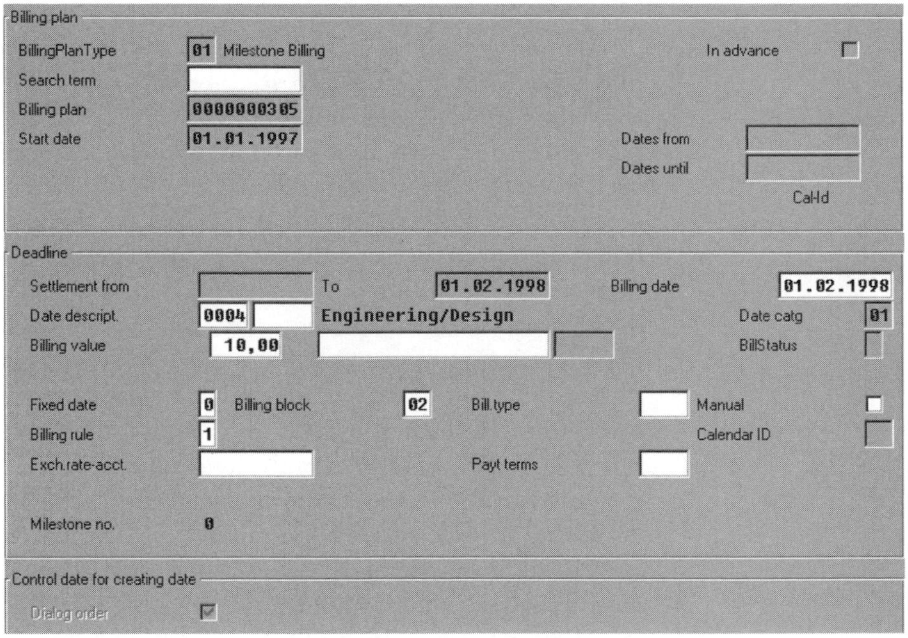

Figure 3-124 The controlling screen for the billing plan

After completing the billing dates, proceed to assign the *billing plan type to sales document types*. This section again is self-explanatory; one merely assigns the relevant billing plan type, be it milestone or periodic billing to the necessary sales document types.

After assignment of the billing plan type to the sales document, proceed to assign the *billing plan types to item categories*. As billing is carried out per item category, one assigns the billing to the sales document item. For example, the standard item category TAN would in most systems use A, which is relevant for delivery-related billing. The SAP standard has item categories MVN, which is used for periodic billing, and item category TAO, which is created for milestone billing. In Figure 3-125, each item category that is relevant for either of the billing plan types must be assigned a billing relevance I, which is relevant for an order-related billing plan. Assigned to the billing relevance would be the billing plan type, such as milestone or periodic billing.

One can define the rules used in the system to define the dates in the billing plans. To define these dates, proceed to define the *rules for determining dates*. This is the same section as previously defined in Chapter 2 under "Rules for Determining Dates." You can create these rules in either section. Please refer to Chapter 2 for details.

Rebate Agreements

A rebate agreement is an agreement between the business and a customer. This agreement takes the form of a special discount paid retroactively to the customer. This discount is based on the sales volume for the customer over a specific time period. The rebate is only relevant if the customer purchases the required sales volume.

Menu Path

The menu path here is IMG, Sales and distribution, Billing, Rebate processing.

The rebate agreement has separate condition records for each product the customer buys. These condition records specify the rebate amount or percentage due to the customer for each product. One can also specify a

ItCa	Description	BillR	BillPlanTy	Billing plan type
LFN	Request billing plan	I	02	Periodic Billing
LKN	SchedAgr w.ExtAgent			
LNN	Ret.Packaging Issue	A		

Figure 3-125 Each item category that is relevant for either of the billing plan types must be assigned a billing relevance I.

pricing scale so that the customer can earn a better rebate by ordering more products. Because rebates are always paid retroactively, the system keeps track of all billing documents that are relevant for rebate processing. This includes standard invoices as well as credit and debit memos related to the rebate.

The system can also post accruals automatically so that the accumulated value of a rebate is recorded for accounting purposes. A rebate agreement is finally settled when a credit memo is issued to the customer for the accumulated rebate total.

Configuration of a Rebate Agreement

The rebate agreement type determines which data the system is to automatically propose for the rebate agreement. The SAP standard has the agreement types shown in Table 3-1

We will use the example, as shown in Figure 3-126, of a customer and material rebate that is rebate agreement type 0002. The rebate agreement has a *validity period*. Thus, it has a valid From and To date rule. The control data of a rebate includes the condition type group assigned to the rebate type. In our example, we use the condition type group 0002.

The *condition type group* is not to be confused with the condition type used in pricing. The condition type group has generally one condition type assigned to it, but it is possible to assign more than one condition type to the condition type group. We will cover this assignment a little later.

The *verification level* is a key indicator that determines the level of detail one sees when displaying totals for a rebate agreement. The *manual accruals*

Table 3-1

Rebate agreement types

Agreement Type	Basis of Rebate	Condition Type
0001	Customer/material %	B001
	Customer/rebate group %	B001
0002	Customer/material quantity dependent	B002
0003	Customer %	B003
0004	Customer hierarchy %	B004
	Customer hierarchy/material %	B005
0005	Sales volume independent	B006

Figure 3-126
Rebate agreement type 0002

Rebate agreement	0002	Material Rebate		
Proposed values				
Proposed valid-from	3	First day of current year		
Proposed valid-to	2	The end of the current year is proposed		
Payment method			Default status	
Control data				
Condition type group	0002	Material		
Verification levels	F	Display totals by payer/material		
☐ Different val.period		Rebate agreement and cond.record have same val.period		
ManAccrls Order type	R4	☑ Manual accruals		
Arrangement calendar				
Manual payment				
Payment procedure	A	Payment allowed up to the accruals value		
Partial settlement	R3	☑ Reverse accruals		
Settlement				
Final settlement	B1		Correction	B2
Minimum status	B	Agreement released for settlement		

order type is actually a sales document type that is assigned to the rebate agreement and is used in the manual accruals in a rebate agreement. Note that the sales document type assigned here should have an order-relevant billing type assigned to it. The SAP standard uses the billing type B4 for the sales document type R4.

Should you want to make *manual payments* of the rebate to the recipient, you can indicate this in the payment procedure. When a manual payment is carried out, the system automatically creates a *credit memo request* of the type specified in the Partial settlement field for the specified amounts. Thus, when the system carries out the final settlement, all partial payments are taken into account, and the remaining balance is paid. Again, make sure there is a order-relevant billing type assigned to the partial settlement sales document type. The SAP standard uses the partial settlement document type R3 and the associated order related billing type B3.

Be sure to indicate that the system must reverse the accruals. This will ensure the system will reverse the accruals up to the amount specified in the manual payment. Should the accruals not be as high as the payment to be made, the system will reverse whatever accruals it has.

In the final settlement area, you must ensure that the credit memo request for the final settlement is assigned to the Final settlement field (again, be sure that this credit memo request has the associated order-relevant billing type assigned to it in the sales document type). The SAP standard uses the credit memo request B1 with billing type B1. One can also assign a *minimum status* that the rebate agreement must reach before the final settlement can be carried out.

NOTE: *You cannot enter the following statuses as a minimum status for final settlement:*

C: Credit memo request already created for settlement

D: Final settlement of agreement already carried out

Now that the rebate agreement type has been defined, proceed to defining the condition type groups.

Condition Type Groups

In this activity, you define the condition type group that is to be assigned to the rebate agreement. Should you need to create your own condition type group, you can copy and change the name, but remember to use the prefix Z.

NOTE: *Should you copy a condition type group, the system does not copy the associated assignments. Thus, you will need to make all the necessary assignments manually.*

Assigning Condition Type/Table to Condition Type Groups

In this activity, one assigns the condition type from the pricing procedure to the condition type group found on the rebate agreement type (see Figure 3-127). The *sequence number* (SqN) column represent the fields in the condition table that determine what the system is to use as the basis for the rebate. In this example, 1 determines that the condition type should use the fields customer and material. The condition type group 0002 will use pricing condition type B002. The pricing procedure and determination will be covered in Chapter 4, "Basic Functions."

CTyGr	Condition type group	Cntr	CnTy	Condition type	SqN	Table
0002	Material	1	B002	Material Rebate	1	Customer/Material

Figure 3-127
Assigning the condition type from the pricing procedure to the condition type group found on the rebate agreement type

ATyp	Agreement type	CTyGr	Condition type group
0002	Material Rebate	0002	Material

Figure 3-128
Agreement type 0002 uses condition type group 0002

Assigning Condition Type Groups and Agreement Types

Here you are presented with a list of agreement types as created in the system and you can assign the relevant condition type group. If you recall, our example agreement type 0002 uses condition type group 0002, as shown in Figure 3-128.

Now proceed with creating and maintaining the condition types and pricing procedures. This is carried out in the *condition technique for rebate processing*. We, however, will not be dealing with the actual configuration necessary here. This is due to the fact that pricing procedures, their determinations, conditions, types, tables, and access sequences should all be dealt with together in detail, which is done in Chapter 4. Also, not many differences exist, other than what is described in the following text, between the determination and maintenance of standard conditions and those used by rebates.

What is important to note here is that on the pricing procedure used with rebates, the condition subtotal SubTo field, which is used as the basis for the rebate, should contain the value 7 that is in the field KOMP-BONBA.

TIP: *This is generally the same subtotal used as the net value for the item.*

The requirement 024 can be assigned to the condition type in the pricing procedure, which determines the condition is only accessed in the billing document. It is not possible to maintain rebate condition types manually in the pricing procedure of sales documents.

Also note the condition types used in rebate processing (in this case, B002) must use condition class C-expense reimbursement. The condition type B002 uses the access sequence B002. The condition types used in rebate processing are slightly different than the standard condition types used for pricing or discounts, in that there is less data to maintain with an inclusion of two rebate indicators (see Figure 3-129).

The rebate procedure indicates if the condition is dependent or independent of the sales volume. The accruals correction procedure indicates if accruals must be corrected when this condition type is accessed.

Account Determination for Rebates Account determination procedures will be dealt with in detail in Chapter 4. There are no significant differences between the standard account determination rules and the assignments for standard condition types and rebates other than the following. Rebate condition types must have an account key assigned to them in the pricing procedure used by the sales document type for orders and billings. One account key is assigned for revenues and the opposite account key is assigned for accruals. These account keys are assigned individual general ledger accounts. The SAP system uses the revenue account key ERB and the accrual account key ERU, as displayed in Figure 3-130.

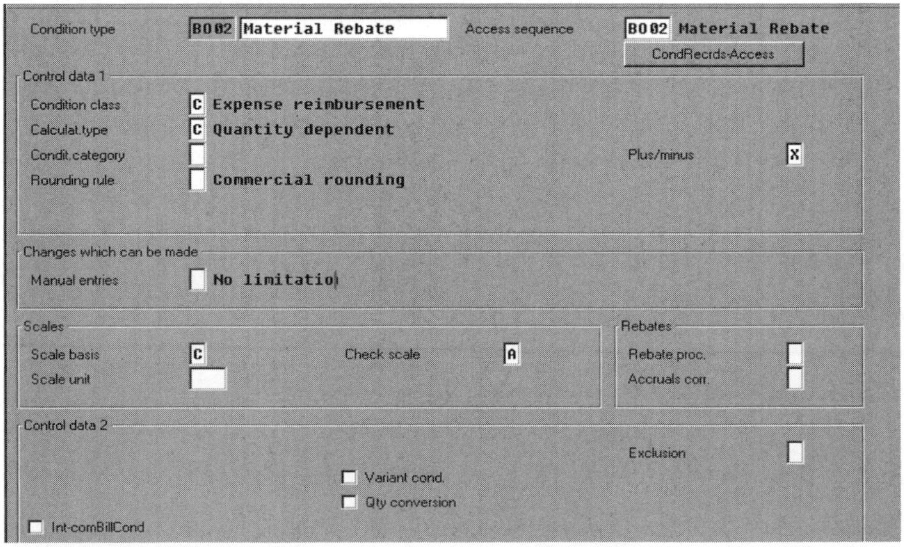

Figure 3-129 The condition types used in rebate processing must use condition class C - expense reimbursement.

Condition type B002 Material Rebate
Access sequence B002 Material Rebate
CondRecrds-Access
Control data 1
Condition class C Expense reimbursement
Calculat.type C Quantity dependent
Condit.category
Plus/minus X
Rounding rule Commercial rounding
Changes which can be made
Manual entries No limitatio
Scales
Scale basis C
Check scale A
Scale unit
Rebates
Rebate proc.
Accruals corr.
Control data 2
Exclusion
Variant cond.
Qty conversion
Int-comBillCond

Proc.	Step	Cntr	CTyp	Name	ActKy	Name	Accrls	Name
RVAA01	901	0	B001	Group Rebate	ERB	Rebate sales dedu	ERU	Rebate sales
	902	0	B002	Material Rebate	ERB	Rebate sales dedu	ERU	Rebate accru
	903	0	B003	Customer Rebate	ERB	Rebate sales dedu	ERU	Rebate accru
	904	0	B004	Hierarchy Rebate	ERB	Rebate sales dedu	ERU	Rebate accru
	905	0	B005	Hierarchy rebate/m	ERB	Rebate sales dedu	ERU	Rebate accru

Figure 3-130
SAP uses the revenue account key ERB and the accrual account key ERU.

SOrg.	Sales org.	Rebate proc.active
3000	USA Philadelphia	☑

Figure 3-131
Activating the relevant sales organizations for rebate agreements

Activating Rebate Processing

Now you activate the relevant sales organizations for rebate agreements, as in Figure 3-131.

Selecting Billing Documents for Rebate Processing

Not all billing documents should be relevant for rebate processing. It would not make sense to indicate a pro forma invoice as relevant for rebates, but it would make sense to indicate the standard billing document types F2 and BV, as well as the associated credit memos, such as G2. You may not want the system to use debit notes for rebate processing or, on the other hand, should you want a debit note to increase the revenue for certain transactions, you can create your own new debit note request as relevant for rebates and create a new debit note billing type. Also ensure this billing type is indicated as rebate-relevant.

Material Rebate Groups

These material rebate groups are merely an additional field SAP offers in order for you to group certain materials together. This grouping of certain materials enables you to use this field and its value in a condition record. The field MVKE-BONUS should be assigned to the Sales organization data 2 view in the material master record. Rebate processing is now configured, so you must proceed to the Logistics screen and maintain the necessary data relevant to rebate agreements.

Create rebate agreements Go to Logistics, Sales and distribution, Master data, Agreements, Rebate agreements, Create. Then enter the agreement type, such as 0002. In the overview screen, enter the necessary details, including the rebate recipient. The system can use the sold-to party or ship-to party as well as the payer as the rebate recipient. However, the system cannot determine an additional alternative partner as the rebate recipient, such as an alternative payer from the customer master record of the sold-to party.

Be sure to indicate on the customer master record that the payer/customer is relevant for rebates. This is done on the billing screen of the customer master record (see Figure 3-132).

Now click on the Conditions button. This will take you to an overview screen where you can enter material descriptions, the rate, and accruals (see Figure 3-133).

You can access an overview of the materials rebate data by selecting the material and pressing Display. In this overview screen, one will find a field

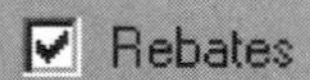

Figure 3-132 The billing screen of the customer master record

Sales organization	3000	USA Philadelphia
Distribution channel	12	Sold for resale
Division	00	Cross-division
Customer	3176	Computer 3000
Validity period	01.01.1997	
To	31.12.1999	

Conditions

Material / Description	Rate / Accruals	Unit	by	UoM	D
R-1000	500,00-	USD	1	PC	
Maxitec-R 375 personal co	500,00-				

Figure 3-133 The conditions overview screen

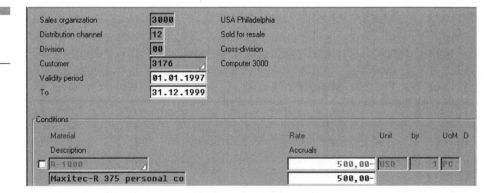

called material for settlement (Matl. f. settl.), as shown in Figure 3-134. This field is important, specifically for rebates that a material is not used for and a material group is used instead.

NOTE: *Should you use a rebate agreement that does not use materials as the basis for the rebate, but instead uses, for example, a customer and material group, you would need to define a material the system can use in order to process the relevant credit memo requests. The system would then take all the necessary data from this material for settlement to create the credit memo requests and subsequent credit memo. This ensures the material for settlement has the correct master data maintained for account assignments, tax determinations, and sales details.*

You then save the agreement and create the sales documents for the sold-to party for which rebates are relevant. In the creation of the sales documents, notice the subtotal value used for the rebate basis (see Figure 3-135). This is the subtotal that had the SubTo field value of 7 assigned in the pricing procedure.

After creating and billing the sales documents, you can proceed back to the rebate agreement and select the Display Business Volume button. This displays all the sales orders created for the associated rebate and all relevant rebate basis figures. By ensuring the status indicator is set to the minimum status required for settlement and by selecting the Execute Settlement button, you can automatically create a credit memo request for the rebate settlement. Then proceed in creating the credit memo, as shown in Figure 3-136 with the pricing in Figure 3-137.

Matl f. settl. R-1000

Figure 3-134
The material for settlement setting

Rebate Basis	7.725,00	USD	1	PC	7.725,00	USD	1

Figure 3-135
The subtotal value is used for the rebate basis.

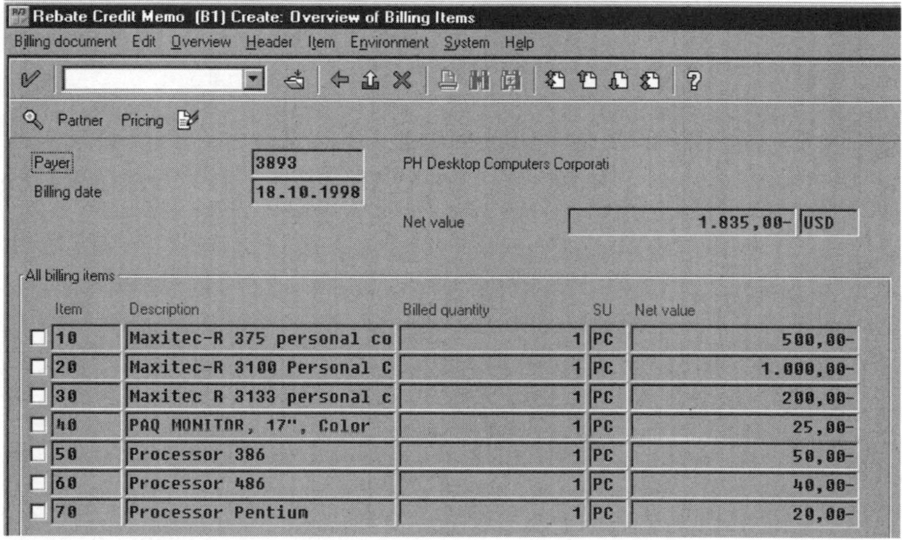

Figure 3-136 Creating the credit memo

Sales | Billing | Financial Accounting | Pricing | Account assignment | Partners | Texts | Purchase order data | Status

Tax 247,73- Net 1.835,00- USD

CnTy	Name	Rate	Curr.	by	UoM	Condition value	Curr.
B002	Material Rebate					1.835,00-	USD
B002	Material Rebate Accr					0,00	USD
UTXJ	Tax Jurisdict.Code					0,00	USD
JR1	Tax Jur Code Level 1					110,10-	USD
JR3	Tax Jur Code Level 3					137,63-	USD

Figure 3-137 Pricing the credit memo

Retroactive Rebate Processing

One can create a rebate agreement with a validity period that has already started. Note that when maintaining a retroactive agreement that the system does not post accruals for billing documents created in the past.

Proceed to *Compare rebate basis and correct accruals* in the IMG. With the report RV15B002, one can check a rebate agreement with regards to the amount due for rebate to the accrual amount posted. These values may differ if one implements rebate processing retrospectively and wants to take into account old billing documents. One can then post a rebate correction request to correct the accruals.

Should one reset rebate processing or alter the pricing procedures, because the subtotals used to calculate the rebate in the billing documents may not be available. If this is the case, you can proceed to *Recalculate subtotals for rebate processing*. This is merely a program RV15B003 that is executed with the selection criteria as the desired billing document number range.

Following this execution of the program, one will need to restructure the billing rebate index. The rebate index is used to settle retroactive rebate agreements. Should you change one of the following determining factors, you will need to restructure the index:

- New rebate relevance of sales organizations
- New rebate relevance of billing types
- New rebate relevance of payers
- Creation or inclusion of new accesses for rebate processing

To recreate the rebate index, proceed to *Create billing index*. Enter the parameters for the desired update, that is, the billing document number range as well as the scheduled run dates. Note that this updates the index of table VBOX, SD Document: Billing Document: Rebate Index. The system uses this index that is updated once the billing document is released to accounting in order to determine all the documents that may be relevant for rebates. The document doesn't need to have a rebate condition at the time of the update.

One can also recreate the setup of statistical data. This is useful if there is an error in the statistical indicator assignments to the customer or material and/or the sales area. Standard SAP uses the information structure S060 for rebates. Proceed to the *Setup of statistical data*.

Intercompany Sales and Business Processing

An intercompany sale transaction occurs when a sale occurs and the selling sales organization belongs to a different company code than that of the delivering plant.

Menu Path

The path here is IMG, Sales and distribution, Billing, Intercompany billing.

An intercompany sale can be best described using Figure 3-138. The customer orders stock from the sales organization, which belongs to a company

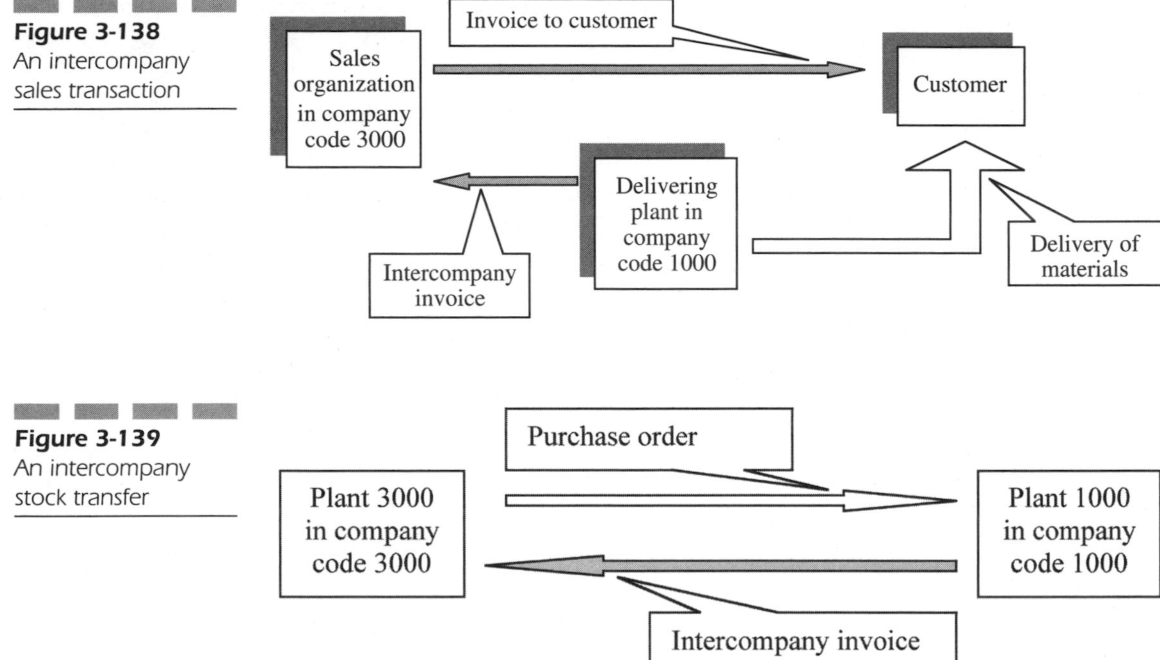

Figure 3-138 *An intercompany sales transaction*

Figure 3-139 *An intercompany stock transfer*

code, such as 3000. The sales organization then creates the sales order and indicates that the delivering plant belongs to a different company code, such as 1000.

The sales organization then invoices the customer for the materials purchased. The system then automatically creates an intercompany billing document at the same time as the customer's billing document is created. This intercompany invoice is sent from the delivering plant to the selling sales organization. This is defined as an *intercompany sales transaction* (see Figure 3-138).

When dealing with different company codes, one may find a need to transfer stock between company codes. Should the stock be transferred within the same company code, there is no need for an intercompany transaction; however, should the stock be transferred between different company codes, a transference of value occurs and is an intercompany sale.

In Figure 3-139, company code 3000, which has plant 3000, creates a purchase order to purchase stock from plant 1000 based in company code 1000. The stock is then delivered to plant 3000. Company code 1000 creates an intercompany invoice and bills company code 3000 for the stock. This process is defined as an *intercompany stock transfer* (see Figure 3-139).

Assigning Order Types for Intercompany Billing

Go to IMG, Sales and distribution, Billing, Intercompany billing, Define order types for intercompany billing. In order for an intercompany sales transaction to be carried out, one needs to define which sales document types can be used in conjunction with intercompany sales. The SAP standard for an intercompany sale billing document type is IV. Thus, should intercompany sales be permitted for sales document type TA, one must assign an intercompany billing type, such as IV, to this sales document.

Assigning Organizational Units by Plant

In this process of assigning organizational units by plant, one assigns a sales area to the delivering plant, as shown in Figure 3-140. A sales area is the combination of a sales organization, distribution channel, and division. The delivering plant then uses this assignment to process the intercompany billing.

Defining the Internal Customer Number by Sales Organization

In this step, one defines the internal customer number that represents the sales organization to be invoiced in intercompany sales processing (see Figure 3-141). This customer number must be created in the system for the sales area specified.

Figure 3-140 Assigning a sales area to the delivering plant

Plnt	Description	SOrg	Sales organization	DstCh	Distrib.channel	Div.	Int.co billing div.
1000	Hamburg	1000	Germany Frankfurt	10	Final customer	00	Cross-division
1100	Berlin	1000	Germany Frankfurt	12	Sold for resale	00	Cross-division
1200	Dresden	1000	Germany Frankfurt	12	Sold for resale	00	Cross-division

Figure 3-141 Defining the internal customer number that represents the sales organization

Sales org.	Sales organization	CustInterC	Cust.inter-co.bill.
3000	USA Philadelphia	3750	New York Plant 3000

For intercompany sales processing to be functional, some master data maintenance must be done. A checklist for intercompany sales processing can be the following:

- The enterprise structure must be maintained correctly; that is, the plants must be assigned to the correct company codes as well as to the correct combination of sales organizations and distribution channels.
- The intercompany customer numbers must be assigned to the relevant sales organizations.
- The delivering plant must be assigned to the sales organization.
- The material to be sold must exist in the original and delivering plant.
- The sales order must be relevant for intercompany sales and have an assigned billing document type.
- The copy control rules must be defined between the standard invoice, such as F2, and the intercompany invoice, such as IV.
- The pricing procedure may have a special condition type assigned to it. This special condition type may represent the price to the intercompany sales organization or it may represent a special discount offered to the intercompany sales organization for the materials sold. The SAP standard system has the following condition types:
- To represent the intercompany price as quantity-dependent
- To represent the intercompany condition as a percentage

Processing an Intercompany Sale

To create an intercompany sales transaction, proceed with creating the standard sales order. In the sales order, change the delivering plant at the line item level and create a delivery for the new shipping point represented for the delivering plant. Proceed with the delivery functions of selecting the packing and posting the goods issue. Then create an external invoice that will be sent to the customer and create an intercompany invoice that will represent the billing document between the delivering plant and the selling sales organization.

An internal intercompany invoice can be created by entering the delivery number again for processing when using transaction [VF01] (Logistics, Sales and distribution, Billing, Billing document, Create). One can also select the documents due for intercompany billing by using the billing due list [VF04] (Logistics, Sales and distribution, Billing, Billing document,

Billing due list). When using the billing due list, be sure to select the intercompany billing documents as the documents to be used (see Figure 3-142).

Intercompany Stock Transfer Orders

Intercompany stock transfer orders are maintained in the system by the materials management module. However, it may be necessary to have an overview of the configuration settings required to maintain this business process. Proceed to IMG, Materials management, Purchasing, Purchase order, Set up stock transport order. You will be faced with an overview screen, as shown in Figure 3-143, where you can proceed with further configurations.

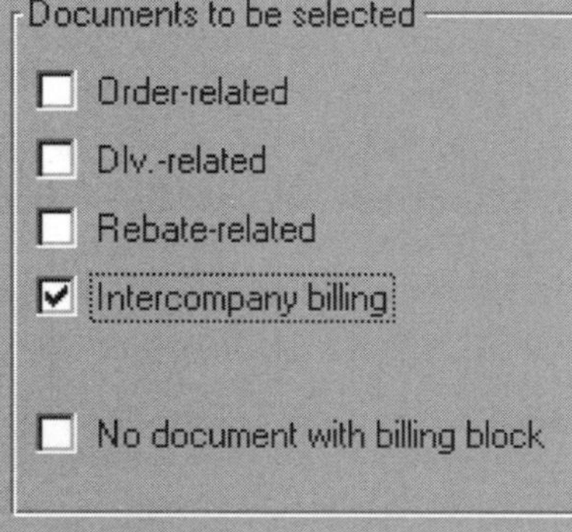

Figure 3-142 Selecting the intercompany billing documents as the documents to be selected

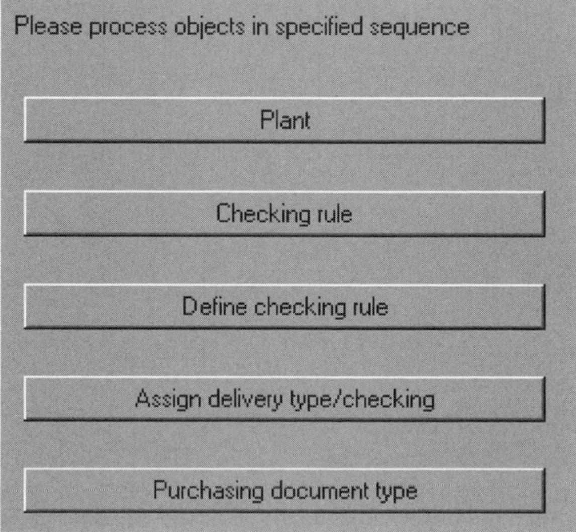

Figure 3-143 Intercompany stock transfer settings within MM

The checking rules have been covered earlier in this chapter. As far as assigning the checking rule to the respective supplying plants and delivery types, this is best left for the materials management team to carry out. We are interested in the assignment of the internal customer number to the plant and the purchasing document type assigned to the respective plants. Select the plant, following by selecting display. One will be faced with the screen shown in Figure 3-144. Assign the customer number representing the plant for the particular sales area. This customer number will be used to represent the plant when an intercompany invoice is created.

Now select the Purchasing document type button in Figure 3-145. This enables you to assign the purchasing document type to the supplying and receiving plants.

The table in Figure 3-146 displays the supplying plant in the initial column, followed by the receiving plant in the adjoining column. The purchasing document type is assigned to this combination. The SAP standard is to use purchasing type UB for stock transport orders. A purchase order is created when the goods movement occurs between plants within the same company code. The SAP standard purchase order document type is NB.

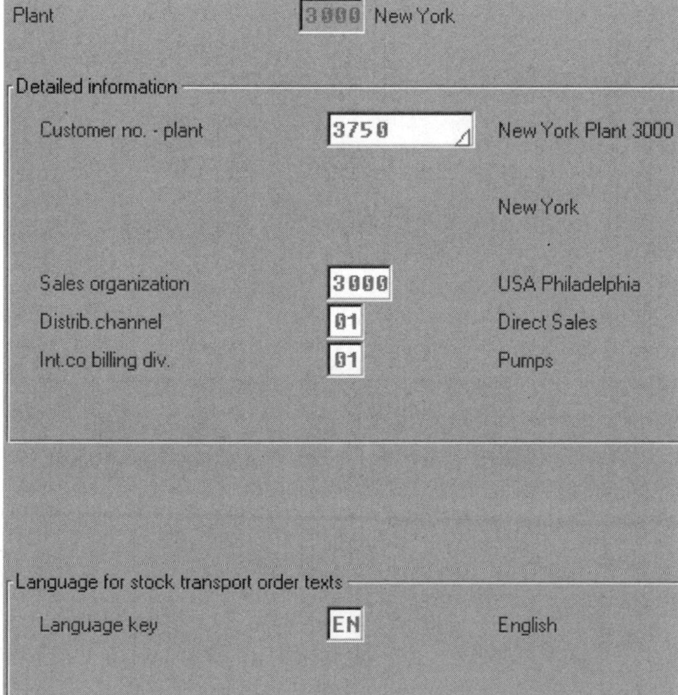

Figure 3-144 Assigning the customer number representing the plant for the sales area

Purchasing document type

Figure 3-145
The Purchasing document type button

Order Types for Stock Transport Order

SPlt	Plnt	Type	One-step
4000	3000	NB	☐
6000	1200	NB	☐
6100	6000	UB	☐
R300	R310	UB	☐
R300	R311	UB	☐

Figure 3-146
Data on the supplying plant and the receiving plant

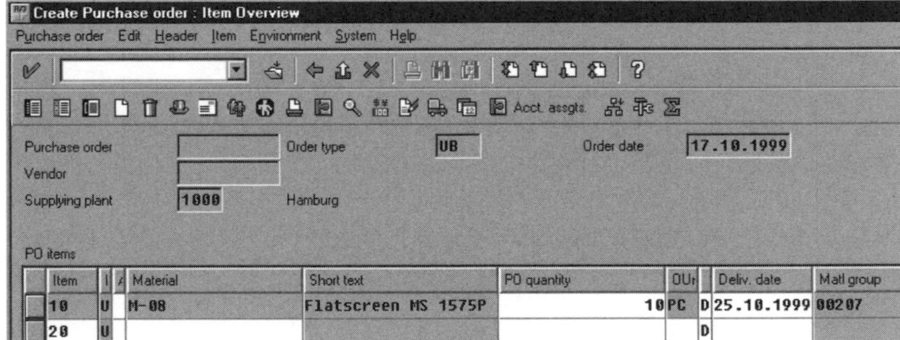

Figure 3-147
Entering the materials and the plant that will receive the items

Processing an Intercompany Stock Transfer Order

Follow the menu path to Logistics, Materials management, Purchasing, Purchase order, Create, Stock transfer [ME27]. Then enter the details of the supplying plant and the organizational data. Press enter and you will be able to enter the materials and the plant that will receive the items (see Figure 3-147). After completion of the stock transfer order, the system process a delivery followed by an intercompany invoice. Do not forget that the material must be created in both sales areas and both plants.

CHAPTER 4

Basic Functions

The Condition Technique as Used in Pricing

The condition technique is the single largest configuration technique used in the *Sales and Distribution* (SD) module. It is used throughout the pricing section. Please refer to the thorough introduction to the condition technique in Chapter 3.

In pricing, a number of alternatives are available to base the price of a product. These alternatives are variables according to specific conditions at the time of the sale. For example, let's say a customer wants to purchase a television. This television has a standard sales price to all customers of $500. However, should the customer be part of a large corporation, a different pricing structure is used, offering lower sales prices, such as $450. This is governed by the condition technique. The condition technique says that if a pricing condition record is found for a particular customer, for example, large corporate customers, they will benefit from a cheaper sales price. However, if no condition record is found, proceed to the next condition, which is merely a standard material price.

What do we know from Chapter 3? We know that a condition record, which is the actual record found on the basis of specific values in fields, is placed in a condition table. The condition table, being the table of fields, is used to find that condition record, and a condition table is placed into an access sequence. An *access sequence* is the sequential placing of condition tables in a logical order to obtain a condition record. An access sequence is assigned to a condition type, and this condition type is placed into a pricing procedure.

In the simple example used above, we could have the following structure:

- A standard **pricing procedure**, such as RVAA01
- Inside this structure, we would have a pricing **condition type** PR00 (the standard price).
- This condition type would use the **access sequence**, PR00 (the standard access sequence for pricing).
- The access sequence would have two steps and **two condition tables** in logical order from the most specific condition to the most general. Thus, the first access would be customer and material, which is the standard condition Table 5. The second condition would be the material only, which uses the standard condition Table 4. (The exclusive indicator is used to ensure no duplicate pricing is carried out. This will be covered later.)
- Two **condition records** would be created, one condition record for the material only and one for the material and customer.

The purpose of this section is to investigate different uses and ensure the optimal performance of condition techniques in pricing.

Menu Path

Starting with the condition types, go to IMG, Sales and Distribution, Basic functions, Pricing, Pricing control, Define condition types.

Transaction Code

The code here is [V/06]. Condition types define pricing elements such as prices, discounts, surcharges, or taxes. They are used in the pricing procedure to define how the condition is going to perform, such as either a percentage or a fixed value. The condition type can be automatic only or it can allow manual changes. By proceeding to "Define condition types," you will find a number of predefined condition types that are standard in the system. Please refer to the following table for a brief example of a few condition types.

Should you want to make any alteration to the condition type or assign a new access sequence to an existing condition type, it is proposed you copy the condition type that represents the nearest outcome you are after and change its key to begin with the letter Z. Then proceed to change the condition type to suit your needs.

There are a number of useful SAP standard condition types you can use to copy from in Table 4-1.

Other condition types are always used, but there is not often a need to copy and alter the condition types, which would fall into the following categories shown in Table 4-2.

The condition types used to determine taxes are country-specific. Thus, I have not selected to display any in the following tables.

For the purpose of this book, we will create a condition type representing a percentage discount from the sales price of a product, based on the sales organization, customer group, and material (this information comes from the sales order). Our access sequence will have a second step of searching for a condition record to offer the discount based on the material only.

We proceed by allocating the closest resemblance to the condition type we are after in the list of standard condition types. This would be the standard condition type K007. In Figure 4-1, you will find the details that define how the condition type is to perform.

Table 4-1

Condition types which are often copied and changed

Condition Type	Description	Condition Class	Calculation Type
BO01	Group rebate	Expense reimbursement	Percentage
BO02	Material rebate	Expense reimbursement	Quantity-dependent
BO03	Customer rebate	Expense reimbursement	Percentage
BO04	Hierarchy rebate	Expense reimbursement	Percentage
HA00	Percentage discount	Discount or surcharge	Percentage
HB00	Discount (value)	Discount or surcharge	Fixed amount
K005	Customer/material	Discount or surcharge	Quantity-dependent
K007	Customer discount	Discount or surcharge	Percentage
KF00	Freight	Discount or surcharge	Gross-weight-dependent
PR00	Price	Prices	Quantity-dependent
R100	100% discount	Discount or surcharge	Percentage
RA00	% discount from Net	Discount or surcharge	Percentage
RA01	% disc. from Gross	Discount or surcharge	Percentage
RB00	Discount (value)	Discount or surcharge	Fixed amount

Table 4-2

Condition types which are not often changed

Condition Type	Description	Condition Class	Calculation Type
EDI1	Cust. expected price	Prices	Quantity-dependent
EDI2	Cust. expected value	Prices	Fixed amount
EK01	Actual costs	Prices	Quantity-dependent
EK02	Calculated costs	Prices	Quantity-dependent
PI01	Intercompany price	Prices	Quantity-dependent
PI02	Intercompany %	Prices	Percentage
VPRS	Cost	Prices	Quantity-dependent
KUMU	Cumulation condition	Discount or surcharge	Formula

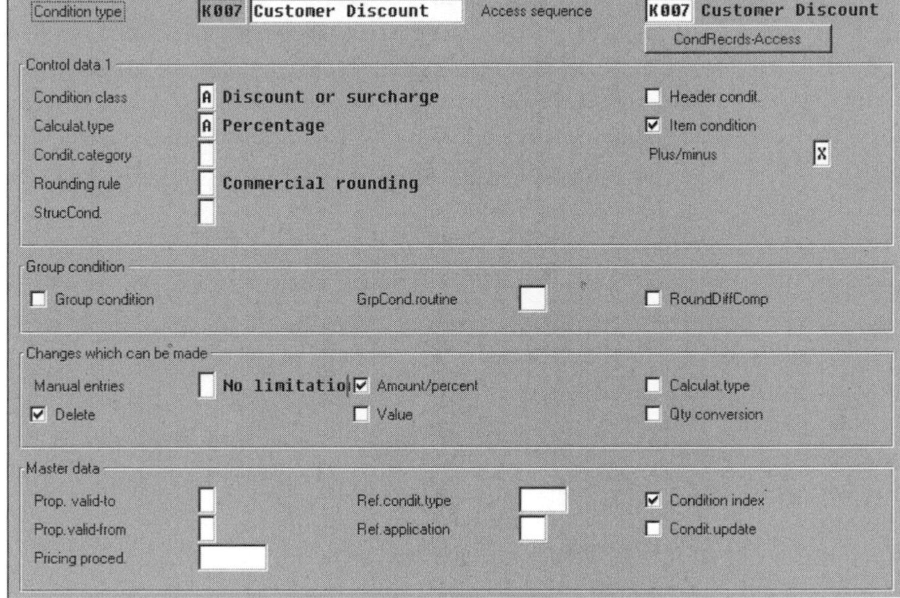

Figure 4-1
Standard Condition type K007

In this figure, we see the condition type is *automatic*; that is, a condition record will be found automatically, if one exists. This is shown by the assignment of an *access sequence*, K007. The *condition class* is A, which determines that the condition type is a discount or surcharge. This condition class is used by the system to determine which conditions it must redetermine and when, for example, a copying rule can indicate that pricing conditions should be copied unchanged and taxes should be redetermined. The system would then use this indicator to determine which conditions are taxes. In copy control pricing, type G is "Copy pricing elements unchanged and redetermine taxes."

The system will redetermine the following condition types:

- Taxes (condition class D)
- Rebate (condition class C)
- Intercompany billing conditions (condition category I)
- Invoice list conditions (condition category R)
- Condition types with condition category L
- Cost conditions (condition category G)
- Cash discount conditions (condition category E)

All other condition types will remain as unchanged.

The *calculation type* is represented by an A. This indicates that the value determined in the condition record will be a percentage. The *condition category* is left blank. This condition category is used by the system to categorize condition types into similar groups, such as all freight or tax conditions. The *rounding rule* is left blank; this indicates the system is to use commercial rounding to find the value of the condition record. The three available rounding rules are

1. **Commercial rounding** A value of less than 5 will be rounded down and a value of greater than or equal to 5 will be rounded up. For example, 10.013 DEM = 10.01 DEM, while 10.019 DEM = 10.02 DEM.
2. **Always round up** The value will always be rounded up, regardless of what the value is. For example, 10.013 DEM = 10.02 DEM and 10.019 DEM = 10.02 DEM.
3. **Always round down** The value will always be rounded down, regardless of what the value is. For example, 10.013 DEM = 10.01 DEM and 10.019 DEM = 10.01 DEM.

The *structured condition* is left blank, which indicates the condition type is not relevant for a cumulation of values of a *bill of materials* (BOM), nor is it relevant to be duplicated across all subitems of a BOM. One then indicates if the condition type is relevant for header pricing or item pricing only. As the K007 discount may be material-specific, the condition should be relevant for the *item level*.

Because the value of the condition record, once it is found, must indicate a discount, we need to indicate that this condition type can only have a negative effect on the price. We assign a X to the *plus/minus* field, indicating that this condition can only result in a minus value from the price. The section on grouped conditions will be covered a little later in this chapter.

Changes which can be made defines what changes are permitted to the condition record. For example, should you allow the condition record of condition type K007 to have its resultant value changed from its initial value according to the condition record, you would set the manual entries to a blank, indicating no limitations, and then indicate that the amount/percent value can be altered. Thus, should the condition record find a discount of 17 percent, one can manually change that value to 20 percent or to 10 percent as the user sees fit.

TIP: *See the section on pricing limits a little later in this chapter.*

Proposed *valid from and to* fields in the condition type indicate the dates when the particular condition type is valid. Note that should you want to limit your price or discount for a specific date range, you can do this at the condition record level [VK11].

If you have more than one condition type that is similar in usage and has the same condition records, yet differs slightly in the description or calculation type, you can set a *reference condition type*. The reference condition type, such as Z007, will indicate that the system is to use the condition records found for Z007 when calculating the conditions of K007. In most instances, however, one would use the same access sequence for the two condition types. Thus, should K007 be similar to Z007, the system can use the same access sequence, K007.

The *scale basis* indicates if the scale is value-based or quantity-based, or if it is based on a formula, as shown in Figure 4-2. *Scale formula* can be utilized by using a routine to determine the scale base value. The *check scale* determines if the scale should always be ascending or descending, or it indicates that the scale is not checked. That is, if it is not checked, the condition scale can be set up to enable the customer to receive a discount of $10 for a purchase of up to 100 items, $20 for a purchase from 101 to 200 items, and $50 for a purchase from 201 to 300 items. The *scale type* is left blank, indicating that the scale can be set up in the condition record. The indicator *currency conversion*, if marked, will cause the system to convert the currency from the condition currency to the document currency after the multiplication of the items. Should the value not be marked, the system converts the currency of the condition into the document currency before multiplying the value for the items.

The date of pricing, that is, the system date that must be used to determine a condition record's validity, must be indicated by the entry in the pricing date. Should you leave this blank, the system will use the standard pricing date KOMK-PRSDT for pricing, but for taxes and rebates, the system will use the date KOMK-FBUDA.

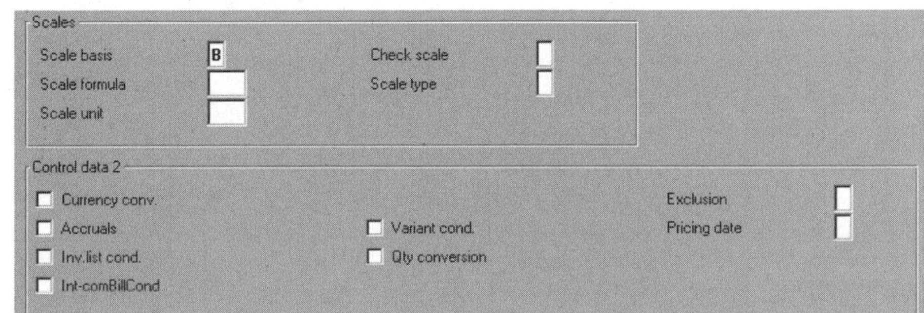

Figure 4-2 Scales and control data of a condition type

Now that we have defined the necessary fields in the condition type, we can copy K007 and change its key to Z007, as shown in Figure 4-3.

We will now create our access sequence. Access sequences should always be maintained from the most specific entry to the most general. Thus, in our example, we will have our first access sequence looking at a condition table that has the sales organization as well as the customer group and material, while the second access will look for a condition based on the material only, as a condition table is placed into an access sequence. We inspect the condition tables first to determine if the two tables we need are in the system.

Menu Path

For condition tables, go to IMG, Sales and Distribution, Basic functions, Pricing, Pricing control, Define price dependencies, Display condition tables.

Transaction Code

The code here is [V/05]. If we use the function key F4, we will be faced with a list of condition tables in which we can see that no condition tables have the fields Sales Organization, Customer Group, and Material. However, there is a standard condition table 004 that we can use for the second step of accessing a record based on the material only. This indicates we will need to create a condition table for our first access. Proceed to Condition, Create. Enter a condition key of three digits with a number above 900. For our example, we will use 901 (see Figure 4-4).

As previously done in Chapter 3, select the fields from the field catalog by double-clicking on them. After you have selected the fields, be sure to give the condition table you are creating a meaningful name, which may assist in quickly identifying the chosen fields later. The final table is shown in Figure 4-5.

Now that we have the two condition tables we will be using in our example, we can define the access sequence.

Figure 4-3
Condition type Z007

Condition type Z007 Customer Discount Access sequence K007 Customer Discount

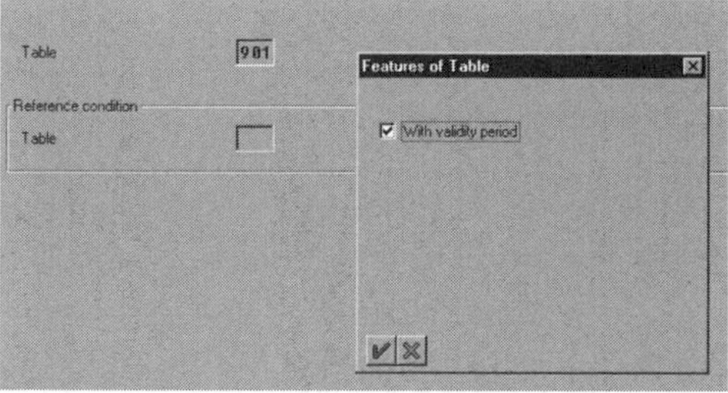

Figure 4-4
Create a condition table for example "901".

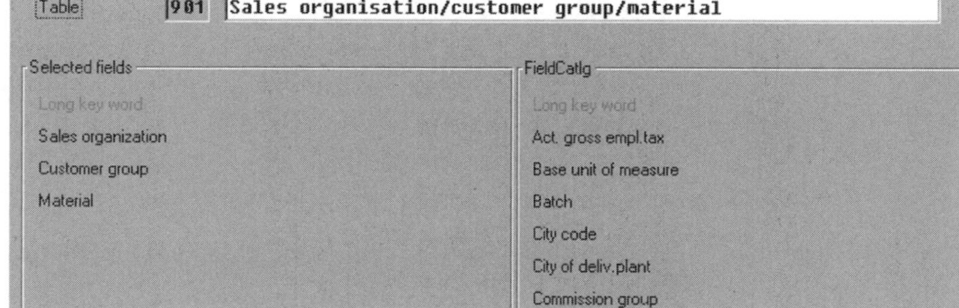

Figure 4-5
Select the fields by double-clicking on the list of available fields on the right.

Menu Path

For access sequences, go to IMG, Sales and Distribution, Basic functions, Pricing, Pricing control, Define access sequences, Maintain access sequences.

Transaction Code

The code here is [V/07]. Again select the access sequence that closely resembles your required access sequence and copy.

TIP: *I find it easier to give the access sequence the same key identification as the condition type to promote ease of use in the system later. Thus, for condition type Z007, we will create an access sequence Z007.*

For the purpose of this example, we will create a new access sequence, Z007. Select the New Entries button and enter the name and description of the access sequence (see Figure 4-6).

Now select the button Accesses. Enter the most specific access table, 901, as access number 10, followed by the next entry of table 004 as access number 20 (see Figure 4-7). Should you want to have a requirement on the access, which must be fulfilled prior to the access being read by the system, you need to enter the requirement in the associated column.

NOTE: *The exclusive indicator should be set. This indicator determines that, if a condition record is successfully found, the system will stop searching for further condition records.*

This access sequence Z007 must now be assigned to the condition type Z007 we created. You can proceed with this by using the transaction code V/06. Now that the condition type is created and the access sequence is created and assigned, we can now assign the condition type to the pricing procedure.

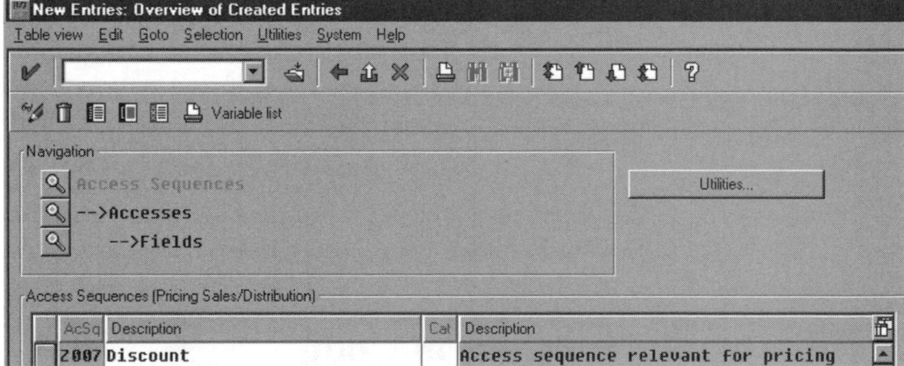

Figure 4-6
Access Sequence—new entries—enter name, Z007

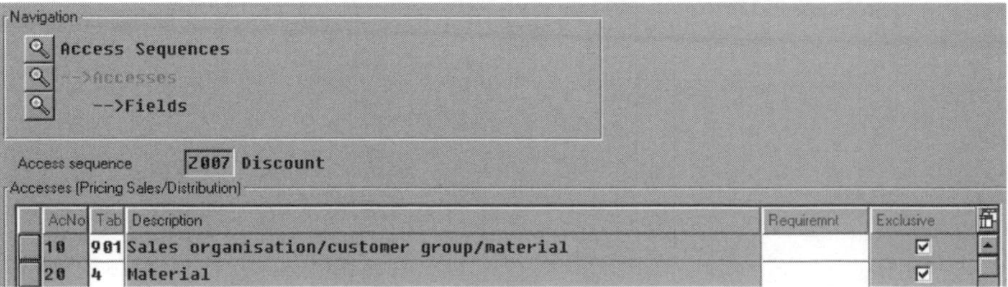

Figure 4-7
After selecting the display accesses button, enter the condition table numbers fom the most specific to the most general.

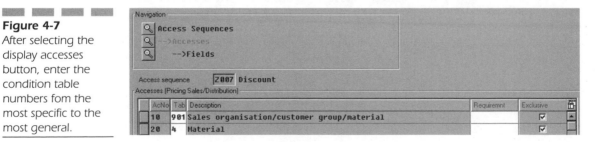

Menu Path

For pricing procedure configuration, go to IMG, Sales and Distribution, Basic functions, Pricing, Pricing control, Define and assign pricing procedures, Maintain pricing procedure.

Transaction code

The code here is [V/08]. The structure of the pricing procedure will be discussed in the section on pricing following this section. However, for the basis of the example we have defined, we will allocate the discount condition type Z007 to a basic pricing procedure consisting of only PR00 (see Figure 4-8).

Before this pricing procedure can be used, one needs to refer to the pricing procedure determination, covered in the next section, to ensure that the combination of sales area, customer *customer pricing procedure* (CuPP), and *document pricing procedure* (DoPP) indicators promote the correct pricing procedure. One must also ensure that the condition records have been maintained correctly. To create a condition record for Z007, proceed as follows: Logistics, Sales and Distribution, Master data, Conditions, Prices, Others, Create (see Figure 4-9).

Figure 4-8 Example pricing procedure

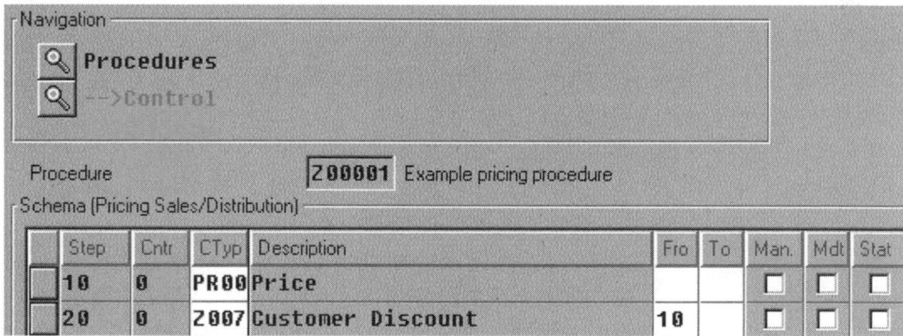

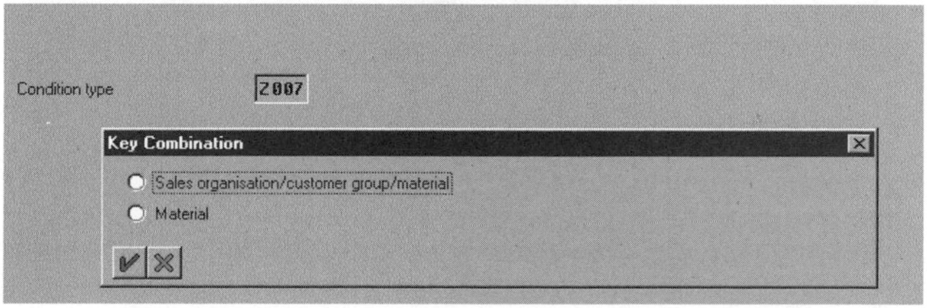

Figure 4-9 Creating a condition record for Z007

Condition type Z007

Key Combination

Sales organisation/customer group/material

Material

For the purpose of our example, we entered a record in sales organization/customer group/material (see Figure 4-10).

We can now create a sales order to see the result of the condition technique in pricing. After creating the sales order, select the line item and select Pricing (see Figure 4-11).

By selecting Analysis, one can see the following data, as in Figure 4-12.

Figure 4-10 Condition record for Sales organization, Customer group and material = 10%–

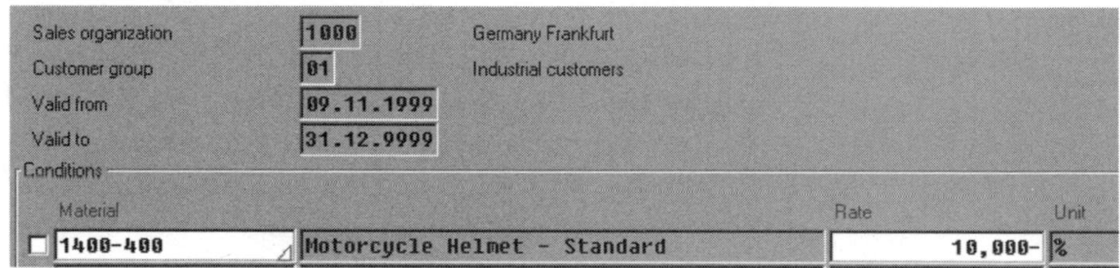

Figure 4-11 Pricing of the line item

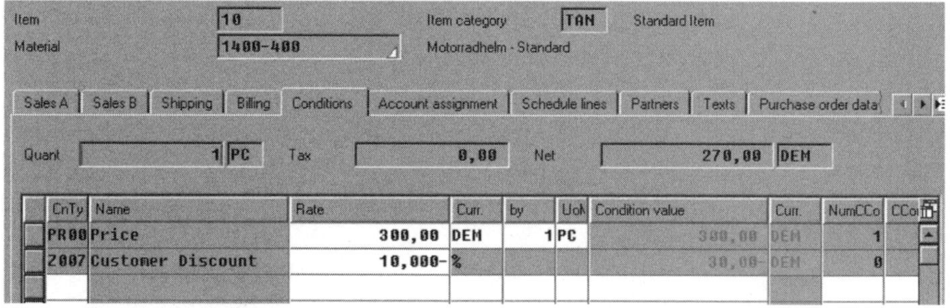

Figure 4-12 Analysis of the Condition type Z007

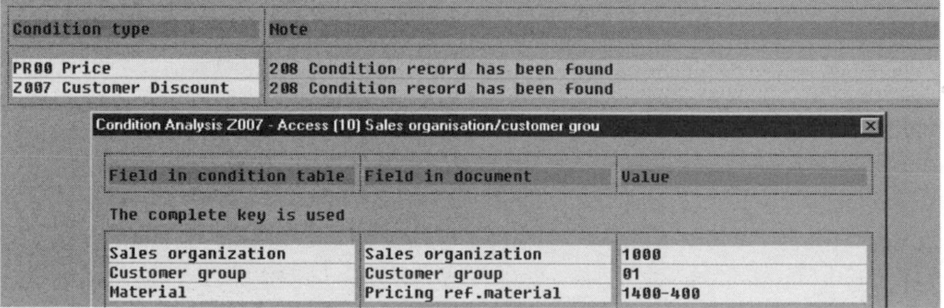

Condition type
Note
PR00 Price
208 Condition record has been found
Z007 Customer Discount
208 Condition record has been found
Condition Analysis Z007 - Access (10) Sales organisation/customer grou
Field in condition table
Field in document
Value
The complete key is used
Sales organization
Sales organization
1000
Customer group
Customer group
01
Material
Pricing ref.material
1400-400

TIP: *Should you create your own access sequences, you may need to initialize the fields of the selected condition table in the newly created access sequence before the system can use the access sequence in pricing. Thus, should you receive an error saying, "no fields exist for access sequence, " this can be fixed by using transaction code V/07 and by selecting the "—> Fields" button, followed by selecting Save.*

Adding Fields to the Field Catalog

When Creating a Condition Table [V/05], one may need additional fields besides what exists in the standard field catalog. As an example, let's say a business no longer wants to have a sales discount based on the sales organization, customer group, and material, but it has decided that the discount should be based on the sales organization, customer group, and ABC indicator of the material master record (this would almost certainly not be the case, as better grouping fields can be used in the material master record, such as material group. I suggest using the ABC indicator field, as it will provide a good example in adding a field to the catalog.) Proceed in checking the field catalog for the particular field, ABC indicator field MAABC. Should it not be in the field catalog, it may be in the list of allowed fields to add into the catalog. The allowed fields can be seen by selecting the downward arrow or in list of available options by pressing F4. Figure 4-13 shows the required field is in the list of available fields to add to the catalog.

If you select the green back arrow, you can click on the button "New entries." You are faced with an empty column. By selecting F4, you can select by double-clicking the field from the list of allowed fields to add to the catalog. Once selected, you can press Save and your field catalog will have the new entry, as shown in Figure 4-14.

One can now create a new condition table, such as 902, with the new field. This can be seen in Figure 4-15.

After adding the table to the access sequence, we will reuse Z007 (where, for the purpose of this example, I removed the previous table 901 from the access sequence and added table 902.) One can save the access sequence, and due to the fact the condition type Z007 is already created, access sequence Z007 is already assigned to it. Condition type Z007 is also already in the basic pricing procedure. We can then proceed straight to creating the necessary condition records, as shown in Figure 4-16.

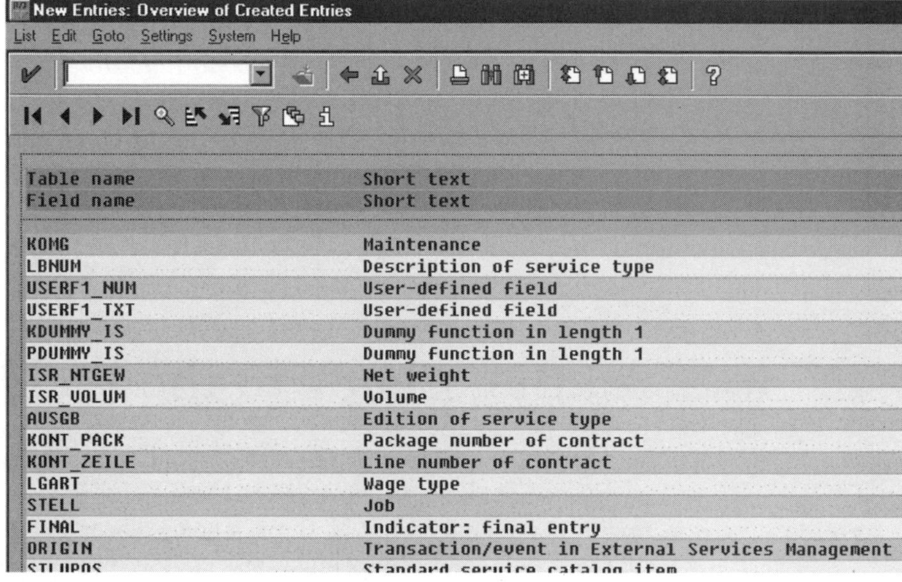

New Entries: Overview of Created Entries

List Edit Goto Settings System Help

Table name Field name	Short text Short text
KOMG	Maintenance
LBNUM	Description of service type
USERF1_NUM	User-defined field
USERF1_TXT	User-defined field
KDUMMY_IS	Dummy function in length 1
PDUMMY_IS	Dummy function in length 1
ISR_NTGEW	Net weight
ISR_VOLUM	Volume
AUSGB	Edition of service type
KONT_PACK	Package number of contract
KONT_ZEILE	Line number of contract
LGART	Wage type
STELL	Job
FINAL	Indicator: final entry
ORIGIN	Transaction/event in External Services Management

Figure 4-13 List of allowed fields to add to the field catalog

Field Catalog (Pricing Sales/Distribution)

Field	Description
RKE_MAABC	ABC indicator
SPART	Division
TAXK1	TaxClass1-Cust.

Figure 4-14 Enter your desired field into the catalog

Condition Edit Goto Environment System Help

Select field Technical view Other description Field attributes...

Table 902 Sales organisation/customer group/ABC indicator

Selected fields	FieldCatlg
Long key word	Long key word
Sales organization	ABC indicator
Customer group	Act. gross empl.tax
ABC indicator	Base unit of measure
	Batch
	City code

Figure 4-15 Create the condition table with the new field

Lastly, ensure the fields in the material master are correctly filled, as in Figure 4-17.

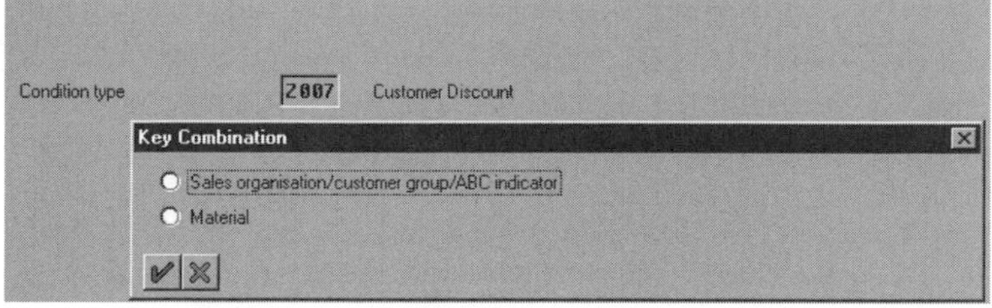

Figure 4-16
Create the condition record

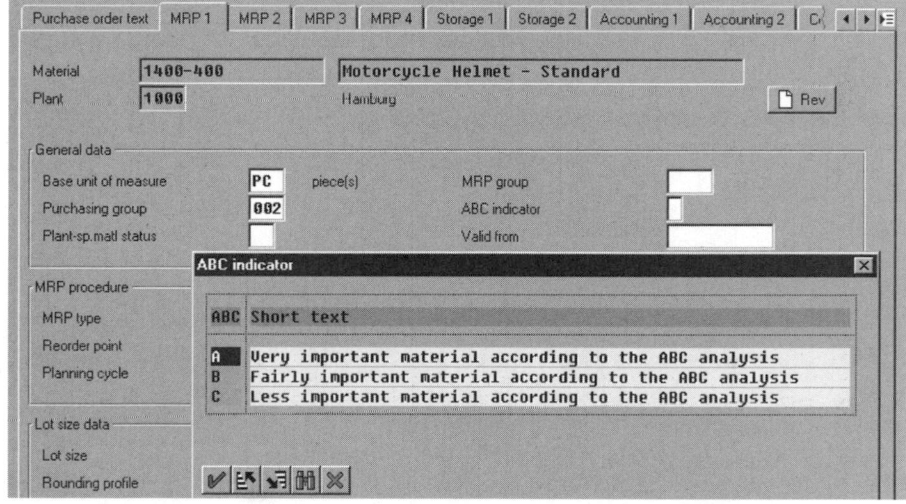

Figure 4-17
Ensure the field "ABC Indicator" has a valid value

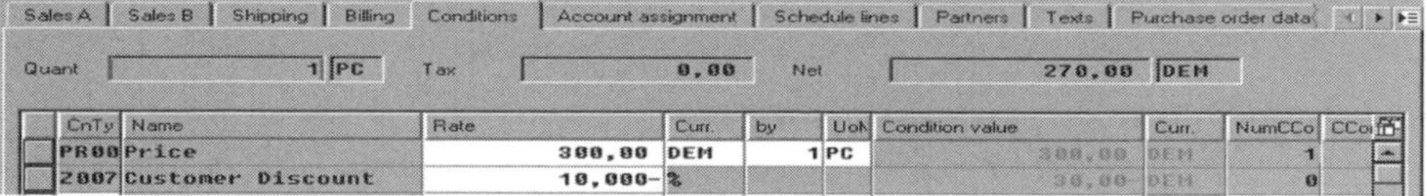

Figure 4-18
Sales order, item pricing

Once the sales order is created, one can now see the discount based on the ABC indicator of the material master record, as in Figure 4-18.

This procedure is fairly simple, as the fields already exist in the list of available fields to be added to the field catalog. Often, however, there may be a need to use a field in the condition technique that is not included in this list of allowed fields. This may be due to the field being newly created. It is possible to add a new field to the list of allowed fields in the field catalog, as this process is slightly more complicated and will be dealt with in Chapter 5, "Cross Functional."

The sequence of creating the discount condition type, which we followed in the example of Z007, is used to assist continuity in thought. However, as in chapter 3, whenever using the condition technique, you may find it easier to use the following sequence when customizing:

1. Put the fields you will need into the field catalog.
2. Create the condition tables.
3. Create the access sequence.
4. Assign the condition tables to the access sequence.
5. Create the condition types.
6. Assign the access sequence to the condition types.
7. Create the determination procedure (if necessary) and assign the condition types to it.
8. Assign the determination procedure.
9. Lastly, create your condition records.

Optimizing Performance in the Condition Technique

Pricing is a function that occurs repeatedly and in great volume. Thus, the maintenance of condition techniques should be strictly governed to ensure the system resources are optimized.

A few tips on ensuring optimal performance in pricing would be the following:

- As standard SAP has pricing procedures with its own pricing condition types, ensure that no unnecessary condition types exist in the pricing procedure. Thus, copy the SAP standard pricing procedure and change it, being sure to delete the unneeded condition types.
- Ensure that only automatic condition types have an associated access sequence, that is, that no manually used condition types have been incorrectly assigned an access sequence that has a resultant condition record that is ignored and overwritten.
- Ensure the access sequence does not have unnecessary access steps. For example, if you have copied a SAP standard access sequence and

the standard has an access searching for "product hierarchy" and you do not use "product hierarchy," be sure to delete the step not required.

- Be sure to use the exclusion indicator in the access sequence, thereby ensuring the system does not search for further condition records after having already found a valid condition record.
- Ensure that the condition table you are using does not have unnecessary searches for fields. For example, if you search for price per material, customer price group, and customer number, you are performing an extra unnecessary step when you should merely search for customer number and material.
- Try to group fields in a condition table by table searched. This will allow the system to not have to fetch and reread tables.
- Be sure to use requirements as much as possible. The higher up in the process, the better. For example, a requirement in the pricing procedure to access a condition type (the highest level) will ensure no unnecessary reading of an access sequence. Thus, no unnecessary reading of all condition tables and all tables and fields in the condition table is carried out. Also, a requirement placed in the access sequence will ensure no unnecessary reading of the access step, and thus no unnecessary reading of all associated tables and fields is carried out.
- Should your business be large enough to warrant it, you may investigate buffering of the prices in your system. This will ensure that all prices are accessed within a faster response time.

TIP: *For further optimization guidelines, you may refer to OSS note 0016430.*

Pricing

Pricing is the combination of creating correct pricing procedures that map the business needs and processes, such as correct pricing and discounting, and keeping to the legal requirements placed on the business, such as adhering to the tax laws of the respective country.

Menu Path

The path here is as follows: IMG, Sales and distribution, Basic functions, Pricing, Pricing control, Define and assign pricing procedures, Maintain pricing procedures.

Transaction Code

The code here is [V/08]. A pricing procedure consists of a list of condition types in a defined order, such as price, less discount, plus tax. Some controls exist in the pricing procedure. For example, you can specify that a condition type is mandatory; it must have an entry defined either automatically or entered manually.

The pricing procedure is also used in account determination. This determines the *general ledger* (GL) accounts to which the prices, discounts, and taxes must be posted. The condition types in the pricing procedure are linked to an account key. This key in turn is linked to the GL accounts. This shows the integration between the pricing in the invoice and the *Financial Accounting* (FI) module.

The SAP standard system includes various standard pricing procedures that can be used as reference models for the pricing procedures you may want to create. It is advisable when creating a pricing procedure to copy a standard, such as RVA001, and then change and delete entries as needed. For the purpose of this book, we will create our own pricing procedure, thus covering as much of this topic as possible.

A pricing procedure is created by selecting new entries and giving the pricing procedure a meaningful key and description. We have already created pricing procedure Z00001. By selecting the pricing procedure and pressing control, you will be faced with an empty structure, as depicted in Figure 4-19.

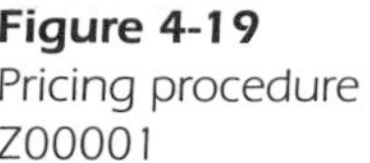

Figure 4-19 Pricing procedure Z00001

You will notice the column *Step*. This indicates the number of the steps in the procedure. For example, the first condition type should be Step 10, the second condition type should be Step 20, and so on. It is possible to number the steps in intervals of 1, but this can make changing the procedure in the future very difficult.

Alongside the column step is the column *Cntr,* the counter. This is used to show a second mini-step within an actual step. For example, you may have all your freight surcharges assigned to Step 100; however, there may be three condition types, each representing a different freight surcharge. Thus, you can assign a freight condition type to Step 100, counter 1; another to step 100, counter 2; another to Step 100, counter 3; and so on.

The column *Ctyp* is the condition type. This is the backbone of the pricing procedure. The condition type is the link from the access sequence all the way to the actual condition record.

When you enter a condition type, the *Description* field is filled automatically with the description from the condition type. If you want to enter a subtotal or total, no condition type applies. In this case, you can enter a description without a condition type, such as net price.

The *Fro* and *To* columns are the From and To columns. These are used in two circumstances:

1. *To define the range for a subtotal* For example, if you want to add up all the condition types from step 10 to 50, you would enter 10 and 50 in the Fro and To columns respectively.
2. *To define the basis for a calculation* For example, if a discount is defined as a percentage, you need to indicate which step must be used as the basis for the calculation. If the calculation must be performed from Step 100, you would enter 100 in the Fro field.

The condition types marked as *statistical* entries affect the pricing procedure in that any entry marked statistical will not be included in the net value calculation for that item. The net value is displayed in the item details of the order and invoice, and the total of all items' net values is displayed on the order and invoice document.

The *Man* column indicates if the condition type it is assigned to is allowed to be processed automatically or only manually.

The *Mdt* column identifies those condition types that are mandatory in the pricing procedure. Mandatory condition types are the sales price or the cost price. Should a mandatory condition not be found in the pricing procedure, the system has an error in pricing and the respective sales order cannot be processed further. No delivery will then be able to be made, for example.

The column *Stat* is used by the pricing procedure to add a value statistically. The value represented in this step will not alter the overall value in the procedure. This can be used to represent the cost price of the material sold.

The thin column that is normally obscured following Stat is labeled *Print*. This column can be made wider, as any of the other columns, by selecting the column-separating line and dragging it wider. This print indicator determines which descriptions and associated values assigned to a step are printed on a document, such as order confirmation.

The *subtotal* field assigns a subtotal key to a step in the pricing procedure. These subtotal fields are then used in other areas of the system, such as in the logistics information system. It is recommended that you assign the subtotal field 4 to the total value in the pricing procedure for Freight.

The column *Reqt* (requirement) is used to assign a requirement to the condition type. This requirement can then be used to exclude the system from accessing the condition type and trying to determine a value. This can be used to specify that the condition type, a discount, should only be accessed if the customer has a low-risk credit group.

The column *AltCty* (alternative calculation type) specifies that the system is to use the formula represented in this column as an alternative in finding the value of the condition type, rather than by using the standard condition technique. This can be used to calculate complex tax scenarios.

The *AltCBV* (alternative condition base value) is a formula assigned to a condition type in order to promote an alternative base value for the calculation of a value. For example, one can specify a formula that uses a subtotal, such as 4, from the Subtotal field, modify it slightly, such as dividing it by 2, and then using the resultant value as a base value for the condition type.

The *ActKey* and *Accrls* (the account key and accruals account keys) are used to assign account keys, which in turn are assigned to GL accounts that are used by the Finance department to register postings.

Now that we know what the columns represent, we need to allocate the condition types for the pricing procedure in the best way possible in order to meet both the needs of the business and the legal requirements. We will create a simple pricing procedure using all the already specified columns.

Start by selecting new entries and enter the price condition type PR00 as Step 10. As this is the price of the item, it should be mandatory, so indicate the condition type as mandatory. As it is quite possible some items are not relevant for pricing, it is advisable to assign a requirement indicating this condition type is not necessary for items not relevant for pricing. This can be done by assigning the requirement 002 to the Reqt column. You can also assign the account key ERL to the Act key column in order to post these values to the revenue account.

Should you not have any further values you want to add to your gross price, you can add a second step, 40 (allow yourself some space between steps at this early stage). In Step 40, do not assign any further condition types, but in the description field, you may specify the description Gross value. In all probability, the customer will want to see this value printed on his documentation; thus, indicate the X in the print column. The gross value may also be used later, so assign the subtotal value 1 in the Sub To column. The initial step in your pricing procedure is shown in Figure 4-20.

TIP: *When using a condition type using condition class B, prices, the system can only use one price per line item. Thus, should the system have a second price in the pricing procedure, it will invalidate all previous pricing conditions. It does not benefit from having more than one price in the pricing procedure.*

Following the pricing procedure, you may want to add extra charges as well as deduct discounts from the value. The discounts we give to the customer should not be deducted from the gross value plus the extra charges. Rather, the discounts offered by most companies are discounts from the gross value with extra charges being added subsequently. For this reason, we now proceed in adding the discount condition types.

Create a Step 50 and assign the newly created discount condition type Z007. Then create a Step 60 and assign another discount condition type, such as K005 (based on the customer and material).

It is possible that you may have a negotiated discount between the sales person and the sold-to party at the time of creating the sales order. For this reason, you may require a manual discount condition type; thus, allocate condition type RB00 to Step 70. For all these steps, the customer would want to see the discount he is obtaining; thus, indicate them relevant for printing. Again, for all these steps, it is advisable to indicate to the system from what value it should offer the discount; thus, specify "40" in the column "from." These condition types are only valid should the item in the sales order be relevant for pricing; thus, assign requirement 002 to the three new discounts. You may assign the GL account key ERS to each condition type.

Figure 4-20
Steps 10 and 40 in pricing procedure Z00001

Procedure Z00001 Example pricing procedure

Schema (Pricing Sales/Distribution)

Step	Cntr	CTyp	Description	Fro	To	Man.	Mdt	Stat	P	SubTo	Reqt	AltCTy	AltCBV	ActKy	Accrls
10	0	PR00	Price			☐	☑	☐			2			ERL	
40	0		Gross value			☐	☐	☐	X	1					

Do not forget condition type RB00 is manual; you should then enable the manual indicator on the pricing procedure. Lastly, one can specify a "total discount" value in Step 100 (again allowing room for further changes). Your pricing procedure should now resemble Figure 4-21.

You can now decide whether the customer should be liable for additional charges such as freight costs. In Step 110, add a condition type KF00 and in Step 120, add HD00. As HD00 is a manual condition type, you should indicate this on the pricing procedure. The values represented by freight should be updated into subtotal field 4 and assign 004 to the Sub To column for both condition types. Both conditions should also be posted to the GL in a specific revenue account for freight. Also assign the conditions the account key ERF. You may now want to have a net value total, so assign the net value description to a new Step 130. This net value should use the net value alternative calculation type 002 as well as subtotal 002. It should also be relevant for printing. Your pricing procedure will now resemble Figure 4-22.

One would now assign the taxes relevant to be levied against the customer and their maintenance will vary from place to place. We will use the basic example of using the condition type MWST to represent our taxes.

Add condition type MWST to Step 140. This condition type is mandatory, so select the mandatory indicator. As the taxes are obtained on the basis of the delivering plant in order to obtain the country delivered from, it is advisable to use the requirement to check if the plant has been maintained in the sales order first. Thus, assign the requirement 010 to Step 140. The

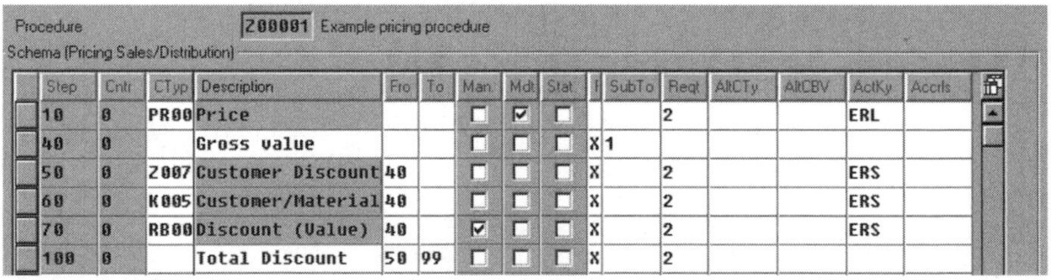

Procedure Z00001 Example pricing procedure

Schema (Pricing Sales/Distribution)

Step	Cntr	CTyp	Description	Fro	To	Man.	Mdt	Stat	P	SubTo	Reqt	AltCTy	AltCBV	ActKy	Accrls
10	0	PR00	Price			☐	☑	☐			2			ERL	
40	0		Gross value			☐	☐	☐	X	1					
50	0	Z007	Customer Discount	40		☐	☐	☐	X		2			ERS	
60	0	K005	Customer/Material	40		☐	☐	☐	X		2			ERS	
70	0	RB00	Discount (Value)	40		☑	☐	☐	X		2			ERS	
100	0		Total Discount	50	99	☐	☐	☐	X		2				

Figure 4-21 Pricing pocedure steps 10 to 100

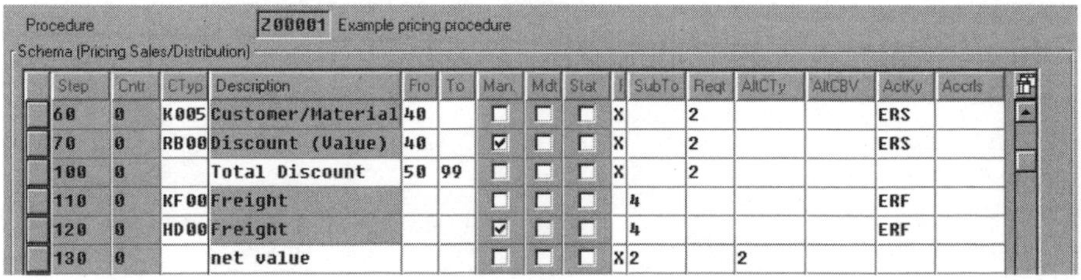

Procedure Z00001 Example pricing procedure

Schema (Pricing Sales/Distribution)

Step	Cntr	CTyp	Description	Fro	To	Man.	Mdt	Stat	P	SubTo	Reqt	AltCTy	AltCBV	ActKy	Accrls
60	0	K005	Customer/Material	40		☐	☐	☐	X		2			ERS	
70	0	RB00	Discount (Value)	40		☑	☐	☐	X		2			ERS	
100	0		Total Discount	50	99	☐	☐	☐	X		2				
110	0	KF00	Freight			☐	☐	☐		4				ERF	
120	0	HD00	Freight			☑	☐	☐		4				ERF	
130	0		net value			☐	☐	☐	X	2		2			

Figure 4-22 Pricing procedure Z00001 up to step 130

alternative condition base value used by the standard system for the MWST is 16. As the revenue for the tax must be posted to a separate GL account, the account key assigned is MWS.

Now that the tax has been added to the net value, the item can now be totaled. Assign a description Total to Step 150 with the subtotal column representing an A, which is the basis for the credit price. The total value can also use the alternative calculation base value of 004, which is the net value plus the tax value.

It is possible you will need to have your cost price represented in the pricing procedure. For this reason, you may enter a Step 160 and assign the VPRS condition type to this step, but do not forget to assign the statistical indicator to this step. This value can be passed into the subtotal column B, which represents the cost price. The standard system has the requirement 004 assigned to the cost price.

The profit margin can now be added in line 170. Add a description "Profit margin" and merely assign alternative calculation type 011 to this step. This alternative calculation type takes the net value and deducts the cost price to determine the profit margin. Your pricing procedure should now look similar to Figure 4-23.

The pricing procedure is now complete. After completing the determination procedures that follow, one can find the pricing procedure after creating a sales order to represent Figures 4–24a and 4–24b.

Here are a few reminders about setting up a pricing procedure:

- *Credit management* The system uses the value as stored in the subtotal A. This will store the value in a special field KOMP-CMPRE (item credit price). Thus, ensure subtotal A is assigned in the correct place in the pricing procedure, usually the net value.
- *Payment terms* Generate a discount if the due amount is paid before a specific date. This is automatically used by the system and requires the condition type SKTV to be in the pricing procedure.

Figure 4-23 Pricing procedure Z00001 up to step 170

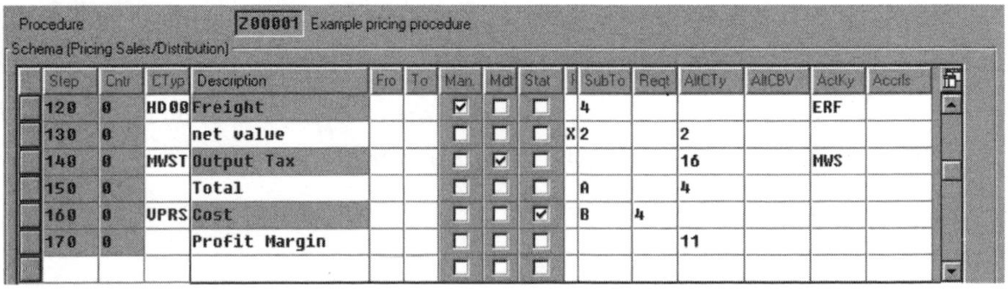

Procedure Z00001 Example pricing procedure

Schema (Pricing Sales/Distribution)

Step	Cntr	CTyp	Description	Fro	To	Man.	Mdt	Stat	P	SubTo	Reqt	AltCTy	AltCBV	ActKy	Accrls
120	0	HD00	Freight			☑	☐	☐		4				ERF	
130	0		net value			☐	☐	☐	X	2		2			
140	0	MWST	Output Tax			☐	☑	☐				16		MWS	
150	0		Total			☐	☐	☐		A		4			
160	0	UPRS	Cost			☐	☐	☑		B	4				
170	0		Profit Margin			☐	☐	☐				11			
						☐	☐	☐							

Figure 4-24a Sales order pricing screen, steps 10–140

Quant 1 PC | Tax 46,80 | Net 312,00 DEM

CnTy	Name	Rate	Curr.	by	Uo	Condition value	Curr.	NumCCo	CCo
PR00	Price	300,00	DEM	1	PC	300,00	DEM	1	
	Gross value	300,00	DEM	1	PC	300,00	DEM	1	
Z007	Customer Discount	10,000-	%			30,00-	DEM	0	
K005	Customer/Material	10,00-	DEM	1	PC	10,00-	DEM	1	
RB00	Discount (Value)	5,00-	DEM			5,00-	DEM	0	
	Total Discount	45,00-	DEM	1	PC	45,00-	DEM	1	
KF00	Freight	7,00	DEM	1	KG	21,00	DEM	1	
HD00	Freight	12,00	DEM	1	KG	36,00	DEM	1	
	net value	312,00	DEM	1	PC	312,00	DEM	1	
MWST	Output Tax	15,000	%			46,80	DEM	0	
	Total	358,80	DEM	1	PC	358,80	DEM	1	

Figure 4-24b Sales order pricing screen, steps 150–170

Quant 1 PC | Tax 46,80 | Net 312,00 DEM

CnTy	Name	Rate	Curr.	by	Uo	Condition value	Curr.	NumCCo	CCo
	Total	358,80	DEM	1	PC	358,80	DEM	1	
VPRS	Cost	45,00	DEM	1	PC	45,00	DEM	1	
	Profit Margin	267,00	DEM	1	PC	267,00	DEM	1	

- *Cost of sales* The system automatically uses condition type VPRS as the condition to represent cost.
- *Rebate* The Rebate condition types are determined if a valid rebate agreement for the material has been created for the customer. The rebates configuration would need to be done and a rebate agreement created for the customer.

SAP will use the rebate agreement to calculate an expected amount that this sale will contribute to the customer's rebate. Accruals can be posted to the GL using these amounts. In this case, the accrual account key ERU must be set up.

NOTE: *Rebate condition types must be defined as expense reimbursements in the condition type record, so that they are not included in the net value.*

Pricing Procedure Determination

The pricing procedure is allocated to the sales document or billing document by a determination rule, similar to other determination rules. The pricing procedure determination is based on the customer master record, the sales document, and the sales area.

Menu Path

Before one can proceed with the determination rules, one needs to maintain the *customer pricing procedure* (CuPP) indicator. This can be done by proceeding to the following menu path: IMG, Sales and distribution, Basic functions, Pricing, Pricing control, Define and assign pricing procedures, Define customer determination procedure.

Transaction Code

The code here is [OVKP]. In this step, one needs to assign a single character alphanumeric key with a short description, as shown in Figure 4-25.

Menu Path

Now one can proceed to define a similar single character alphanumeric key with a short description to represent the document type. The menu path is as follows: IMG, Sales and distribution, Basic functions, Pricing, Pricing control, Define and assign pricing procedures, Define document determination procedure.

Figure 4-25
Customer pricing procedure indicator

CuPP	Description
1	Standard
2	Stand.incl.Sales Ta
3	International
4	MT
Z	Example

Figure 4-26 Document pricing procedure indicator

DoPr	Description
A	Standard
B	Plants Abroad
C	Free
I	IB Sales
L	Subcontracting

Transaction Code

The code here is [OVKI] (see Figure 4-26). Simply copy or create your own DoPP indicator as required.

After the DoPP indicator has been created, one must assign it to the sales document types. This will ensure that, for example, all sales orders created using a standard sales order type TA, which has been assigned a DoPP of 1, will all use the same pricing procedures if created in the same sales area and with the same CuPP. In some instances, you may not want to have the same pricing procedure for a sales document as you may want in a billing document. For this reason, you may allocate a different DoPP to a billing document. Don't forget to assign the CuPP indicator to your customer master record in the sales screen.

Menu Path

To assign these DoPP indicators to the sales documents, proceed as follows: IMG, Sales and distribution, Basic functions, Pricing, Pricing control, Define and assign pricing procedures, Assign document pricing procedure to order types.

Transaction Code

The code here is [OVKJ] for order types.

Menu Path

To assign these DoPP indicators to the billing documents, proceed as follows: IMG, Sales and distribution, Basic functions, Pricing, Pricing control, Define and assign pricing procedures, Document pricing procedure—assign billing types.

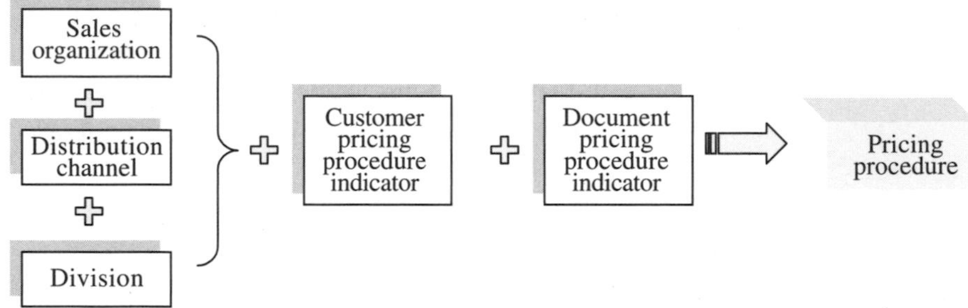

Figure 4-27 Pricing procedure determination

Figure 4-28 Pricing procedure determination

SOrg.	DChl	Dv	DoPr	CuPP	PriPr.	Pricing procedure	CnTy	Condition type
0001	01	01	A	1	RVAA01	Standard	PR00	Price
0001	01	01	A	2	RVAB01	Tax Included in Price	PR01	Price incl.Sales Tax
0001	01	01	C	1	RVCA01	Standard - Free with F		
0001	01	01	C	2	RVCA02	Standard - Free w/out		
0001	01	01	P	1	RVPS01	PS: Order, billing doc		
0001	01	01	P	2	RVPS01	PS: Order, billing doc		
0001	01	01	V	1	PSER01	Periodic Billing	PPSV	Service Price Item
0001	01	01	V	2	PSER01	Periodic Billing	PPSV	Service Price Item

Transaction Code

The code here is [OVTP] for billing types. Once this data has been maintained, the determination rules can be laid out. The pricing procedure determination is as stated in Figure 4-27.

Thus, assign your pricing procedure to the combination of sales area as well as CuPP and DoPP (see Figure 4-28).

Pricing Limits

Condition types offer an automatic or manually determined value according to their determination. Condition types can also be manually altered, enabling the user the opportunity to overcharge or undercharge a customer. For example, should we have a discount and do not govern its limit, the user may incorrectly offer a 100 percent reduction. For this reason, we govern the condition type with a limit.

Menu Path

The path here is IMG, Sales and distribution, Basic functions, Pricing, Pricing control, Define condition types, Define upper and lower limits for conditions.

Transaction Code

The code here is [OVB2]. As we can see in Figure 4-29, should one have a condition type that can be altered manually in the sales document, one needs to ensure that there is no room left for abuse. In our example, we have added condition type K005, which is the customer- and material-based discount. This discount in Figure 4-29 has a upper limit of 1 DEM and a lower limit of 10 DEM. Thus, the user is unable to offer a discount lower than 10 DEM.

NOTE: *The condition type's calculation type controls the calculation type of the limit. Thus, should the calculation type for the condition be a percentage, the limit will also be based in percentage terms.*

TIP: *It is often better to keep discounts percentage-based, as these discounts are easier to maintain. For example, governing a value-based condition type with a limit does not take into account the volume of items purchased in the sale. However, placing a five percent limit on the discount will remain in proportion regardless of the quantity purchased.*

If you have a maximum surcharge on freight, for example, regardless of the quantity purchased, it would obviously be better to use a fixed value as the basis for the condition type, and thus the basis for the limit. Should the user try to create a condition that falls outside of the limited range, he will receive an error, as in Figure 4-30.

Figure 4-29
Condition type limit

Variable list

CTyp	Condition type	CalTy	Unit	Lower limit	Upper limit	by	UoM
K005	Customer/Material	C	DEM	10,00-	1,00-	1	PC

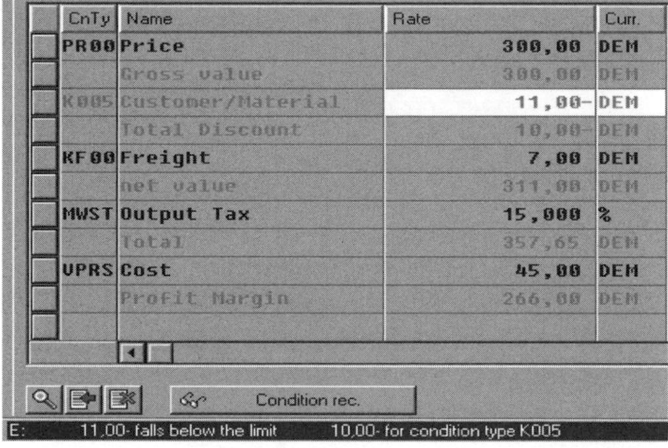

Figure 4-30
The error received in a sales order—should a condition record fall out of a range for a limit

Define Pricing by Item Category

Here you can define per item category if the item in the sales order is relevant for pricing, statistics, and costing.

Menu Path

The path here is IMG, Sales and distribution, Basic functions, Pricing, Pricing control, Define pricing by item category, Activate pricing for item categories.

Transaction Code

The code here is [OVK0]. You are faced with a table as in Figure 4-31. For each item category, you can define if the item should be relevant for pricing. Should the items not be relevant for pricing, these items can be indicated with a blank. Should standard pricing be carried out for the item, you can indicate these item categories with an X. The statistical value column adjoining the pricing column represents if the item must be used for statistical purposes, that is, in updating the logistics information system (sales information systems and so on). An blank entry indicates that the item is relevant for statistics updating and the value of the item will be added to the header totals. Items that would not be relevant for pricing would be text items.

Figure 4-31 Define pricing per item category

ItemCat	Description	Pricing	Statistical value
0001	Requisition		
AFC	Configuration	X	
AFN	Inquiry Item	X	
AFNN	Free of Charge Item		
AFX	Inquiry Item	X	

Figure 4-32 Determine cost per item category

ItCa	Description	Prcg.	DCost
0001	Requisition		
AFC	Configuration	X	X
AFN	Inquiry Item	X	X
AFNN	Free of Charge Item		X
AFTX	Text Item		
AFX	Inquiry Item	X	

Menu Path

To activate cost determination for item categories, proceed as follows: IMG, Sales and distribution, Basic functions, Pricing, Pricing control, Define pricing by item category, Activate cost determination for item categories.

Transaction Code

The code here is [OVKL]. By referring to Figure 4-32, you can determine if pricing is carried out for the particular item category while determining if the item should be relevant for cost determination. If you want the cost of the item to be determined, you must indicate that the item is relevant with an X.

TIP: *The cost of the item will only be available should you have a condition type in the pricing procedure that determines cost, such as the SAP standard condition type VPRS. The cost of the item is taken automatically by the system from the fixed cost price of the material in the material master record. Should the material not have a fixed cost, the system will then take the cost price from the moving average price in the purchase information record.*

The purchase information record, however, belongs to the Materials Management module. Thus, we will not be covering it, other than to say that if you want to access one, use the following transaction code [ME13] or go to Logistics, Materials management, Purchasing, Master data, Info record, Display.

TIP: *Do not forget to use the OSS note 0024832, as discussed in copying rules in Chapter 2, which outlines condition types that are redetermined according to the pricing type in copying.*

TIP: *For the same reason, if the condition type in the pricing analysis says in a billing document that the "condition is found and set," and one is using the condition requirement number 024 (which only determines the price in billing document) yet still has to do new pricing in order to obtain the condition record, the fault would be that the condition category on the condition type should be equal to L.*

That way, when copying into a billing document, the requirement says "proceed with determining the value for the condition type" and the system does new pricing for that condition record due to the category being an L and thus finds a record. Should the condition category be blank, the system would propose the message "condition is found and set" but does not provide an actual condition record.

Condition Exclusion Groups

It is quite possible that you may have more than one condition type in your pricing procedure offering a discount to a customer. Should the discounts be automatically determined, there is the risk that the customer will receive all the relevant discounts and thus purchase the product lower than he should. By using condition exclusion groups, you can ensure the customer does not receive all discounts, but instead only receives, for example (the best of the four discount condition types).

Menu Path

The path here is IMG, Sales and distribution, Basic functions, Pricing, Pricing control, Condition exclusion, Condition exclusion for groups of conditions, Define condition exclusion groups.

Transaction Code

The code here is [OV31]. A condition exclusion group is merely a grouping of condition types that are compared to each other during pricing and result in the exclusion of particular condition types within a group or entire groups.

There are four possible methods of using the condition exclusion groups:

- Selection of the most (or least) favorable condition type within a condition exclusion group
- Selection of the most (or least) favorable condition record of a condition type, if more valid condition records exist (such as selection from different condition records of the condition type PR00)
- Selection of the most (or least) favorable of the two condition exclusion groups (in this case, all condition types of the two groups are cumulated and the totals are compared)
- An exclusion procedure in which if a condition type in the first group exists in the document, all condition types in the second group are set to inactive

We will use the example of the most (or least) favorable condition type within a condition exclusion group as an example, using the two discount condition types K005 and our created Z007. Thus, we will place both these condition types in an exclusion group.

Proceed by defining an exclusion group by using a four-character alphanumeric key. In our example, we will call our group Z100 (see Figure 4-33).

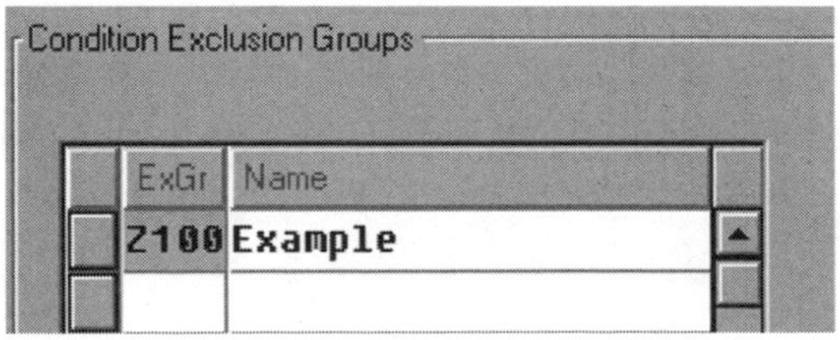

Figure 4-33
Condition Exclusion Group

Menu Path

One now proceeds to assign the condition types to the exclusion group. Go to IMG, Sales and distribution, Basic functions, Pricing, Pricing control, Condition exclusion, Condition exclusion for groups of conditions, Assign condition types to the exclusion groups.

Transaction Code

The code here is [OV32]. As in Figure 4-34, assign the relevant condition types to the condition exclusion group.

Menu Path

After completing the assignment of the condition types to the exclusion group, proceed with assigning the condition exclusion group to the pricing procedure as follows: IMG, Sales and distribution, Basic functions, Pricing, Pricing control, Condition exclusion, Condition exclusion for groups of conditions, Maintain condition exclusion for pricing procedures.

Transaction Code

The code here is [VOK8]. After selecting the pricing procedure for which you want the condition exclusion to be active, select the button "—> Exclusion." This will take you to Figure 4-35.

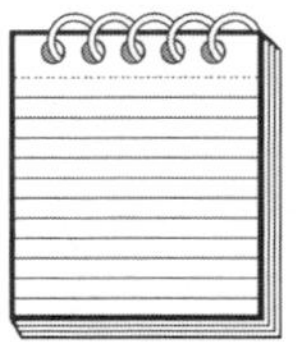

NOTE: *Do not forget the condition types that you want the system to compare must exist in the pricing procedure and have valid condition records created for them.*

ExGr	Cond.exclusion group	CTyp	Condition type
Z100	Example	K005	Customer/Material
Z100	Example	Z007	Customer Discount

Figure 4-34
Assign the condition types to the Condition exclusion group

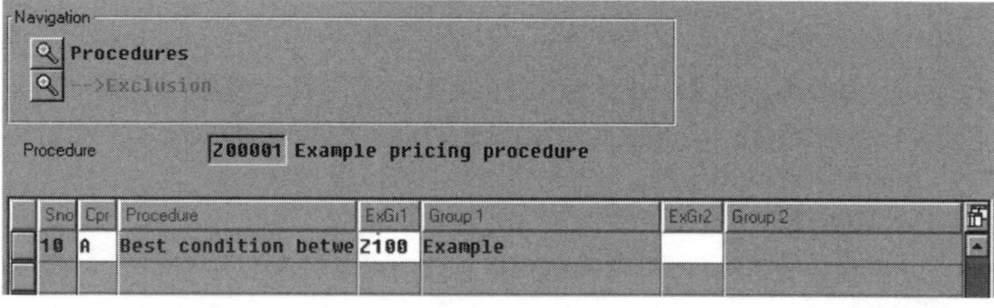

Figure 4-35 Assign the condition exclusion group to the pricing procedure

Sales A | Sales B | Shipping | Billing | Conditions | Account assignment | Schedule lines | Partners | Texts | Purchase order data

Quant 1 PC   Tax 43,65   Net 291,00 DEM

CnTy	Name	Rate	Curr.	by	UoM	Condition value	Curr.	NumCCo
PR00	Price	300,00	DEM	1	PC	300,00	DEM	1
	Gross value	300,00	DEM	1	PC	300,00	DEM	1
Z007	Customer Discount	10,000-	%			30,00-	DEM	0
K005	Customer/Material	10,00-	DEM	1	PC	10,00-	DEM	1
	Total Discount	30,00-	DEM	1	PC	30,00-	DEM	1

Figure 4-36 Condition type Z007 offers a 30 DEM discount whilst K005 offers a 10 DEM discount

If you now create a sales order using the same pricing procedure that the exclusion group is assigned to, you will find that the condition offering the most favorable discount to the customer is represented in the pricing procedure (see Figure 4-36).

One can see in Figure 4-36 that the condition type Z007 has offered a discount of 10 percent off the sale price or a real value of 30 DEM, while condition type K005 has offered a real value discount of 10 DEM. The system then takes the best discount for the customer between the two, which is Z007, and makes the other discount, K005, inactive. This can be seen by double-clicking on K005. You will then be faced with the screen in Figure 4-37. Note the entry "Inactive A condition exclusion item."

It is possible to see the advantages of the exclusion groups in the previous example. Imagine the product has a lower sales price of, say, 90 DEM per item. The result would be that condition type Z007 offers a 10 percent discount, which is a real value of DEM, while K005 still offers a discount of 10 DEM. In this case, Z007 would be inactive and the system would use K005.

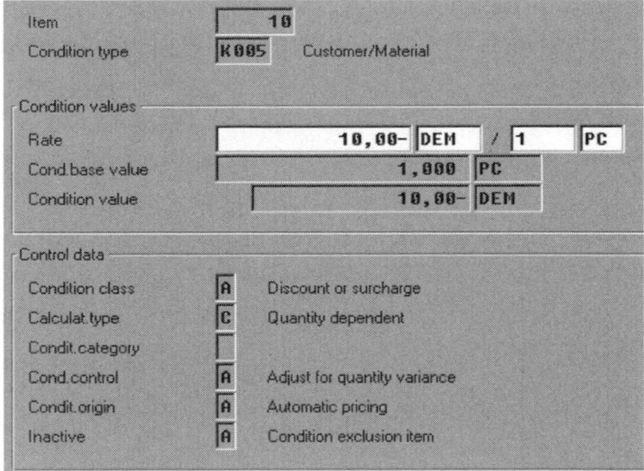

Figure 4-37 Condition type K005 is inactive.

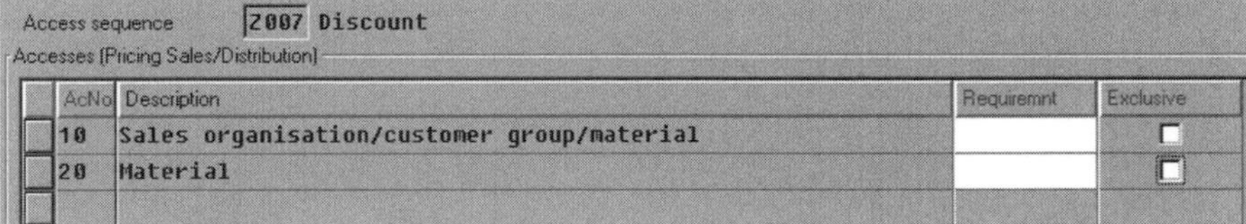

Figure 4-38 The Exclusive indicator on Z007 is unchecked.

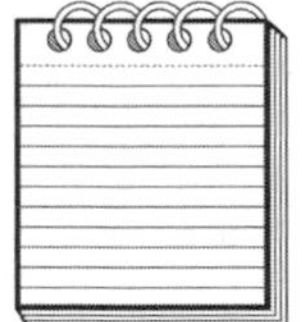

NOTE: *When using the best condition record within a condition type, only use one condition type in the exclusion group. Also note that you must deactivate the Exclusive indicator on the access sequence assigned to that condition type. Otherwise, the system will merely find the first condition record and stop searching for other records.*

For example, we will modify the already-created condition exclusion group Z100 in order so that the only valid condition type assigned to it will be our discount condition type of Z007. After removing the exclusive indicators from Z007, the access sequence is as follows in Figure 4-38.

If the standard determination uses the condition technique, should the exclusion indicators be set, the system will find a record for the first access and not proceed further. However, should one set the condition type in the exclusion group as Z007 only, and set the search of the exclusion, as in Figure 4-39, to the the best record within a condition type, the result would be as follows in Figure 4-40.

In Figure 4-40, we can see the system has found both records, but the initial record of 10 percent deduction for Z007 has been set as inactive. Instead, the system uses the record of 15 percent deduction. The condition type K005 is still active, as it is no longer part of a condition exclusion group, but merely part of the standard pricing procedure.

NOTE: *If the exclusive indicators are not set, but condition record exists for the condition tables in the access sequence, and no condition exclusion group exists for the condition type, the system will bring all valid condition records into the sales document, such as in Figure 4-41.*

Procedure Z00001 Example pricing procedure

Sno	Cpr	Procedure	ExGr1	Group 1	ExGr2	Group 2
10	B	Best condition withi	Z100	Example		

Figure 4-39
Exclusion indicator now searches for the best record within a condition type.

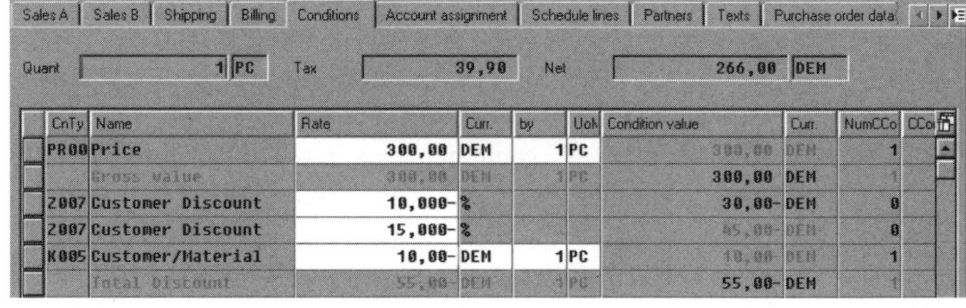

Sales A | Sales B | Shipping | Billing | Conditions | Account assignment | Schedule lines | Partners | Texts | Purchase order data

Quant 1 PC Tax 39,90 Net 266,00 DEM

CnTy	Name	Rate	Curr.	by	UoM	Condition value	Curr.	NumCCo	CCo
PR00	Price	300,00	DEM	1	PC	300,00	DEM	1	
	Gross value	300,00	DEM	1	PC	300,00	DEM	1	
Z007	Customer Discount	10,000-	%			30,00-	DEM	0	
Z007	Customer Discount	15,000-	%			45,00-	DEM	0	
K005	Customer/Material	10,00-	DEM	1	PC	10,00-	DEM	1	
	Total Discount	55,00-	DEM	1	PC	55,00-	DEM	1	

Figure 4-40
The second condition record for Z007 is used now offering a discount of 45 DEM.

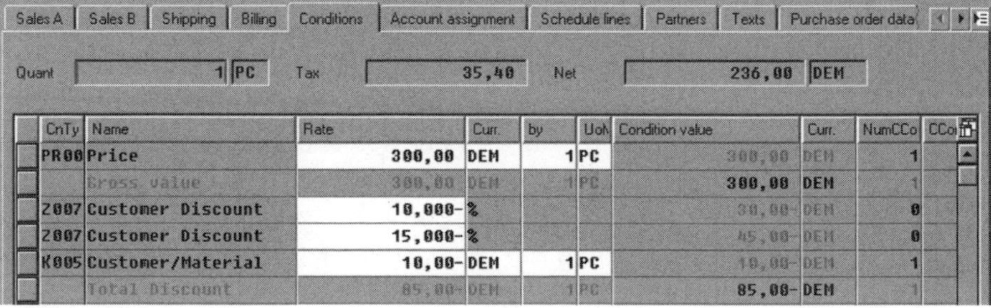

Sales A | Sales B | Shipping | Billing | Conditions | Account assignment | Schedule lines | Partners | Texts | Purchase order data

Quant 1 PC Tax 35,40 Net 236,00 DEM

CnTy	Name	Rate	Curr.	by	UoM	Condition value	Curr.	NumCCo	CCo
PR00	Price	300,00	DEM	1	PC	300,00	DEM	1	
	Gross value	300,00	DEM	1	PC	300,00	DEM	1	
Z007	Customer Discount	10,000-	%			30,00-	DEM	0	
Z007	Customer Discount	15,000-	%			45,00-	DEM	0	
K005	Customer/Material	10,00-	DEM	1	PC	10,00-	DEM	1	
	Total Discount	85,00-	DEM	1	PC	85,00-	DEM	1	

Figure 4-41
All valid condition records are found.

Price-Relevant Master Data

Due to the many different requirements in business for pricing and the complexities of these requirements, SAP has a number of fields by which one can group both customers and materials. These additional groups are the customer price list type, the customer pricing group, and the material group. One can use these groups as key fields in condition tables. All resale prices, that is, condition type PR00, can be based on the customer price list type.

Menu Path

The path here is IMG, Sales and distribution, Basic functions, Pricing, Maintain price relevant master data fields, Define price list types for customers.

Transaction Code

The code here is [OVSI]. Create your customer price list type to meet the business requirements by entering a two-character field and a short description, such as in Figure 4-42.

After the creation of the data that fills this field, one can assign the newly created data to the customer master record in the Sales area view, as in Figure 4-43.

Menu Path

To create the data for the customer pricing group, you can proceed as follows: IMG, Sales and distribution, Basic functions, Pricing, Maintain price relevant master data fields, Define pricing groups for customers.

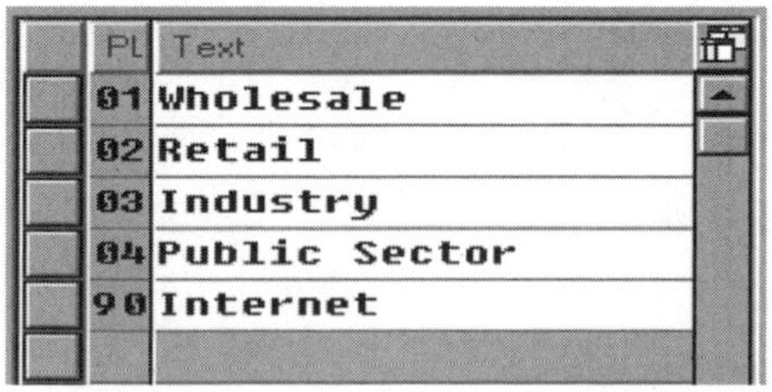

Figure 4-42
Customer price list type

PL	Text
01	Wholesale
02	Retail
03	Industry
04	Public Sector
90	Internet

Transaction Code

The code here is [OVSL]. As in Figure 4-44, you can define your pricing groups with a two-character key and a short description. After the creation of the group, you can assign the data again to the sales view of the customer master, as in Figure 4-43.

Menu Path

To proceed with the definition of the material group, proceed as follows: IMG, Sales and distribution, Basic functions, Pricing, Maintain price-relevant master data fields, Define material groups.

Transaction Code

The code here is [OVSJ].

As shown in Figure 4-45, assign the two-character key a short description. Then proceed to assign this data to the Sales Organization 2 view of the material master records (see Figure 4-46).

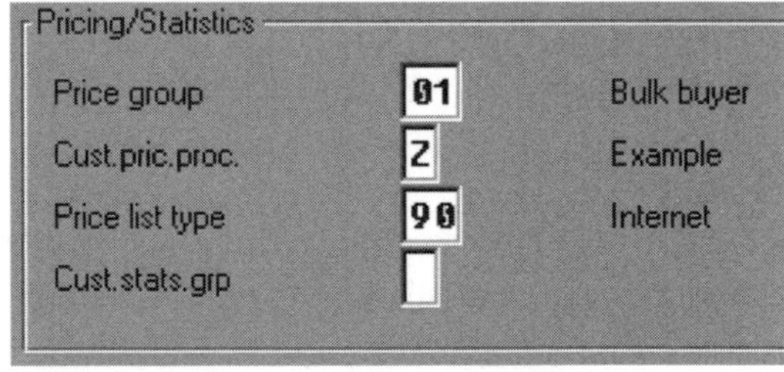

Figure 4-43 Customer master record sales view, pricing section

Price grp	Description
01	Bulk buyer
02	Occasional buyer
03	New customers

Figure 4-44 Price group

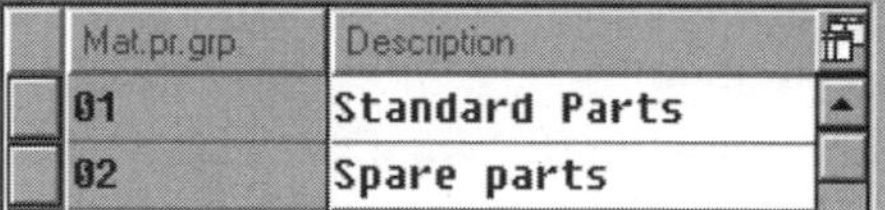

Figure 4-45 Material pricing group

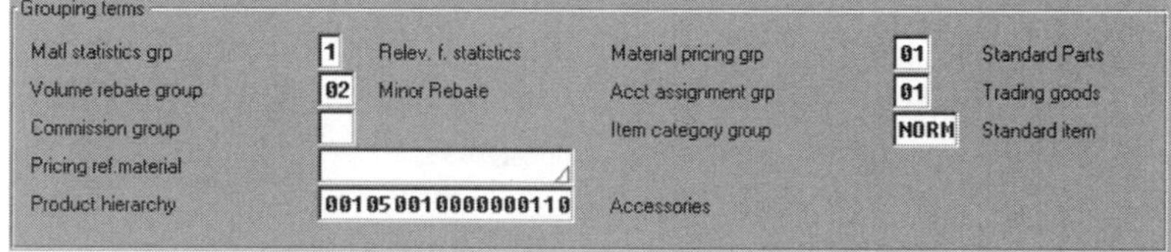

Figure 4-46 Material master record sales organization 2 view

Condition Supplements

A *condition supplement* is a group of conditions that should be applied every time a certain condition is found. For example, if you define a material price, you would enter condition records for every material and the associated price for those materials. If, for one of those materials, you also wanted to include a discount every time that price is determined, you can enter the additional condition type discount as a condition supplement. When SAP determines the condition record in the pricing procedure, it will automatically also include the discount condition record.

Procedure

1. Create the condition types that are to be defined as condition supplements, such as all the discounts, surcharges, and related pricing elements that must be included in the condition type.
2. Create a pricing procedure and list all the conditions that are to form the condition supplement in this procedure.

In the condition type that the supplement applies to, enter the pricing procedure one has just defined from step 2 in the *Master data*—> Pric.Procedure field of the condition type [V/06]. When you create the pricing condition in the master data, you need to enter the condition supplements that go with that condition in the condition record. Enter the condition record and then use the menu path *Goto*—> Condition supplement. You can enter the condition supplements for all the condition types defined in the pricing procedure from Step 2 in the configuration process. The result would now be that the conditions you enter here will automatically be included in the pricing procedure when this condition record is determined.

Tax Determination

The SAP R3 system automatically determines and calculates taxes based on the organizational structure, country, region, or city of delivering plants and country or receiving customer in combination with tax relevancy indicators on the customer and material master records. Prior to maintaining this section, one needs to ensure that one's plants and country or geographical areas, such as regions and cities, are maintained.

Menu Path

The path here is IMG, Sales and distribution, Basic functions, Taxes, Define tax determination rules.

Transaction Code

The code here is [OVK1]. When determining taxes, one should always maintain the data relevant to taxes in consultation with the FI module. The business requirements should also be strictly administered by an experienced accountant who represents and knows the business procedures.

TIP: *One should carefully consider the tax implications in the business blueprint of a project prior to creating an organizational model. It is only necessary to maintain the tax relevant data for foreign countries with which you do business.*

The system automatically determines the relevant taxes according to the country of the delivering plant, plus the country of the customer receiving the goods in combination with the tax indicator of the customer master record and the tax indicator of the material master record. As in Figure 4-47, one must assign the relevant tax condition types to the country key. The system will only list condition types that are regarded as "taxes" in the condition class of the condition type.

After assigning the tax condition type or "tax category" to the country key, one needs to specify if more than one tax is required and in which order the system is to access the condition records. This is done by assigning the relevant tax condition types to the relevant country keys and by assigning an access sequence number. In Figure 4-47, Canada has a GST tax and a PST tax.

After one has assigned the tax condition types or categories, one must ensure that the condition types are placed into the relevant pricing procedures. Also ensure the associated tax condition records are created and maintained. As some countries may have county or regionalized taxes, it is possible to state specific regions within a country code. For example, in Figure 4-48, Great Britain is subdivided into further regions.

Menu Path

Stating specific regions within a country code is maintained by following IMG, Sales and distribution, Basic functions, Taxes, Define regional codes,

Figure 4-47 Tax condition types are assigned to a country key.

Tax count.	Name	Seq.	Tax categ.	Name
AT	Austria	1	MWST	Output Tax
AU	Australia	1	ATX1	Output Tax
BE	Belgium	1	MWST	Output Tax
CA	Canada	1	CTX1	GST (Canada)
CA	Canada	2	CTX2	PST (Canada)
CA	Canada	3	CTX3	PST-Que & Mar(Base+)
CH	Switzerland	1	MWST	Output Tax

Figure 4-48 Defining regions within a country code

Country	Region	Description	County cde	Description
GB	AV	Avon		Avon
GB	BE	Bedfordshire		Bedfordshire
GB	BK	Berkshire		Berkshire

Define county codes. It is also possible to define city codes in the IMG by following IMG, Sales and distribution, Basic functions, Taxes, Define regional codes, Define city codes.

Currently, only the US requires a tax based on the city level. Thus, it is possible to subdivide a country code further into city codes, as shown in Figure 4-49.

Menu Path

As the delivering plant must be assigned to a country, region, and/or city code for tax purposes, one needs to make this assignment in the IMG. Go to IMG, Sales and distribution, Basic functions, Taxes, Assign delivering plants for tax determination. As displayed in Figure 4-50, Plant 2200 is assigned to country France and region 75–Paris.

Menu Path

After assigning the delivering plant, one needs to create the indicators that are represented in the customer and material master records. This is done by going to IMG, Sales and distribution, Basic functions, Taxes, Define tax relevancy of master records, Customer taxes.

It is important to specify if the customer is liable for taxes or not. One can then assign a relevancy indicator to the tax condition type or "tax category" in this menu option. For example, in Figure 4-51a, four indicators are assigned to the Canadian tax category CT×1. Any of these four can be assigned to a customer master record.

Figure 4-49 Defining city codes within a region and country code

Country	Region	Description	City code	Description
US	AK	Alaska	0001	City code in AK
US	AL	Alabama	0001	City code in AL
US	AR	Arkansas	0001	City code in AR
US	AS	American Samoa	0001	City code in AS
US	AZ	Arizona	0001	City code in AZ

Figure 4-50 Plants are assigned to a country code.

Plnt	Country	Name	Region	Description	County cde	City code
2200	FR	France	75	Paris		
2300	ES	Spain	08	Barcelona		
3000	US	United States	NY	New York	001	0001

The system then uses the indicator as found in the Billing view of the customer master record, shown in Figure 4-51b.

Now proceed to create the material tax indicators.

Menu Path

The menu path here is IMG, Sales and distribution, Basic functions, Taxes, Define tax relevancy of master records, Material taxes.

Here one assigns a tax relevancy indicator to the tax condition type or "tax category," which will later be assigned to the material master record. This is shown in Figure 4-52a.

This indicator is then assigned to the material master record in the Sales organization 1 view (see Figure 4-52b).

Tax categ.	Name	Tax class.	Description
CTX1	GST (Canada)	0	Tax exempt
CTX1	GST (Canada)	1	GST Only
CTX1	GST (Canada)	2	GST & PST(Ont & West
CTX1	GST (Canada)	3	GST & PST (Que &Mar)

Figure 4-51a Tax classification for customer's master records

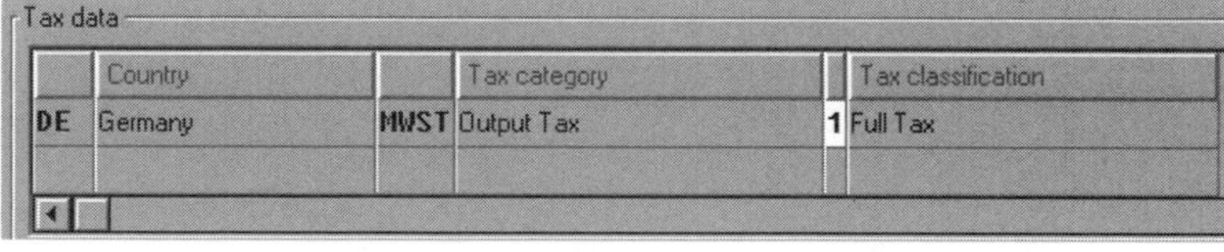

Tax data

	Country		Tax category		Tax classification
DE	Germany	MWST	Output Tax	1	Full Tax

Figure 4-51b Tax classification assigned to the customer master record, billing view

Tax categ.	Name	Tax class.	Description
CTX1	GST (Canada)	0	No tax
CTX1	GST (Canada)	1	Full Tax

Figure 4-52a Tax classification for material master records

Tax data

	Country		Tax category		Tax classification
DE	Germany	MWST	Output Tax	1	Full Tax

Figure 4-52b Tax classification assigned to the material master record, sales organizaton 1 view.

Tax/VAT Registration Number Determination in Sales and Billing Documents

This section is important as the tax classification or tax indicators can be taken from a different customer master record than that of the sold-to party. The same rule that defines how the system is to determine the tax classification number also defines how the system is to reproduce the tax or VAT registration number from the customer master record into the sales documents.

Menu Path

The path here is IMG, Sales and distribution, Basic functions, Taxes, Maintain sales tax—Identification number determination.

Three available options can be assigned to each sales organization. It is recommended that in order to keep consistency throughout the system, use the same determining rules across all sales organizations. The first is determination rule A, which indicates that the tax number and tax indicator classification are generally taken from the sold-to party customer master record. Determination rule B indicates that the tax number and tax classification are generally taken from the customer master record of the payer. Finally, if the field is left blank, the system determines the tax number and the tax classification according to the following sequence:

1. If the payer has a VAT registration number and is identical to the sold-to party, the tax number and tax classification are copied from the payer (in this case, the ship-to party is not relevant). The tax number is copied according to the country of destination relevant for taxes.
2. If 1 does not apply, the ship-to party has a VAT registration number, and the sold-to party does not, the tax number and tax classification are copied from the ship-to party.
3. If 2 does not apply, the tax number and tax classification are copied from the sold-to party.

TIP: *Generally, the VAT registration number on the customer master record will be 11 characters long and begin with the country's ISO code. For example, Germany is DE123456789.*

Figure 4-53a
Select country and tax category

Tax records

Country relev.for tax		Seq.	Tax category
AT	Austria	1	MWST Output Tax
AU	Australia	1	ATX1 Output Tax
BE	Belgium	1	MWST Output Tax
CA	Canada	1	CTX1 GST (Canada)
CA	Canada	2	CTX2 PST (Canada)
CA	Canada	3	CTX3 PST-Que & Mar(Base+)
CH	Switzerland	1	MWST Output Tax
CN	China	1	MWST Output Tax

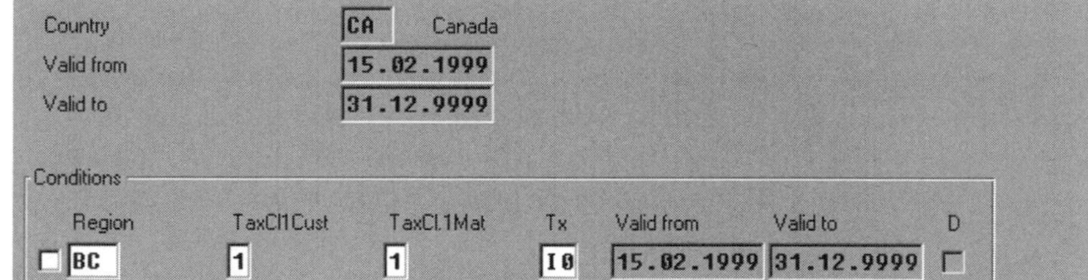

Figure 4-53b
A tax condition record

Do not forget to create the condition records for the tax condition type. These can be created by following the menu path from the logistics overview screen as follows: Logistics, Sales and distribution, Master data, Conditions, Taxes, Create. You will reach the overview screen shown in Figure 4-53a.

Select the country and tax condition type that you want to create the tax condition records for by double-clicking on the entry. For example, in Figure 4-53b, we have created a condition type for Canada's British Columbia. The tax classification in the customer master record equals 1, the tax classification in the material master record equals 1, and the assigned tax code equals IO.

Plants Abroad

The Plants Abroad section needs only to be maintained if your company has one or more plants in a different country from where you are operating. The goods movements between plants across these borders for which no actual sale occurs requires tax postings as well as INTRASTAT entries (or intra-European trade statistics). Examples of stock movements that fall into this category are stock transfers and consignment fill-ups.

Menu Path

The menu path here is IMG, Sales and distribution, Basic functions, Taxes, Plants abroad, Maintain and assign pricing procedure.

Because Germany, France, and Austria are all members of the EU, if any movement of goods happens between their borders for the purpose of consignment to a customer or stock transfer, the sale must be relevant for INTRASTAT and taxes. However, should a consignment stock transfer or stock transfer happen between Austria and South Africa, for example, the stock fill-up sale is not relevant for INTRASTAT.

The pricing procedure used in stock transfers (the standard SAP version uses RVWIA1) must have the following tax condition types:

WIA1 Input tax in the country of destination. The tax indicator for the tax determination procedure of the country of departure must correspond with the tax indicator of the country of the company code. This is because the system uses the country of the company code to access the tax indicator during the transfer to FI. You must maintain the reporting country field (that is, the country of destination) for the tax indicator characteristics.

WIA2 Output tax in the country of departure (0 percent for deliveries within the EU).

WIA3 Output tax in the country of destination. The tax indicator for the tax determination procedure of the country of departure must again correspond with the tax indicator of the country of the company code for the same reasons as in WIA1.

Note that the billing document only needs to represent a value of zero, as no sale is actually taking place. Rather, the goods are passing between storage facilities and are still owned by the holding company. Even in the case of a consignment fill up, the goods still belong to the issuing plant until a consignment issue consumes them.

Figure 4-54 Example of plant structure in a company

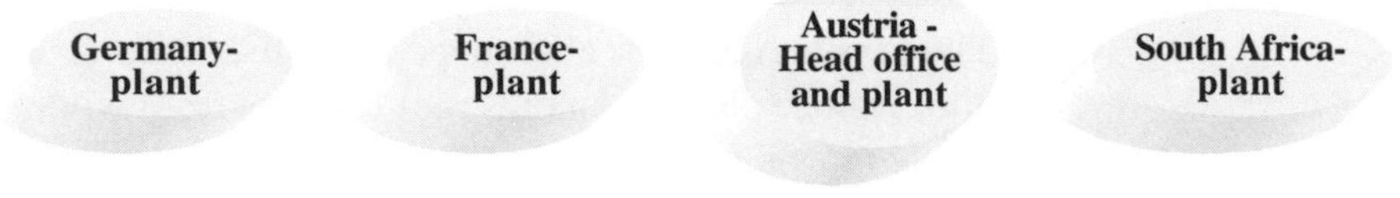

The standard pricing procedure RVWIA1 results in a billing document of zero value, as it contains a condition type that creates a 100 percent discount (condition type R100). The pricing procedure determination used to obtain RVWIA1 as a billing DoPP uses the CuPP indicator of 1 and the DoPP indicator of B, which can be assigned to the billing document.

In the IMG activity of maintaining and assigning the pricing procedure, one can copy the standard pricing procedure, rename it, and make the necessary alterations.

Menu Path

The menu path here is IMG, Sales and distribution, Basic functions, Taxes, Plants abroad, Maintain billing type and billing type proposal.

The standard system has a predefined billing type WIA, which is used for plants abroad. This billing type proposes the billing pricing procedure. In this IMG activity, one can copy and rename the billing type WIA and then assign it to the sales document types as required.

Menu Path

The path here is IMG, Sales and distribution, Basic functions, Taxes, Plants abroad, Maintain copying control.

In the copying control between the sales document, delivery document, and the billing document, you must be sure to set the pricing indicator at the item level to B to ensure the system carries out new pricing and thus obtains the RVWIA1 (or substitute).

Menu Path

The path here is IMG, Sales and distribution, Basic functions, Taxes, Plants abroad, Maintain billing relevance for item categories.

The SAP system has a unique indicator at the item category level that determines if the item is relevant for billing or not. This indicator can be set to a J, which determines the item is only relevant for billing across EU borders. If the customer is not within an EU country, the item category will not be relevant for billing (see Figure 4-55).

Relev. for billing J

Figure 4-55
Item category relevance for billing

This billing-relevant indicator is designed for the stock replenishment and consignment process, which uses the following item categories:

- NLN, replenishment
- KBN, consignment fill-up
- KAN, consignment pick-up

Menu Path

The menu path here is IMG, Sales and distribution, Basic functions, Taxes, Plants abroad, Assign G/L account to account key.

This area is described in the following section, but it is worthwhile noting that the system pre-allocates both PR00 and the 100 percent discount R100 the account key UML. This account key is then assigned a GL account that should always have a balance of zero.

Menu Path

The path is IMG, Sales and distribution, Basic functions, Taxes, Plants abroad, Maintain declaration numbers.

Two assignments need to be maintained here. First, the country that your foreign plant resides in must be given an INTRASTAT number. Secondly, the foreign plant must be given a VAT registration number for tax purposes. This can be assigned by creating an intercompany stock transfer partner that has a customer master record similar to the sold-to party, but this customer master record resembles your foreign plant and must have the VAT registration number correctly assigned to it. After creating this master record, you must ensure it is assigned to the plant in the following menu path: IMG, Materials management, Purchasing, Purchase order, Set up stock transport order, Plant. Double-click on the plant and enter the customer master record number that identifies the plant.

Account Assignment

The condition technique is also used in account determination in order to allocate the correct GL account to the account key, as assigned in the pricing procedure. Whenever a sale is posted to accounting, SAP must find (or determine) the account where the revenues and discounts should be posted. Therefore, a determination procedure is used to find the accounts, the account determination procedure. This procedure contains a condition type to find which account to post to based on the conditions of the sale. The condition type searches all the records that contain accounts for conditions that match the sale in the order of the access sequence. As soon as it finds a record that matches the conditions, it returns a condition value, in this case the GL account.

The condition technique is used to post to different accounts under different conditions. For example, sales of a certain material can go to one revenue account, sales of other materials to a different account, export sales can go to another, and local sales to yet another. Depending on all these conditions (the material, types of sale, and so on), SAP can find a different account. The condition technique is used to find the right account under the right conditions.

Menu Path

The path here is as follows: IMG, Sales and Distribution, Basic functions, Account assignment, Revenue account determination, Check master data relevant for account assignment.

Because the configuration is similar between revenue account determination and reconciliation account determination, we will be focusing on the revenue account determination for the purposes of this book. Please note this section is highly integrated with the FI and Cost Accounting (CO) modules.

Through Check master data relevant for account assignment, one has the opportunity to create account assignment grouping criteria. This grouping criteria provides the system with an extra variable in determining the required account number. For example, by selecting Check master data relevant for account assignment in Materials: account assignment goods, one can specify, as in Figure 4-56, whether a material should be classified as a

- Trading item (material type HAWA)
- Service item (material type DIEN)
- Finished product (material type FERT)

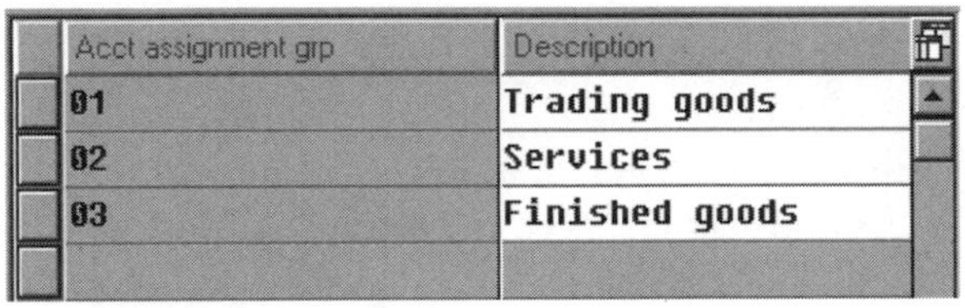

Acct assignment grp	Description
01	Trading goods
02	Services
03	Finished goods

Figure 4-56
Account assignment group

Material pricing grp	01	Standard Parts
Acct assignment grp	01	Trading goods
Item category group	NORM	Standard item

Figure 4-57
Account assignment group is assigned to the material master record

To recreate new entries, you can copy the existing standard and rename the entry using an alphanumeric key of two characters with a short description. After the creation of these account keys, ensure that they are assigned to the material master record (see Figure 4-57).

The same is true for the customer account keys. You can select the following: Check master data relevant for account assignment, and Customers: account assignment groups.

Again, to recreate new entries, one can copy the existing standard and rename the entry using an alphanumeric key of two characters with a short description. These account assignment keys are useful in grouping account determination. For example, a business may want domestic sales to be posted into account X, while international sales may have to be posted into account Y.

As account determination follows the condition technique, it is understandable that there may be a need to change the condition table that is used in the access sequence to find the correct condition record (that is, the correct account number).

Menu Path

Account determination is possible by going to IMG, Sales and Distribution, Basic functions, Account assignment, Revenue account determination, Define dependencies of revenue account determination. Here one can create or change a condition table, but one must be careful, as there are not many fields one can select from in order to create this condition table.

TIP: Please refer back to the section on pricing in this chapter for more information on creating and changing condition tables.

After ensuring your condition tables exist as required, ensure that the access sequence and condition types are maintained as required too.

Menu Path

The path here is IMG, Sales and Distribution, Basic functions, Account assignment, Revenue account determination, Define access sequences and account determination types.

The standard system has an account determination type with the key KOFI. Create the necessary access sequence first, followed by an account determination type (condition type). The condition type is nothing more than a four-character alphanumeric key with no additional control features. The KOFI access sequence has five condition tables assigned to it (see Figure 4-58).

This KOFI access sequence can be used for most businesses, with the possible exception being that maybe not all the condition tables will be used. If this is the case, it will be recommended to copy the access sequence and rename it; then allocate this new access sequence to the relevant account determination type (condition type). Within the new access sequence, one would now be able to delete condition tables that are not being used, thus improving on system performance response times.

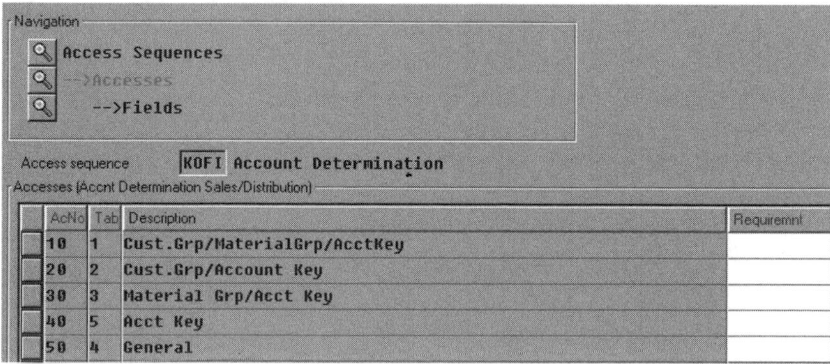

AcNo	Tab	Description	Requiremnt
10	1	Cust.Grp/MaterialGrp/AcctKey	
20	2	Cust.Grp/Account Key	
30	3	Material Grp/Acct Key	
40	5	Acct Key	
50	4	General	

Figure 4-58 Account Determination type KOFI has an Access Sequence KOFI with assigned condition tables

As in the standard condition techniques, one can assign a requirement to the condition tables within the access sequence if necessary. Now you can create the account assignment procedure.

Menu Path

The menu path here is as follows: IMG, Sales and Distribution, Basic functions, Account assignment, Revenue account determination, Define and assign account determination procedures, Define account determination procedure.

The standard system has an account determination procedure, KOFI00, which has the account assignment condition types KOFI and KOFK assigned to it. The procedure performs in the same way as the standard procedure used in the pricing condition technique, with the only obvious exception being that there is more control data in pricing at the condition type level than at the condition type level in the pricing procedure for account determination, which only has an allocation allowed for a requirement. This can be seen in Figure 4-59.

Menu Path

The account determination procedure is then assigned to a billing type. This can be done as follows: IMG, Sales and Distribution, Basic functions, Account assignment, Revenue account determination, Define and assign account determination procedures, Assign account determination procedure.

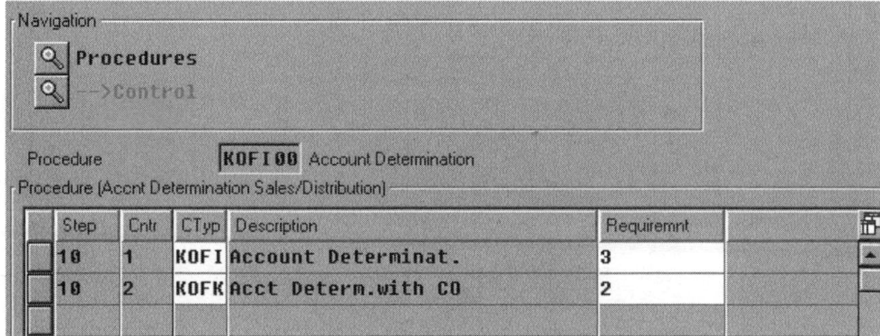

Figure 4-59 Account Determination procedure

The account determination procedure is assigned to the billing document type, as shown in Figure 4-60.

The column described as "CaAc" represents the cash allocation key, which causes the system to post directly into a GL account for the cash entry, rather than into a receivables account. Thus, in Figure 4-60, the system will use the EVV key to post the cash sale.

One now needs to create the account keys that are going to be used in the system. This is possible by following the IMG to Define and assign account keys, Define account key. Here one can create an account key as one determines, which is a three-character alphanumeric key with a short description. An example of this is shown in Figure 4-61.

The assignment of the account key (IMG, Assign account keys) is the actual process of assigning the account key to the condition type, as done in the pricing procedure maintenance.

TIP: *By referring back to the section on pricing and viewing the pricing procedure Z00001, you can see the account key assignments. These assignments can also be carried out in an account assignment, as displayed in Figure 4-62.*

Figure 4-60 The account determination procedure is assigned to the billing type.

BillT	Description	ActDPr	Description	CaAc	Name
BV	Cash Sale	KOFI00		EVV	Cash clearing
F1	Invoice	KOFI00			
F2	Invoice	KOFI00			

Figure 4-61 Account keys

ActKy	Name
B01	Purch.acct.provsns
B02	Prchacct rebate rev
ERB	Rebate sales deduct
ERF	Freight revenue
ERL	Sales revenues
ERS	Sales deductions

Proc.	Step	Cntr	CTyp	Name	ActKy	Name	Accrls
Z00001	10	0	PR00	Price	ERL	Sales revenues	
	50	0	Z007	Customer Discount	ERS	Sales deductions	
	60	0	K005	Customer/Material	ERS	Sales deductions	
	70	0	RB00	Discount (Value)	ERS	Sales deductions	
	110	0	KF00	Freight	ERF	Freight revenue	
	120	0	HD00	Freight	ERF	Freight revenue	
	140	0	MWST	Output Tax	MWS	Taxes on sls/purch.	
	160	0	VPRS	Cost			

Figure 4-62 Account Key assignments to Condition Types within a pricing procedure

All that remains is the assignment of the GL accounts to the condition table, as specified in the access sequence.

Menu Path

The path here is IMG, Sales and Distribution, Basic functions, Account assignment, Revenue account determination, Assign G/L accounts.

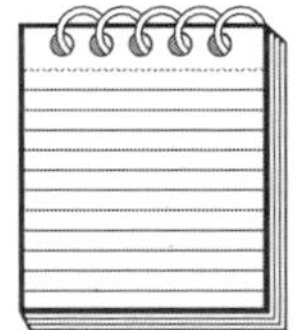

NOTE: *Before the GL accounts can be assigned, the FI module must have finished creating the chart of accounts and the GL accounts.*

An example of the assignment of the GL accounts to the Account key condition table/field overview would be as follows in Figure 4-63.

TIP: *Should you have an account determination error in the goods issue of a delivery, it is likely the error is in the materials management account assignment. This account assignment can be displayed via the transaction code [OBYC] or by following the menu path Materials management, Valuation and account assignment, Account determination, Account determination without wizard, Create automatic postings.*

Figure 4-63 Assignment of GL account to the account key

App	CndTy.	ChAc	SOrg.	ActKy	G/L acct	G/L acct
V	KOFI	CAFR	0001	ERL	701100	
V	KOFI	CAFR	0001	EVV	580000	
V	KOFI	CAFR	0001	MWS	445710	
V	KOFI	CAFR	2200	ERF	708500	
V	KOFI	CAFR	2200	ERL	701100	
V	KOFI	CAFR	2200	ERS	709100	
V	KOFI	CAFR	2200	EVV	531100	
V	KOFI	CAFR	2200	MWS	445710	

Sales Incompletion Logs

As the sales, delivery, and billing data is recorded into the system through the data entered in the sales, delivery, and billing documents, it is imperative that specific control is maintained. The data maintained in the sales document is passed through to the delivery and finally the billing document. Thus, it is the sales document data that is used as a backbone in sales and distribution processing. In some instances, a delivery document may also need specific data to be maintained. For this reason, SAP has an incompletion structure that can be maintained to highlight missing data in sales and delivery documents as well as sales activities and partner functions.

Menu Path

The path here is IMG, Sales and Distribution, Basic functions, Incompletion control for sales documents, Define status groups.

Transaction Code

The code here is [OVA0]. An incompletion process inspects the object, such as a sales document line item, and inspects specific fields in order to see if data has been maintained in these fields. Should data not be maintained in these specified fields, the system is told how to respond, that is, does it or does it not give a warning message and to what extent does it allow further processing of the document.

The incompletion log cannot register what data is maintained in the specified field and compare it to data that should be in the specified field. For example, should a sales document header have a purchase order number, the system will check to see if data is maintained in VBKD-BSTKD (sales document header—purchase order number). The standard system cannot check to see if the entry, however, in the field is equal to a specific value, for example, 10002. One can create incompletion logs for the following:

- Sales document header data
- Sales document item data
- Sales document schedule line data
- Sales activity data
- Partner data in sales documents, deliveries, and sales activities
- Delivery header data
- Delivery item data

First, one needs to define the status groups. This can be done by using the menu path as described previously. These status groups are eventually assigned to the specific field in the incompletion log. Thus, it is possible to specify in a sale document that field A may be incomplete, but not hinder the document from being processed further, while field B may be incomplete and be the cause of the same document being blocked for further processing. The status groups in Figure 4-64 will be assigned to a field in the sales incompletion log.

The statuses group settings are

- *General* Setting this status in the status group and assigning the status group to a field in the incompletion procedure will cause the sales document to be incomplete, but will allow the document to be processed further.
- *Delivery* Setting this status in the status group and assigning the status group to a field in the incompletion procedure will cause the sales

Figure 4-64 Status groups

StatusGr	General	Delivery	BillingDoc	Price	Goods mov.	Picking	Pack
00							
01	X						
02	X	X					
03	X		X		X		
04	X	X	X		X		
05	X		X	X	X		

document to be incomplete for further processing; that is, the creation of a delivery will not hinder the creation of a billing document, should the field not be filled and the delivery document be rendered as incomplete for further processing, such as saving the delivery document.

- *Billing document* Setting this status in the status group and assigning the status group to a field in the incompletion procedure will cause the sales document and delivery document to be incomplete for further processing, that is, the creation of the billing document should the associated field not be filled.
- *Price* Setting this status in the status group and assigning the status group to a field in the incompletion procedure will cause the sales document to be incomplete for further processing should pricing not have been carried out.
- *Goods movement* Setting this status in the status group and assigning the status group to a field in the incompletion procedure will cause the delivery document to be incomplete for further processing, that is, for goods movement, should a field not be filled, such as quantity picked.
- *Picking* Setting this status in the status group and assigning the status group to a field in the incompletion procedure will cause the delivery document to be incomplete for further processing, that is, picking, should a field not be filled, such as serial numbers.
- *Packing* Setting this status in the status group and assigning the status group to a field in the incompletion procedure will cause the delivery document to be incomplete for further processing, that is, packing, should a field not be filled, such as quantity picked.

Should you wish to change a status group, be sure to copy the status group that closely resembles your requirements, change its name, and continue to change this new status group's assignments in order to ensure you do not change the SAP standard. In our example, we will be using the Status group 01, which has a general status. Now we can proceed to define the incompletion procedures.

Menu Path

The menu path here is IMG, Sales and Distribution, Basic functions, Incompletion control for sales documents, Define incompletion procedures.

Transaction Code

The code here is [OVA2]. By referring to Figure 4-65, one can see the incompletion groups one is able to maintain.

By selecting Group A—Sales Header and then selecting the display button -> procedures, you can see the incompletion procedures. Note that the incompletion procedures are assigned to the various sales document types and sales document item categories. Thus, Figure 4-66 displays a selection of incompletion procedures that can be assigned to sales document headers.

NOTE: *It is not possible to create your own error group, such as a copy of group A—Sales header.*

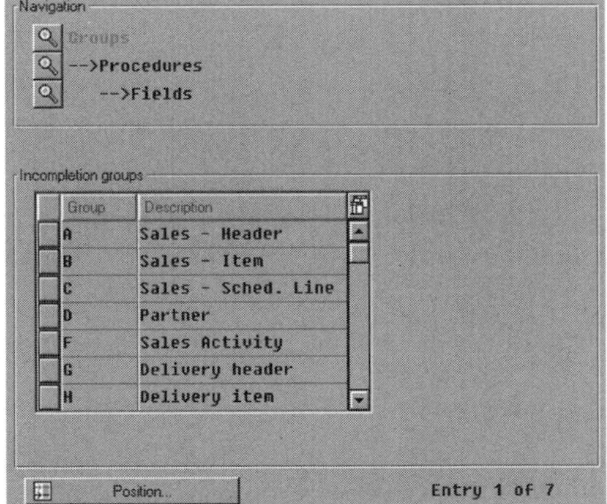

Figure 4-65 Incompletion groups

Error group: A

Incompletion procedures

InProc	Description
10	Inquiry/Quotation
11	Sales Order
12	Outline Agreement
13	Order w/o charge
14	Credit memo
15	Debit Memo
16	Product proposal

Figure 4-66 Incompletion procedures

However, should one need to change the SAP standard by adding or deleting entries in a procedure, you can create a copy of the assigned procedures to the error group, such as a copy of the standard procedure 11—Sales order.

To create your own incompletion procedure, select the Change Display button or simply press the control key on your keyboard plus F1. Then proceed as usual in copying the incompletion procedure and renaming it. The system will ask if you want to copy the dependent entries, as shown in Figure 4-67. These dependent entries are the assigned incompletion fields and associated assigned status groups. You can select the Copy all button.

By selecting the incompletion procedure, such as ZS—"Copy of Sales order," one can assign new entries or delete nonrequired entries, as shown in Figure 4-68.

One can see the table names with the assigned field name and a description of that field. In Figure 4-68, the purchase order number is relevant as incomplete. The assigned screen "KBES" is the screen that the system takes the user through in order to complete the missing data. Assigned to

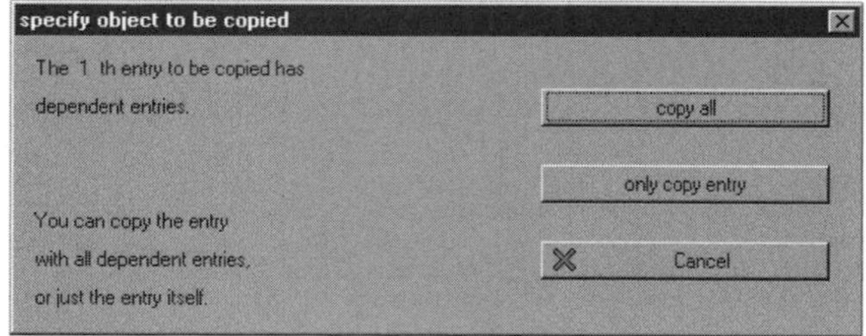

Figure 4-67
Option to copy all dependent entries

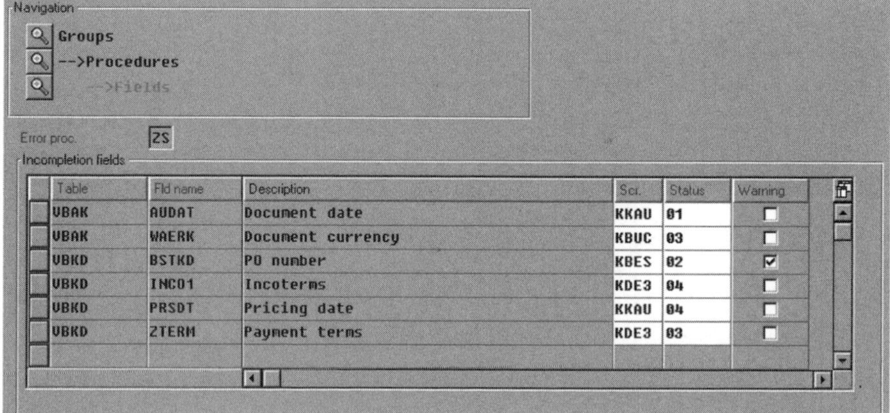

Table	Fld name	Description	Scr.	Status	Warning
VBAK	AUDAT	Document date	KKAU	01	☐
VBAK	WAERK	Document currency	KBUC	03	☐
VBKD	BSTKD	PO number	KBES	02	☑
VBKD	INCO1	Incoterms	KDE3	04	☐
VBKD	PRSDT	Pricing date	KKAU	04	☐
VBKD	ZTERM	Payment terms	KDE3	03	☐

Figure 4-68
Option to alter fields and associated entries

the purchase order number is the status group 02, which we have defined as general, and delivery will render the document incomplete for further delivery, but not billing processing. Finally assigned to the purchase order number is an indicator saying the system must display a warning message in the sales order at the time that the system checks to see if the data is maintained for the purpose of the incompletion log.

Should no warning message be assigned at the time of saving, the system will merely indicate the sales document is incomplete and offer an option, as displayed in Figure 4-69. This enables the document to be saved as incomplete and disallows any further processing or the data to be maintained prior to saving. Thus, once fully maintained, the sales document will be able to be processed further.

Should one select to maintain the data, one will be faced with an overview screen with a list of errors shown in Figure 4-70. If you select the error followed by the Complete Data button, you will be taken to the overview screen shown as assigned in Figure 4-68, where you will be able to complete the missing data.

Figure 4-69
Sales order incomplete document message

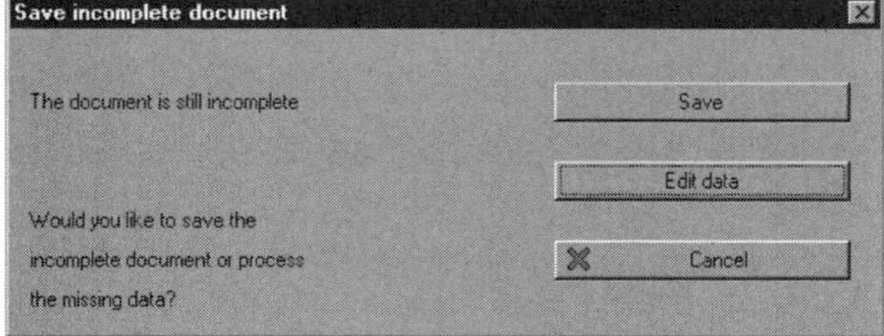

Figure 4-70
Sales Incompletion Log

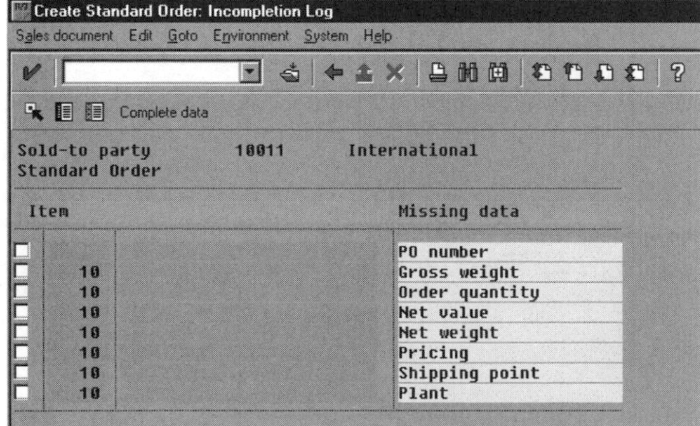

One can see in Figure 4-70 that the purchase order number is incomplete, as it has no associated item number. One knows it is at the header level, whereas item 10 is missing a plant in the same sales order.

TIP: *The tables that can be used in the maintenance of the incompletion procedure are as follows:*

VBKD	*Business data*
VBAK	*Header data*
VEDA	*Contract data*
VBAP	*Item data*
VBKA	*Sales activities*
VBEP	*Schedule line data*
VBPA	*Partner*
LIKP	*Delivery: Header data*
LIPS	*Delivery: Item data*
LIPSD	*Delivery: Item data (dynamic/online)*
LIPSVB	*Delivery: Item data (LIPS 1 LIPSD)*
V50UC	*Delivery: Dynamically generated data (item and header)*
FMII1	*Funds management account assignment data*

Now that the incompletion procedure is created, one needs to assign the incompletion procedure to the object, such as the sales document header.

Menu Path

This can be done as follows: IMG, Sales and distribution, Basic functions, Incompletion control for sales documents, Assign incompletion procedures, Assign procedures to the sales document types.

Transaction Code

The code here is [VUA2]. One can assign the procedure to each object that resembles an incompletion error group, such as Group A—Sales header. You could assign the procedure ZS to the sales document type ZSQ (see Figure 4-71).

SaTy	Description	Proc.	Description	Incomplet.messages
ZSQ	Standard Order	ZS	Copy of Sales order	☑

Figure 4-71
Assign incompletion procedure to the sales document type

TIP: *Should one not require the pop-up box, as displayed in Figure 4-69, but merely allow the document to be automatically saved, even though it will still be blocked for further processing if incomplete, one can select the indicator "incomplete messages." This, however, is not all that helpful, as one will still proceed through to the incompletion screen. The only benefit is missing out on a pop-up box.*

TIP: *Should you have inconsistencies between the header and item incompletion statuses of a sales document, you can create and run a special report via [SE38] called SDVBUK00. This is highlighted in SAP OSS note 0088511. This report will align the incompletion status in tables VBUK and VBUP.*

Partner Determination

Partners such as the sold-to party, the bill-to party, and the payer are a necessary in the majority of document processing. Automatic partner determination happens in the sales document, delivery and billing documents, sales activities, and the customer master record. This automatic partner determination is configurable in this section along with the control data behind the partner eligibility. For example, a ship-to party can use the same account group as a sold-to party.

Menu Path

The menu path to follow is IMG, Sales and distribution, Basic functions, Partner determination, Define partner functions.

Transaction Code

The code here is [VOPA].

TIP: *By referring back to master data in Chapter 1, we see that each customer master record is created on the basis of a specific account group. For example, sold-to parties use account group 0001.*

We also note the four basic partner functions:

SP	*Sold-to party*	*(German—AG)*
SH	*Ship-to party*	*(German—WE)*
BP	*Bill-to party*	*(German—RE)*
PY	*Payer*	*(German—RG)*

Each partner function can be assigned a partner type. This partner type specifies whether the partner is a customer, contact person, or vendor. The overview screen, as shown in Figure 4-72, displays the available options when configuring the partner determination. By selecting "customer master" and then selecting the Partner functions button, one can specify all the partner functions that are acceptable (see Figure 4-73). In this figure, one can see the sold-to party is partner type KU—customer.

Although the incompletion procedure assigned to the SP partner function is 07, this incompletion procedure is used by the system to register partner fields that are not filled at the time of creating the sales order. We will cover the higher-level function as well as the customer-hierarchy type a little later in customer hierarchies.

Figure 4-72
Partner functions per partner object

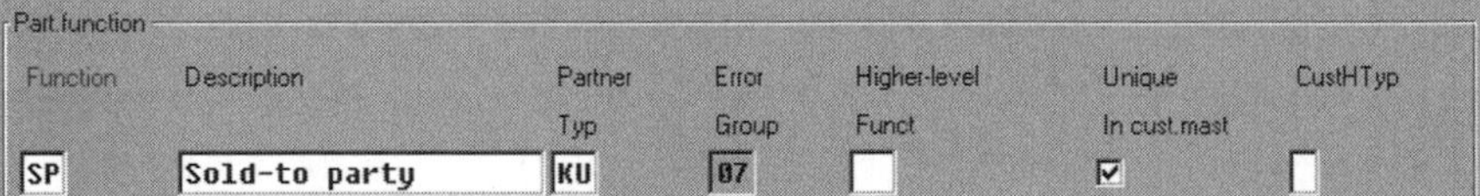

Figure 4-73 Partner Function-SP-sold to party

Allowed account groups for each partner function

Funct	Description	Account grp	Description
SP	Sold-to party	0001	Sold-to party
SP	Sold-to party	0005	Prospective customer
SP	Sold-to party	0007	Sales partner
SP	Sold-to party	0099	One-time account

Figure 4-74 Account group assignment to partner functions

The unique customer master indicator is set for the sold-to party; this indicates that the system must only enable one entry of this partner function in the customer master record. From this view in Figure 4-73, should one select environment, Account group assignment one will be faced with an assignment table, as in Figure 4-74.

TIP: *Should one create a new customer account group, such as a copy of 0001, do not forget to assign the new account group to the list of allowed account groups for partner determination.*

Before one can make any partner determination maintenance, one must ensure the partner functions that are to be used in the partner determination procedures, exist in the list of allowed partner functions.

Now one can proceed with the assignment of the partner functions to a partner determination procedure. We will proceed with two examples:

Example A: Creating partner determination for a customer master record

1. Select the radio button for the customer master.
2. After ensuring all necessary partner functions have been maintained correctly, one can select the button "Partner procedures."
3. Create a new procedure key that is four characters in length with a short description, such as "ZS" (see Figure 4-75).

Figure 4-75
Partner determination procedure

Procedure details Procedure assignment

Partner procedures

Proc.	Description
ZS	Sold-to Party

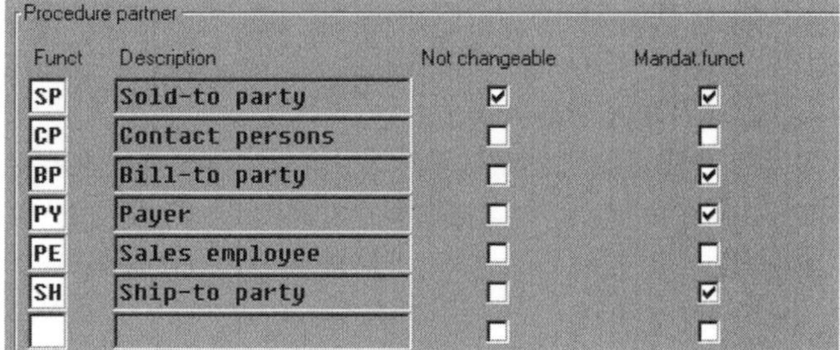

Procedure partner

Funct	Description	Not changeable	Mandat.funct
SP	Sold-to party	☑	☑
CP	Contact persons	☐	☐
BP	Bill-to party	☐	☑
PY	Payer	☐	☑
PE	Sales employee	☐	☐
SH	Ship-to party	☐	☑
		☐	☐

Figure 4-76
Assigned partner functions

4. Select the newly created procedure and select the Procedure details button. You will be faced with a screen where you assign the associated partner functions that you permit and/or require to be placed in the customer master record. For example, we select the basic four partner functions, SP, SH, BP, and PY, as well as the contact person CP and sales employee PE. All four basic partner functions we want to make mandatory, but we only want the sold-to party to be unchangeable. These settings are displayed in Figure 4-76.
5. Once the procedure has been created and the partner functions have been assigned, it is necessary to assign this partner procedure to an account group, as displayed in Figure 4-77. This is carried out by selecting the Procedure assignment button.

One can now create the customer master records in this example using account group 0001. The result would be that the system allows one single entry for partner function SP while permitting multiple entries for partner functions SH, BP, PY, CP, and PE, as well as ensuring the partner functions SP, SH, BP, and PY are mandatory.

Figure 4-77 Assign the partner procedure to the account group.

Account grp	Description	Proc.	Description
0001	Sold-to party	ZS	Sold to party

Example B: Creating partner determination for a sales document header

1. Select the radio button for the sales document header. After ensuring all necessary partner functions have been maintained correctly, hit the Partner procedures button.
2. Create a new procedure key four characters in length with a short description such as "ZOR."
3. Select the newly created procedure and hit the Procedure details button. You will be faced with a screen where you now assign the associated partner functions that you permit and/or require to be placed in the Sales document header. In Figure 4-78, one can see that the assigned partner function sold-to party is not changeable and is a mandatory function, whereas the bill-to party, payer, and ship-to party are mandatory yet are changeable.
4. Once the procedure has been created and the partner functions have been assigned, it is necessary to assign this partner procedure to a sales document type, as displayed in Figure 4-79. This is carried out by selecting the Procedure assignment button.

Should you now create a sales document that uses the assigned partner determination procedure, you would be restricted to only enter the partners. The only available partners for selection are shown in Figure 4-80.

The fields for source and sequence are used when the system needs to obtain a partner record from any associated partner in the sales document, other than that of the sold-to party. If a partner is a buyer partner function BU and the record of the buyer is not assigned to the sold-to party, but to the bill-to party, the source field may be assigned "BP" for the bill-to party and the sequence number must come after that of the bill-to party. Thus, should the bill-to party have a sequence of blank or 0, the sequence for the buyer may read 1.

Procedure partner

Funct	Description	Not changeable	Mandat.funct	Source	Seq.
SP	Sold-to party	☑	☑		
BP	Bill-to party	☐	☑		
PY	Payer	☐	☑		
SH	Ship-to party	☐	☑		
		☐	☐		

Figure 4-78
Assigned partner functions

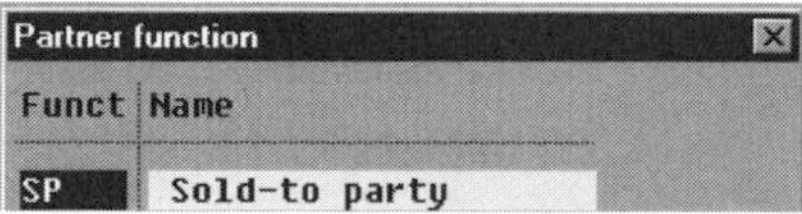

Figure 4-79
Assign the partner procedure to the sales document type.

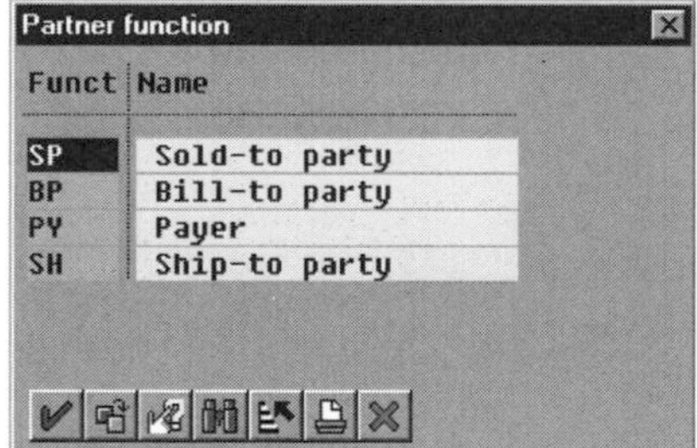

Figure 4-80
List of allowed partners

TIP: *One needs to save one's entries after each section of data has been maintained. For example, in customer partner determination, after creating a partner procedure, one cannot assign the partner functions, save only the partner functions, and then try to assign the procedure to an account group. Instead, one needs to save the partner procedure first and then assign and save the partner functions. Only after saving each step of the determination can you proceed to assign the procedure to an account group.*

Text Determination

Text forms a basic but essential need within document processing. Using text determination, one can automatically copy a text line from one text object to another, such as from a customer master record to a sales document.

Menu Path

The path here is IMG, Sales and distribution, Basic functions, Partner determination, Define partner functions.

Transaction Code

The code here is [VOTX].

The sales and distribution module is used in the text determination for the following text objects (see Figure 4-81):

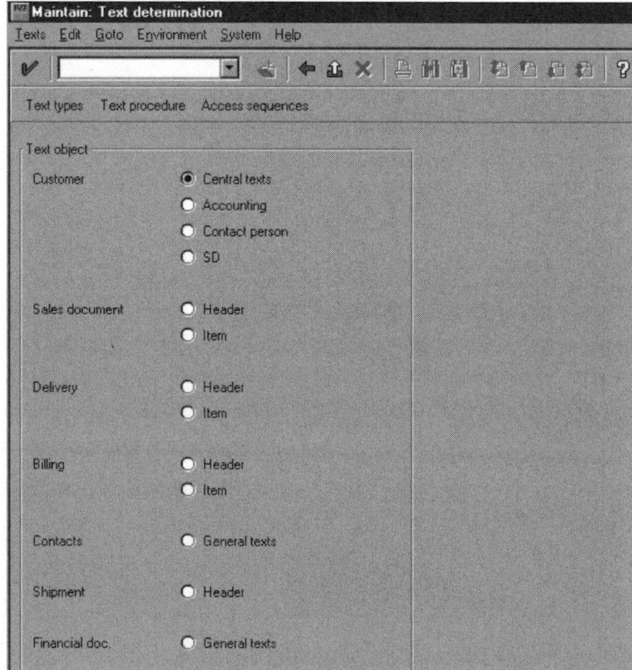

Figure 4-81 Maintain Text determination text objects

Customer

- Central texts
- Accounting texts
- Texts concerning the contact persons
- Sales and distribution texts

Sales document

- Header texts
- Item texts

Delivery:

- Header texts
- Item texts

Billing document

- Header texts
- Item texts

By selecting one of the text objects and selecting the button "Text types," one can define the permitted text types for the text object. We will maintain the text determination in the customer master record and the sales document header as examples.

Example A: Text determination for the customer master record

1. Select the text object radio button "Customer—SD." This is the text object. Then select the button text types.
2. You will be faced with an overview as in Figure 4-82. It is here that you define the different text types you want to have in the customer master record and a short description for each of them. For example, entry "ZEXM" is used as "customer's text."

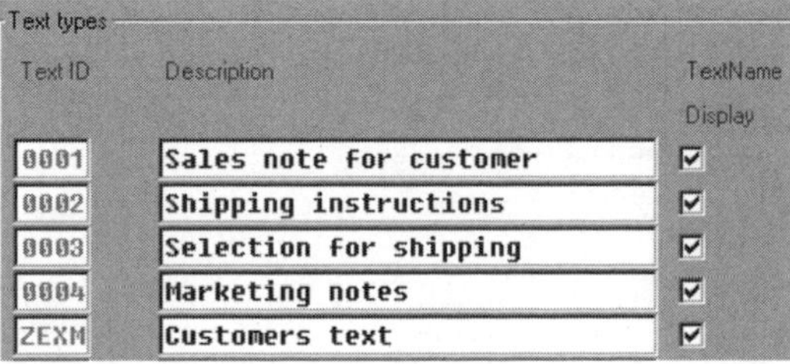

Text types

Text ID	Description	TextName Display
0001	Sales note for customer	☑
0002	Shipping instructions	☑
0003	Selection for shipping	☑
0004	Marketing notes	☑
ZEXM	Customers text	☑

Figure 4-82
Text types

TIP: *If you have difficulty creating new text types, it is possible to overwrite an existing text type entry and description. The system will then proceed in automatically creating a new entry while leaving the previous text type unchanged.*

Once the text type has been created, one needs to define the access sequences. However, the access sequence is not necessary for the customer master record text, as the customer master record is the highest level possible in text determination.

3. After creating the access sequences, one then proceeds to create the text procedure by selecting the Text procedure button (see Figure 4-83). Create a two-character key with a short description.
4. After the procedure has been created, one can proceed to assign the text types to the procedure. This can be done by selecting the button "Texts in procedure." It is here you assign the actual text types you would like to have assigned to the customer master record. There is the four-character key ID and the short description. In our example, we have added our text type, ZEXM—Customers text, to the list.
5. Once the text has been assigned to the procedure, it is time to assign the procedure to the customer's account group. This is done by selecting the button Text proc. assignment from the procedure overview. In our example, all the account groups have been assigned to the text procedure 01.

After completion of the customer account group assignment, it is now possible to create the text in the customer master record. The customer master record has four text objects, as we have previously seen. The sales and distribution text object is accessible from the Sales view of the customer master record and by selecting Extras, Texts. This is displayed in Figure 4-84. Note the description in the text as we will be using that for our next example.

Figure 4-83
Text procedure

Texts in procedure | Text proc.assignment

Text proc.

Proc.	Description
01	Customer sales texts

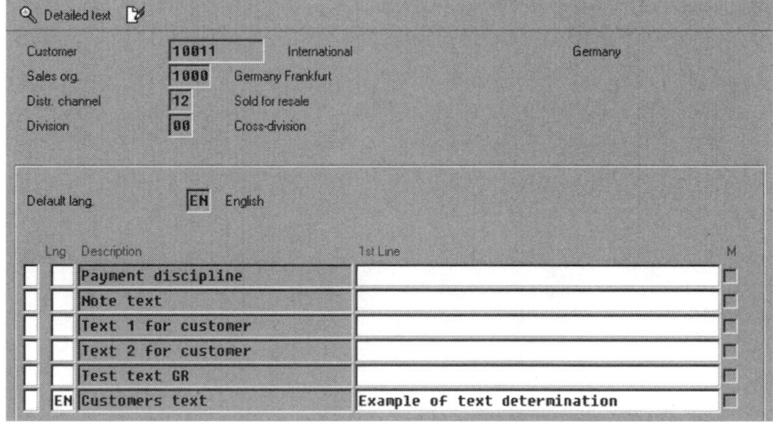

Figure 4-84 Customer master record texts

Example B: Text determination for the Sales document header

1. Select the text object radio button "Sales document—header." This is the text object. Then select the button text types.
2. You will be faced with an overview as in Figure 4-82. It is here that you define the different text types you want to have in the sales document header and a short description for each of them. For example, entry "Z000" is used as "Text from customer master."
3. Once the text type has been created, define the access sequences. This is done by selecting the Access sequences button from the text object overview. To create a new access sequence, enter an access sequence number and a short description, such as "501—Customer to Sales." Then hit the Access sequence button (see Figure 4-85).

1. One is now faced with an empty access sequence. Although the appearance is different than the standard pricing access sequences, the usage by the system remains the same. One must first assign the text object where the text is originating from in order for it to be placed in the sales document header. In our example, the text is originating from the customer master record. Thus, the text object is the customer master record and is thus KNVV. One must now assign the text ID as used in the customer master record; since we are copying text ID or text type ZEXM, we enter KNVV — ZEXM.

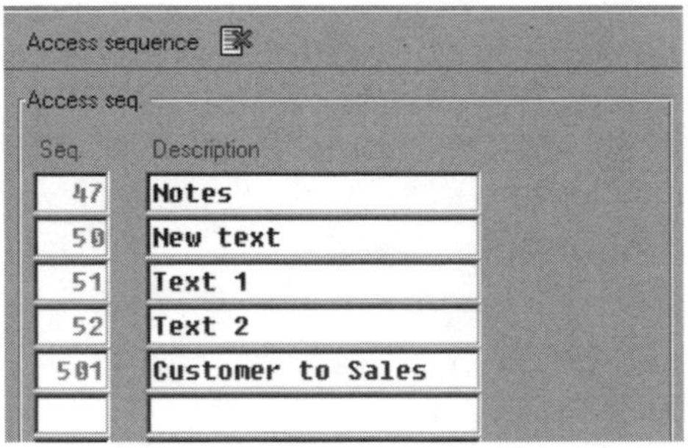

Figure 4-85
Text determination access sequences

Access sequence

Access seq.

Seq.	Description
47	Notes
50	New text
51	Text 1
52	Text 2
501	Customer to Sales

2. We also indicate that the customer master record that must be used is the SP sold-to party. One can select all languages or specify a specific language from a partner function. If a specific text is to be used by the ship-to party only, and the ship-to party speaks a different language to the other partners, it is possible to specify the language as that of the ship-to party.
3. Finally, one can specify the language of the sales organization. Thus, if we indicate the language of the sales organization, only those texts that are maintained in the language of the sales organization will be copied. One can then specify a requirement for the text determination to check if a condition exists, such as if a previous document exists before copying the text. Last, one can specify a routine that can be used in defining the text origination; this determines if it is possible to use a user exit to define alternative sources for texts. After completing the access sequence and saving it, the system will prompt you to generate the access sequence. Figure 4-86 shows the access sequence we will be using in order to transfer the text from the customer master record into the sales document header.
4. After creating the access sequences, create the text procedure by selecting the Text procedure button. Create a two-character key with a short description. We will use the standard procedure "01—Sales header" for this example.
5. After the procedure has been created, assign the text types to the procedure. This can be done by selecting the button "Texts in procedure." It is here you assign the actual text types you want to have assigned to the sales document header with the four-character

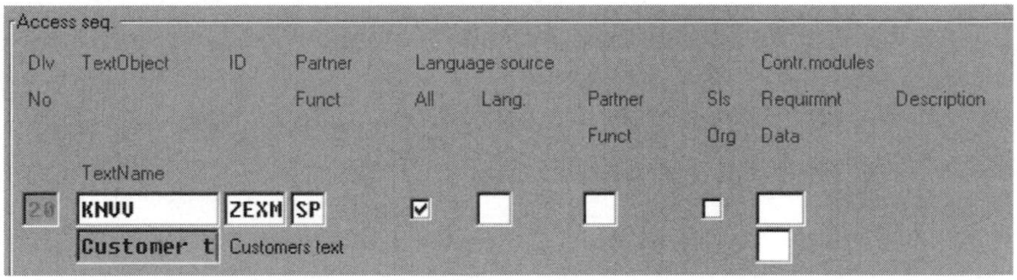

Figure 4-86 Access sequence transferring text from customer master records into sales document header

Access seq.

Dlv No	TextObject / TextName	ID	Partner Funct	Language source All	Lang.	Partner Funct	Sls Org	Contr.modules Requirmnt / Data	Description
20	KNVV	ZEXM	SP	☑			☐		
	Customer t	Customers text							

key ID and the short description. In our example, we have added our text type, "Z000—Text from customer master" to the list.

Now you can assign the access sequence that must be used by the system in obtaining this text. Thus, you assign the access sequence we created, number 501.

You can also specify if the text is to be mandatory or not. If the text is specified as mandatory and does not exist in the sales document, the system will place an entry in the sales incompletion log.

Note the reference/duplication rule: If you select copy, the system will copy the text from one document into the other where it can be changed and edited. If you do not select copy, the system does not copy the text. Instead, the system references the text from the previous document and displays it in the editor. Obviously, because the text does not belong to the document, it cannot be changed. To change it, you need to change it in the original document. Since the text is referenced, these changes will be visible in the reference documents immediately. Figure 4-87 shows the text type Z000 using access sequence 501, which has been assigned to the text procedure 01.

6. Once the texts have been assigned to the procedure, it is time to assign the procedure to the sales document types. This is done by selecting the Text proc. assignment button from the procedure overview. In our example, the standard sales order document type OR has been assigned to the text determination procedure.

We can now create the sales order. By selecting Goto, Header, Texts, you can see that the customer-specific text has been automatically copied from the customer master record into the sales document header (see Figure 4-88).

Do not forget that by selecting the Analysis button, one can find any errors or if the determination is correct (see Figure 4-89).

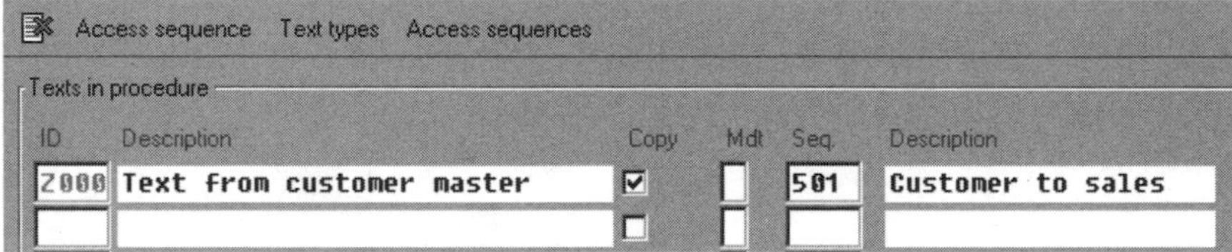

Figure 4-87
Assignment of the access sequence to the text type

Sales | Shipping | Billing | Payment cards | Financial Accounting | Pricing | Account assignment | Partners | Texts | Purchase or

Default language DE German

Language	Description	L	First line
	Contract riders (clauses)		
	Selection		
	Other contractual stipulations		
EN	Text from customer master		Example of text determination

Figure 4-88
Sales document texts

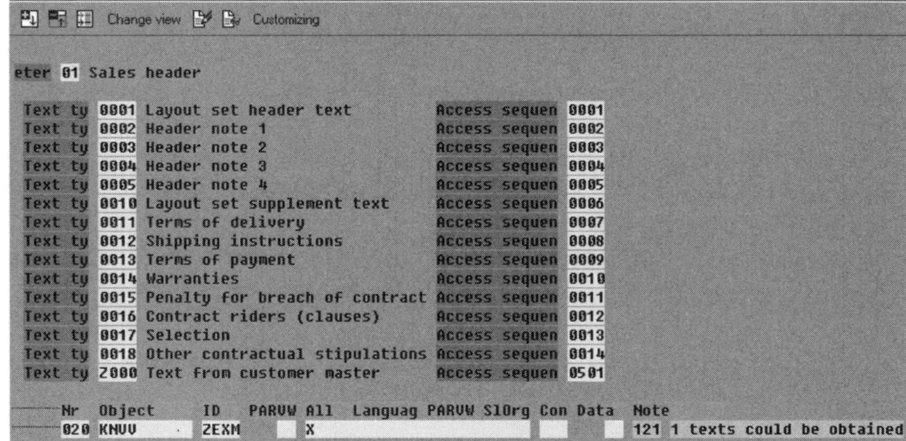

Figure 4-89
Sales document text analysis

TIP: *Do not forget the* Materials Management module (MM) *has text determination too. These are split up into the different document types that are used in the MM module, such as the purchase order and the contract or scheduling agreement. This is accessible by following the menu path IMG, Materials management, Purchasing, Scheduling agreement, Define rules for copying (adoption of) text.*

TIP: *In the maintenance of access sequences, it is useful to know the different text objects. The most common are as follows:*

- ***KNVV:*** *Customer sales texts (texts entered in Extras–.Texts) in the customer master from one of the sales screens*
- ***KNA1:*** *Customer master central texts (texts entered in Extras–.Texts) in the customer master from one of the general screens*
- ***KNB1:*** *The accounting texts*
- ***KNMT:*** *Texts defined for the customer material information record*
- ***KNVK:*** *Texts from the contact person's screen in the customer master (Extras–.Texts from the contact person's screen of the customer master)*
- ***MVKE:*** *Texts from the sales text screen in the customer master record. For MVKE, there is only one text ID — 0001 that refers to the text in the material master sales text screen.*
- ***VBBK:*** *The preceding sales document where the text is defined as header text. For example, if the preceding document is a quote copied into a delivery, then VBBK refers to the quote. If it is a order copied to a delivery, then VBBK refers to the order. If a delivery is copied to an invoice, then VBBK is the delivery.*
- ***VBBP:*** *Preceding sales document ITEM where the text is defined at the item level*
- ***TEXT:*** *This refers to standard text that applies across the system (that is, it is not specific to a document, customer, or material). The text ID in this case must be ST. When you select this text object in the access sequence, an additional field will open for you to enter the name of the standard text. This is the name you give the text when you create it in the SAPScript editor. To create standard text from the Logistics screen, proceed to Tools, Word Processing, Standard text [SO10].*

Output Determination

Output is a form of media from a business to one of its business partners. The possible media forms are printouts, faxes, telexes, e-mails, and *electronic data interchange* (EDI). The output can be sent to any of the partners defined in the document. Outputs are usually in the form of order confirmations, delivery notes, invoices, and shipping notifications.

Menu Path

The menu path here is IMG, Sales and distribution, Basic functions, Output, Output determination.

An *output type* is simply a type of output and it contains all the control features for the output. For example, it defines the kind of output (order confirmation, invoice, and so on), which business transaction it applies to, which business partner receives the output, how the output is sent (the media), and the print program and SAPScript layout to use in formatting the output. The output type is thus the central component of the output determination.

Output determination can be maintained as originating from the customer master record or as originating by using the condition technique. It is advisable to use the condition technique for the process of output determination, as this will enable greater flexibility than by using the customer master record as the source. However, in order for you to understand the differences between the two techniques, we will introduce the output proposal from the customer master record. We'll also provide examples of creating the output determination using the condition technique.

Output Proposal from the Customer Master Record

The menu path here is IMG, Sales and distribution, Basic functions, Output, Output determination, Output proposal from the customer master record, Define output.

In this option, one creates output types, such as BA00 (order confirmation). After creating the output type, one assigns the output type to an output procedure, such as DB0001 (output for customer master record). After the assignment of the output types to the procedure, the output procedure is then assigned to the customer account group. This is a simple procedure and results in the output that is placed on the customer master record being copied into the sales document.

TIP: *You can only define output on the customer master record should the output determination procedure be assigned to the customer's account group in transaction V/37. Should no output determination procedure be assigned, the system will not enable any data to be entered in the customer master record for output. This can be seen by comparing Figure 4-90a with Figure 4-90b (the output determination procedure has been assigned to the customer master account group in Figure 4-90a). The view shown in both figures is the Change Customer Master Record—transaction [VDO2].*

One main difference between the two determination procedures is that the output proposal from the customer master record is specifically dependent on the customer master record, whereas the output determined via the condition technique is specifically determined by the action, such as the creation of a sales order. The second and biggest difference between the two determinations is that the condition technique assigns an access sequence to the output type, whereas the output type proposed from the customer master record does not have the benefit of using an access sequence.

Figure 4-90a Output determination procedure is assigned to the customer master account group.

Sales area data
Sales
Shipping
Billing
Partner functions

Figure 4-90b Output determination procedure is not assigned to the customer master account group.

Output Proposal Using the Condition Technique

The menu path to follow here is as follows: IMG, Sales and distribution, Basic functions, Output, Output determination, Output proposal using the condition technique, Maintain output determination for sales documents.

It is possible to maintain the output determination for eight activities using the condition technique that is used for the following:

- Sales activities
- Sales documents
- Deliveries
- Picking lists
- Shipping units
- Groups (type of collective processing)
- Shipments
- Billing documents

Because the determination techniques used in output determination are the same, we will focus on the particular example of output determination for the sales documents.

As we know from pricing and the condition technique, when using the condition technique, one should follow the maintenance activities in sequence:

1. Put the fields you will need into the field catalog.
2. Create the condition tables.
3. Create the access sequence.
4. Assign the condition tables to the access sequence.
5. Create the condition types.
6. Assign the access sequence to the condition types.
7. Create the determination procedure (if necessary) and assign the condition types to it.
8. Assign the determination procedure.

Last, create your condition records. The output determination is no different. Steps 1 and 2 are identical and are accessible by following the menu path to Maintain output determination for sales documents, Maintain condition tables.

Step 3 and 4 are also identical, in that one follows the same customizing steps as used in pricing in creating the access sequence. This is available by following the menu path to Maintain output determination for sales documents, Maintain access sequences (see Figure 4-91).

Step 5 and 6 are identical in theory and usage, in that one assigns an access sequence to the output condition type, except that the output condition type controls different data. The output condition type is accessible by going to Maintain output determination for sales documents, Maintain output types. The output type represents different forms of output such as order confirmations, sales quotations, and so on. The output type is shown in Figure 4-92a and Figure 4-92b. You can access the output type settings by selecting the output type, such as BA00, and selecting the Display button (the magnifying glass).

You can see in Figure 4-92a that the access sequence is assigned to the output type. In the General data area, you can determine if the output is to be proposed from the customer master record or the condition technique. This is done by setting the indicator access to conditions.

You can also set an indicator allowing the output type to be manually changed during processing. It is also possible to determine if the output must be partner-independent. You can also set an allowance for multiple issuing, allowing the output type to be reissued in the sales documents for each change in the sales document.

The condition record proposal is one of the most important areas of output determination. It is here that one assigns the transmission medium, that is, how the output is to be sent. Is it to be a fax, a printout, or sent via *electronic data interchange* (EDI)? It is here that one sets the partner function allocated to the specific output type as well as the processing time for the physical output to be created. For example, this physical output can be created by batch job overnight or immediately in the application update.

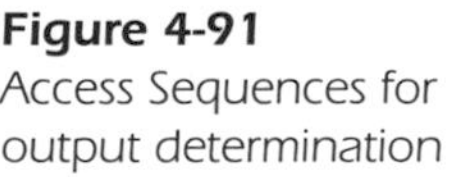

Figure 4-91
Access Sequences for output determination

Navigation
Access Sequences
-->Accesses
-->Fields
Utilities...

Access Sequences (Output Sales)

AcSq	Description	Description
0001	SalesOrg/DistrCh/Div/Customer	
0002	Order Type	
0003	SalesOrg/Customer	
0004	SalesOrg/Sales Order Type	

Figure 4-92a
Output type (view 1)

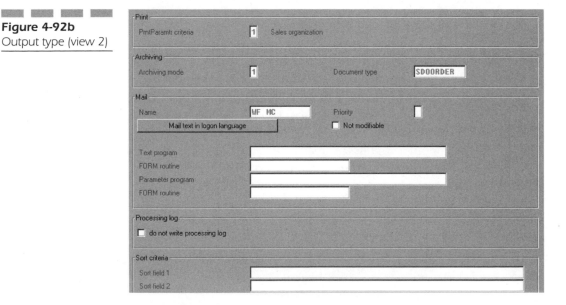

Work area
Output type BA00 Order Confirmation
Access sequence 0002

General
☑ Access to conditions
☐ CannotBeChanged
☐ Partner-indep.output
☐ Multiple issuing

Condition record proposal
Transm. medium 6
Part.funct. SP
Time 4
Processing program
Partner definition

Time of dispatch
☑ Dispatch time 1 not allowed
☐ Dispatch time 2 not allowed
☐ Dispatch time 3 not allowed
☐ Dispatch time 4 not allowed
Output timing prg
FORM routine

Changed output
Changed output prog.
FORM routine

Figure 4-92b
Output type (view 2)

Print
PrntParamtr criteria 1 Sales organization

Archiving
Archiving mode 1
Document type SDOORDER

Mail
Name WF MC
Priority
Mail text in logon language
☐ Not modifiable
Text program
FORM routine
Parameter program
FORM routine

Processing log
☐ do not write processing log

Sort criteria
Sort field 1
Sort field 2

NOTE: *The values entered for the output type and the time and partner functions for the condition record proposal data are automatically transferred as default values when creating a condition record by an output condition.*

You must understand that the output is automatically proposed and processed according to the rules governed in output determination. However, the user can still reprint or change the printing specifications online in the sales document. For example, the order confirmation could be printed overnight and posted to the customer the following day, but the customer may explicitly request that his order confirmation is handed to him immediately. Thus, the user would change the output processing time to a 4—immediately.

The business, however, may not want the user to have this authority on all output types. For example, the order confirmation may be printed on a special printer with special paper, and should only be done via a batch job at night. Thus, you can specify that specific times for dispatches are not allowed. This is set by indicating, for example, time of dispatch 4—not allowed. You can also set the print parameter, as shown in Figure 4-92b. These criteria can be set as the sales organization or sales office, for example.

It is also possible to print and archive a document automatically by setting the Archiving mode to 3 and assigning the correct archiving document type. This field identifies whether the archived document is an invoice, quotation, or order confirmation. The archiving object of outgoing documents begins with SD0. Prior to completing Step 7, follow this menu path: Maintain output determination for sales documents, Assign output types to partner functions.

One can assign the allowed output types and processing medium to the partner functions. For example, one can assign the order confirmation as a printout to the sold-to party and the order confirmation as a fax to the sold-to party (see Figure 4-93).

Step 7 is also identical and is accessible via the following menu path: Maintain output determination for sales documents, Maintain output determination procedure.

One has an output determination procedure with the output condition types assigned to it. The condition types also have a requirement that can be assigned, restricting any access to the output type as well as access to

Figure 4-93 Output Control, assigning Output Types to Partner Functions

Output Control: Output By Partner Function

Outp	Med	Funct	Name	Name
BA00	1	SP	Order Confirmation	Sold-to party
BA00	2	SP	Order Confirmation	Sold-to party
BA00	6	SP	Order Confirmation	Sold-to party
BA00	A	SP	Order Confirmation	Sold-to party

the access sequence and condition records, unless specific conditions in the requirement have been fulfilled (see Figure 4-94).

After completing the assignment of the condition type to the procedure, proceed to Step 8, where you assign the procedure. The assignment is achieved in the following menu path: Maintain output determination for sales documents, Assign output determination procedures. This assignment of the output occurs at the header and item level for sales documents. This assignment is shown in Figure 4-95a for the header level and Figure 4-95b for the item level.

Finally, one can now create the condition records necessary for output determination (see Figure 4-96). This can be done by going to Logistics, Sales and distribution, Master data, Output, Sales document, Create.

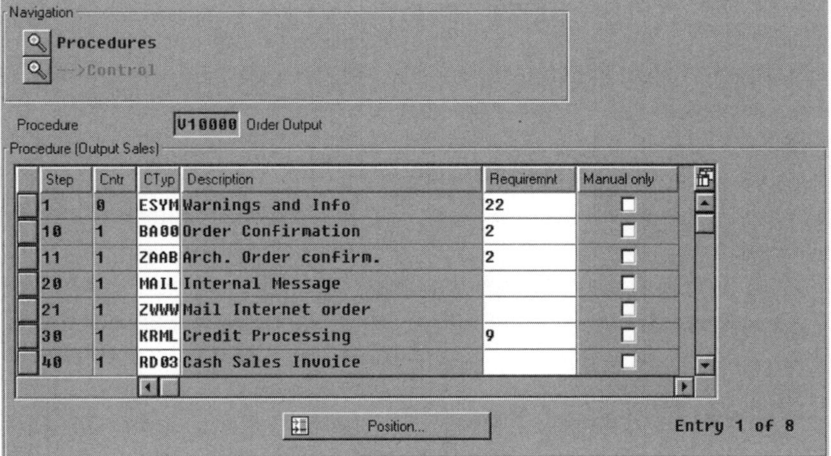

Navigation
Procedures
--->Control

Procedure V10000 Order Output

Procedure (Output Sales)

Step	Cntr	CTyp	Description	Requiremnt	Manual only
1	0	ESYM	Warnings and Info	22	☐
10	1	BA00	Order Confirmation	2	☐
11	1	ZAAB	Arch. Order confirm.	2	☐
20	1	MAIL	Internal Message		☐
21	1	ZWWW	Mail Internet order		☐
30	1	KRML	Credit Processing	9	☐
40	1	RD03	Cash Sales Invoice		☐

Position... Entry 1 of 8

Figure 4-94 Output types within an output determination procedure with assigned reqirements

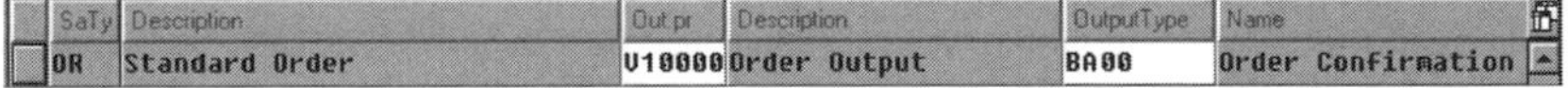

SaTy	Description	Out pr	Description	OutputType	Name
OR	Standard Order	V10000	Order Output	BA00	Order Confirmation

Figure 4-95a Output assignment at header level

Output View TVAP

Item category	Description	Item output proc.
TAN	Standard Item	

Figure 4-95b Output assignment at item level

Figure 4-96
Output condition record

Figure 4-97
Output condition, communication data

Sales document type
OR

Printing Information

Output device	LP01	Print immediately
Number of messages	1	Release after output
Spool request name	SD_003	
Suffix 1	BA00	
Suffix 2	ORDER_CONFIR	
SAP cover sheet		
Recipient		
Department		
Text for cover sheet		
Authorization		

Figure 4-98
Output is now shown in the sales order.

Communication method Processing log Further data Repeat output Change output

Standard Order

Statu	Output type		Medium		PartFi	Partner	Langu	Change	Processing
	BA00	Order Confirmatic	1	Print output	SP	10011	EN		

One assigns the output type, partner function, transmission medium (1 = printout), timing of the output (4 = immediately), and the language, English. By selecting communication, as in Figure 4-97, one can assign the output device (due to the transmission medium being a printout), the number of messages, and whether the output must be printed immediately.

If you now create a sales order with document type OR (English), the system will automatically propose an output type BA00 based on the output determination as set in the above steps. This is seen in Figure 4-98.

The buttons in the sales order output are the communication methods that identify the details as set in the communication area of the condition record, such as printer name and so on. The view is similar to that as shown in Figure 4-97.

Processing log records a log of the output already processed in the sales document.

Further data determines if the output has been processed as well as the timing data, that is, the output to be processed immediately or in batch.

Repeat output can be used to repeat already-processed output.

Change output can be used to change the output.

This completes the maintenance of the output determination as required in the system. However, there is a lot of additional data that pertains to output that you should be aware of. These details are as follows.

Brief Overview of a Layout Set and Its Assignment to Output Types

Layout sets and SAPScript do not fall within the scope of this book, but it is beneficial for one to understand how the sales and distribution module integrates with the layout set and SAPscript.

How does output work? Each output type is linked to a processing print program and a layout set. For example, in the SAP standard, the output type BA00 (order confirmation) is linked to processing program RVADOR01 and layout set RVORDER01. When the user enters the output type in the business transaction and then selects to print it, SAP calls the print program. The print program reads the business transaction and collects all the information that needs to be printed on it. It puts this information into structures defined in the data dictionary. The fields in these structures are used in the SAPScript layout to define what data must be printed and where it must be printed.

The print program then opens the SAPScript layout and calls each of the elements in the layout. The layout takes the information from the data dictionary structures as well as all the formatting information and then formats it for the printer, fax machine, or e-mail. Finally, the SAP system sends the output to the necessary device (printer, fax, or mail server).

In the order example, when the user enters the output type BA00 in the order transaction and then issues the output, SAP calls the print program RVADOR01. This program reads the sales order and related information and transfers it into the structures VBDKA (header information), VBDPA (item information), KOMK (pricing information), and others. It calls SAPScript, printing the relevant elements. SAPScript uses the information in the structures and formats the output to be printed.

When SAP sends the output to the printer, it is printed with the information collected by the print program in the format defined in the layout set. The output type is linked to a layout set. A layout set in SAPScript is used for the control layout of the page. As described previously, this is linked by the output being processed by a program that processes the output and calls up the layout set or form. This processing program calls up a routine and form, as shown in Figure 4-99.

Menu Path

This link is assigned in the following menu path: IMG, Sales and distribution, Basic functions, Output, Output determination, Process output and forms, Assign forms and programs, Assign to sales documents.

Once the link has been done, the layout set may need to be examined. This is possible by going to IMG, Sales and distribution, Basic functions, Output, Output determination, Process output and forms, Define forms. It is here that one enters the name of the form or the layout set and displays the required data, as shown in Figure 4-100.

The layout set is divided up into six elements, namely:

Header data General information about the layout set, such as the user who is responsible for creating it and a short description of the layout set.

Paragraphs This defines the paragraph styles used in the layout and defines how the paragraph will print. For example, must the paragraph be right- or left-justified?

Character strings These define the styles for a string of characters. For example, should a word be printed as bold, underlined, or italic?

Figure 4-99 Output type, linked to Program and FORM routine

Output: Processing Programs

Outp	Name	Med	Program	FORM routine	Form
BA00	Order Confirmation	1	RVADOR01	ENTRY	RVORDER01
BA00	Order Confirmation	2	RVADOR01	ENTRY	RVORDER01
BA00	Order Confirmation	5	RVADOR01	ENTRY	RVORDER01
BA00	Order Confirmation	6	RSNASTED	EDI_PROCESSING	
BA00	Order Confirmation	A	RSNASTED	ALE_PROCESSING	

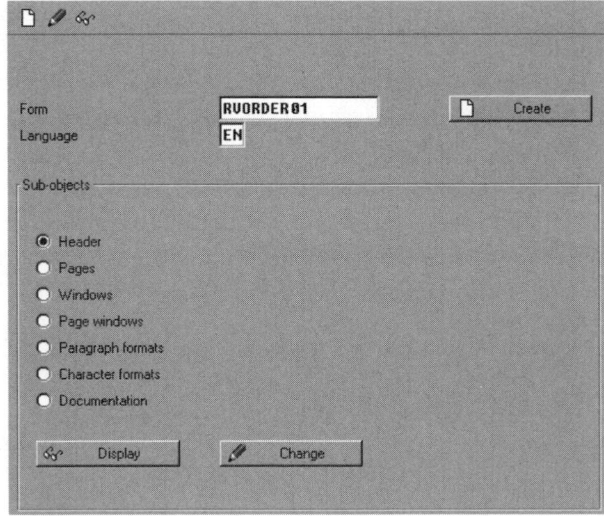

Figure 4-100 Layout set/form objects

Windows Windows are separate sections on the page. For example, you could have a header window for a company log and a footer window for the page footer. The most important window is the Main window where the items are printed. You specify the text and fields to be printed in the layout set in the different windows.

Page This defines the pages in your layout. You may have a first page containing a lot of header information, but the following pages contain the overflow from the Main window.

Page windows In this section, you arrange the windows you defined in the Windows section on the pages. You specify which windows are on each page and the positions they occupy on the page.

Menu Path

One can also define specific form texts for the sales organization, sales office, or shipping point by going to IMG, Sales and distribution, Basic functions, Output, Output determination, Process output and forms, Assign form texts. These specific texts are the address text, letter header, letter footer text, and greeting text (see Figure 4-101). One can specify the position of these texts within the output document.

Figure 4-101
Assign specific form texts

SOrg	Name	Address text	Letter header	Footer text li	Greeting text
0001	Sales Org. Germany	ADRS_SENDER	ADRS_HEADER	ADRS_FOOTER	ADRS_SIGNATURE

TIP: *Output processing via a batch is explained in Chapter 5.*

The "number of copies" allocation to the customer master record output and the condition technique output is a bit of a red herring in that, in most instances, one will not be able to create more than one output (see OSS note 0003748), unless one dedicates a printer to print a specified number of outputs as a default for all outputs on that printer. The only alternative options are to manually reprint a specific output or to create a copy of the output type. For example, allow two order confirmations to be automatically determined by the system for specific conditions, thus causing two printouts.

TIP: *One can view printer details and output specific data by using the transaction code* Spool Administration (SPAD) *and branching off to view necessary data, such as output devices and spool servers.*

TIP: *Should one need to reprint a number of documents, such as billing documents, one will have to create a new specific print program in SAP version 2. However in version 3 and above one may use the menu path: Logistic, Sales and distribution, output, billing documents*

Transaction code
VF31—Billing documents
VT70—Shipping and delivery documents

One must enter the number range of documents that must be printed, the output type, and the transmission medium and set the process mode, for example, to reprocess.

Customer Hierarchies

Customer hierarchies are used when a customer has a complex chain or organizational structure in which all or some of the parts of this structure will benefit from an agreement made for the customer's company as a whole. For example, a large customer may have dependent offices, each responsible for their own purchasing, and as individuals, they would not benefit from a global pricing scheme. However, as part of a customer's hierarchy, they would still benefit from being associated with the larger parent company.

Before setting out and maintaining a customer hierarchy, one needs to determine what the requirement for the hierarchy is. If the requirement is a report, such as reporting bookings or billings for global customers within a hierarchy, this can be done using a standard reporting hierarchy within the sales information system, which will be covered in Chapter 5. Should the desire be merely to offer prices according to a specific group, one could think about using a customer group on the customer master record, rather than a customer hierarchy.

If, on the other hand, one wants to have a customer hierarchy in order to offer special price agreements or rebates across a customer's organization on a global level, which may not be covered by a standard grouping, this can be covered by using the customer hierarchy.

The customer hierarchy integrates and relies on the partner determination in conjunction with the customer hierarchy settings in order to promote the linking between the customers. The partner determination causes the customer hierarchy to be represented in the sales document. The customer hierarchy is a hierarchical organizational structure that consists of higher and lower level nodes. Each node is assigned within the structure to form a graphical diagram of the customer's organization.

A node is represented by an account group. A node can be a customer, such as a sold-to party, thus account group 0001. A node could also be a platform or merely an organizational department; thus, we have account group 0012. A customer hierarchy can only have a maximum of 26 hierarchy levels. One creates a customer hierarchy by first defining the hierarchy type.

Menu Path

The menu path here is IMG, Sales and distribution, Master data, Business partners, Customers, Customer hierarchy, Define hierarchy types.

Transaction Code

The code here is [OVH1].

In Figure 4-102, we have a customer hierarchy type A. This is assigned to the partner function 1A, which is the highest node of the partner represented in the hierarchy. There should not be a need for you to create more than one hierarchy type, as you can only assign one hierarchy type per sales document type, which we will see later. The only time you may need a new hierarchy type is when one uses a different hierarchy for different business transactions.

One can now proceed to create the associated partner determinations for customer hierarchies.

Menu Path

Creating the associated partner determinations for customer hierarchies can be done by going to IMG, Sales and distribution, Master data, Business partners, Customers, Customer hierarchy, Set partner determination for hierarchy categories.

Transaction Code

The code here is [VOPA].

One can assign partner functions up to 26 levels, from 1A through to 1Z. This may be seen in Figure 4-103. It is advisable to set the partner function

Figure 4-102 Customer Hierarchy Type

CustHType	Name	PartFunct.	Name
A	Standard Hierarchy	1A	Customer hierarchy 1

Figure 4-103 Partner determination assign partner functions

Procedure partner

Funct	Description	Not changeable	Mandat.funct	Source	Seq.
1A	Customer hierarchy 1	☑	☐	B	
1B	Customer hierarchy 2	☑	☐	B	
1C	Customer hierarchy 3	☑	☐	B	
1D	Customer hierarchy 4	☑	☐	B	

as not changeable and one also needs to maintain the source as a B, representing a customer hierarchy. This should be carried out for the sales document header and the billing document header, as one may need the hierarchy to be represented in both document types.

Be careful also to maintain enough partner determination levels as are needed to represent the customer's structure. For example, let's say the customer's company had seven levels in the hierarchy, and we only maintained five levels in the partner determination. The system would only copy data relevant to the five maintained levels into the sales document, and thus would only search for condition records up to the five levels of partners.

After the partner determination has been maintained, one needs to maintain the association between the higher and lower level customer account groups. As we know, the hierarchy is formed by a linking of account groups, and we need to maintain what account groups are to be linked.

Menu Path

The menu path here is IMG, Sales and distribution, Master data, Business partners, Customers, Customer hierarchy, Assign account groups.

Transaction Code

The code here is [OVH2].

Here one assigns which account group can be assigned to a higher level account group, per the customer hierarchy type. For example, in Figure 4-104, we can see for hierarchy type A that a sold-to party (0001) can be assigned to another sold-to party (0001), while a sold-to party (0001) can also be assigned to a payer (0003) and a hierarchy node (0012). Further down the table, we see that a hierarchy node (0012) can also be assigned to a sold-to party. This is logically assigning account groups, but if we do not introduce some form of organizational definition, the hierarchy could easily run out of control, especially

Figure 4-104 Account group assignments allowed in the customer hierarchy

CustHType	Name	Acct group	Description	HgLvAcctGr	Description
A	Standard Hierarchy	0001	Sold-to party	0001	Sold-to party
A	Standard Hierarchy	0001	Sold-to party	0003	Payer
A	Standard Hierarchy	0001	Sold-to party	0012	Hierarchy node
A	Standard Hierarchy	0003	Payer	0012	Hierarchy node
A	Standard Hierarchy	0012	Hierarchy node	0001	Sold-to party
A	Standard Hierarchy	0012	Hierarchy node	0003	Payer
A	Standard Hierarchy	0012	Hierarchy node	0012	Hierarchy node

because the system would not have a definitive organizational path to follow for condition records. Thus, one needs to assign lower level sales areas to higher level sales areas.

Menu Path

Assigning lower level sales areas to higher level sales areas is done through IMG, Sales and distribution, Master data, Business partners, Customers, Customer hierarchy, Assign sales areas.

Transaction Code

The code here is [OVH3]. One can see in Figure 4-105 that the sales area 1000/12 /00 has been assigned to itself as well as to sales area 1020/20 /00.

Now that all the master data is maintained, other than the creation of the actual hierarchy itself, one needs to assign the hierarchy type to the actual sales document type.

Menu Path

The path here is IMG, Sales and distribution, Master data, Business partners, Customers, Customer hierarchy, Assign hierarchy type for pricing by sales document type.

Transaction Code

The code here is [OVH4]. This simple assignment of the hierarchy type, such as "A" to a sales document type "OR," (or "TA") means that you cannot have more than one hierarchy type per sales document, but you can have more than one customer hierarchy within the hierarchy type. The only step to be carried out is the creation of the hierarchy to match that of the customer.

Figure 4-105 Sales area assignments allowed in the customer hierarchy

CustHType	Sales org.	Distr. chl	Division	HgLvSlsOrg	HLDstrCh	HgLvDivis.
A	1000	12	00	1000	12	00
A	1000	12	00	1020	20	00
A	1020	20	00	1020	20	00

Let's use the example that our customer "International" is a global account with branches represented in Africa, the Americas, Europe, Asia, and Australia. Each branch in these areas is further broken down into a national office and a subsequent regional office. Due to the size of the customer, we offer all "International" regional offices across the globe the same pricing discount of 10 percent off all our products. This would be represented in a hierarchy.

Menu Path

To create this hierarchy, go to Logistics, Sales and distribution, Master data, Business partners, Customer hierarchy, Change.

Transaction Code

The code here is [VDH1]. Do not forget to create the customer hierarchy nodes in the same way that you would create all customer master records either using [VD01] with the account group 0012 or using the path. Got to Logistics, Sales and distribution, Master data, Business partners, Hierarchy nodes, Create transaction code [V−12].

Also do not forget to indicate the customers or nodes as relevant for customer hierarchy-specific pricing and/or rebates. This is done by setting the indicators on the billing screen of the customer master as in Figure 4-106.

I have created the following nodes and customers:

Customer:	10011—Munich Regional office of International	Account group 0001
Node:	10051—Germany–National office	Account group 0012
Node:	10052—Europe	Account group 0012
Node:	10054—Africa	Account group 0012
Node:	10055—Americas	Account group 0012
Node:	10056—Asia	Account group 0012
Node:	10053—International—Global account	Account group 0012

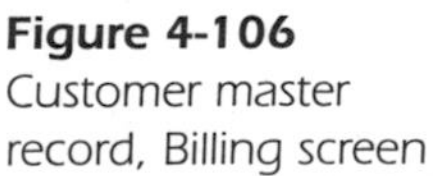

Figure 4-106 Customer master record, Billing screen

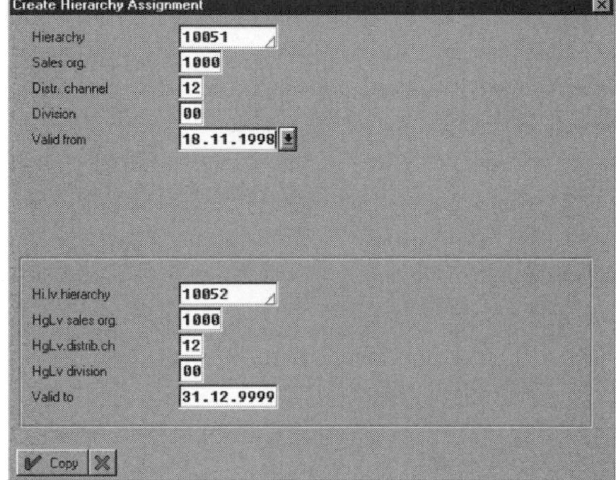

Figure 4-107 Assignment of a lower level node to a higher level node

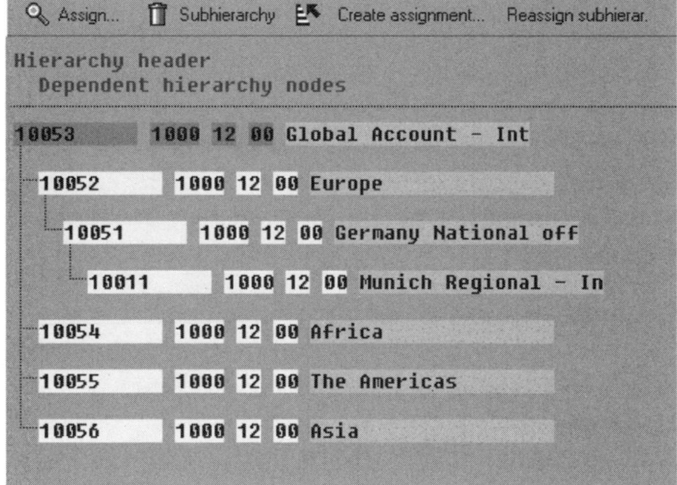

Figure 4-108 Hierarchy structure

On creation of the hierarchy node using transaction code [VDH1], one must select the Create assignment button and then enter the higher level and the assigned lower level node, as shown in Figure 4-107.

Thus, the structure that meets the requirement of our International customer is now seen in Figure 4-108.

When creating a sales order, one can clearly see the customer hierarchy in the partner's overview, as shown in Figure 4-109.

If you do not initially see the hierarchy, note the four buttons at the bottom of the display, as shown in Figure 4-110. Select "Show all partners."

Sales | Shipping | Billing | Payment cards | Financial Accounting | Pricing | Account assignment | Partners | Texts | Purchase ord

All partners in the doc. header

	Partner function	Partner	Name	Part
1B	Customer hierarchy 2	10051	Germany National office	
1C	Customer hierarchy 3	10052	Europe	
1D	Customer hierarchy 4	10053	Global Account - Internationa	
SP	Sold-to party	10011	Munich Regional - Internation	
BP	Bill-to party	10011	Munich Regional - Internation	
PY	Payer	10011	Munich Regional - Internation	
SH	Ship-to party	10011	Munich Regional - Internation	

Figure 4-109 Hierarchy structure as represented in the partners screen of the sales document

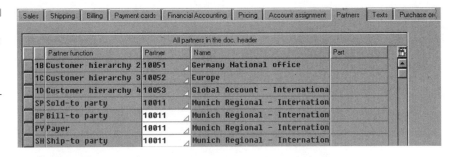

Figure 4-110 Select show all partners

This concludes the determination of the customer hierarchy. Its usefulness remains in that it can be used in conjunction with the condition technique to offer discounts, surcharges, or special pricing. Do not forget that if the sole purpose of your customer hierarchy is to report bookings or billings in a hierarchical form, this can be done by using the standard *logistics information systems* (LIS) hierarchies, which will be described in Chapter 5.

Product Hierarchies

Product hierarchies are the domain of materials management, but it is beneficial for the SD module to know they exist, what they are, and where they are maintained. A product hierarchy like a customer hierarchy has an automatic "family tree" linking it back to a certain grouping of products.

Menu Path

The menu path here is IMG, Logistics general, Logistics basic data: Material master, Material, Data relevant to sales and distribution, Define product hierarchies.

Transaction Code

The code here is [OVSV]. A product hierarchy is assigned to the material master record. This hierarchy is broken down into specific levels, each level containing its own characteristics. A product hierarchy is recorded by the sequence of digits within a hierarchy number. This hierarchy number can have a maximum of 18 digits with a maximum number of nine levels.

For example, a material can be classified as a laptop computer with an active screen. Such a product hierarchy with three levels is as follows:

Computer	00001
Laptop	00002
Active screen	00000100

Thus, by assigning the hierarchy number 000010000200000100 to the material, one can determine a classification of the material. This hierarchy can be used in pricing with each level being used as a field in the condition technique. Thus, it is possible to say all materials with a product hierarchy level 1 equal to 00001 can have a 10 percent discount. Each of these levels can also be used as fields for reporting purposes in the LIS; thus, it is possible for one to report on the number of computers sold by selecting all materials with level 1 equal to 00001.

The SAP standard system has a product hierarchy structure consisting of three levels. These three levels are broken down into two levels of five digits each and one level of eight digits. Should this hierarchy structure meet the requirements of your business, one can proceed straight through to the maintenance of the hierarchy in transaction [V/76].

If, however, one needs to create a new hierarchy structure, one can proceed by following these steps:

1. One needs to maintain the product hierarchy structure — PRODHS. The maintenance of structures does not fall within the scope of this book, but there is clear documentation in the system on how to perform this step. This structure defines each level and the length of digits permitted for each level, as shown in Figure 4-111.
2. One can create a template that represents the product hierarchy. This template should have placeholders defined by an underscore and separators defined by a forward slash or a colon. Thus, a template of five, five, and eight digits will look as follows: _____/_____/________.

3. One can then create the product hierarchy as used by the system (see Figure 4-112).
4. Now that the hierarchy and the template with the entries allowed in the hierarchy are created, you merely need to ensure that the hierarchy levels are in the field catalog used in pricing as well as in the field catalog in the LIS (see Figure 4-113).
5. Last, one must ensure that the material master record has the product hierarchy assigned to it in the Basic data 1 view under General data (see Figure 4-114).

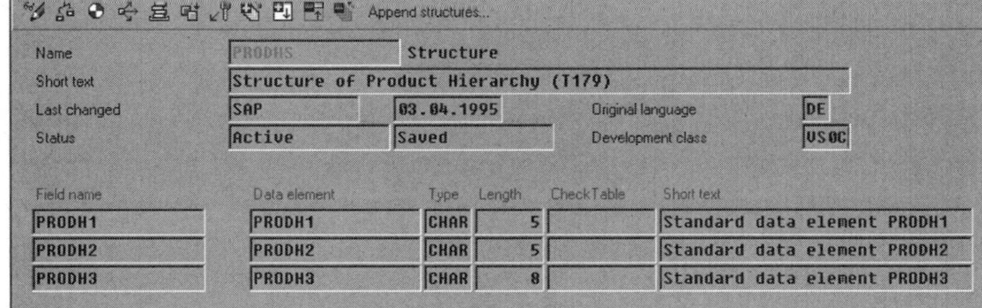

Append structures...

Name: PRODHS Structure
Short text: Structure of Product Hierarchy (T179)
Last changed: SAP 03.04.1995 Original language: DE
Status: Active Saved Development class: VSOC

Field name	Data element	Type	Length	CheckTable	Short text
PRODH1	PRODH1	CHAR	5		Standard data element PRODH1
PRODH2	PRODH2	CHAR	5		Standard data element PRODH2
PRODH3	PRODH3	CHAR	8		Standard data element PRODH3

Figure 4-111 Field names within the structure "ProdH5"

Product hierarchy	Level no.	Description
00145	1	Foods
0014500100	2	General foodstuffs
001450010000000100	3	Soup
0014500105	2	Luxury foods
001450010500000100	3	Chocolate
001450010500000105	3	Wafer
001450010500000110	3	Cookie
0014500110	2	Drinks

Figure 4-112 Create the actual Product hierarchy

Field Catalog (Pricing Sales/Distribution)

Field	Description
PRODH	Product hierarchy
PRODH1	Main group
PRODH2	Group
PRODH3	Subgroup

Figure 4-113 Ensure product hierarchy fields are in the Field Category for pricing

Prod.hierarchy 00145001050000000100

Figure 4-114
Material master record basic data 1 screen

Credit Management

Most transactions in SAP enable customers a time period in which to pay their accounts. These time periods are shown via the payment terms as assigned to the customer master record. Should a customer not pay his outstanding amounts by the end of his allowed payment term, he is defaulting on his agreement and the company will need to govern his allowed credit more closely.

In order to manage these situations, SAP has developed a complex credit management solution that enables, among other things, the maintenance of set credit limits per customer as well the maintenance of the system responses, should a customer's credit limit be exceeded.

Before we proceed with credit management, we need to discuss certain master data. For example, a credit limit may be a *customer's credit limit*, which is the permitted limit of the value of open items, such as invoices not yet paid, plus the value of open sales orders. The customer's credit limit is assigned to the customer by going to the Logistics overview screen, Accounting, Financial accounting, Accounts receivable, Master records, Credit management, Change.

A *credit control area* is an organizational unit that is comprised of one or more company codes. A company code can have no more than one credit control area. These credit control areas are maintained and assigned as follows.

Menu Path to Create a Credit Control Area

The path to follow is IMG, Enterprise structure, Maintain structure, Definition, Financial accounting, Maintain credit control area.

Transaction Code

The code here is [OB45] (see Figure 4-115).

Menu Path to Assign a Credit Control Area to a Company Code

The path is as follows: IMG, Enterprise structure, Maintain structure, Assignment, Financial accounting, Assign company code to credit control area.

Transaction Code

The code here is [OB38] (see Figure 4-116).

TIP: *It is possible to assign a credit control area to a sales area (a combination of a sales organization, distribution channel, and division). This is a more specific assignment than the assignment to the company code.*

A customer's *risk category* is a grouping category that controls the credit checks when automatic credit control takes place. Thus, one can assign high-risk customers to risk category, for example, A01, medium-risk customers can belong to B01, and low-risk customers can belong to group C01. We will use this category and define its assignment later.

A credit check can only occur in three places: the sales order, the delivery, and the goods issue. The system can use a *simple credit check*, a *static credit check*, or a *dynamic credit check*.

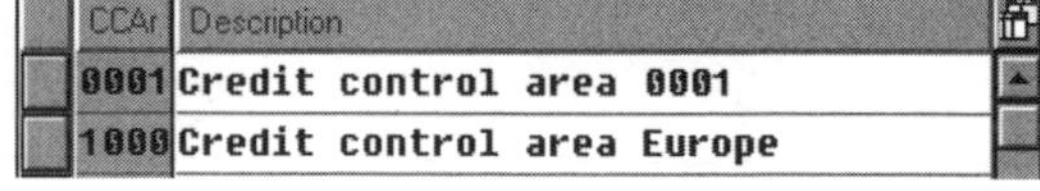

CCAr	Description
0001	Credit control area 0001
1000	Credit control area Europe

Figure 4-115
Credit Control Areas

CoCd	Company name	City	CCAr	C
0001	SAP A.G.	Walldorf		
1000	IDES AG	Frankfurt	1000	

Figure 4-116
Assigning a credit control area to a Company Code

The simple credit check compares the *payer* customer master record's credit limit to the total of the net document value and the value of all open items. Should the value of the document and open items be greater than the credit limit permitted, the system may respond with a warning message in the sales order, a warning message and a delivery block (which will allow the order to be taken but will block it for delivery), or an error message that will cause the document not to be saved. This setting for a simple credit check is set at the document type level; thus, the system will use this simple check for all sales orders created for this particular sales document type. The system will perform the simple credit check for all created and changed sales documents.

Menu Path for a Simple Credit Check

The path is as follows: IMG, Sales and distribution, Basic functions, Credit management/Risk management, Simple credit limit check.

Transaction Code

The code here is [OVAK]. One can now assign the credit limit check to the sales document type:

A Run a simple credit limit check and a warning message.

B Run a simple credit limit check and an error message.

C Run a simple credit limit check and a delivery block.

As it is generally not beneficial to treat all customers the same way as far as credit management is concerned, SAP enables a dynamic and static credit check according to a customer's risk category. Thus, one can differentiate that if a good customer with a low-risk credit rating exceeds his credit limit, the sales order can still be created and not blocked. However, should a high-risk customer with a high-risk credit rating exceed his credit limit using the same sales document type, the system can block the sales document from being processed further. This credit management control is maintained by using the automatic credit control functionality.

The automatic credit control divides the sales document types, the delivery document types, and goods issue into specific credit groups. It also uses the customer's risk category as assigned to the customer master record of the payer and assigns an outcome procedure to the combination of the above two objects, that is, the credit group and the customer risk category, along with the credit control area. The definition of the customer's risk category is carried out in the Financial accounting module.

Menu Path

The path here is IMG, Financial accounting, Accounts receivable and accounts payable, Credit management, Credit control account, Define risk categories.

Transaction Code

The code here is [OB01]. As a tip, it is advisable to be as simplistic as possible when defining the credit risk categories and document credit groups. Due to the number of combinations, one can perform with these two groupings. The risk categories are shown in Figure 4-117.

Now that the risk category has been defined, it is possible to proceed with the settings for the automatic credit control.

Menu Path

The path here is IMG, Sales and distribution, Basic functions, Credit management/Risk management, Credit management, Define credit groups.

Transaction Code

The code here is [OVA6]. One merely creates a credit group for each differentiation in the document type (see Figure 4-118).

Figure 4-117 Credit Risk Categories and associated credit control

Risk category	CCAr	Name
001	1000	Low risk
001	3000	Low risk
001	5000	Low risk
002	1000	High risk
002	3000	High risk
002	5000	High risk
004	1000	Medium risk
004	3000	Medium risk
004	5000	Medium risk
100	1000	New customers
100	3000	New customers

Should you create a different credit group, such as if you want to perform the credit check differently for standard sales orders, as one does for scheduling agreements, you can create and assign the credit group to this table. You then need to assign the credit groups to the sales document and delivery document types.

Menu Path

The menu path is IMG, Sales and distribution, Basic functions, Credit management/Risk management, Credit management, Assign sales documents and delivery documents, Credit limit check for order types, Credit limit check for delivery types.

Transaction Code

The code here is [OVAK] for order document types and [OVAD] for delivery document types. As in Figure 4-119, one can assign the sales document type OR, the check credit indicator D to determine the automatic credit control, and the credit group 01. Determining this automatic credit control is carried out for a sales order.

Figure 4-118 Credit groups

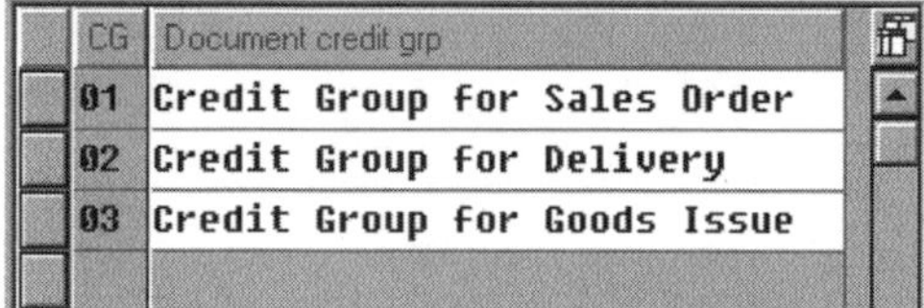

CG	Document credit grp
01	Credit Group for Sales Order
02	Credit Group for Delivery
03	Credit Group for Goods Issue

Figure 4-119 Automatic credit control determination, document type and automatic check indicator and credit group

SaTy	Description	Check credit	Credit group
OR	Standard Order	D	01

Menu Path

One can now define the automatic credit control settings. This is maintained by proceeding as follows: IMG, Sales and distribution, Basic functions, Credit management/Risk management, Credit management, Define automatic credit control.

Transaction Code

The code here is [OVA8]. One now assigns settings to the combination of the credit control area, the customers risk category, and the credit group, as shown in Figure 4-120.

One can see in the previous example that we have automatic settings for a low-risk customer, a medium-risk customer, and a high-risk customer in a sales order. One has already assigned the credit control area as well as the credit group; all that is remaining is the assignment of the risk category to the customer master record. This risk category assignment occurs in the same place as the customer's credit limit, which is the Customers credit management screen. That is, the risk category is assigned to the customer by Finance by going to the Logistics overview screen, Accounting, Financial accounting, Accounts receivable, Master records, Credit management, Change, or to transaction code [FD32] (see Figure 4-121).

One can also assign various other credit settings in relation to the customer master record here. This customer credit master record is divided up into five views:

Figure 4-120 Credit control area plus customers Risk Category plus credit group

CCAr	Risk cat.	CG	Credit control
1000	001	01	Low Risk Sales Orders
1000	001	02	Low Risk Deliveries
1000	001	03	Low Risk Goods Issue
1000	002	01	High Risk Sales Orders
1000	002	02	High Risk Deliveries
1000	002	03	High Risk Goods Issue
1000	004	01	Medium Risk Sales Orders
1000	004	02	Medium Risk Deliveries
1000	004	03	Medium Risk Goods Issue
1000	100	01	Orders: New customer
1000	100	02	Deliveries: New customer

Figure 4-121
Customer master credit settings

Customer 10011 Munich Regional - International
Credit control area 1000 Credit control area Europe DEM

Credit limit data
Credit limit 100.000,00 Receivables 0,00
Credit account 10011 Special liabil. 0,00
Order value 0,00
Credit limit used 0,00 % Credit exposure 0,00
A/R summary Sec.receivables 0,00

Internal data
Risk category 001 Low risk Blocked
Credit rep.group Texts exist
Cust.cred.group Texts
Customer group Last int.review
Reference date Next int.review

- The **overview** gives an overview of the credit settings in relation to the customer, including his credit limit, the credit exposure, the percentage of the credit limit used, his payment data, and his risk category.
- The **address** view gives the customer's address details as they appear on the customer master record.
- The **central data** is a view that shows the total credit limit the customer can receive across all credit control areas as well as the maximum limit he can receive in one credit control area. For example, he may be allowed to purchase in more than one company code, and thus may be allowed to purchase in more than one credit control area. However, the business may want to limit their overall exposure to the customer and may assign a maximum limit pertaining to the sum of individual limits across all credit control areas. The business may go further and assign a maximum limit allowed in any one credit control area.
- The **status** view shows the customer's actual individual details according to the particular credit control area being investigated. This includes his credit limit, the percentage used, the credit exposure, the risk category, whether he is blocked due to credit or not, and so on.
- The **payment history** view displays the payments made by the customer for a particular credit control area where a company code is assigned (as payments are made within a company code).

We can now maintain the settings for the automatic credit control. These settings may take the form of a static check or a dynamic check. The static credit limit check is a check comparing the credit limit assigned to the customer to the total value of open sales orders, plus the total value of open deliveries not yet invoiced, plus the total value of open billing documents not yet passed on to accounting, plus the total value of billing documents that have been passed on to accounting, but which have not yet been paid by the customer.

The dynamic credit check is a check comparing the customer's credit limit to the total of open sales orders not yet delivered, plus the total value of open deliveries not yet invoiced, plus the total value of open billing documents not yet passed onto accounting, plus the total value of billing documents that have been passed onto accounting, but which have not yet been paid by the customer. This dynamic check has an attached time period that states that the system is not to include sales orders in the total of outstanding items created after the specified time period. For example, the time period may be two months; thus, when the system defines the credit amount used by a customer, it includes all open items in sales orders, but does not include open items with a shipping date of two or more months in advance.

These are the two main types of checks, but one can also require additional checks to be performed in combination with the dynamic or static credit checks or require these additional checks to be used on their own. These additional checks perform the following tasks:

- A credit check when the maximum document value is exceeded. This check is performed when a document value in the currency of the credit control area is exceeded. For example, the company may want all sales orders exceeding a value of $10,000 to be automatically blocked and released by a credit manager.
- A credit check when changing critical fields. It is possible to institute a recheck of the credit, should certain customer master record fields that are credit-relevant be altered in the sales order from those in the master record. An example would be the customer's payment terms.
- A credit check at the time of the next internal check. This activates the credit check to be performed on a certain date. All preceding sales orders are not relevant for credit checking.

- A credit check on the basis of overdue open items. The credit check is based upon the ratio of open items that are overdue by a certain number of days and the customer's balance, which must not exceed a certain percentage.
- A credit check on the basis of oldest open items. This check enables the oldest open item to be only a certain number of days overdue.
- A credit check against the maximum-allowed dunning levels. This check allows the dunning level of the customer to only reach a specific value.
- Customer-specific credit checks. These credit checks are self-definable and can be created in the user exits LVKMPTZZ and LVKMPFZ1.

These settings can be seen in Figure 4-122.

Figure 4-122 Automatic Credit Control settings

Change View "View for Maintenance of Automatic Credit Control": Detail

Table view Edit Goto Selection Utilities System Help

New entries Variable list

CCA RkC CG Credit control Curr. Update

1000 001 01 Low Risk Sales Orders DEM 000012

Document controlling

No credit check

[x] Item check

Released documents are still unchecked

Deviation in %

Number of days

Credit limit seasonal factor

% Minus From To

Checks in financial accounting/old A/R summary

[ ] Payer

Permitted days Permitted hours

Checks

Reaction Status/Block

[ ] Static [ ] Open orders [ ] Open deliveries

[x] Dynamic A [x] Horizon 2 M

[ ] Document value Max.doc.value

[ ] Critical fields

[ ] NextReview date No of days

[ ] Open items Max.open.item % NoDays openI

[ ] OldestOpenItem Days oldestItem

[ ] High.dunn.level High.dunn.level

[ ] User 1

The credit relevant data is updated into an information structure, where it is accessed and updated. Thus each automatic credit control must be assigned an update group. The system allows for no update, and update group 000012, 000015 and 000018. The difference between the three update groups is as follows:

- **Update group 000012**
  - Sales order: Increases the open order value from delivery-relevant schedule lines
  - Delivery: Reduces the open order value from delivery-relevant schedule lines and increases the open delivery value
  - Billing document: Reduces the open delivery value and increases the open billing document value
  - Financial accounting document: Reduces the open billing document value and increases open items
- **Update group 000015**
  - Delivery: Increases the open delivery value and increases the open billing document value
  - Financial accounting document: Reduces the open billing document value and increases open items
- **Update group 000018**
  - Sales order: Increases the open delivery value
  - Billing document: Reduces the open delivery value and increases the open billing document value
  - Financial accounting document: Reduces the open billing document value and increases open items

The decision on which update group to use is based upon the business requirements; however, update group 000012 is thorough and used in most businesses. Should the customer then exceed his credit limit or fail a credit check, and a warning has been assigned to that check, the system will use a pop-up box, as shown in Figure 4-123. To warn the user when creating the sales order, this pop-up is detailed in that it explains which check the customer failed by indicating a NOK (not OK) assigned to the failed check.

In order to release these sales orders or delivery documents from credit blocking, one can use the transaction code [VKM3] for sales documents and transactions [VKM5] for delivery documents, or [VKM4] for both sales documents and delivery documents. One can proceed with the menu path from the logistics screen by going to Accounting, Financial accounting, Accounts receivable, Environment, Credit management, Sales and distribution data, Sales and distribution docs, All. One can then see the offending document as in Figure 4-124. Note on the right-hand side, the Status field. This shows the check the document failed. If this field is empty, the document did not fail a credit check, even though it may be in the list of SD documents that are "required to be released."

To release the document, one indicates the document to be released and then clicks the Release button. The result is the offending document entry, highlighted green. One then proceeds to save, after which you are informed that the document number "xyz" has been released.

TIP: *To view the customer's credit master sheet, proceed from the logistics screen and go to Accounting, Financial accounting, Accounts receivable, Environment, Credit management, Check, Credit master sheet [F.35].*

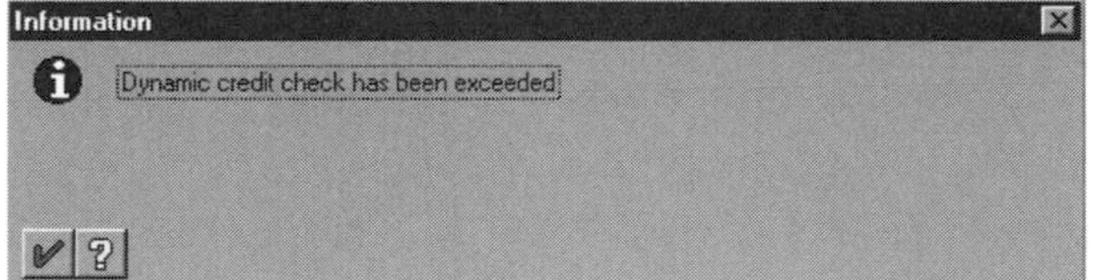
Information
Dynamic credit check has been exceeded

Figure 4-123 Warning message, as shown in a sales document

Disp.var. ... Release Reassign Reject Forward Forward to authorization

CreditAcctArea 1000 Credit control area Basic list
CredRepGroup

	ShipDate	Credit Account	Document	Credit Val	Curr.	Use	TPay	RCa	T	Status
☐	29.11.99	Munich Regional	5636	12.650,00	TDEM	000	0001	001	B	Dynamic check

Figure 4-124 Offending document which failed the credit check—note the status field.

This master sheet offers all necessary credit data that can be used in viewing the customer's overall credit status. This includes the total credit limit used and the open order, delivery, and receivable values, as shown in Figure 4-125a and 4–125b.

Figure 4-125a The customers credit master sheet (view A)

Line items Account analysis Customer Payment history Texts

Central FI Syst Credit Master Sheet Time
- Deutschland RFDK

NORMAL

Balance			
Control area 1000 Credit control area Europe			
Balance	0,00	DEM	
Highest balance at end of 6 months	0,00	DEM	00 11 1999
Highest balance at end of 12 months	0,00	DEM	00 11 1999
Sales from current year	0,00	DEM	
Previous year sales	0,00	DEM	

Days in arrears by cash disc.due date
Customer 0000010011

Control area 1000 Credit cont	Due since	Due in
0 - 030	0,00	0,00
031 - 060	0,00	0,00
061 - 090	0,00	0,00
091 - 120	0,00	0,00
121 - 150	0,00	0,00
> 150	0,00	0,00
Total DEM	0,00	0,00

Figure 4-125b The customers credit master sheet (view B)

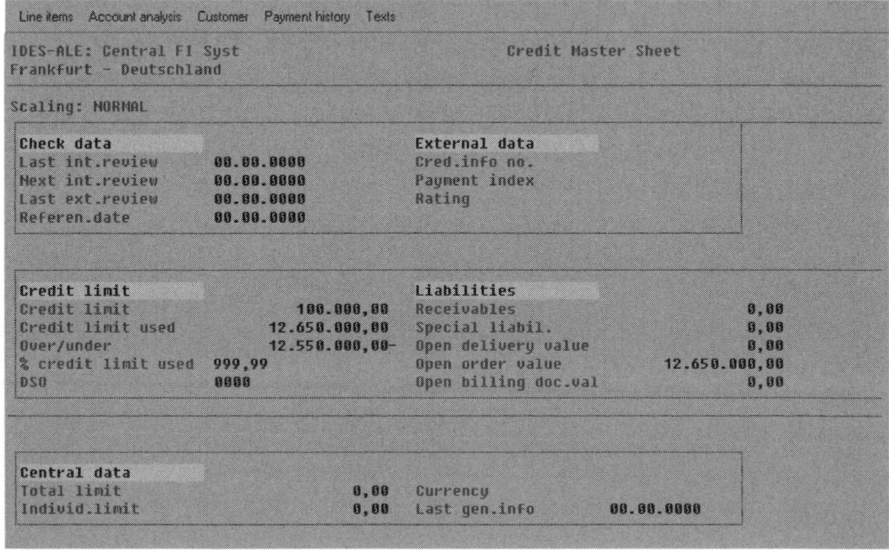

Line items Account analysis Customer Payment history Texts

IDES-ALE: Central FI Syst Credit Master Sheet
Frankfurt - Deutschland

Scaling: NORMAL

Check data		External data	
Last int.review	00.00.0000	Cred.info no.	
Next int.review	00.00.0000	Payment index	
Last ext.review	00.00.0000	Rating	
Referen.date	00.00.0000		

Credit limit		Liabilities	
Credit limit	100.000,00	Receivables	0,00
Credit limit used	12.650.000,00	Special liabil.	0,00
Over/under	12.550.000,00-	Open delivery value	0,00
% credit limit used	999,99	Open order value	12.650.000,00
DSO	0000	Open billing doc.val	0,00

Central data			
Total limit	0,00	Currency	
Individ.limit	0,00	Last gen.info	00.00.0000

Decentralized Sales Processing with Central Financial Accounting

When using decentralized sales processing, a business may have four offices within a country, but each of the four offices are not linked to a central online computer. However, each of the four offices gives credit to customers and operates as one unit as far as the financial accounting view goes.

In this case, there are a few guidelines one should adhere to:

- Each company code must have its own credit control area.
- Each decentralized computer represented by a decentralized sales organization must be assigned to a company code.
- All credit master records, all credit checks, and all management releases are carried out on the decentralized sales computer.

TIP: *You may want to assign the partner functions KB—Credit representation and KM—Credit manager to the sales document in order to send internal mail to them if required.*

The credit management system uses the information structure S066 to record the monthly update of outstanding order values, as used in automatic credit control.

Credit management should be guarded by authorization objects. The following authorization objects are available:

- V_VBUK_FRE
- V_KNKK_FRE
- F_KNKA_KKB
- F_KNKA_MAN
- F_KNKA_AEN

When creating the customer's risk category, it is useful to create a blank risk category and assign it new customers. The reason for this is that when a new customer is created, his risk category will not yet be allocated, and thus he will automatically have a blank as a default. One may want all new customer's sales orders to be blocked and released. Thus, it is worthwhile setting a maximum document value of, say, 100 to the credit check as well for this "new customer" assignment.

Blocking Customers

It is often necessary to block specific customer master records. This may be due to the fact that one has blacklisted a customer or there may be an embargo against the country in which the customer resides. Whatever the reason, it is possible to block customer master records from creating either sales orders, deliveries, or billing documents in specific sales areas or all of them.

Menu Path

The menu path is Logistics, Sales and distribution, Master data, Business partners, Sold-to party, Block/unblock.

Transaction Code

The code here is [VD05]

These blocking reasons are assigned to the customer master record, as shown in Figure 4-126, and one can assign the blocking reason to the selected sales area or for all sales areas for sales orders, deliveries, billings, or for sales support. The blocking reasons are each created in the individual path in the IMG.

Menu Path

For the blocking of a customer master record for delivery, proceed as follows: IMG, Sales and Distribution, Shipping, Deliveries, Define reasons for blocking in shipping. In Figure 4-127, we have created a delivery block called ZG.

Once this delivery block has been created, it must be assigned to a delivery document type, as shown in Figure 4-128.

After the delivery document types have been assigned, you can assign the blocking reason to the customer in transaction [VD05].

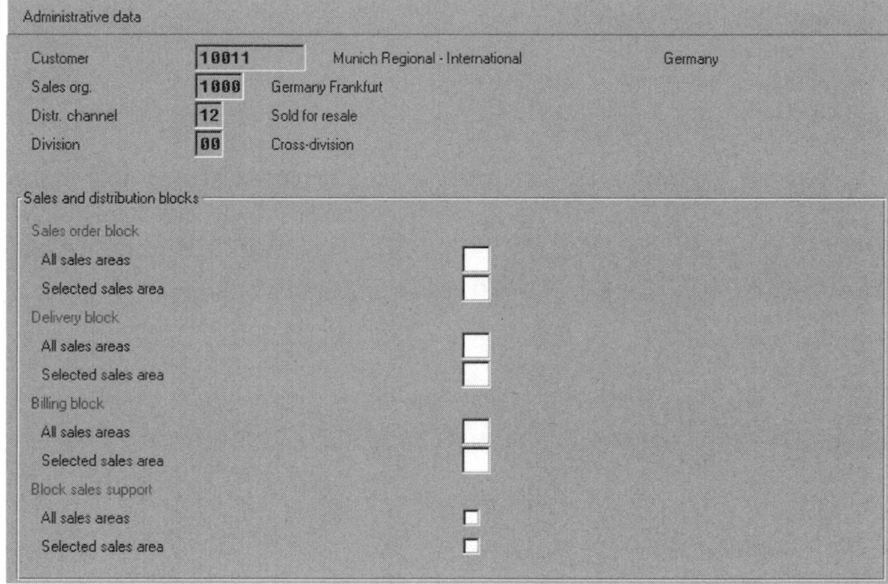

Administrative data

Customer 10011 Munich Regional - International Germany

Sales org. 1000 Germany Frankfurt

Distr. channel 12 Sold for resale

Division 00 Cross-division

Sales and distribution blocks

Sales order block

All sales areas

Selected sales area

Delivery block

All sales areas

Selected sales area

Billing block

All sales areas

Selected sales area

Block sales support

All sales areas

Selected sales area

Figure 4-126 Assign blocking reasons to the customer master record

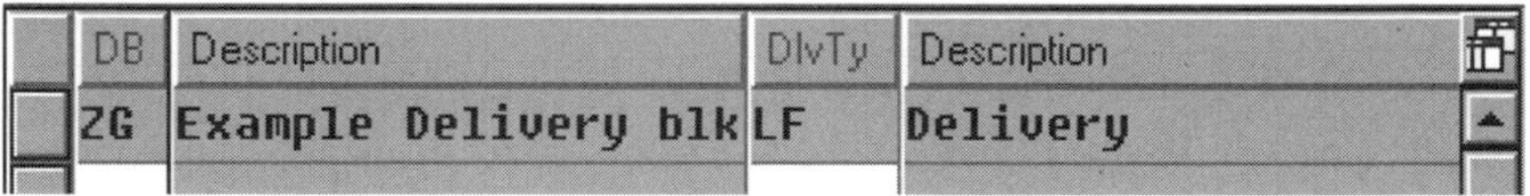

DB	Description	Order	Conf.	Print	DDueList	SpKom	SpWag
ZG	Example Delivery blk	X	X	X	X		

Figure 4-127 Delivery block

DB	Description	DlvTy	Description
ZG	Example Delivery blk	LF	Delivery

Figure 4-128 Delivery block assigned to the delivery type

Menu Path

Thus, to create the blocking reasons for the sales documents, continue with the same procedure as above, starting on the menu path as follows: IMG, Sales and Distribution, Sales, Sales documents, Define and assign reasons for blocking.

To create the blocking reasons for the billing documents, continue with the same procedure as before, following this menu path: IMG, Sales and Distribution, Billing, Billing documents, Define blocking reasons for billing.

These blocking reasons are automatically copied into the sales document during creation. A message will appear at the base of the document explaining, for example, that the customer has a delivery block. One will also be able to find this delivery block copied into the sales document (the shipping view of the sales order line item and shipping header) where it can be removed by an authorized user.

Factory Calendars

Factory calendars specify the work days at a customer's site. These calendars are used to determine when a delivery must take place in order for it to reach the customer's site on a work day when it can be received. We also use factory calendars in consolidated invoicing. That is, if we specify that only one day a week is a working day for our customer, the billing documents are only to be created for that one day each week, causing delivery documents to be consolidated into one billing document. Factory calendars are used throughout the system, and we will focus on the creation and maintenance of the customer's shipping calendar.

Menu Path

The menu path is IMG, Sales and distribution, Master data, Business partners, Customers, Shipping, Define customer calendars.

Transaction Code

The code here is [OVR3].

Two calendars must be maintained: the holiday calendar and the factory calendar, which is created on the basis of the holiday calendar. For the purpose of this book we will create a Factory calendar called "ZG" that is "the International company working calendar."

Step 1 is to create the public holidays. This is done by selecting the Public holidays radio button on the initial screen, as in Figure 4-129, selecting the Change button, and then by selecting the New button or by pressing Shift + F1 on the next screen. This creates a pop-up box, as in Figure 4-130.

Select a fixed date and press enter. One is now faced with a screen in which settings are be made that define this holiday, as shown in Figure 4-131.

You can see the fixed day, 30, and the month, 10, as well as the Guaranteed section describes that if this holiday falls on a Saturday or Sunday, the holiday will automatically be moved to the next working day. The holiday is described as a national celebration. After pressing Enter, you can see the public holiday is not yet assigned to the holiday calendar, as shown in Figure 4-132.

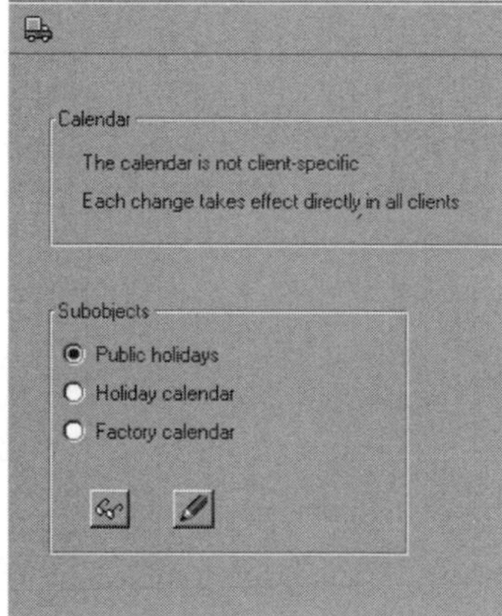

Figure 4-129
Select public holidays calendar

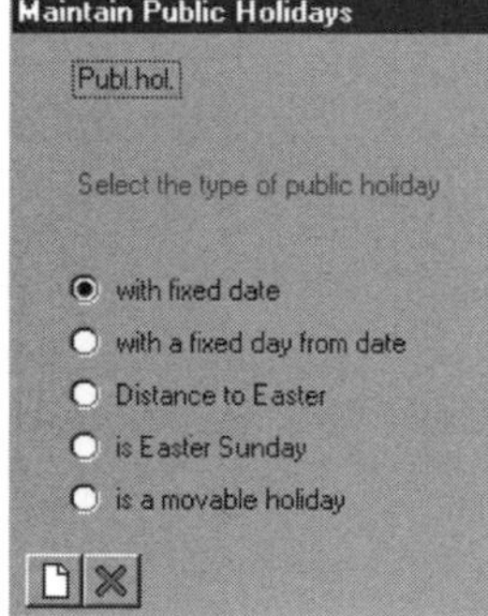

Figure 4-130
Pop-up box to maintain the public holiday calendar

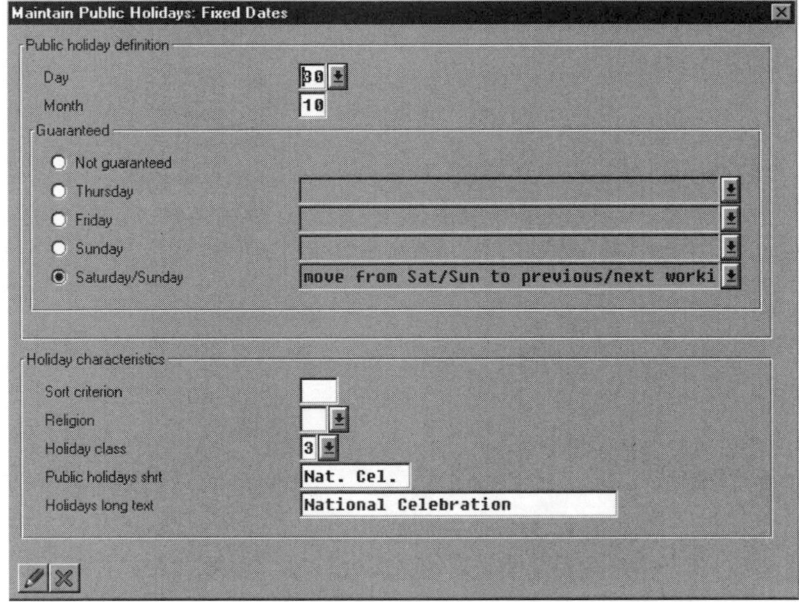

Figure 4-131 Define the Public Holiday

Text	Used in publ. holiday calendar
☐ National Celebration	
☐ New Year (2nd day)	X
☐ Spring Festival, 3rd Day	X
☐ New Year's Day	X

Figure 4-132 The public holiday is not yet assigned to the public holiday calendar

Now select the Holiday calendar radio button and then the Change button. Then select Create or press Shift + F1. Enter a calendar ID, such as "ZG," with a description and a validity period. By selecting the Assign button, you can select the public holidays as maintained previously, as shown in Figure 4-133.

After assigning the public holidays to the holiday calendar, save your work, and you'll be presented with a list of the public holiday calendars and whether they are used or not (see Figure 4-134).

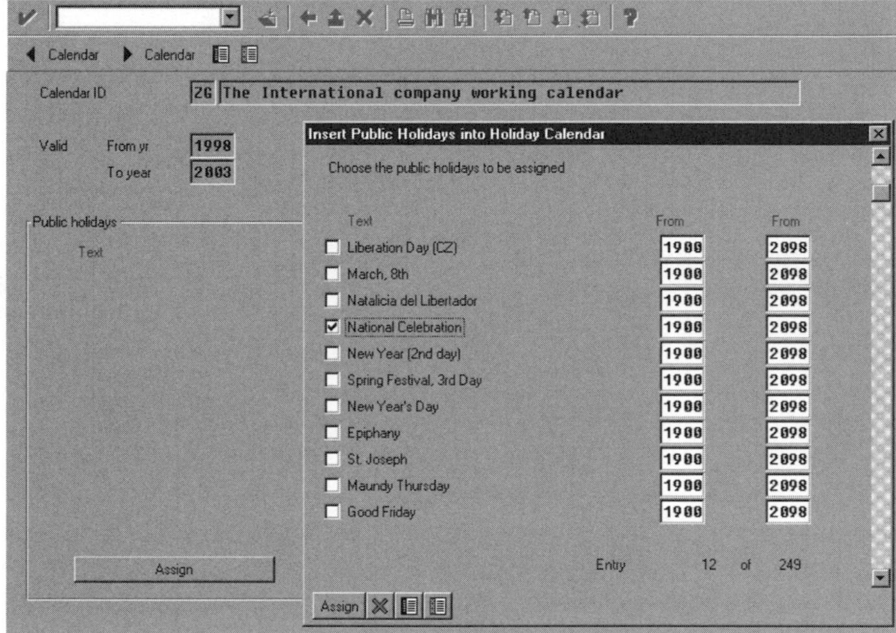

Figure 4-133 Select the Public Holiday for the Calendar

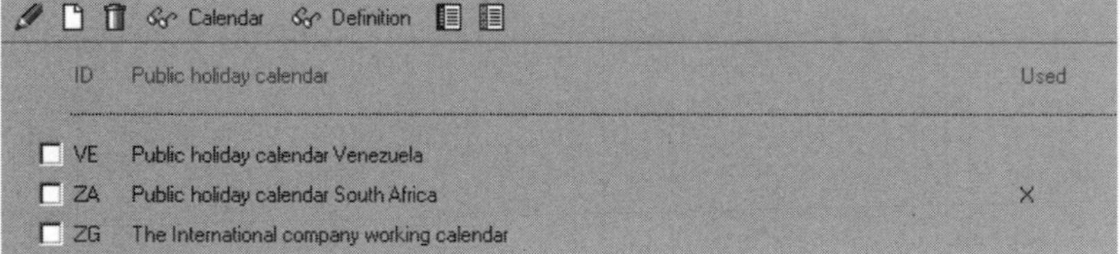

Figure 4-134 List of used/unused Public holiday calendars

Now create a factory calendar by selecting the Factory calendar radio button from the initial maintenance screen and select the Change button. You are now able to specify a factory calendar ID with a short description as well as assign the holiday calendar that must be used. This factory calendar then has a validity period and most importantly specifies what days of the week are working days (see Figure 4-135).

Last, now that the customer-specific calendar has been created, do not forget to assign the calendar to the specific master data, such as the unloading points assigned to the customer master record, as in Figure 4-136.

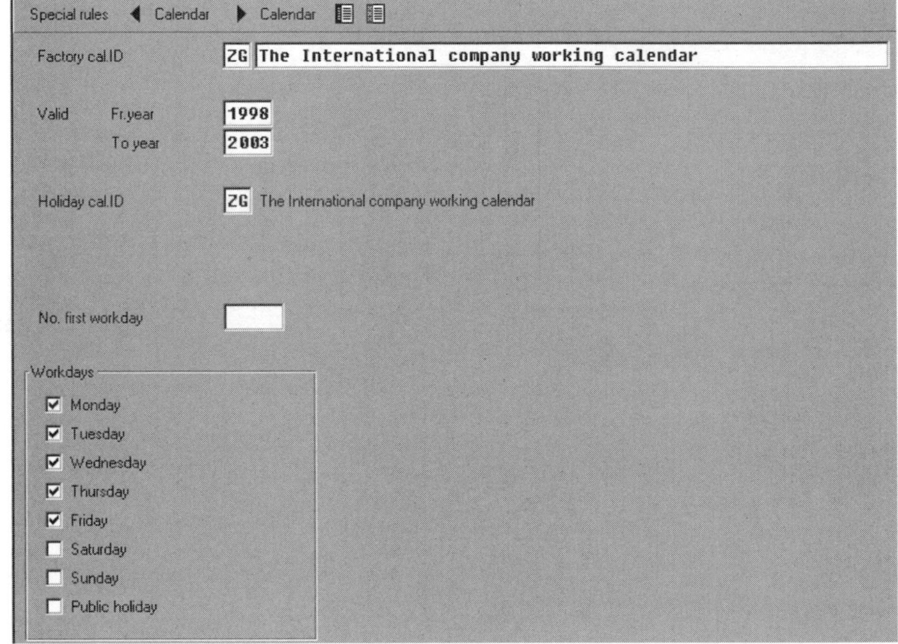

Figure 4-135
Create a facory calendar and assign a holiday calendar in the settings.

Figure 4-136
Assign the factory calendar to the necessary master records.

NOTE: *When transporting changed factory calendars, such as increasing the factory calendar's validity date from one system client to another, be sure to check the transport of the changed calendar in all servers. On numerous occasions I have found the calendar only transports correctly into each server individually. That is, it is no good merely setting up the transport from one client to the other.*

Requirements, Copying Requirements, Data Transfer Routines, and Pricing Formulas

The use of requirements, copying requirements, data transfer routines, and pricing formulas occurs throughout the system. Requirements are represented by FORM routines in the ABAP code. Requirements check for certain criteria during the execution of functions. Copying requirements are used in the same way as standard requirements by the system; they check for certain criteria as preconditions for carrying out the copying function. Data transfer routines are used during copying control to fine-tune which data is necessary to transfer between documents. These transfer routines may also alter the copied data. Formulas are also represented by FORM routines in ABAP code. Formulas are used in pricing and influence the determination of prices.

Menu Path

The path here is IMG, Sales and Distribution, System modification, Routines, Define copying requirements.

Transaction Code

The code here is [VOFM]. All requirements and formulas are maintainable from this code. The copying requirements are divided up into the following:

- Orders
- Deliveries
- Billing documents
- Sales activities
- Texts

The data transfer routines are divided up into

- Orders
- Deliveries
- Billing documents
- Sales activities
- Shipping units
- Texts
- Text names

The requirements are divided into

- Pricing
- Output control
- Account determination
- Material determination
- Material listing and exclusion
- Free goods
- Risk management
- Credit checks
- Card authorization
- Transfer of requirements/availability
- Purchase requisitions/assembly for order
- Delivery due index
- Picking
- Packing
- Goods issue

The Formulas are divided into

- Scale base
- Condition base value
- Condition value
- Structure of group key
- Rounding rule
- Calculation rule for rebate in kind

Naturally, we cannot provide an example of each of these special requirements and formulas, but we will focus on the creation of one specific copying requirement. It is useful to know where requirements and data transfer routines are available to be assigned within the system.

Here are some general rules of thumb: Copying requirements are available to be assigned when transferring data between documents and texts. Data transfer routines are available when copying between documents and texts. Requirements are available to be assigned to any access sequence (or where a determination procedure is used) as well as prior to any material movement or function in relation to a material. Formulas are used generally in pricing determination.

The Creation of a Copying Requirement

In our example, the business requires that when creating a sales order from a quotation, the system must not copy the schedule lines or the order quantity of the line items, but merely the header and line item data. One would then proceed to [VOFM] and select Copying requirements, Orders.

You would then be faced with a list of routine numbers with a short description. You can enter a routine number between 600 and 999 with a short description. In our example, we have created 601, as shown in Figure 4-137. Because the "business requirements" in the example is similar to copying routine 502, you can copy routine 502 and rename it with a different key. You can also copy a routine by entering a key ID over the original, such as overwriting 502 with 601.

TIP: *To create the routine, one would specifically require an access key for the object.*

In the newly created routine, you can change the ABAP code if we have an access key to meet the business requirements (see Figure 4-138).

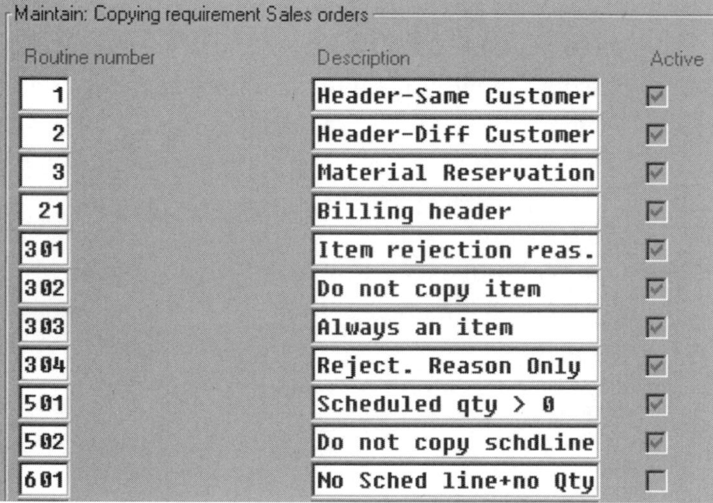

Maintain: Copying requirement Sales orders
Routine number
Description
Active
1 Header-Same Customer
2 Header-Diff Customer
3 Material Reservation
21 Billing header
301 Item rejection reas.
302 Do not copy item
303 Always an item
304 Reject. Reason Only
501 Scheduled qty > 0
502 Do not copy schdLine
601 No Sched line+no Qty

Figure 4-137 Maintain Copying requirements

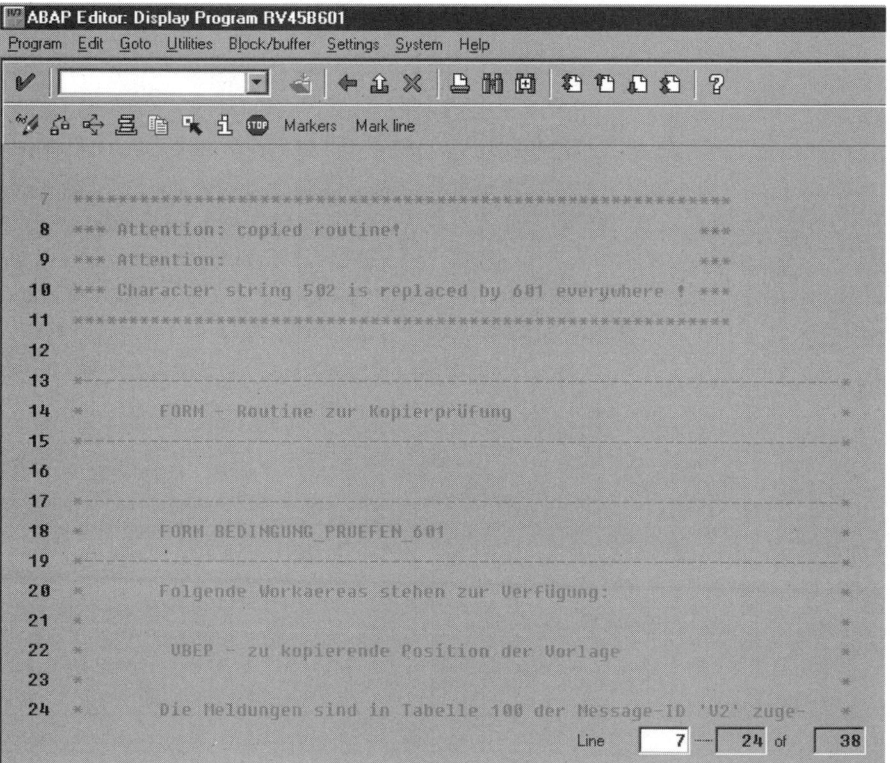

ABAP Editor: Display Program RV45B601
Program Edit Goto Utilities Block/buffer Settings System Help
Markers Mark line
*** Attention: copied routine! ***
*** Attention: ***
*** Character string 502 is replaced by 601 everywhere ! ***
* FORM - Routine zur Kopierprüfung *
* FORM BEDINGUNG_PRUEFEN_601 *
* Folgende Workaereas stehen zur Verfügung: *
* VBEP - zu kopierende Position der Vorlage *
* Die Meldungen sind in Tabelle 100 der Message-ID 'V2' zuge- *
Line 7 24 of 38

Figure 4-138 Create the new routine in ABAP.

Once the requirement is correctly created, you can perform the following tasks:

1. You can generate the routine by selecting Program, Generate from the screen as in Figure 4-137.
2. You must activate the requirement, which is done by proceeding back to the overview screen and by selecting Edit, Activate.
3. Now you need to determine if the routine is found within the main program. This is done by selecting Utilities, Main programs from the screen in Figure 4-138. If you receive a message, "Main program for include not found," you'll need to generate the main program.
4. To generate the main program, proceed back to the overview screen and select a SAP standard routine, such as 001. Again select Utilities, Main programs and then proceed to select the main program and select the Generate button, as shown in Figure 4-139.
5. After generating the main program, proceed back to the routine in Figure 4-138 and again select Utilities, Main programs. One should now see the main program has been found.

The routine or copy requirement is now created and can be assigned to the copying rules between a sales document QT (quotation) and a sales document OR (order).

TIP: *When transporting any new routine or formula between system clients, be sure to transport the table entry, which is the Figure 4-137 entry, and the ABAP code, which is the Figure 4-138 entry, in the same transport. Should you transport the two individually, you may receive problems, especially if the ABAP code goes through to the new client without a table entry.*

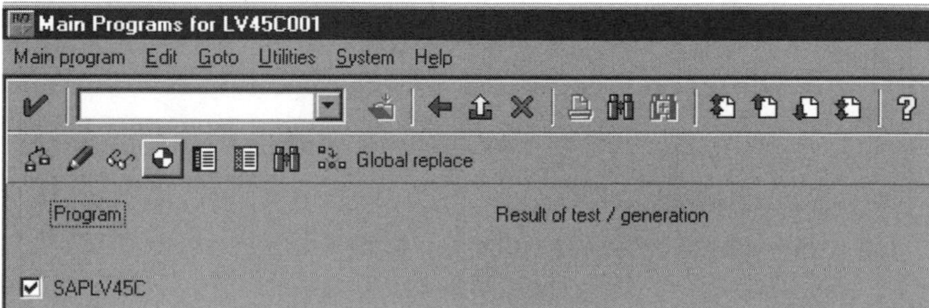

Figure 4-139 Select the program and select the generate button.

CHAPTER 5

Cross Functionality

Online Service System (OSS)

SAP has a vast reference library of solutions for system bugs as well as advice on the creation and maintenance of certain functions, such as pricing. This library of advice and solutions is called the *online service system*.

Transaction Code

The online service system is reachable via the transaction code [OSS1]. When logging on, you will be prompted to select a group from a list of available groups. Select Public, then Continue, and you will then need to enter your user name and password. After your user name and password have been validated, you will be logged on to the online service system.

This online service system, which is constantly being upgraded by SAP, performs two main functions. The first main function is to search for previous notes on a subject you select. This search will then list all correspondence from SAP with regard to that particular subject. The search page can be accessed via the overview or inbox page, shown in Figure 5-1.

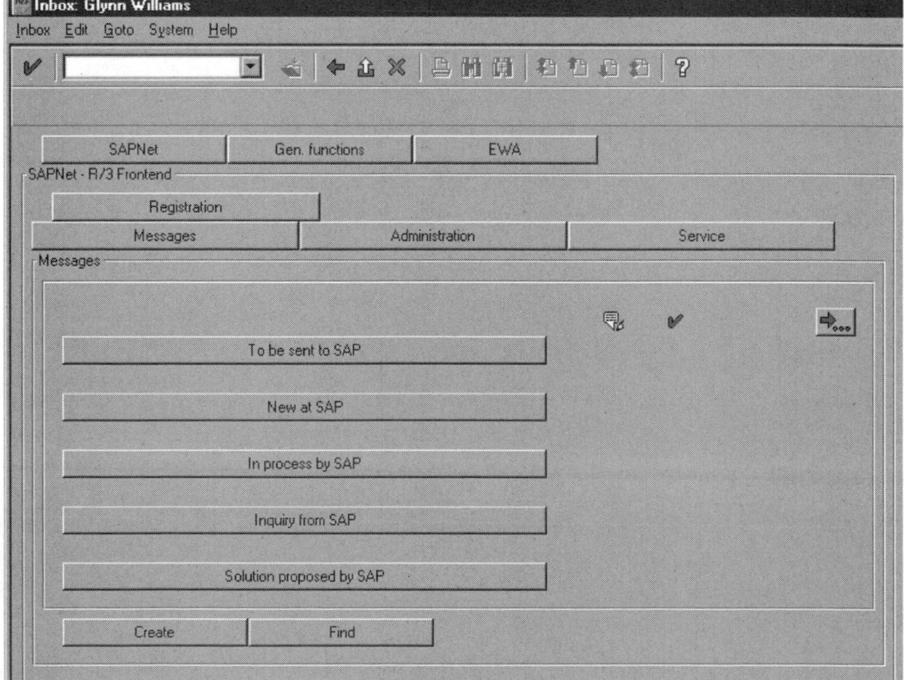

Figure 5-1 Online Service System Inbox

Should one hit the General functions button, followed by the Find button, one will be faced with a selection screen in which one can enter data to be used as a parameter to search. Naturally, the more specific the search criteria, the fewer entries will be found. Thus, if you search for pricing subtotals, for example, from release 4.0b and component SD-BF-PR, *Sales and distribution* (SD); *Basic functions* (BF); *Pricing and conditions* (PR), the selection screen would look like Figure 5-2.

By hitting Enter, we find three entries that match the specific selection criteria (see Figure 5-3). You can then sift through the entries by description until you find the note you're looking for.

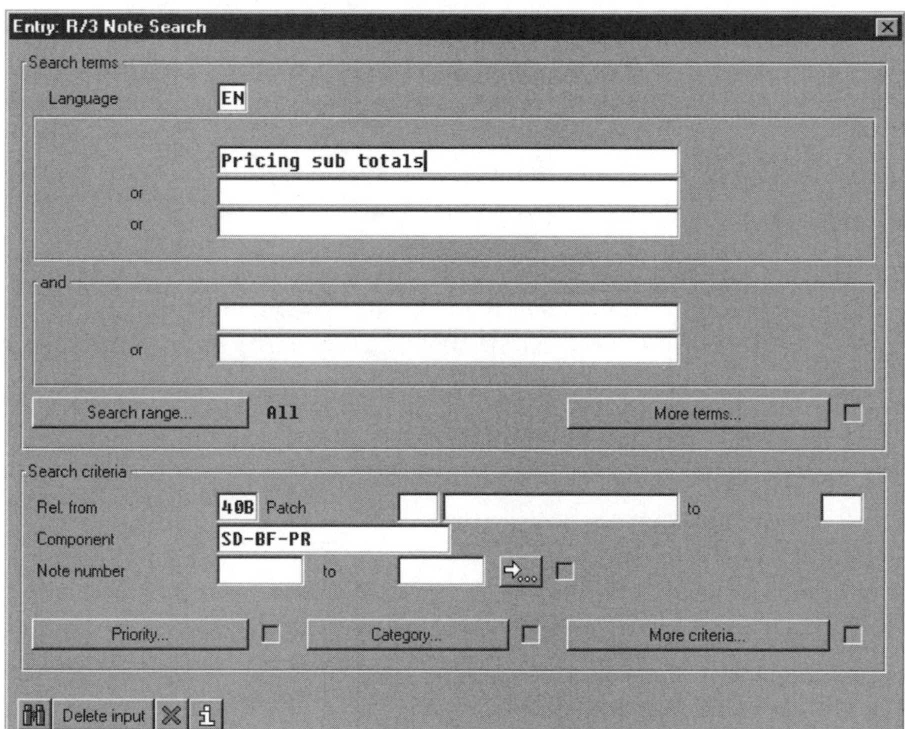

Figure 5-2 Search terms and criteria in OSS

Figure 5-3 Results of a search

Notes List selection

Display variant: List

M	Component	Number	Vers	Rankg	Short text	Min	Max
	SD-BF-PR	0130742	0004	0.780	Roundings in subtotal lines	30F	45A
	SD-BF-PR	0155932	0002	0.760	Net value, net price or subtotal is incorrect	30F	45B
	SD-BF-PR	0162423	0001	0.700	Structure conditions with price source	40A	46A

Note that by paging a little to the right, you can see if the note relates to a program error or a consulting issue, due to the additional text description.

The second function of OSS is to provide a form of communication between the business and SAP. If you experience a problem in SAP (such as a bug) and you cannot find an existing note to solve the problem, you can create an OSS note and send it to SAP.

We will proceed with an example of sending SAP an OSS note on a fictitious problem in pricing subtotals. Select the Create button from the initial inbox view, as shown in Figure 5-1. You will be prompted with an overview of the different clients and instances. For example, if the specific problem you are having is in the development client, you could select the Dxx client along with the associated system and platform.

After selecting the client, one is faced with a "Create message" screen. This is broken into three sections. The top left-hand section represents the person reporting the problem, with the company name, installation number, and telephone numbers. The data at the top right represents the system details, that is, the operating system and database server, as well as the system being reported with the fault, such as the development system. The central section represents the actual message to SAP, as shown in Figure 5-4.

The first line of text on the actual border of the message, just above the Component field, is the message number. The component is the same as in the search SD-BF-PR. The priority may be one of four options:

- *Very high* Only for system or application shutdowns in your productive system or in a non-productive system in a critical project phase

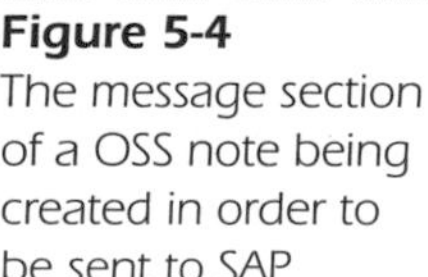

Figure 5-4 The message section of a OSS note being created in order to be sent to SAP

- *High* When important applications or subprograms fail or for a system shutdown in a non-productive system
- *Medium* For error situations with less serious consequences than the above two cases; operation of the productive system is not seriously affected
- *Low* For minor errors, such as errors in documentation or typos

One can then write in as much detail as needed about the problem. Should you not have enough space to write, proceed to Edit, Description. You will then be faced with a screen where it is possible to create additional lines. Thus, your message may look similar to Figure 5-5.

After completing the message and saving it, do not forget to send it to SAP. This can be carried out by selecting "Yes" when prompted to send it to SAP, or by selecting "Send to SAP" from the Message creation screen.

All messages sent to SAP proceed to a support desk that is responsible for investigating already-created OSS notes that may solve the problem. Thus, nine times out of 10, you will receive a message back from SAP to investigate a number of OSS notes as possible solutions. After you have investigated these notes, and you are certain they cannot assist you, one can reply and explain you need further help. This new message will then proceed back to SAP to a support desk, which will forward the message to a functional consultant who will look at the problem and proceed to give you a solution. You can see the progress of the message by selecting the Action log button.

Figure 5-5 Example of a OSS note ready to be sent

```
Delete  Continue replace  Concatenate  Split line

       ....+....1....+....2....+....3....+....4....+....5....+....6....+....7..
000010 System-ID   : DEE    System Patch : SAPKE40B24      Kernel Rel.: 40B
000020 Transaction : V/08   Program      :  SAPL080M  Screen      : 40
000030 Error message   .. ...
000040 Good day,
000050 We are having problems with the sub totals in pricing.......
000060 The error message we receive is V...  and reads ".........
000070 We have looked at OSS notes ........ and they do not help us.
000080 We have set up a remote connection for you to investigate this problem.
000090 The application server is ....The system number is ...
000100 Please phone me for your password. My telephone number is.........
000101 Many thanks
000102 Glynn Williams
000110
```

Logistics Information System (LIS)

The *logistics information system* (LIS) is a central integrated information system where one can create specific tables that are updated at specific stages and that can be used to report on values contained in specific fields. This allows the information systems to be used for controlling, monitoring, and planning purposes.

The LIS can be broken down into each logistics application's individual information system, such as the *sales information system* (SIS). The other logistics applications that have their own information systems yet contribute to the LIS are as follows:

- Inventory management
- Purchasing
- Shop floor control
- Plant maintenance
- Quality management
- Retail information system

An example of where an LIS structure is used for planning is in product allocation. Product allocation uses a structure to allocate limited stock to a customer (the SAP standard has an example of S140 with planning type COMMIT, viewable from [MC94]). This enables the customer to purchase specific stock up to the amount allocated to him in the planning structure for that specific time period.

In theory, how this happens is that the structure is created, allocating the quantity of specific stock the specific customer is allowed to order for a specific time period. When a sales order is created, the system updates this structure with the called-off quantity. Should the called-off quantity exceed the allowed quantity, the system then determines the remaining amount to be called off and prompts the user to change his order quantity to match the available amount.

SAP has *standard sales information structures* (SIS) that are already configured in the system; these information structures are used for reporting purposes.

Menu Path

These standard information structures can be accessed via the following menu path: Logistics, Sales and distribution, Sales information system, Standard analysis.

The reports use the following characteristics:

- Customer
- Material
- Sales organization
- Shipping point
- Sales employee
- Sales office

Thus, should one want to use the standard reports, one can follow the above menu path and select one of the above characteristics as the basis for the report.

Should one use a standard report, one must ensure the report is activated in customizing. One must also ensure that the statistics group in the customer master (sales screen) and material master (sales org. 2 screen) must be set and relevant for updating these structures in the updating control. You will then be faced with a screen where you can enter more restrictive settings for the Reports selection. By pressing Excecute, you are faced with the data that matches the selection criteria and that has been specifically updated into the standard information structure. This will be explained in more detail a little later.

Should these standard reports not report on the fields and values you require, it is possible to create a "self-defined analysis" information structure. In our example of using the LIS, we will create such an information structure for reporting purposes.

Menu Path

The menu path here is IMG, Logistics general, *Logistics information system* (LIS), Logistics data warehouse.

The logistics data warehouse is divided into two main sections: Data basis and Updating. Data basis is responsible for the actual design of the information structure, that is, what key fields are reported on or displayed.

It is broken down into further sections that we will deal with individually. Updating is responsible for the updating rules used by the system, determining how the information structure is to be updated, and when this updating is to take place. It is also broken down into further sections that we will deal with individually.

The information structure itself is a group of fields that can be updated at specific intervals. This information structure can be used for analysis and planning purposes. Each *information structure* consists of the following:

- A period unit, which allocates a reference to time.
- Characteristics, which display cumulated values.
- Key figures, which are the actual cumulated information assigned to a characteristic, such as a sales order value.

TIP: *Key figures can always be cumulated, such as a value or a quantity. Although characteristics cannot be cumulated, they represent the object that the cumulation is happening for, such as a sales office or a sold-to party.*

In our example, we are required to create a simple information structure that can be used to report on the net value of sales orders per sales organization, broken down further by customer and again by material group. (We are merely using this simple structure in order to demonstrate the different processes required in creating an LIS report.) The net value is a key figure. The Characteristics are the sales organization, customer, and material group.

Menu Path

The menu path here is IMG, Logistics general, *Logistics information system* (LIS), Logistics data warehouse, Data basis, Field catalog, Maintain self-defined field catalog, Create.

Transaction Code

The code here is [MC18]. We know from the condition technique that a field catalog is a grouping of fields that may be used later. (In the condition technique, the fields used in the condition table must first have existed in the field catalog.)

TIP: *One does not need to create a field catalog, as one can use those already provided by SAP. However, it is useful to place all the fields you will be using into one, self-created field catalog, as this provides ease of use later.*

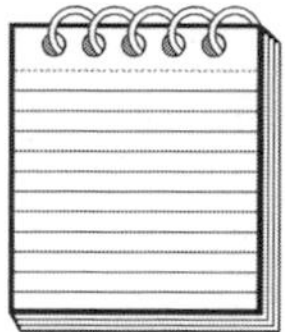

NOTE: *The source tables used in the LIS are required by the system in order to interact between document processing and the updating of the statistical data. The LIS uses different datasets than those used in document processing. It instead uses communication structures, which are automatically supplied with the document data when the documents are posted. The use of communication structures is beneficial, as it enables the statistics updating to be done at a separate time than the document updating. The communication structures also contain fewer fields than the document and thus have a faster response time in transferring data to the LIS. These communication structures are used in the source tables beginning with "MC." Thus, the original table VBAK will use the source table in LIS of MCVBAK.*

One can now create a field catalog by entering a four-character alphanumeric key beginning with Z and a short description. Application 01 represents *Sales and Distribution* (SD) and the catalog category can be selected as the characteristics catalog. You are then presented with the screen shown in Figure 5-6.

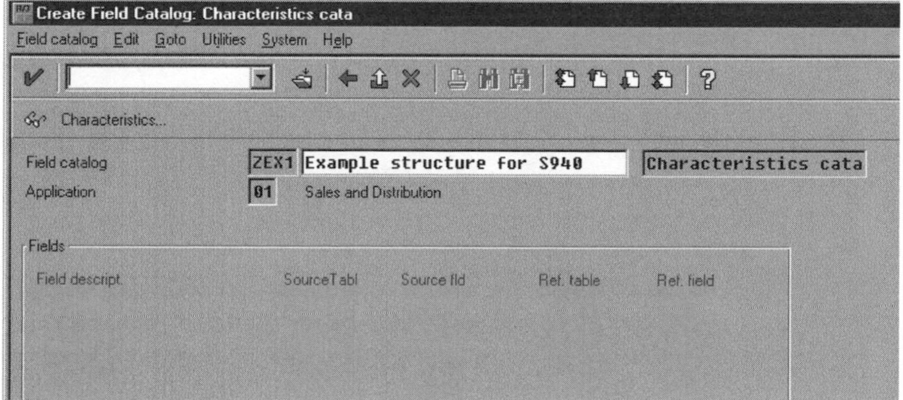

Figure 5-6
Create Field Catalog for Characteristics

Select the Characteristics button. One is then presented with the screen in Figure 5-7.

The source table is in the right-hand column with the fields from the source table in the left-hand column. Because the structure we are creating is only concerned with the sales order, we can select the sales document's header data source table and then select the sales organization and sold-to party by double-clicking on the two fields of the left-hand column. We can then proceed to select the sales document's item data source table and select the Material group field. It is possible to have as many characteristics as you want in the field catalog, but you are restricted to nine characteristics in the actual information structure, which we will get to later.

After selecting the fields, press the "Copy and close" button, followed by hitting the Copy button. You are then presented with the field catalog of selected fields, as shown in Figure 5-8.

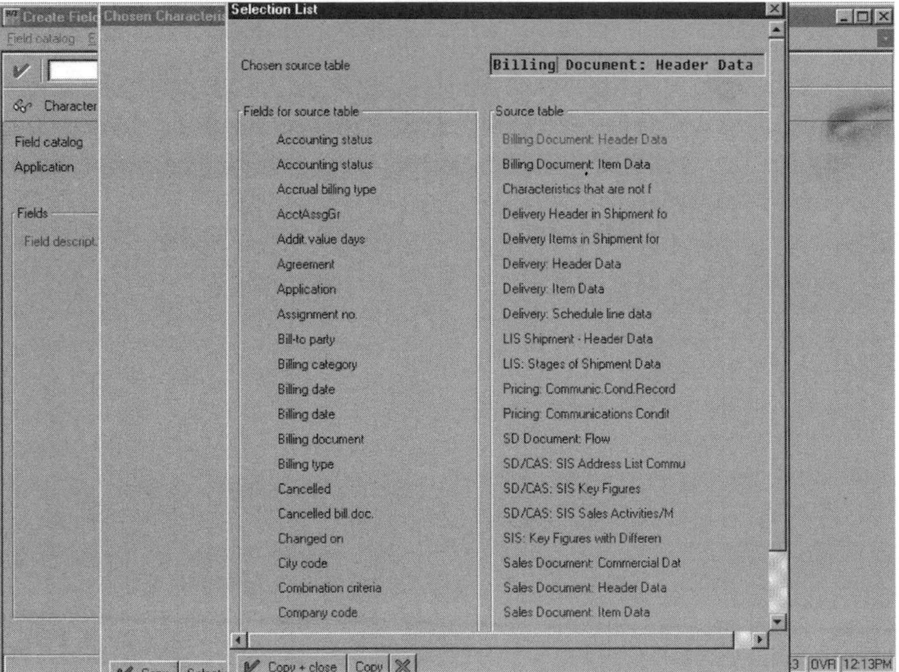

Figure 5-7
Source table and related fields

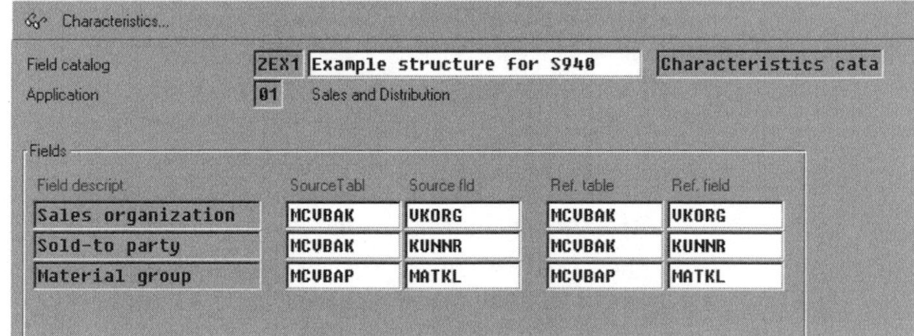

Figure 5-8
Field catalog of selected fields

Should one require a specific field to be a characteristic or key figure that is not in the list of available fields as assigned to a source table, one can select any field from the list of allowed fields and then overwrite it with the needed field and table names.

Let's say we could not find a field for the additional data customer group 1, and we are required to report on it from the sales order. We could select the sales organization, MCVBAK-VKORG. By changing the field name in both the source and reference fields to KVGR1 (as found by selecting F1 and then F9 on the field in the sales order), we would see the field description change to represent "Customer group 1." This assumes that KVGR1 is in the table MCVBAK; we can check this with transaction code [SE11].

Now that the characteristics field catalog has been created, you can create a field catalog for your key figures the same way you did for the characteristics.

Menu Path

The menu path here is IMG, Logistics general, *Logistics information system* (LIS), Logistics data warehouse, Data Basis, Information structures, Maintain self-defined information structures, Create.

Transaction Code

The code here is [MC21]. In Figure 5-9, we can see the creation of an information structure. Self-defined information structures must be created with a key ranging from S501 and S999. Note that you can only change or delete an information structure should no data be in it. Once data is in the information structure, you must delete this data first before deleting the structure.

After pressing Enter, you can then select a list of characteristics by selecting the Choose characteristics button. This provides a pop-up menu of a number of field catalogs with the associated fields represented in them. As we have already created our field catalog, this process is simply completed by selecting the three fields assigned to the field catalog named "Example structure for S940." Then select the Copy and Close button, followed by the Copy button (see Figure 5-10). Note that you can have a maximum of nine characteristics in an information structure.

The key figure "sales orders—net value" can be selected from an already-created field catalog. This can be selected from the field catalog, SD: Values, prices (order), or by selecting the Net Value field.

The information structure is nearly complete; all that remains is the assignment of a unit to the key figure. We have assigned the unit representing the document currency. After saving the structure, we need to gen-

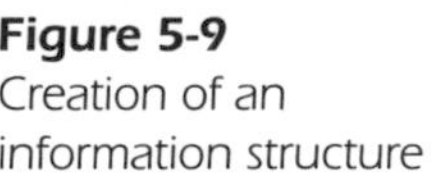

Figure 5-9 Creation of an information structure

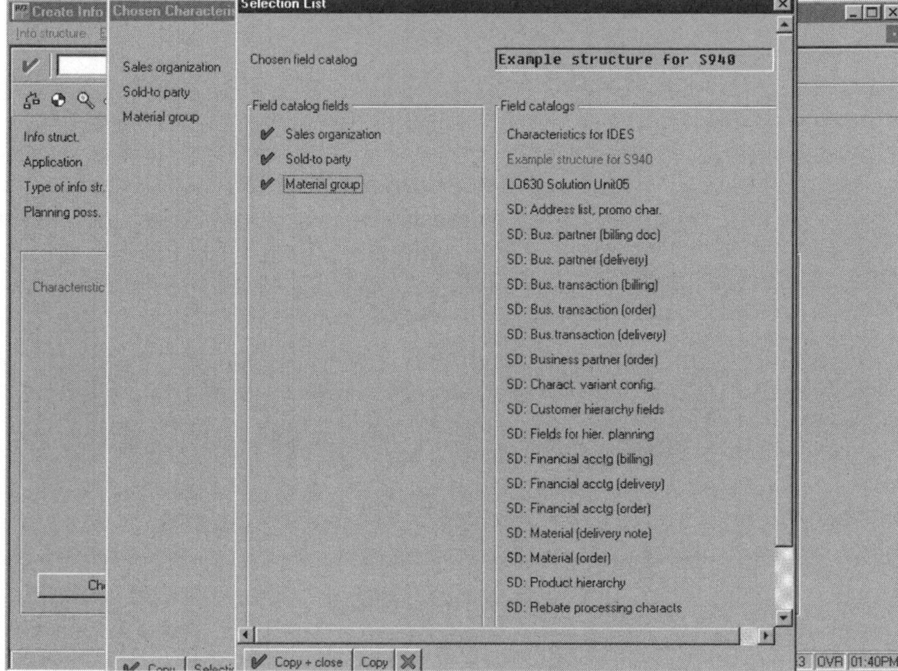

Figure 5-10
Creating the information structure by selecting the characteristics from the field catalog

erate the structure. This is carried out by selecting the Generation button (or by pressing Shift + F8).

Now that the information structure has been created, one needs to define how the updating is to perform. The updating of the information structure can be divided into two sections, the first being the updating rules. The updating rules are the actual control of the updating of the information structure at a higher level. These include the creation and assignment of requirements for updating or formulas in updating. The second section is the updating control. This section is at a lower level in the controlling of the update in the information structure. It is this level that defines which document types are included in the update.

Menu Path

The path here is IMG, Logistics general, *Logistics information system* (LIS), Logistics data warehouse, Updating, Updating definition, Specific definition using update rules, Maintain update rules.

Transaction Code

The code here is [MC24]. Here one enters the information structure for creating the *update rules* as well as assigning the relevant update group to the structure.

The update groups are used as a global grouping at the business transaction level, allowing one to group the update of standard sales into one group while allowing one to group the update of returns into another group. The usage of these groups will be seen again later.

The reason why one can define the update rules by information structure plus update group is due to the fact that you may want certain key figures to be updated differently according to the update group. For example, you may have a situation where you want to update a business transaction differently. In this case, you would create an update group for this business transaction. For all your standard sales, you want to add the net value of the sales document, but for your returns, you want to subtract the net value. In this case, you need two update groups: one to add the net value that operates for all the standard sales and one to subtract the net value for all returns sales. Later on you will see how to associate these update groups with the different sales transactions. As in Figure 5-11, the system will show a list of key figures used in the information structure. By selecting the Rules for key figures button, one can assign the general rules for the key figure "Net value," as shown to the right of the figure.

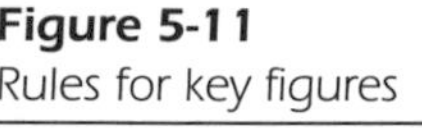

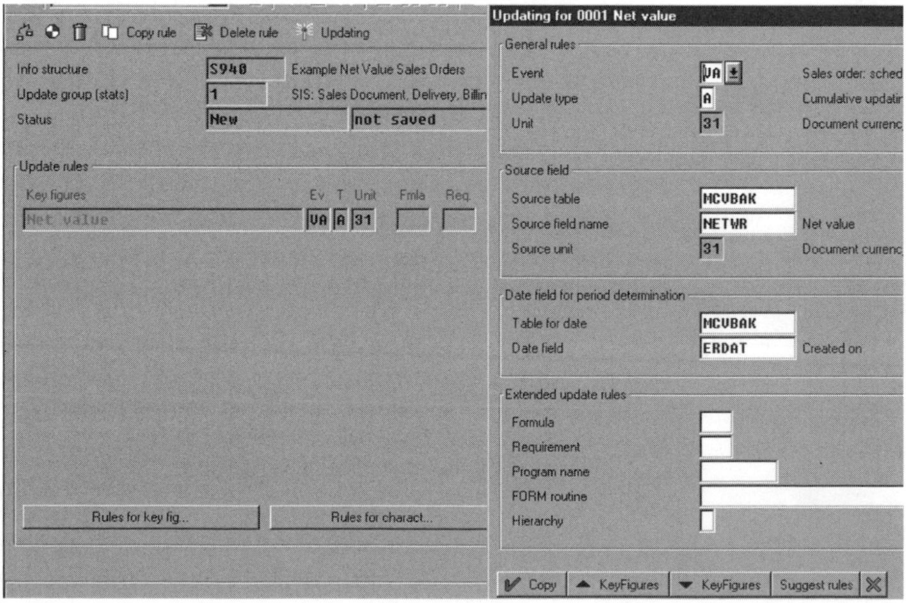

Figure 5-11
Rules for key figures

The rules for the key figure Net value state that the update must happen at the event VA—sales order.

The update type equals A—cumulative updating (values are added together for each update.) The two other options are *data transfer* only, which determines that only the last value to be updated is shown in the structure; that is, the value is constantly being overwritten. This would be used if one wanted to report on the current sales price. The third update type is used as a *counter*, where a value of one is added to the remaining value in the information structure each time the information structure is updated. The *unit* is preassigned from the unit specified in the information structure, that is, the document currency.

The *date* field for period determination can be any of the available date fields. In this example, we have selected the document header, "Created on." One can then assign a requirement to the update, specifying that certain preconditions must first be met before an update can happen. One can also specify a formula to the update, causing the updated value of the key figure to be manipulated if required.

Both the requirements and formulas can be created using transactions codes [MC1B] and [MC1D] respectively. This requires a prior knowledge of ABAP. Remember that a requirement can be used to stop the record from being updated. For example, you could create a requirement to exclude all sales for a particular material type.

A formula can be used to get the value for the characteristic/key figure from a source other than the source fields. For example, you could write a formula to read the customer master record and get the field value Transport zone, which is not available in the MCVBAK/MCVBAP tables.

The next step is to maintain the update rules for the characteristics. This is done by clicking the key figure and then selecting the Rules for characteristics button.

TIP: *The offset / length field is available should one not require the entire contents of the field to be updated in the structure. This can be used in the product hierarchy. For example, the SAP standard product hierarchy has a length of five, five, and eight characters, but one requires these characteristics to be used in reporting or planning. Thus, one can specify that the source table and field is*

MCVBAP-PRODH offset 00 length 05 for the first characteristic

MCVBAP-PRODH offset 05 length 05 for the second characteristic

MCVBAP-PRODH offset 10 length 08 for the third characteristic

NOTE: One must maintain the rules for the characteristics of each key figure. Thus, should you have four key figures, you will need to select "Rules for characteristics" for each of the key figures in the update rule for key figures. If you specify an update type "Counter," a formula, or an external routine as a source, you do not have to specify a source table or source field. However, you do have to specify a source unit, as this unit may not be determined automatically. You must also specify a hierarchy. The hierarchy defines the level at which the requirement will run. If you are using the requirement to update a header field, the hierarchy level must be a header, as SAP will run this requirement at the header level. It makes no sense to try and run a formula at the header level when the information used in the formula is at the item level.

One can then check one's entries by selecting the Check icon button, followed by saving the updating rules. Once this has been done, generate the updating rules, followed again by selecting the Activate updating button. After doing so, you will come across a screen similar to Figure 5-12. You can activate the pop-up menu by double-clicking on the information structure needing the updating.

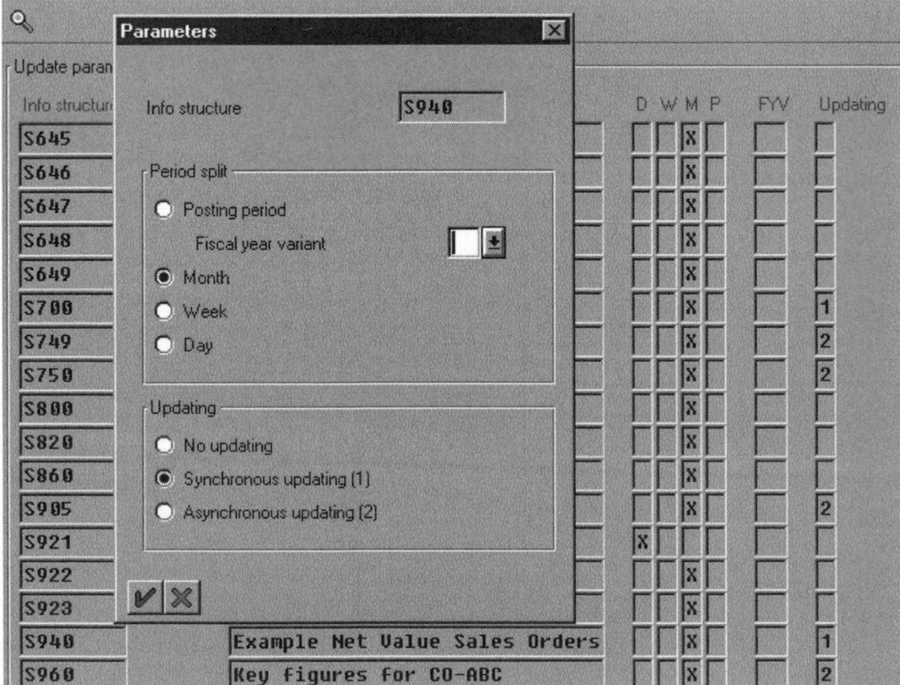

Figure 5-12 Activate the Updating of an Information structure

Three types of updating can be assigned:

- *Synchronous updating* This type of updating happens at the same time as the document update. Should there be a problem in the statistics update, the document itself will not be able to be updated and thus will need to be re-entered into the system.
- *Asynchronous updating* This type of updating occurs slightly later than the document update. Thus, the document will be able to be updated, regardless of whether the statistics update may fail or not.
- *No updating* This is assigned if you want updating to be deactivated for a particular information structure.

After maintaining the settings, one must save one's data.

Menu Path

These settings are also maintainable through this menu path: IMG, Logistics general, Logistics information system (LIS), Logistics data warehouse, Updating, Updating control, Activate update.

Transaction Code

The code here is [OMO1]. All that remains to be completed is the assignment of the grouping criteria and the determination procedures.

Three grouping options are possible:

- Customer statistics groups
- Material statistics groups
- Document statistics groups

Menu Path

The *customer statistics group* is created by proceeding to IMG, Logistics general, *Logistics information system* (LIS), Logistics data warehouse, Updating, Updating control, Settings sales, Statistics groups, Maintain statistics groups for customers.

Transaction Code

The code here is [OVRA]. It is advisable to have at least two entries for both the customer and material statistics groups. Those two entries should be at least "relevant for updating" and "not relevant for updating." This is due to the fact that it would be advisable to make the updating statistics group indicators on the customer and material master record mandatory entries. If you have a material or customer for which no updating is to be carried out, you will still need to assign an update group. If you do not make the update groups on the material and customer master record mandatory entries, a user could create a master record and forget to assign an update group, resulting in missing updates and incorrect data in information structures. The customer statistic group is assigned to the customer master record in the sales screen under the area on pricing/statistics.

Menu Path

The *material statistics group* is created by proceeding to IMG, Logistics general, *Logistics information system* (LIS), Logistics data warehouse, Updating, Updating control, Settings sales, Statistics groups, Maintain statistics groups for material.

Transaction Code

The code here is [OVRF]. The material statistic group is assigned to the material master record, Sales—sales organization 2, under the area on grouping terms.

Menu Path

The *document statistics group* is created by proceeding to IMG, Logistics general, *Logistics information system* (LIS), Logistics data warehouse, Updating, Updating control, Settings sales, Statistics groups, Maintain statistics groups for sales documents.

Transaction Code

The code here is [OVRN]. The document statistics groups are assigned to each sales document type [OVRH], sales document item category [OVRI], delivery document type [OVRK], and delivery item category [OVRL].

The reason one needs to set the document statistic group at the delivery level is due to one being able to create deliveries without reference to the order.

The updating group is in field STAFO on VBAK/VBAP and is copied to the delivery and billing document. You can see what update group is active using [SE16] for table VBAK/VBAP. If there is no preceding sales order, SAP must use the delivery to find STAFO; thus, there is the need to specify the update indicators for the delivery.

The billing document types that need to be updated can be indicated as well. However, it is not possible to assign an update group to the billing document, as the system will automatically determine the update group via the reference to the sales order or delivery document.

Finally, determine the update groups. This is carried out at the item and header levels.

Menu Path

One can proceed in the assignment at the item level by going to IMG, Logistics general, *Logistics information system* (LIS), Logistics data warehouse, Updating, Updating control, Settings sales, Update group, Assign update group on item level.

Transaction Code

The code here is [OVRP]. This is the assignment of the sales organization, the distribution channel, the division, the customer statistics group, the material statistics group, the sales document type statistics group, and the statistics group for the item category to the update group. This is shown in Figure 5-13.

Menu Path

One can assign the update group at the header level by going to IMG, Logistics general, *Logistics information system* (LIS), Logistics data warehouse, Updating, Updating control, Settings sales, Update group, Assign update group on header level.

Transaction Code

The code here is [OVRO]. Now that the settings have all been made, we can determine if our information structure is being populated.

TIP: *In order to determine what information structures are being populated and with what values, proceed to enter the parameter "MCL" with associated value "X" under your own user profile. To do this, proceed from the Logistics overview screen to System, User profile, Own data, and, under the Parameters tab, place the entries (see Figure 5-14).*

After creating a sales order, use transaction code [MC30] in order to see what information structures have been updated and with what values (see Figure 5-15). Here one can also see that the information structure has been updated.

By selecting the Details button, you can see the value being updated into the key figure, as shown in Figure 5-16, as well as an updating log for each key figure and characteristic by selecting the Key Figures or Characteristic buttons respectively.

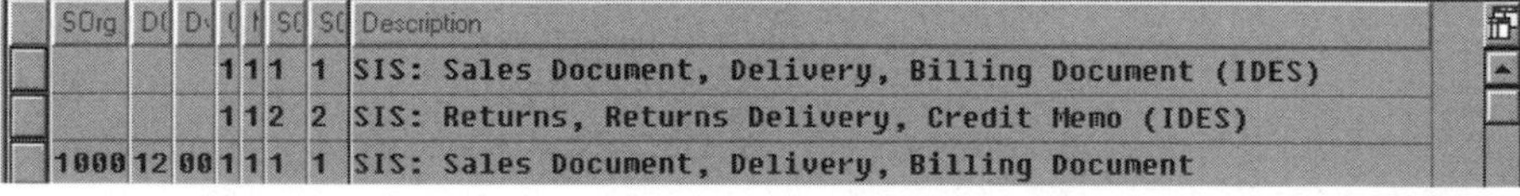

SOrg	DC	Dv	(	I	SC	SC	Description
			1	1	1	1	SIS: Sales Document, Delivery, Billing Document (IDES)
			1	1	2	2	SIS: Returns, Returns Delivery, Credit Memo (IDES)
1000	12	00	1	1	1	1	SIS: Sales Document, Delivery, Billing Document

Figure 5-13 Update determination

Address | Defaults | Parameters

Parameters	Value	Text
MCL	X	

Figure 5-14 Update the user profile

Figure 5-15
With an updated user profile, one is able to view the updates to Information Structures via transaction [MC30]

Details Analysis

Info Struc.	UpdGrp	Document	U	Description
S001	1	0000005637	X	Customer
S002	1	0000005637	X	Sales office
S003	1	0000005637	X	Sales organization
S004	1	0000005637	X	Material
S006	1	0000005637	X	Sales employee
S008	4	0000005637		RK/P bridge
S009	7	0000005637	X	CAS: Last sales promotion
S014	7	0000005637	X	CAS document information
S066	12	0000005637		Open orders: credit mgmt
S067	12	0000005637		Open deliveries/billing docs
S123	1	0000005637	X	Customer / Material Group
S124	1	0000005637	X	Customer / Material
S126	1	0000005637		Open Variants - Basis 1
S131	12	0000005637		Letter of credit
S132	12	0000005637		Open values - document
S160	1	0000005637		Perishables
S749	1	0000005637	X	JS Test - Doc #
S940	1	0000005637	X	Example Net Value Sales Orders

Figure 5-16
Detailed view of the update shows the values of the Key figures

Key figure... Characteristics...

Info structure S940 Day Document no. 0000005637
Update Group 1 Event Sales order: sched.a

UpNo	Key figure	Contents	O/N	Item
0001	Net value	11000.00	New	10

One can view the information structure as a report by going to Logistics, Sales and distribution, Sales information system, Standard analysis, Self-defined analysis or [MCSI], and then selecting the information structure required, such as S940. The system will then automatically propose a selection screen where you can define which characteristics must be looked at (see Figure 5-17).

After pressing Enter, one will be faced with the updated data for the highest characteristic level, which in our example is the sales organization (see Figure 5-18).

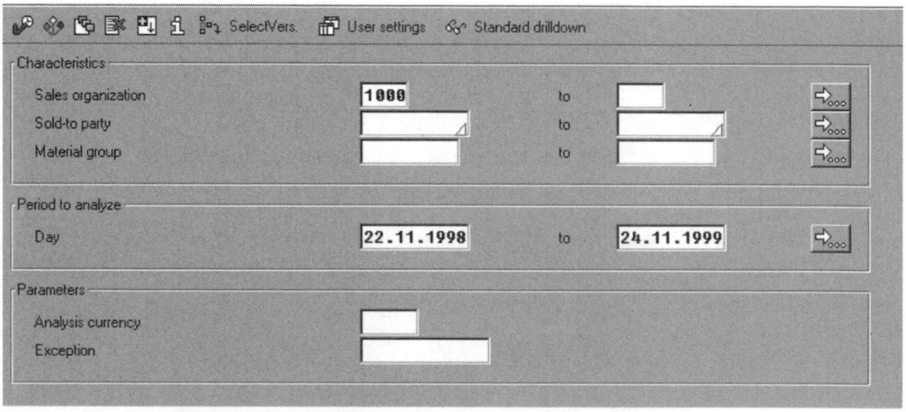

Figure 5-17 Viewing data in an information structure—selection screen

SelectVers. User settings Standard drilldown

Characteristics
Sales organization 1000 to
Sold-to party to
Material group to

Period to analyze
Day 22.11.1998 to 24.11.1999

Parameters
Analysis currency
Exception

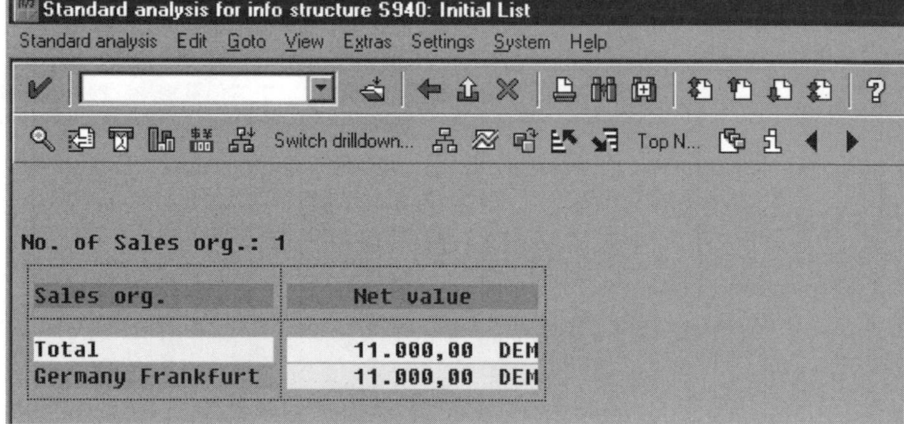

Figure 5-18 Updated data within the information structure

By double-clicking on the characteristic, one can see the next level in the characteristic breakdown. Thus, we see the totals of the net value for each sales organization. This is then broken down for each sold-to party, which is then broken down further into each material group.

Due to this customer master record also having a customer hierarchy, one can add the customer hierarchy as a "higher level of characteristic;" one can view the Net value now in relation to the level of the hierarchy. This can be done by selecting the characteristic "Frankfurt, Germany" (sales organization), for example, and then by selecting View, Hierarchy drill down, and then "Customer hierarchy," as shown in Figure 5-19.

One then selects the hierarchy type; in our example, the hierarchy type is A. After pressing Enter, you can inspect the net value for the sales organization broken down per hierarchy node, that is, "Global account—International," followed by the net value for "Europe," the net value for "Germany National office," and then "Munich regional—International," until finally one again reaches the bottom of the structure, the Material group. This is shown in Figure 5-20.

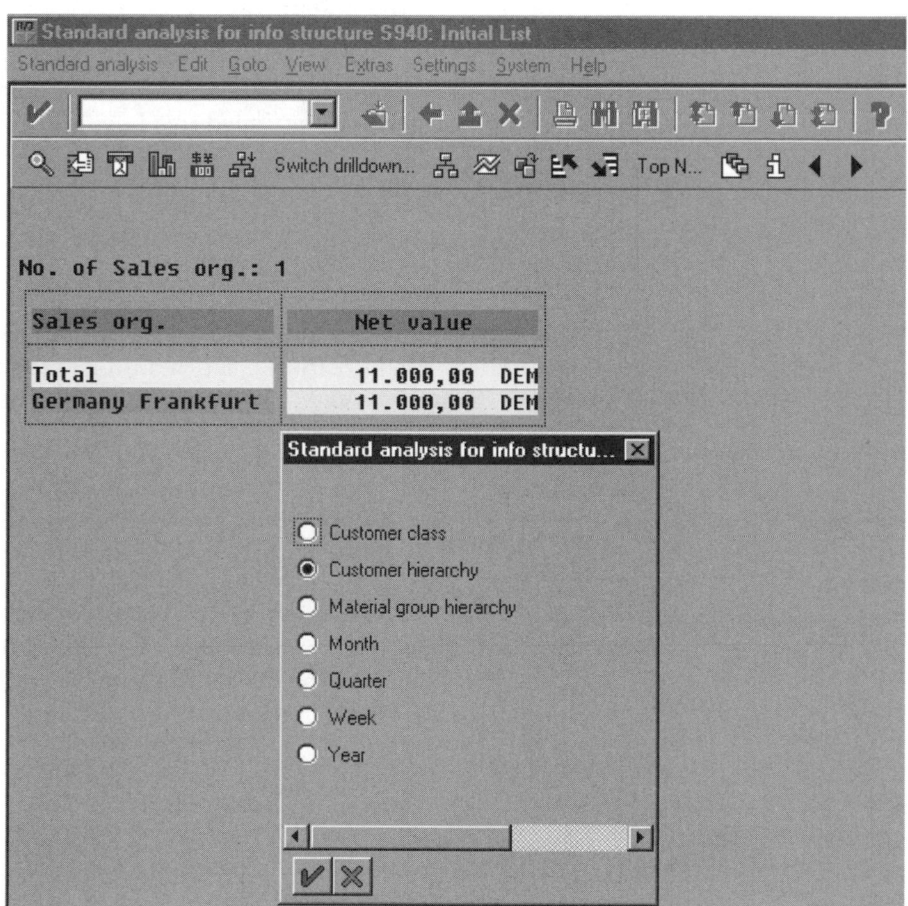

Figure 5-19 Customer hierarchy within the info structure

Sales org. Germany Frankfurt Customer hier. Global Account - Inte
Customer hier. Europe Customer hier. Germany National offi
No. of Material group: 1egional - Int

Material group	Net value
Total	11.000,00 DEM
Accessories	11.000,00 DEM

Figure 5-20 Lowest characteristic

Statistics Currencies

Currencies in information structures may not always be equal, and document currencies may differ, as may currencies of sales organizations or company codes. Thus, if one creates an information structure that accumulates values in different currencies, the system may not know which currency to use as the basis of the information structure. For this reason, the system can enable one to specify a statistics currency to be used as the basis for all information structures. This statistics currency is assigned to a sales organization, and it can also be assigned to a key figure in the definition of the information structure.

Menu Path

To assign the statistics currencies, proceed to IMG, Logistics general, *Logistics information system* (LIS), Logistics data warehouse, Updating, Updating control, Settings sales, Change statistics currency for each sales organization.

Transaction Code

The code here is [OVRB]. Once the currency has been assigned, when one accesses the information in an information structure, the system will use the statistics currency as the default. This currency can be overwritten in the information structure, if needed.

Creating a General Hierarchy for the Purpose of Using LIS/SIS

As discussed previously, one does not need to create a customer hierarchy within the customer master data for the purpose of reporting in LIS, as described in Chapter 4. Rather, that hierarchy should be created when the business offers pricing or rebates on a global scale. Should one require a customer hierarchy for the sole purpose of reporting, one can create this hierarchy using the General Hierarchy feature in the SIS.

Menu Path

This can be done by following the menu path from the Logistics screen as follows: Logistics, Sales and distribution, Sales information system, Environment, General hierarchy, Create.

Transaction Code

The code here is [MCK1]. To create a general hierarchy, you must assign a hierarchy name and a short description. Then specify a characteristic that is obtainable in an information structure as the data element key, such as the customer KUNAG.

The hierarchy can also consist of nodes and customer numbers, like the customer hierarchy. However, the node does not have to be represented by a customer master record, nor is the node or any part of this general hierarchy used anywhere else but in the LIS. Thus, it is not possible to do pricing according to this hierarchy, nor is it possible to see this hierarchy from the sales document.

To create a hierarchical structure, one must assign nodes and customers. There are no rules in creating this hierarchy, other than one cannot have more than one node with the same name.

In order to keep a differentiation between the customer hierarchy and the general hierarchy, the general hierarchy represents the organizational structure of a fictitious company called "Worldwide." This hierarchy is shown in Figure 5-21.

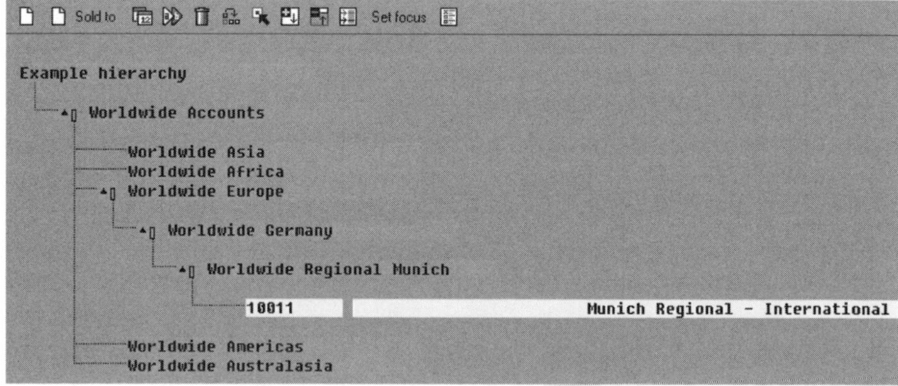

Figure 5-21 An example of a general hiearchy in the LIS

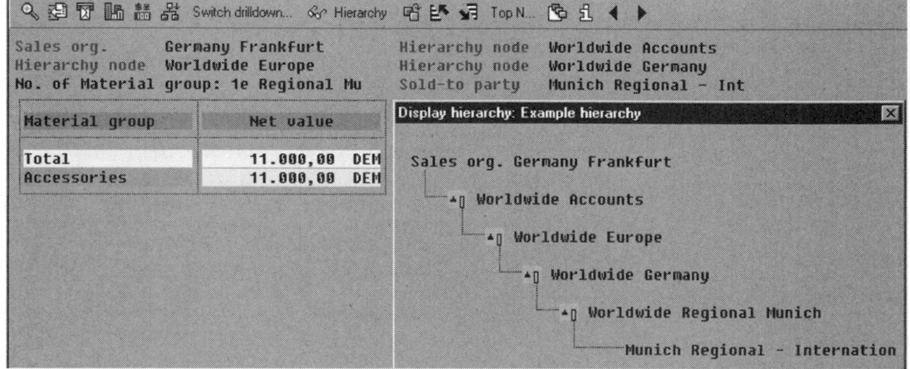

Figure 5-22
Using the general hiearchy with the LIS

After the completion of the hierarchy, proceed back to the self-defined information structures. [MCSI] can be found by proceeding back to the selection of the hierarchy drill-down. One can select the hierarchy just created (an example hierarchy) as the basis for the drill-down reporting. This can be seen in Figure 5-22.

TIP: *Should one create an LIS structure and discover it is not being updated correctly, the structure must be cleared and re-updated. This is also necessary should one create a new structure and require historical data to be updated into it. OSS note 0064636 explains the methods of proceeding with this statistical update.*

Number Range Buffering

As discussed in Chapter 4, one can follow various procedures with regards to improving system performance and response times. One of these methods is to use number range buffering, which enables the faster allocation of numbers to objects, such as sales documents. It reduces the possibility of bottlenecks occurring between the assignment of the number to the document and the COMMIT, where the numbers are allocated.

The buffering of number ranges has been enhanced from 3.0b and now enables the number ranges to be buffered on each application server (instance). This enables each server to be allocated a portion of numbers. In the creation of a sales order, each server can have, for example, 100 numbers in memory. Thus, when each sales order is created, the system does not have to access a number for the sales order from one exclusive place. Rather, each server can allocate numbers. A database block or exclusive lockwait can only occur within an instance that is no longer systemwide.

One must note the following when buffering document number ranges:

- Document numbers cannot be allocated in ascending order according to time. Thus, it is possible for a sales order to be created with a document number of "100" at 10:00 am, while at 10:30 am a sales order can be created with the number "82."
- It is possible to "lose" numbers; thus, not all numbers may be sequential. This may happen if the system crashes and thus a server may lose its previously assigned numbers.

Naturally, it is not beneficial for all documents to be buffered according to the number range. For example, a legal requirement in Italy is that all billing documents are sequential, and that no billing document numbers can be mislaid. In some countries, it is important that delivery numbers are sequential and that no delivery numbers are missing. Due to these requirements, SAP specifies that OSS note 0023835 must be implemented up to release 4.5A. This OSS note prevents the buffering of deliveries and billing documents.

Transaction Code

The code here is [SNRO]. To set the buffer of SD documents, enter the object name, RV_BELEG, and select "Change," as shown in Figure 5-23.

Proceed by selecting Edit, Set up buffering, Main memory (see Figure 5-24).

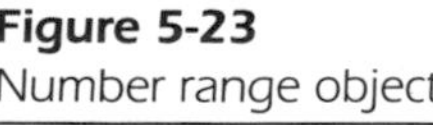

Figure 5-23
Number range object

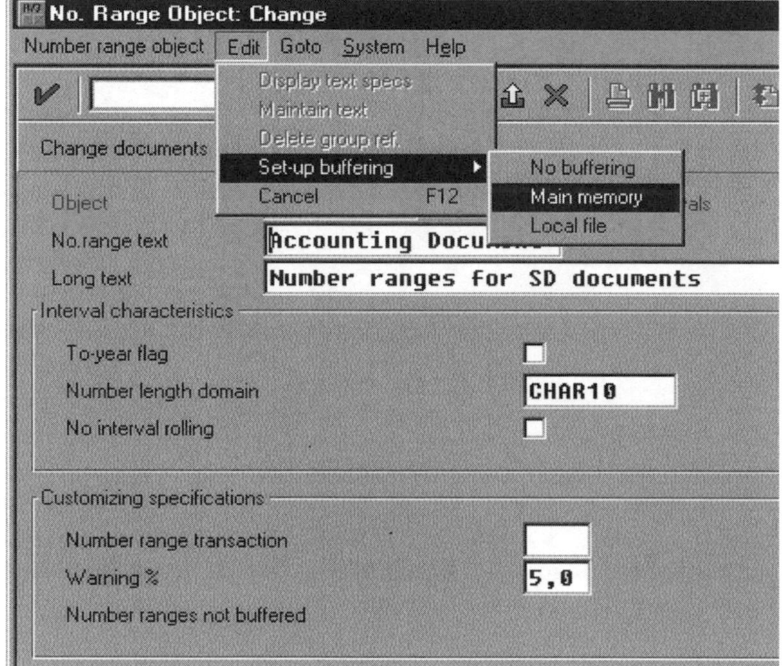

Figure 5-24
Set up buffering

You will now be prompted to set up the numbers you would like the system to use in the buffer. This depends on the size of the business and the amount of transactions happening. Thus, enter a number that you feel would adequately cover the business requirements, such as in the range from 50 to 5,000. Remember that too small a number may actually mean the number range buffer has no affect on the system at all, as the numbers will have to be allocated to the servers, and thus a lock situation could occur on the table NRIV (number range interval). Do not forget to install the OSS note 0023835.

TIP: *You can display the number range buffering including the buffer times and server times by using transaction code [SM56].*

Batch Inputs

The batch input facility in SAP is a convenient tool for capturing data into SAP or updating large amounts of information in SAP transactions. For example, you may wish to change the customer pricing procedure indicator on the customer master record for a list of customers. One could use batch input to make the changes or upload prices into the SAP database tables.

Menu Path

The Batch input tool is available from the Logistics screen, Services menu: System, Services, Batch input, Edit.

Transaction Code

The code here is [SM35]. This section is divided into two parts:

- Recording a batch input
- Running the batch input

In this documentation, we define and run a batch input to change the customer pricing procedure indicator on the customer master sales screen.

Process Overview

Using batch input to capture and change data in SAP involves the following steps:

1. First you record the batch input for the transaction you use to enter the data in SAP.
2. Then you export the batch input recording to a text file.
3. From the recording, you know what data is required. Create a spreadsheet or word processor document for all the data to be captured or changed.
4. Then mail merge the exported text file (from 2) with the data (from 3) in a word processing program (such as Microsoft Word).

5. Import the mail merged file.
6. Upload the file into SAP.
7. Execute batch input in SAP.

Part 1: Recording the Batch Input

Follow these steps to record the batch input:

1. Record the batch input.
2. Export the batch-input-recording format to a text file.
3. Create the data to be used in the batch input.
4. Merge the format with the data.
5. Upload the merged file. The data is now in the format that the batch input requires.

After uploading the recording with the data, you can run the batch input.

Step 1: Recording the Batch Input

To record the batch input, use the menu path: System, Services, Batch input, Edit. Then hit the Recording button (or select Goto, Recording from the menu). Alternatively, you can use Transaction code [SHDB]. The following screen then appears, as shown in Figure 5-25.

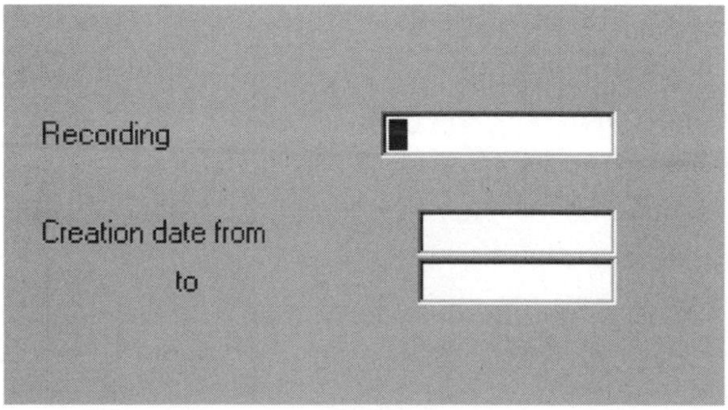

Figure 5-25 Recording a batch input

Recording

Creation date from
to

Enter a name for your recording and press the Create button ( ). Enter the transaction code you will use to update or capture the data. (Refer to Chapter 1 for more information on how to find the transaction code for a SAP transaction.)

Since we will be changing the customer pricing procedure in the customer master sales screens, we will enter transaction code [VD02]. After you have entered the transaction code, SAP will run the transaction as if you selected to run the transaction through the normal menus.

Enter the data in the screens as if you were changing the data online in normal business processing. In other words, make the changes as if you were changing the data online. Be sure to use each of the fields that you want to include in the recording. I recommend that you use a genuine customer master record for creating the recording that you would use in the batch input. This ensures that you include all the fields and menu options in the batch input recording that you need. In our example, we will change the customer pricing procedure indicator on the sales screen of the customer master record.

When the customer change transaction appears for the batch input recording, enter the customer number and the sales area. This information is needed to access the sales screen. Then select the sales screen and press Enter. The sales screen will then appear. Change the customer pricing procedure field to the value you want and press the Save button ( ). Note that these are the exact same steps as changing the pricing procedure indicator manually.

After pressing Save, the transaction ends and you are returned to the Batch Input: Recording screen. This screen shows all the screens and fields you accessed in the transaction and the values you entered in each. The result of our recording is visible in Figure 5-26.

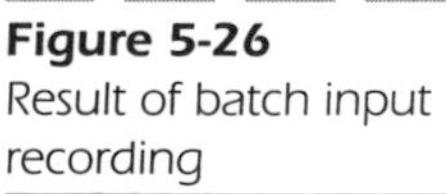

Figure 5-26
Result of batch input recording

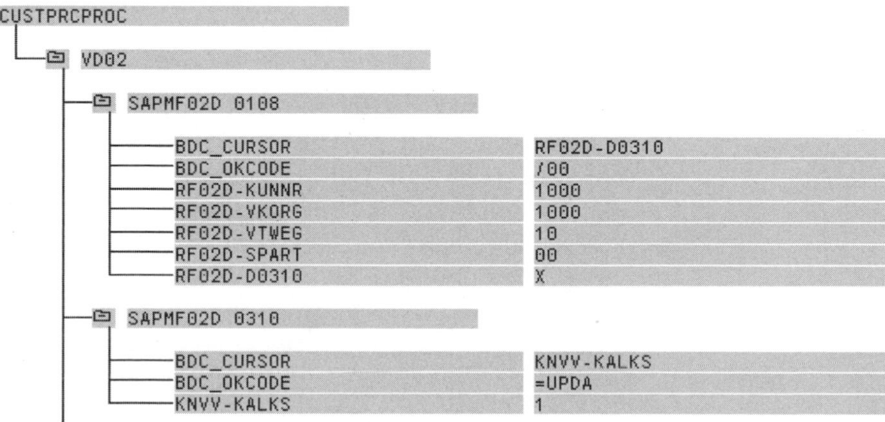

This screen represents the batch input recording. Note all the fields that are accessed and the values entered in each. If you remember, when you are on a field, you can press the F1 key and then the F9 key to see the SAP screen field name. The field names in this recording are the same as the field names in the help screens.

SAP has recorded each screen we accessed (such as screen 0108 in program SAPMF02D), each field we accessed (such as RF02D-KUNNR, the customer number field), and the values entered in each (such as 1000, the customer number). To save the recording, press the Save button.

You now have a recording of all the steps required to change the customer pricing procedure in the customer master sales screen. You can use the same procedure to make changes to any of the fields in any of the SAP transactions. This procedure is especially useful for making changes to master data like the customer and material master.

Step 2: Exporting the Format of the Recording to a Text File

Once you have made the recording, you must export the format to a text file for use in a mail merge program or word processor. Go to the Batch input transaction system, Services, Batch input, Edit. Press the *Recording* button or select Goto, Recording from the menu. Alternatively, use transaction code [SHDB].

From the screen, enter the name you gave the recording in step 1 and press the Overview button. Alternatively, you can enter a date range and press the Overview button( ). This will display all recordings made in that date range.

After pressing the Overview button, the screen in Figure 5-27 is displayed listing all the batch input recordings for the name and date range you entered.

Select the recording you made in step one and press the Change button( ). You will see the recording displayed (just as it was displayed after you finished recording it in step 1). Then select the Editing button. Alternatively, select Edit, Editing from the menu. The batch input recording is displayed in Figure 5–28. This recording is in the format that SAP needs to access the screens and fields and process the transaction.

Figure 5-27
List of all batch input recordings for name and date range

Recording	Date	Time	Created by	Trans	Scree
CUPRCPROC	29.11.1999	08:05:35	G0013	1	2

Figure 2-28
Batch input recording

	Program	Scr.	S	Fld name	FldValue
1			T	VD02	BS
2	SAPMF02D	108	X		
3				BDC_CURSOR	RF02D-D0310
4				BDC_OKCODE	/00
5				RF02D-KUNNR	1000
6				RF02D-VKORG	1000
7				RF02D-VTWEG	10
8				RF02D-SPART	00
9				RF02D-D0310	X
10	SAPMF02D	310	X		
11				BDC_CURSOR	KNVV-KALKS
12				BDC_OKCODE	/00
13				KNVV-KALKS	3

Figure 2-29
Export the recording format to a text file.

Transfer to a Local File

File name	H:\CUPRCPROC.TXT
Data format	DAT

Transfer

Press the *Export* button ( ) to export the recording format to a text file, as shown in Figure 5–29.

In the screen displayed, type the file name and the file type. In this example, we will use the file type DAT for ASCII text separated by tab columns, but you may also want to use WK1 for a spreadsheet format. The DAT format is most convenient for mail merge programs. You now have the format you need to put your data in so that SAP can use it in the batch input recording.

Step 3: Create the Data to be Used in the Batch Input

The next step is to create the data that will be used in the batch input. In our example, this is a list of all the customers, their sales areas, and the customer pricing procedures for each one. We will be using Microsoft Word to create a merged file of the format we created in step 2 with the data we create in this step. We will create the data for our batch input in an Excel spreadsheet. The spreadsheet will have five columns: the customer number, sales organization, distribution channel and division, and the customer pricing procedure. Each of the rows will be a customer record. Note that each of these columns represents the fields that we typed in when we did our batch input recording.

NOTE: *You can use an ABAP query (discussed later in this chapter) to create a query to list all the customers, sales areas, and their existing customer pricing procedures. You can then run the query and export it to a spreadsheet. You can use this spreadsheet to change the customer pricing procedures for each customer and sales area.*

In the example on ABAP queries later in this chapter, we use an ABAP query to create the customer list from table KNVV. This list contains the field's customer name, sales organization, distribution channel, division, and customer pricing procedure. The query has been run for the selection list and the result is displayed as a table (see Figure 5-30).

After exporting the table to an Excel spreadsheet, use List, Spreadsheet and then Excel display from the menu. The spreadsheet in Figure 5-31 is the result.

Customer sales screens data

Customer	SOrg	D(	D	(
1000	1000	10	00	3
1001	1000	12	00	1
1002	1000	12	00	1
1010	1000	10	00	1
1012	1000	12	00	1
1020	1000	10	00	1
1032	1000	10	00	1
1032	1000	14	00	1
1033	1000	12	00	1
1034	1000	10	00	1
1034	1000	14	00	1

Figure 5-30
List of customers with their sales areas and customer pricing procedure indicator

Figure 5-31 Excel spreadsheet of data

	A	B	C	D	E
1	Customer numbe	Sales organizatio	Distribution chann	Divisior	Pricing procedure assigned to this custo
2	1000	1000	10	00	3
3	100016	1000	10	00	1
4	100016	1000	12	00	1
5	100026	1000	10	00	1
6	100027	1000	12	00	1
7	1001	1000	12	00	1
8	1002	1000	12	00	1
9	1010	1000	10	00	1
10	1012	1000	12	00	1
11	1020	1000	10	00	1
12	1032	1000	10	00	1
13	1032	1000	14	00	1
14	1033	1000	12	00	1

One can now use this spreadsheet to change the pricing procedure to 2 for all entries using the Excel search and replace tools. After one has made all the changes, the spreadsheet can be saved. One now has the data for the batch input.

Step 4: Merge the Data with the Format for the Batch Input Recording

When we created the batch input recording, we were recording each of the actions in the transaction we wanted to process. By recording these actions, they can be executed again and again to get the same result.

For example, we can run the batch input recording we created again. SAP will then use this recording to execute the actions in exactly the same way as when we executed the actions during the recording. This means that if we change the data in the recording, we can run the recording again for the new data. We could change the customer number in the recording and then run it again. It will make the same changes to the customer master for this new customer number. We already exported this recording to a text file and created a separate spreadsheet with a list of all the customers we want to change. If we create a recording for each of the customers in the spreadsheet, then SAP will run the recording for each of the customers.

We have the format and the customers, so we can use any method to create a copy of the recording for each of the customers in the spreadsheet (for example, use a program, copy and paste, or use the Microsoft Word mail merge facility). We will use Word for our example.

The Text File—Creating the Mail Merge File After opening the file you created in step 2 in Word, you will see Figure 5-32. Note that this mirrors the recording you created in step 1.

You now need to use this structure to define the fields in the mail merge. The fields that can change are the values next to KUNNR, VKORG, VTWEG, SPART, and KALKS. We need to define these as mail merge fields. If you do not know how to use mail merge in MS Word, please use the MS Word help for directions.

Here is a quick-step guide:

1. Open the text file you exported to the recording format.
2. Select Tools, Mail merge from the Word menu (see Figure 5-33).
3. For the main document, press Create, choose the Catalog mail merge type, and then choose the existing (Active) window as the mail merge document.
4. For the data source, press the Get data button and then Open data source. Select the Excel spreadsheet you created in step 3 and you will see the screen in Figure 5-34.
5. Go back to the main document section, press the Edit button to edit the mail merge document, and insert the merge fields. You will see the Mail merge tool bar is active, as in Figure 5-35. Note that in the Insert Merge field menu, the columns from your spreadsheet are listed.

Figure 5-32 Text file in Microsoft Word

```
        0000    T       VD02   BS
SAPMF02D        0108    X
        0000            BDC_CURSOR   RF02D-D0310
        0000            BDC_OKCODE   /00
        0000            RF02D-KUNNR  1000
        0000            RF02D-VKORG  1000
        0000            RF02D-VTWEG  10
        0000            RF02D-SPART  00
        0000            RF02D-D0310  X
SAPMF02D        0310    X
        0000            BDC_CURSOR   KNVV-KALKS
        0000            BDC_OKCODE   /00
        0000            KNVV-KALKS   3
```

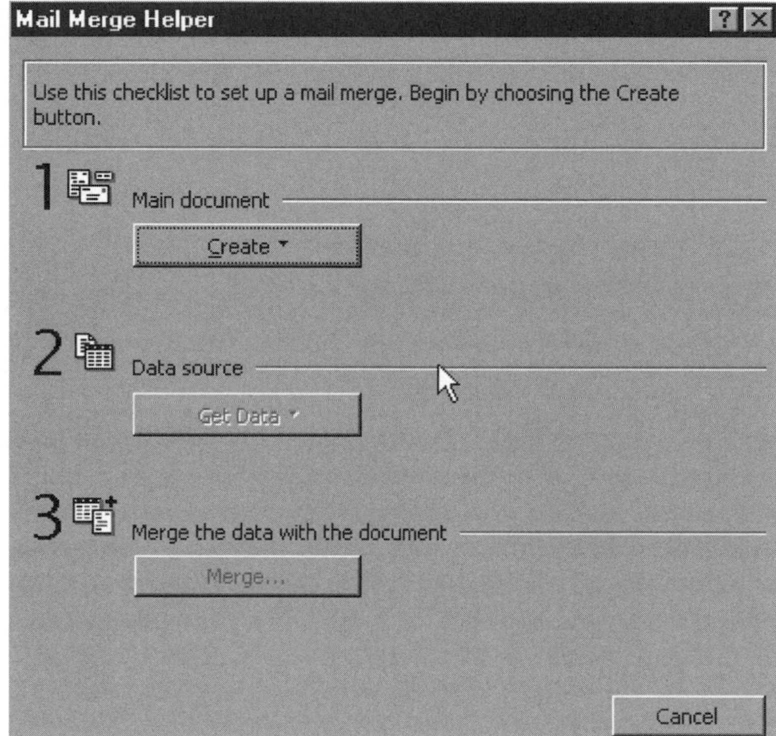

Figure 5-33 Mail merge helper in Microsoft Word

Then select the area where the data must be placed and choose Insert Merge field and the merge field to replace it. The selected area is replaced with the merge field name. Do this for each of the fields that are to be replaced. After inserting the mail merge field, the selected area is replaced with the mail merge field name, as in Figure 5-36.

6. Once you have placed all the mail merge fields from the spreadsheet, you can merge the spreadsheet with the Word document. Select Tools, Mail merge from the Word menu, and then press the Merge button. Execute the merge in a new document. A new window will be opened in Word with the result. You will see that for every record in the spreadsheet, the text from the recording has been duplicated with the spreadsheet data.
7. Save the document as a text-only document. You now have a batch input recording for each record in the spreadsheet.

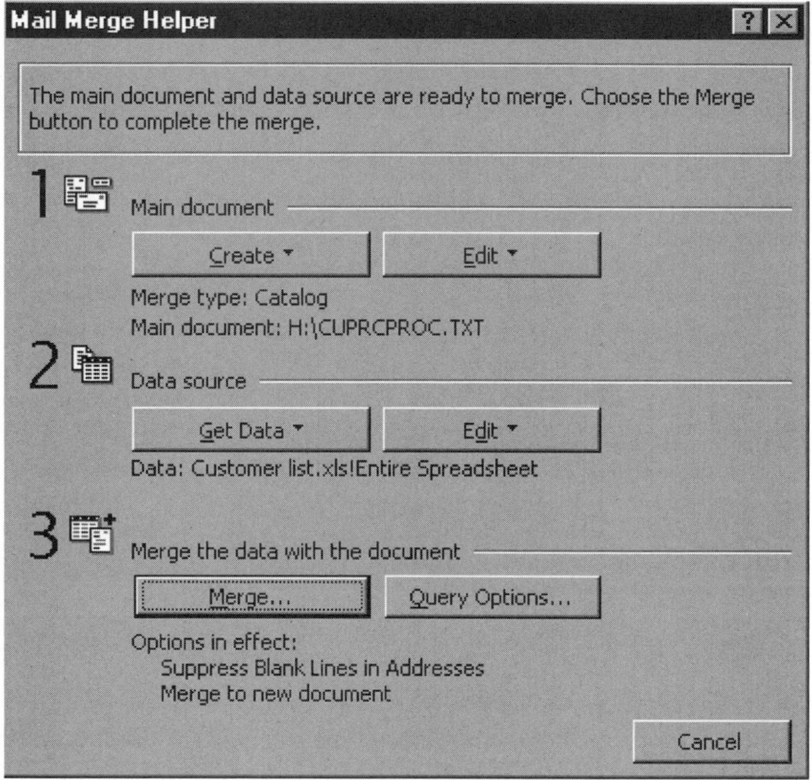

Figure 5-34
Ready to merge the Word document and the Excel document

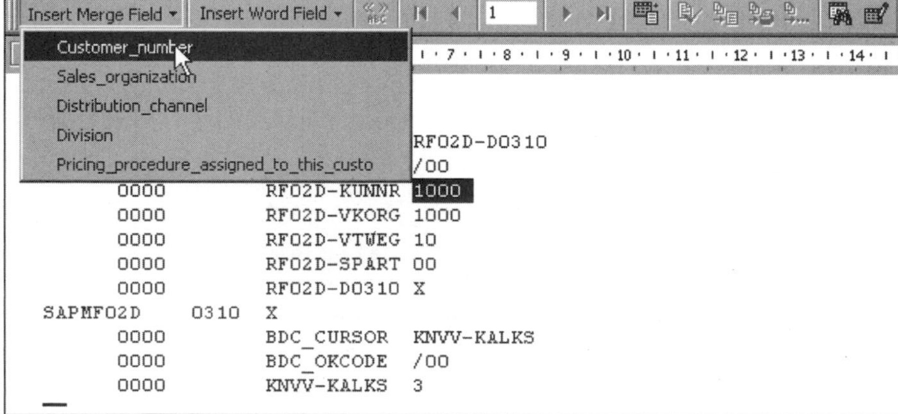

Figure 5-35
The columns for the spreadsheet are listed.

Step 5: Upload the Merged File

The final step in creating the batch input is uploading the merged file. Go to the batch input recording (transaction SHDB) and the editing screen where you exported the format in step 2 (press the Editing button or select Edit, Editing from the menu).

Press the Import button ( ) to import the new recording with the merged data (see Figure 5-37).

Enter the file name that you saved in step 4 and select the format DAT. After importing the data, the batch recording will be replaced with the data from the file, as in Figure 5-38. Note that the number of records in the recording has increased (the bottom right of the screen shows there are now 1,177 records in this recording).

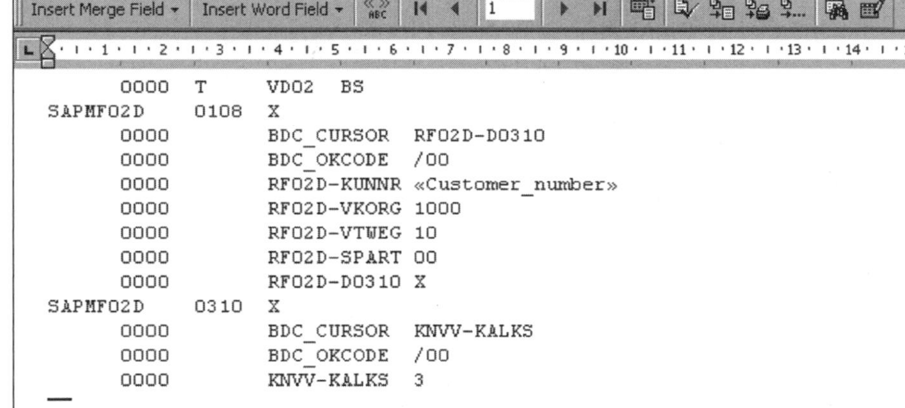

Figure 5-36 The selected area is replaced with the mail merge field name.

Import from a Local File
File name H:\MERGEDLIST.TXT
Data format DAT
Transfer

Figure 5-37 Import the new recording with the merged data.

	Program	Scr.	S	Fld name	FldValue
1			T	VD02	BS
2	SAPMF02D	108	X		
3				BDC_CURSOR	RF02D-D0310
4				BDC_OKCODE	/00
5				RF02D-KUNNR	1000
6				RF02D-VKORG	1000
7				RF02D-VTWEG	10
8				RF02D-SPART	00
9				RF02D-D0310	X
10	SAPMF02D	310	X		
11				BDC_CURSOR	KNVV-KALKS
12				BDC_OKCODE	/00
13				KNVV-KALKS	1
14	SAPMF02D	108	X		
15				BDC_CURSOR	RF02D-D0310
16				BDC_OKCODE	/00
17				RF02D-KUNNR	100016
18				RF02D-VKORG	1000
19				RF02D-VTWEG	10
20				RF02D-SPART	00
21				RF02D-D0310	X

Line 1 — 21 Fr. 1177

Figure 5-38
The batch recording now has data from the merged file.

Press the Save button ( ) to save the new recording. You can now run this recording in the following section.

Part 2: Executing the Batch Input

Once you have created a recording, you can execute it. To run the batch input, you must create a batch input session and then execute this session.

1. Create the batch input session.

   To run the batch input, you must create a batch input session from the recording you made in the previous section. To create the session, use the menu path System, Services, Batch input, Edit. Then select the Recording button or Goto, Recording from the menu. Alternatively, use transaction code [SHDB].

   Enter the batch input recording name (or a date range) and then press the Overview button ( ). The recording (or the recordings you have created for the date range) are displayed on the screen in a list.

Select the recording you want to create a batch input session for and press the Generate session button ( ). Enter the session name and the user ID of the person whose authorization profile SAP must use to process the session.

Select the Keep session flag, as seen in Figure 5-39, if you do not want SAP to delete the session after successfully executing it. Now that the session has been created from the recording, you can execute it. (See Figure 5-40.)

Figure 5-39
Create a Session

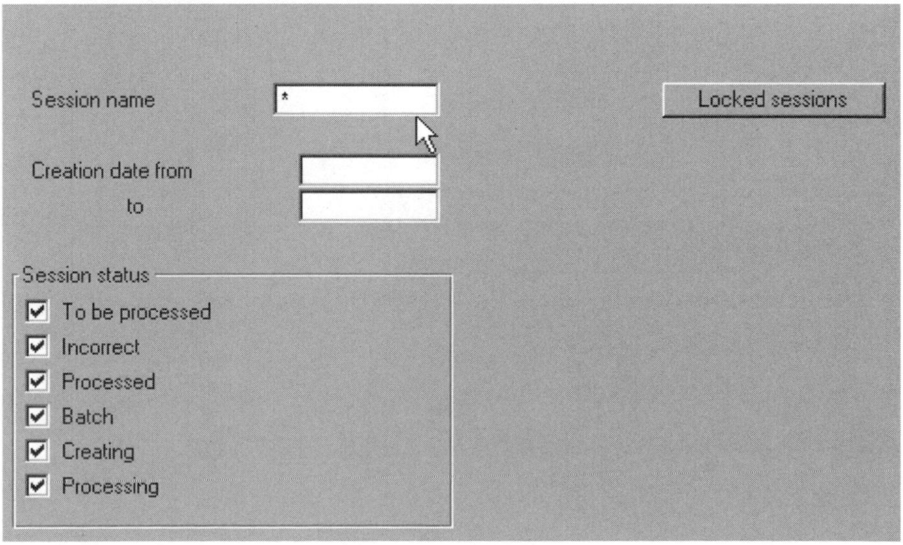

Figure 5-40
Selecting Sessions

2. Execute the batch input session.

   To execute the batch input session you created, use the menu path System, Services, Batch input, Edit. Alternatively, use transaction code [SM35]. Enter the name of the session you created in the previous section or a date range. Go to the overview screen (press the Overview button).

The sessions you have created will be displayed as in the following list in Figure 5-41:

Select the session you want to execute and press the Execute button (icon). The screen in Figure 5-42 then appears.

Figure 5-41 List of created sessions

Sessions still to be processed

Session	Date	Time	Locked	Created by	Tran.	Screen	Authorizatio
CPRCPROC_01	29.11.1999	13:42:29		G0013	1	196	G0013

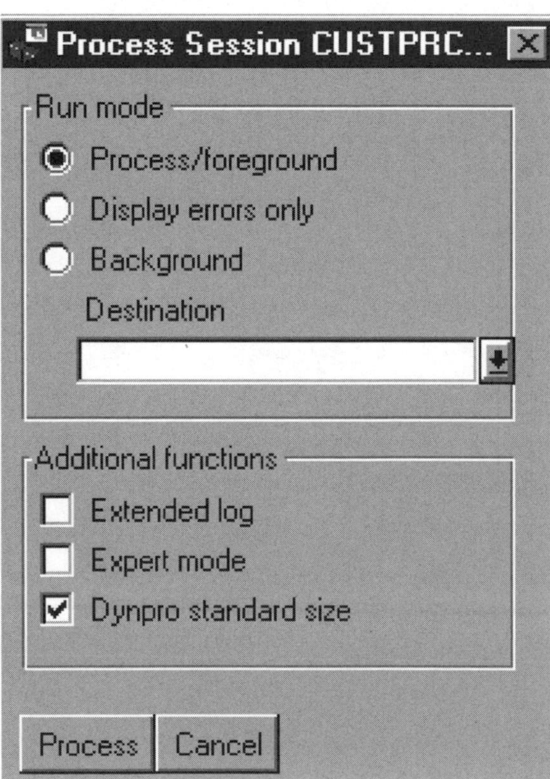

Figure 5-42 Exeuting the selected session

Processing Modes

Three processing modes are used by SAP:

- *Process / foreground* With this option, SAP will run the recording online, but you must press Enter for each action in the recording. This is fine for testing, but for long recordings, this is very tedious.
- *Display errors only* With this option, SAP will run each action in the recording. If SAP encounters an error, it will stop and open the transaction screen (in our example, the change customer transaction VD02) for you to correct the error. After correcting the error, the process will continue.
- *Background* With this option, SAP runs the recording in a batch session on the server. You will not be notified of errors, but you can check the batch input log to see if the session was processed correctly. We will look at the batch input log later. This is the recommended method.

Dynpro standard size is an additional function. Select this option to use the standard screen size.

NOTE: *When it comes to executing batch input sessions, users can change their system settings, such as the screen size and fonts. This may change the screen size and the number of screen fields on a screen (especially in screens where there are table structures, like the order entry screen).*

If SAP tries to run a recording for a batch input where the screen sizes are different, it may not be able to find the field in the recording. For example, if the table has five lines in one screen size and 10 in another, and if you created a recording for the screen size with 10 lines and tried to run it with a screen size of five lines, an error will occur when SAP tries to place the sixth line on the screen with only five lines.

To prevent this, always create the batch input recordings with the standard screen, and always run the batch input with the standard screen size. If you created the batch input recording on the same computer as you are running it, and you are running the batch input in the foreground, this is not a consideration.

The Batch Input

If you selected the processing mode *in the foreground*, you would need to step through each of the actions in the recording. If you selected Processing and Displaying *errors only*, your screen will wait until each record in the batch input has been processed. If there is an error, the transaction will be displayed (as if you were processing in the foreground) and you can correct the error before continuing. Your dialog session is held up by the batch input as SAP processes the batch input using your dialog session. In this example, we have a recording that has a customer pricing procedure '6,' but this has not been defined. The batch input stops on the screen shown in Figure 5-43.

You can now change the field value to a correct entry and then press Enter. After changing it to a correct value, the batch input session continues until the next error. At the end of the session, the screen in Figure 5-44 appears.

Press the *Resume* button to return to the batch input screen. If you selected *background* processing, SAP will create a job for the batch input session and run it on the server, immediately freeing up your dialog session for you and other people using SAP to continue with other transactions.

Figure 5-43 An error needing correcting during a session

Figure 5-44 Batch input completed

NOTE: From the point of view of system performance, this is the most efficient processing option because the dialog session is not tied up by a single operation. For very long batch inputs, you should always run them in the background to optimize performance.

If errors occur in a batch input run in the background, you need to process these after the whole batch session is complete.

NOTE: A batch input session can also be created by an ABAP program. If you hand the recording made for a transaction to an ABAP programmer, the programmer can use the recording to write a program to perform the batch input.

Jobs

A job is a specific background task for the server to carry out. When you create and execute a batch input session, you are giving the server a job.

Menu Path

You can see the jobs you have created using the menu path System, Services, Jobs, Job overview.

Transaction Code

The code here is [SM37]. The job overview screen is displayed in Figure 5-45. Press Enter to see a list of jobs. The screen shows the background job created for our example.

Figure 5-45
Job overview screen

Job name	Scheduled	Released	Ready	Active	Finished	Cancelled
CPRCPROC_01					X	

You can see a list of all the background jobs you created and their status. In this case, the job is finished and we can check it for errors. If the job is still running on the server, it will be marked as *Active*. If it is still waiting in the job queue, it will be marked as *Ready*. Jobs that are cancelled by the system administrator are marked as *Cancelled*.

Processing Errors from Background Sessions

Once a batch input or any other job that you executed in the background has been completed, it needs to be checked for errors. To do so, go to the batch input screen using the menu path System, Services, Batch input, Edit, or use the transaction code [SM35]. Enter the name of the session (the name you created the session with) and press the Overview button. If the session is processed without errors, it will be displayed in the section, Processed sessions. If there are errors, the session will be displayed in the section, Errors in sessions, as in Figure 5-46. All the records with errors in them are placed in this batch input session.

Viewing the Errors

To view the errors, select the session and press the Log button. The log will be displayed, as in Figure 5-47.

The field entry 6 does not exist for the customer pricing procedure.

Press the green back arrow ( ) to return to the session overview screen.

Correcting the Errors

To correct the errors, select the session from the session overview screen and press the Execute button ( ). You are faced with the same screen that appeared when you first selected to execute the batch input session.

Figure 5-46
Errors in sessions

Errors in sessions

Session	Date	Time	Locked	Created by	Tran.	Screen	Authorizatio
C_01	29.11.1999	14:45:00		G0013	1	196	G0013

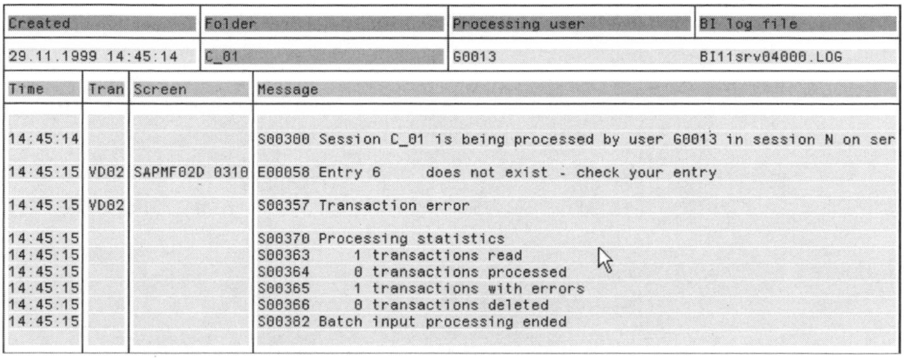

Figure 5-47
Error log

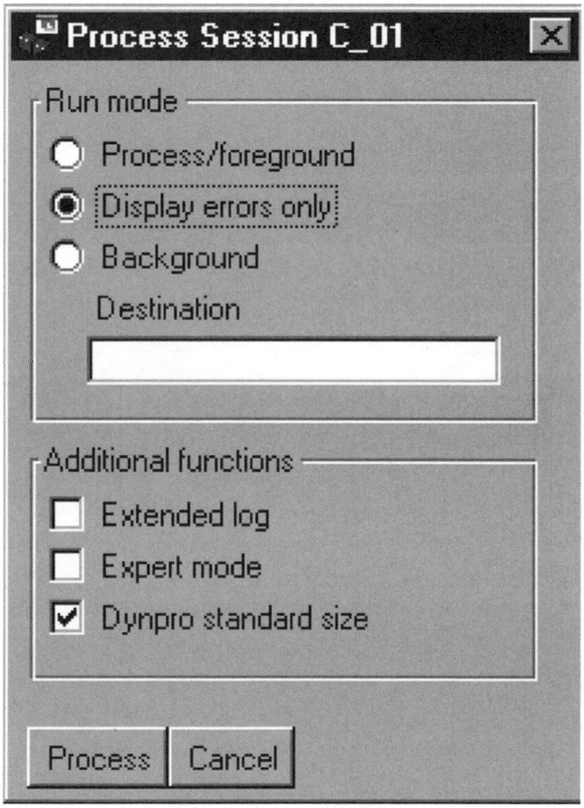

Created	Folder	Processing user	BI log file
29.11.1999 14:45:14	C_01	G0013	BI11srv04000.LOG

Time	Tran	Screen	Message
14:45:14			S00300 Session C_01 is being processed by user G0013 in session N on ser
14:45:15	VD02	SAPMF02D 0310	E00058 Entry 6 does not exist - check your entry
14:45:15	VD02		S00357 Transaction error
14:45:15			S00370 Processing statistics
14:45:15			S00363 1 transactions read
14:45:15			S00364 0 transactions processed
14:45:15			S00365 1 transactions with errors
14:45:15			S00366 0 transactions deleted
14:45:15			S00382 Batch input processing ended

Figure 5-48
Process the session with display errors only

Process Session C_01
Run mode
Process/foreground
Display errors only
Background
Destination
Additional functions
Extended log
Expert mode
Dynpro standard size
Process
Cancel

In this case, process the session with the Display errors only option so that you can correct the error, as seen in Figure 5-48.

Variants

It is possible to assign a background job a variant. What one actually does is make a particular program that has a specific variant assigned to it only use the selection or processing options as laid out in the variant each time the program is run. This is done by the following procedure.

Menu Path

From the Logistics screen, select Tools, ABAP workbench, and then select the ABAP Editor button or use the transaction code [SE38]. One then proceeds to enter the program name that requires a variant. In our example, we will create a variant for the print program RSNAST00. One can then enter the program name followed by selecting the Variants button (see Figure 5-49).

One then selects the Change button, which will bring up the screen in Figure 5-50. In this screen, one must assign the variant name, which can be an alphanumeric key. It is advised to make this a meaningful, descriptive key, for ease of use when reading from the batch job log. We have called the variant in our example ZRD00-Daily.

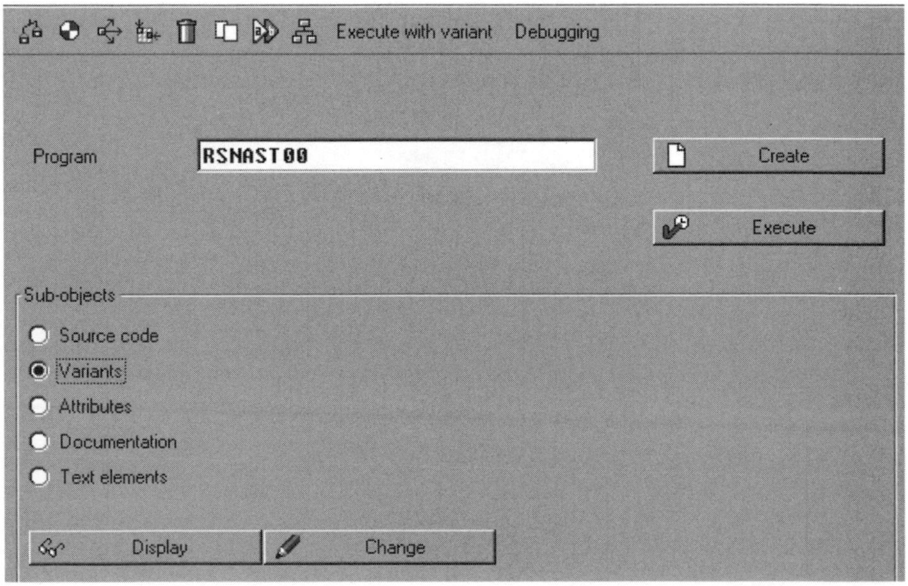

Figure 5-49
Create a Variant for a Program

Then select the Create button. You will receive a selection screen where it is advisable to enable the variant to be created for all selection screens of the report. Press Enter and then enter the variant attributes (see Figure 5-51).

Program
RSNAST00
Variant
ZRD00-Daily
Create
Sub-objects
Values
Attributes
Display
Change

Figure 5-50
Name the variant and select "create."

Maintain Variants: Report RSNAST00, Variant ZRD00-DAILY
Variant Edit Goto System Help
Continue
Selection parameter
Output application
V3
to
Object key
to
Output type
RD00
to
Transmission medium
to
Send again
Sort
Parameter for calling up the processing program
Printer default
Spool: Suffix 2

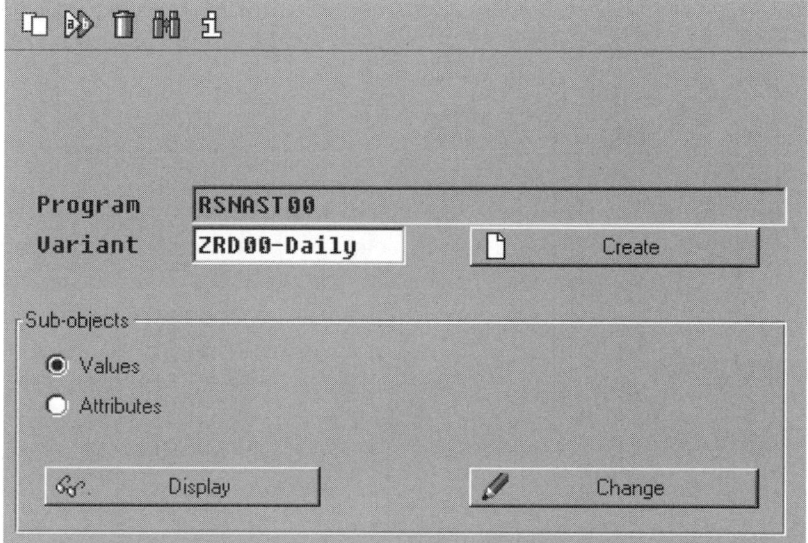

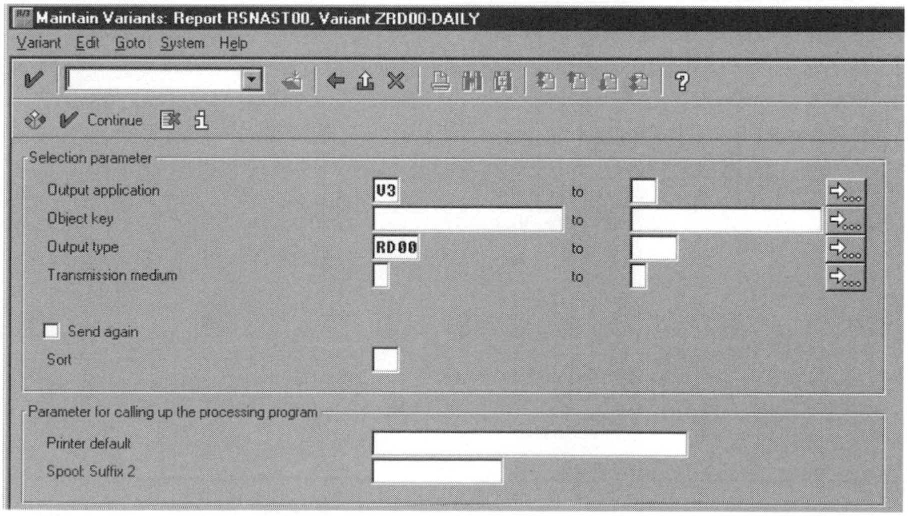

Figure 5-51
Maintain the variant's attributes.

You can then select the Continue button, and will be faced with the overall control selections of the variant. In our example, we have protected the variant from being changed by anyone other than the user who created the variant (see Figure 5-52). We have also protected the variant from being allowed to be changed during runtime.

You can now save the variant. Now that the variant is created, you need to use the variant when processing a job in batch mode.

Menu Path

To create a job, one needs to proceed along the following menu path. From the Logistics screen, select System, Services, Jobs, Define Job. Alternatively, you can use transaction code [SM36]. Then enter a job name as well as a class and target host, after which the entry will be similar to Figure 5-53.

The class is important, as you can use the class to sequence jobs. For example, one may want the delivery due list to be carried out in batch before the posting of goods issue in batch. Thus, one can assign the delivery due list the class A, while the posting of goods issue can be assigned class B. The basis team can then use these classifications to know when to process or schedule the background jobs. Then hit the Start date button, following which one can select, for example, the button "Immediate." You will

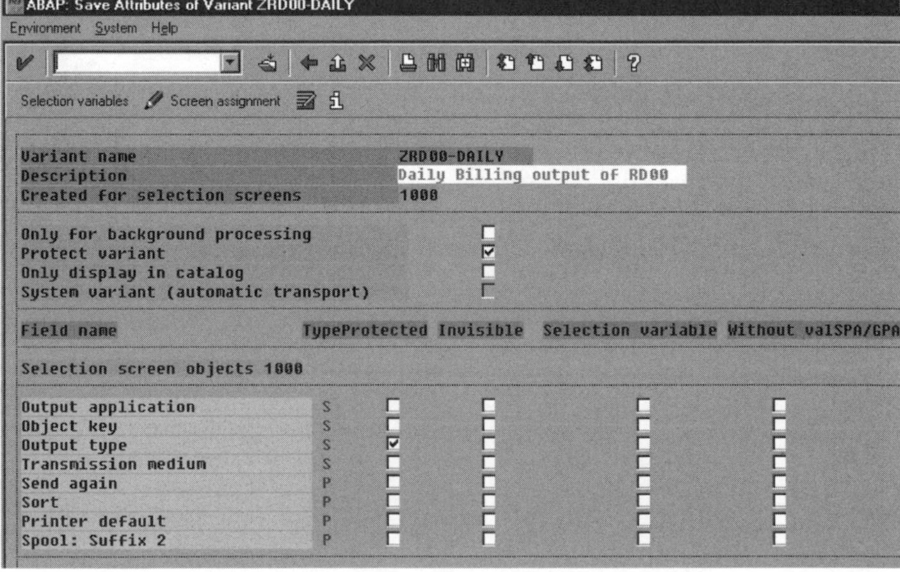

Figure 5-52 Attributes of the variant are saved and protected.

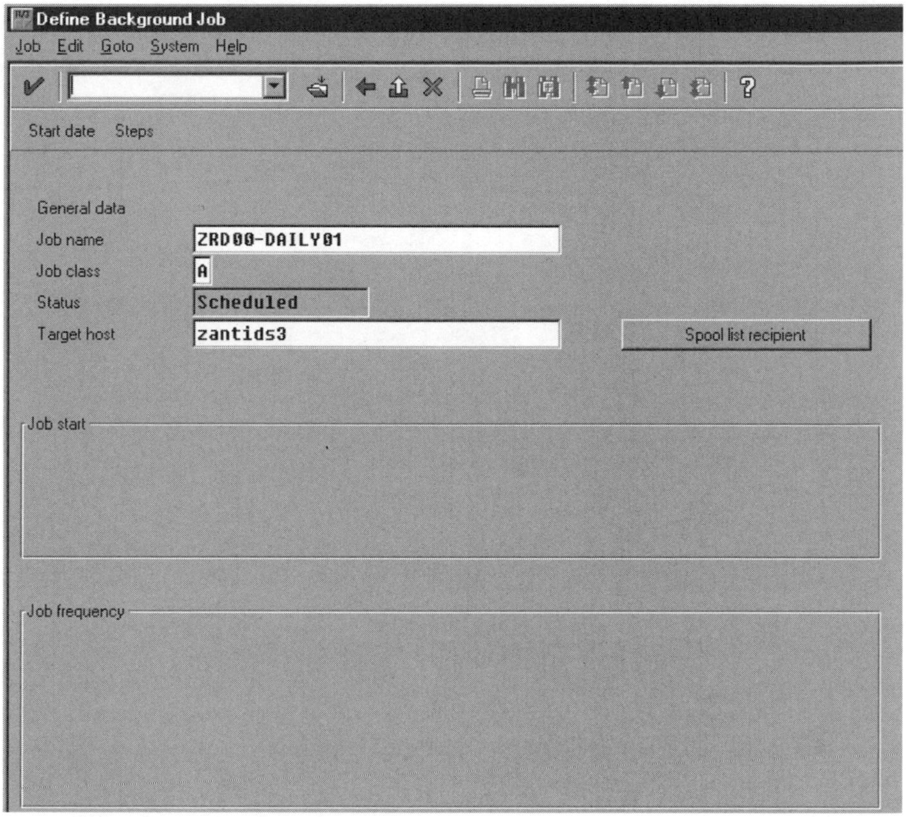

Figure 5-53
Define a background job.

notice the periodic indicator at the base of the selection screen, shown in Figure 5-54. By selecting this indicator, you can select the Period values button. After selecting it, you can select the period, such as "daily."

Then press Save. You will receive an overview screen where you will see the assignment of the daily period. You can select Save here also, which brings up the screen in Figure 5-55 where you can enter the associated variant you just created. After saving the variant, it will finally be assigned to the batch job you created.

Should you proceed to [SM37], you will find the job overview screen, where you can select background jobs. You can select the job by using the job name and then view the job, as shown in Figure 5-56.

Should you want to see a log of the selected job, press the Job Log button, which will show the results in Figure 5-57.

Start Time
Immediate
Date/Time
After job
After event
At operation mode
>>
Date/Time
Immediate
Period Values
Hourly
Daily
Weekly
Monthly
Other period
Check
After job
At operation mode
After event
Periodic job
Check
Period values
Restrictions

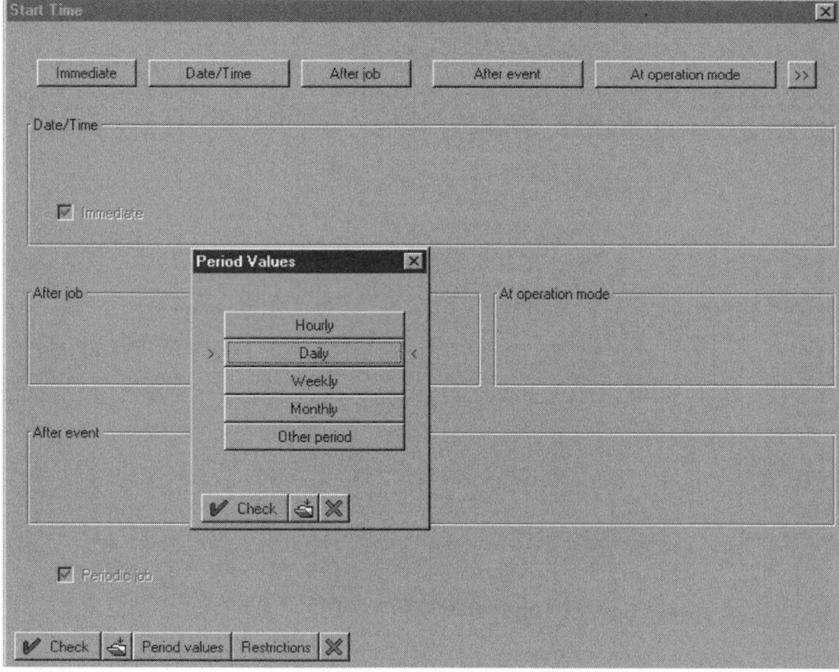

Figure 5-54
Notice in start time the Check box for Periodic job.

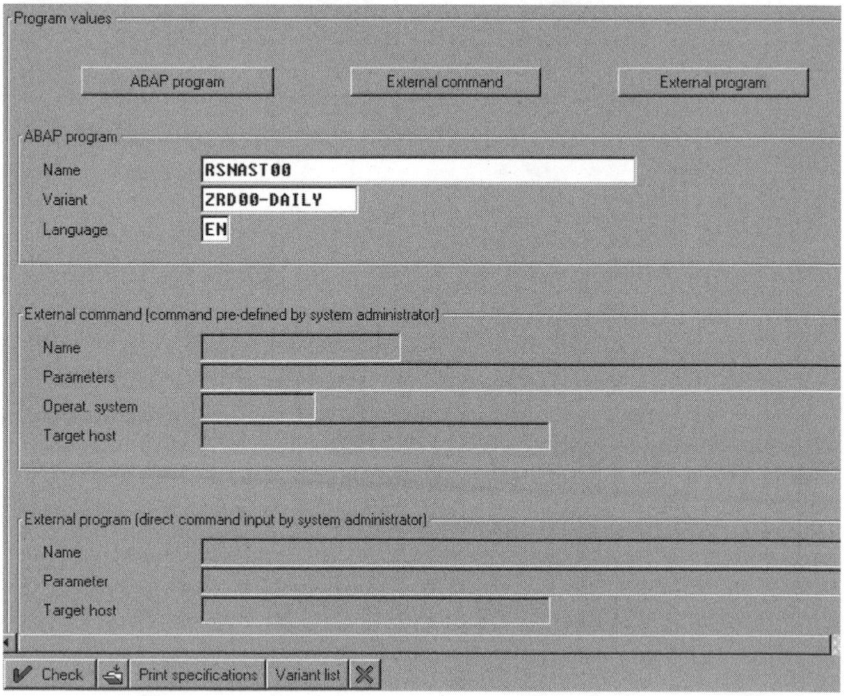

Program values
ABAP program
External command
External program
ABAP program
Name
RSNAST00
Variant
ZRD00-DAILY
Language
EN
External command (command pre-defined by system administrator)
Name
Parameters
Operat. system
Target host
External program (direct command input by system administrator)
Name
Parameter
Target host
Check
Print specifications
Variant list

Figure 5-55
You may assign the variant to the program.

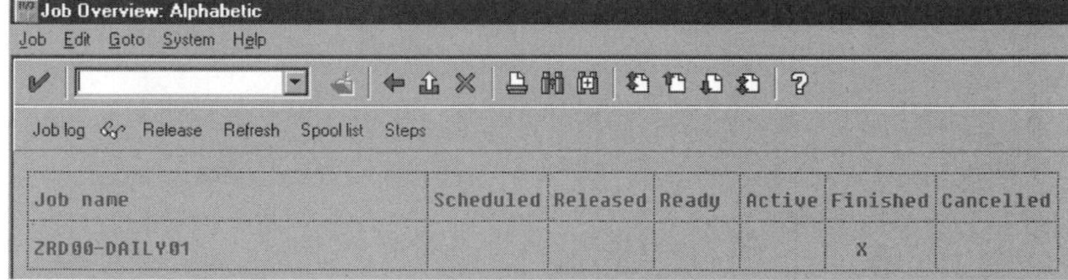

Figure 5-56
View the job in the job overview.

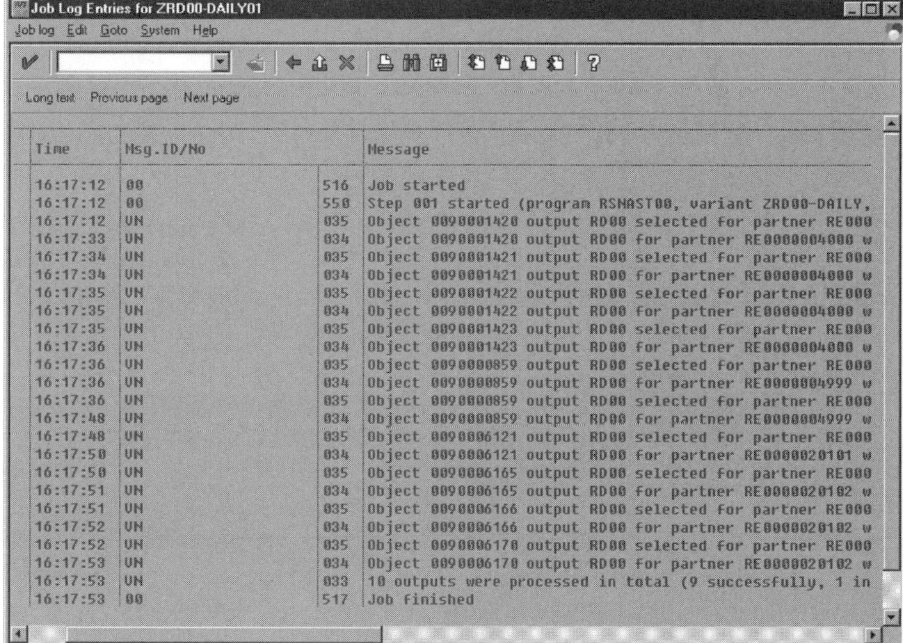

Figure 5-57
Job log of the selected job as previously seen in the job overview.

ABAP Enhancements: User-Defined Transaction Codes

It is quite possible that an implementation will run specially created reports or programs performing specific functions. Generally, these reports or functions will need to be accessed by a large number of people on a frequent basis.

For this reason, SAP enables the creation of user-defined transaction codes. Thus, by creating a transaction code, you can speed up access to specific reports/programs, as the user no longer needs this capability. To access a program, for example, use transaction code [SA38], followed by entering the program name and pressing Excecute. The user can then simply use a transaction code that will automatically open the program.

Menu Path

From the Logistics screen, select Tools, ABAP/4 workbench, Development, Other tools, Transactions.

Transaction Code

The code here is [SE93].

Background We saw in Chapter 1 how to access the transaction code of a screen. Should you want to have a list of transaction codes and their descriptions, one can access the table TSTC using [SE16]. This will provide a list of all the transaction codes in the system.

Procedure One can create one's own transaction code by proceeding along the earlier menu path. One will be faced with the screen in Figure 5-58.

One can enter a four-character alphanumeric key, beginning with the letter Z, such as ZD40.

After entering the transaction code, select the Create button ( ). You will then be presented with a selection box of transaction types (see Figure 5-59).

The transaction type with parameters is very useful. For example, let's say you wanted to create a transaction code for each of the order types in

Figure 5-58 Maintain Transaction code

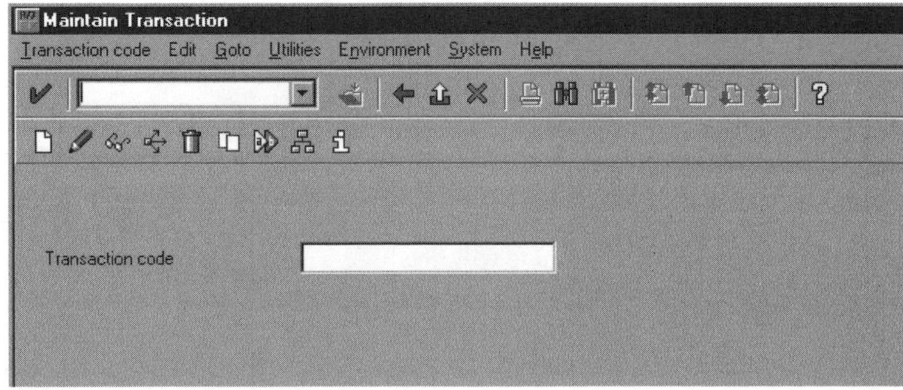

your business. Instead of the user selecting transaction VA01 and typing in the order type each time, you can create a number of transactions (ZVA01_OR as the standard order, for example) for each order type and define these as parameter transactions. You can then enter the parameters for the transaction and select the option "Skip first screen," as in the following example (see Figure 5-60a).

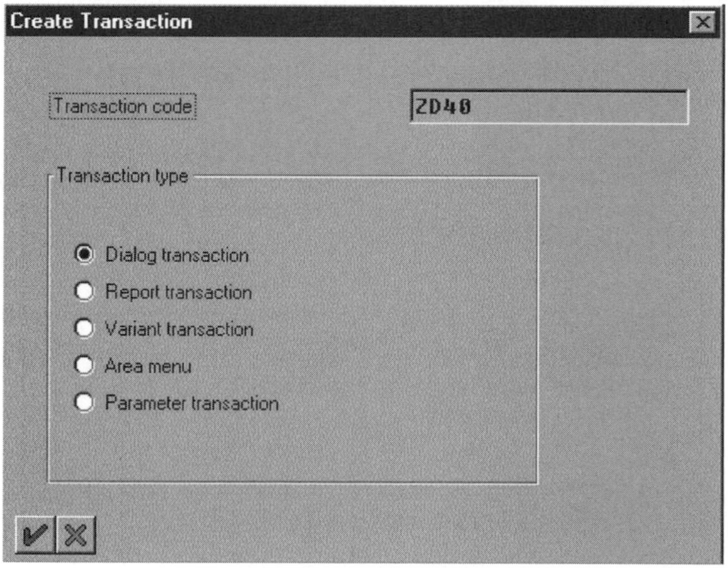

Figure 5-59
Create a Transaction code and assign Transaction types.

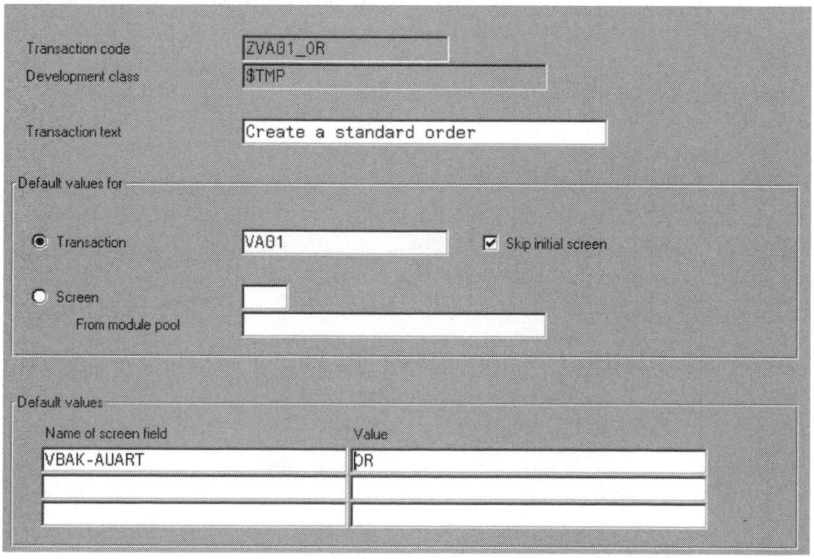

Figure 5-60a
Parameters for the Transaction

When the user runs this transaction, SAP will go directly to the order entry screen, assuming the order type is OR. You can do this for all the order types, CR, DR, and so on, and place them in an area menu so that you get the effect shown in Figure 5-60b.

For the purpose of this example, we will merely use the same details necessary to create a list of sales orders as if one is using the transaction code [VA05]. Naturally, there is no need to create another transaction code for a SAP standard program, but it is useful for the purpose of an example.

After selecting the transaction type that suits your needs (we have selected "Dialog transaction"), press Enter and the screen in Figure 5-61 appears, where one is prompted for a program name, screen number, and transaction text. You can also assign an authorization object to the transaction code, thus restricting authority on its usage. After entering the data, as shown in Figure 5-61, you can save.

Now proceed back to the Logistics screen [S000] and enter your newly created transaction code into the command line. The system will automatically call up the assigned program and screen, as in Figure 5-62. Note that the normal transaction code to display a list of sales orders is [VA05]. This list was obtained by transaction code [ZD40].

ABAP Area Menus

Using the ABAP/4 workbench, you can create your own menus that branch into user-defined or SAP standard transactions. In SAP, these menus are called *area menus*. Area menus are useful for grouping transactions that belong to a process, task, or work area in one place.

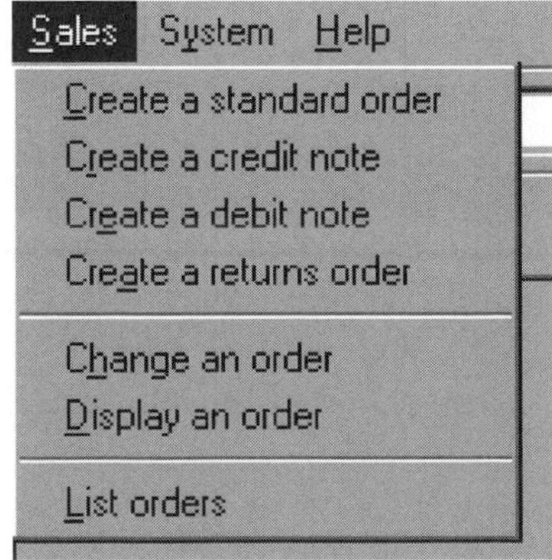

Figure 5-60b Example of usage in an area menu

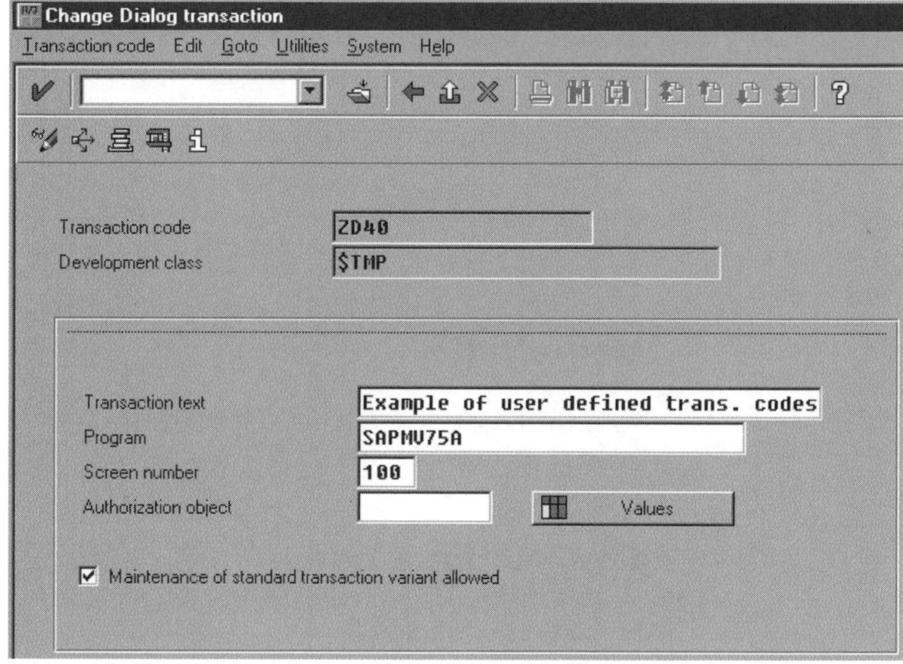

Figure 5-61
When creating the transaction code enter in the required program name, screen number, etc.

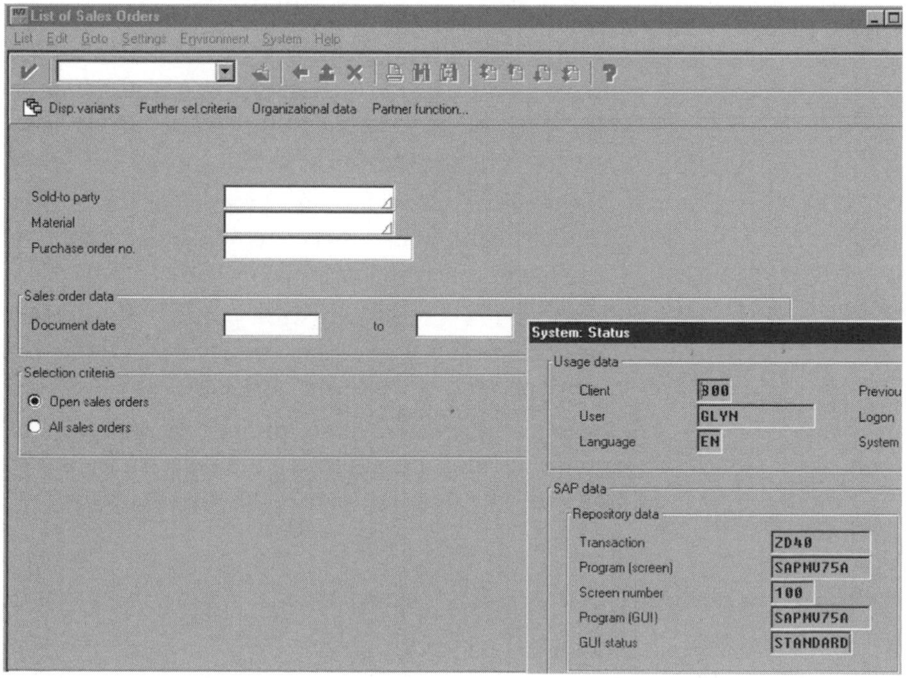

Figure 5-62
The settings for the new transaction code are complete. When used, the systm will verify the new details should one select System → Status

An area menu can be created for customer services, for example. This menu can contain all the transactions that relate to customer services, such as order lists, delivery lists, invoice lists, and any other lists you have created in ABAP/4. These lists are normally accessed through different menus in SAP; using an area menu they can be accessed through one single menu.

The user can access the area menu automatically when he logs on to SAP or by typing the transaction code for the area menu in the command line. An area menu can call other transactions or other area menus.

Menu Path

From the Logistics screen, select Tools, ABAP/4 workbench, Development, Other tools, Area menus.

Transaction Code

The code here is [SE43].

The advantages of area menus are as follows:

- Area menus enable you to define a grouping for transactions used in a process or work area. In other words, they are self-documenting and self-explanatory.
- Area menus provide easy access to a number of related transactions. The user has to remember one code to access all transactions that are used in a process or work area.
- Area menus speed the work process. An area menu contains all the transactions the user needs in one place without the need to memorize and follow many menu paths or transaction codes.
- Area menus simplify the work process, as only relevant transactions are included. This removes the need to tell the users about standard menu options in S000 that are not used.
- Area menus enable you to provide menu access to customer-written programs and reports that would otherwise have to be accessed through the standard transaction code [SA38].

Process

By following the menu path stated earlier, you will be faced with the screen in Figure 5-63.

Enter a four-character alphanumeric key beginning with the letter Z and select the Create button. In our example, we are creating ZD41.

NOTE: ZD41 is the transaction code that will be used to gain access to this particular area menu.

One will be faced with a box needing a short text. In our example, we entered "Lists available for use." Press enter and you will be faced with the screen in Figure 5-64.

Enter a title bar, such as "Area menu ZD41—SD Lists available for users." By selecting the menu bar, one can enter up to six menu path starting bars. Then enter a text for each menu bar, as in Figure 5-65.

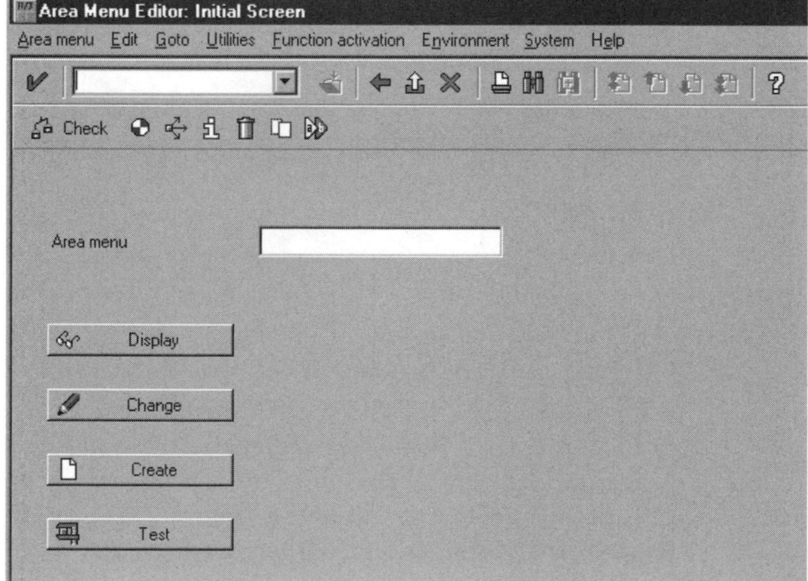

Figure 5-63 Create Area Menu Initial Screen.

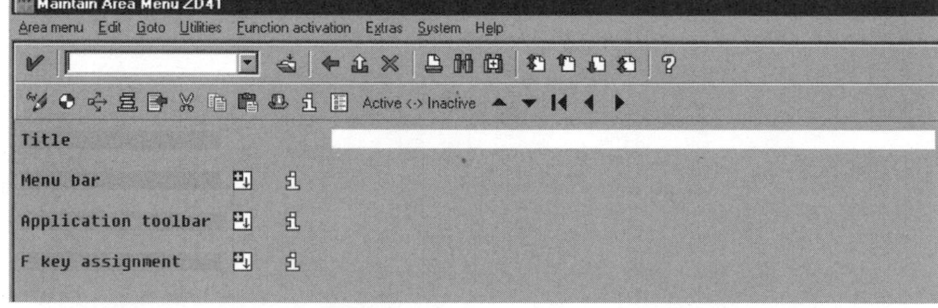

Figure 5-64 Maintain Area Menu—overview

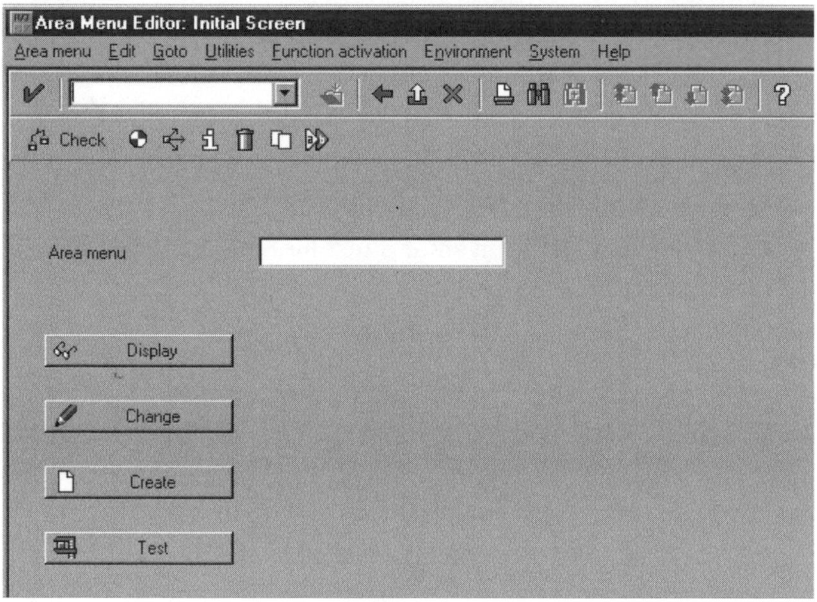

Figure 5-65 Maintain Area Menu—Menu bar

Now assign the associate transaction codes to the menu bar headings. In our example, we will assign transaction codes associated with lists, which is done by double-clicking the menu bar. You can then assign the transaction codes with a short text name. This is shown in Figure 5-66.

You will notice in the above diagram that the first five entries under *Sales and Distribution* (SD) have transaction codes assigned on the left with a short text on the right. Underneath the fifth entry (VA45 Contract list), there is a separator line. This separator line is created by proceeding from the menu bar to Edit, Insert, Separator line.

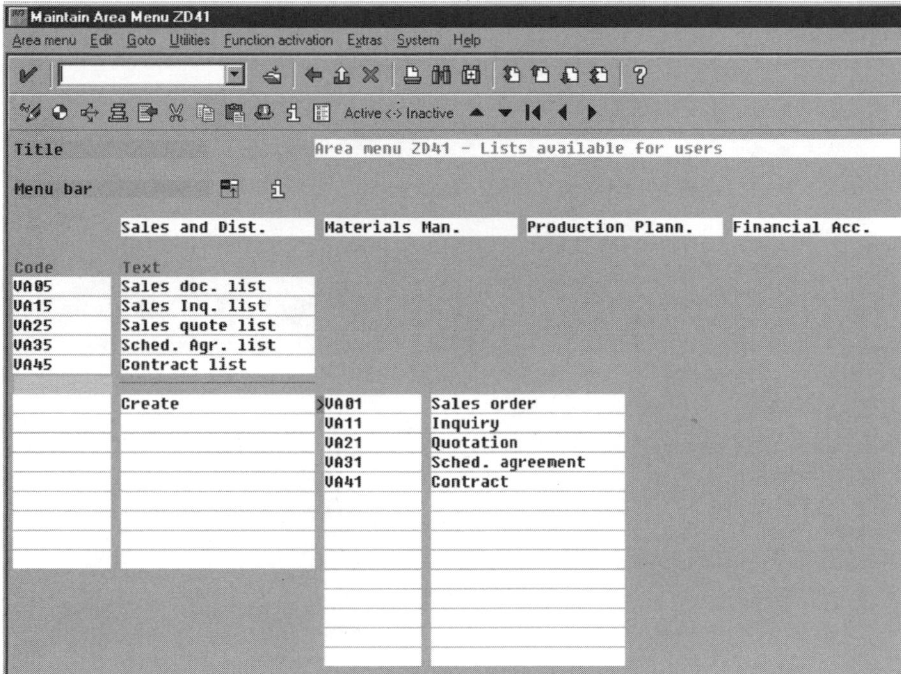

Figure 5-66
Submenu

Also notice the submenu assigned to the text "Create." This is maintainable by typing in a short text without an assigned transaction code. The system will automatically prompt a ">" sign. Should you click on this sign, you will be able to enter further transaction codes and texts as a submenu, shown earlier in Figure 5-66.

Note that you now need to activate the functions. This is done by selecting (single-clicking) the transaction code and pressing the "Activate/Inactivate" button ( ). Alternatively, you could also select the "Function activation" menu bar followed by "In function list" and then selecting the function codes to be activated. Inactivated transactions codes are represented by red text, while activated transaction codes are represented by black text.

After activating the function code, proceed with selecting the area menu test, which will demonstrate a test screen of the settings created. Should you be satisfied with the results, select Save and then the Generate button ( ). You can then use the transaction code. Using [ZD41], for example, will now prompt the screen in Figure 5-67.

Area menu ZD41 - Lists available for users

Sales and Dist. Materials Man. Production Plann. Financial Acc. System Help

Sales doc. list F1
Sales Inq. list
Sales quote list
Sched. Agr. list
Contract list
Create
Sales order
Inquiry
Quotation
Sched. agreement
Contract

Figure 5-67
Menu is usable.

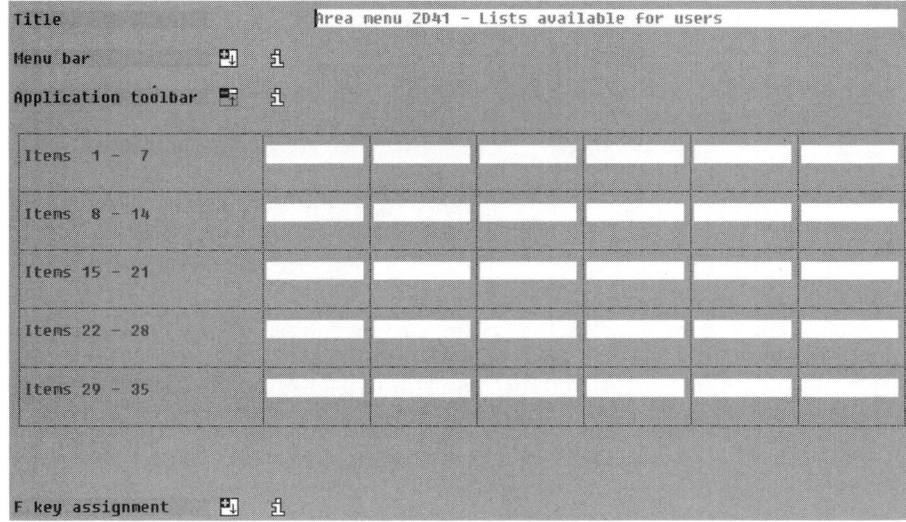

Figure 5-68
Select Application toolbar

Should you now want to add function key commands (the keys on a keyboard with F as a prefix, such as F1) to your area menu items and create fast access buttons, proceed as follows. Select the heading application toolbar by double-clicking on it, as in Figure 5-68.

In the blank space, enter the transaction code you have used in the earlier menu path, such as [VA21], Create quotation. Now double-click on the entry VA21. You will be faced with a pop-up box that assigns a function key that has not yet been assigned in this screen to the transaction VA21. In this example, we selected F2 (see Figure 5-69).

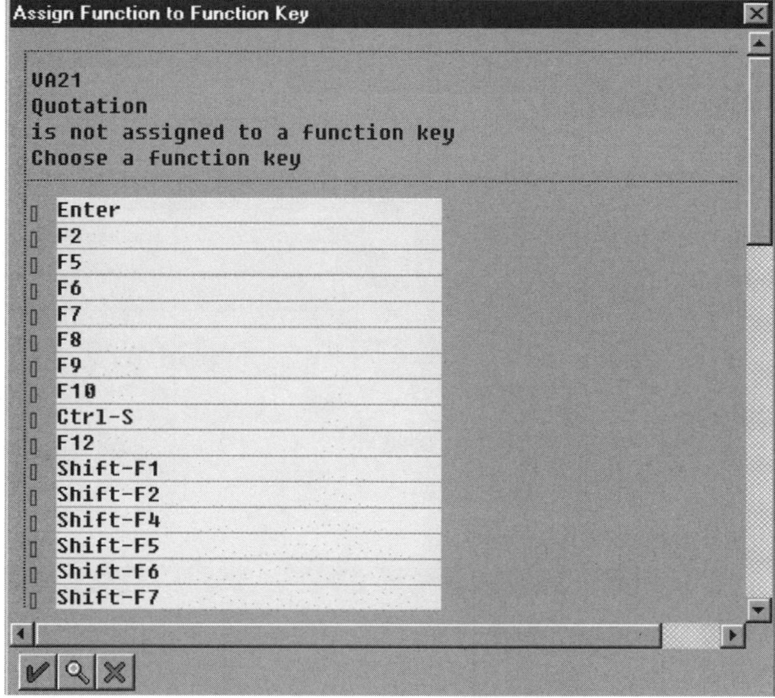

Figure 5-69
Assign a Function to a Function Key.

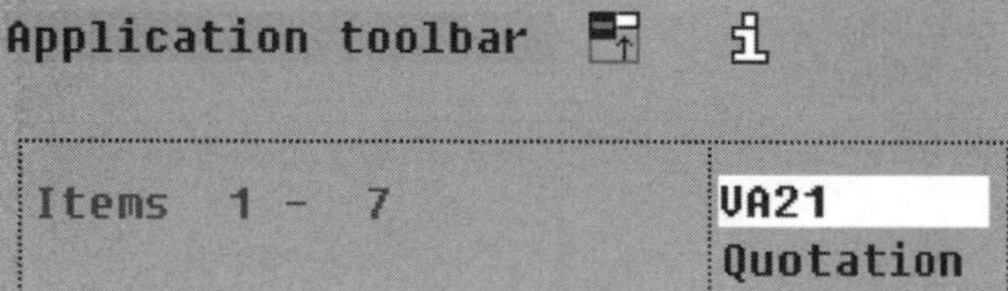

Figure 5-70
Quotation has now been assigned.

You now have a display similar to Figure 5-70.

If you double-click the entry VA21, as in the earlier figure, you will receive a pop-up box, as in Figure 5-71.

Now you must select whether to have an icon button representing the function or a text button with an attached icon. For the purpose of this example, we will create a text button with an icon. You can select an icon from the list of available icons in the system that is obtainable by selecting F4. In our example, we have selected the icon with the name ICON_SYSTEM_FAVORITES.

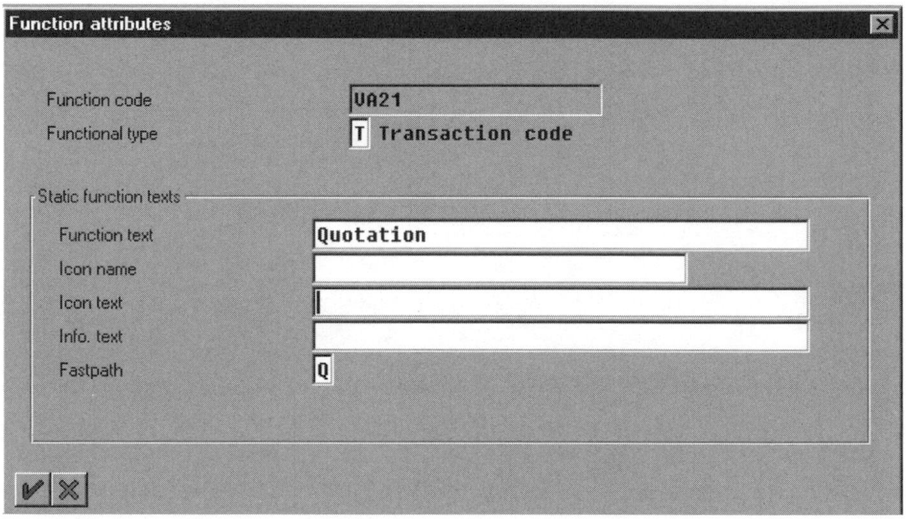

Figure 5-71
Function attributes

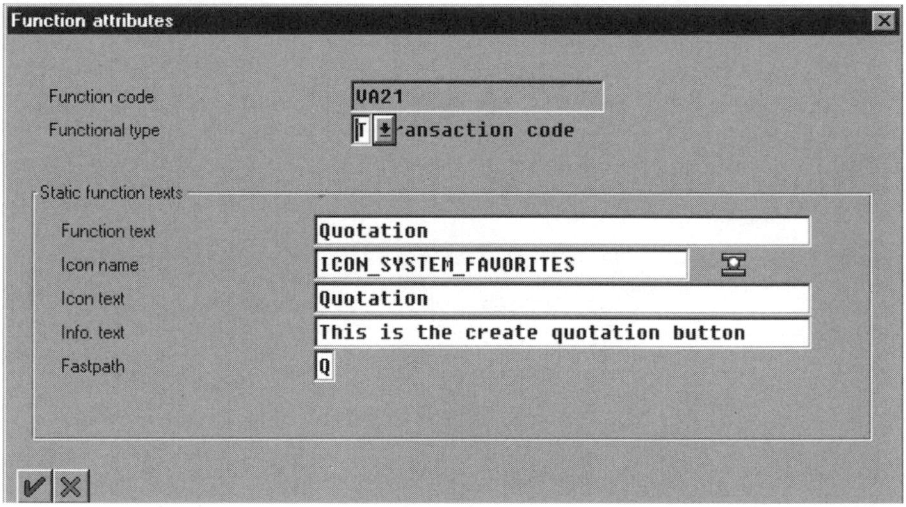

Figure 5-72
Function attributes

The icon text can be entered as well. In this example, we have selected "Quotation." The function attribute screen is shown in Figure 5-72. A list of commonly used icons may be found in the Appendix if this book.

By selecting Enter, one can see that the display in Figure 5-70 has been changed to represent the new attributes. Should one now select the "F Key assignment," one will see a list of assigned function keys and the assigned key F2 to transaction code VA21—Quotation (see Figure 5-73).

If you do not require a button and a function key assignment, you can merely assign a function key to the transaction code by typing in the transaction code beside the desired function key.

Note the standard toolbar represented by the green, yellow, and red arrows ( ). You will notice that [%BCK] has been assigned to them. This is a command used by the system to move the user back to the previous screen. At this point, save and select the Generate button.

Now you can use the area menu that has been created. This is done by using the transaction code created in the first step, ZD41. The result is as follows in Figure 5-74. The area menu has now been created.

Here are some area menu tips:

- Try to keep the area menu clearly focused on a particular work area or personnel group, rather than on more than one work area or group.
- Try not to create too many area menus; there should be only one area menu per work area or personnel group.

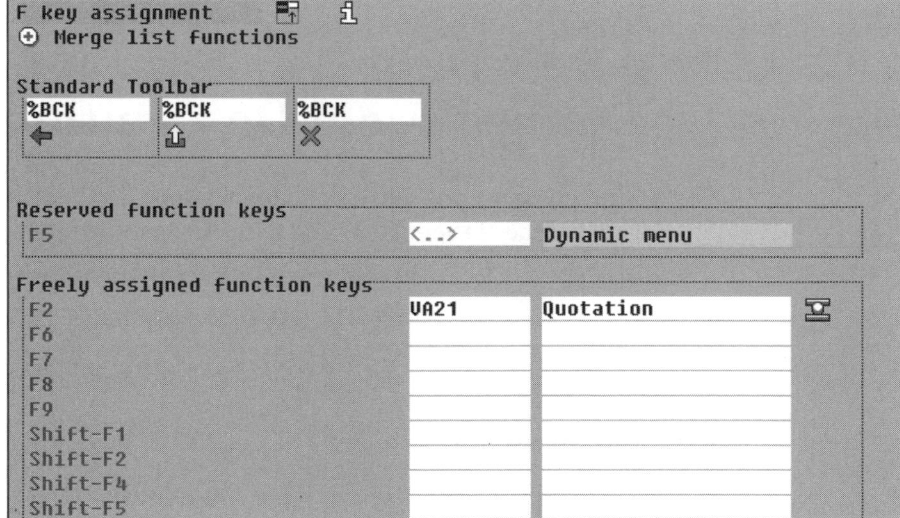

Figure 5-73 List of assigned function keys with icons

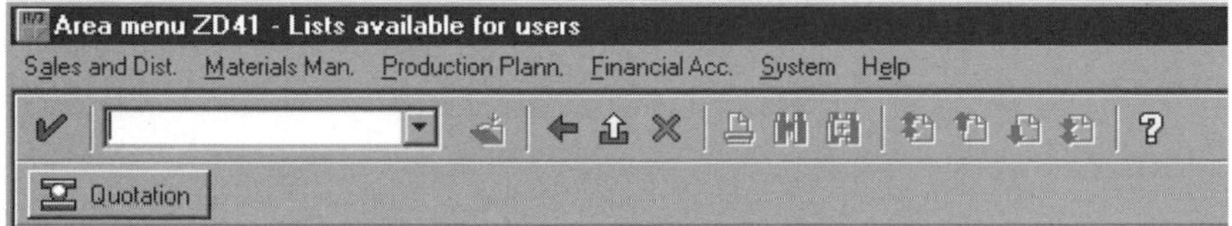

Figure 5-74 The area menu is now created with the quotation and icon assignment.

- Try not to let area menus overlap. For example, try not to create two area menus that do the same task with only minor differences.
- Include as many logically related transactions as possible without cluttering up the area menu. For example, it is always a good idea to include an Environment menu option. Under this option, frequently used tasks not immediately related to the area menu can be accessed. You could include the sales lists under the Environment menu option, even though the area menu relates to delivery processing, for example.
- Include access to the related SAP standard menu. For example, if your area menu deals with order processing, include the SAP standard menu VA00 (order processing) in the menu, possibly under Environment.
- Divide the area menu logically. Use the bar menus like main headings. These can be tasks (such as orders, deliveries, billing) or types of tasks (such as create, change, list, processing).

ABAP Data Elements and User-Defined Field Descriptions

One can create one's own field descriptions for the fields in the SAP screens. This is done without changing the SAP standard code, data dictionary, functions, or screens.

Why Change a Field Description?

There may be many reasons to change the field description of a field:

- The field is used differently in the implemented system than that described by the SAP standard description.
- You would like to conform a field description to the description in the legacy system.
- The field is of such importance that you want the description of its use to be explicit to your company. This is frequently the case with fields in the customer and material master (such as wanting the SAP term "Material" to be called a "Service" since you only sell services).
- You would like to enhance the meaning of the SAP field (usually the case in changes to SIS fields).

NOTE: Try not to change fields where the change has no material impact on the use of the system. For example, you do not need to change "Tax Code" in the standard "Tax ID."

Also be careful when changing field descriptions. Be aware of the true meaning of the field and do not change it if the meaning is central to the SAP concept. For example, exercise caution when changing something like Sold-to Customer. Sold-to has a more specific meaning than customer because the ship-to party, bill-to party, and payers are also customers.

Changing Field Descriptions When you change a field description, you are not changing the description of the field, but the description of the data element for that field. In SAP, a *data element* defines a type of field (for example, a character or numeric field) and the field description. For every data element, there is a short, medium, and long description as well as a column header. These are used in the SAP screens and reports.

When a field is defined, it is defined in a table or structure in relation to a data element. You can thus have many fields in many tables using the same data element. In this way, there is a standardization of the field descriptions across all the tables.

A data element can have many fields, but a field cannot have more than one data element. In this case, it will be defined with two different characteristics. For example, it cannot be called "Sales office" and "Sales region" at the same time.

Fields always refer to a data element to obtain the field description. Thus, when you change a field description in the SAP enhancement concept, you are really changing the data element's description. Before changing the description of a data element (or field), make sure that all the fields that use the data element will use the new description. Also make sure that the new description is appropriate to all fields defined for the data element, so that "sales office" in the customer master record is also "sales office" in the sales order, for example.

In general, you can safely assume that a field will be defined for a data element and used in the same way as described by the data element. Thus, if the field XYZ in table TX01 uses data element VKBUR (Sales office), you can be sure that SAP intends to use this field to record a sales office. Thus, if you want to change the meaning of Sales office to Sales region, you can change the data element. However, if you want to change the description of field XYZ in table TX01 only, you must not change the descriptions for the data element, because this will change the descriptions for all the fields. It is not possible to change the descriptions of a single field in a table only.

NOTE: *You can check which fields will be affected by a change to the data element's description by using the Where-used facility for the data element. Use transaction SE11 to display the data element. Then select the Where-used menu option (or press the Where-used button). A list of all the fields in all the tables that use the data element will be displayed. Check that you want all these fields to use the new description.*

Menu Path

From the Logistics screen, select Tools, ABAP Workbench and select the Dictionary button.

Transaction Code

The code here is [SE11].

How to Determine the Data Element

You can identify the data element for a field by going to the field, pressing the F1 key, and then the F9 key (the Technical information button in the Field help screen). Then double-click on the field name to drill down to the SAP R/3 ABAP dictionary. The column headed "Data element" indicates the data element for the field.

You can further drill down to the data element definition by double-clicking on the data element. From this screen, you can use the Where-used button to see all the fields that use the data element. Once the data element has been found, such as BZIRK of KNVV-BZIRK, that is, the Sales district, and after following through the above mentioned menu path, one will be faced with the screen in Figure 5-75.

After selecting the Change button, you will be prompted to enter an access key, which is obtainable from the Basis team. You will then be faced with the screen in Figure 5-76.

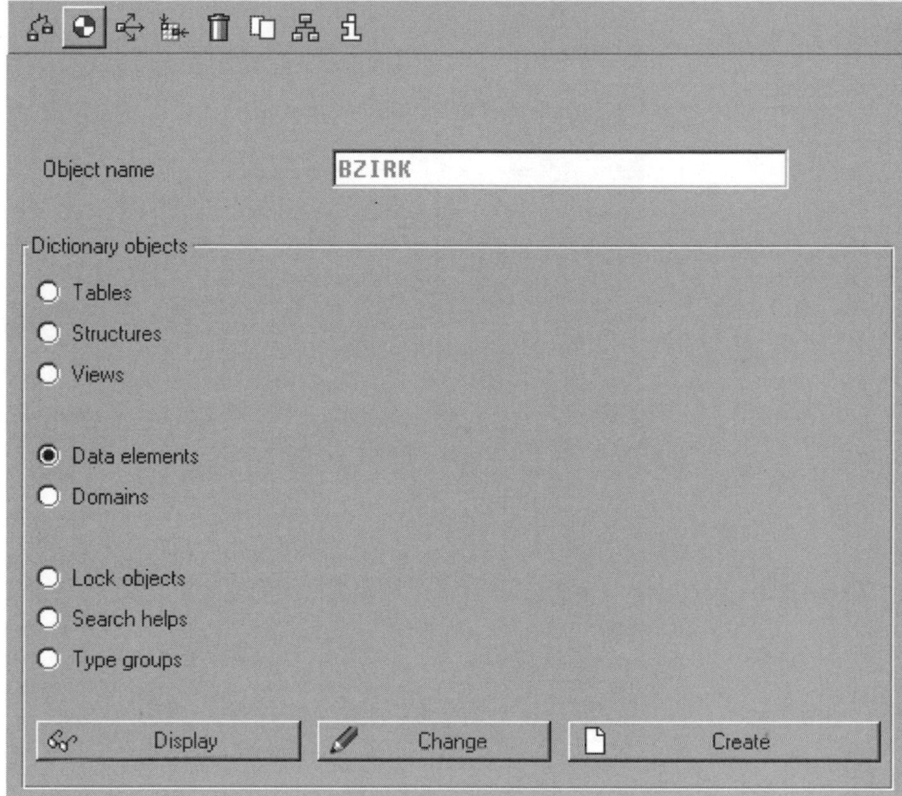

Figure 5-75 Enter the object name. Select data element followed by the change button.

One can determine where this data element is used by selecting the Where-used list button ( ). If you are satisfied that by changing the description of the data element, the description will be changed in all the associated tables fields and structures as well, continue with the process.

One can now change the short, medium, and long text descriptions, such as by changing District to Region. Keep to the original field label length:

Short = 10 Characters

Medium = 15 Characters

Long = 20 Characters

After changing the text, you can save the data element and activate it.

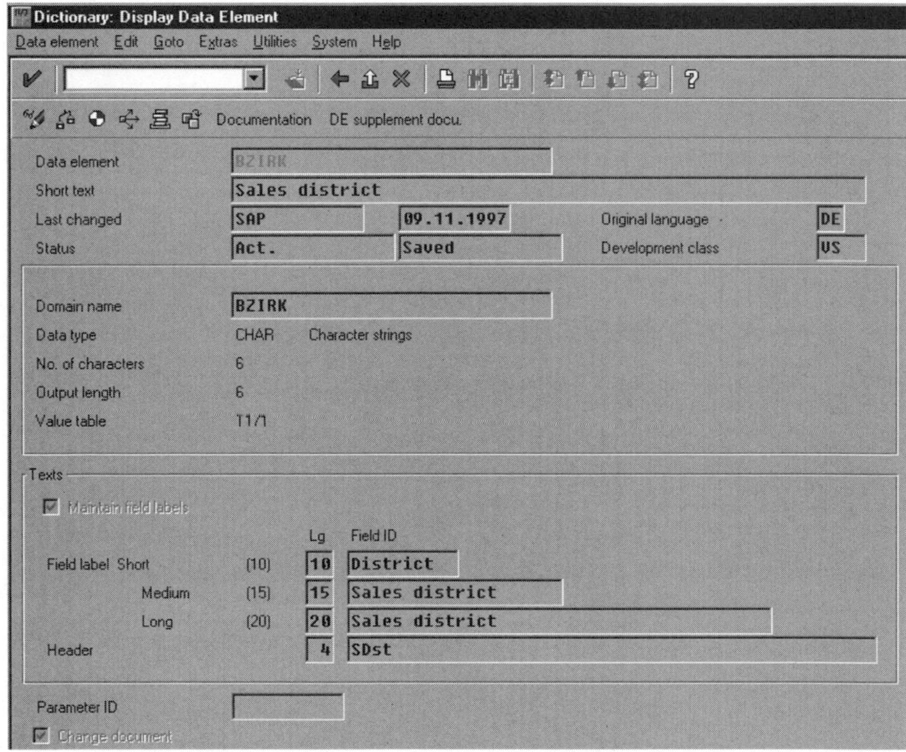

Figure 5-76
Data element characteristics

User Exits

User exits are provided in various places throughout the system in order to allow system modifications and enhancements. There are countless reasons why a user exit should be utilized in a system. For example, one can use a user exit to fill a specifically created table during sales order processing and then later use a requirement to read from that table before carrying out a specific function like the creation of the delivery. However, while one cannot provide examples of all such reasons to use them, it is useful to know what user exits are available in the system and where they are.

Menu Path

The menu path here is IMG, Sales and distribution, System modification, User exits.

User exits in SD are available for the following processes:

- User exits for price determination
- User exits for credit checks and risk management
- User exits in sales
  - User exits in sales document processing
  - User exits for contract processing
  - User exits for product allocation processing
  - User exits for availability checking
  - User exits for component supply processing
  - User exits for product selection
  - User exits for billing plan
- User exits for shipping
- User exits for transportation
- User exits for billing
- User exits for general billing interface
- User exits for sales support
- User exits for lists

The topic of user exits is a subject that concerns ABAP development, and extensive experience in ABAP is required to understand and use the user exits. SAP provides guidelines for the user exits in the IMG menu path described earlier. This documentation is available from the IMG, if installed, by selecting the text of the selected step.

Menu Path

One can also select the user exits by using the following menu path. From the Logistics screen, proceed as follows: Tools, ABAP Workbench, Repository browser and enter the development class as VMOD, as shown in Figure 5-77.

By selecting Display, the object types associated with the development class VMOD appear. By selecting Includes, one will be faced with all the includes where user exits exist (see Figure 5-78).

The most difficult part of using the user exits is understanding how they perform and how they are used within the program that calls them. To get a better understanding of this, it is a good idea to put a break point in the user exit and then run the transaction. The ABAP programmer can then look at the data that is available in the user exit and see if it can meet his requirements.

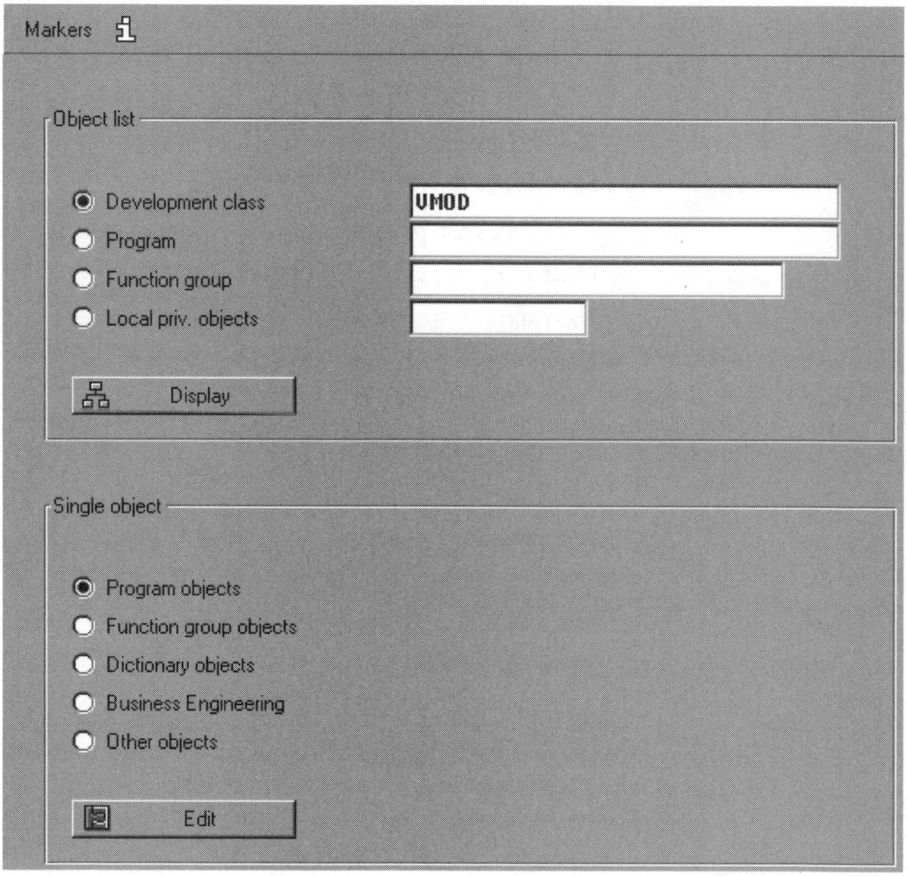

Figure 5-77
Development class VMOD

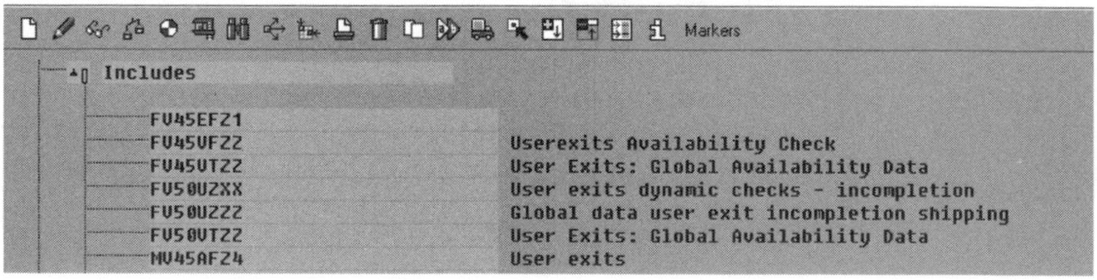

Figure 5-78
Display of Includes where user exits exist

The following example illustrates the complexities of using the user exits and provides some tips and guidelines of how you and an ABAP programmer can go about looking for the information you will need to use in the user exits. Hopefully, these ideas will provide you with the skills you need to find the right user exit.

For example, let's say we wanted to check a user's authorization before allowing him to remove the billing block. We now have the problem, which user exit do we use for this? We can try the exit "userexit_save_document_prepare" in MV45AFZZ, since this seems to be the most logical place to make the check. But first, we need to see if the billing block data is available at the time of this exit and if this user exit is run every time the order is saved, so that the check can be made.

To check this, we put a break point in this user exit. First, use transaction SE38 to display the program code for MV45AFZZ. Then go to the section "userexit_save_document_prepare," as in Figure 5-79.

We now create an order using VA01, put a billing block on, change the order with VA02, and try and remove the billing block. If the user exit is called when we save our changes, the breakpoint will branch from the transaction VA02 to the ABAP screen above after we have pressed the Save button. If it is not, the break point will have no effect and we will have to search for another user exit to do what we need.

We now know that this user exit is run when the user presses the Save button and only if there has been a change to the data in the order. In our case, when we changed the billing block and pressed the Save button, the user exit was called, so we can use this user exit. Now we need to know if we can see the field contents for the billing block, and if we can see the field contents before any changes were made at the time of this user exit. In the break point field, we can enter the field name to see the contents shown in Figure 5-80.

If the field is not available, SAP will display the icon on the left of the field, and we will know that this information is not available in this user exit. We would then have to look for another one, but fortunately, our billing block information is available.

Now a look at the data definitions in the order entry program SAPMV45A in the include MV45ATOP and the include VBAKDATA might tell us what data is available at this time as well. Note that there is a structure called YVBAK (see Figure 5-81).

Figure 5-79
Set a breakpoint in the selected user exit.

```
form userexit_save_document_prepare.


endform.
```

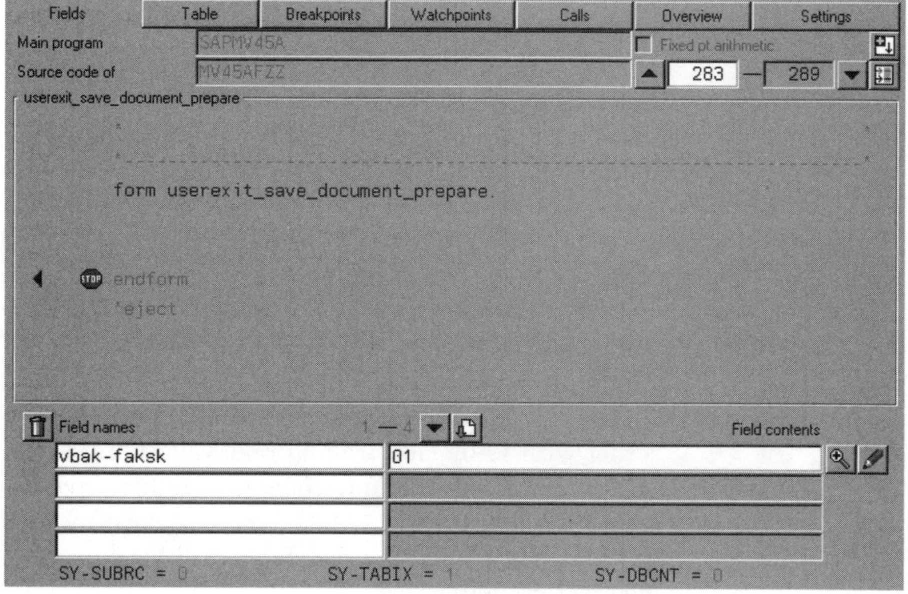

Figure 5-80
Enter the field name to see the contents shown.

```
* Alter Tabellenstand beim Ändern
data:    begin of yvbak.
           include structure vbak.
data:    end of yvbak.
```

Figure 5-81
Structure yvbak is called up.

A little help from our German dictionary shows that this table is relevant "before changes." We can now go back to our debugging screen and enter the field YVBAK-FAKSK to see if it is available. Change the order with a billing block by removing the billing block and then save. When the user exit comes up in the debugging screen, enter the field YVBAK-FAKSK (see Figure 5-82).

In this case, we see that the billing block used to be 01 (YVBAK-FAKSK) and is now SPACE (VBAK-FAKSK). We now have enough information to say that this user exit will be suitable for our requirement.

We can write the ABAP code in this user exit as follows: If VBAK-FAKSK is not equal to YVBAK-FAKSK, then the billing block has been changed by the user and we must perform an authorization check. To do that, we need to create our own authorization object in the ABAP repository and assign it

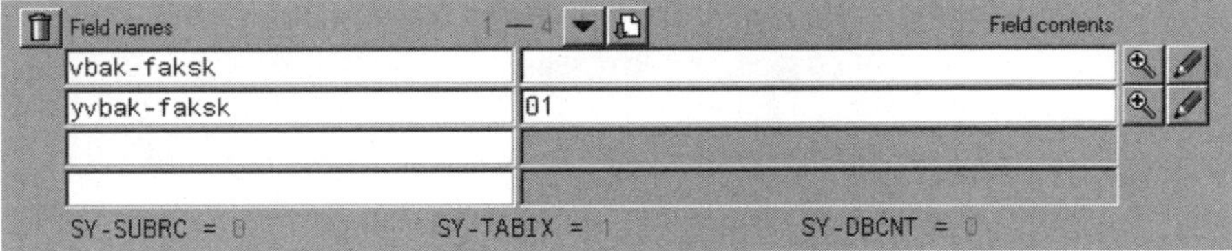

Figure 5-82
Enter the field names to see the contents shown.

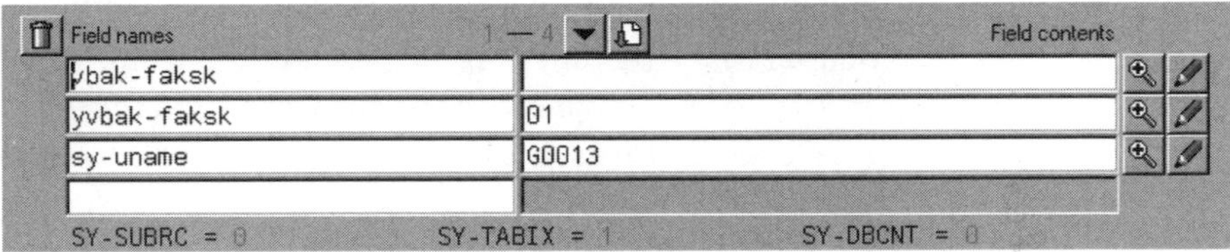

Figure 5-83
Field sy-name shows the user id.

to the user. To use the authorization check function, we need to know the user ID, so again we check if this is available. Fortunately, it is available in the field SY-UNAME, as shown in Figure 5-83.

We make the check in the user exit ABAP code, and if it fails, we send an warning message from the user exit to tell the user the change is not authorized. Then we reset the billing block so that VBAK-FAKSK equals YVBAK-FAKSK, and the document is saved without that change.

ABAP Queries

An ABAP query is a convenient tool to access the SAP database tables. It can be used to provide basic lists to the system users (such as a list of customers) and complex queries to facilitate testing and using the system.

Menu Path

From the Logistics screen, select System, Services, ABAP Query.

Transaction Code

The code here is [SQ00]. This section is divided into two parts:

- Creating an ABAP query
- Using an ABAP query

In this documentation, we will define and run an ABAP query for a list of customer addresses.

Definitions The following terms are used:

An *ABAP query* is a tool that reads and displays selected data from the SAP database tables. For example, you may have a query to list customers and their telephone numbers.

A *functional area* is a group of related queries. For example, all the queries related to the customer master data could comprise a functional area.

A *functional area* also includes the tables to be used in a query.

A *user group* is a group of users who are allowed to use the ABAP queries. You assign the SAP user IDs to a user group, and assign the user group to a functional area. Using these assignments, SAP can determine which queries the user is permitted to run.

First Steps

When you access the ABAP query tool, a list of the existing queries for the current user group and functional area is displayed. This screen is displayed below in Figure 5-84.

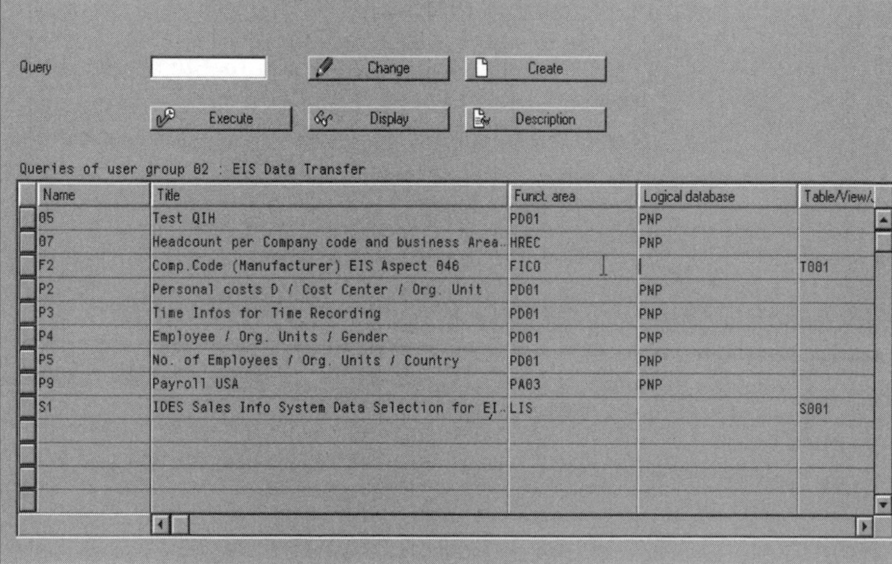

Query
Change
Create
Execute
Display
Description
Queries of user group 02 : EIS Data Transfer
Name | Title | Funct. area | Logical database | Table/View/
05 | Test QIH | PD01 | PNP
07 | Headcount per Company code and business Area | HREC | PNP
F2 | Comp.Code (Manufacturer) EIS Aspect 046 | FICO | | T001
P2 | Personal costs D / Cost Center / Org. Unit | PD01 | PNP
P3 | Time Infos for Time Recording | PD01 | PNP
P4 | Employee / Org. Units / Gender | PD01 | PNP
P5 | No. of Employees / Org. Units / Country | PD01 | PNP
P9 | Payroll USA | PA03 | PNP
S1 | IDES Sales Info System Data Selection for EI | LIS | | S001

Figure 5-84
List of existing queries

From this screen, you can

- Execute an ABAP query.
- Create or change an ABAP query.

To execute a query, you can

- Select one of these queries by pressing the selection box on the left-hand side of the screen and the hitting the Execute button.
- Type the query number and press the Execute button.

You may want to select a query from a different user group and functional area. In this case, go to Edit, Other user group. We will look at executing an ABAP query in more detail after describing how to create an ABAP query.

Part 1: Creating an ABAP Query

Follow these steps in creating an ABAP query:

1. Create the user group.
2. Create the functional area.
3. Assign the user group to the functional area.
4. Create the query.

Step 1: Creating the User Group

From the ABAP query screen, go to Environment, User groups. User groups use the transaction code [SQ03], which will provide the screen as shown in Figure 5-85.

1. Enter the user group name in the User group field and select Create to create a user group. (If you want to change or display a user group, select Change or Display.)
2. Enter a description for the user group and press Save.
3. After entering a description for the user group, enter the user ID in the User field and press Change. A screen appears showing all the existing user groups. The user group this user belongs to will be marked. You can also see if the user has the authorization to make changes to the queries assigned to this user group.

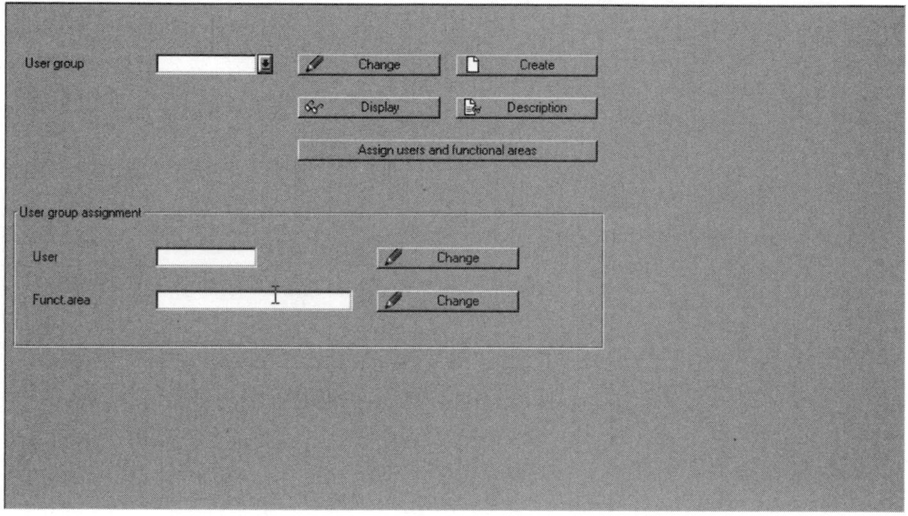

Figure 5-85
Enter the user group.

To assign the user to the user group you created in step 1, mark the user group you created and then press Save ( ). This user is now assigned to the user group you just created.

4. Repeat these steps for all the users you want to assign to this user group.

Deleting a User Group You can delete a user group by entering the user group name and selecting User group, Delete. Alternatively, press Delete ( ).

Copying a User Group You can copy a user group by entering the user group name and selecting User group, Copy. Alternatively, press Delete ( ).

Renaming a User Group You can rename a user group by entering the user group name and selecting User group, Rename. Alternatively, press the Rename button ( ).

Step 2: Creating the Functional Area

Remember that a functional area is a group of SAP tables that is used by a group of ABAP queries. In other words, a functional area consists of the tables that the ABAP queries access and the queries that access them.

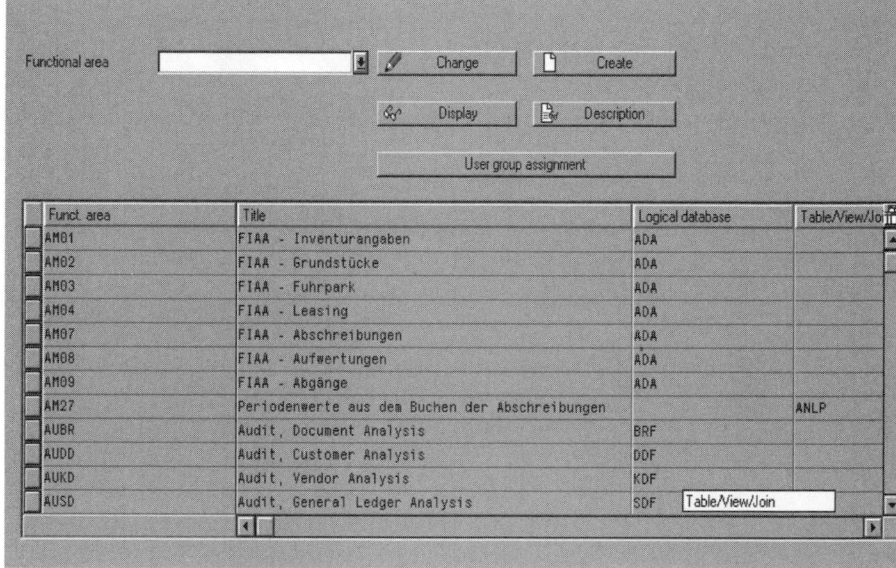

Functional area
Change
Create
Display
Description
User group assignment
Funct. area
Title
Logical database
Table/View/Join
AM01 FIAA - Inventurangaben ADA
AM02 FIAA - Grundstücke ADA
AM03 FIAA - Fuhrpark ADA
AM04 FIAA - Leasing ADA
AM07 FIAA - Abschreibungen ADA
AM08 FIAA - Aufwertungen ADA
AM09 FIAA - Abgänge ADA
AM27 Periodenwerte aus dem Buchen der Abschreibungen ANLP
AUBR Audit, Document Analysis BRF
AUDD Audit, Customer Analysis DDF
AUKD Audit, Vendor Analysis KDF
AUSD Audit, General Ledger Analysis SDF

Figure 5-86 Functional area screen

When you create a functional area, your primary concern is selecting the database tables that you will need for your ABAP queries. You need to select the tables that contain the information that will be displayed in your query. From the ABAP query screen, use the menu path: Environment, Functional areas. Functional areas also use the transaction code [SQ02], which will bring up the screen shown in Figure 5-86.

1. Enter the functional area name in the Functional area field and select Create to create a functional area. If you want to change or display a functional area, select Change or Display.
2. The screen in Figure 5-87 then appears.

   Enter a long name for the functional area. You can also enter an authorization group. Only users with this authorization group can use the queries in this functional area.

   A logical database is an ABAP construct that links together a number of ABAP tables into a database using the relationships between the tables. For example, the orders table is linked to the customer master table by the customer number. It is also linked to the order items table by the order number. These three tables can make up a logical database.

Figure 5-87 Change a Functional area.

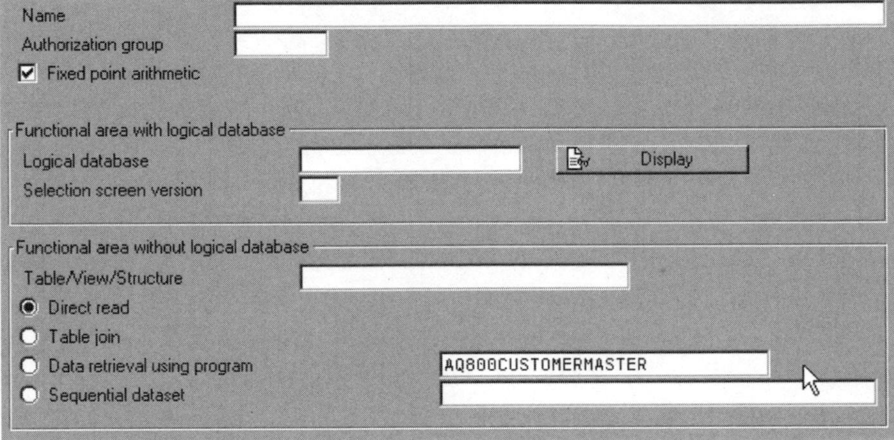

Logical databases are very efficient in system processing, so if the information you require can be found in a logical database, you should use this for your ABAP query. An example would be VAV. This is the logical database for sales documents (inquiries, quotes, orders, and contracts).

NOTE: *To view a logical database and the tables in it, use transaction code [SE36]. Go to Tools, ABAP workbench, Development, Programming environment, Logical databases. You can also create your own logical databases in the ABAP repository, or copy existing ones and make the changes you require. It is not recommended that you change the SAP standard logical databases.*

If you do not use a logical database, you need to select the SAP table or tables to use in your query. We will use our example of a list of addresses from the customer master. The customer central data is stored in table KNA1. All the information we require is in this table, so we will enter table KNA1 in the Table/View/Structure field and select Direct read.

You can use the direct read method of accessing data that is in a single table or tables that are unrelated to one another by the key.

If you required data from more than one table, and they are related by a key, you could link the tables using their keys with the *Table join* option. For example, if we wanted a list of customers and the customer pricing procedure indicators they use, we would need to use table KNA1 to get the customer name, and KNVV to get the sales area information. These tables are related with the key customer number (KUNNR). Select KNVV as the table you wish to read, and then the *Table join* option. Enter table KNA1 as the join table, as shown in Figure 5-88.

Press the *Define condition* button. The tables will be linked based on the key fields in each.

3. After selecting the tables for this functional area, you need to choose which fields you want to use from the tables. Figure 5-89 appears after you have selected the tables.

   Within the functional area, you create a *functional group*, which is a group of fields from the tables that you want to use in the functional area.

Figure 5-88 Joined tables

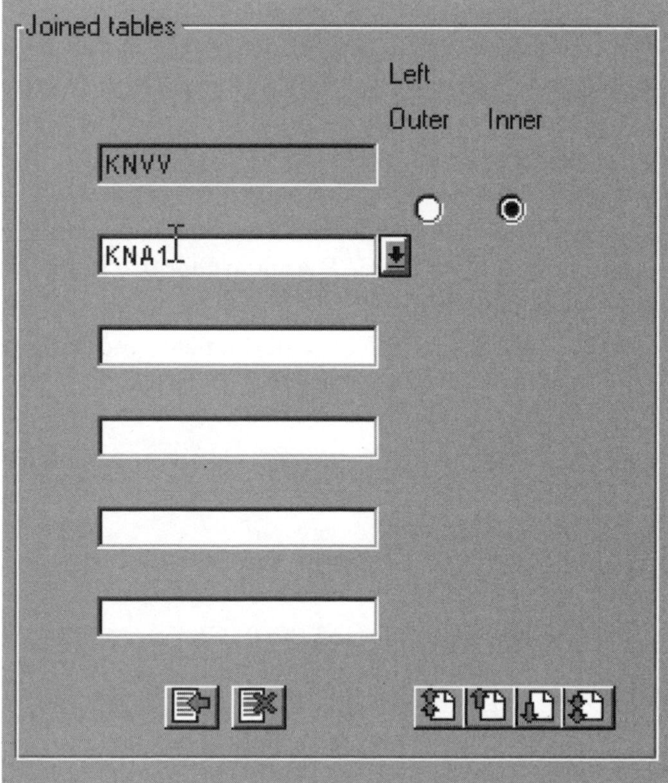

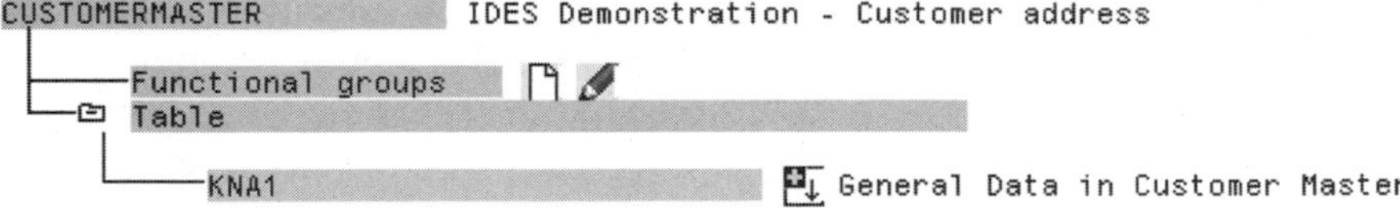

Figure 5-89
Display following the Table selection

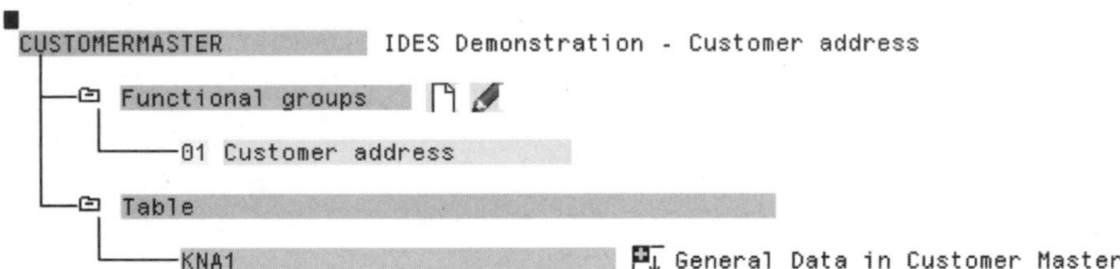

Figure 5-90
Display after creating a Functional group

Select the Create button ( ) to create a functional group. Alternatively, you can select the Change button ( ) to change a group. After creating a functional group to group all the fields related to the customer address, the screen will look like Figure 5-90.

Select the functional group by double-clicking on it (it is possible to have more than one functional group of fields). Then press the button to list the fields in the table. Click on the icon to include the field in the functional group. The icon changes to indicate that the field is in the functional group. By clicking on these icons, you can alternatively add and remove the field from the functional group.

By double-clicking on the field, you can change the field description and title from the SAP standard for use in this functional area only (see Figure 5-91).

When you have selected all the fields you need to use in this table, the screen will look similar to Figure 5-92.

NOTE: *The fields selected have a number next to them. This is the functional group that you created.*

4. After you have selected the fields, you need to generate and save the functional area.

   To generate the functional area, press the Generate button ( ) or select Functional area, Generate from the menu. Press Save ( ) to save the functional area and exit this transaction.

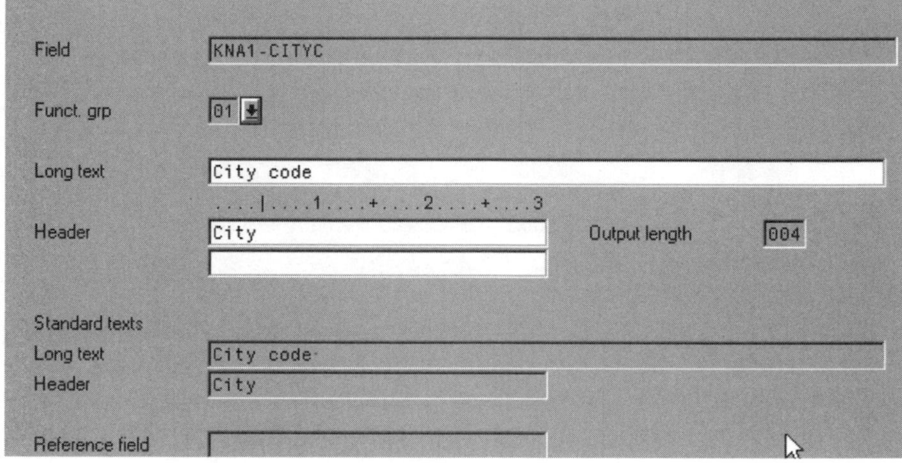

Figure 5-91 One is able to change the description.

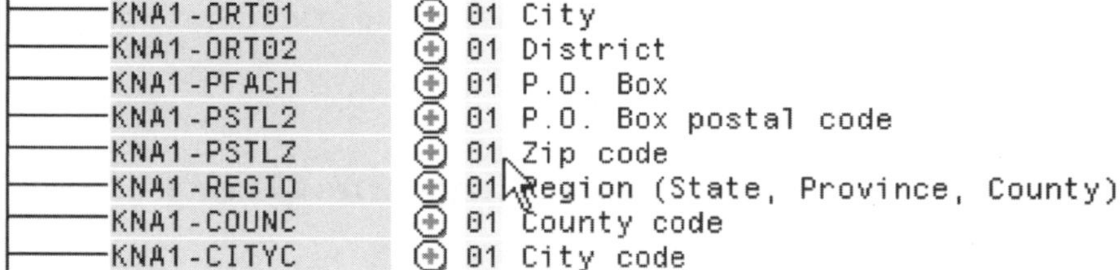

Figure 5-92 Fields which have been selected

You can delete a functional area by entering the functional area name from screen [SQ02] and selecting Functional area, Delete from the menu. Alternatively, press the Delete button ( ).

You can copy a functional area by entering the functional area name and selecting Functional area, Copy from the menu. Alternatively, press the Delete button ( ).

You can rename a functional area by entering the functional area name and selecting Functional area, Rename from the menu. Alternatively, press the Rename button ( ).

Step 3: Assign the User Group to the Functional Area

From the ABAP query screen, use the menu path: Environment, User groups. User groups also use the transaction code [SQ03]. One will then be presented with the screen in Figure 5-93.

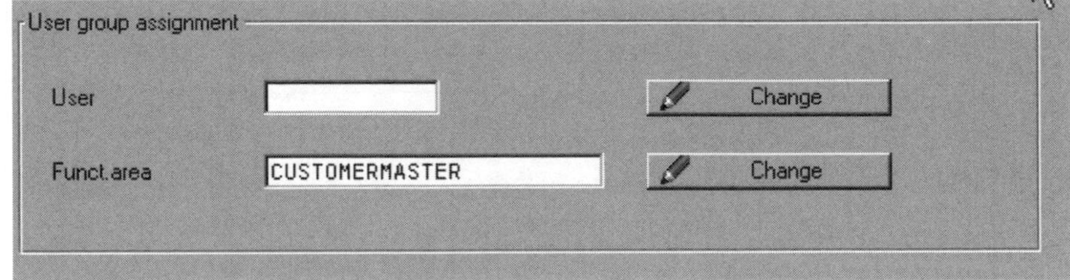

Figure 5-93
User group assignments

Enter the user group to which you want to assign the functional area. In the User group assignment screen section, enter the functional area in the Funct.area field and press Change. You can assign functional areas to the selected user group in the same way as you assigned users to the user group.

After pressing the *Change* button, a list of user groups is displayed. Mark those user groups you want to assign this functional area to and then save your work.

Step 4: Creating the Query

You need to create the query for the right user group, so you must select the user group before creating the query. From the ABAP query screen, use the menu path: Edit, Other user group. To access the list of user groups, select one of the user groups. The queries created for this user group will then be displayed onscreen.

Steps in Creating a Query

1. Enter a query name and select the functional area. In the Query field, enter the name for your query and then press the Create button. If you want to change a query, press the Change button. After pressing Create, a list of functional areas assigned to this user group is displayed. Select the functional area that contains the tables for which you want to define the ABAP query. You will now be passed through a number of screens in which you define the query.
2. Enter a title and description for your query in the Title screen (see Figure 5-95). For the moment, you do not need to consider the other fields on this screen. When you have finished, press the Next Page button ( ).

Title Customer addresses
Notes

Figure 5-95
Enter the Title of the query.

Figure 5-96
Select the Functional group screen

3. Select the Functional Group screen. In this screen, as shown in Figure 5-96, select the functional group. Remember that the functional group is a list of fields you selected within the functional area. Only the fields you selected in this group are available for this query. Press the Next Page button to continue.

NOTE: *You can use the Previous Page button ( ) to go backwards.*

4. Select the Field screen. This screen displays all the fields you selected in the functional group when you created the functional area (see Figure 5-97). From this list, select the fields you want to display in the query. For the purposes of this example, we will only select the postal address. Press the Next Page button to continue.

5. In the Selections screen, define which of the fields can be used to select the data for the query (see Figure 5-98) or, in other words, the fields for which the user can enter a display range. For the purposes of this example, we will use the customer number, name, and city. You have now defined all the elements of the query. You must now define the list layout.

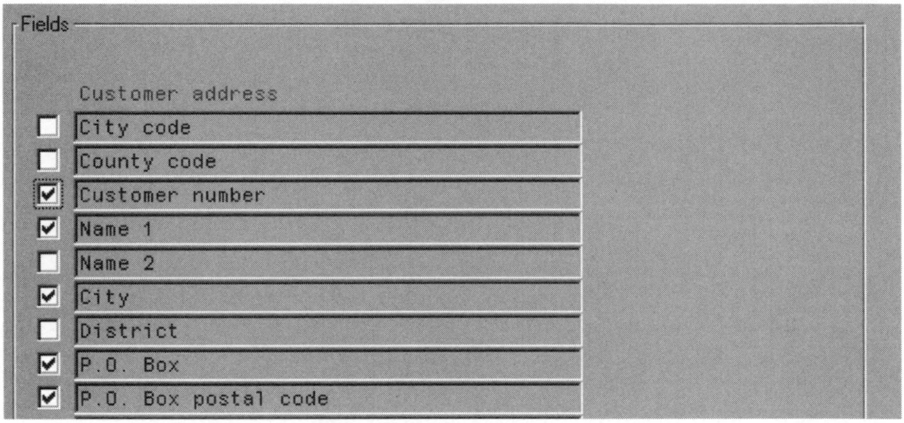

Figure 5-97
Select the Fields

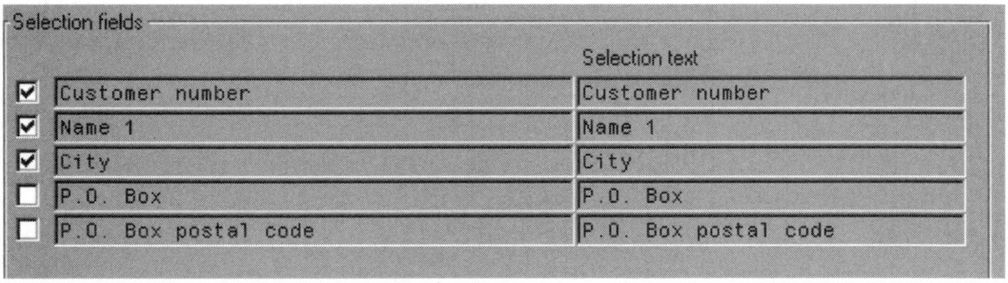

Figure 5-98
Select the Selection fields

6. Press the Basic List button. The basic list line structure screen is where you define the list layout (see Figure 5-99). The Line column defines the line where the field is displayed. If the list has only one line, you would enter 1 in this column. If the list has two lines, you would indicate in this column whether the field is displayed on line 1 or 2 of the report. The Sequence column defines the order that the field appears in from left to right. The Sort column is used to sort the list.

   Figure 5-100 shows the results of the list definition. We have a report with one line displaying the customer number, name, PO box, postal code, and city. We have sorted the list by city, customer name, and customer number.

7. After defining the query, press Save. You can now run the query.

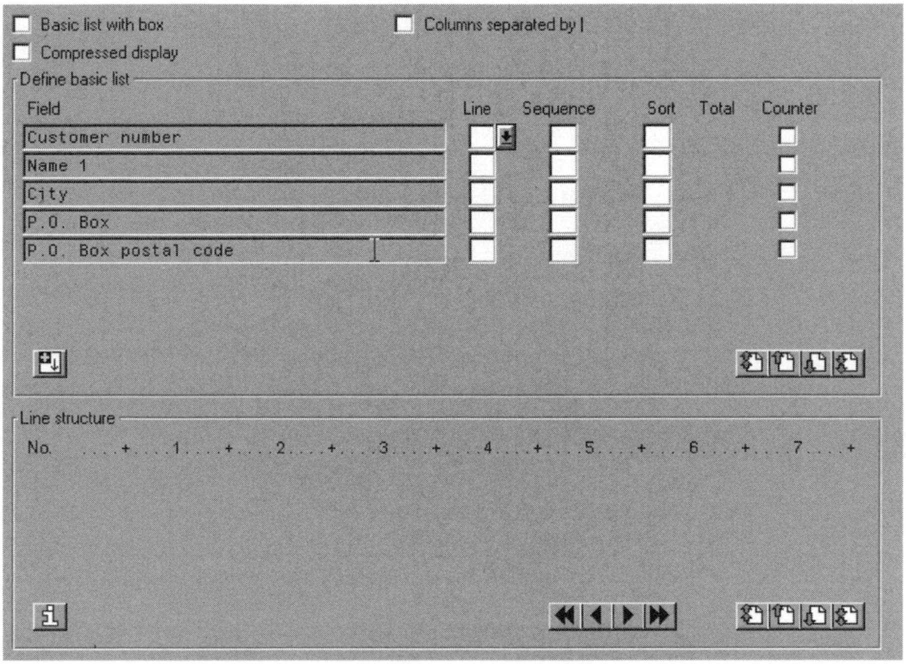

Figure 5-99
Define the list layout.

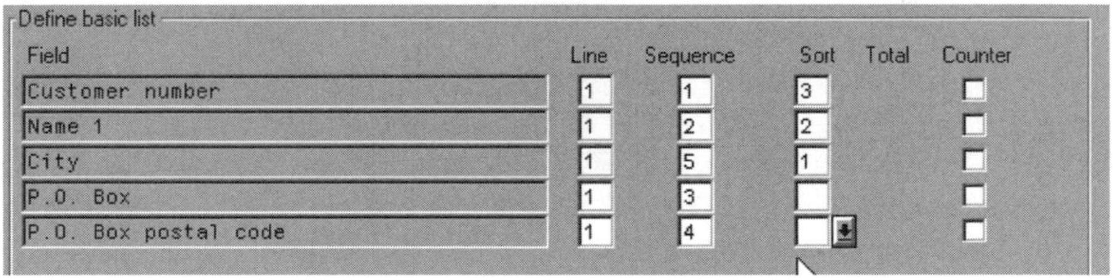

Figure 5-100
Define basic list settings.

Part 2: Using an ABAP Query

Once an ABAP query has been created, the system users can make use of it through these steps:

1. Selecting the user group.
2. Selecting and running the query.
3. Using the query.

Step 1: Selecting the User Group

To run an ABAP query, use the menu path System, Services, ABAP Query. Alternatively, use the transaction code [SQ00] that displays Figure 5-101. You may be faced with a list of queries that belong to a different user group. You can see the user group onscreen.

If the wrong user group is displayed, you can change it by going to Edit, Other user group. Select the user group you require and the queries for this user group will be displayed.

Step 2: Selecting the Query

You can select the query by using the Select box on the far left of the screen or by typing the query name in the Query field. Press the Execute button to execute the query. The query selection screen is displayed in Figure 5-102. The fields you selected when creating the query are displayed here along

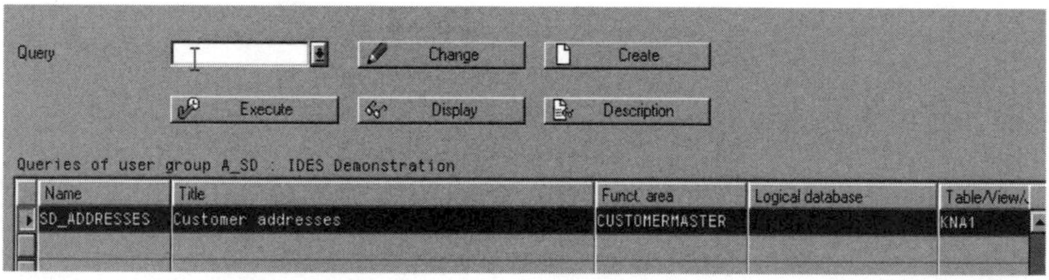

Figure 5-101 List of queries per user group

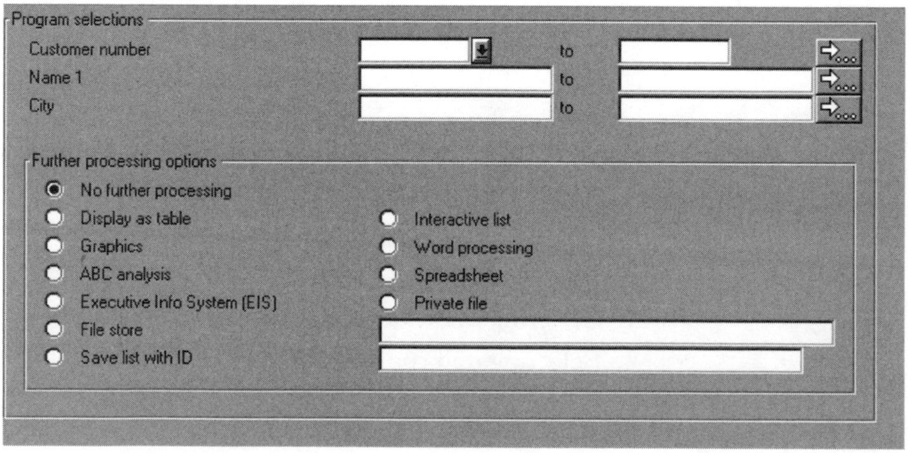

Figure 5-102 Program selections

with the processing options. Enter the selection range. We will display the results in a table, so select Display as table, under the section Further processing options.

After entering your selections, press the *Execute* ( ) button. The results are displayed in a table, as shown in Figure 5-103. You have now successfully created and run an ABAP query.

Step 3: Using the Query

Once you have executed the query, you can

- Print it (select List, Print from the menu, or press ( )).
- Convert it to a spreadsheet (select List, Spreadsheet from the menu).
- Use it in a mail merge (select List, Word processing from the menu).
- Save it to a file (select List, File store from the menu, or press ( )).

You can also transfer the query into the SAP ABAP list format. Select Edit, Interactive list from the menu or press (Insert list icon here). The query is displayed as a list. The user can use the SAP standard Settings menu available in many ABAP lists within the system to change the column settings.

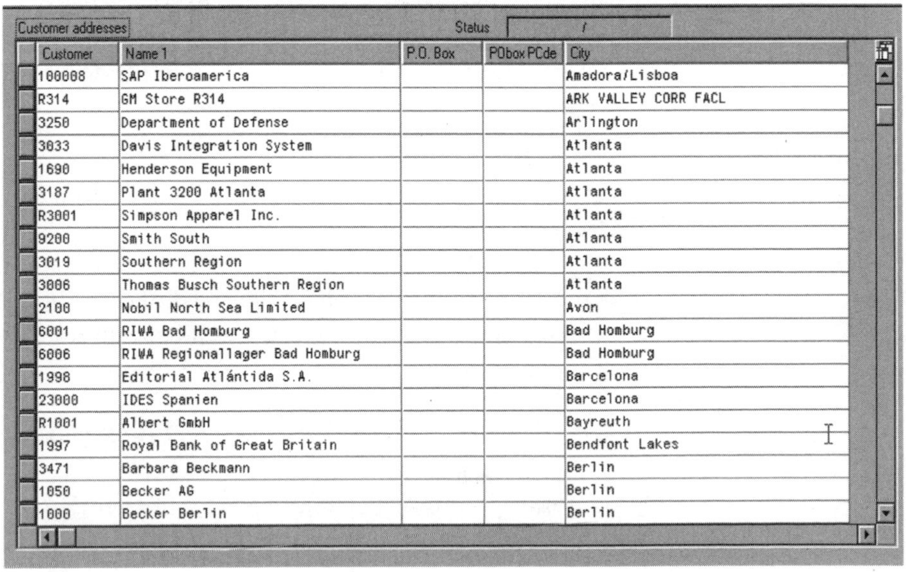

Figure 5-103
Results of an ABAP query

Customer addresses   Status /

Customer	Name 1	P.O. Box	PObox PCde	City
100008	SAP Iberoamerica			Amadora/Lisboa
R314	GM Store R314			ARK VALLEY CORR FACL
3250	Department of Defense			Arlington
3033	Davis Integration System			Atlanta
1690	Henderson Equipment			Atlanta
3187	Plant 3200 Atlanta			Atlanta
R3001	Simpson Apparel Inc.			Atlanta
9200	Smith South			Atlanta
3019	Southern Region			Atlanta
3006	Thomas Busch Southern Region			Atlanta
2100	Nobil North Sea Limited			Avon
6001	RIWA Bad Homburg			Bad Homburg
6006	RIWA Regionallager Bad Homburg			Bad Homburg
1998	Editorial Atlántida S.A.			Barcelona
23000	IDES Spanien			Barcelona
R1001	Albert GmbH			Bayreuth
1997	Royal Bank of Great Britain			Bendfont Lakes
3471	Barbara Beckmann			Berlin
1050	Becker AG			Berlin
1000	Becker Berlin			Berlin

New Fields in Pricing

To use a field in pricing, one creates a condition table. This condition table is created using the allowed fields from the field catalog. Should the fields one requires not be included in the list of allowed fields, one can add the fields from the list of available fields. However, one may find that a new field may not be in the list of available fields. For this reason, one must create new fields for pricing. The document and item data in SD is stored in data tables, such as VBAK and VBAP (for the order transaction). Many of the fields from these tables are available in the field catalog.

The field catalog is a structure (KOMG) that consists of two tables (KOMK and KOMP). These tables contain the header and item data for pricing respectively. They are called KOM "x" because they are communications structures used to communicate the transaction data with the pricing procedure. Table KOMG contains the fields of tables KOMK and KOMP.

If you require a field that is not in KOMG, it means that it is not in KOMK or KOMP. This means that the field you require cannot be used in pricing because there is no communication of this field from the transaction to the pricing procedure via the communication structures.

To use a field not defined in the field catalog, you need to add this field to the KOMK or KOMP structures, and then write the ABAP code to transfer the data in the field from the transaction tables to the communication structure. Follow these steps:

1. Create the field in the KOMK (header data) and KOMP (item data) tables using the standard includes provided for this requirement.
2. Write the code in the user exit to read the transaction data and transfer it to the KOM "x" structures.

Menu Path

The menu path here is IMG, Sales and distribution, System modification, Create new fields (using the condition technique), New fields for pricing.

Adding the Field to KOMK and KOMP

This process requires some knowledge of the ABAP dictionary and how to use the ABAP dictionary to create and change fields and tables. You may have to use an ABAP skill to assist you. If the field is from the header table (for example, the order table VBAK), you'll need to add it to the include table KOMKAZ in table KOMK. If the field is from the item table (for example, the order item table VBAP), you'll need to add it to the include table KOMPAZ in table KOMP.

Let's say you need to use the "base material" to define a price and the base material is not in the pricing field catalog. The base material is a field on the material master basic data screen and is defined as MARA-WRKST. Since this relates to the material, it is at the item level, so you would add the field to the KOMPAZ include table.

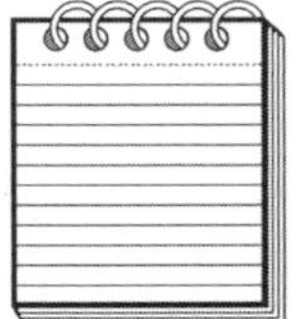

NOTE: *When you add a field to these tables, it must start with "ZZ." Therefore, the field you add would be ZZWRKST. In ABAP, when you add the field, use the same domain as in the field in the original table MARA-WRKST.*

After adding the field, generate the structure KOMP. This field is not available in the field catalog and can be used in condition tables.

Writing the ABAP Code

The field in the communications structure will be blank unless the ABAP code transfers the data from the material master to the field KOMP-ZZWRKST. Pricing occurs in the order and in the invoice, so you need to put this code in both places. For the order transaction, write the ABAP code in user exit USEREXIT_PRICING_PREPARE_TKOMP in include program MV45AFZZ. For the billing transaction, write the ABAP code in user exit USEREXIT_PRICING_PREPARE_TKOMP in RV60AFZZ.

NOTE: *The TKOMP is for the item level. If you are writing the code for a field at the header level, you would use the user exits that end with TKOMK. The ABAP code would select the Base material field from the material master table using the material from table VBAP/VBRP. It would then transfer this field to the structure TKOMP from MOVE MARA-WRKST to TKOMP-ZZWRKST.*

Sundry Tips

One often collects a number of tips that cannot be categorized in a single process, but are valuable time-savers in their own right. This is a short list of such time saving tips:

- Transaction code [SM13] can be used to view the update error log. This is useful for looking at terminated updates.
- Transaction code [ST22] will also give you a list of system dumps. This is very useful in investigating system problems.
- Should one want to find a more detailed description or log when processing a list, such as a delivery due list [VL04], in order to find out why certain deliveries were not created, use the transaction code [V.20], which issues logs of a collective run.
- Should one be working with IDocs, one can use transaction [WEDI] to call up the IDoc type and EDI basis screen. One may also find transaction code [WE02] useful in listing IDocs.
- Should one want to see the changes made to documents, use the Data browser [SE16] with tables CDHDR—for change header and CDPOS—for change item. Be sure to enter as much selection criteria as possible to narrow down the selection, as these tables are very big and may sap resources.
- Should you need to compare entries in tables across clients in a system, use handy transaction code [OY19]. You then select View/Compare table. You will then be required to log on to the comparison system. Once logged on, you can display all entries or merely what the differences are between the two tables. This is useful when transporting tables across clients, such as from a test client into a production client.
- Should one need to close a period for the material master records, use the transaction code [MMPV]. This is useful when creating material stock by creating a goods receipt using [MB1C].
- Should one want to access the user maintenance screen, use transaction code [SU01].
- It is useful to investigate which user is locking a table entry. This can be done by using the transaction code [SM12].
- Should one want to see a list of the users on a system and the number of sessions they have open, use the transaction [SM04].

- Do not forget that your transports between instances are controlled by transaction code [SE01], followed by selecting either workbench or customizing overviews.
- A logical database is available to investigate associated tables and fields within a process. This is obtainable by using the transaction code [SE80] and selecting the Other objects button followed by hitting the Edit button. You then select the Logical database button and can use the matchcode to select a logical database that you are searching for. In the matchcode, select the Information system button, followed by selecting Enter to obtain a list of logical databases.
- Often, when creating a sales order, one may want to know where the system is obtaining information. This is especially true when trying to ascertain the cause of a problem. For this reason, SAP provides the use of a *Structered query language* (SQL) trace. A SQL trace records all open, prepared, fetched, and excecuted statements, as well as actual SQL statements and the duration time for each step in a procedure.

A SQL trace can be used by selecting System, Utilities, SQL trace, or by using transaction code [ST05]. One then proceeds to select the SQL trace button, followed by the button "Trace on" (traces are requested per user). One can then proceed to another session and carry out the process that requires recording.

After finishing the process, proceed back to the SQL trace session or back to [ST05] where you select Trace off. To view the trace, select List trace. By selecting the indicator Show SQL trace and selecting Excecute (all other entries required for selection should be present automatically by default), one will see the results of the trace.

- When using output and spools, it is useful to know of transaction code [SPAD], which is the spool administration overview screen. This screen transfers the investigation into spools as well as output devices and requests for output.

APPENDIX

System Icons and Their Usage

ICON	Description	Name
	Select mode; select	ICON_SYSTEM_MARK
	Select all	ICON_SELECT_ALL
	Select block	ICON_SELECT_BLOCK
	Deselect all	ICON_DESELECT_ALL
	Cut	ICON_SYSTEM_CUT
	Copy	ICON_SYSTEM_COPY
	Paste	ICON_SYSTEM_PASTE
	Undo	ICON_SYSTEM_UNDO
	OK; continue; choose <value>	ICON_OKAY
	Cancel	ICON_CANCEL
	Previous screen	ICON_PREVIOUS_OBJECT
	Next screen	ICON_NEXT_OBJECT
	Extreme left; first . . .	ICON_TOTAL_LEFT
	Page left	ICON_PAGE_LEFT
	Column left; previous . . .	ICON_COLUMN_LEFT
	Column right; next . . .	ICON_COLUMN_RIGHT

ICON	Description	Name
	Page right	ICON_PAGE_RIGHT
	Extreme right; last . . .	ICON_TOTAL_RIGHT
	First page	ICON_FIRST_PAGE
	Previous page	ICON_PREVIOUS_PAGE
	Next page	ICON_NEXT_PAGE
	Last page	ICON_LAST_PAGE
	Other <object>	ICON_OTHER_OBJECT
	Header; basic data	ICON_HEADER
	Overview; overview; list screen	ICON_OVERVIEW
	Detail view	ICON_DETAIL
	Period screen; time breakdown	ICON_PERIOD
	Change	ICON_CHANGE
	Create	ICON_CREATE
	Display	ICON_DISPLAY
	Display change	ICON_TOGGLE_DISPLAY_CHANGE
	Refresh	ICON_REFRESH
	Execute <object>	ICON_EXECUTE_OBJECT
	Choose detail; detail screen	ICON_SELECT_DETAIL

ICON	Description	Name
	Print	ICON_PRINT
	Replace	ICON_REPLACE
	Expand all	ICON_EXPAND_ALL
	Expand; enlarge	ICON_EXPAND
	Compress; reduce	ICON_COLLAPSE
	Compress all	ICON_COLLAPSE_ALL
	Export	ICON_EXPORT
	Import	ICON_IMPORT
	Filter	ICON_FILTER
	Emphasize	ICON_INTENSIFY
	Copy <object>	ICON_COPY_OBJECT
	Delete	ICON_DELETE
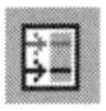	Position; other entry	ICON_POSITION
	Sort in descending order	ICON_SORT_DOWN
	Sort in ascending order	ICON_SORT_UP
	Find	ICON_SEARCH
	Continue search	ICON_SEARCH_NEXT
	Sum	ICON_SUM

ICON	Description	Name
	Subtotal	ICON_INTERMEDIATE_SUM
	Skip	ICON_SKIP
	Rename	ICON_RENAME
	Convert	ICON_CONVERT
	Compare	ICON_COMPARE
	Move	ICON_MOVE
	Insert line	ICON_INSERT_ROW
	Delete line	ICON_DELETE_ROW
	Restore	ICON_RETRIEVE
	Selection	ICON_SELECTION
	Exit recording	ICON_SYSTEM_STOP_RECORDING
	Dynamic selections	ICON_FENCING
	Text	ICON_CHANGE_TEXT
	Create text	ICON_CREATE_TEXT
	Display text	ICON_DISPLAY_TEXT
	Note; remark	ICON_ANNOTATION
	Create note	ICON_CREATE_NOTE
	Display note	ICON_DISPLAY_NOTE

ICON	Description	Name
	Address	ICON_ADDRESS
	Bar chart graphic; plan. board	ICON_PLANNING_TABLE
	Graphics	ICON_GRAPHICS
	Information	ICON_INFORMATION
	Costing	ICON_CALCULATION
	List	ICON_LIST
	Variants	ICON_VARIANTS
	Tools	ICON_TOOLS
	Failed	ICON_FAILURE
	Locked; lock	ICON_LOCKED
	Free; unlock	ICON_UNLOCKED
	Next value; previous entry	ICON_NEXT_VALUE
	Previous value; next entry	ICON_PREVIOUS_VALUE
	Previous hierarchy level	ICON_PREVIOUS_HIERARCHY_LEVEL
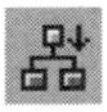	Next hierarchy level	ICON_NEXT_HIERARCHY_LEVEL
	Previous node	ICON_PREVIOUS_NODE
	Next node	ICON_NEXT_NODE
	Hierarchy	ICON_TREE

ICON	Description	Name
	Insert dependency	ICON_INSERT_RELATION
	Multiple selection (active)	ICON_DISPLAY_MORE
	Multiple selection	ICON_ENTER_MORE
	Select: Equal	ICON_EQUAL_GREEN
	Select: Not equal	ICON_NOT_EQUAL_GREEN
	Select: Not equal	ICON_EQUAL_RED
	Do not select: Not equal	ICON_NOT_EQUAL_RED
	Release	ICON_RELEASE
	Activate	ICON_ACTIVATE
	Foreign key	ICON_FOREIGN_KEY
	Generate	ICON_GENERATE
	Check	ICON_CHECK
	Stack	ICON_STACK
	Test	ICON_TEST
	Transport	ICON_TRANSPORT
	Where-used list	ICON_REFERENCE_LIST
	Debugger, single step	ICON_DEBUGGER_STEP_INTO
	Debugger, execute	ICON_DEBUGGER_STEP_OVER

ICON	Description	Name
	Debugger, back	ICON_DEBUGGER_STEP_OUT
	Debugger, continue	ICON_DEBUGGER_CONTINUE
	Save	ICON_SYSTEM_SAVE
	Help	ICON_SYSTEM_HELP
	Repeat	ICON_SYSTEM_REDO
	SAP function set	ICON_SYSTEM_SAP_MENU
	Company menu	ICON_SYSTEM_COMP_MENU
	User menu	ICON_SYSTEM_USER_MENU
	User favorites	ICON_SYSTEM_FAVORITES

INDEX

A

B

C

J–K

L

M

P

T

U

V

W-Z

ABOUT THE AUTHOR

Glynn Christopher Williams was born in England, and educated in South Africa. He is a Christian and loves life. Currently based in South Africa he is a SAP SD consultant, with international experience, having worked on projects in South America and Europe. He has had the opportunity of working on implementations within some of the world's largest companies, the most recent implementing SAP across 12 countries in Europe.

His extensive experience and knowledge of the SD module allows the sharing of fantastic time saving tips, as well as easy to understand assistance in implementing SAP Sales and Distribution.